AUTOCOURSE

Publisher: Richard Poulter
Editor: Maurice Hamilton
Assistant Publisher: Liz Wagstaff
French Editor: José Rosinski
United States Editor: Gordon Kirby
Chief Photographer: Nigel Snowdon
Design and Production: Jim Bamber
Lap Charts: Angela Poulter
Results and Statistics: John Taylor

The illustration on the dust jacket is by Jim Bamber and depicts the 1981 World Champion, Nelson Piquet, and the 1951 World Champion, Juan Manuel Fangio.

AUTOCOURSE is published by Hazleton Publishing
3 Richmond Hill, Richmond, Surrey TW10 6RE
Printed in Holland by drukkerij de Lange/van Leer b.v., Deventer
Typesetting by C. Leggett & Son Ltd, Mitcham, Surrey, England

UK distribution by
Seymour Press Limited
334 Brixton Road, London SW9 7AG

United States distribution by
Motorbooks International
Publishers & Wholesalers Inc.
Osceola, Wisconsin 54020, USA

ISBN 0 905138 17 1

Contents

Photographs published in *Autocourse* 1981/82 have been contributed by:
Bernard Asset, A&P
Diana Burnett
Rodger Calvert
Mark Clifford
Daytona International Speedway
Mike Doodson
Michael Gehrke
Geoffrey Goddard
Bruce Grant-Braham
Dennis Honeywell
Jeff Hutchinson, International Press Agency
David Hutson
Charles Knight
Lasercolor, Bill Stahl
Mike Levasheff
David J. Martin
Don Morley, All-Sport
Jean-Yves Ruszniewski, Agence Vandystadt
Jad Sherif, International Press Agency
Nigel Snowdon
Sports Graphics
Keith Sutton
David Winter

ACKNOWLEDGEMENTS

The Editor of *Autocourse* wishes to thank the following for their assistance in compiling the 1981/82 edition:
Canada: Canadian Automobile Sports Club. France: Automobiles Ligier, Renault Sport, Seita. Great Britain: Arrows Racing Team, ATS Engineering, Autosport, Cosworth Engineering, Ensign Racing, Fittipaldi Automotive, Alan Henry, Denis Jenkinson, Edgar Jessop, Brian Lisles, McLaren International, March Grand Prix, Motor Racing Developments, Team Lotus, Theodore Racing, Toleman Motorsport, Tyrrell Racing Organisation, Williams Grand Prix Engineering. Italy: Autodelta SpA, Ferrari SpA SEFAC, Osella Squadra Corse, Giorgio Piola, Brenda Vernor. United States of America: Championship Auto Racing Teams, Daytona International Speedway, International Motor Sports Association, NASCAR News Bureau, Sports Car Club of America, United States Auto Club.

VALVOLINE PROTECTS MORE GRAND PRIX ENGINES THAN ANY OTHER MOTOR OIL.

There's a good reason why more Grand Prix teams choose Valvoline® Racing Motor Oil. Valvoline gives them the kind of protection that keeps their engines running smooth and cool—on the world's most demanding circuits.

You, too, can get the same kind of engine protection for your everyday driving.

Because Valvoline is not just for winning races. There's a Valvoline® Motor Oil for every kind of car and every kind of driving.

Valvoline®

Winning the world over since 1866.

Foreword
by Nelson Piquet

"When you don't win the Championship, you tend to shrug it off and say 'well, you know, it really doesn't matter that much'. But we all know that it does – and that's what we're all ultimately racing for. So I'm obviously delighted to have achieved a very personal ambition by winning the 1981 title.

"But you've got to remember that winning in Formula One is very much a team effort. So I've relied on my mechanics, my designer Gordon Murray, Bernie Ecclestone and a lot of other people to provide me with such a good car as the Brabham BT49C. Alright, so I've won the Championship, but I was given good equipment to do the job.

"I owe a great deal to the people who've encouraged me, in both Brazil and Europe. I've had the benefit of a lot of helpful advice on my way to Formula One and I want those people to know I appreciate their assistance. I hope they now think I've done a good job! Now I've got to put 1981 behind me and start planning for 1982. I'll be driving for Brabham once more – my fourth straight year – and I can only say I'm delighted.

And I hope I'll be writing the foreword to AUTOCOURSE again in 12 months time!"

Introduction

Welcome to the 30th anniversary edition of *Autocourse*. With the luxury of additional pages this year, we have allocated space for special features by Doug Nye and Denis Jenkinson as they take a stroll back to 1951. You may or may not agree with their sentiments (particularly those of the small, bearded gentleman from *Motor Sport*) but a theme which occurs time and again is that 'nothing changes....'

In October 1951, Formula 1 visited the Pedrables street circuit in Barcelona; in October 1981, the World Championship was settled in a car park in Las Vegas. The contrast could not be more complete yet, at the end of the day, we had practice, a race and a winner. The Caesars Palace zig-zag could scarcely be called a top line circuit but, in its own way, the track proved demanding and, regrettably, it's a sign of the times as motor racing moves firmly into the Eighties and provides material for television rather than the much-maligned spectator. Although, if the BBC's *Grand Prix* series in 1981 was anything to go by, then there is much to be said for television – and James Hunt's pithy comments – as a means of spreading the sport's appeal.

One of the highlights on the silver screen was Patrick Uden's superb documentary filmed around the Williams team. Apart from explaining Grand Prix racing in a concise manner, the second and final programme gave an interesting illustration of Carlos Reutemann and Alan Jones as they waited for the start of the British Grand Prix. Jones sat in his car, chatting quietly with Patrick Head and generally preparing himself mentally for the start. Reutemann, on the other hand, was pacing round his car, prodding tyres and working himself into a negative state of mind.

On that basis, Carlos hardly deserved to win the championship although the fact that he did not has gone down badly in the offices of *Autocourse*. Contrary to what certain individuals may think, we were great fans of the talented Argentinian, the colour proof of page 107 watching over the desk of Liz Wagstaff, our Assistant Publisher! We regret his retirement as we went to press did not permit a more fitting tribute; anyone who has savoured 'Lole's' flowing style could not fail to have been impressed; equally, anyone who watched him talk himself down the field at Las Vegas could not say they had seen a champion at work.

Although the championship was fought to the bitter end, it was not a memorable one. Nonetheless, Nelson Piquet scored more points than anyone else and brought the title to Brabham. That, at least, has been just reward for Bernie Ecclestone, Gordon Murray and Mike 'Herbie' Blash who have worked solidly towards that goal for 10 seasons. For Murray and his mechanics, of course, the real prize is the Constructors' Cup (won this year by Williams) and, with Riccardo Patrese joining Piquet in 1982, the hard-working team from Chessington must have an excellent chance. Which driver will score the most points is another question entirely....

In 1951, *Autocourse* carried an advertisement from B.R.M. It referred to the fledgling company as a 'Symbol of Britain' as they produced a racing car 'that will be another example and ambassador of British engineering skill'. In October 1981, the remaining green cars were sold by Christie's although, happily, Tom Wheatcroft's mighty cheque book ensured that the majority will stay in Great Britain, the country they symbolised so effectively at the height of their success. In 1981, Frank Williams received the Queen's Award for Industry and, while nothing may change in this world, we hope Frank's racing years do not suffer the same embarrassing and sad decline.

Apart from the additional features, there are few changes to the familiar format of *Autocourse*. Alan Henry takes a look at the new World Champion; Nigel Roebuck reviews the Formula 1 season; Doug Nye talks to the teams about a most confusing and complicated year for the designers. It's pleasant to record that British drivers fared well in Formula 2 and Formula 3, Ian Phillips and David Tremayne analysing the respective series. With the temporary demise of the British Formula 1 series, we have expanded Quentin Spurring's Sports Car Review to keep in step with the growing status of the revised series. Mike Doodson kindly stepped in at the last minute to provide a profile of Alan Jones which, even if he does not retire, will remain as a fitting tribute to the man who, in our opinion, was the Driver of the Year. Eoin Young, better known as a purveyor of rare motoring books than a writer these days, has been persuaded to pick up the pen and write about his personal memories of the late Mike Hailwood. The style of racing in the Fifties would have suited Mike admirably even though, by his own admission, he was never a truly great driver. Just who was the greatest during the past 30 years is difficult to analyse but John Taylor, our statistician, fuels the arguments with interesting facts on page 60.

In closing his first editorial, Stanley Sedgwick said of *Autocourse* Volume 1, Number 1: 'We think it is good and we hope you agree.' Nothing changes.

Maurice Hamilton
Dorking
Surrey

October, 1981

Caesars Palace, Las Vegas. The shape of things to come? *(right)*. Nelson Piquet was helped by attention to detail and meticulous preparation by the team. Chief Mechanic, Charlie Whiting, works through a pre-race check list *(below, far right)*.

Years of perseverance by Bernie Ecclestone and Gordon Murray paid off with the 1981 Driver's Championship for Nelson Piquet *(below right)*.

Photo: Nigel Snowdon

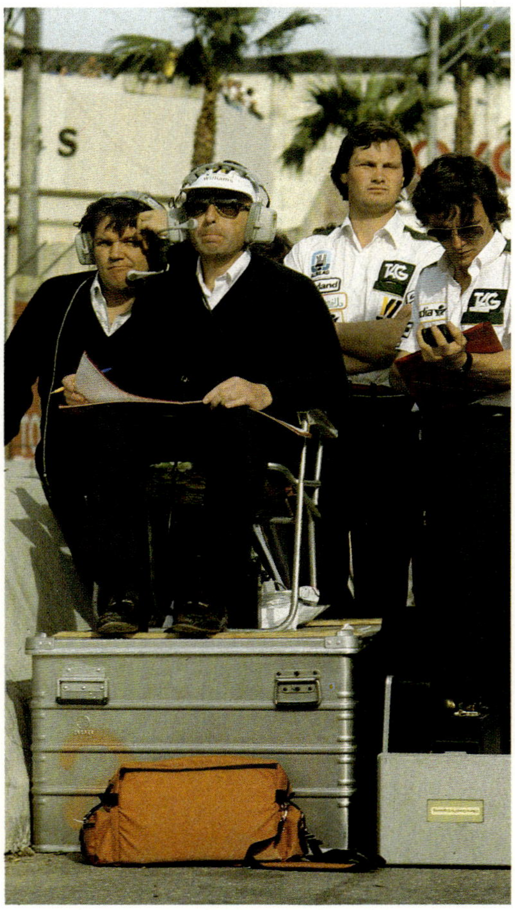

Frank Williams enjoyed another successful season in 1981 although the team were not without their problems. Frank is surrounded by key men Patrick Head (left), Frank Dernie and Jeff Hazell.

Photo: Nigel Snowdon

Following pages:
The Penthouse sponsored Arrows of Riccardo Patrese took pole position for the first Grand Prix of the season at Long Beach.
Lasercolor: Bill Stahl

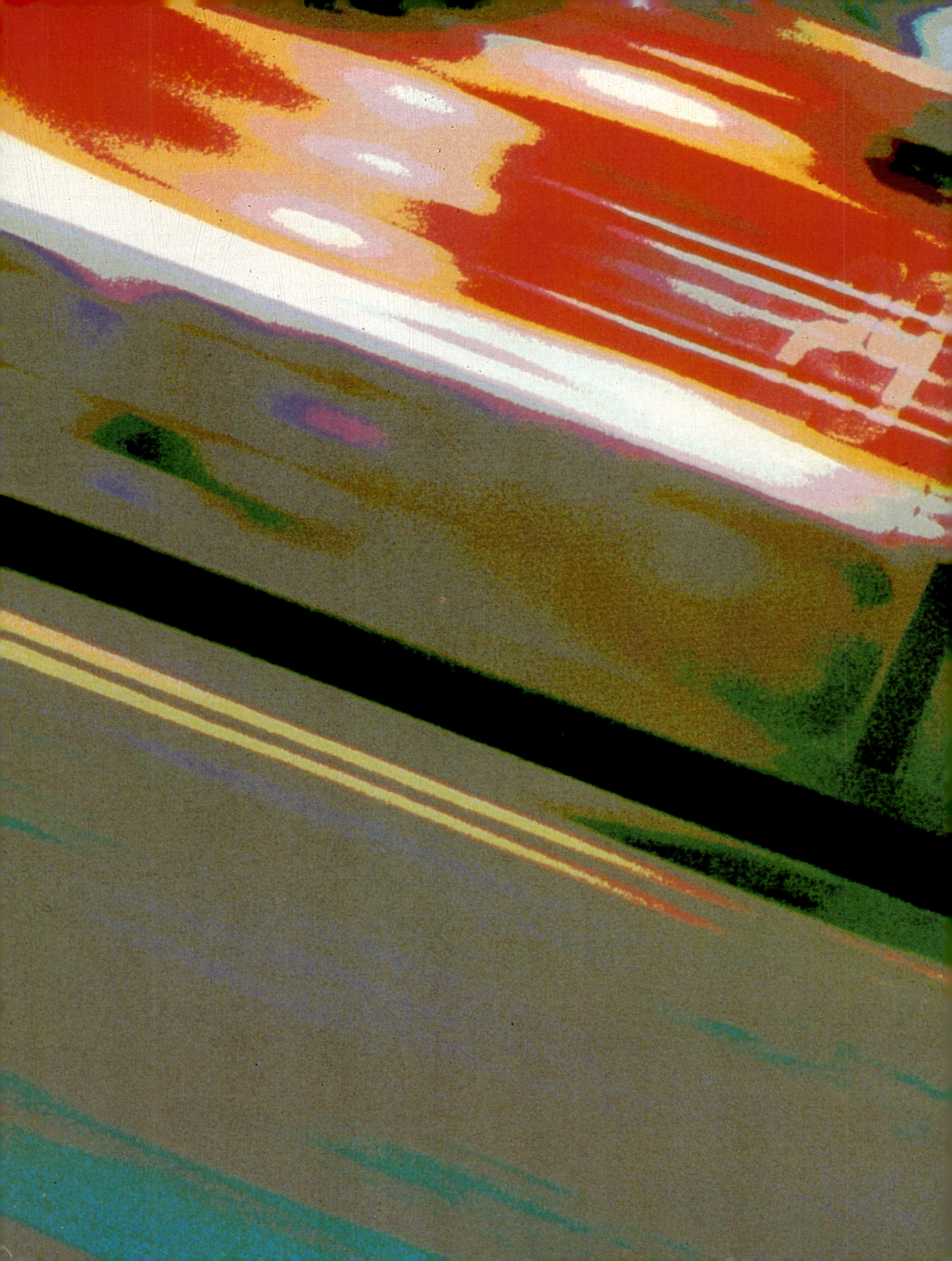

PENTHOUSE

The Top Ten The Editor's evaluation of the leading Grand Prix drivers in 1981

1 Alan Jones

When Alan Jones spun off at Kyalami in March, it seemed he would be playing out the familiar role of a reigning World Champion, his competitiveness blunted by success and large amounts of money. Happily, nothing could have been further from the truth. In 1981, Jones was outstanding, his racing instincts sharper than ever, his driving confident and aggressive. You could say that he made mistakes (Spain) and overtaxed his tyres (Zandvoort), but that happened because he was racing – at the front. His final race was brilliant from start to finish; a yardstick for those struggling in his wake to win the championship. The fact that Jones didn't take the title was the one major flaw in a memorable season for the Australian and those who appreciate the essence of motor racing.

2 Alain Prost

Alain Prost's exceptional all-round ability in only his second season of Formula 1 was a revelation. 1980 had shown him to be promising but his speed and confidence this year exceeded every expectation. Mistakes were few and his coolness under relentless pressure from Jones marked him as a tough but fair opponent; a future champion. Indeed, had he not been let down in England and Austria, the championship story might have been different and his drive in the wet at Montreal proved that such success would have been due to more than turbocharged power.

3 Gilles Villeneuve

As ever, there were complaints about Gilles Villeneuve's burning desire to win races. They said he lacked intelligence; held up others; acted like a 'rock ape'. However, given half a chance, there is hardly a team manager who would not sign Gilles tomorrow. Driving a car which was hopelessly outclassed, Villeneuve might have been excused for losing heart this year. But the fact that his raw enthusiasm for the business of driving cars quickly did not diminish made up for moments of questionable behaviour. His position on the front of the grid not withstanding, Gilles was ready to take the lead at Monaco when others would have been cruising and consolidated second place and, similarly, he was leading four drivers who had qualified ahead of him when Jones threw away the Spanish Grand Prix. That was just as important as the subsequent drive which demonstrated such remarkable natural ability.

4 Nelson Piquet

It would be easy to say we predicted Nelson Piquet's championship but his results did not come in the manner anticipated. Without detracting from the importance of his achievement, there was little to suggest that Nelson had *outstanding* ability at the wheel. That may be a side-effect of running for the championship under the present system. Indeed, his mature drives at Zandvoort, Monza and Montreal were dictated by championship points – which was not a bad thing considering his surprising fit of temper in May. As he sat in the pressroom in Las Vegas and talked easily about the championship, it seemed he had matured three years in an afternoon. With the pressure and worry removed from his young and comparatively inexperienced shoulders in 1982, we hope to watch Nelson's flair dispel the nagging doubt that perhaps the Brabham BT49C was even better than the Brazilian made it look.

JOHN
WATSON
Marlboro
Marlboro
Marlboro

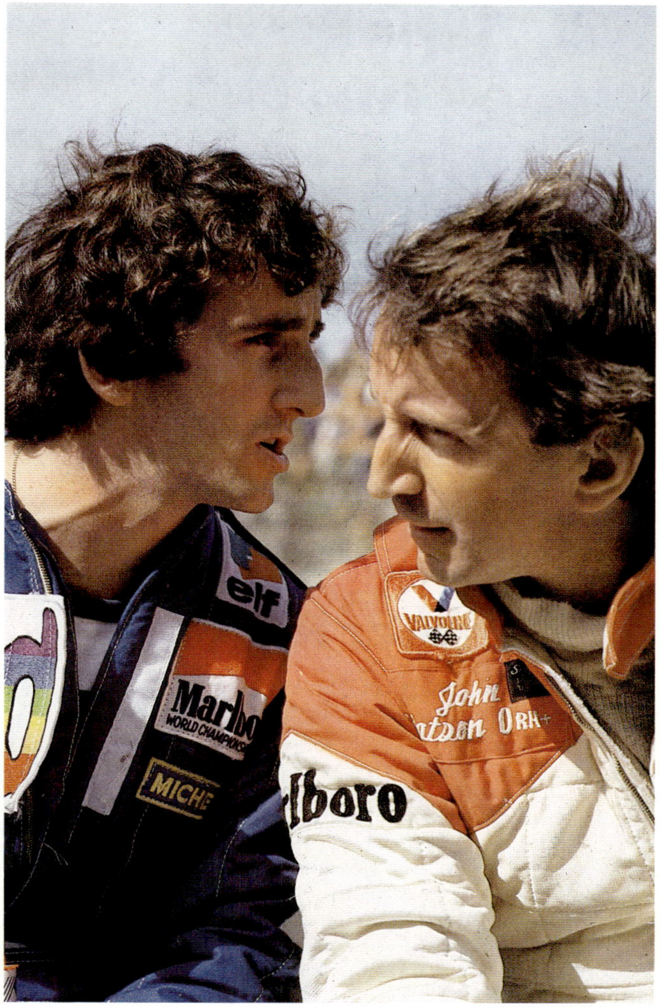
elf
John

Marlboro
WORLD CHAMPIONSHIP TEAM
HELADERAS
PEABODY
TAG
LEYLAND
TRACTORS
Marlboro
WORLD CHAMPIONSHIP TEAM
GAREF
CHAMPION

5 Carlos Reutemann

It's hard to believe that a survey at mid-season placed Carlos Reutemann among the top two drivers of 1981. His driving was better than ever; his confidence soared as he reeled off technically brilliant practice laps and followed them up with a succession of well-earned results. After Silverstone, he had a seemingly unassailable 17-point lead but a change from Michelin to Goodyear seemed to unsettle him. The car was no longer as he would have liked it and, while the shattering practice laps continued, his race performances slumped. Everyone committed errors in 1981 and Reutemann made his at Long Beach and Zandvoort but his drive at Las Vegas showed that he lacked a fighting spirit unless, of course, his car was perfect. But was the Williams really *that* bad at Las Vegas?

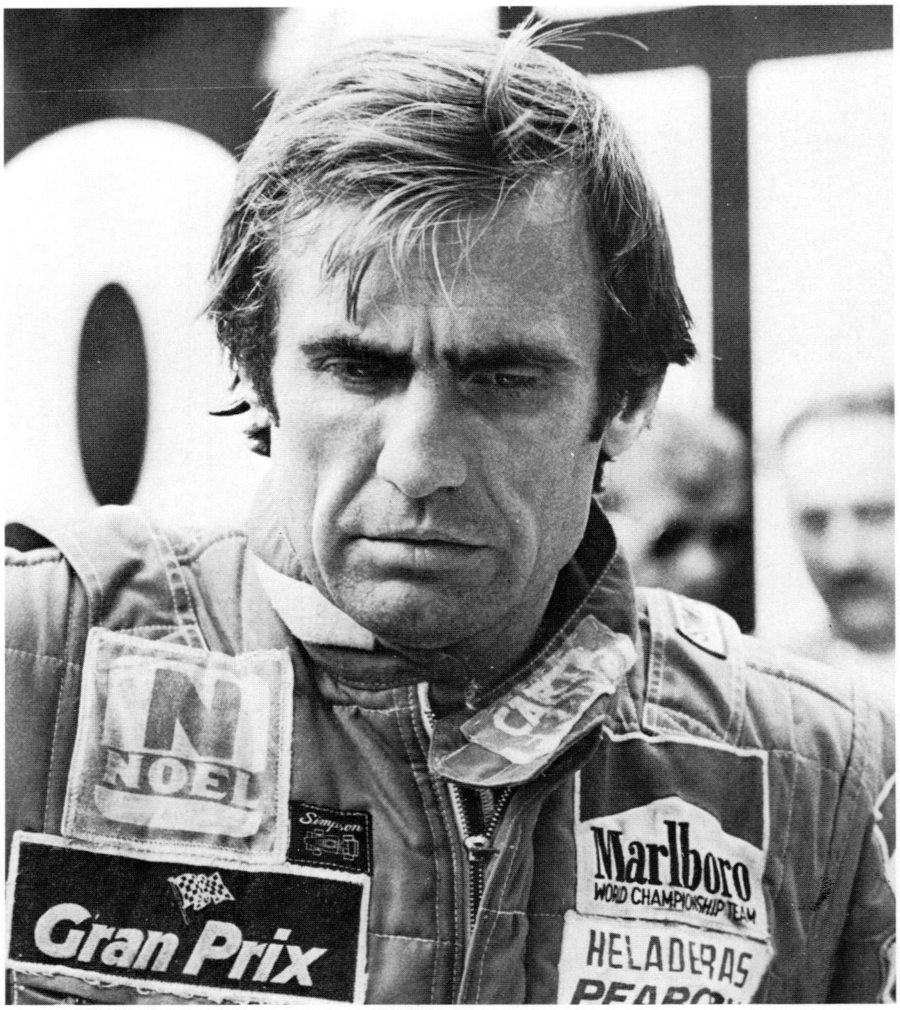

6 Didier Pironi

Considering he had Gilles Villeneuve as a partner in a team hamstrung by an appalling chassis, Didier Pironi has had an impressive year. Undaunted by consistent mechanical failures and a number of accidents, Pironi continually worked his car towards the front of the field as he found his own high level of competitiveness and refused to be ruffled by the speed and results achieved by his team-mate. Pironi at Imola, Monza and Montreal illustrated that he remains a world class driver, one who will be hard to beat if the turbo V6 finds its way into a decent chassis.

SUNBEAM
The New Talbot
Sunbeam Lotus.
TALBOT
ON THE MOVE.

7 Jacques Laffite

Typical Laffite; a steady season rather than a spectacular one. His performances early on were restricted as the Talbot-Ligier team became familiar with a new car/engine combination although Jacques didn't help matters with a misjudgement at Long Beach. He leapt up the championship table through consistency and made his late season bid with excellent drives in Austria, Italy and particularly Canada. It was his final charge in Las Vegas, however, which illustrated the Frenchman's ability to go motor racing when the need arose.

8 John Watson

John Watson insists that he has been driving as well as ever, it's just that he had the right equipment in 1981. That may be true but there's no denying that such a good car, particularly mid-season, gave 'Wattie' the necessary confidence boost which polished a fine edge on his natural ability. Occasionally there were uncharacteristically aggressive moves in races and too much fiddling around during practice, but Watson deserved to score more championship points than ever before and rejoin the Top Ten after a two year absence.

9 René Arnoux

A major disappointment. After two seasons of promise, René Arnoux lost form completely during the first half of the year and was overshadowed by Prost throughout. As a result, his driving became untidy and mistakes continued to creep in although his confidence had returned by Dijon. Four pole positions and a couple of press-on performances showed Arnoux is still a charger if no longer championship material – for the time being.

10 Elio de Angelis

Apart from an increasingly rare over-reaction at Silverstone, Elio de Angelis's season has been notable for quick and consistent performances. The various Lotus chassis have been far from suitable yet Elio's enthusiasm and class remained, particularly when it came to racing. There may have been problems enticing the Italian to go testing but he performed when it mattered most, bringing his car home in the points on eight occasions. His drive at Kyalami (on slicks in the wet) and a charge through the field at Buenos Aires were memorable even if he was psyched by Mansell occasionally.

If Alain Prost was the sensation of 1981 then Nigel Mansell was the Find of the Year. His attitude towards racing cannot be questioned and the Lotus driver's almost overwhelming determination was characterised by his performance at Zolder where he finished third in his seventh Formula 1 race.

Of the rest (as they appeared on the entry lists), Eddie Cheever got down to business straightaway with the Tyrrell team although his slow progress thereafter was probably caused by the team's financial problems. Of the newcomers, Michele Alboreto showed great promise, the Italian containing a natural aggression and refusing to overreach himself at this important stage. While accepting that Hector Rebaque found his way into the Brabham team by financial means rather than ability, the Mexican proved to be a stubborn little charger although the car appeared to be exceptionally forgiving during some hairy moments.

Talking of spectacular performances leads to Andrea de Cesaris. He's fast, there's no question about that, but his apparent refusal to adopt the Alboreto approach and learn from mistakes leaves his future career in doubt. Slim Borgudd improved gradually although, judging by the sound handling qualities of the ATS, Jan Lammers, Borgudd's predecessor, would have been a better choice had he found suitable backing. Marc Surer came out of his shell in 1981 and grabbed his opportunity with Ensign and Theodore. His determination to succeed resulted in some superb efforts, particularly in the rain at Rio and during practice at Monaco.

Derek Daly was forced to take a step backwards and suffered accordingly as the March team found their feet. His year was highlighted by 100% effort during the races he

started, regardless of grid position, and the rain at Montreal left no doubt that his skill had not diminished. Eliseo Salazar partnered Daly at March but the Chilean got a chance to surprise everyone with hard-working and aggressive performances in the Ensign, his drives at Hockenheim, the Österreichring and Zandvoort being particularly impressive.

Keke Rosberg calmed down but his equipment was no match for the ability and confidence which he struggled to maintain during an extremely difficult year. It's impossible to assess Chico Serra for the same reasons except to say that his early races were mature and steady – just what you would expect from a novice number two. Mario Andretti had a good season considering the equipment and confusion emanating from Alfa Romeo before the arrival of Gerard Ducarouge. With the exception of Austria, perhaps, he drove as quickly as ever and outclassed Bruno Giacomelli who didn't seem to have his heart in his racing – certainly not by the standards set at the end of 1980.

For Patrick Tambay, it was a joyful comeback to Formula 1 as he drove some fine races in the uncluttered atmosphere of the Theodore team. His move to Talbot-Ligier brought a return to the Big Team politics and pressures which had dogged his career previously and, once again, an underestimated talent was lost. After seasons of acrimony, there was hardly a complaint voiced against Riccardo Patrese in 1981. The Italian appeared to relax more and his driving followed its smooth, natural course although he was let down badly by a switch to Pirellis after an impressive start to the season. Siegfried Stohr, Patrese's partner at Arrows, did not look like getting to grips with Formula 1. Beppe Gabbiani never had a chance – and, towards the end of the season, never gave himself a chance – to follow up the ability shown in Formula 2. He was pushed into the background when Jean-Pierre Jarier joined Osella, the Frenchman doing the inspired job you would expect after being snubbed by Ligier.

Quite how Toleman drivers Brian Henton and Derek Warwick kept smiling remains a mystery. After a successful season in Formula 2, when the front of the grid and a victory rostrum to follow were commonplace, 1981 was character building to put it mildly with neither driver giving anything less than his best. With an experience like that behind them, anything 1982 has to offer will be straightforward by comparison.

ALAN JONES
MARIO ANDRETTI
NIKI LAUDA
JAMES HUNT
GOODYEAR
parmalat
PEMEX
5 parmalat
GOOD
THE CHOICE

JACKIE STEWART

DENNY HULME

JACK BRABHAM

EMERSON FITTIPALDI

YEAR

F CHAMPIONS

A year of mistakes

Long Beach: Alan Jones. Las Vegas: Alan Jones. If the 1981 World Championship had within it any logical strain, it was that its bookends were provided by the great Australian. Indisputably the driver of the year, Jones should by rights have filled most of the shelf between his North American victories. As it was, they were his only chart-toppers, and others – textbooks from Alain Prost, thrillers from Gilles Villeneuve and Jacques Laffite, steady sellers from Carlos Reutemann and Nelson Piquet, a romance from John Watson – occupied the number one position through the summer.

On overall sales, Jones was beaten by Piquet and Reutemann. On the sheer quality of his work, he was far ahead of everyone, better even than in his World Championship year of 1980.

After the fiasco of the FISA-FOCA war which preceded it, the 1981 Grand Prix season was, perhaps inevitably, something of a mess. Indeed, when the FOCA teams presented themselves at Kyalami in February, the rowing was still not done. For the South African race, the 'manufacturers' stayed away, but the event served two useful purposes: it showed the world that half a grid did not a race make, and it brought home to the likes of Renault and Fiat that all-important television exposure was being lost.

The approach of Long Beach was the clincher. While Jean-Marie Balestre and his FISA cronies seemed content to let Rome burn, sacrificing races until FOCA was brought to heel, for Renault the problem was now rather more pressing. Beckoning was the vast North American market place. They *needed* to compete at Long Beach.

Compromise wheels, dragging FISA along behind, were set in motion, and eventually came the Concorde Agreement. FISA had their way on the sliding skirts ban, and FOCA kept control of the all-important 'commercial side'.

Miraculously, then, all the teams went to California, and we had what seemed to be a sane breed of Formula 1 car, devoid of skirts, enjoyable and satisfying for the driver.

This happy state remained for just one race. Thanks to sloppy wording in the regulations, for a designer of Gordon Murray's calibre to drive a coach and horses through their intent. At Rio, the scene of round two, Piquet's Brabham BT49 precisely conformed to the new six-centimetre minimum ground clearance rule while stationary (when the gap could be checked), but the car's unique hydraulic suspension system allowed it to sink at speed – to the point that its skirts were all but in contact with the ground.

To keep these fixed skirts from destroying themselves on the tarmac, phenomenally stiff springs were the order of the day. It was the beginning of the go-kart syndrome, the start of a Formula 1 fad which made the cars unnecessarily dangerous for those who drove, laughable for those who watched.

Undeniably, however, the system provided a lot more downforce, and – after a cantering victory by Piquet at Buenos Aires – other constructors were up in arms, demanding a FISA ruling on the matter. When it came, most racing people were stupefied. Yes, said the men in Paris, the Brabham was 'legal'. Hydraulic suspension systems were acceptable – provided, of course, that they did not allow the car to breach the six-centimetre ground clearance rule!

People scratched their heads in amazement. It was as if the Vatican had okayed the Pill – so long as you didn't use it to keep from getting pregnant . . .

It was a staggering decision, and one which found very little favour. But it left the other teams with no option: they had to follow the Brabham's lead, or get blown away. And in Grand Prix racing, everything is secondary to competitiveness.

Soon, the sublety of Murray's original concept was lost. As teams got to work on 'refining' the hydraulic systems, air pressure ceased to be the lowering trigger, replaced by a simple driver-operated switch. And so we had the absurd spectacle of lunar vehicles staggering in and out of the pits (where their ground clearance was checked), and rock-hard race cars jumping around on the track.

Ealing comedy, nothing more.

Hand in hand with the giggles went the threat of tragedy. Balestre, in his obsessive drive to ban sliding skirts, had always cited safety as his motivation. Now, by ratifying hydraulics and solid skirts, he had given the green light to an infinitely more lethal machine than that he had banned.

Consider: with barely an inch of conventional suspension movement available (as opposed to the six or seven inches on the sliding skirt cars), suspension arms and tyre sidewalls took over the job of shock absorption. Being so stiffly set up, the cars did not corner consistently, for when they leapt over a bump, ground effect was temporarily lost. Unimaginable momentary forces were put through suspension and tyre, neck and spine. At the end of a race, drivers were fatigued as never before. They *hated* these cars with a passion, both for their lack of feel, and also for the physical discomfort of driving them. Jacques Villeneuve, after testing one for the first time, said it felt like a truck compared with his regular Formula Atlantic car.

As well as that, they proved to be virtually as quick as their sliding skirt predecessors. What a triumph for Balestre and FISA! A little slower, but a lot less progressive and safe. *Formidable*!

So it was that we went through a Grand Prix season knowing not whether to laugh or cry, with 24 'illegal' cars on the grid. During practice and race they would come by the pits, shaving the ground, with officialdom looking on approvingly, but woe betide them if they dared to enter the pits in that condition. Illegal! Throw that man out! In the course of the year, many a hapless driver sweated for a time, then saw it discounted because his car had failed The Test. And who can calculate the cost over the season of overheating damage to engine and clutch as the cars queued for this farce?

How we used to laugh at Peter Ustinov's brilliant 'Grand Prix of Gibraltar' record, fell about when Jose Julio Fandango went down the escape road, crossed the Spanish frontier and was arrested for so doing without his passport. In the context of 1981, Ustinov's script smacks more of documentary then satire. A man ahead of his time, perhaps?

Throughout his battle with FOCA, Balestre had, of course, relied heavily on the support of the 'manufacturers', the grandee constructors who felt they could ill afford to break away from the governing body. Feeling that he had the war almost won, the controversial FISA President was less than delighted when looming Long Beach spurred some of the grandees to seek compromise with Bernie Ecclestone's camp. Indeed, some have cynically suggested that here lay the reason for his apparently unfathomable decision to ratify hydraulic suspensions and solid skirts. Whatever his motive, it is undeniable that this effectively negated all the grandees' winter testing, which had been conducted in cars running without skirts – in some cases, designed specifically to do so. Renault's RE30, for example, although it emerged as the dominant car of the second half of the season, was seriously delayed by this sudden rewriting of the rule book.

If we accept, then, that the season was played out in silly cars, and that a consequent increase in driving errors was inevitable, which best came through it?

Among the drivers, Alan Jones was the consistent star. Vociferous in his condemnation of this new breed of Grand Prix car, Jones nevertheless buckled down to the job, showing far more aggression and fire than is usual for a reigning World Champion. Only a quirky fuel system problem kept him from victory at Monaco and Hockenheim, and these points would have given him another title by a considerable margin. Conversely, a driving error lost him the race at Jarama, and nine points there would also have made him World Champion again. But Alan made very few mistakes in 1981, and consistently drove as if for his life. His pursuit of Piquet at Monte Carlo was chilling in its intensity, and he alone fought strenuously with Prost's Renault at Hockenheim and Zandvoort.

At Las Vegas, apparently his swansong in a Formula 1 car, the Australian was quite simply in a different class from his rivals. On good terms with neither of the South Americans going for his title, Jones utterly humiliated Reutemann and Piquet. It was a victory in the Clark tradition, and should have been rewarded by the clinching of a second championship.

Carlos Reutemann was magnificent during the first half of the year, leaner and fitter than ever, looking set to take the title. But there was controversy from the start. In Brazil he led all the way in wet conditions, ignoring pit signals demanding that he cede his position to Jones. And that set the tone for the balance of the year. Thereafter, Carlos and Alan were not team mates, but merely two individuals who happened to operate out of the same pit.

From the Argentine we had all the usual deftness and elegance of style, a whole series of explosive qualifying laps, the sheer quality of an enormously gifted natural driver. But Reutemann had two weaknesses: he was too easily disheartened, and he was not strong in a fight. At Montreal, having qualified superbly as usual, he dithered over tyre choice before the wet race. You saw him sitting on the grid, shaking his head, and you knew he was not going to be a factor. Nor was he. I remain baffled by a man capable of splitting the Renaults during Monza practice (the most impressive single lap of the entire year?), yet allowing three cars by on the first lap of the title decider at Las Vegas.

If they did not produce the World Champion driver in 1981, the Williams team nevertheless comfortably took a second consecutive Constructors' title. There was more pressure on them this year, and their legendary reliability inevitably suffered. The mid-season switch from Michelin to Goodyear was a gamble, and one which did not find total favour from the drivers. They did not adapt their car from French radials to American cross-plies as quickly as Brabham. But, race for race, Frank's outfit was the most consistently competitive of the season, ambition unblunted by triumphs past. Patrick Head remains the best on-circuit witch doctor in the business.

Nelson Piquet had a peculiar season, albeit one which ultimately made him World Champion. The Brabham team was first into the hydraulic suspension act, giving the Brazilian an embarrassingly untroubled win in Argentina, but an extraordinary decision to run slicks in the rains of Rio had already cost him one victory.

At Imola Nelson produced a sensational drive after a poor start, scything through with quick, slashing, passing strokes to win comfortably in treacherous conditions. Thereafter, however, his composure went temporarily to pieces. An altercation with Jones at Zolder brought threats to put the Australian into the barriers next time. Spurred by certain of his coterie, Piquet's remarks were hysterical and immature. At Monaco, he paid the price, particularly relentless pressure from Jones putting *him* into the barrier.

Germany brought a lucky win after a good drive in a damaged car, and thereafter consistency paid off. If Nelson matches his fitness to his talent, he will win better World Championships in the future. He was in a state of collapse at the end of the Las Vegas race. One more lap would have made seventh, rather than fifth, and the title would have been lost.

Hector Rebaque's insistence on returning home to Mexico between races meant that the first day of practice was sometimes a total loss, with Hector tired and off the pace. Many of his race performances, however, were a revelation in their aggressiveness. Rebaque overtakes well, but makes unnecessary work for himself by qualifying poorly.

Alain Prost was sensational in this, only his second season of Grand Prix racing. From the beginning he was markedly quicker than René Arnoux, particularly in the crucial early laps of a race. Quite often, Arnoux – with his boost a little higher? – was a fraction quicker in practice, but invariably Prost was ahead by the first corner, there to stay.

It took Renault some little time to get their hydraulic suspension and skirts working well, but the RE30 was undoubtedly the star of the 'second half'. Going to

The responsibility of supplying Williams, among others, from mid-season weighed heavily on Leo Mehl of Goodyear.

Watson: his best season ever in terms of results *(far left)*. Nigel Mansell's performances gave Lotus hope in a season interrupted by Colin Chapman's obsession with the 88 *(left)*.

in
itgang.
MIC
MICHELIN
de Carbon
FACOM
15
europcar
UREFLEX
MICHEL BAULE
FACOM
RENAUL
PROS

CHELIN
elf
FERODO

Previous pages: Michelin received full praise for their efforts when they supplied every team at the beginning of the season. The French company went on to dominate the results and scored their second win with Renault at Zandvoort.
Photo: Nigel Snowdon
'Prost made few mistakes, even under pressure from Alan Jones' *(right)*.
Piquet and Jones at Monte Carlo; a pursuit chilling in its intensity *(below)*.
"I've whacked him on the head, Teddy. Now what do I do?" Andrea de Cesaris tried the patience of John Barnard and the McLaren team *(below right)*.
Eliseo Salazar: one of the revelations of 1981 in the Ensign *(bottom)*.
A familiar sight in 1981: mechanics on their hands and knees replacing a skirt during practice *(opposite)*.

Dijon, Prost had only four points. After Las Vegas he had 43, thanks to three wins and two seconds.

Alain is a tough little man, a fighter, yet one with a lovely, flowing style. He makes very few mistakes, even under pressure from a man like Jones. His victories at Zandvoort and Monza were decisive, but what was more impressive than taking the turbo into the lead during the early monsoon at Montreal? In 1981, Prost stood second only to Jones.

Arnoux, by contrast, was a great disappointment. His opening races were disastrous, and he frankly admitted to a loss of confidence. Once in Europe – particularly at the faster tracks – he came more into his element, but nearly always he started badly, and left himself with too much to do.

The great turnaround in the season came at Dijon, where Goodyear returned to supply Williams and Brabham. And then Lotus. And then one half of the Tyrrell team. Until then, Michelin had had a virtual monopoly of the field, with Avon on the fringes.

Unquestionably, the French manufacturer had played the game honourably, filling the Goodyear breach, supplying everyone with identical tyres – to the great distress, incidentally, of some of their originally-contracted teams. With no opposition on the horizon, compounds were conservative, and for a little while, thankfully, we had some stability in the world of Formula 1 tyres.

At the French Grand Prix, though, Goodyear returned. And Michelin, highly resentful in the belief that they had been used, threw everything into this new war, introducing a bewildering selection of compounds and bringing back qualifying tyres.

To the end of the season, the Williams drivers would maintain that, all things considered, they would have been better off with Michelin for the balance of the year. Too much time was lost in converting their chassis for the switch.

For all that, the Americans' return served to remove a large chunk of opposition to the leading British teams. The last couple of races before the French Grand Prix, Monaco and Spain, had been won by Ferrari, by an inspired Gilles Villeneuve.

It had been the old story from Maranello: a magnificent engine in a poor chassis. Ferrari's 126C had maintained the tradition. It handled appallingly,

more so even than its predecessor, the T5. But it had two brilliant drivers, and also a devastatingly effective new V6 turbo engine.

No one was surprised about the horsepower. Ferrari's great strength has always lain in its ability to develop new racing engines, to extract a lot of reliable power in a short time. Totally unexpected, however, was the speed with which the Italians solved the perennial turbo throttle lag problem. After four years of Formula 1, Renault were still troubled by it. But it was apparent from the 126C's first race that the car got away from the line – and out of corners – as no Renault ever had.

So long as everyone ran hard Michelins, Villeneuve and Didier Pironi were competitive. Gilles inherited victory at Monte Carlo, but the really significant point of the weekend was that he qualified the car second. That made the Cosworth teams nervous.

At Jarama Villeneuve won again, holding off a queue of faster cars. Seventh fastest in practice, he was second by lap two, first when Jones went off the road. Thereafter, the Ferrari proved impossible to pass, clear vindication of the French-Canadian's philosophy of going hard from the start.

For sheer bravura, Gilles was again the star of the year. The Spanish victory was completely against the run of play, but thereafter the Ferrari challenge deteriorated, the cars destroying their tyres and skirts with regularity. At 'downforce circuits' like Silverstone, they were outclassed. Rain, the great equaliser, allowed a charging drive from Villeneuve in front of his home crowd, but after four years with Ferrari he is becoming impatient. Next year, perhaps, with turbo power allied to a Postlethwaite chassis?

Most drivers suffer by comparison with Villeneuve, but Pironi was far from outclassed. He drove a sensational race at Imola, and was consistently impressive through the year. Like Gilles, Didier is a born Ferrari driver, and has slid smoothly into Maranello ways. His best times are ahead.

The 12-cylinder teams provided the surprise of 1981. We all knew – did we not? – that Alfa Romeo, after their storming finish to the previous season, would be front runners. And Talbot-Ligier, by leaving Cosworth for Matra, were obviously in for strife.

On both counts, the pundits were wrong. Mario Andretti's Alfa debut, at Long Beach, was strong and gave hope for the future. The Ligiers were off the pace. But during the long European season, roles reversed. The Italian team, enthusiastic but disorganised as ever, slid from contention, utterly incapable of making their 179 chassis behave under the revised 'hydraulic' rules. At the same time, Ligier began to come good. If the Matra V12 was barely the equal of a good Cosworth, it was at least reliable, and the JS17 chassis progressed well.

At mid-season, Gerard Ducarouge was fired from the French team, to be replaced by Jean-Pierre Jabouille, who retired from the cockpit after the Spanish Grand Prix. Alan Jones has said that Jabouille knows more about racing cars than any other driver, and the quiet man's influence began to exert itself. In Austria Laffite drove a storming race, chasing the Renaults, winning fair and square – and this in a car which had struggled to qualify in South America! Laffite, gamey as ever, also won superbly at Montreal, and went to Las Vegas with a tilt, albeit a small one, at the World Championship. And there, unlike his rivals, Piquet and Reutemann, he at least went for it, running second before stopping for tyres. Imagine a driver with Laffite's determination and Reutemann's raw talent! You might argue, of course, that in Jones, Villeneuve and Prost, we have three such . . .

While Laffite went from strength to strength, Alfa Romeo progressed but slowly. After his dismissal from Ligier, Ducarouge joined them, and made good short-term progress, but his efforts were hampered. A man called Ducaroni might have succeeded, but Carlo Chiti had no enthusiasm for a Frenchman on his staff, and petty jealousies constantly intruded upon the business of making the car quick. Andretti ran well throughout the year, but suffered from a series of heartbreaking and trivial reliability problems. By the end, his patience was spent.

Only towards season's end did we see anything like the best of Bruno Giacomelli. Was this really the man who dominated so at Watkins Glen in 1980? For most of the season he was right out of it, beset by a multitude of psychological troubles. Simply, his driving lacked confidence and conviction, and it showed.

The victories were taken by Williams (four), Brabham and Renault (three), Ferrari and Ligier (two) and McLaren (one). Undoubtedly the most beautiful car of 1981, John Barnard's McLaren MP4, with its revolutionary carbon-fibre monocoque, should have had more success. Through the fast swerves of Dijon, for example, it looked like a masterpiece, almost uncannily smooth and progressive and – logical. It made you wonder why all cars did not behave that way.

Thereafter, though, it never quite lived up to its promise, and John Watson's car, in particular, suffered from a mysterious porpoise-like lurching which made it almost undriveable on occasion. It took a long time to rectify the problem.

In terms of results, Watson had his best season ever, including that highly emotional victory at Silverstone. Yes, is came only because the Renaults expired, but no matter. If ever a man was in line for a good break, it was John Watson. Consistently among the front runners, he did much to wipe away the memory of disappointments past. And it took a very resilient man – and a brave one – to step from that horrifying wreckage at Monza and put on a display such as he did at the next race, Montreal.

By contrast, his team mate had a season of almost unparalleled disaster. Andrea de Cesaris, young, fast and rich, crashed so often during the year as to bring his mechanics close to tears. Worse, he showed absolutely no sign of learning from his mistakes. Other drivers frankly admitted to a fear of going near him on the track. In all, it was a very sad saga, for the young

Italian has a genuine talent, obliterated by his lack of maturity. When he kept it on the road, as at Imola, his aggression and sheer speed were very impressive.

There, then were the teams which did the winning, and most of the men who made the news. Of the rest, we must first mention Lotus.

When FISA announced that hydraulic suspension and solid skirts were 'legal', none had more reason to feel aggrieved than Colin Chapman. All Balestre and his men were saying, after all, was that it was permissible to circumvent the rules in a certain way. Chapman, looking for innovation, as ever, thought he had found a loophole with the 'twin-chassis' Lotus 88. In truth, this car, with its conventionally-sprung traditional monocoque and 'floating' bodywork, was a much more elegant solution to the minimum ride height regulation – and potentially a safer one, too.

Most of the other constructors did not agree, however, and the car was repeatedly thrown out at scrutineering after their protests. A slightly revised version, the 88B, was accepted by Silverstone officials, who were then crudely overruled by the autocratic Balestre. The affair was a disgrace to the sport.

Chapman's obsession with the 88 – not at all shared by its unenthusiastic drivers – inevitably detracted from the Lotus season. But the 'back-up' 87 made a fantastic debut at Monaco, where Nigel Mansell qualified third. The car was always at its best on tight, twisty, circuits, having the traditional Lotus bugbear of poor straightline speed, but Mansell and Elio de Angelis worked hard through the year, and both are undoubtedly future stars. Nigel's third place at Zolder, in the old 81, was one of the season's great performances.

Arrows, their revamped A3 working superbly on Michelins, were front runners in the early races, Riccardo Patrese taking the pole at Long Beach, and leading the race until retirement. But gradually the orange and white cars slipped down the grid, and a change to Pirelli at mid-season made little difference.

For Ken Tyrrell, it was another year of disappointment. Money was short, and Eddie Cheever made no progress at all. Michele Alboreto, the team's number two for most of the year, looked distinctly promising by the end of it.

Not until Adrian Reynard joined John MacDonald's March team did we see Derek Daly's traditional grin. Then, and only then, did the team begin to qualify regularly. Major changes to the car made it a midfield runner, and Daly had two really strong drives, at Monza and Montreal.

In the early races, Derek was partnered by Eliseo Salazar, who eventually left to join Ensign. In Mo Nunn's car, the Chilean emerged as one of the revelations of 1981. Here was no mere South American rich kid, but a distinctly promising Grand Prix driver. He worked well with Morris, and together they quite often humbled bigger-buck operations.

ATS were considerably strengthened by the arrival of Alastair Caldwell, who took control and made sure that Gunther Schmid palyed no more team manager games. By the time of Caldwell's arrival, however, Jan Lammers had been sent packing, and Slim Borgudd was in the cockpit.

Only when Jean-Pierre Jarier joined the team, did Osella start to make any progress. The Frenchman always charges when clutching at straws, and he returned from the wilderness in good form, hurrying the Italian car along at a pace which it found a little breathless, being more familiar with the touch of Beppe Gabbiani.

For Fittipaldi, 1981 was a nightmare of financial problems, non-qualifying and internal disputes. Keke Rosberg became understandably disheartened as yet another year of his career went down the tubes, and new boy Chico Serra seemed bemused by it all.

Patrick Tambay returned to Formula 1 with the Theodore team, and several sparkling drives made him the obvious choice for Ligier when Jabouille decided to quit. In the French car he also acquitted himself well, but banknotes saw him removed at the end of the year in favour of Eddie Cheever. Tambay is one of those men perpetually on the fringe, like Marc Surer, who replaced him at Theodore. Both are highly underrated.

And . . . the Tolemans. Impressive sponsorship backed this new British team, which chose a mighty difficult route, with new turbocharged Hart four-cylinder engine and Pirelli tyres. Disheartened they may have been by constant non-qualification, but they plugged away, and Brian Henton made the race at Monza, Derek Warwick at Las Vegas. Statistically, it was hardly an impressive record, but it *was* a triumph over considerable adversity.

"If the race had been one lap longer," said someone after Las Vegas, "Reutemann would have been World Champion. Laffite and Watson would have passed Piquet on the last lap, making him seventh rather than fifth."

Fine. But you can continue this indefinitely. *If* Reutemann had not made a silly mistake at Long Beach, letting Jones through, he would have had three more points, enough to give him the title. *If* he hadn't driven into Laffite at Zandvoort, he would have scored points. *If* Jones had not gone off the road at Jarama, he would have won the race – and the World Championship. *If* Piquet had not hit the wall at Monaco, he would almost certainly have got nine points – and he also threw some away at Jarama.

And all this takes no account of mechanical failures, car problems.

In the end, Nelson Piquet, exhausted, lasted just long enough at Las Vegas to clinch it. Two miles more would have meant two points less – and no title.

Most telling of all, perhaps, recall the words of Gilles Villeneuve after the Spanish Grand Prix: "I won because Reutemann had a poor opening lap. I could see Jones disappearing into the distance, and I knew I had to get Carlos before he settled down. I was amazed that I was still on his tail at the end of the first lap, and I was able to get him on the straight. Another lap, with all those tight corners, and I would have had no chance. If he had gone with Alan, he would have walked the race . . ."

A single lap in a single race. Little things can mean a lot in a Grand Prix season.

1981: LAP OF LUXURY.

It saddened us that they weren't able to test the BMW 735i Special Equipment that you see here.

Its refinements would surely have ensured BMW took the first three places.

For along with its computer controlled engine, it has a computer controlled braking system that can not only stop you up to 40% faster. It also lets you steer and brake safely at the same time. (Predictably it's a system BMW pioneered on the race track.)

Another computer located in the cockpit, feeds you vital information about your journey.

Even to the point of warning you if the outside temperature drops below 3° C, so you know if black ice is likely.

Such innovations conform precisely with BMW's definition of a luxury saloon.

Which is not to build a wallowing limousine that hauls you impassively from appointment to appointment.

But to create a system of luxury where every creature comfort is designed to improve the driving experience, not isolate you from it.

And if you do choose to take a back seat, you'll find that BMW haven't forgotten you. Even the rear seat is electrically adjustable to suit your needs.

It's a combination of virtues that must surely place the BMW 7 Series laps ahead of every other car on the road.

THE ULTIMATE DRIVING MACHINE

TELEPHONE: 01-897 6665. (LITERATURE REQUESTS ONLY). FOR TAX-FREE SALES: 56 PARK LANE, LONDON W1. RING 01-629 9277.

World Champion – and still improving

Nelson impressed the Formula 1 world with his first Grand Prix drive in an Ensign at Hockenheim in 1978 *(right)*. Piquet signed for Brabham in 1979 and learnt about Formula 1 at the wheel of the hefty BT48-Alfa Romeo *(middle right)*. Nelson has a keen sense of humour – particularly after winning races *(below)*. His win at Hockenheim was the result of a mature and tenacious drive which typified the latter half of his championship year *(bottom right)*.

by Alan Henry, Grand Prix Correspondent, *Motoring News*

"He has a Latin temperament, that's for sure, but I've had plenty of experience working with that sort of character. Nelson can be excitable, a bit like Carlos Pace. That's a fairly typical South American trait. But there is another side to Nelson which has endeared him to the team. He fits in well, not only when he's doing his work in the cockpit, but also when he's off duty. People like Reutemann and Lauda worked very well with our team when we were on-track, but they tended to be a bit detached when they were away from the car. Nelson has a great sense of humour, loves practical jokes and that's why the mechanics have such a high opinion of him . . ."

Those words were spoken by Brabham designer Gordon Murray a few days after his number one driver had clinched the 1981 World Championship for Drivers at Las Vegas. Fifth place, exhausted and aching, was sufficient to guarantee the 29-year old Brazilian the title in his third season of full-time Grand Prix racing, and thereby defeat his arch-rival Carlos Reutemann, ten years his senior, by a clear point.

In assessing Piquet's achievement, it should perhaps be emphasised just how varied are the attitudes towards Formula One accomplishments these days. Observers tend to be more critical of any achievement than ever before. A man is seldom hailed, indisputably, as World Champion and there are always reservations. In 1981 there were four, possibly five, contenders for the World Championship crown. Until late in the season, the balance might have been tipped in the favour of any one of them. But one by one they were eliminated from the contest until the last race saw Reutemann and Piquet standing alone. And at the end of the day it was a conservative drive, spiced with a dash of good fortune, that earned Nelson Piquet his title.

He won three World Championship Grands Prix. The critics would say that it should have been only two, but his ardent supporters suggest that only bad luck and bad judgement prevented it from being five. "But that Brabham, with its hydro-pneumatic suspension was illegal at Buenos Aires!" scream the detractors, pointing to Hector Rebaque's apparent superiority over Reutemann in the same race, "he just walked away without trying." Nelson's fans say he would have walked the Brazilian race if he hadn't been party to that amazing decision to run on slicks from pole position in the rain. And he would have taken the British at Silverstone if a tyre failure had not sent him into the retaining wall and all but broken one of his ankles. But dispassionately, one cannot get involved in such complicated 'ifs and buts'. Nelson won, and won well, at both Imola and Hockenheim. And if these other reservations are to be held against Piquet, then one must cite Jones's driving error at Jarama and Reutemann's lacklustre outings at Montreal and Las Vegas as equally persuasive arguments against either of the Williams drivers deserving the title. Objectively, Piquet drove well. Whether or not his will be regarded as an epic victory in the World Championship matters very little. Just as Lauda did in 1977, Nelson Piquet won the title by the points system that prevailed at the time. And if his sheer hunger for outright victory appeared to dim slightly towards the end of the year, who can blame a man for driving 'strategically' when so much prestige, financial gain and esteem is associated with winning the World Championship. I say it again; Nelson drove well. Any criticism of the way in which he won his title is a criticism of the system, not the competitor.

Nelson Piquet came to Europe from his native Brazil in the wake of Emerson Fittipaldi's trail-blazing efforts which re-established South America firmly on the motor racing map at the start of the 1970s. By the time he arrived in England he had already done sufficient racing at home (karting and formula Vee) to persuade him to compete under an assumed name. His father, a successful lawyer, had attempted to persuade Nelson that tennis was a far more rewarding and less hazardous pursuit to follow. Nelson felt otherwise and, in order to stay anonymous, discarded his Souto Maior family name and substituted his mother's maiden name Piquet. This was to guarantee him the eventual distinction of being the first man to win the World Championship under what amounted to be an assumed identity!

Emerson's friends and colleagues gave him a lot of valuable racing advice in Brazil; and it all amounted to 'get over to Britain as fast as you can'. He did just that, running European Formula 3 in 1977 and then moving to dominate the British Championships the following year. Even at that early stage, Nelson Piquet was showing signs of the quietly shrewd side of his character. A monumental degree of bitter rivalry was blowing up between Nelson and his compatriot Chico

Serra. And when Serra proved unable to beat Piquet's Ralt regularly in his March, Chico began moaning about it in the Brazilian press.

Nelson grins mischievously as he recalls it: "Chico's mother worked for TV Globo in Brazil and helped him with a great deal of publicity. Chico would moan that I had better engines than he had, but he wouldn't do that in the *British* press because he knew people wouldn't take him seriously. He also knew that the British press knew the truth. So I had all the articles in *Motoring News* and *Autosport* translated and sent back to Brazil – that proved the real story!"

What's more, in the split-second world of Formula 3, Piquet turned situations to his advantage – even after he'd quit the formula at the end of '78 to take in some GP outings in a B.S. Fabrications McLaren M23. "We had a lot of help from Ralt with our car", he admits appreciatively, "but we eventually took it away and did all our own modifications which gave us a bit of an edge. We were naturally reluctant to share these with anybody else. But, just to teach Chico a lesson, when I moved into F1 I gave all my Ralt chassis settings to Derek Warwick to help him keep on top of Serra. Derek is a really good driver, particularly in the wet, but I don't think he was too good at setting a car up. The information we gave him was enough for him to win the other British Championship and beat Chico!"

Piquet's early pace in that old McLaren held everybody's attention. By the end of the year he had come to an arrangement with the equally shrewd Bernie Ecclestone to drive for Brabham alongside Lauda in 1979. "You've got to understand that this was something very special for me," he reflects with a tinge of emotion, "some people see Ferrari and Lotus as the 'classic' teams for whom they'd like to drive. But ever since I started out with my sights set on Formula One my dream was to drive for Brabhams. And this was my chance!"

Driving the bulky, thirsty BT48-V12s, we saw a true measure of Piquet's form throughout 1979. The benefits of serving a season as Lauda's team mate are still paying off, according to Piquet. "He was an honest, open and sincere man to deal with. If he thought you were a fool, or had done something stupid, he would tell you so. Direct and to your face. There was no messing around with Niki. He had a keen sense of humour and I learned a great deal about testing from him. Not merely how to drive the car, but how to be selective about the information collected during a test session."

Gordon Murray echoes the value of Lauda's tutoring. "Technically, I think that Nelson is getting better all the time. Unquestionably, he learnt a lot of his craft from Niki. Even by the end of the 1979 season I could see the sort of progress he was making. He wasn't afraid to make suggestions and he quickly found out what *I* wanted to know from *him*. In the past year he has progressed to the point where he always gives me accurate and relevant information. He appreciates precisely what I need to know to take a step forward in setting up the car. He gives me this and doesn't waste time with superfluous information."

Piquet signed a three year deal with Brabham, appending his signature to a contract which paid him a nominal 50,000 dollars per year. Of course, that is nowhere near an accurate reflection of the amount of money earned by the cheerful Brazilian. Prize money, additional support from Parmalat, lucrative fees from BMW for driving in selected long distance events plus considerable personal sponsorship have ensured that Piquet is a wealthy man. But when he walked away from his blown-up Brabham BT49 at Montreal in 1980, he hardly looked bothered at his failure to win the World Championship. Grinning sheepishly, he remarked "there's no way I can vary my contract for 1981 if I had won this time. Now, of course, if I win next year . . ."

One must inevitably speculate as to Niki Lauda's feelings as he watched Nelson establish a front-running reputation in the Brabham-Cosworth BT49 – the car which the Austrian had tried for a few laps at Montreal before announcing his abrupt retirement the previous autumn. It didn't take Piquet long to get into his stride and his wins at Long Beach, Zandvoort and Imola were achieved in highly impressive style. "That Cosworth was *amazing* after a season with the Alfa," grins Nelson, "that V12 was awful. Rough and unresponsive. Everybody was telling me 'ah, a 12 should be smooth and silky, you'll find the V8 very rough by comparison.' But that wasn't the case. I don't know what other 12 cylinders are like, but that Alfa was rough. The Cosworth was smooth, progressive and predictable by comparison."

Throughout 1981 Nelson matured as a Grand Prix driver, although some critics feel that his season-long 'needle match' with Alan Jones poses something of a question mark over his ultimate temperament. Ever

since Jones and Piquet collided on the first corner at Montreal last year, Nelson has felt irritated. "I think Jones should have come and apologised to me," he insists. Then came Zolder, this year, when Jones clipped Nelson's Brabham twice during the frantic tussle in the leading bunch, the second time hard enough to send the BT49C off the circuit. Nelson was livid. "If he ever comes near me again, I'll send him off the track," he fumed shortly afterwards. The whole affair blew up out of all proportion. "Why isn't he man enough to come and apologise to me?" asked Piquet to anybody who would listen. Jones, who found it increasingly difficult to hide his dislike of both Piquet and team mate Reutemann beneath a thin veneer of jocularity, simply ignored him. "I've got no problem, so what's he worrying about?" he once snapped to an idle press inquiry on the matter!

At Monaco Piquet qualified on pole position, as always to the accompaniment of accusations that Brabham's spare 'qualifying car' was dramatically under-weight. The Brabham team reacted to these allegations with as much attention as Jones paid to Nelson's complaints. In other words, they treated them with disdain. Nelson made a good start, but eventually Jones gobbled up his advantage to the point where the Australian driver was looking over Nelson's shoulder into the Brabham's cockpit at a couple of places round the circuit. Nelson fought back and just as he'd opened a gap to the Williams, he misjudged things as he came up to lap Cheever and Tambay. He slid into the guard rail and out of the race. Knowledgeable observers shook their heads sagely; "he can't stand the pressure, poor lad" they agreed. Nelson simply replied "OK, so I made an error. But I was trying to demoralise Jones by getting ahead of those slower cars and making a couple of seconds on him in one lap. For sure, there was no way he was going to *pass* me, pure and simple."

In the second half of the season, the trend seemed to be going Piquet's way within the ranks of the Cosworth cars. The Brabham wasn't always the quickest in practice, but their race set-up inevitably seemed to be better than the Williams FWO7Cs. Hockenheim provided a somewhat fortunate victory to make up for the massive accident at Silverstone, caused by a tyre deflation. "I reckon I could have won the British, *with* a pit stop for tyres. I was going to stop next time round, but that cover simply exploded just as I was snatching fourth and from then on I was a passenger. Then I ruined a skirt in Germany when I hit some debris on the return straight. I was really lucky there. The piece of aluminium went between the monocoque and the wheel, otherwise I'd have had another blow-out for sure!"

Austria brought a third place, Zandvoort, a well-judged second and then he was equal with Reutemann's points score at they went to the line at Monza. But an engine blow-up thwarted his challenge – the only mechanical failure all season which is a great testimony to the mechanics. Then came a superb fifth at Montreal – the first Goodyear runner to finish in the streaming rain, and the title was finally sealed with a quite calculating drive at Las Vegas, capitalising on Reutemann's lowly showing.

"I get an enormous amount of pleasure from my racing" says this quiet and shy Brazilian who almost shuns attention and is extremely reserved with people he hasn't got to know well, "but I find some of the other aspects of F1 very irritating. I don't like the politics, I don't like the hassle surrounding the travel. Airports, waiting for luggage – that sort of thing. It's not a happy life style in many ways. It's too rushed, too intense . . ."

Nelson Piquet admits that he can see that the day will arrive when he no longer wants to race. "I can imagine myself in a country house somewhere with a big garage, looking after a collection of nice cars," he smiles. But his star is still very much in the ascendent. Gordon Murray considers that his talent is still very much on the upswing. The only real question hangs over his physical fitness. "I admit that I don't train. But I don't smoke, don't drink and I do get lots of sleep." To judge by his totally drained state at Las Vegas, this may not be *quite* sufficient for this small, jockey-like driver.

But Nelson Piquet seems to have got his temperament pretty well under control now. If he can only get his physical fitness sharpened up then he may peak out in a couple of year's time as indisputably the best Grand Prix driver of the bunch. Says Gordon Murray, "in the last few races this year he's been more relaxed than I've ever seen him before – and more confident. At Zandvoort he played it cool, really looking after his tyres. At Monza he went hard in the rain – when he knew Reutemann would slow up. I think he was brilliant in the rain at Montreal and in Las Vegas he did precisely what we wanted of him.

"In terms of talent and promise I think he'll just go on and on improving, peaking out in about two season's time. And by then he'll be very, very good!"

A Championship in one's third full year of Grand Prix racing. A fine achievement and, perhaps, only a portent of the great things to come from the quiet man from Brazil who changed his name. He still remains a slight enigma to many but then that's part of his fascination as a driver. Time alone will tell whether he becomes numbered amongst the great ones.

When you choose Duckhams you can be sure you're choosing a truly remarkable oil.

Choose Duckhams and you'll be using the same oil as the Rothmans Rally Team use in their Ford Escorts.

Duckhams are the oil specialists – with over 80 years' experience of creating the world's finest oils.

Duckhams' unique formulation goes on giving protection when other oils are past their best.

Quite simply, Duckhams won't break down as quickly.

That's why you get extra protection from one oil change through to the next – however gruelling the conditions.

Like the Rothmans Rally Team, make sure you choose the right oil: pure, green protective Duckhams.

Duckhams: the utmost care.

Pure, green protection.

1981 Formula 1 car specifications

Full details of every car which took part in World Championship events

By relying on further development of their 1979 FWO7 design and the performances of two top drivers, Williams won the Constructors' Championship for the second year in succession. Although they won five races (including the non-championship South African Grand Prix), Williams' season was far from smooth, the team losing points mid-season with an engine misfire which took a long time to cure.

Brabham lost the Constructors' Championship by having just one top driver, Nelson Piquet. The Brazilian's BT49C displayed excellent reliability throughout its second full season and won three Grands Prix.

Renault also won three Grands Prix but would have taken at least two more had it not been for continual reliability problems. Indeed, the French team, in their fourth full season of turbocharging, were embarrassed by the advances made by Ferrari with their turbo. The Italian team won two races although those results were due to Villeneuve's skill and tenacity rather than power from the V6.

Alfa Romeo failed to live up to the promise shown at the end of 1980 but the new Talbot-Ligier-Matra liaison made rapid progress and won two races. Similarly, the revamped McLaren team improved towards mid-season and won one race.

The few remaining assets of the Shadow team formed the basis of the Theodore team; John Macdonald's team, formerly RAM Racing, took charge of March's return to Formula 1 and the Toleman team joined Grand Prix racing at the beginning of the European season.

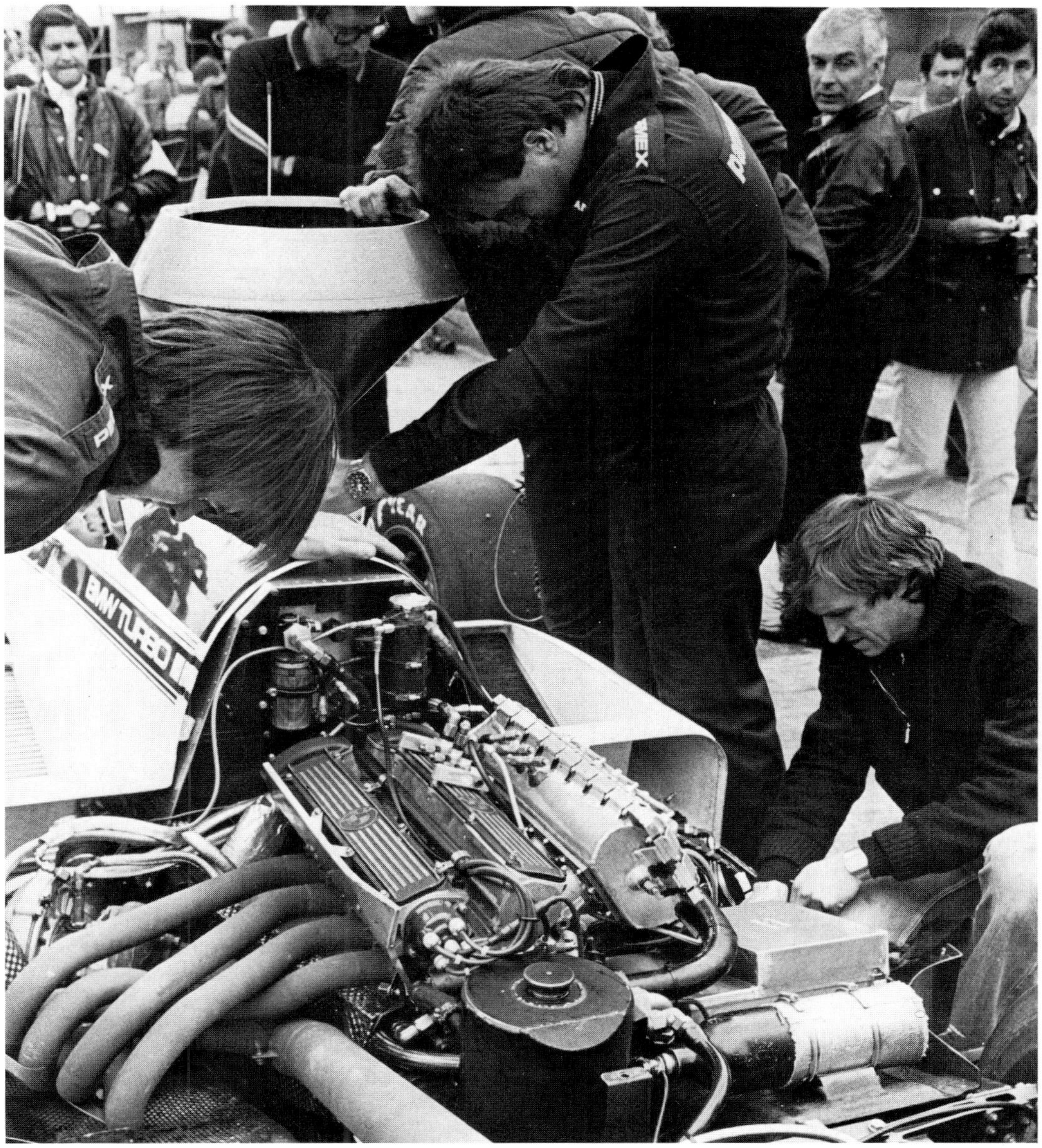

The engines

With the addition of Ferrari's V6 plus the Hart and BMW in-line 4s to the Renault V6, turbocharging became entrenched more strongly during 1981. The Ford-Cosworth DFV, scoring its 144th win at Las Vegas, may have dominated the results but the turbos made their mark with two wins for Ferrari and three to Renault.

The Matra V12 returned for the first time since 1978 and powered the Talbot-Ligier to two victories while, predictably, the Hart 415T encountered many teething troubles. The BMW turbo was tested continually by Brabham and showed remarkable speed at its one public outing during practice for the British Grand Prix. Development continued on the turbo Alfa Romeo V8 but the engine did not appear at any races.

	Ford-Cosworth DFV	Renault EF1 Turbo	Ferrari 126C Turbo	Alfa Romeo 1260	BMW M12/13 Turbo	Hart 145T Turbo	Matra MS81
No of cylinders	V8	V6	V6	V12	4-in line	4-in line	V12
Bore and stroke	85·6 mm x 64·8 mm	86 mm x 42·8 mm	81 mm x 48·4 mm	77 mm x 53·6 mm	89·2 mm x 60 mm	88 mm x 61·5 mm	79·7 mm x 50 mm
Capacity	2993 cc	1492 cc	1496 cc	2995 cc	1499 cc	1494 cc	2993 cc
Compression ratio	12:1	6·8:1	6·5:1	11·5:1	6·7:1	7·1:1	11:1
Maximum power	470 bhp (minimum)	540 bhp	560 bhp	540 bhp	557 bhp	540 bhp (minimum)	510 bhp (average)
Maximum rpm	11,100	11,500	11,500	12,000	9,500	10,500	13,000
Valve sizes	34·5 mm x 2	–	–	30 mm x 2	35·8 mm x 2	–	33 mm x 2
	29 mm x 2			25 mm x 2	30·2 mm x 2		27·2 mm x 2
Valve lift	10·4 mm	–	–	9 mm	–	–	9·5 mm
Valve timing	102°	–	–	50-70/70-50	–	–	85/65, 60/80
Pistons and rings	Cosworth	Mahle/Goetze	Mahle	Mahle	Mahle	Mahle/Goetze	Eaton Nova/Goetze
Bearings	Vandervell	Glyco	Clevite/Vandervell	Clevite	–	Vandervell	Vandervell
Fuel injection	Lucas	Bosch-Kugelfischer	Lucas/Ferrari	Lucas	Bosch	Lucas	Lucas/Matra
Ignition system	Lucas/Contactless	Magneti Marelli	Marelli	Marelli Dinoplex	–	Lucas	Marelli Dinoplex
Turbocharger(s)	–	2 KKK	KKK	–	KKK	Garrett Airesearch	–
Weight	360 lb/163 kg	397 lb/180 kg	140-150 kg	–	–	300 lb (less intercooler)	361 lb/164 kg-350 lb/159 kg

Formula 1 Car Specifications

	Alfa Romeo 179	Arrows A3 - Cosworth	ATS D4 - Cosworth
Sponsor(s)	Alfa Romeo/Marlboro	Ragno/Beta	ATS Wheels/Abba
Designer(s)	Carlo Chiti	Dave Wass	Gustav Brunner/Tim Wardrop
Team manager(s)	Carlo Chiti/Gerard Ducarouge	Alan Rees	Jo Ramirez/Roger Heavens
Chief mechanic(s)	—	Dave Luckett	G. Richter/John Redgrave
No. of chassis built	6	5	6
ENGINE			
Type	Alfa Romeo 1260	Ford-Cosworth DFV	Ford-Cosworth DFV
Fuel and oil	Agip	—/Valvoline	Shell
Sparking plugs	Champion	Champion	Champion
TRANSMISSION			
Gearbox/speeds	Alfa Romeo (5)	Arrows/Hewland FGB	Hewland (5)
Drive-shafts	Alfa Romeo	Arrows	ATS/Löbro
Clutch	Borg & Beck	AP	Borg & Beck
CHASSIS			
Front suspension	Top rocker arms, lower wishbones, inboard springs	Top rocker arms, lower wishbones, inboard springs	Top rocker arms, lower wishbones, inboard springs
Rear suspension	Top rocker arms, lower wishbones, inboard springs	Top rocker arms, lower wishbones, inboard springs	Top rocker arms, lower wishbones, inboard springs
Suspension dampers	Koni	Koni	Koni
Wheel diameter	13 in front	15 in front	13 in front
	13 in rear	15 in rear	13 in rear
Wheel rim widths	11 in front	11 in front	10 in front
	18 in rear	16 in rear	16 in rear
Tyres	Michelin	Michelin/Pirelli	Michelin/Goodyear
Brakes	Lockheed	Lockheed	Lockheed
Brake pads	Ferodo	Ferodo	Ferodo
Steering	Alfa Romeo/Cremagliera	Knight/Arrows	ATS
Radiator(s)	Serck	Serck/VW	Sofica/Serck
Fuel tank	Superflexit	Aerotech	Marston
Battery	Marelli	Yuasa	Yuasa
Instruments	Veglia	Smiths	Smiths
DIMENSIONS			
Wheelbase	108 in/2740 mm	102 in/2591 mm	105 in/2667 mm
Track	—	68 in/1727 mm front	69 in/1753 mm front
	—	62 in/1575 mm rear	64 in/1626 mm rear
Gearbox weight	—	95 lb/43 kg	110 lb/50 kg
Chassis weight (tub)	—	85 lb/39 kg	82 lb/37 kg
Formula weight	1312 lb/595 kg	1290 lb/585 kg	1312 lb/595 kg
Fuel capacity	44 gall/200 litres	43 gall/195 litres	38 gall/173 litres
Fuel consumption	—	5·6-6 mpg/ 47-50 litres/100 km	—

Alfa Romeo 179

Arrows A3

ATS D4

	ATS HGS 1 - Cosworth	Brabham BT49C - Cosworth	Brabham BT50 - BMW
Sponsor(s)	ATS Wheels/Abba	Parmalat/Pemex	Parmalat/Pemex
Designer(s)	Tim Wardrop/Hervé Guilpin	Gordon Murray/David North	Gordon Murray/David North
Team manager(s)	Roger Heavens/Alastair Caldwell	Herbie Blash/Bernard Ecclestone	Herbie Blash/Bernard Ecclestone
Chief mechanic(s)	John Redgrave	Charlie Whiting	Charlie Whiting
No. of chassis built	3	14	2
ENGINE			
Type	Ford-Cosworth DFV	Ford-Cosworth DFV	BMW M12/13 Turbo
Fuel and oil	Shell	Elf	Elf
Sparking plugs	Champion	Champion	Champion
TRANSMISSION			
Gearbox/speeds	Hewland (5)	Hewland/Alfa Romeo/Brabham (5 or 6)	Hewland/Alfa Romeo/Brabham (5 or 6)
Drive-shafts	ATS/Löbro	Brabham	Brabham
Clutch	Borg & Beck	Borg & Beck	Borg & Beck
CHASSIS			
Front suspension	Top rocker arms, lower wishbones, inboard springs	Double wishbones, semi-inboard springs.	Double wishbones, semi-inboard springs.
Rear suspension	Top rocker arms, lower wishbones, inboard springs	Double wishbones, semi-inboard springs.	Double wishbones, semi-inboard springs.
Suspension dampers	Koni	Koni	Koni
Wheel diameter	13 in front 13 in rear	13 in/15 in front 13 in/15 in rear	13 in/15 in front 13 in/15 in rear
Wheel rim widths	10 in front 16 in rear	11 in front 16 in rear	11in front 16 in rear
Tyres	Michelin/Goodyear/Avon	Michelin/Goodyear	Goodyear
Brakes	Lockheed	Brabham/Girling/AP/Hitco	Brabham/Girling/AP/Hitco
Brake pads	Ferodo	Ferodo/Hitco	Ferodo/Hitco
Steering	ATS	Brabham	Brabham rack and pinion
Radiator(s)	Sofica/Serck	Serck/SMS	Serck/SMS
Fuel tank	Marston	ATL	ATL
Battery	Yuasa	Yuasa	Yuasa
Instruments	Smiths	Veglia	Veglia
DIMENSIONS			
Wheelbase	104 in/2642 mm	107 in/2718 mm	108 in/2743 mm
Track	67 in/1702 mm front 64 in/1626 mm rear	68 in/1727 mm front 64 in/1626 mm rear	68 in/1727 mm front 64 in/1626 mm rear
Gearbox weight	110 lb/50 kg	110 lb/50 kg	110 lb/50 kg
Chassis weight (tub)	94 lb/43 kg	97 lb/44 kg	97 lb/44 kg
Formula weight	1312/595 kg	1279 lb/580 kg (unballasted)	1301 lb/590 kg
Fuel capacity	38 gall/173 litres	38 gall/173 litres	48 gall/218 litres
Fuel consumption	—	5-6 mpg/47-57 litres/100 km	—

ATS HGS 1

Brabham BT49C

Brabham BT50

Formula 1 Car Specifications

	Ensign N180B - Cosworth	Ferrari 126C	Fittipaldi F8C - Cosworth
Sponsor(s)	Tecfin/Din/Toyota/Lucas/Champion/Koni	Fiat	Pastamatic/Pioneer
Designer(s)	Ralph Bellamy/Nigel Bennett	Ferrari	Gary Thomas
Team manager(s)	Morris Nunn	Enzo Ferrari	Peter Warr
Chief mechanic(s)	Daryl Kincade	Scaramelli/Bellentani	Sho Fujiike
No. of chassis built	2	5	3
ENGINE			
Type	Ford-Cosworth DFV	Ferrari 126CK	Ford-Cosworth DFV
Fuel and oil	—/Valvoline	Agip	—
Sparking plugs	Champion	Champion	Champion
TRANSMISSION			
Gearbox/speeds	Hewland (5)	Ferrari (5)	Hewland (5)
Drive-shafts	Ensign	Löbro/Ferrari	Fittipaldi
Clutch	AP	Borg & Beck	Borg & Beck
CHASSIS			
Front suspension	Top rocker arms,	Top rocker arms,	Top rocker arms,
	lower wishbones,	lower wishbones,	lower wishbones,
	inboard springs	inboard springs	inboard springs
Rear suspension	Top rocker arms,	Top rocker arms,	Top rocker arms,
	lower wishbones,	lower wishbones,	lower wishbones,
	inboard springs	inboard springs	inboard springs
Suspension dampers	Koni	Koni	Koni
Wheel diameter	13 in front	13 in front	13 in front
	13 in rear	13 in rear	13 in rear
Wheel rim widths	11·5 in front	10 in/12 in front	11 in front
	18 in rear	16 in rear	16/18 in rear
Tyres	Michelin/Avon	Michelin	Michelin/Avon/Pirelli
Brakes	AP	Brembo	Lockheed
Brake pads	Ferodo	Fèrodo	Ferodo
Steering	Knight	Ferrari	Knight
Radiator(s)	Serck	Valeo/Ferrari	VW
Fuel tank	Marston	Pirelli	Marston
Battery	Yuasa	Varley	Yuasa
Instruments	Smiths	Borletti/Farem	Veglia
DIMENSIONS			
Wheelbase	104 in/2642 mm	107·1-112·2 in/2720-2850 mm	103 in/2616 mm
Track	69 in/1753 mm front	66·93-68·89 in/1700-1750 mm front	68 in/1727 mm front
	63 in/1600 mm rear	63·8 in/1620 mm rear	64 in/1626 mm rear
Gearbox weight	—	97 lb/44 kg	102 lb/46 kg
Chassis weight (tub)	105 lb/48 kg	84 lb/38 kg	88 lb/40 kg
Formula weight	1300 lb/590 kg	1345 lb/610 kg	1268 lb/575 kg
Fuel capacity	38·5 gall/173 litres	46·2 gall/210 litres	41 gall/186 litres
Fuel consumption	6 mpg/47 litres/100 km	—	6 mpg/47 litres/100 km

Ensign N180B

Ferrari 126C

Fittipaldi F8C

	Lotus 81 - Cosworth	Lotus 87 - Cosworth	Lotus 88/88B - Cosworth
Sponsor(s)	John Player/Essex/Tissot/NGK	John Player/Essex/Tissot/NGK	John Player/Essex/Tissot/NGK
Designer(s)	Colin Chapman/Martin Ogilvie	Colin Chapman/Martin Ogilvie	Colin Chapman/Martin Ogilvie
Team manager(s)	Peter Collins	Peter Collins	Peter Collins
Chief mechanic(s)	Bob Dance	Bob Dance	Bob Dance
No. of chassis built	4	5	3
ENGINE			
Type	Ford-Cosworth DFV	Ford-Cosworth DFV	Ford-Cosworth DFV
Fuel and oil	—	—	—
Sparking plugs	NGK	NGK	NGK
TRANSMISSION			
Gearbox/speeds	Lotus/Hewland (5)	Lotus/Hewland (5)	Lotus/Hewland (5)
Drive-shafts	Löbro	Löbro	Löbro
Clutch	Borg & Beck	Borg & Beck	Borg & Beck
CHASSIS			
Front suspension	Top rocker arms,	Top rocker arms,	Top rocker arms,
	lower wishbones,	lower wishbones,	lower wishbones,
	inboard springs	inboard springs	inboard springs
Rear suspension	Top rocker arms,	Top rocker arms,	Top rocker arms,
	lower wishbones,	lower wishbones,	lower wishbones,
	inboard springs	inboard springs	inboard springs
Suspension dampers	Koni	Koni	Koni
Wheel diameter	13 in/15 in front	13 in/15 in front	13 in/15 in front
	13 in rear	13 in rear	13 in rear
Wheel rim widths	11 in front	11 in front	11 in front
	16 in rear	16 in rear	16 in rear
Tyres	Michelin/Goodyear	Michelin/Goodyear	Michelin/Goodyear
Brakes	Lockheed	Lockheed	Lockheed
Brake pads	Ferodo	Ferodo	Ferodo
Steering	Knight	Knight	Knight
Radiator(s)	Serck	Serck	Serck
Fuel tank	Aerotech	Aerotech	Aerotech
Battery	Yuasa	Yuasa	Yuasa
Instruments	Smiths/Veglia	Smiths/Veglia	Smiths/Veglia
DIMENSIONS			
Wheelbase	111 in/2819 mm	107 in/2718 mm	107 in/2718 mm
Track	66 in/1676 mm front	70 in/1778 mm front	70 in/1778 mm front
	64 in/1626 mm rear	63 in/1600 mm rear	63 in/1600 mm rear
Gearbox weight	—	—	—
Chassis weight (tub)	85 lb/39 kg	75 lb/34 kg	75 lb/34 kg
Formula weight	1290 lb/585 kg	1290 lb/585 kg	1290 lb/585 kg
Fuel capacity	35·5 gall/161·4 litres	42 gall/191 litres	42 gall/191 litres
Fuel consumption	5-6 mpg/47-57 litres/100 km	5-6 mpg/47-57 litres/100 km	5-6 mpg/47-57 litres/100 km

Lotus 87

Lotus 88

Formula 1 Car Specifications

	March 811 - Cosworth	McLaren M29F - Cosworth	McLaren MP4 - Cosworth
Sponsor(s)	Guinness/Rizla	Marlboro/Unipart/Valvoline	Marlboro/Unipart/Valvoline
Designer(s)	Adrian Reynard/Alan Mertens	Gordon Coppuck/John Baldwin	John Barnard
Team manager(s)	John Macdonald	Ron Dennis/Teddy Mayer	Ron Dennis/Teddy Mayer
Chief mechanic(s)	Ray Boulter	Phil Sharp	Phil Sharp
No. of chassis built	6	3	5
ENGINE			
Type	Ford-Cosworth DFV	Ford-Cosworth DFV	Ford-Cosworth DFV
Fuel and oil	Valvoline	Valvoline	Valvoline
Sparking plugs	Champion	Champion	Champion
TRANSMISSION			
Gearbox/speeds	Hewland FGA (5)	Hewland/McLaren (5)	Hewland/McLaren (5)
Drive-shafts	March	McLaren/Löbro	McLaren/Löbro
Clutch	AP	Borg & Beck	Borg & Beck/AP
CHASSIS			
Front suspension	Top rocker arms,	Top rocker arms,	Top rocker arms,
	lower wishbones,	lower wishbones,	lower wishbones,
	inboard springs	inboard springs	inboard springs
Rear suspension	Top rocker arms,	Top rocker arms,	Top rocker arms,
	lower wishbones,	lower wishbones,	lower wishbones,
	inboard springs	inboard springs	inboard springs
Suspension dampers	Koni	Koni	Koni
Wheel diameter	13 in front	13 in front	13 in front
	13 in rear	13 in rear	13 in rear
Wheel rim widths	11 in front	11 in front	11 in front
	16 in rear	16 in rear	16 in rear
Tyres	Michelin/Avon	Michelin	Michelin
Brakes	AP	Lockheed	Lockheed
Brake pads	AP/Ferodo	Ferodp	Ferodo
Steering	March	McLaren	McLaren
Radiator(s)	Serck	Marston	Marston
Fuel tank	ATL	Marston	ATL
Battery	Yuasa	Furukawa	Furukawa
Instruments	Veglia/Smiths	Smiths	Smiths
DIMENSIONS			
Wheelbase	106 in/2692 mm	108 in/2743 mm	105·1 in/2669·5 mm
Track	68 in/1727 mm front	68 in/1727 mm front	71 in/1803 mm front
	63·25 in/1607 mm rear	62 in/1575 mm rear	66 in/1676 mm rear
Gearbox weight	115 lb/52 kg	125 lb/57 kg	120 lb/54 kg
Chassis weight (tub)	109 lb/50 kg	85 lb/39 kg	80 lb/36 kg
Formula weight	1393-1321 lb/632-599 kg	1320 lb/599 kg	1300 lb/590 kg
Fuel capacity	40 gall/182 litres	40 gall/181 litres	42 gall/191 litres
Fuel consumption	5·5-6 mpg/47-51 litres/100 km	—	—

March 811

McLaren MP4

	Osella FA1B - Cosworth	Osella FA1C - Cosworth	Renault RE 25B-27B
Sponsor(s)	Denim/SAIMA	Denim/SAIMA	Elf
Designer(s)	Enzo Osella/Ing Valentini	Ing Valentini	Renault Sport Design Team
Team manager(s)	Gianfranco Palazzoli	Gianfranco Palazzoli	Gerard Larrousse/Jean Sage
Chief mechanic(s)	—	—	Daniel Champion
No. of chassis built	4	1	3
ENGINE			
Type	Ford Cosworth DFV	Ford-Cosworth DFV	Renault EF1
Fuel and oil	Valvoline	Valvoline	Elf
Sparking plugs	Champion	Champion	Champion
TRANSMISSION			
Gearbox/speeds	Hewland FGB (5)	Hewland	Hewland FGA 400 (5)
Drive-shafts	Osella	Osella	Renault
Clutch	Borg & Beck	Borg & Beck	AP
CHASSIS			
Front suspension	Top rocker arms,	Top rocker arms,	Top rocker arms,
	lower wishbones,	lower wishbones,	lower wishbones,
	inboard springs	inboard springs	inboard springs
Rear suspension	Top rocker arms,	Top rocker arms,	Top rocker arms,
	lower wishbones,	lower wishbones,	lower wishbones,
	inboard springs	inboard springs	inboard springs
Suspension dampers	Koni	Koni	De Carbon
Wheel diameter	13 in front	13 in front	13 in front
	13 in rear	13 in rear	13 in rear
Wheel rim widths	11 in front	11 in front	240 mm front
	16·5 in rear	16·5 in rear	16·5 in rear
Tyres	Michelin	Michelin	Michelin
Brakes	Brembo	Brembo	AP
Brake pads	Ferodo	Ferodo	Ferodo
Steering	Osella/Knight	Osella/Knight	Renault
Radiator(s)	Osella (water)/Ipra (oil)	Ipra	Secan/Chausson
Fuel tank	Pirelli	Pirelli	Superflexit
Battery	Magneti Marelli	Magneti Marelli	Marelli
Instruments	Smiths	Smiths	Contactless/Poinsot
DIMENSIONS			
Wheelbase	103·94 in/2640 mm	104 in/2640 mm	112·6 in/2860 mm
Track	68·11 in/1730 mm front	68 in/1730 mm front	67 in/1706 mm front
	65·75 in/1670 mm rear	66 in/1670 mm rear	60 in/1531 mm rear
Gearbox weight	126 lb/57 kg	102 lb/406 kg	102 lb/46 kg
Chassis weight (tub)	88 lb/40 kg	—	106 lb/48 kg
Formula weight	1301 lb/590 kg	1321 lb/600 kg	1356 lb/615 kg
Fuel capacity	41 gall/185 litres	39·6 gall/180 litres	49·5 gall/225 litres
Fuel consumption	4·9-6 mpg/47-57 litres/100 km	—	5·6-4·2 mpg/50-62 litres/100 km

Osella FA1B

Renault RE27B

Formula 1 Car Specifications

	Renault RE 30-35	Talbot Ligier-Matra	Theodore TY01 - Cosworth
Sponsor(s)	Elf	Gitanes/Elf	Teddy Yip
Designer(s)	Renault Sport Design Team	Gerard Ducarouge/Michael Beaujon	Tony Southgate
Team manager(s)	Gerard Larrousse/Jean Sage	Guy Ligier	Dave Simms/Jo Ramirez
Chief mechanic(s)	Daniel Champion	Lionel Hublet	Terry Gibbons
No. of chassis built	5	5	3
ENGINE			
Type	Renault EF1	Matra MS81	Ford-Cosworth DFV
Fuel and oil	Elf	Elf	—/Valvoline
Sparking plugs	Champion	Champion	Champion
TRANSMISSION			
Gearbox/speeds	Renault type 30/Hewland	Hewland (5)	Hewland FGB (5)
Drive-shafts	Renault	Citroën	Theodore
Clutch	AP	Borg & Beck	Borg & Beck
CHASSIS			
Front suspension	Top rocker arms, lower wishbones, inboard springs	Top rocker arms, lower wishbones, inboard springs	Top rocker arms, lower wishbones, inboard springs
Rear suspension	Top rocker arms, lower wishbones, inboard springs	Top rocker arms, lower wishbones, inboard springs	Top rocker arms, lower wishbones, inboard springs
Suspension dampers	De Carbon	Koni	Koni
Wheel diameter	13 in front 13 in rear	13 in front 13·5 in rear	13 in front 13 in rear
Wheel rim widths	240 mm front 16·5 in rear	11 in front 16·5 in rear	10 in front 18 in rear
Tyres	Michelin	Michelin	Michelin/Avon
Brakes	AP	Lockheed	Lockheed
Brake pads	Ferodo	Ferodo	Ferodo
Steering	Renault	Ligier/Crémaillère	Knight/Theodore
Radiator(s)	Secan	Chausson/Serck	Serck
Fuel tank	Superflexit	ATL	Marston Excelsior
Battery	Marelli	Varley	Yuasa
Instruments	Contactless/Poinsot	Jaeger/Smiths	Smiths
DIMENSIONS			
Wheelbase	107·5 in/2730 mm	109 in/2780 mm	109 in/2769 mm
Track	68·5 in/1740 mm front 64·1 in/1630 mm rear	67 in/1710 mm front 62 in/1577 mm rear	68 in/1727 mm front 63 in/1600 mm rear
Gearbox weight	95 lb/43 kg	134 lb/61 kg	—
Chassis weight (tub)	99 lb/45 kg	99 lb/45 kg	—
Formula weight	1334 lb/605 kg	1312 lb/595 kg	1269 lb/576 kg
Fuel capacity	49·5 gall/225 litres	45 gall/203 litres	40 gall/181 litres
Fuel consumption	4·2-5·6 mpg/50-62 litres/100 km	4·7-5·1 mpg/55-60 litres/100 km	5·4-6·2 mpg/46-52 litres/100 km

Renault RE33

Talbot-Ligier JS17

Theodore TR3

	Toleman TG181 - Hart	Tyrrell 010 - Cosworth	Tyrrell 011 - Cosworth	Williams FW07C - Cosworth
Sponsor(s)	Candy/SAIMA/Diavia	Imola Ceramica/Pastamatic	Imola Ceramica/Pastamatic	TAG/Leyland Vehicles/Saudia Airlines/Mobil
Designer(s)	Rory Byrne/John Gentry	Maurice Phillippe	Maurice Phillippe	Patrick Head/Frank Dernie
Team manager(s)	Roger Silman	Ken Tyrrell	Ken Tyrrell	Frank Williams/Jeff Hazell
Chief mechanic(s)	Jim Vale	Roger Hill	Roger Hill	Alan Challis
No. of chassis built	6	6	3	6
ENGINE				
Type	Hart 415T	Ford-Cosworth DFV	Ford-Cosworth DFV	Ford-Cosworth DFV
Fuel and oil	BP	Valvoline	Valvoline	Mobil
Sparking plugs	Champion	Champion	Champion	Champion
TRANSMISSION				
Gearbox/speeds	Hewland/Toleman (5)	Hewland/Tyrrell (5)	Hewland/Tyrrell (5)	Hewland/Williams (5)
Drive-shafts	Toleman	Tyrrell/Löbro	Tyrrell/Löbro	Williams
Clutch	Borg & Beck	AP	AP	AP
CHASSIS				
Front suspension	Top rocker arms, lower wishbones, inboard springs	Top rocker arms, lower wishbones, inboard springs	Top rocker arms, lower wishbones, inboard springs	Top rocker arms, lower wishbones, inboard springs
Rear suspension	Top rocker arms, lower wishbones, inboard springs	Top rocker arms, lower wishbones, inboard springs	Top rocker arms, lower wishbones, inboard springs	Top rocker arms, lower wishbones, inboard springs
Suspension dampers	Koni	Koni	Koni	Koni
Wheel diameter	15 in front 15 in rear	13 in/15 in front 13 in/15 in rear	13 in/15 in front 13 in/15 in rear	15 in front 13 in rear
Wheel rim widths	11·5in front 17 in rear	11 in front 16 in rear	11 in front 16 in rear	10 in front 16 in rear
Tyres	Pirelli	Michelin/Goodyear/Avon	Goodyear/Avon	Michelin/Goodyear
Brakes	Lockheed	AP	AP	Lockheed
Brake pads	Ferodo	Ferodo	Ferodo	Ferodo
Steering	Knight	Knight	Knight	Knight
Radiator(s)	Toleman/Serck	Serck/Sofica	Serck/Sofica	Serck/Sofica
Fuel tank	Marston	Aerotech	Aerotech/Marston	ATL
Battery	H&S	Yuasa	Yuasa	Panasonic
Instruments	Smiths	Smiths/Contactless	Smiths/Contactless	Contactless
DIMENSIONS				
Wheelbase	106 in/2692 mm	106 in/2692 mm	106 in-108 in/2692-2743 mm	106 in/2692 mm
Track	67 in/1702 mm front 66·3 in/1684 mm rear	67 in/1702 mm front 63·5 in/1613 mm rear	68 in/1727 mm front 63·5 in/1613 mm rear	68 in/1727 mm front 65 in/1651 mm rear
Gearbox weight	85 lb/39 kg	112 lb/51 kg	112 lb/51 kg	110 lb/50 kg
Chassis weight (tub)	68 lb/31 kg	80 lb/36 kg	90 lb/41 kg	90 lb/41 kg
Formula weight	1327 lb/602 kg	1290 lb/586 kg	1290 lb/586 kg	1290 lb/585 kg
Fuel capacity	48·5 gall/220 litres	40 gall/181 litres	40 gall/181 litres	39 gall/177 litres
Fuel consumption	4·5-5·5 mpg/42-52 litres/100 km	5-6 mpg/47-57 litres/100 km	5-6 mpg/47-57 litres/100 km	5·5 mpg/51 litres/100 km

Toleman TG181

Tyrrell 011

Williams FW07C

For us, of course, the Championship was never in any doubt.

After a nail-biting finish, congratulations to Nelson Piquet for taking the 1981 World Driver's Championship by one point from Carlos Reutemann, and Alan Jones in third place.

Congratulations as well to the Saudia Leyland Williams team for winning the Constructor's Championship.

For AP, of course, it was a foregone conclusion. All the cars in the Championship were fitted with Borg & Beck clutches and the majority were fitted with Lockheed brakes. So with all due modesty, we must admit it came as no surprise that we chalked up yet another victory.

ap RACING

AP Racing,
a division of Automotive Products Ltd.,
Leamington Spa, Warwickshire.
Tel: 0926 27000 Telex: 311571.

AP Racing produce components for virtually every form of Motor and Motor Cycle Sport. So, whatever the event, AP Racing can help you win.

Thirty years of change

by Doug Nye

There is a likeable little bearded man who appears in my garden, up at the head of our valley, after each Grand Prix, who accepts a cup of coffee – with two sugars and a sweet biscuit – and tells me amongst great guffaws just what has been going on – the story inevitably punctuated by regular cries of "Nothing changes!" . . .

What doesn't change is inevitably the double-dealing, wheeler-dealing, poor showings by moribund teams with no-hope drivers, and the heroic exploits of the genuine aces – no matter how poor their cars might have become, or sometimes how good. The best man in the best car will always lead – the luckiest man in the most reliable good car will often win. But to finish first, one must first finish. That certainly will never change.

Now that *Autocourse* can so justifiably celebrate its 30th anniversary issue, it is time to ponder awhile on just what has changed in those unprecedented thirty years of unbroken Grand Prix competition from 1951 to 1981, and in terms of the nuts and bolts, and the circuits used, those changes are immense and enthralling, if in some ways appalling too . . .

Look at the first annual volume of *Autocourse*, covering the 1951 season, and you will see photographs of the great Grand Prix cars and drivers of the time. There they are, high-built cars with much-louvred aluminium bodyshells, spindly-tyres, engines up front, drum brakes, slithering wildly around the Grand Prix circuits of the world with their uncertain suspension geometries setting wheels at all angles and pointing in all directions . . . In the roomy space-wasting cockpits are their muscle-bound linen-helmeted heroic drivers, clearly visible from the waist up, gritting their teeth and hanging on tight. Just looking at the photographs, one can imagine the wailing superchargers and deafening engine notes as those tortured rear tyres slip-grip-slip in tread-destroying wheelspin. It really was a different age. Incredibly primitive, rooted in pre-war practice; compare those cars with the early jet aircraft of the time – the comparison of Lago-Talbot and DH Comet is stunning!

But then through 1952-53 there is the demise of supercharged Formula 1 and the adoption of relatively dull unblown 2-litre Formula 2 racing to qualify for the World Championship. It looks pedestrian and dull in comparison – as indeed it was. These cars really did lack technical sophistication and certainly charisma, and that was not to return until 1954-55 when the new 2½-litre unsupercharged Formula 1 took effect and Mercedes-Benz – as usual – stood the racing world on its ear.

Their *Silberpfeile* W196 cars set new standards with their lightweight multi-tubular triangulated space-frame chassis, initially all-enveloping but always streamlined low-drag, relatively louvre-free bodies, and powerful fuel-injected slant-eight engines.

After Mercedes' withdrawal at the end of 1955 the Italian old guard returned to dominance, Ferrari then Maserati, but the British challenge was growing from humble beginnings just postwar. Now chassis power was becoming as important as had been engine power, and here in England were the men to grasp Grand Prix racing by the scruff of the neck and who, in general terms, still have firm hold today.

Under their bidding, front-engined cars discovered low-drag aerodynamics. Cockpits became enclosed until only the driver's bare face and shoulders were allowed to protrude. Louvring disappeared and properly airflowed NACA ducts were used only in the most advantageous places.

Then the regulations changed again. People speak today of 'the old 2½-litre Formula' and they mean the whole racing period from 1954 to 1960. But in truth 2½-litre racing was divided most distinctly into two parts, and the break came on January 1, 1958. From

Vanwalls, pictured at Aintree in 1957, led the way in low-drag aerodynamics for front-engined cars *(below)*.
Colin Chapman demonstrates the 'laid back' driving technique required by his monocoque Lotus 25 *(bottom)*.

The Lotus 72, with its low unsprung weight and inboard brakes, made a stunning impression in 1970 in the hands of Jochen Rindt *(below)*. The roller-bearing Honda V12: 'big enough to live in... *(bottom)*.'

that date the traditional old alcohol-based fuel brews were banned and AvGas aviation gasoline or 'petrol' became mandatory. I often wonder if the regulators on the CSI committee which bowed to oil company pressure to make that change, ever appreciated just what sweeping revolution they were about to unleash.

The point was that fuel consumption is high when alcohol brews with nitro-methane oxygen-liberating additives are used. That means a large fuel load to be carried when one is attempting a 500km Grand Prix with just one refuelling stop. If the fuel load is large and heavy then the car frame to carry it must be robust to match, and the bodywork capacious to enclose the tanks. Everything gets bigger, brakes grow to slow efficiently the greater mass, transmission demands are high, components big and strong enough to cope.

Then came January 1, 1958, and at a stroke not only did we have to run aviation petrol but race distances were also slashed by 200kms. Now fuel tankage could be much reduced, frames, suspensions, transmissions could all be lighter and more compact. Formula 1 had become closer to the existing 1500cc Formula 2, and it was from Formula 2 that the rear-engined Coopers grew to colonise the Grand Prix class.

Their proprietary Coventry Climax engines grew in sympathy, and Jack Brabham's 1959 World Championship for the Cooper Car Company proved that a specialist chassis builder could succeed in Formula 1 using engines and transmissions virtually off the shelf from outside suppliers.

Now the traditional ways of Grand Prix racing were dying fast. Only Ferrari and BRM survived as teams building their own engines, chassis and transmissions in-house. Not for nothing does Mr Ferrari today describe his own Fiat-backed team, Renault and Alfa Romeo as the *'Grande Costruttori'* while referring contemptuously to the proprietary Cosworth-engined brigade as *'Assemblatori'* . . . but the fact remains that the assemblers, special builders, kit car manufacturers – describe them as you will – have produced the more effective and usually very sophisticated answers to the Formula 1 problem for two decades past . . .

In 1961, the controversial 1½-litre unsupercharged Formula took effect and it ran until 1965. Today it is regarded with a kind of patronising condescension by many, but it was still the Formula which perfected modern all-independent suspension systems and found the answers to most problems of their geometry. It was also the Formula which threw-up the monocoque stressed-skin form of chassis construction as a worthwhile and workable solution, the Formula which accelerated development of the ultra high-speed high-efficiency internal combustion engine, and the Formula which proved the use of a fully-stressed engine crankcase as an integral part of the chassis structure rather than as mere stiffening for some other suspension-carrying medium. It was also the Formula which laid drivers down to work, and slashed frontal area to the absolute minimum.

By 1965 the American tyre companies of Firestone and Goodyear were embroiled in the Formula 1 fray with Dunlop's very British stiff upper lip quivering in financially out-gunned indignation as its long-held monopoly was chewed away. During the Dunlop monoply years 1100lb 1500cc Formula 1 cars raced 200-mile Grand Prix events on tyres designed to support a 2,000lb 3- or 4-litre sports-prototype car for 24-Hours at Le Mans! In 1963 Jimmy Clark's dominant Lotus 25 completed four GPs on the same set of tyres . . . they were competitive against their peers, and simply would not wear out.

Now the tyre war has broken out in earnest and, as in any war, development was forced on at fearsome pace. Rim and tread widths grew, tyre carcass designs, tread patterns and compounds all came under minute scrutiny. Immense strides began to be made. Lap times tumbled as tyres developed and grew, and then the 3-litre Formula was upon us, taking effect on January 1, 1966 . . .

There's a funny story about how 3-litre racing came about, and it sounds so typical of the way regulatory changes are made that it is surely true. When the CSI convened their Formula 1-change meeting in Paris to discuss the new rules for 1966, the British constructors had a prior meeting to discuss their preferences. Clearly 1½-litre racing was not as popular as it could have been, but neither BRM nor Coventry Climax – the main British engine builders – was interested in the capital investment, time and trouble of producing completely new power units.

The ideal would be a 2-litre Formula, for then all existing engines could be relatively simply developed and enlarged to meet the new requirement. But the Brits didn't dare lay their cards on the table in French and Italian company. "No" they said, "Let's suggest 3-litres, and the CSI will throw their hands up and say 'No, too big, too powerful, too fast' and will cut it down from there. They can't go to 2½-litres because that's what we had from '54 to '60, and they can't go to 1½-litres because that's what we have now. So" said British logic, ". . . they must go for 2-litres, which will suit us just fine . . ."

Consequently perfidious Albion presented this united 3-litre front at the Place de la Concorde meeting of the CSI committee. When asked for their proposals, the 3-litre recommendation went forward, and in effect the CSI's men looked at Ferrari's representative, and said "3-litres, OK?" and he – mindful of the well-stocked redundant parts store back at Maranello and all those 3-litre V12 sports car bits – could only beam like the Cheshire cat and say "Sure – that suits me". The Chairman's gavel fell, the meeting closed and a bemused group of British representatives trailed home leaving the French confounded by their gloom at having their own suggestion so readily accepted . . .

As it was, Coventry Climax opted-out of further Formula 1 engine development after seven supremely-successful years, and BRM embarked on parallel and highly-costly programmes for their H16 and V12-cylinder engines. The former Coventry Climax users were in a quandary, eventually Lotus promoting the Cosworth-Ford deal which spawned the epochal DFV engine, while Cooper turned to Maserati (and laid-in a stock of lubricating oil) and Brabham, wily as ever, took on the misleadingly humble Australian-built, Oldsmobile F85-derived, Repco V8. Ferrari, of course, riffled along the parts shelf, and put together a

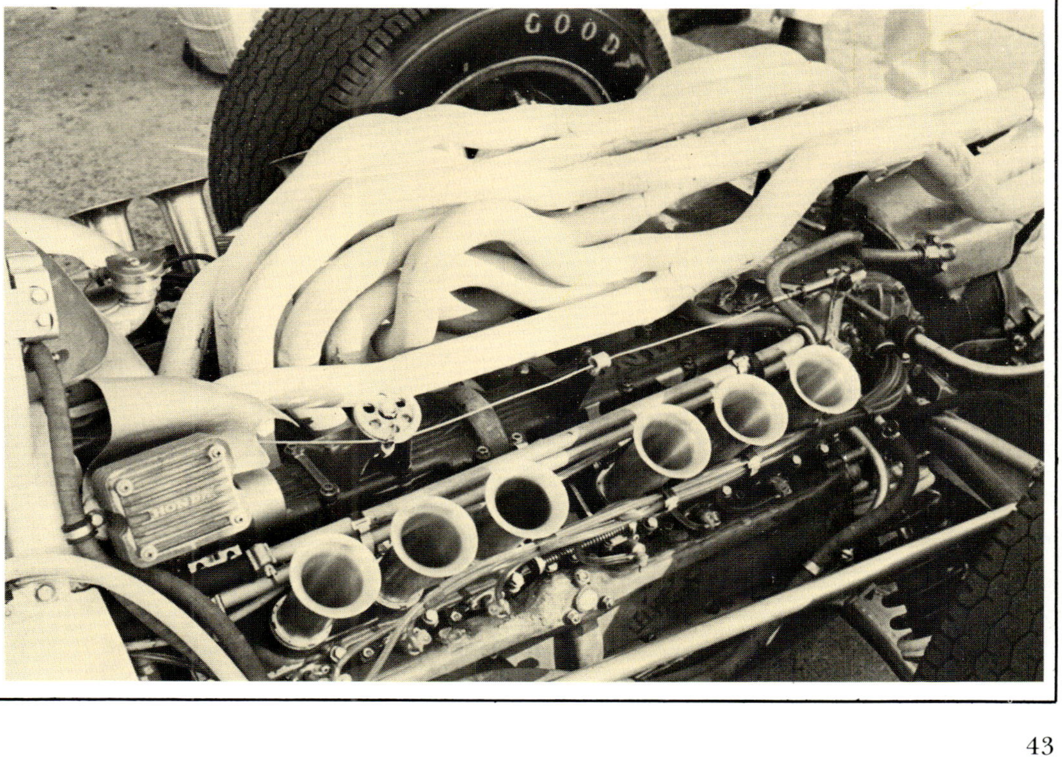

th hush.

18 Turbo

Will it keep going? Carlos Reutemann took the Ford-Cosworth DFV to its 141st World Championship Grand Prix victory in Belgium.
Photo: Charles Knight

fine V12, and Honda of Japan showed their relative inexperience by constructing a huge roller-bearing V12 'big enough to live in . . .'.

Promoters began a love affair with the 3-litre Formula by promoting it initially as the 'Return of Power'. Jack Brabham and Denny Hulme won the Formula's first two Championship titles with the least powerful engine of them all in the best-handling, neatest and lightest full 3-litre chassis. It was a multi-tubular spaceframe of the type pioneered in Grand Prix racing by Mercedes-Benz in 1954-55, using all-independent coil-spring, wishbone, link and radius rod suspension of the type pioneered by the British engineering coterie of Chapman, Broadley and Rudd, and so well-developed by Ron Tauranac, the British-based Australian.

Meanwhile it was an historical fact that Ferrari's great racing ethic was to build an engine of great power and oh yes we'll have to have a chassis to put it in as well . . . To Mr Ferrari the engine was everything, the chassis incidental, but with the appointment of *Ingennere* Mauro Forghieri as Chief Engineer in 1962, change even penetrated the hallowed halls at Maranello. British-type chassis and suspensions were toyed with. John Surtees had joined the team ex-Lola in 1963 and his modern British suspension knowledge was avidly absorbed. Mike Parkes – taken on as a full-time development engineer and part-time works sports car driver – also greatly assisted the operation, and by 1964 Ferrari chassis were handling well enough on their British-type suspension systems to take on the best that BRM, Lotus and Brabham could throw at them, and still steal the World Championships.

Ferrari's failure in the Championships of 1966-67 was more due to internal politics than any lack of engineering skill, and it was to be some years before a Ferrari chassis was once more so demonstrably ill-handling or low-performing relative to the opposition, as it became in 1981, with turbo power.

Perhaps the most significant season in all this past thirty year period was 1967, for the Dutch Grand Prix that year saw the stunning, victorious debut of Keith Duckworth's DFV V8 engine in the stern of Jimmy Clark's Team Lotus 49. For anyone not around at the time, the impact of that event should be underlined, for not only did the new engine win in Clark's car, it also set pole position time in Graham Hill's sister car, which led the opening stages and set fastest lap. Overnight a whole new performance standard had been set which Ferrari, BRM, Maserati, Repco and the rest had to attempt to emulate, and when the DFV was made available to approved customers other than the number one, Team Lotus, the Formula 1 cake was evidently going to be sliced exceeding thin for those non-Cosworth users.

This was the most significant revolution in Grand Prix racing since the engine had been moved from ahead of the driver's toes to behind his shoulders in 1959-60. With a common engine used by the most accomplished chassis and suspension specialists, and a tyre war still being fought white hot between Firestone, Goodyear and Dunlop – who were still doing quite well, but were running out of breath, and bread – performance curves simply took off.

At Spa-Francorchamps in 1967 Brabham had experimented with tiny aerodynamic 'dive-planes' or tabs to anchor their BT20 and BT24 spaceframe cars through the superfast curves around that valley in the Ardennes. Come 1968 and Ron Tauranac and his BAC-trained aerodynamicist advisor, Ray Jessop, had evolved a tiny strutted wing standing proud on the rear of the BT26 chassis, and coincidentally Mauro Forghieri of Ferrari had produced a similarly tentative strutted device. The concept was new to Formula 1 but not new to motor racing, and despite the non-enclosing bodywork and the inevitable turbulence of open cockpits, unfared suspensions, wheels and the more private parts of an F1 engine, it worked.

Before the end of 1968 strutted aerofoil aids had grown and multiplied, with Colin Chapman and Lotus enthusiastically leading the way, mounting their 'wings' high on struts anchored directly to the suspension uprights at front and rear.

In this way dynamic loads were transferred direct to the road wheels and therefore to the tyre contact patch upon the roadway. Traction under acceleration, cornering and braking was hugely enhanced without the penalty of a static 200lb weight bolted to the chassis . . . which would have been another – though self-defeating – way of achieving similar tyre loading.

Initially the extra traction destroyed transmissions as the safety-valve of wheelspin was drastically restricted. Gearbox internals, and particularly half-shaft universal joints, had to be improved and redesigned and into 1969 some cars were just ready to make the most of the high-wing technology when the crunching Lotus accidents at Barcelona set the CSI regulators racing to the scene and hastily devising wing height and width restrictions which killed the high-level clean-air system dead before anyone else got hurt.

Coincidentally the newfound power and torque of the Cosworth engine and of Ferrari's developing 36- and 48-valve V12s had been exceeding chassis roadholding capabilities for the first time in many long years. It was exciting to watch the cars cornering again. The wing thing had been a worthy palliative, but coincidentally four-wheel drive experiments to handle

Renault had their fair share of problems with the turbo V6 *(below)*.
Photo: Bernard Asset/A&P
Ferrari took up the turbocharged option in 1981, Gilles Villeneuve winning rounds six and seven of the championship *(bottom)*.
Photo: Nigel Snowdon

all that power were begun for 1969 by Lotus, McLaren, Matra and Cosworth themselves, but not – significaly, by BRM, who had been down that road in 1964 and knew it ended in a brick wall which for all practicable purposes was not worth penetrating.

The development of wings, even the CSI-regulated type, successfully side-stepped the requirement for four-wheel drive, which proved a blind alley due to excessive weight, excessive power loss and more importantly excessive understeer accompanied by nasty messages to the poor driver whenever anything like a worthwhile front-wheel torque split was employed. Matra, who had also experimented with hydraulic hub-motor drive at this time, came closest to success with their MS84 four-wheel drive spaceframe exercise, but by the end of the season it was running 100 per cent rear/0 per cent front power-split (a fact which nobody bothered to transmit to driver Johnny Servoz-Gavin) and so was merely a 100lbs-odd overweight rear-wheel drive car. Cosworth had the best idea. Keith Duckworth and Mike Costin recognised that aerodynamic developments had rendered four-wheel drive unnecessary, and they cut their losses and sold their car to a private collector without ever racing it . . .

Into 1970 fuel tank sheathing regulations made the monocoque chassis universal, and Ferrari launched its *boxer* flat-12 engine which would, had the late races of 1970 and the early races of 1971 all fallen into the same calendar season, have won an immediate World Championship. As it was the low centre of gravity engine and the combination of its effect upon chassis handling, high power and good torque, was not to be recognised until 1975-6-7 when Ferrari achieved that memorable hat-trick of Formula 1 Constructors' World Championship titles with Niki Lauda, Clay Regazzoni and Carlos Reutemann doing the driving.

During this period the death of the Cosworth V8 engine had been announced several times. It is ironic to recall how even Keith Duckworth was expounding the virtues of a flat engine at the time when Ferrari was on the crest of the flat-12 wave with the 312T and 312T2 cars, and from many interested engineers' comments it seemed highly likely that a flat-8 Cosworth would be the result, and BRM had actually – and literally – laid down a flat-12 design using their existing V12 components.

During this period Team Lotus had drifted into the doldrums of the geriatric Lotus 72 which had made such an impression when new in 1970 with its ultra-low unsprung weight, and all-inboard brakes to minimise tyre heating and therefore make it possible to run what were soon to be called 'qualifying' tyres through a race distance. The succeeding designs from Lotus proved woefully unsuccessful until Colin Chapman produced a study document suggesting to his engineers, headed by Tony Rudd, veteran ex-BRM Chief Engineer and lately Lotus Director of Engineering, that airflow beneath the Formula 1 car should be investigated with a view to harnessing it to generate added downforce.

The result was the seminal Lotus 78 design with its wing pods and underskirts, which dominated so many races in 1977 and lost so many through failure of its Cosworth 'development' engine – tweaked to match Ferrari horsepower – and suffering suspect reliability in consequence. With the Lotus 78 there dawned the age of the ground-effects car, which in turn suffered that all-too-familiar set-back during the winter of 1980-81 as FISA – the CSI by another name – regulated skirts into limbo, and in consequence Gordon Murray of Brabham forced through hydropneumatic jacking suspension to even the score.

By this time chassis power was again being occasionally outstripped by sheer horsepower with the advent of 1500cc turbocharged engines, taking up the little-used alternative offered under the Formula. The Régie Renault took the brave step into Formula 1 in 1977 after agonising for long months over whether they should or should not take the plunge. Their problem was "If we win, who will we beat – If we lose, will it make headlines?" They took the brave step, and lost with remarkable Gallic consistency until 1979 when victory came at last with their twin-turbo cars in the best place possible – the French Grand Prix at Dijon-Prenois. More success followed, but even the mighty Régie was unable to win with authority against Ferrari and especially against the British *Assemblatori* – despite what the Brits saw as French rule-juggling to load the dice.

Then for 1981 Ferrari took up the turbocharged option with the 126Cs and within mere months Gilles Villeneuve was winning. Renault's years of struggle looked rather sorry in comparison, until Ferrari reverted to their historical norm of having supreme power in a D-minus chassis, and in this age there is no room for notable weakness – and quick as a flash the opposition were In! Competitiveness, waste not an hour, never miss a trick – it's the name of the game.

Thirty years ago, when *Autocourse* 1951 was published, a whole era of forced-induction Grand Prix racing had just come to an end. Today, after this long litany of sensational development and immense progress, a new era of forced-induction racing might just be on the painful verge of blossoming. In that respect the wheel has perhaps come full circle.

So we enthusiasts sit in the sun, sip our coffee, and look out over the peaceful valley.

Nothing changes . . .

SUPERCAT. THE NEW XJS-H.E.

Take the world's most civilised supercar. Add 23% improved fuel economy.* Add even more performance. Even better looks. Even surer road-holding. Even greater luxury. And you've got Supercat – the new Jaguar XJS-H.E.

A revolutionary new "fireball" cylinder head gives better performance and outstanding fuel economy.

(In a Motor magazine test,** the XJS-H.E. averaged 21.9 m.p.g. between Munich and Calais at an average speed of 62.6 m.p.h.)

Wider section Dunlop D7 radials on new alloy wheels deliver even more cat-like grip.

A dozen subtle styling changes combine to give a distinctive new look to a classic Jaguar body design.

Inside, you are surrounded by a new and even more luxurious driving environment.

Almost everything you see is trimmed in finest hide, enhanced – on the dashboard and doors – by the beauty of genuine elm burr veneer.

And the interior, like the body, is available in a complete new range of colours.

There are many other improvements, including a substantially reduced recommended price of £18,950. The one thing we haven't changed is the unique blend of searing performance and uncanny smoothness and silence.

For confirmation, simply take one for a purr round the block.

The new leather and elm burr trimmed interior.

Official fuel consumption figures for Jaguar XJS-H.E.: urban cycle 15.6 m.p.g. (18.1 L/100 km); constant 56 m.p.h. 27.1 m.p.g. (10.4 L/100 km); constant 75 m.p.h. 22.5 m.p.g. (12.6 L/100 km). *23% improvement over 1980 model at constant 56 m.p.h. **Issue dated 18th July 1981.

Only the icing and the frills have changed

by Denis Jenkinson, Grand Prix Correspondent *Motor Sport*

During the past season the Editor mentioned to me that *Autocourse* was in its thirtieth year and that I must have been around Grand Prix racing consistently during that period. He was quite correct, for indeed I was in the thick of Grand Prix racing when *Autocourse* began, just as I still am as it completes its thirtieth year of publication.

My involvement over that period has been to report on Grand Prix races and Formula 1 for the monthly magazine *Motor Sport*, and when Vol 1 No.1 of *Autocourse* appeared I had already a number of seasons of Grand Prix racing behind me. I might add that at that point, in 1951, *Motor Sport* was already twenty-seven years old! On the face of things there have been vast changes to the Grand Prix scene since 1951, and people who cannot keep pace with today like to loom over me, with misty eyes, and say "ah, things aren't like they used to be". This sort of remark always revs me up, and depending on who makes it, I either say "no, thank goodness" or "yes, they are exactly the same", either way seems to befuddle the misty-eyed old bore more than ever.

If challenged on either statement I can always defend myself, and looking at Vol 1 No.1 of *Autocourse* I see that Silverstone was being lapped at 93 mph, which is approximately 150 kph. For this years's Grand Prix at Silverstone you could almost use the kph figures of 1951 and substitute mph! On a lap approaching 150 mph average, today's Formula 1 car never drops anywhere near as low a speed as the 1951 average. Today we would find 1951 very boring, but of course, at the time it was exciting. A remarkable happening at Silverstone in 1951 was that the International Trophy for the current Formula 1 was stopped because of torrential rain. In 1981 the French Grand Prix was stopped because of torrential rain. Nothing changes, does it? At that time two of the leading protagonists in Grand Prix racing were Alfa Romeo and Ferrari, just like today, and then Ferraris were red, as they are today.

While all the foregoing is fact, it is not strictly true to say nothing has changed over thiry years. There have been enormous changes in all directions, and vast additions to the overall scene, some good, some bad, but basically Grand Prix racing has not changed. We are still racing for the same reasons and winning is still the name of the game, while the basic ingredients for success are the same. I liken the scene to a rich plum cake, which we all enjoy eating. The cake is the same, but today there is more icing on it, and some rather bitter marzipan beneath, and on top of the icing there are a myriad of fairies and pixies, but remove all this and deep down it is still good, solid, plum cake. Occasionally the whole thing gets wrapped up in a layer of frilly tinsel, but the heart inside it all is just the same. One of the highlights of today is to see Gilles Villeneuve make a meteoric start, like the memorable one in Austria in 1979; thirty years ago young Alberto Ascari was making similar meteoric starts, both drivers in Ferraris oddly enough, and such starts can still be all-important to the outcome of a race, as we saw in Spain this year. When *Autocourse* began we had just passed through a traumatic period in driver relationships within the Alfa Romeo team, which upset a lot of people. Jean-Pierre Wimille was undoubtedly the fastest driver in the Milanese team, but under team-orders he had to let the older, and slower, Achille Varzi win on occasions. There was a coolness within the team, just as there has been this year between Alan Jones and Carlos Reutemann in the Williams team, over team-orders.

In the forefront of Grand Prix racing it has always been the strong teams with a lot of research and development behind them, and they always make sure they employ the best drivers. Equally, the best drivers always ensure that they are employed by the best teams, though evaluation of 'best drivers' is an open question. There never have been more than a handful of super-aces in any period of Grand Prix racing, for it is not an easy game at which to excel, the requirements being very exacting. In 1951 we had Farina, Gonzalez, Fangio and Ascari. In 1961 we had Moss, Clark, Brabham and Graham Hill, while in 1971 we had Stewart, Ickx, Fittipaldi and Amon, and today we have Villeneuve, Piquet, Jones and Reutemann. If you want to add more names to these lists you have to 'um' and 'ah' a bit. If you want to go down to six or ten best drivers of an era, as some people like to do, you have to start scratching about in the bottom of the barrel. Yet we have a regular thirty or more drivers ready to compete in Grand Prix events, and in 1951 there were twenty in the British Grand Prix. We have been through some doldrums when there were only 12 or 15 aspirants, but such moments did not last, I am happy to say.

While the front of the field is relatively unchanged, with the best drivers in the best cars, the rear half has seen great improvements, for at one time a happy-go-lucky private-owner could buy an old Grand Prix car and take part on a minimal budget, or even build his own 'special' and take part, not with any hope of success but just for fun. A more serious private-owner

Alfa Romeo, leading protagonists in 1951, were racing in 1981. (Okay, we're cheating. This is Farina at Silverstone one year before the period in question but we couldn't resist using this wonderful shot from the files of Geoffrey Goddard!)

The drivers' apparel may have changed but there are never more than a handful of 'super-aces' in any given period. Stirling Moss and Gilles Villeneuve; drivers from different eras but 'super-aces' none the less.

could buy an up-to-date Grand Prix car, not quite as good as the works cars, and take part with good prospects of a reasonable result, while a local or national driver could reckon to participate in his home Grand Prix as an addition to a works team, or a works-supported team. All that has changed and the private-owner now has to buy his way into a lesser team who needs money to keep going. It always did cost the private-owner a lot of money to take part in a Grand Prix, and still does, but whereas he used to buy a car from a factory like Ferrari, Maserati or Talbot-Lago, and the money went into the factory team, now he has to finance a complete team of his own, or a ready-made one that lacks a driver, and has to commit himself to a full season of events, not just his home event. Those drivers today in one-car teams, such as Salazar, Daly and Borgudd would have spent their money, or someone else's that they had acquired, on buying either an ex-works Grand Prix car, or a production one like a Talbot-Lago or a Maserati. There have always been those sort of drivers on the grid, hoping to get up into the big factory teams, but it is a bit more costly and complicated to do so today.

Over the thirty years we are looking at we have experienced five Grand Prix Formulae, and whereas it used to be changed drastically every three or four years, we have now reached a state of continual change, which at times is so gradual that you would think there has been no change, but a detail study of the Formula 1 rules would soon prove that this is not so. In 1951 the existing Formula 1 was at its peak, with supercharged 1½-litre cars vying with unsupercharged 4½-litre cars, and the odds were even. Overnight, due to various vicissitudes and some political manoeuvring, this Formula stopped and was replaced by the existing Formula 2, which was for unsupercharged 2-litre cars. It was a temporary measure for two years, before the start of a brand new Formula in 1954 for unsupercharged 2½-litre cars and supercharged ¾-litres. This was a four year plan and was very successful, and with modifications to suit vested interests, it was extended for another three years. Then a minor revolution broke out and more political skulduggery produced a new Formula limited to 1½-litres and for five years we were in a bit of a doldrum, but sanity prevailed and in 1966 the unsupercharged 3-litre Formula was introduced, with provision for supercharged 1½-litres to run on equal terms, though no-one took advantage of this until recently.

Since 1966 this basic Formula has remained in force, but along the way restrictions and mandatory items have been added which have had the effect of introducing new breeds of cars, but powered by the same basic engines. There are now so many rules concerning the construction of a Formula 1 car, something like 91 detail requirements, that it is difficult to conceive a car that is radically different from the rest. A Formula 1 car of 1966 could not take part in Grand Prix racing today, even though it has a 3-litre engine, as there as so many detailed regulations that it could not comply with, nor be modified in order to comply. Tubular space-frames are out, welded alloy fuel tanks are out, sixteen cylinders are out, rear-mounted oil tanks are out and so on. So you see for fifteen years we have had the same Formula 1 but always with a difference, the changes being continuous and gradual. Only this year all the 1980 Formula 1 cars were made obsolete by the banning of sliding side-skirts. The 1982 rule about the construction of the front of the monocoque with added foot protection for the driver, will rule out most of this year's cars.

During this thirty years I have seen the passing of many things that I regret, though I am lucky to have seen them, like the passing of the single and two-stage superchargers, and the banning of methanol and nitro-methane fuels in 1958. Although nitro-methane made your eyes water if you stood behind the exhaust pipes, there was something fascinating about an engine running on a nitro mixture for it moved it into a different world from the engines in our normal cars. Then there was the totally enveloping bodywork, like the W196 Mercedes-Benz, the B-series Connaught and the Vanwall and Maserati experiments, all of which stopped in 1958 when officialdom saw the fully enclosed Copper-Climax weaving up the straight at Reims because the aerodynamics were all wrong. A pity, for there were some interesting fully-streamlined projects in the pipe-line for use on high-speed circuits. The advent of aerofoils was another enjoyable land-mark and especially the driver-controlled movable aerofoils, while even better were the fully automatic ones which 'feathered' down the straights, went to maximum drag under braking, and optimum down-force for cornering. Anyone who saw Jim Hall's Chaparral 2F being driven correctly by Phil Hill and Mike Spence must have realised what a fascinating world we were moving into in Formula 1 when the designers cottoned on to what Jim Hall was doing.

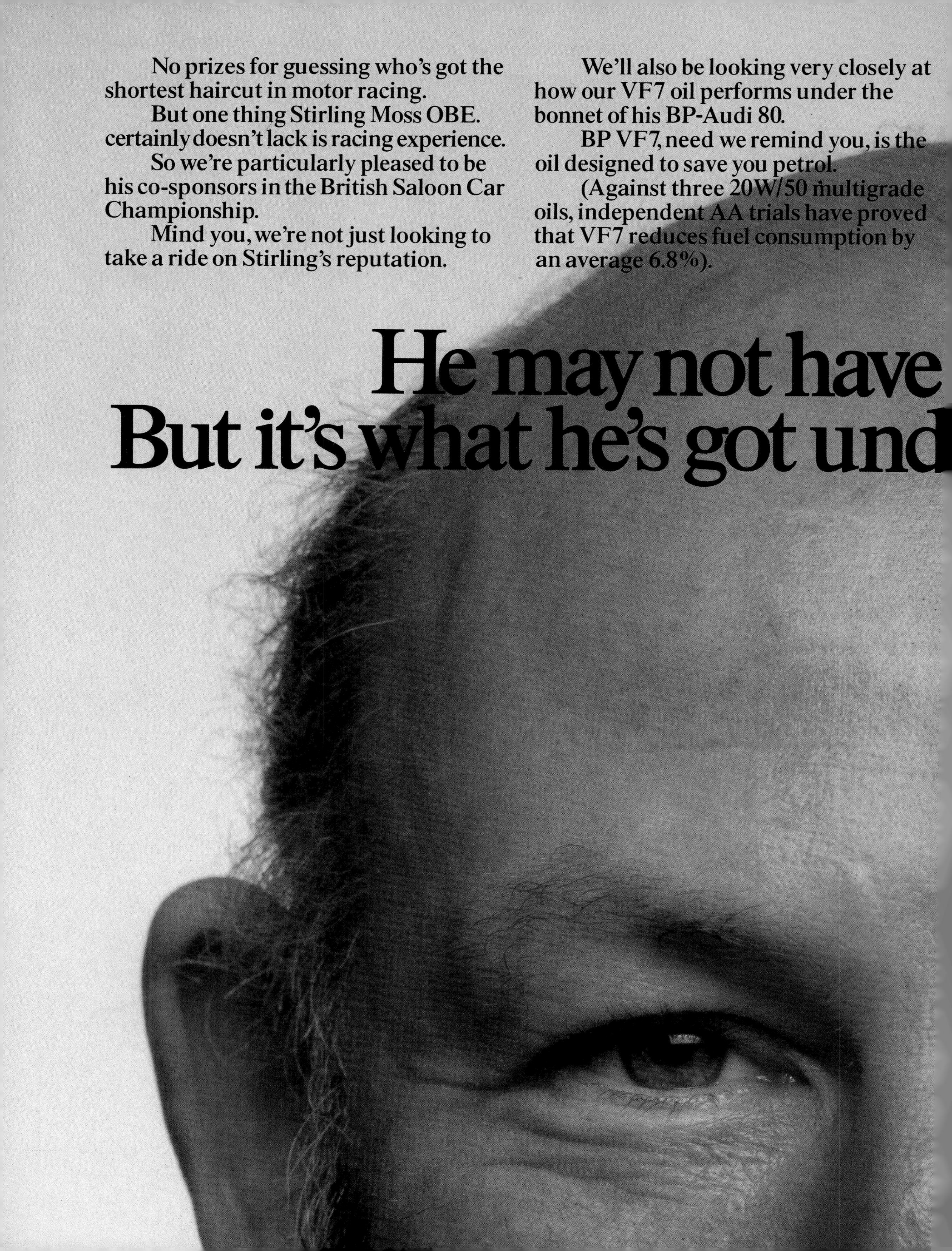
No prizes for guessing who's got the shortest haircut in motor racing.
But one thing Stirling Moss OBE. certainly doesn't lack is racing experience.
So we're particularly pleased to be his co-sponsors in the British Saloon Car Championship.
Mind you, we're not just looking to take a ride on Stirling's reputation.
We'll also be looking very closely at how our VF7 oil performs under the bonnet of his BP-Audi 80.
BP VF7, need we remind you, is the oil designed to save you petrol.
(Against three 20W/50 multigrade oils, independent AA trials have proved that VF7 reduces fuel consumption by an average 6.8%).
He may not have
But it's what he's got und

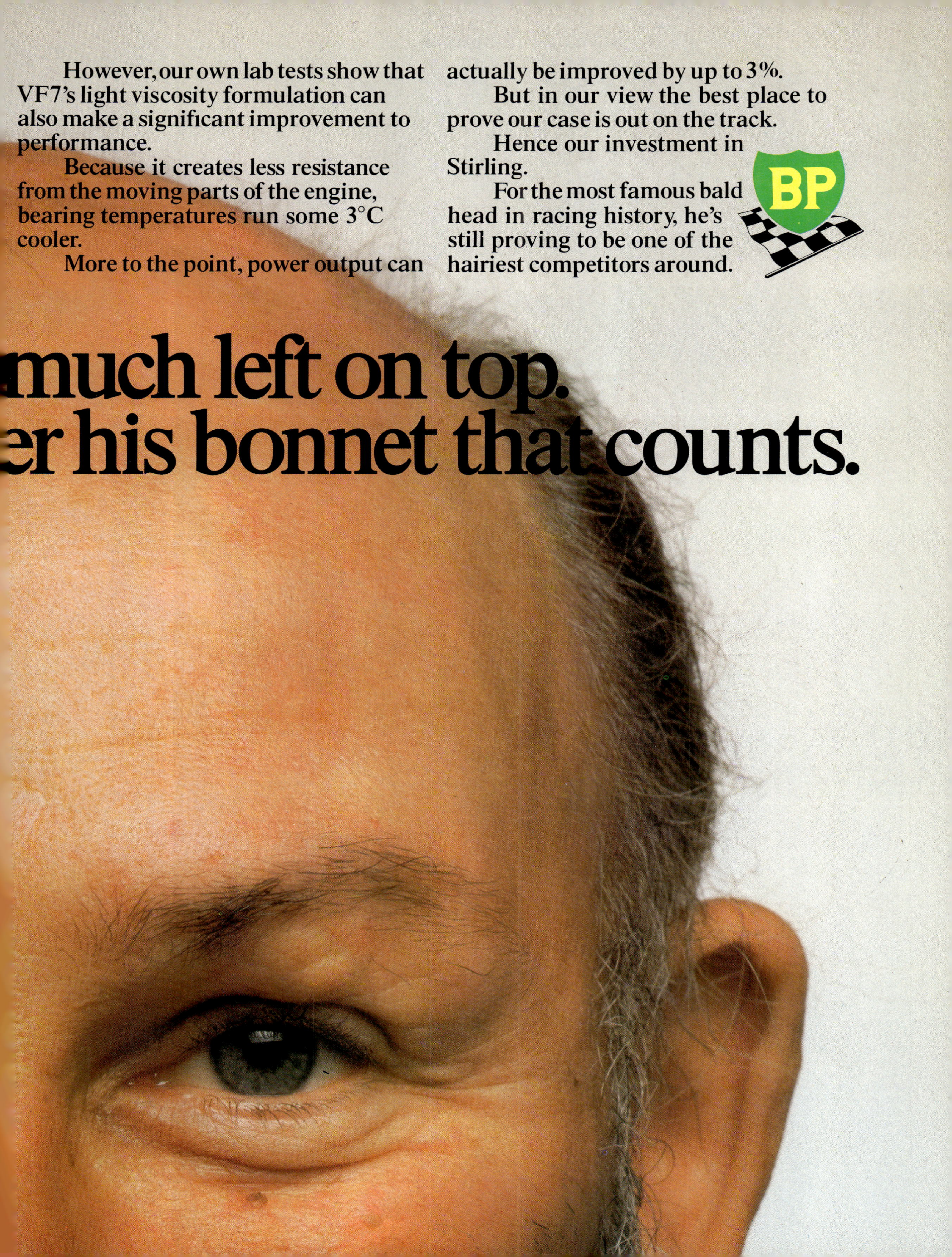
However, our own lab tests show that VF7's light viscosity formulation can also make a significant improvement to performance.
Because it creates less resistance from the moving parts of the engine, bearing temperatures run some 3°C cooler.
More to the point, power output can actually be improved by up to 3%.
But in our view the best place to prove our case is out on the track.
Hence our investment in Stirling.
For the most famous bald head in racing history, he's still proving to be one of the hairiest competitors around.
BP
much left on top.
er his bonnet that counts.

The current 3-litre Formula has been in force since 1966 but Jack Brabham's championship winning BT20 of that year would not have been eligible to take part in races against the 1981 Brabham BT49C of Nelson Piquet.

Alas, officialdom saw some breakages on Brabhams, and accidents to Lotus, before their very eyes and banned movable aerofoils instantly.

In the overall scene a major change that has come about has been the formation of multi-national teams in addition to the National ones. At one time Grand Prix teams were strictly national and virtually represented their country, allied to a major motor manufacturer or a major engineering industry and cars were painted in national colours, red for Italy, white for Germany, blue for France and green for England. With the advent of world-wide air travel and a greater ease of moving about, big influences came upon the European scene from America, Argentina, Brazil, South Africa, Australia, New Zealand and Japan and we saw the formation of new teams and firms that had no fixed identity. They were truly multi-national with, for example, American money, English brains, South African and Japanese mechanics, Australian administration and Brazilian drivers, so what national colour could such a team take? The only thing to do was to take the nationality of the entrant, but this was a misnomer as he might be an American born in Paris and living in Switzerland. The problem was solved, or alleviated, with the introduction of advertising into Grand Prix racing, directly on the cars, drivers and teams, for this brought in multi-national advertising money, so the whole polyglot had no real identity and could take the colours of the sponsoring firm which invariably bore no connection to anything at all, except perhaps the ad-man's distorted vision of 'impact'.

Freedom to advertise on racing cars saw a really big change to the icing on the cake, but it did not alter the cake. With it came all the tinsel, the fairies, the pixies, the coloured lights, artificial snow and the razzmatazz, along with vulgar music and brash showmanship of the world of advertising. Just occasionally some good taste in advertising would appear, like that of Yardley, Martini, Gulf or ELF which kept one sane, but by and large, the advertising scene around Formula 1 has lost control. It comes and goes and usually that which comes in with the greatest noise disappears the soonest without a sound. It is an amusing after-dinner past-time to reflect on 'what ever happened to . . .' Take it all away and underneath we still have the good old solid plum cake of Grand Prix racing, the art of racing the motor car in its ultimate form. We had Ascari, Fangio, Moss, Stewart and we still have Villeneuve, Piquet and Jones, and we have always had Ferrari.

The circuits. Now there we have seen some changes for even those that are still in use after thirty years, such as Monza, Silverstone, Monaco and Zandvoort have been altered almost beyond recognition. One disease that we still suffer from, and always have suffered from, is the addition of 'chicanes' to slow the cars down. The concept of racing has always been to go faster than before, and it always will be, so there is a never-ending battle between those racing and those administrating to maintain some degree of compromise. Artificial 'chicanes' have sprouted at Monza, Silverstone and Zandvoort, while the rebuilt portion of Monaco is one big 'chicane', but at least we are still racing at these venues. Ove the years we have lost a lot of circuits but they have been replaced by others, and some of them, like the Osterreichring and Dijon-Prenois have more than made up for those we lost. Others, like Paul-Ricard, Jarama, Zolder, Hockenheimring are a mere shadow of those that have gone. For as long as I can recall people have been saying "don't you regret the passing of such-and-such circuit?" There is no point in regretting such things, time is ever changing, and I was sad to see the going of the Bremgarten circuit in Berne, the Montesilvano circuit at Pescara, the Spa-Francorchamps circuit in Belgium, the Nürburgring, Rouen-les-Essarts and all those smaller circuits like Naples, Bari, Siracuse, Lake Garda, Genoa, Bordeaux, Aix-les-Bains, Caen, Solitude just as I have been sad to see the passing of Mike Hawthorn, Jean Behra, Luigi Musso, Jim Clark, von Trips, Lorenzo Bandini, Jochen Rindt, Ronnie Peterson, and Patrick Depailler. I was also sad to see the passing of the Connaught team, of Mercedes-Benz, Lancia, BRM and so on. Time is always changing and you cannot stop it, but I am very happy that I have been able to see it all passing and to still be involved as deeply, some thirty years or more later. I was not sad to see the passing of the Nivelles autodrome in Belgium for that was a bad nightmare that could have caught on and changed the Grand Prix scene. It was the classic example of an Autodrome constructed from scratch, what the Americans call a 'racing facility', in which more time, money and effort went into the amenities than on the actual circuit on which the cars raced. If there was ever a prime example of getting your priorities wrong the Nivelles Autodrome was it.

The changing face of life throughout Europe has outlawed the use of public roads for Grand Prix racing, as was inevitable if you looked at it dispassion-

ARE YOU WELL BRED FROM AN IMPRESSIVE STABLE? DO YOU LEAP INTO LIFE FIRST THING IN THE MORNING?

COAST OVER PROBLEMS WITHOUT A MURMUR? TAKE A LARGE BOOT SIZE?

HAVE A SILKEN FEEL AND A PLEASING EXTERIOR?

ENJOY THE CHALLENGE OF A LONG AND WINDING ROAD? ARE YOU ROUGH ON THE OPPOSITION AND SMOOTH ON YOUR FRIENDS?

DOES YOUR MECHANISM RESPOND TO THE FAINTEST TOUCH OF A FEMININE HAND?

ARE YOU SOBER, UPRIGHT, RESTRAINED AND HONEST?

AND COULD YOU WIN AN EXECUTIVE OF THE YEAR AWARD FOR TWO YEARS RUNNING?

VOTED BY 'WHAT CAR?' BEST EXECUTIVE SALOON FOR TWO YEARS RUNNING.

PEUGEOT 505

TAKE PRIDE IN PRECISION

For the address of your nearest dealer check Yellow Pages. Diplomatic, Nato and personal export inquiries Peugeot Park Lane 63/67 Park Lane, London W1Y 3TE. Tel: 01-499 5533.

UNIPART The answer is yes. Now what's the question?

ately, so that artificial autodromes were the only hope of survival for an activity that is noisy and anti-social to the majority of people if it happens to be on their doorstep. Television coverage has now brought Grand Prix racing into their living rooms in a peaceful and quiet manner, which they seem to enjoy, but it is no substitute for 'being there' amidst all the noise and confusion. One satisfaction that I have is having stood alongside an Alfa Romeo 158, a Mercedes-Benz W196, a V12 Maserati, a Honda V12, a BRM 16 cylinder, a Matra V12 and a turbocharged Ferrari and enjoyed the sounds from their exhaust pipe, untrammelled by silencers or baffles. The sounds have been thrilling and make the adrenalin flow; they have also made me go deaf, but it has been worth it.

Two other aspects which must be mentioned are the media and the politics, both being closely allied to each other. Thirty years ago both were there, but were unobtrusive. I can recall being at races where I was one of six English journalists, whereas now there can be sixty. I have stood on corners to watch the racing with perhaps one photographer, now there are so many photographers that there is hardly room for me to stand with them. A Press tribune for two dozen people, with a couple of telephones, used to be adequate, now you need space for 200 and 20 telephones and a dozen telex machines is not enough. The whole world has become hungry for news, and Formula 1 has become so big that it is news-worthy and that gives work for a great number of people, so we must not complain, but at times I do wonder if we have not lost control and give thought to a single central news agency and a single central photographic agency, but that would then lead to a single central racing team, and that would not be a good thing.

All this media cover is aimed at one thing, 'who is the winner'. Winning is still the name of the game, and always will be and the bigger the prize the more people prepared to have a go at winning it. And to win it you still need the best of everything, the best driver, the best car, the best designer, the best mechanics, the best management, the best research and development, the best equipment. The ingredients of that lovely succulent plum cake have not changed. Scrape away the icing and the tinsel, remove the fairy from the top and get down to basics and the basics were never more prevalent than when the starting signal is given and twenty-four Grand Prix drivers let in their clutches and floor their throttle pedals. And first across the line is the winner, providing he plays according to the rules.

At the moment Formula 1 is in a bit of a turmoil within its administration as various people vye with each other for control, either to impose their own ideas on the scene or to implement the ideas of their backers, or to prevent someone else having their way. It was ever thus. The main difference now is that with so many media people about things are said and heard and get reported where they should be ignored. Advertising brought with it 'big-business' ethics, or the lack of them, and its follow-up and cover-up activities and nowadays far too much attention is paid to what are, in effect, the rantings and ravings of small-time politicians and barrack-room lawyers. There were always such people behind the scenes, but thirty years ago the few journalists who were in Grand Prix racing were only interested in the racing and the cars, so they did not go poking about behind the scenes, especially if the end result was satisfactory. Who, for example, made the decision to equate supercharged 1½-litre cars with unsupercharged 4½-litre cars in 1947? Who decided over-night that Formula 2 would take over the World Championship Grand Prix races? Who decided to ban methanol fuel and restrict engines to pump fuel? Who imposed the 1½-litre Formula in 1961, against the wishes of most of the people taking part? Who banned movable aerofoils? These things were done by someone, they did not just happen. In 1980, sliding side-skirts were banned, but we all think we know who did that. The present crop of small-time politicians in the racing administration are quite good ones and know how to manipulate the media to their own ends, or to cover-up what is really going on, and the media fall for it hook, line and sinker. It all seems to be part of the game of the nineteen-eighties. There were similar games being played in the nineteen-fifties if you cared to look close enough.

Thirty years seems a long time, but on reflection it has passed very quickly, with very few dull moments and the fact that my adrenalin flows every time I hear a Grand Prix race start even now, would suggest that the basic name of the game has not changed. I was moved by the sight and sound of 158 Alfa Romeos, 4½-litre Ferraris, 4 CLT Maseratis and Lago-Talbots surging away from the start-line at Monza in 1951, just as I am moved by the sight and sound of turbo-Ferraris, turbo-Renaults, Cosworth-Williams, Brabhams, and V12 Alfa Romeos surging away from the start at Monza in 1981. I hope I shall still be able to say the same thing in the year 2011, but I have a nasty feeling that there may not be any Grand Prix racing by that time. Let us enjoy it while we can.

"I have stooc on corners to watch the racing with perhaps one photographer . . .
. . .now there are so many photographers there is hardly room for me to stand with them."

Mike Hailwood — Memories of the Legend

By Eoin S. Young

Mike Hailwood was one of those rare racing men whom other racing men regarded as great and that regard was more than merely for the best motorcycle racer in living memory. Perhaps ever. The news of his Ducati win on the Isle of Man in 1978 came through on the morning of the Spanish Grand Prix at Jarama and you could literally see the news flickering along the pit lane with drivers and mechanics wreathed in smiles as they heard that Mike had made it. You could lipread "Good old Mike" on a hundred mouths as the word was passed along over the noise of the Grand Prix engines.

Other men fortunate enough to know Mike Hailwood, knew him as an expansive personality, explosive fun to be with, totally competitive, very much a man's man. Yet the comment that keeps cropping up after his death is that nobody knew Mike completely . . . nobody knew every side of "Mike the Bike" because there were so many sides, so many facets. The fans, who could only marvel at him from the other side of the leathers or the Nomex, knew they had a real hero. Mike wasn't your 10-speed bike and Muesli breakfast sports star. He was the sort of knockabout chap enjoying a drink at the bar with his mates after the race.

Nobby Clark, the Rhodesian mechanic who worked closely with Mike for several seasons, recalled in 'Motorcycle Racing' how Mike was a rider that mechanics loved working for. "Mike never expected the impossible. He had ideas about what he wanted of a machine, but if it meant that the mechanics would be up all night working, he would say 'Oh, don't bother then – I'll manage.' The thing was though, because it was Mike, people were *prepared* to work all night. There was no suggestion of 'good night chaps, I'll see you in the morning.' "

I was privileged to know Mike before I realised how fortunate I was and that was probably fortunate for me because Mike was not greatly in favour of people who wished to be known as people who Knew Mike Hailwood. That's why this profile isn't a record of race wins. It's a memory of the Mike Hailwood I knew, and I'm sure there are hundreds of other people who prefer to enjoy their own private stories of Mike rather than remembering him as simply a man on a motorcycle. I rented one of two apartments he had bought in a high-rise apartment block not far from the roar of the M4 motorway at Heston on the flightpath to Heathrow. Mike was installed on the second floor and we were on the ninth. At the time I was working at McLaren Racing and Mike was racing bikes and cars. Phone calls more often than not signalled an impromptu party downstairs. There were other times when it was quieter with Chris Barber on the hi-fi and Mike on the clarinet. These talents were the private talents and the better to remember him by.

Mike retired from Honda with a golden handshake that amounted to a lot of money *not* to ride for anyone else, so he grabbed the opportunity to switch over to cars and began the long hard slog on four wheels. He never enjoyed that same magical winning streak that made him a legend twice over on two wheels. The fluid style and the magical balance that won him a string of TT victories and World Championships, simply didn't translate into cars.

Hailwood's talent on two wheels was something God gave out sparingly as I'm sure earlier and later two-wheel racing greats will agree. He switched from motorcycle racing with an urge to race cars at a time when it was regarded as something of a challenge. He had reached the point where there was nothing left to win and it was only news when he lost. Not a climate for a man like Mike to enjoy, so he opted for the gamble. Men like Nuvolari and Rosemeyer had done it. Geoff Duke had failed. John Surtees had succeeded. Agostini and Ceccotto would struggle against failure in Formula 2. It wasn't a logical progression.

Even Mike's fiercest fans would confess that Mike never really made it in cars, certainly never enjoyed that total command of his environment he had on bikes. There were times when he was good, better than those about him, and he won the Formula 2 Championship for John Surtees in 1972 but although he drove Formula 1 cars for Surtees too, John and Mike never 'clicked' on personality or performance. Perhaps it was wrong for either of them to have expected it. John was the motorcycle world champion who led Ferrari to win the car World Championship in 1964, but their personalities were poles apart. Mike was essentially a social person with his sport as an extension of his personality; John was sternly serious where Mike was always ready for a laugh. John regarded Mike's 'sport' as a business and was perhaps unable to always cope with Mike's cavalier attitude, much as he may have tried.

I can still think back to the fun of the incidents when he shared a rambling old house in Ditton Road, Surbiton, with Peter Revson, Tony Maggs and Chris Amon. They were all anxious to break into Formula 1 and they were christened 'The Ditton Road Fliers'. It was combined bachelordom taken to its wildest extreme. Like the wet weekend when Mike stayed at home and painted his third-floor room – with every wall a garishly different colour! There were his cowboy boots under the bed, stuffed with wads of every known currency after motorcycle race wins, Mike safe in his supposition that no burglar could possibly take an interest in his boots!

Mike never forgot his way around the Isle of Man TT course, a track so frightening in its raw speed over country lanes that many men can never learn it properly; some 'champions' prefer not to even try... Mike's first taste of the TT was in 1958 when he finished up with a 3rd, a 7th, a 12th and a 13th placing in each class he contested from 125cc to the 500cc 'Senior'. The Senior became Mike's goal. It was THE race. It lured him back again 20 years after his first race there.

In some ways Mike's crash in the German Grand Prix in 1974 at the Nürburgring was a mixed blessing. His McLaren landed badly off a bump and slammed into the guardrailing. He survived the crash but he never had the full use of his right leg for the subtle but vitally important swivelling between brake and accelerator. Mike and Pauline were married with a young daughter Michelle, and would later have a son David, but retirement held little attraction for Mike. He was restless. The family tried new countries, living for a time in South Africa and then in New Zealand, but he was still drawn back to Britain.

Then came the decision – born perhaps of boredom? – to have another go at the Isle of Man. Hailwood fans and friends around the world were amazed, delighted and appalled, generally in that order as the significance of Mike's announcement sank in. How could he possibly go back to the world's most dangerous racing circuit after all those years and expect to foot it with the younger stars? This aspect had either not occurred, or didn't bother Mike. It bothered him a little more as the day of the first race of his 'comeback' drew nearer. But he was equal to the occasion when it arrived. He won the 'Formula 1' race on a more or less production Ducati but failed in his bid for the Senior on a works Yamaha. In 1979 he was back again, tempting fate still further to achieve his goal and win the coveted Senior TT on a Suzuki. This time he succeeded. I think if he had been able to win the Senior the year before, he would have retired for good, as sensationally as he had returned.

John Wyer has always been regarded as a careful picker of talent for his long-distance cars over the years, and the fact that he picked Mike indicates that he saw more in Hailwood than he had been able to demonstrate in Formula 1 cars. Wyer demanded total obedience from his team and the rigid discipline he exerted probably resulted in most of his success. Mike was always Wyer's despair, a tearaway in his team, but a driver whose wry sense of humour could even appease the gimlet-eyed Wyer on occasion.

One year during the 1000 Kilometre race at the Nürburgring, Mike's Gulf-Mirage had come to a stop out on the circuit and he had made his way back to the pits on the back of a motorcycle. After the race, the car was brought in and the trouble diagnosed as some minor malfunction of, I think, a fuel pump. "But why didn't you open the bonnet and check about to see if you could find out what the problem was?" asked a slightly miffed Wyer. "Check around?" retorted Mike. "Check around? I don't even know how to open the bloody bonnet!"

He won the George Medal for bravery after rescuing Clay Regazzoni from his blazing BRM at Kyalami. Mike was almost embarrassed at the acclaim, saying that anyone else would have done the same thing. It was just that he had happened to be the first person on the scene. He couldn't accept that what he had done was anything out of the ordinary. Courage was simply a necessary part of his makeup and he wasn't aware that not everyone had the same measure...

'Mike the Bike' is a collection of memories for his friends all round the world, and every memory is a pleasant one. Which makes it all the harder to accept his tragic death together with little Michelle that wet afternoon last March when his Rover skidded under a turning lorry. To have survived many a tumble on two wheels and four on race tracks internationally and then be claimed on a dual carriageway close to his home, is almost impossible to accept. But Mike is succeeded by his legend, a legend that will be embellished in the re-telling wherever motor sporting people gather for a drink and the conversation gets around to whatever happened to the 'real characters' in racing. Because Mike was one.

Grand Prix Statistics

by John Taylor

In an effort to equate driver performances over the 32 years of the Drivers World Championship, total points scored have been divided by the number of races started by every driver who scored 20 or more points. This system is quite simple but has some flaws. It tends to include some freak averages like Luigi Fagioli's whilst excluding such luminaries as Olivier Gendebien (average 1.286) and Eugenio Castellotti (average 1.393).

Not included in the survey, although it was a Championship round from 1950 to 1960, is the Indianapolis 500. The reason for this is that the race never had any bearing on the outcome of the Championship and the cars raced at Indy never bore much resemblance to Grand Prix cars. Only three drivers ever made the cross over whilst the race counted for the Championship. Alberto Ascari took part in the Indy classic in 1952 and both Troy Ruttman (France 1958) and Roger Ward (USA 1959) took part in a Grand Prix.

Also not included in the survey are starts in Formula 2 events which were run as a separate race within a Grand Prix. These starts are noted however in the starts column as a grand total in brackets.

In the columns covering 1st to 6th places no mention is made of shared drives as this would have complicated the chart and is reflected in the points scored anyway. In the 1956 Monaco event Fangio actually drove both 2nd and 4th place cars but only received 3 points for the shared 2nd place.

Where drivers were officially placed in scoring positions but were awarded no points due to an infringement of the rules the placing is still included in the relevant column. Thus Moss and Trintignant both show a 3rd place from Argentina in 1960 for which they received no points, shared drives being outlawed from the end of 1958. Where drivers were completely disqualified from the results after an event no placing is recorded, only the start.

Fastest laps are as the official results although these are often not too reliable. The only time official fastest lap is not used is for Monaco 1980 when it is generally considered that Reutemann did fastest lap and not Patrese as the results state.

Position	Name	Nationality	Starts	Points	1st	2nd	3rd	4th	5th	6th	Pole	F. Lap	Points Average
1	Juan Manuel Fangio	RA	51	$277\frac{9}{14}$	24	9	1	6	–	–	28	23	5·444
2	Luigi Fagioli	I	7	32	1	4	1	–	–	–	–	–	4·571
3	Alberto Ascari	I	31	$140\frac{1}{7}$	13	4	–	2	1	1	14	12	4·521
4	Giuseppe Farina	I	33	127⅓	5	9	6	3	2	1	5	6	3·859
5	Jim Clark	GB	72	274	25	1	6	4	3	1	33	28	3·806
6	Jackie Stewart	GB	99	360	27	11	5	6	5	3	17	15	3·636
7	José Froilan Gonzalez	RA	26	$77\frac{9}{14}$	2	7	6	2	1	–	4	6	2·986
8	Mike Hawthorn	GB	45	$127\frac{9}{14}$	3	9	6	7	2	3	4	6	2·837
9	Stirling Moss	GB	66	$186\frac{9}{14}$	16	5	3	3	2	1	16	20	2·828
10	Niki Lauda	A	113	292½	17	15	7	3	5	3	24	16	2·588
11	Piero Taruffi	I	18	41	1	3	1	2	2	1	–	1	2·278
12	Jody Scheckter	ZA	112	251	10	14	9	9	7	4	3	6	2·241
13	Denny Hulme	NZ	112	248	8	9	16	11	8	9	1	9	2·214
14	Nelson Piquet	BR	49	107	6	3	4	4	3	1	6	3	2·184
15	Jack Brabham	AUS	123(126)	261	14	10	7	13	5	7	13	11	2·122
16	Carlos Reutemann	RA	144	304	12	12	20	11	11	7	6	6	2·111
17	Alan Jones	AUS	96	202	12	7	5	7	5	1	6	13	2·104
18	Phil Hill	USA	47(48)	98	3	5	8	2	–	3	6	6	2·085
19	Wolfgang von Trips	D	27	56	2	2	2	3	4	3	1	–	2·074
20	Richie Ginther	USA	52	107	1	8	5	6	4	4	–	3	2·058
21	Peter Revson	USA	30	61	2	2	4	3	3	–	1	–	2·033
22	Bruce McLaren	NZ	99(101)	196½	4	11	12	7	11	5	–	3	1·985
23	Tony Brooks	GB	38	75	6	2	2	1	3	–	3	3	1·974
24	Emerson Fittipaldi	BR	144	281	14	13	8	9	5	8	6	6	1·951
25	James Hunt	GB	92	179	10	6	7	7	2	3	14	8	1·946
26	François Cévert	F	46	89	1	10	2	2	2	2	–	2	1·935
27	Alain Prost	F	26	48	3	2	1	–	1	3	2	1	1·846
28	Luigi Musso	I	24	44	1	5	1	1	1	–	–	1	1·833
29	Jochen Rindt	A	60	109	6	3	4	6	1	1	10	3	1·817
30	Ronnie Peterson	S	123	206	10	10	6	5	7	4	14	9	1·675
31	Graham Hill	GB	175(176)	289	14	15	7	9	7	9	13	10	1·651
32	Jacques Laffite	F	108	177	6	8	12	4	6	3	7	5	1·638
33	John Surtees	GB	111	180	6	10	8	5	8	3	8	11	1·622
34	Clay Regazzoni	CH	132	212	5	13	10	8	9	7	5	15	1·606
35	Gilles Villeneuve	CDN	63	101	6	4	2	2	3	3	2	6	1·603
36	Jacky Ickx	B	114(116)	181	8	7	10	4	7	4	13	14	1·588
37	Luigi Villoresi	I	31	49	–	2	6	2	3	4	–	1	1·581
38	Dan Gurney	USA	86	133	4	8	7	2	5	5	3	6	1·547
39	Patrick Depailler	F	93	141	2	10	7	6	6	5	1	4	1·516
40	Peter Collins	GB	32	47	3	3	3	1	1	1	–	–	1·469
41	Mario Andretti	USA	125	176	12	2	4	7	7	5	17	10	1·408
42	Lorenzo Bandini	I	42	58	1	2	5	2	4	3	1	2	1·381
43	Pedro Rodriguez	MEX	54(55)	71	2	3	2	4	4	7	–	1	1·315
44	René Arnoux	F	48	57	2	4	1	2	2	1	9	7	1·188
45	Tony Maggs	RSR	25	26	–	2	1	1	2	3	–	–	1·040
46	Didier Pironi	F	60	62	1	1	5	3	6	6	2	3	1·033
47	Gunner Nilsson	S	31	31	1	–	3	1	3	1	–	1	1·000
48	Jean Behra	F	52	$51\frac{1}{7}$	–	2	7	2	4	6	–	1	0·984
49	Innes Ireland	GB	50	47	1	2	1	4	4	2	–	1	0·940
50	Jean-Pierre Beltoise	F	84(85)	77	1	3	4	3	10	5	–	4	0·917
51	John Watson	GB	122	108	2	4	6	8	5	8	2	3	0·885
52	Maurice Trintignant	F	82	72⅓	2	3	5	4	8	3	–	1	0·882
53	Chris Amon	NZ	96	83	–	3	8	4	7	7	5	3	0·865
54	Carlos Pace	BR	72	58	1	3	2	5	3	2	1	5	0·806
55	Mike Spence	GB	36	27	–	–	1	3	6	2	–	–	0·750
56	Piers Courage	GB	27(28)	20	–	2	–	1	2	1	–	–	0·741
57	Jochen Mass	D	96	71	1	1	6	7	4	9	–	2	0·740
58	Elio de Angelis	I	41	30	–	1	–	4	4	4	–	–	0·731
59	Jo Siffert	CH	96	68	2	2	2	7	2	5	2	4	0·708
60	Harry Schell	USA	55	32	–	1	1	3	7	4	–	–	0·582

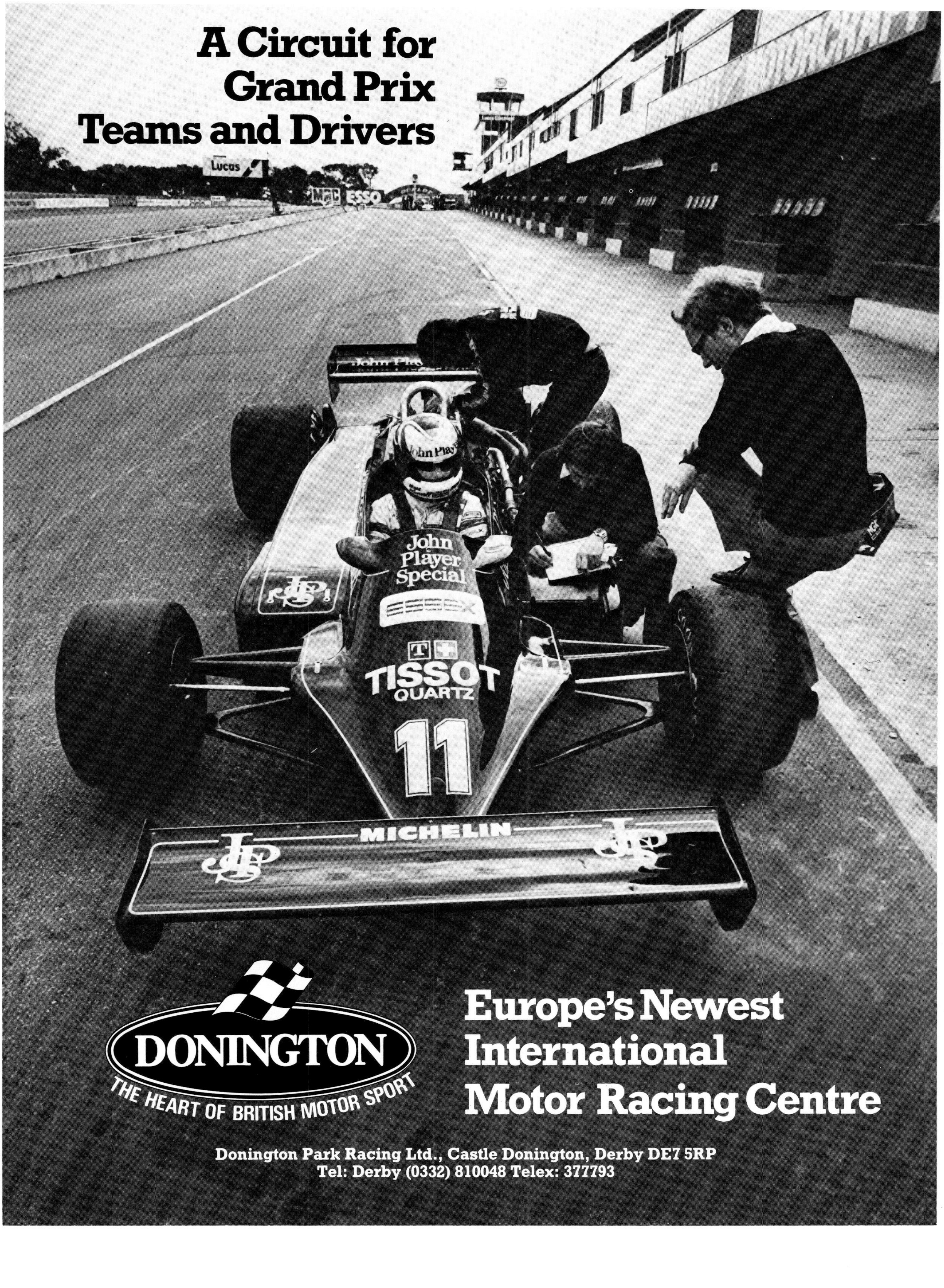
A Circuit for Grand Prix Teams and Drivers
Lucas
ESSO
MOTORCRAFT
John Player Special
ESSEX
TISSOT QUARTZ
11
MICHELIN
JPS
DONINGTON
THE HEART OF BRITISH MOTOR SPORT
Europe's Newest International Motor Racing Centre
Donington Park Racing Ltd., Castle Donington, Derby DE7 5RP
Tel: Derby (0332) 810048 Telex: 377793

Carlos Reutemann

Carlos Reutemann announced his retirement as we closed for press. It has been impossible to prepare a suitable feature on the Argentinian but we offer this collection of photographs as a tribute.

After several seasons of racing saloons and sports cars in Argentina, Carlos came to Europe in 1970 with a Formula 2 team sponsored by the Automovil Club Argentino. He is pictured at Brands Hatch in 1971 with his Brabham BT36 before going on to finish second in the European Championship the following year *(left)*.

In 1972, he caused a sensation by taking pole position, driving a Brabham BT34, for his first Grand Prix, the Argentine.

Carlos was to continue with Brabham for six seasons, driving the BT37 in the 1972 British Grand Prix *(right)*.

He won his first Grand Prix in South Africa with the BT44 in 1974 and went on to win in Austria *(left)* and at Watkins Glen .

Reutemann is pictured *(right)* leading Niki Lauda in Austria and he joined the Austrian driver at Ferrari in 1977 before enjoying a successful season the following year with four victories. In 1979, he moved to Lotus for one year and, finally, joined Williams for two seasons, losing the 1981 championship by one point.

1981 Formula 1 Drivers' Statistics

During 1981, 41 drivers from 17 countries participated in the season's 16 Formula 1 races including the non-championship South African Grand Prix. They were seen in 17 different makes of car powered by seven makes of engine.

Alan Jones, Riccardo Patrese, Nelson Piquet, Carlos Reutemann and John Watson took part in all 16 races.

In 1980, 43 drivers from 18 countries participated in the season's 15 Formula 1 races in 15 different makes of car using four makes of engine.

Driver	Nat	Date of Birth	Car	United States West	Brazil	Argentina	San Marino	Belgium	Monaco	Spain	France	Great Britain	Germany	Austria	Holland	Italy	Canada	Las Vegas	World Championship Points	No. of Grands Prix started	Placings in GPs 1st	2nd	3rd	No. of Grand Prix pole positions	South Africa
Michele Alboreto	I	23/12/56	Tyrrell-Cosworth	–	–	–	R	12	R	NQ	16	R	NQ	R	9*	R	11	NC	0	10	–	–	–	–	–
Mario Andretti	USA	28/2/40	Alfa Romeo	4	R	8	R	10	R	8	8	R	9	R	R	R	7	R	3	125	12	2	4	17	–
Elio de Angelis	I	26/3/58	Lotus-Cosworth	R	5	6	W	5	R	5	6	R	7	7	5	4	6	R	14	40	–	1	–	–	3
René Arnoux	F	4/7/48	Renault	8	R	5	8	NQ	R	9	4	9*	13	2	R	R	R	R	11	48	2	4	1	8	–
Slim Borgudd	S	25/11/46	ATS-Cosworth	–	–	–	13	NQ	NPQ	NQ	NQ	6	R	R	10	R	R	NQ	1	7	–	–	–	–	–
Andrea de Cesaris	I	31/5/59	McLaren-Cosworth	R	R	11	6	R	R	R	11	R	R	8	DNS	7*	R	12	1	16	–	–	–	–	R
Eddie Cheever	USA	10/1/58	Tyrrell-Cosworth	5	NC	R	R	6	5	NC	13	4	5	NQ	R	R	R	R	10	25	–	–	–	–	7
Kevin Cogan	USA	31/3/56	Tyrrell-Cosworth	NQ	–	–	–	–	–	–	–	–	–	–	–	–	–	–	0	0	–	–	–	–	–
Derek Daly	IRL	11/3/53	March-Cosworth	NQ	NQ	NQ	NQ	NQ	NPQ	16	R	7	R	11	R	R	8	NQ	0	44	–	–	–	–	11
Giorgio Francia	I	8/11/47	Osella-Cosworth	–	–	–	–	–	–	NQ	–	–	–	–	–	–	–	–	0	0	–	–	–	–	–
Beppe Gabbiani	I	2/1/57	Osella-Cosworth	R	NQ	NQ	R	R	NQ	NQ	NQ	NQ	NQ	NQ	NQ	NQ	NQ	NQ	0	3	–	–	–	–	–
Piercarlo Ghinzani	I	16/1/52	Osella-Cosworth	–	–	–	–	13	NQ	–	–	–	–	–	–	–	–	–	0	0	–	–	–	–	–
Bruno Giacomelli	I	10/9/52	Alfa Romeo	R	NC	10*	R	9	R	10	15	R	15	R	R	8	4	3	7	39	–	–	1	1	–
Miguel-Angel Guerra	RA	31/8/53	Osella-Cosworth	NQ	NQ	NQ	R	–	–	–	–	–	–	–	–	–	–	–	0	1	–	–	–	–	–
Brian Henton	GB	19/9/46	Toleman-Hart	–	–	–	NQ	NQ	NPQ	NQ	NQ	NQ	NQ	NQ	NQ	10	NQ	NQ	0	5	–	–	–	–	–
Jean-Pierre Jabouille	F	1/10/42	Talbot Ligier-Matra	–	W	NQ	NC	R	NQ	R	–	–	–	–	–	–	–	–	0	49	2	–	–	7	–
Jean-Pierre Jarier	F	10/7/46	Talbot Ligier-Matra Osella-Cosworth	R	7	–	–	–	–	–	–	8	8	10	R	9	R	R	0	105	–	–	3	3	–
Alan Jones	AUS	2/11/46	Williams-Cosworth	1	2	4	12	R	2	7	17	R	11	4	3	2	R	1	46	86	12	7	5	6	R
Jacques Laffite	F	21/11/43	Talbot Ligier-Matra	R	6	R	R	2	3	2	R	3	3	1	R	R	1	6	44	108	6	8	13	7	–
Jan Lammers	NL	2/6/56	ATS-Cosworth	R	NQ	12	NQ	–	–	–	–	–	–	–	–	–	–	–	0	20	–	–	–	–	R
Geoff Lees	GB	1/5/51	Theodore-Cosworth	–	–	–	–	–	–	–	–	–	–	–	–	–	–	–	0	3	–	–	–	–	R
Nigel Mansell	GB	8/8/54	Lotus-Cosworth	R	11	R	W	3	R	6	7	NQ	R	R	R	R	R	4	8	16	–	–	1	–	10
Riccardo Patrese	I	17/4/54	Arrows-Cosworth	R	3	7	2	R	R	R	14	10*	R	R	R	R	R	11	10	65	–	3	1	1	6
Nelson Piquet†	BR	17/8/52	Brabham-Cosworth	3	12	1	1	R	R	R	3	R	1	3	2	6*	5	5	50	49	6	3	4	6	2
Didier Pironi	F	26/3/52	Ferrari	R	R	R	5	8	4	15	5	R	R	9	R	5	R	9	9	60	1	1	5	2	–
Alain Prost	F	24/2/55	Renault	R	R	3	R	R	R	R	1	R	2	R	1	1	R	2	43	26	3	2	1	2	–
Hector Rebaque	MEX	5/2/56	Brabham-Cosworth	R	R	R	4	R	NQ	R	9	5	4	R	4	R	R	R	11	41	–	–	–	–	–
Carlos Reutemann	RA	12/4/42	Williams-Cosworth	2	1	2	3	1	R	4	10	2	R	5	R	3	10	8	49	144	12	12	20	6	1
Keke Rosberg	SF	6/12/48	Fittipaldi-Cosworth	R	9	R	R	R	NQ	12	R	R	NQ	W	NQ	NQ	NQ	10	0	36	–	–	1	–	4
Eliseo Salazar	RCH	14/11/54	March-Cosworth Ensign-Cosworth	NQ	NQ	NQ	R	NQ	NPQ	14	R	NQ	NC	R	6	R	R	NC	1	9	–	–	–	–	R
Chico Serra	BR	3/2/57	Fittipaldi-Cosworth	7	R	R	NQ	R	NQ	11	DNS	NQ	NQ	W	NQ	NQ	NQ	NQ	0	5	–	–	–	–	9
Siegfried Stohr	I	10/10/53	Arrows-Cosworth	NQ	R	9	NQ	R	R	R	NQ	R	12	R	7	NQ	–	–	0	9	–	–	–	–	R
Marc Surer	CH	18/9/51	Ensign-Cosworth Theodore-Cosworth	R	4	R	9	11	6	–	12	11*	14*	R	8	NQ	9	R	4	23	–	–	–	–	R
Patrick Tambay	F	25/6/49	Theodore-Cosworth Talbot Ligier-Matra	6	10	R	11	NQ	7	13	R	R	R	R	R	R	R	R	1	35	–	–	–	–	–
Gilles Villeneuve	CDN	18/1/52	Ferrari	R	R	R	7	4	1	1	R	R	10	R	R	R	3	R	25	63	6	4	2	2	–
Jacques Villeneuve	CDN	4/11/55	Arrows-Cosworth	–	–	–	–	–	–	–	–	–	–	–	–	–	NQ	NQ	0	0	–	–	–	–	–
Emilio de Villota	E	26/7/46	Williams-Cosworth	–	–	–	–	–	–	W	–	–	–	–	–	–	–	–	0	2	–	–	–	–	–
Derek Warwick	GB	27/8/54	Toleman-Hart	–	–	–	NQ	NQ	NQ	NQ	NQ	NQ	NQ	NQ	NQ	NQ	NQ	R	0	1	–	–	–	–	–
John Watson	GB	4/5/46	McLaren-Cosworth	R	8	R	10	7	R	3	2	1	6	6	R	R	2	7	27	122	2	4	6	2	5
Desiré Wilson	ZA	26/11/53	Tyrrell-Cosworth	–	–	–	–	–	–	–	–	–	–	–	–	–	–	–	0	0	–	–	–	–	R
Ricardo Zunino	RA	13/4/49	Tyrrell-Cosworth Brabham-Cosworth	–	13	13	–	–	–	–	–	–	–	–	–	–	–	–	0	10	–	–	–	–	8

† Nelson Piquet used a Brabham-BMW during practice for the British Grand Prix.

* Retired but classified as a finisher. DNP = Did not practise.
DNS = Qualified, did not start.
NC = Running at finish, not classified. NQ = Did not qualify. R = Retired.
W = Entry withdrawn. NPQ = Did not qualify in pre practice.

As if we had only ourselves to beat.

In '81 Jimmy McRae's Opel Ascona narrowly beat Tony Pond's Chevette 2300 HSR to win the Rothman's RAC British Open Rally Championship.

Mind you, Tony wasn't too upset because Vauxhall won the Manufacturers' Championship. Just beating, you've guessed it, Opel.

What's more, Brian Wiggins drove off with the Group One, 1300cc class in his Astra 1300S. And Jimmy McRae clinched the Irish Tarmac Championship for the second year running.

An extraordinarily successful season for the Vauxhall-Opel dealer teams.

But hardly surprising with them all driving cars engineered by General Motors; sturdy cars, built to win in the toughest driving conditions as well as being a delight to drive.

Which you will find out for yourself when you go along to your Vauxhall-Opel dealer and take a test drive.

Then you'll know what it feels like to be part of a winning team.

VAUXHALL-OPEL GM

BACKED BY THE WORLDWIDE RESOURCES OF GENERAL MOTORS.

For the record

Regrettably, the chassis log book is rather sketchy in parts. The Editor's notes were stolen in Monza and we would like to express our sincere thanks to Denis Jenkinson, Giorgio Piola and the various designers and team managers who came to our aid and helped to ensure the publication of the following facts:

Alfa Romeo

Impossible to list the chassis used (with or without our notes!) since the same three identification plates were used at random throughout the season. Six 'C' specification cars were built in 1981 but the team reverted to 1980 'B' chassis from time to time. A 'C' chassis was modified to 'D' specification mid-season, the team returning to 'C' spec after two cars were badly damaged at Zandvoort. An 'E' specification was constructed but proved unsatisfactory and did not practise or race. A carbon fibre chassis was completed but was never used.

Arrows

No new cars in 1981. Raced modified 1980 A3 (2), (3), (5) and (6).

2 Spare car throughout season.

3 For Patrese in Kyalami, Long Beach, Rio and Buenos Aires. For Stohr in Hockenheim, Österreichring, Zandvoort, and Monza. For J. Villeneuve in Montreal and Las Vegas.

5 For Patrese in Imola, Zolder, Monaco, Jarama, Dijon, Silverstone, Hockenheim, Österreichring, Zandvoort, Monza, Montreal and Las Vegas.

6 For Stohr in Kyalami, Long Beach, Rio, Buenos Aires, Imola, Monaco, Zolder, Jarama and Silverstone.

ATS

Built new chassis D4 (05) and retained 1980 model (04).

04 Spare car in Kyalami, Long Beach, Rio and Buenos Aires.

05 For Lammers in Kyalami (new), Long Beach, Rio and Buenos Aires and Imola. Spare car in Zolder, Monaco, Jarama, Dijon and Silverstone.

Built new chassis HGS (1)

1 For Borgudd in Imola (new), Zolder, Monaco, Jarama, Dijon, Silverstone and Hockenheim. Spare car in Österreichring, Zandvoort, Monza, Montreal and Las Vegas.

2 New in Hockenheim as spare for Borgudd. For Borgudd in Österreichring, Zandvoort, Monza, Montreal and Las Vegas.

Brabham

Began season with modified 1980 cars, BT49 (7), (9) and (10).

7 B-spec for Rebaque in Kyalami.

9 C-spec spare car in Long Beach, Rio, Buenos Aires, Imola, Zolder, Monaco, Jarama, Dijon, Österreichring, Zandvoort, and Monza.

10 B-spec for Piquet in Kyalami. C-spec spare car for Rebaque in Monaco. Spare car in Silverstone and Hockenheim.

11 C-spec for Piquet in Long Beach (new), Rio, Buenos Aires, Imola, Zolder, Monaco, Jarama, Dijon and Silverstone.

12 C-spec for Rebaque in Long Beach (new), Rio, Buenos Aires, Imola, Zolder, Monaco, Jarama, Dijon, Silverstone, Hockenheim, Österreichring, Zandvoort, Monza, Montreal and Las Vegas.

13 Number not allocated.

14 C-spec for Piquet in Hockenheim (new), Österreichring, Zandvoort and Monza. Spare car in Montreal and Las Vegas.

15 C-spec for Piquet in Montreal (new) and Las Vegas.

Built BT50 for BMW 4-cylinder turbo.

1 Practised by Piquet at Silverstone.

Ensign

Updated 1980 chassis N180 (MN14) to B-spec and renumbered N180B (MN15).

15 For Surer in Kyalami, Long Beach, Rio, Buenos Aires, Imola, Zolder and Monaco. For Salazar in Jarama, Dijon, Silverstone, Hockenheim, Österreichring, Zandvoort, Monza, Montreal and Las Vegas.

12 Tub brought to Hockenheim. On its wheels by the Österreichring but never actually completed.

Ferrari

Modified 126C (049), first seen during practice for 1980 Italian Grand Prix. Built new chassis (050) and (051) for Long Beach.

049 For Pironi (but raced by Villeneuve) in Long Beach. Spare car in Rio and Buenos Aires. Spare car in Monaco and Monza (raced by Pironi). For Pironi in Montreal and Las Vegas.

050 Spare car in Long Beach (raced by Pironi), Jarama, and Dijon. For Pironi in Rio, Buenos Aires, Imola, Zolder, and Monaco. Uprated to B-spec for Villeneuve in Österreichring, Zandvoort and Montreal.

051 For Villeneuve in Long Beach, Rio and Buenos Aires. Spare car in Imola, Zolder and Monaco. Uprated to B-spec and used as spare car in Silverstone, Hockenheim. For Pironi in Österreichring and Zandvoort. For Villeneuve in Las Vegas.

052 For Villeneuve in Imola, Zolder, Monaco, Jarama, and Dijon. Spare car in Monza, Montreal (raced by Villeneuve) and Las Vegas.

053 For Pironi in Jarama (new), Dijon, Silverstone and Hockenheim. For Villeneuve in Monza.

054 For Villeneuve in Silverstone (new) and Hockenheim. For Pironi in Monza. Spare car in Österreichring and Zandvoort.

Fittipaldi

Began season with new chassis F8C (3) and 1980 chassis F8 (2).

2 For Serra in Kyalami. Spare car in Long Beach, Rio, Buenos Aires, Imola, Zolder, Monaco, Jarama, Dijon, Silverstone, Hockenheim, Zandvoort and Monza.

3 For Rosberg in Kyalami, Long Beach, Rio, Buenos Aires, Imola, Zolder, Monaco, Jarama, Dijon, Silverstone, Hockenheim, Zandvoort, Monza, Montreal and Las Vegas.

4 New monocoque taken to Kyalami. Built to C-spec for Serra at Long Beach, Rio, Buenos Aires, Imola, Zolder, Monaco, Jarama, Dijon, Silverstone, Hockenheim, Zandvoort, Monza, Montreal and Las Vegas.

Lotus

Began season with 1980 chassis 81 (1), (2) and (3).

1 Spare car in Kyalami. For Mansell in Zolder.

2 For Mansell in Kyalami, Long Beach, Rio and Buenos Aires. Spare car in Zolder, Monaco, Jarama and Dijon.

3 For de Angelis in Kyalami, Long Beach, Rio, Buenos Aires and Zolder.

Built new chassis 87 (1) and (2).

1 For Mansell in Monaco, Jarama and Dijon.

2 For de Angelis in Monaco, Jarama and Dijon. Spare car in Hockenheim, Österreichring, Zandvoort, Monza, Montreal and Las Vegas. (For Silverstone, see 88B(2).)

3 For de Angelis at Silverstone, Hockenheim, Österreichring, Zandvoort, Monza, Montreal and Las Vegas.

4 Converted from 88B (4) for Mansell in Hockenheim, Österreichring, Zandvoort and Monza.

5 Spare car in Monza (new). For Mansell in Montreal and Las Vegas.

Built twin chassis 88 (1) which was used by de Angelis in between protests during practice in Long Beach, Rio and Buenos Aires. Converted to B-spec.

1 Spare car in Silverstone.

2 Converted 87 (2) to 88B (2) for Mansell in Silverstone and converted back to 87 (2) for second practice.

4 For de Angelis in Silverstone but converted from 88B (4) to 87 (4) for Mansell in Hockenheim.

March

811 (RM01) built for testing during winter.

01 For Daly in Buenos Aires and Imola. Spare car in Zolder.

02 For Daly in Kyalami (new), Long Beach and Rio.

03 For Salazar in Kyalami (new), Long Beach, Rio, Buenos Aires and Imola.

04 For Salazar in Zolder (new) and Monaco. For Daly in Jarama and Dijon.

05 For Daly in Zolder and Monaco. Spare car in Jarama, Dijon, Silverstone, Hockenheim, Österreichring, Zandvoort, Monza, Montreal and Las Vegas.

06 For Daly in Silverstone, Hockenheim, Österreichring, Zandvoort, Monza, Montreal and Las Vegas.

McLaren

McLaren Racing merged with Project Four Racing at the end of 1980. New car known as Marlboro MP4 designed and produced over winter. Took 1980 McLarens M29C (2), (4) amd (5) to first race at Kyalami.

2 Spare car at Kyalami. Uprated to F-spec. Spare car in Long Beach and Rio. For Watson in Buenos Aires.

4 For Watson in Kyalami. Uprated to F-spec. Spare car in Long Beach. For Watson in Rio. For de Cesaris in Imola and Zolder. Spare car in Monaco and Jarama.

5 For de Cesaris in Kyalami. Uprated to F-spec. For de Cesaris in Long Beach, Rio and Buenos Aires.

MP4 (1) introduced at Long Beach

1 For Watson in Long Beach (practice only) and Buenos Aires. Spare car in Imola and Zolder. For de Cesaris in Monaco, Jarama, Dijon, Silverstone, Hockenheim, Österreichring, Zandvoort, Monza, Montreal and Las Vegas.

2 For Watson in Imola (new), Zolder, Monaco, Jarama, Dijon, Silverstone and Hockenheim. Spare car in Österreichring, Zandvoort, Monza, Montreal and Las Vegas.

3 Spare car in Dijon (new) and Silverstone. For Watson in Hockenheim (practice only), Österreichring, Zandvoort and Monza.

4 For Watson in Montreal (new) and Las Vegas.

Osella

Introduced new cars FA1B (3) and (4) for Long Beach. 1980 chassis FA1B (1) uprated and retained.

1 Spare car in Long Beach, Rio, Buenos Aires, Imola, Zolder, Monaco, Jarama, Dijon, Silverstone, Hockenheim, Österreichring, Zandvoort and Monza.

3 For Gabbiani in Long Beach (new), Rio, Buenos Aires, Imola, Zolder, Monaco, Jarama, Dijon, Silverstone, Hockenheim, Österreichring and Zandvoort.

4 For Guerra in Long Beach (new), Rio, Buenos Aires and Imola. For Ghinzani in Zolder and Monaco. For Francia in Jarama. Spare car in Dijon. For Jarier in Silverstone, Hockenheim, Österreichring and Zandvoort. For Gabbiani in Monza, Montreal and Las Vegas.

Introduced new model FA1C in Monza.

1 For Jarier in Monza (new), Montreal and Las Vegas.

Renault

Retained 1980 chassis RE22 and uprated to B-spec. Dismantled RE23 and RE25 and rebuilt using numbers RE26B and RE27B.

22B Spare car in Long Beach (raced by Prost), Rio (raced by Prost), Buenos Aires, Imola (raced by Prost) and Zolder (raced by Prost).

26B For Prost in Long Beach, Rio, Buenos Aires and Imola. Spare car in Zolder and Monaco.

27B For Arnoux in Long Beach, Rio, Buenos Aires and Imola. Spare car in Jarama.

Introduced new model RE30 in Zolder.

30 For Prost in Zolder (new). Destroyed in testing accident at Dijon.

31 For Arnoux in Zolder (new) and Monaco. Spare car in Dijon, Silverstone, Hockenheim and Österreichring.

32 For Prost in Monaco (new), Jarama, Dijon, Silverstone, Hockenheim, Österreichring. Spare car in Zandvoort, Monza, Montreal and Las Vegas.

33 For Arnoux in Jarama (new), Dijon, Silverstone, Hockenheim,

Österreichring, Zandvoort, Monza and Montreal.
34 For Prost in Zandvoort (new), Monza, Montreal and Las Vegas.
35 For Arnoux in Las Vegas (new).

Talbot-Ligier

Began season with new chassis to accept Matra V12 engines, JS17 (01), (02) and (03).
01 Spare car in Long Beach, Rio, Buenos Aires, Imola, Zolder and Monaco.
02 For Laffite in Long Beach (new), Rio, Buenos Aires, Imola, Zolder and Monaco. Spare car in Jarama, Dijon, Silverstone, Hockenheim, Österreichring, Zandvoort, Monza, Montreal and Las Vegas.
03 For Jabouille in Long Beach (new), for Jabouille and Jarier in Rio, for Jabouille in Buenos Aires, Imola, Zolder, Monaco and Jarama. For Tambay in Dijon, Silverstone, Hockenheim and Österreichring.
04 For Laffite in Jarama (new), Dijon, Silverstone, Hockenheim, Österreichring and Zandvoort.
05 For Tambay in Zandvoort and Monza (raced by Laffite). For Laffite in Montreal and Las Vegas.
06 For Laffite in Monza (new), for Tambay in Montreal and Las Vegas.

Theodore

A new team set up by Teddy Yip and using ex-Shadow equipment at beginning of season. Took Shadow DN12/1 (renumbered TR2) to Kyalami for Lees to race. Designed new car TR3 (TY 01).
01 For Tambay in Long Beach (new), Rio, Buenos Aires, Imola and Zolder. Spare car in Monaco, Jarama and Dijon. For Surer in Zandvoort, Monza, Montreal and Las Vegas.
02 For Tambay in Monaco (new) and Jarama. For Surer in Dijon. Spare car in Silverstone and Hockenheim. For Surer in Österreichring. Spare car in Monza, Montreal and Las Vegas.
03 For Surer in Silverstone (new) and Hockenheim.

Toleman

Joined Formula 1 in Imola with 1981 chassis TG181 (01) and (02).
01 For Warwick in Imola (new), and Monaco. Spare car in Silverstone. For Henton in Hockenheim and Österreichring. Spare car in Zandvoort and Monza.
02 For Henton in Imola (new), Monaco, Jarama, Dijon and Silverstone.
03 For Warwick in Jarama (new) and Dijon.
04 For Warwick in Silverstone, Hockenheim, Österreichring, Zandvoort, Monza, Montreal and Las Vegas.
05 For Henton in Zandvoort, Monza, Montreal and Las Vegas.

Tyrrell

Modified 1980 chassis 010 (1), (2/2) and (3/5).
1 For Wilson in Kyalami. For Cogan in Long Beach. For Zunino in Rio and Buenos Aires. For Alboreto in Imola, Zolder, Monaco, Jarama and Dijon.
2/2 Spare car in Kyalami (raced by Cheever), Long Beach, Rio (raced by Cheever), Buenos Aires (raced by Zunino), Imola, Zolder, Monaco, Jarama, Dijon, Silverstone (raced by Cheever), Hockenheim, Österreichring, Zandvoort, Monza, Montreal and Las Vegas.
3/5 For Cheever in Kyalami, Long Beach, Rio, Buenos Aires, Imola, Zolder, Monaco, Jarama and Dijon. For Alboreto in Silverstone, Hockenheim and Österreichring.
Introduced new model 011 (1) at Silverstone.
1 For Cheever in Silverstone, Hockenheim, Österreichring, and Zandvoort. For Alboreto in Monza, Montreal and Las Vegas.
2 For Alboreto in Zandvoort (new). For Cheever in Monza, Montreal and Las Vegas.

Williams

Took 1980 cars FW07B (8) and (9) plus new (10) to South Africa.
8 Spare car in Kyalami.
9 For Jones in Kyalami.
10 For Reutemann in Kyalami. Spare car in Long Beach, Rio and Buenos Aires.
Built new C-spec cars FW07C (11) and (12).
11 For Jones in Long Beach, Rio, Buenos Aires, Imola, and Zolder. Spare car in Dijon (raced by Jones). For Jones in Silverstone.
12 For Reutemann in Long Beach, Rio, Buenos Aires, Imola, Zolder, Monaco, Jarama, Dijon and Silverstone. Spare car in Montreal and Las Vegas.
13 Number not allocated.
14 Spare car in Imola (new), Zolder, Monaco, Jarama and Silverstone. For Reutemann in Hockenheim and Österreichring.
15 For Jones in Monaco (new), Jarama and Dijon. Spare car in Silverstone, Hockenheim (raced by Reutemann), Österreichring, Zandvoort, Monza, Montreal and Las Vegas.
16 Originally planned as D-spec chassis for six-wheeled project. For Jones in Hockenheim (new), Österreichring, Zandvoort, Monza, Montreal and Las Vegas.
17 For Reutemann in Zandvoort (new), Monza, Montreal and Las Vegas.

Leyland Vehicles

A winning combination – what

more could a sponsor ask for?

The Nuts and Bolts of '81

by Doug Nye

"You can do what you can get away with, and what you can get away with seems to depend upon who you are . . ." Peter Wright, the Lotus aerodynamicist and true originator of the modern ground-effects Grand Prix car, was commenting on the state of Formula 1 technology through 1981 . . .

That was the way the season developed, with certain engineers venturing far into the misty frontiers of inadequately-worded, essentially over-complex regulations; some having their wrists smacked for venturing too far, but others slipping equipment through and finding the governing body accepting the *fait accompli* with which they were confronted. By the time of the Dutch Grand Prix, FISA President Jean-Marie Balestre could state before a bemused press conference: "The cars are not illegal, but they do not conform to Formula 1 rules . . ."

It had all begun way back, as Formula 1 regulations became increasingly complex and all-embracing. The more regulations intruded, the more inexactitudes emerged in translation from the governing body's original French to the majority of the competing teams' English. Blatant disregard of the regulation stability rules by the governing body – who began attempting to alter major technical regulations by decree without notice rather than with logical discussion and adequate warning – created intense friction between FOCA and FISA. Matters came to a head at the 1980 Spanish Grand Prix which FISA declared a 'pirate race' and from which major-manufacturer teams like Ferrari (representing Fiat) and Renault and Alfa Romeo withdrew in order to protect their parent industry's wide-ranging relationships with the FIA.

Mr Ferrari began speaking of his own company, plus Renault and Alfa Romeo, as the *Grande Costruttori*

> **"You can do what you can get away with, and what you can get away with seems to depend upon who you are . . ."**
> **PETER WRIGHT**

– 'The Great Constructors' – while referring disparagingly to the proprietary-engine teams as mere *Assemblatori* – more or less, 'The Kit-Builders'. This dichotomy provided the basis of the FISA/FOCA dispute of the winter months preceding this past season. Most *Grande Costruttori* could not afford to be at odds with the FIA through FISA – the subsidiary body to which the FIA had delegated control of motor sport. Most *Assemblatori* saw their future with FOCA, and that future seemed distinctly threatened by what FISA was proposing . . .

So why should a ban on sliding skirts and other changes, such as the increase in minimum weight, appear such a threat? In essence it was attacking the whole basis of the Cosworth-engined brigade's competitiveness. They were outgunned for sheer power by the expensive turbocharged engines long-raced by Renault and under test for Ferrari and Alfa Romeo, and had compensated by their greater chassis expertise, especially in their appreciation of aerodynamic downloading and how it could be harnessed to improve car performance. Through 1980 the sliding-skirted ground-effects cars from Williams, Brabham and Ligier had proved intensely competitive with the aerodynamically less-effective but powerful Renaults while Ferrari – with their wealth of engine experience – would clearly pose a supreme threat, but their chassis engineering in general and their grasp of aerodynamic effect in particular had for years been highly suspect.

Now Ferrari especially had been pressing for a sliding skirt ban, and through their 1979 World Champion driver Jody Scheckter had orchestrated apparent driver opposition to this system which was vital to enhance ground-effect loadings.

The theory seemed to be that if the *Assemblatori* lost their sliding skirts their chassis power would be hamstrung. Their ageing Cosworth V8 engines could never match turbo power. On the *Grande Costruttori* side turbo horsepower was there to play with, they would have the power to pull big conventional nose and tail wings through the air, to harness the big wings' download and never mind their drag; what's another 50hp between turbocharged friends? The Cosworth brigade, near the ragged edge on power output, could never afford to absorb precious horsepower through similar big-wing drag. So a ban on sliding skirts would close the chassis performance gap quite dramatically, and an increase in minimum weight – from a figure which the hefty Renaults and Ferraris had never been able to approach – would further handicap the Cosworth brigade, to the *Grande Costruttori*'s advantage. Added weight is lap time lost; ballast lengthens acceleration and braking times. The bolt-on weights added to Williams and Brabham chassis for example would rest in a mechanic's hand as tangible evidence of chunks of time given to the overweight opposition . . .

But all that the winter of discontent achieved for FOCA's *Assemblatori* was Goodyear's withdrawal from the scene and much development time wasted on skirted cars. Yet it's a measure of their engineers' deep understanding of their machines that at Long Beach the new 6cm clearance cars from Williams finished 1-2, and at Rio repeated that result, and Brabham were right there too . . .

But while most teams had taken a simple view of the new regulations, Gordon Murray of Brabham had looked hard at the letter of the law. His soft air-spring lowering suspension for the Brabham BT49C allowed it to assume the required 6cm ride height at very low speed and when stationary in the pit-lane, but as speed increased so aerodynamic download would crush the car down much closer to the road surface where its ground-effect underbodies could approach sliding-skirt efficiencies.

A similar ideal was approached from a different direction by Lotus with their allegedly 'twin-chassis' Type 88, but before it could demonstrate its actual capabilities it was banned – while the Brabham suspension system (despite most bitter protest) was accepted.

No serious Formula 1 team can afford to let its rivals move far ahead and while the Brabham system made its (unsuccessful) debut in practice at Long Beach, by Brazil Williams had their own version under development while giving notice that they would protest if Brabham ran lowered in BA. But FISA turned a blind eye to all protests, except those directed at the Lotus 88, and the Brabhams dominated in Argentina as what Gordon Murray vociferously protested they had always been – as totally legal Formula 1 cars . . .

Imola was the most contentious Grand Prix yet as all teams appeared with some form of lowering suspension system to retrieve sliding-skirt style ground-effect, and then at Zolder driver-switched lowering and jacking systems – as distinct from those in which soft springs naturally returned the chassis to a legal ride height as speed and download decreased – became tacitly accepted, since the scrutineers turned to FISA and explained that this silly regulation was impossible to police. Later in the year the 6cm ground clearance regulation was no longer worded to apply "at any moment when the car is in motion" which in

> **"If you excite any system at its natural frequency it just becomes more and more excited until it goes out of control . . ."**
> **PATRICK HEAD**

essence had given it practical racing significance. Now it had been clarified to warn merely that all cars should have a 6cm ground clearance *at the point of measurement* in the pit lane! Out on circuit anything goes . . . It takes a fleet-footed scrutineer to measure the ground clearance of a 180mph motor car.

But the effect of such farcical rulings was far from funny. The true clearance cars of the early-season races had carried 'rigid' brief side skirts to manage underbody airflow as best they could with a nominally 6cm gap. Then the lowering suspension ploy appeared and fixed skirts dropped closer to the road. Since the old sliding skirt with its ceramic running skids was now illegal, underbody airflow – and therefore downloading – could no longer be adequately controlled as the cars rose and fell on their suspension. What was needed was a fixed skirt system

The Williams FWO7C-Cosworth DFV in French Grand Prix specification *(above)*.
The beginning of the end for the success of the 6cm rule. Nelson Piquet demonstrates the effect of aerodynamic download on his BT49C in Brazil, the car riding high at slow speeds but dropping closer to the track when motoring quickly *(right)*.
Gordon Murray has his cake and eats it... *(far right)*.

Photo: David Winter

Ikebana. The Japanese art of flower arranging.
HONDA PRELUDE 2 + 2. FOR THE NAMI

Honda. The Japanese art of car making.
HONDA
Made with pride, driven with pride.
AND ADDRESS OF YOUR NEAREST HONDA DEALER CONTACT HONDA (UK) LIMITED, POWER ROAD, CHISWICK, LONDON W4 5YT.

which would react to suspension movement to some degree, and which would not contact the road surface self-destructively. The most logical method to achieve this survival was to limit suspension movement, while some form of skirt flexion would take up what movement inevitably occurred as the car bounced from bump to bump.

When the Brabhams dominated in Buenos Aires they ran 3mm thick plastic underskirts with a thicker block of the same material on the bottom edge for an added degree of abrade resistance. This set the other teams wittering and caused intense acrimony. Twin-material abrade resistant skirts were tried by some engineers, and hinged part-pliable part-hardened skirts appeared while arguments raged about what is 'rigid'. Eventually a skirt regulation clarification was issued which insisted upon the use of a single material throughout the 'rigidly attached' skirt which must be no more than 6cm deep and must have a uniform thickness of between 5mm and 6mm. This latter restriction prevented a lengthwise slot being machined along the skirt to form a hinge.

The favourite skirt emerged as a curtain of very floppy polyurethane which could roll in beneath the lowered car, its bottom edge actually riding clear of the road on the shallow cushion of air bleeding into the underbody low-pressure area from normal atmospheric pressure around the car. This thin air-cushion effect protected the skirt from damage against the road but to achieve a consistent gap and to balance air-bleed against optimum aerodynamic download became a tricky problem which few mastered.

Suspension movement had to be minimised – if 'the gap' should gape then download would be lost, fine adjustment and fine balance became vital. Now stiff suspensions were required not merely to withstand the high downloadings of a ground-effect car, but actually to optimise those downloadings in cars robbed of sliding skirts . . . The new regulations had spiralled in on themselves and produced the most uncomfortable Grand Prix cars in modern history.

To all this technical drama the season added tyre problems, with Michelin keeping Formula 1 running during Goodyear's defection by supplying a restricted tyre range to all teams in the early events before the Akron giant, plus Pirelli plus Avon returned to the fray. Early suspicion among the *Assemblatori* that Michelin could dictate the course of the World Championship gave way to universal admiration for the French company's products and fair-minded conduct before Goodyear returned. Michelin benefitted too. In Brazil two leading British engineers were approached by a worried Michelin tyre chief after practice asking what their tyre problems had been? "None at all" they replied, "they're very fine tyres." The Michelin man looked puzzled, distressed; these engineers were holding out on him. "But you must have problems," he insisted "Ferrari and Renault – they always have problems . . ." Good tyres on fine chassis had worked perfectly – now the Continental chassis engineers had to look for other straws . . .

It was an absorbing season. How did the leading teams view it technically?

Patrick Head, of Williams, looks back on it like this: "We ran to the regulations as written in the first two or three races, then the Brabham success in Argentina really started the hydraulic suspension set-ups, and we all had to have them. Imola was an odd race with all the shouting and arm-waving, everyone tried lowering systems, some of which worked and some of which didn't. At Zolder everyone had their systems more or less sorted out, we discovered what was acceptable and

from then on we were back on a par with Brabham again . . .

"Then we started running the cars really low to achieve more ground-effect and we got into a very bouncy situation. What had happened was that any car has a natural frequency of bounce on its springs and tyres, and as our cars rebounded from the road so ground-effect diminished, then as the gap closed-up it increased, so you had this ground-effect input increasing and decreasing at the same frequency as the natural frequency of the car. If you excite any system at its natural frequency it just becomes more and more excited until it goes out of control.

"We had really made the wrong technical judgment when we started using inward-facing flexible skirt edges to improve the balance of the cars . . .

"At Dijon and Silverstone we were frankly off the pace, back on at Hockenheim and very quick in Austria but the cars were by this time so stiff that they were very uncomfortable for the drivers under full tanks.

"At Zolder . . . all our advantage had been taken from us, months of work had been wasted and driver-control as a short cut let everybody else catch up."
GORDON MURRAY

"Our mid-season misfire problem probably cost wins for Alan at Monaco and Hockenheim, and a probable third or fourth at Dijon for Carlos. We never really got to the root of the problem, but by changing components which had otherwise worked reliably since 1979 – like the fuel feed and collector pot – we managed the late season races without further trouble."

Gordon Murray was the engineer whose lead everyone else followed during the year. It was Brabham's most competitive season ever under the Ecclestone-Murray regime, but often an intensely irritating and frustrating one: "Really the whole season was overpowered by the regulations. We were forced to make continual development changes around them, rather than being able to follow a smooth and logical policy. The year broke-up into several phases . . .

"Initially we thought we would be running sliding skirts, so the 49C was drawn that way. We hadn't tested at all without skirts or with a nominal gap before the ban. After Kyalami we had to rush through a new car layout for the 6cm gap and that was pretty complicated but it *was* legal – I'm totally sure of that. We used soft air-springs which the aerodynamic load compressed as speed rose to give us our running height, and as speed dropped away into the pits so the car automatically rose up again. We tried it at Long Beach but it didn't work properly, so we took it off and lost the race. It was very difficult to get it working well in Brazil, Argentina and Imola, despite the Argentine win.

"We had a lead over the rest until Zolder, when it was all set free and driver-controlled systems were accepted. By that time we had got our automatic system working properly and at a stroke all our advantage had been taken from us, months of work had been wasted and driver-control as a short cut let everybody else catch up.

"Then there were stories that Ligier was running illegal skirts of different hardness material, with a non-abrade edge at the bottom, since Spain, and FISA just accepted it. This was a whole new ball-game and I felt we were being screwed . . .

"Zolder was the low point of our season. At a stroke everybody had caught us up and then Nelson was pushed off in the race . . .

"Then came the return of Goodyear tyres. Michelin were not prepared to service everybody much longer, and they weren't prepared to give us a contract, so Goodyear came back in. But they had been out of racing and had no experience of modern skirtless cars and that lost us Dijon and Silverstone. Nelson had been leading at Dijon but at the restart Goodyear had no tyres soft enough for the final sprint, and Michelin had a mountain of alternative compounds. Then we had the Silverstone tyre failure that put Nelson into the bank, and in Montreal we had a hard wet and a soft wet tyre available to us and both were far too hard for the conditions. Nelson said it was like driving on an ice rink.

"But generally it was our best-ever season. We looked like winners everywhere except the turbo circuits in terms of relative car performance, but made the wrong tyre choice in Brazil, there were the incidents at Zolder and Monaco and the blow-out at Silverstone. The only mechanical failure on Nelson's car was the blow-up with a mile to go at Monza."

The Talbot-Ligier team, meanwhile, proved the dark horse of the season after an indifferent start with their Georges Martin-designed Matra V12 engines – now basically fourteen-years old. "We started the

Driver operated ride-height control lever (left) on the Williams.

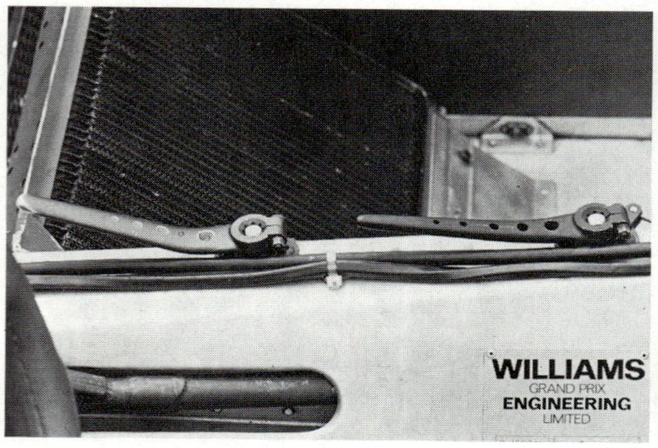

Renault's answer to the critics who suggested their turbo power was available at the turn of a screw....

season very bad, following the regulations as written while lots of the other works cars were not right . . . When we tried lowering suspension we tried two springs end-to-end on the same damper, the softer spring collapsing to give ride height, then recovering as the speed fell and the download come off. At Imola we have the hydro-pneumatic suspension like the Brabham and then came the problem of new skirts to work with this suspension. We tested literally dozens of different skirts and found the best was one material throughout, not two different materials . . .

"Matra provide our engines and for Spain they have a new one, 500rpm more. We used to race 12,300rpm and only test to 12,800rpm but from Spain we can race 12,800. It gives a bigger range for the driver to use, you can gear the car so that there are more revolutions ahead of you when you take the next one . . .

"Jacques likes Jarama and with the new suspension and the modified engine it seemed we could win races again – we were very 'appy, five cars together and all the same performance. Then we win in Austria after more testing and more learning, it was a win for the car. Montreal was super – a win for Jacques the driver, after Monza and Zandvoort where we thought we could win and didn't . . .

"At Zandvoort Jacques was amazed by what Carlos did to 'im. He told us afterwards 'Incredible Carlos should try to do it there, no way 'e could stay on the

" . . . in April, FISA decide the Brabham suspension is legal and we are 'orrified . . ."
MARIE-CLAUDE BEAUMONT

road. If I thought 'e would try it I would 'ave stop on the left of the road and watch 'im go by into the fence' – it was desperate points to lose, for both of us . . ."

During the season the Talbot-Ligier team used five chassis, badly damaging one of them, and Matra provided something between 15 and 20 engines, the team's Cosworth inventory in 1980 having totalled 17. The Ligier équipe has always been the best of the Continentals aerodynamically, using the *Institute des Arts et Metiers* wind tunnel at St Cyr as do Renault, with less evident result. "Is a great advantage being with Talbot for Talbot is with Peugeot, Citroen and Matra and if we 'ave a specialist problem we take it to them and in one of the companies they 'ave the man, and the equipment, to find us the answer . . ."

Renault is similarly well-equipped, in even greater depth, and after their 1980 successes were looking seriously towards this season as being their World Championship year. During the winter battles the FOCA-aligned British teams talked bitterly of the "Bloody Frogs", hinting darkly that Régie Renault and the French-dominated FISA were tampering with the regulations to bring France the World Championship she had never won. In fact, Renault Sports has been as embarrassed by FISA's misrule as most British teams . . .

Marie-Claude Beaumont: "We started the season with the long-wheelbase RE20B, developed from the 1980 RE20 to run without skirts while the new RE30 had been designed and was being built to the new regulations. We really would have been happy to continue with sliding skirts because we needed them to help put our power down, but after the affair in Spain last year Renault had to support the FIA position through FISA and so we accepted their decision through the winter . . .

"Then in the first races Brabham produced the

The 312B of Clay Regazzoni in the 1970 Dutch Grand Prix; the last truly integrated Ferrari chassis/engine design *(top left)*.
The performance of the carbon-fibre MP4 silenced critics in every respect *(top)*.
Riccardo Patresse and the Arrows team were on pole at Long Beach but their fortunes dipped as the tyre war developed *(above)*.
Photos: Nigel Snowdon
Alfa Romeo chopped and changed their suspension continually *(left)*.

parmalat
Marlboro
Marlboro
TEXACO
33

14

video specialists special offers!

Grand Prix 1978/79
1978 Grand Prix plus achievement of Ferrari.

Grand Prix 1976/77
James Hunt in '76, plus Niki Lauder in '77.

Grand Prix 1974/75
Award Winning '74 film, plus McLaren in '75 season.

Grand Prix 1972/73
Fittipaldi wins Monza, Jackie Stewart in '73.

Grand Prix 1970/71
'70 season, plus Jackie Stewart in '71.

Grand Prix of the Decade '70/79
Winner of World Championship of the Decade.

Nurburgring 1000Kms 1956
Monaco Grand Prix 1957
Moss, Fangio and the Aston Martin team.

Grand Prix Trio 1955
Grand Prix d'Europe 1958
Moss, Fangio, Hawthorn and Brooks.

A fast drive in the country
Le Mans, hosted by James Coburn.

If you're not winning...you're not trying
Colin Chapman and John Player Team Lotus.

The Fastest Man of Earth
Pursuit of Speed, narration by Robert Vaughan.

La Ronde Infernale
Le Mans 1969.

Mountain Legend
Targa Florio in Sicily.

Rouen Round 1962
Brands Hatch Beat 1964
Hill, Clark, Surtees, McLaren and Salvidori.

Goodwood Nine Hours 1955
Final Victory 1959
Moss, Chapman, Sobell and Aston Martin Team.

A Time of Change
Appointment of Penha
'76 Rally season, plus Rallye de Portugal.

Stages to Victory
1976 Castrol/Autosport Rally Championship.

Racecraft – Collision Course
Frank Gardner and Camaro, plus Daytona 500.

Avon Motor Tour of Britain '74/75
Avon Tour of Britain 1974 and 1975.

Scottish Rally 1973
72 Hours in Argyll – 1974
Scottish Rally 1973 plus Burma Rally '74.

A dash of the Irish Road Time
'71 Irish Road Race with Paddy Hopkirk and '73 Monte Carlo.

Inca Road Scene '72 – Take 7
Los Caminos del Inca Road Race.

The Flying Finns
The Golden Age of Rallying
Mikkola, Makinen, plus '58-'68 decade of rallying.

Please complete your order form in BLOCK CAPITALS and send your remittance to:
IPC VIDEO, Surrey House, Throwley Way, Sutton, Surrey.

Name ____________________
Address ____________________
____
Postcode ____________________
Phone ____________________

Description	How Many	Beta-max	VHS	Price each £ p	Total Price £ p
		Please tick			
Grand Prix 1978/79					
Grand Prix 1976/77					
Grand Prix 1974/75					
Grand Prix 1972/73					
Grand Prix 1970/71					
Grand Prix of Decade '70/79					
Nurburgring '56/Monaco '57					
G.P. Trio '55/G.P. d'Europe '58					
A Fast Drive in the Country					
If you're not winning...					
The Fastest Man on Earth					
La Ronde Infernale					
Mountain Legend					
Rouen '62/Brands Hatch '64					
Goodwood '55/Final Victory '59					
Time of Change/Penha					
Stages to Victory					
Racecraft/Collision Course					
Avon Tour of Britain '74/'75					
Scottish Rally '73/Argyll '74					
Dash of Irish/Road Time					
Inca Road/Scene '72-Take 7					
Flying Finns/Golden Age of Rallying					
Total no. of items				Total	

I enclose cheque/P.O. no. ____________________
Please cross /& Co/ and make payable to IPC BUSINESS PRESS.

M9.

ipc VIDEO

Hydrop-nermatique suspension. We were sure FISA would ban Brabham but in April they decided the Brabham suspension is legal and we are 'orrified. Now the cars could run low and run skirts and our RE30 was being built around a no-skirts design so we are in trouble.

"We are struggling to perfect new aerodynamics and the hydrop-nermatique at Zolder and poor René fails to qualify 'is car then is arrested, at least after 'e has not qualified! It was our low point in the season, but the RE30 did take a long time to become competitive.

"For Silverstone we introduced a new small rear wing in place of the big 'U'-wing we had always used before and from then to Monza the cars ran unchanged really, always fast, the most pole positions and two wins.

"At Silverstone we were running the engine flat-out for longer periods than anywhere else and full-charge on the engine burned the valves. It was a problem our engineer Bernard Dudot understood. In Austria there was the wrong tyre choice and then at Montreal for the first time we have a car under 600kg, Prost's RE30 with the carbon-fibre rear wing and new 'oneycomb sides, and a new injection system, not the electronic we are testing for '82.

"Michelin tyres were very good, very safe all season. In Holland for the first time we run TRX tyres on the front wheels as well as the back, but we were running big front brakes in 15-inch wheels so we had perhaps not the best aerodynamics. Then at Montreal we ran 13-inch front wheels for the first time with smaller brakes, it saved some weight too, but in the rain the front brakes on Alain's car ran too cold and 'e fall back . . ."

"It got to the point where you just didn't look forward to going to the races anymore . . ."
DAVE WASS

During the season the Renaults suddenly developed the speed off the startline they had traditionally lacked. How? "The RE30 engine is much better in fuel consumption so the cars start with less fuel and the car is lighter than ever before anyway, the chassis is good, the tyres good and the power goes down well . . ." It is also possible that they have used smaller low-inertia turbine wheels in their KKK turbochargers, these small-diameter lightweight wheels reacting much more rapidly to driver command and so minimising throttle lag. The smaller wheels have to spin faster to move the same volume of gas as a larger wheel, so have to endure higher temperatures. If you have the metallurgy you can make them survive, Renault and KKK certainly have it . . .

The RE30 obviously works well and chassis engineer Michel Tétu is able to tune it most adequately to various circuits, but the British opposition in particular finds Renault's high skirt gap, relatively high ground clearance and big wings rather surprising – power remains their main advantage and their engines have proved generally very reliable.

As have Ferrari's in mechanical terms although they have massacred their KKK turbochargers – after setting aside the pressure-wave mechanically-driven BB Comprex system early in the year. Ferrari stunned many observers by achieving competitiveness with their 1500cc turbo within six months of introduction, but none should under-estimate Maranello's understanding of the internal combustion engine, nor their resources. They had also had a good look at Renault's wrong-turns during Michelin testing . . . But historically Ferrari has regarded the engine as all-important and the chassis as an irritating minor necessity to carry wheels, fuel and the man. Possibly the last truly integrated Ferrari engine/chassis design was the beautiful 312B of 1970, and the inelegant 126C with its after-thought brackets adding weight and complication and its messy engine installation attracted little beyond satisfied smirks from the opposition. But engineers like Head, Murray and John Barnard of McLaren all warn: "If they ever put that engine in a halfway reasonable chassis we'll never see which way they've gone . . .". Mid-'81 saw Maranello take on Dr Harvey Postlethwaite to help them do just that for the coming year . . .

But Didier Pironi was explaining early in '81 how "people say it's our chassis that's at fault, but it's our aerodynamics" and certainly the Italian team's skirts seemed unduly vulnerable and they never came to grips with a hydro-pneumatic lowering system. At Zolder Villeneuve's front suspension jammed up, and stayed there throughout the race. A mid-season strengthening programme added even more weight, the team winning some sort of heavyweight prize at Hockenheim – a normal Ferrari weight being 640kg or thereabouts . . .

Barnard's largely carbon-fibre moulded monocoque McLaren MP4 design silenced its critics not only with John Watson's Silverstone victory but also with its resilience in a torrid series of accidents. But looking back on '81 John considers: "Dijon was our best race as far as I'm concerned because we set the car up just right and with minimal practice changes it was very quick. Silverstone was a sweetener, not expected but appreciated, though I was disappointed because in testing John had been able to do anything he liked with

Talbot-Ligier proved to be the dark horse of the season.
Photo: Diana Burnett

the car, and for the race we couldn't get it quite so well balanced.

"Having to run super-stiff suspension made us re-examine the whole package stiffness, we had some damper problems and then got into a bounce problem which proved quite major. We're the only Cosworth team contracted to Michelin and in some ways have suffered because of that. Our requirements are not the same as Ferrari or Renault, their big problem is sufficient traction, and that's not our's but that's the way tyre development goes. Sometimes by using different construction tyres we could minimise the bounce, we have much more downforce than Renault and certainly more than Ferrari, but they have much more power . . . We really have to think towards a turbo package for the future, partly in fact because turbocharged racing is so expensive, the investment so vast, that it must mean more stability in the regulations – it will be too expensive to keep ringing the changes . . ."

Lotus suffered for much of the season. Peter Wright: "The first concept for the twin-chassis prototype Type 86 started in October 1979 but it was delayed by problems with the 81. It first ran fully-skirted in November 1980 but ran only three times enabling us to establish its capabilities before the rules were changed. Then we developed the 88 with the different moulded tub and running gear and, once that design was complete, we then drew a conventional Type 87 car on the same tub and running gear as a contingency because as we realised for the first time at Long Beach, we were in deep legal trouble.

"Once the size of the opposition to the 88 was established, the first three races at which the 88 was banned were very upsetting, particularly for Geoff Hardacre and Nigel Stepney, the two mechanics who'd run the build of the prototype car and who were beavering away all hours to get it running . . .

"We had retained the 86, the first 88 survives as an 88 and the two 88Bs were converted to 87s – body panels are the only major difference . . . The 88 didn't run after South America until only 3 or 4 weeks before the British GP when the RAC indicated we could pick it up again. It did what it set out to do, but there were problems, particularly in engine installation/power production. The 87 cheered us all up with Nigel's performance at Monaco, but the 88 business put us behind and we had to run harder ever after just to keep up. Then we lost four or five races to development of the 87 through confusion over the change from Michelin to Goodyear tyres. There is a big difference, but it's difficult to assess. We had never run the 87 on Goodyears before we tried to qualify them in second practice at Silverstone, and again we spent the rest of the season catching up . . . Really the high point of the season for us was I suppose the return of John Player for three-and-a-half years' sponsorship!"

In recession, sponsorship of Formula 1 magnitude is difficult to find. Arrows had adequate funding from Ceramica Ragno but fell foul of the tyre situation. Their experience is typical of the smaller teams.

Dave Wass: "For us the season went with the tyres. At the start when everybody was running on Michelin we were very competitive, look at Riccardo at Long Beach . . . but when neither Michelin nor Goodyear wanted to supply us we went onto Pirelli, who really only wanted to service Toleman and learn their way.

"The Pirelli steel-belted radials were always just too heavy, despite late-season attempts to develop a Kevlar-belted alternative. A set of four Pirelli wets on rims weighs about 50lbs more than a comparable set of Michelins and that puts you into a major inertia problem. Heavier wheels and tyres don't want to change direction on bump as rapidly as the lighter sort, and so you can't run as stiff springs as you'd like and can't run the skirts as close to the ground as you like and so don't generate competitive downloads. It's a vicious circle. It got to the point where you just didn't look forward to going to the races anymore, you knew you had no chance on the tyres you were going to get . . "

For the grossly-underfinanced teams like Tyrrell the situation was even worse. Ken Tyrrell: "We couldn't afford a new car until too late in the season, couldn't afford to go testing, couldn't afford to make all the modifications we would have liked. We ran a restricted season strictly budgeting what funds were available – we could no longer use what we wanted, we had to use what we could afford. Our staff contracted from about 42 to 26, we had to buy our tyres, from

"High spot? What d'you mean high spot?"
KEN TYRRELL

Avon eventually, so you didn't just throw different tyres on the car as you felt fit, you used as few as possible.

"High spot? What d'you mean high spot? Our least low point in the season was Long Beach, where Eddie qualified well and finished fifth. Things looked promising, then came the suspension and skirt business and that sank matters because we didn't have the budget. It was all a fight for survival but Eddie I am convinced is a future Formula 1 star, and Alboreto did a very fine job for us and progressed very well indeed, with no testing at all, he only drove his car at the races. What they both need now is a better car . . ."

But Ken raised a fascinating point in comparing his own perhaps £500,000 maximum budget with that of Alfa Romeo which was possibly twenty times larger. The Italians scored no points at all between Long Beach and Montreal while Tyrrell notched 10 and Mo Nunn's tiny one-car Ensign concern took five . . . "It's an interesting comparison of cost-effectiveness" Ken grunted; the bottom line on an expensive season for all concerned . . . With the turbos on the march, 1982 will cost even more . . .

The Champion quits, still on top

by Mike Doodson, Sports Editor *Motor*

It was the Canadian Grand Prix in Montreal that finally put paid to Alan Jones's already slim chances of winning the 1981 world championship. The reigning champion was as relaxed as he'd ever been while he waited 90 minutes before the race day warm-up for some wrangle over insurance problems to be sorted out. But as he watched the rain tumble down he knew from a glance at the times in the warm-up session that he didn't have a chance in hell of beating the Michelins on the soaking Ile Notre Dame track.

He cracked another joke before climbing into his Williams for the final extra ten minute warm-up on the soaking track. It took him only half a lap to confirm that the car was not a race winner.

Yet Alan Jones – even the Alan Jones who had announced his pending retirement from Formula 1 only ten days earlier – doesn't give up easily. His hopes were raised when the rain had eased a bit before the long-delayed start of the race. Maybe he would find that the shallow-block pattern on his tyres would suit those conditions. So, in a phrase which he uses frequently, he "went for it." He swooped off his second row grid position as the light went green, gobbled up Nelson Piquet and drew level with his own team mate, Carlos Reutemann. The two cars touched on the way to the first corner, and the one who emerged in front of the race was Alan.

"Going for it" is an activity in which Alan has excelled throughout his racing career. No matter that in Canada it rained again, obliging Alan to concede his lead and eventually (after a pit stop) to pack it in for the day ("it didn't seem worth the risk of putting it in the fence when you're in 103rd place"). It was obvious that he was just as much a fighter in his last but one Grand Prix as in any race he's ever done.

Jones could never be described as a popular driver. He's loyal and attentive to the few people whom he knows and respects, but has no time at all for what he calls "time wasters." That phrase has included people who have paid him large sums of money for endorsing their products, and it encompasses virtually every Frenchman except the one who makes his racing boots from genuine kangaroo skin dyed a bilious green.

The French, especially the French press, will be happy to see the back of Alan Jones. "Boorish and uncultured," wrote one columnist, "his language comes from the farmyard," and went on to cite (incorrectly) "dangerous behaviour on the race track." But there will be many thousands who have thrilled to his sideways style even in the era of ground effect. "I've only seen one other man drive like Alan did today," said Frank Williams, after the Long Beach GP of 1979, "and that was Ronnie Peterson." There have been dozens of other occasions since. And Alan beamed with genuine pleasure when he was told about the parallel.

I have to confess my own partiality for Jones. I first met him at the beginning of 1971, when he was racing his Formula 3 Brabham in the Brazilian Torneio. He hadn't done much that was noteworthy in his first British season of F3, and he didn't have much to be proud of in Brazil until the last race, where more in desperation than anything else he brought out his spare engine . . . and immediately started to go respectably well. One of the people who took a sudden interest in Alan Jones's new-found speed was Lotus racing boss Peter Warr, who suspected some sort of illegality. As Alan tells in his book (*Driving Ambition*, Stanley Paul, £6.95), his father chased Warr out of their garage with his walking stick, a not inconsiderable achievement, for Stan Jones had already been seriously incapacitated by a stroke.

Stan Jones died a couple of years later, in England, and his body went back to Australia for burial with the laurels from Alan's first major Formula 3 victory inside the coffin. As Alan said later, he would probably never have been a racing driver if his father hadn't been one too. And he would certainly not have been as motivated as he is if his father hadn't mismanaged his own financial affairs.

"Yes, I had a lot of heartbreak and sacrifice," confessed Alan to an interviewer last year. "It is not commonly known that my father was a very wealthy man in Victoria, so money was not completely unknown to me. It is even worse when you've been accustomed to money and then your father goes broke and you move to a strange country."

He's more than made up the family losses. Six years in Formula 1, the last two at the very top of the tree, have generated the means to buy property on three continents, a flotilla of expensive cars, a helicopter, all the trappings of wealth. But most of all there is his farm, 75 minutes' drive from Melbourne, over a thousand acres of grazing for his pure bred Simmenthal cattle and a flock of Merino sheep. "My bolt hole from the world," he called it at first: "Beverley, my wife, and our son Christian can go there even if everything else turns to rubbish. There's plenty of firewood to keep us warm, and enough to eat just so long as the animals keep on making love to each other."

On the way to affluence, though, there have been some remarkably hard times. The first two or three years of married life found Alan and Beverley running a rooming house in North London. And the charm which enabled Alan to cajole eight times what he had been paid in 1978 from Frank Williams in 1981 got him a bank overdraft for which he had no visible means of support.

Alan's personal horizons have changed just as fast as the escalation in his salary. Two years ago, the acquisition of a clifftop house in Palos Verdes, a Los Angeles suburb, represented success at its most worthwhile. Four classic Ferraris in England were his pride and joy. But he abruptly sold them, house and cars, when he discovered that he had a natural aptitude for farming. And when the time came to return to racing at the beginning of 1981, he admits that he was "sorely tempted" to stay in Australia. Despite the virtual purdah which his career attracted from the Australian press, at least until 1980, he holds his country dear: "it's the only place now where I would seriously consider living. And the prospects are endless...."

The decision to retire crept up on him almost before he realised it had happened. "I never actually sat down to work out all the permutations," he confessed, though there were many factors which contributed. The Cosworth engine, for example, may at last be eclipsed ("it was only Renault's incompetence, not our brilliance, which prevented them from winning the championship this year") and it will be two or three years before Frank Williams has a viable turbo engine of his own.

There were other things which niggled him, like the stiffly-sprung racing cars which threatened to do physical harm to their driver's spines. He tends to get little bouts of flu in Europe which resist any amount of medication. He wants to watch Christian grow up. And the farm is prospering: one of his Simmenthal bulls won a prize at the Melbourne Show one week before Alan announced retirement, and he found that gave him more pleasure than being outgunned by that monotonously powerful Renault at Monza. The writing was on the wall.

Much more than Hunt and Scheckter, the two champions who retired before him, Alan Jones was still as quick and determined at the end of his career as at any time during it. He will continue to race touring cars in Australia, and the tin-top heroes out there stand to have their reputations seriously dented. Whether this and the farming will satisfy Alan Jones's ambitions, only time will tell. Not everyone is sorry to see him go, but he is a serious loss to the sport none the less.

Alan Jones

1946	Born in Melbourne, Australia on November 2.
1963/4	Raced karts and Minis in Australia.
1970	Arrived in England to race Formula 3.
1974	Competed in Formula Atlantic with March 74A.
1975	Made Grand Prix debut in Spain with privately entered Hesketh 308.
	Won two races in British Formula 5000 series with March 75A V6.
1976	Joined Surtees Formula 1 team.
1977	Won Austrian Grand Prix for Shadow.
1978	Won CanAm Championship with five victories in Lola T333CS.
	Joined Williams Grand Prix Engineering.
1979	Won German, Austrian, Dutch and Canadian Grands Prix.
1980	World Champion: won Argentine, French, British, Canadian, United States (East) and non-championship Spanish Grands Prix.
1981	Won United States Grand Prix (West).
	Retired from Formula 1.

When the Champions go racing they go with Champion.

Saudia Leyland Williams, 1981 Formula I World Constructors' Champions.

Nelson Piquet, 1981 Formula I World Champion Driver in his Brabham Cosworth Ford.

Wolfgang Schütz Renault 5 Turbo Cup Champion.

Mauro Baldi, Formula 3 European Champion in a March–Alfa Romeo.

Lancia Beta Monte Carlo, winner of the World Championship for makes.

Tommy Byrne, Formula Ford 2000 Euroseries Champion in his Van Diemen Ford.

In 1981 – yet again – top teams in Formula I, Endurance Racing, Rallies and Marque Racing, chose Champion because Champion Spark Plugs give outstanding performance and dependability.

That's why you'll find Champions in Ferrari, Alfa Romeo, Talbot Ligier Matra, Ford, Cosworth, Renault and Lancia engines.

And it's through working closely with these big names in motor sport that Champion technology produces the right plugs for your car, too.

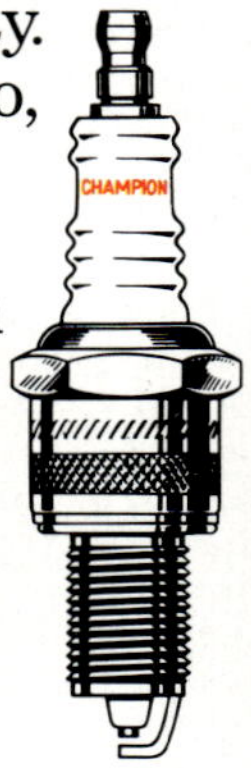

CHAMPION®

Follow the Champions

GRANDS PRIX 1981

Toyota Grand Prix of the United States (West)

You couldn't help but notice a certain smug feeling surrounding the victory podium at Long Beach. After a winter of fierce and continual hostility between the sport's governing body (FISA) and the Formula One Constructors Association (FOCA), agreement had been reached just 10 days before the opening round of the championship in California.

Skirts would, after all, be banned and the FOCA teams switched immediately to 'Plan B' as they adapted their cars to suit. The FISA-aligned teams, meanwhile, continued their test programmes without skirts in the happy knowledge that they had been right all along. Having already wasted valuable time racing with skirts in a non-championship race in South Africa, the FOCA teams would clearly be in trouble at Long Beach. What's more, they had run Goodyears at Kyalami but the Akron company's decision to withdraw from Formula 1 would come into force at Long Beach. Everyone would have Michelins and that seemingly was another point in favour of Renault and Ferrari, the two teams contracted to the French tyre company in 1980.

At the end of the weekend, however, Alan Jones and the Saudia-Leyland Williams team proved that little had changed in Grand Prix racing. The reigning World Champion and Carlos Reutemann took up where they had left off at Watkins Glen by finishing 25 seconds ahead of Nelson Piquet's Parmalat Brabham.

Piquet was no match for the new FW07Cs but, equally, the Williams team could not cope with Riccardo Patrese in the Ragno-Beta Arrows. It was the one surprise element as Patrese led from pole and drove with consumate ease until cruelly sidelined by a blocked fuel filter at one-third distance.

Inbetween the bouts of arguing over the winter, there had been the usual shuffling of contracts and Long Beach represented new hope for several drivers. Mario Andretti finished an excellent fourth in his first race for Marlboro Alfa Romeo; Eddie Cheever, having switched to Tyrrell, was overjoyed with his first championship points and Patrick Tambay cocked a snook at the establishment with a splendid sixth place in the brand new Theodore. Ferrari, now firmly committed to the turbocharged route, ran strongly before Gilles Villeneuve and Didier Pironi were forced to retire.

Only eight cars finished and, once again, the tricky street circuit provided few pointers towards the outcome of the championship save to say that Williams were still on top, regardless of the new regulations. Unfortunately, the slack wording of those rules led to an unhappy dispute surrounding the new Lotus 88. Colin Chapman's car featured a controversial 'double chassis' and, after much discussion and ill-feeling, the car was finally excluded – a melodrama which confirmed that little had changed in the competitive world of Grand Prix racing.

JANUARY:

Jody Scheckter fined £1,000 and given a two month suspended sentence following a traffic offence in Nice.

Representatives from every Formula 1 team meet in Maranello and produce 'Maranello Agreement' for presentation as peace initiative to FISA.

Avon tyre company announce plans for a return to Grand Prix racing.

Emerson Fittipaldi formally announces his retirement from motor racing.

FEBRUARY:

Carlos Reutemann, driving a Williams with sliding skirts, wins non-championship South African Grand Prix at Kyalami. Ferrari, Renault, Alfa Romeo, Talbot-Ligier and Osella do not attend pending outcome of peace talks between FISA and FOCA.

Jody Scheckter becomes World Superstars Champion.

MARCH:

Peace agreement in Paris between FISA and FOCA.

Michelin announce plans to supply every Formula 1 team for first three races.

ENTRY AND PRACTICE

The pit lane was positively gleaming as 16 teams rolled out their pristine machinery and 29 drivers prepared to go motor racing for championship points at last. There had been occasions during the preceding five months when it seemed there might be a fragmented championship at best and a complete absence of Grand Prix racing at worst. But, at 10 a.m. on Friday, March 13, the streets of Long Beach echoed with that familiar strident sound as the sport showed every sign of surviving one of its bitterest conflicts.

The upshot of hours of arguing and yards of telex was an agreement, among other things, to run without skirts and increase the minimum weight limit. It was back to Square One as designers threw away the time and money consuming flexible side-skirts and thought about ways of overcoming a mandatory six centimetre gap between the bodywork and the track – applicable only while the car was stationary. Brabham came up with a hydro-pneumatic suspension, Williams had variable-rate springing and then, of course, there was the Lotus 88 – but that's another story.

As if adapting to a new design formula on the streets of Long Beach was not difficult enough, a further complication was added by the fact that 90% of the teams were running Michelin radials for the first time. Both FISA and FOCA may have scored points in the battle for control of the sport but both sides lost heavily when Goodyear cried enough and pulled out of Formula 1 at the end of 1980.

The war may have been over but the sniping continued in other directions as Frank Williams took aim at the Lotus 88 on the day before official practice: "If that car passes scrutineering, I will withdraw my cars," he said with a sense of purpose and pomp which obviously came with winning the championship. The Lotus *did* pass scrutineering and, of course, Frank was at his usual place by the pit wall when practice commenced.

Working with rather less fuss at the far end of the pit lane were the Arrows team, resplendent in their orange and white livery in deference to their new sponsors, Ragno tiles and Beta tools. After much indecision, Riccardo Patrese eventually rejoined the Milton Keynes company for another year and, by the end of practice, he was probably relieved he had done so.

For the first time in his Grand Prix career, the Italian was on pole after reeling off neat and consistent laps with a car weighing some 40 lbs less thanks to new carbon fibre bodywork and aluminium radiators. The rear wing was mounted further forward and, clearly, the Arrows without side skirts and Goodyears worked well.

"I suppose it shows how badly our skirts were working," said Dave Wass, the team's unassuming designer. In truth, part of the team's advantage was Wass's redesigned rear suspension and Patrese's experience with Pirelli radials during his races with the Lancia Group 5 car in 1980.

Siegfried Stohr had joined the team from Formula 2 and, after a decent performance at Kyalami, the Italian psychoanalyst was totally at sea amid the Long Beach concrete walls. The Arrows rarely appeared on the same line and Siegfried rearranged the rear suspension pick-up point when he tapped a wall. His chances of qualifying were ruined finally by an engine failure on the spare car after one lap of the last practice session.

After five weeks of flat-out activity at their Didcot factory, the Williams team arrived at Long Beach with two new cars for Jones and Reutemann. The FW07C was more than an update on the original FW07 chassis, the 'C' featuring a wider front track, slimmer monocoque, revised bodywork (including a return to kick-ups in front of the rear wheels) and variable rate springing, the idea being to have the car sit closer to the track while on the move. That was abandoned after the first day's practice and Jones went all out to take pole from Patrese on Saturday. Alan tried just a shade too hard and touched a wall on the exit of the corner leading on to the pit straight. He immediately jumped into the spare FW07B but the set-up was not to his liking and Patrese retained pole by a scant one-hundredth of a second.

Reutemann did his usual thorough job and collected third place on the grid although Carlos said he had slight understeer turning into the slow corners on the Michelin radials. Jones overcame the same problem by turning in while braking and provoking the same tingling attitudes witnessed two years previously with the non-ground effects FW06.

The new rules increased the weight limit from 580 kg to 585 kg, a change which found little favour with the top teams. "It's ridiculous," said Frank Dernie of Williams. "The absence of skirts gives a weight reduction before you start and then the additional five kilos means we are carrying something like a 20 lb penalty. This is all in the interests of safety supposedly but, when you think about it, the most reliable and the safest cars are well engineered and light – and therefore penalised."

Alan Jones was rather more direct in his comments: "What it means is that we have handed the FISA teams a Christmas present in the form of lead strapped to our gearbox . . . ."

Gordon Murray shut himself off from the whole affair by playing John Lennon on his Sony headset. As it was, the Brabham designer had enough on his plate with an ingenious hydro-pneumatic system of ride height control. The system proved troublesome on

Alan Jones enjoys the trappings of success. Apart from the Michelin cap, little had changed *(right)*.
'Unaccustomed as I am....' Riccardo Patrese became the centre of attention when he took his first pole position *(below)*.
"I thought all Alfas were supposed to have adjustable back-rests." Mario Andretti finished an encouraging fourth in his first Grand Prix for Alfa Romeo *(below right)*.

Patrese kept Reutemann at bay until the Arrows stopped with a blocked fuel filter. The Williams driver then threw the lead away with an uncharacteristic mistake *(below)*.
Eddie Cheever was delighted with his first championship points. The Tyrrell driver finished fifth after a busy race *(bottom left)*.

Friday which meant a return to convention and, in effect, one day for Piquet to set the car up and claim a good grid position. With that in mind, the Brazilian did an excellent job to take fourth place. Hector Rebaque had missed the South African Grand Prix due to a bout of hepatitis but the Mexican had recovered sufficiently to take his seat at Long Beach and put the chassis with the Weismann gearbox halfway up the grid.

It was clear from the Ferrari pit that the team were committed to the V6 engine and various forms of forced induction. The turbo had appeared briefly at the Italian Grand Prix the previous September and, for 1981, Gilles Villeneuve and new recruit Didier Pironi were hoping to make the most of a busy winter testing both a KKK turbocharger and a Brown Boveri Comprex system. The cars had been tidied up in all departments including the bodywork, exhausts and a revised transverse gearbox. Initially, the race cars were fitted with Comprex superchargers while the spare carried the KKK system but a hectic two days of practice saw the drivers and engines swap chassis at a bewildering rate. Villeneuve was forced to use the spare car on Friday after a drive belt to the supercharger broke and the French Canadian was soon lapping faster than before with the KKK. Mauro Forghieri took note and Gilles's race car had a turbo fitted for Saturday practice while Pironi switched to the T-car. All that went awry, however, when Gilles's engine holed a piston and he was obliged to use the Comprex abandoned by Pironi while mechanics swapped engines in time for a few laps at the end of official practice. Those few laps, however, were ruined by a misfire and Villeneuve did a spectacular job taking a place on the third row. Pironi was not without his problems either, his gearbox (T-car) having lost all of its oil on Saturday morning and the Frenchman could manage no better than a position six places behind his team-mate. None the less, it was an encouraging start even if the handling was horrible thanks to a lack of chassis development and a high centre of gravity brought about by the tall plumbing required by the turbos. But at least the red cars were quickest in a straight line; faster, even, than the powerful Alfa Romeos.

Mario Andretti, shining with enthusiasm in his new Misura overalls, was raring to go racing for the first time with the Marlboro sponsored team. There were three cars on hand, developments of the 1980 chassis with stiffer monocoques and slots in the side-pods to direct air downwards in the hope that it might act like a skirt and form a curtain. Practice had barely begun when Giacomelli came trailing into the pits with his nose wing wrapped around the cockpit. Large front wings had become the fashion to balance the loss of skirts and Bruno had not made allowances for the large front appendage. The unfortunate Italian later tangled with Patrese and dislodged an oil line. The resulting fire brought practice to a halt and the foam-covered Alfa Romeo back to the pits on the end of a rope. Andretti, meanwhile, was enjoying the torque of the V12 and took sixth place ahead of Nigel Mansell.

The Englishman tackled the race in his customary professional and determined manner. Never having seen the circuit before, Mansell spent hours studying videos of previous races and by the time he reached Long Beach, he knew the track from every angle. Such dedication paid off when he set ninth fastest time on Friday and improved to seventh place the following day. Mansell simply got on with the job in his 81 and let the turmoil surrounding the Lotus 88 pass over his head.

Poor Elio de Angelis was not so fortunate, hopping from one car to the other. The 88 did not reach the pit lane until Friday afternoon when it completed a handful of laps before the drive to the fuel pump, of all things, brought the technological wonder to a halt. Elio was beginning to get down to serious motoring on Saturday morning when the car was black-flagged and he had to be content with 13th place in his 81.

The Tyrrell team, struggling throughout 1980, surprised other teams – not to mention themselves – when they removed skirts from the 010 chassis, bolted on Michelins and immediately set competitive times during winter tests at Paul Ricard. Tyrrell had let Jarier and Daly go in favour of Eddie Cheever who was more than happy to accept the offer after a hard year

CHEEVER

saudia
dallah
AVCO

MICHELIN
28
LONGINES
Agip
olivetti

Marlboro
SCAINI
Marlboro
MICHELIN
MICHELIN
22
Ron Rock

saudia
1
CHAMPION

Previous pages:
Eddie Cheever finished fifth in the Tyrrell despite gearbox trouble *(left)*.
Photo: David Winter
Didier Pironi and the turbo Ferrari showed an amazing turn of speed *(top right)*.
Photo: Nigel Snowdon
Mario Andretti made an encouraging debut with the Marlboro Alfa Romeo team *(below right)*.
Photo: Don Morley – All Sport
Alan Jones and the Saudia-Leyland Williams; a familiar combination – a familiar result *(bottom left)*.
Photo: David Winter

with Osella. His enthusiasm showed at Long Beach with a place on the fourth row and he became the unsponsored team's only representative when Kevin Cogan failed to qualify. The American Formula Atlantic driver brought along money from Michelob but spent the weekend disagreeing with the gearbox on his black car.

Another frequent visitor to Ricard had been the reshaped Ligier team. Talbot had stepped in to add more than just their name and, as a result, the Ford-Cosworth DFV had been abandoned after two years and the Matra V12 revived pending a turbo V6 later in the year. Pironi's departure made the way clear for Jean-Pierre Jabouille but the Frenchman was still recovering from his broken leg sustained during a heavy shunt in his Renault during the Canadian Grand Prix five months previously. Jean-Pierre Jarier stepped in to take his place and the beautifully turned out cars occupied the middle of the grid despite severe understeer and, in Jacques Laffite's case on Friday, a sticking throttle.

Considering the Renault-Elf team's encouraging winter tests with the revised RE 20Bs and Arnoux's front row position the previous year, it was surprising to find the turbos so far down the grid. After much legal discussion with McLaren and Marlboro, Alain Prost got his way and joined René Arnoux for a season which started badly when he clipped the wall on Friday. Prost was in the spare car during the afternoon and again on Saturday after gearbox trouble with his regular car. Both drivers complained of poor grip and understeer so it was obvious that having run Michelins in 1980 was not such an advantage after all.

"It's because Michelin have agreed to service every car," said Jean Sage, the Renault team manager. "Obviously, I understand why they are doing it because Renault does not want to race against an empty grid but we are not at all happy about the individual effect it has had on us. In normal circumstances we could have had every tyre we wanted but at the moment we are bound to use only the four sets allowed to everyone else."

The Fittipaldi team, sponsorless and virgin white, brought revised F8s for their regular driver Keke Rosberg and Chico Serra, the replacement for Emerson Fittipaldi who had finally announced his retirement at the beginning of the season. Rosberg bent a rear rocker arm and lost 20 minutes on Saturday afternoon while Serra, driving a brand new car, had gearbox trouble after bending two selector rods in succession on Friday. "He's stronger than we thought. . . ." muttered Peter Warr who, generally, was very pleased with the Brazilian's mature and careful approach to Grand Prix racing.

There weren't many pundits willing to put money on the new Tony Southgate designed Theodore which was completed for Patrick Tambay on the Monday before the event. Teddy Yipp, patron of the reshaped team, brought relief from the bickering when he launched the car in style with a couple of hundred of his closest friends on board the *Queen Mary*. Part of the razzmatazz included a tribal dance to ward off evil spirits and, while some doubters may have smiled quietly, it was the Hong Kong entrepreneur who had the last laugh when Tambay showed splendid style and determination to take 17th place on the grid.

Marc Surer and Jan Lammers had switched teams during the winter, the Swiss joining Ensign while Lammers returned to ATS at the scene of his great practice effort in 1980. The same form could not be found 12 month later unfortunately and the Dutchman finished two places behind Surer in a revised model of the 1980 Ensign. An indication of Mo Nunn's dire financial problems was the presence of sliding skirt attachments, the team being unable to afford new side-pods.

McLaren International brought their new carbon fibre Marlboro MP4 along and Ron Denis's immaculate preparation won the *Concours*. It was to be the high point of the weekend. The MP4 had not had sufficient testing and fuel pressure problems coupled with the wrong choice of springs and exhausts which burnt the bodywork forced Watson to use the stand-by M29 during Saturday afternoon and take a place behind his team mate, Andrea de Cesaris, at the back of the grid.

The final qualifier was Beppe Gabbiani in a new Osella. The Italian team tackled their second season of Grand Prix racing with two new cars for the novice drivers but Miguel-Angel Guerra failed to qualify. John Macdonald had regrouped to form March Grand Prix which, in effect, was a combination of the efficient Londoner's preparation and Robin Herd's design work, handled by Derek Daly and Eliseo Salazar. The March 811s had shown promise at Kyalami in spite of the expected teething troubles but the cut and thrust of a full blown Grand Prix practice took its toll regardless of Daly's gritty struggle with the ill-handling car.

RACE

The Arrows team, bemused but determined to take their new found status in their stride, calmly prepared for the start. The car, according to Patrese, was perfect during the warm-up and the team gave the A3 a final check before the 2 p.m. start.

The morning session, though, had not been without its dramas as Mansell nudged the inside wall at Queens Hairpin. The team had cured an understeer problem rather too well and the Englishman bent a rear top link which was changed in time. Prost, however, reluctantly prepared to race the spare Renault after the engine in his usual car developed a misfire.

The cars completed a slow lap before gathering on the pit straight. Patrese was surrounded by mechanics in orange and white shirts and blue Michelin hats while ex-Penthouse Pet, Dominique Maure, posed alongside in something rather more appealing. Williams, accustomed to that sort of thing, watched quietly from behind; Piquet and Murray thought about what might have been had they not wasted two days testing and a full timed practice session with the new suspension system; Villeneuve wondered whether his turbo would last as temperatures hovered at the 70°F mark; Andretti was still raring to go racing and Mansell prepared for a slow getaway by the turbo Ferrari in front and over exhuberance from the Tyrrell and Alfa Romeo drivers at his rear.

The 80,000 crowd whooped and hollered as the field set off towards the start line on Shoreline Drive; 24 cars formed without fuss and lit up their tyres as the 1981 Grand Prix season well and truly got under way. Patrese made the most of his opportunity but Jones was slow off the mark and Reutemann took up the challenge as the cars swept through the right-hander and aimed for Queens Hairpin.

Patrese had the line and Reutemann was consolidating second place when Villeneuve rushed down the outside to take the lead briefly on the very edge of control. The Ferrari driver braked a fraction too hard and too late and gathered himself together as he took a wide line while the Arrows and both Williams slipped through in a more orderly manner. Villeneuve elbowed his way in front of Piquet, Cheever, Pironi, Andretti, Laffite, de Angelis, Giacomelli, Mansell, Jarier and Rosberg. Behind the Fittipaldi, however, the now traditional Long Beach shunt for the benefit of the army of photographers was taking place as de Cesaris made a nonsense of his braking and punted Prost sideways before launching Rebaque into the air. The McLaren and the Renault were out then and there but Rebaque (now running a Hewland gearbox) continued ahead of Tambay (taking it easy in his first Grand Prix in over 12 months), Serra, Surer, Arnoux, Watson and Gabbiani.

As Patrese confidently opened a small gap over the Williams, Villeneuve lost ground when he ran wide at the left-hand hairpin leading towards the straight and let Pironi and Piquet through. Rosberg had quickly worked his way into 10th place but his team-mate had been struck from behind by Lammers when the ATS driver forgot about the large nose wing while slip-streaming the Fittipaldi. Serra continued but Lammers was the first pits visitor on lap five with Watson following three laps later. The Ulsterman was to retire with engine trouble on lap 16. Rebaque, unaware that de Cesaris had broken the Brabham's rear anti-roll bar, called at his pit to say the handling was evil and the team, short on ideas, changed all four tyres. Arnoux was next to pit with a complaint about vibrations from the front of his Renault (discovered later to have been caused by a faulty shock absorber).

While the Renault mechanics were inspecting the car, their Lotus colleagues watched helplessly as de Angelis limped along the pit straight, his rear suspension buckled after clouting the wall at the exit of the preceding corner. The team's hopes faded completely on lap 26 when Mansell's 81 inexplicably slid into a wall down on Pine Avenue – possibly a legacy of his shunt earlier in the day.

The major drama of the moment, however, concerned the leaders. On lap 24, Patrese felt his engine hesitate and the ever-present Reutemann was soon alongside. The Arrows recovered but, a lap later, the same thing happened and Reutemann was through followed, on lap 26, by Jones. Patrese tore into the pit lane and almost reached third gear before halting at his pit. The team, desperately searching for the cause of the misfire, asked Riccardo if his fuel pressure was satisfactory. The Italian said it was and,

Elio de Angelis (foreground) was forced to use the Lotus 81 after the 88 had been excluded. Nigel Mansell put his 81 on the fourth row of the grid but both drivers were to hit the wall during the race *(left)*.
Patrick Tambay made a brilliant comeback to Formula 1 in the brand new Theodore and gave the new team a championship point *(bottom)*.
New noises. The Talbot-Ligier team replaced the Ford Cosworth DFV with the Matra V12. Ferrari were committed to their V6 engine in both turbocharged and supercharged forms.

with that fault apparently ruled out, the mechanics changed the black box. Four laps later, Patrese was back with the same problem and he retired on lap 33.

In his excitement, the distraught Patrese had looked at the wrong gauge and the problem was indeed connected with fuel. It was thought initially that the petrol had affected the resin on the glass-fibre pipes leading to the collector in the fuel tank and, as a result, the filter had blocked but a stray piece of raw glass fibre led the team to reach other conclusions . . . . Patrese could merely reflect sadly on a lead that he had held with ease.

Reutemann, who said later he had driven ten-tenths to keep the smooth Arrows in sight, now relaxed slightly although Jones was not far behind and wondering if Reutemann would let the number one driver through. The question of contracts was shelved until a later date when Reutemann made a potentially disastrous error on lap 32. The Argentinian had just lapped Marc Surer as he left Queens Hairpin and, two corners later, Reutemann locked his brakes and went wide before bouncing across a kerb and back onto the track. Surer couldn't believe his eyes and swerved almost to a standstill while Jones, seeing his opportunity, accelerated past them both.

Reutemann soon regained his composure and a pit signal to hold station sealed the outcome of the race. The Williams, running like clockwork, were some 30 seconds ahead of Nelson Piquet who had eventually got the better of Pironi on the dash up the hill before the pits. Piquet, struggling with a stiff gearchange and a blistered hand, was unable to do anything about the fleeing Williams and Pironi gradually dropped back as attention focused on a changing battle for fifth place.

Villeneuve had retired on lap 17 with a broken drive-shaft and Cheever was going strongly although Andretti was not far behind. Laffite was catching them both and he moved ahead of the Alfa Romeo on lap 35 and set after the Tyrrell. In his impatience to get by, Laffite totally misjudged his braking at the end of the pit straight and bent the front of his Ligier against the rear of the Tyrrell. As Jacques crawled round to the pits, he unwittingly caused the demise of Lammers and Giacomelli as they came upon the stricken Ligier. Lammers darted one way, backed off when he got onto the loose and Giacomelli then ran over his rear wheel as he tried to squeeze between the two cars. Suddenly there seemed to be more traffic in the pit lane than on the track as the three cars filed nose-to-tail into retirement. At the same time, Rosberg stopped with engine trouble after dropping back down the field with oversteer.

Cheever, possibly because of Laffite's dodgem tactics, was finding difficulty selecting second gear and Andretti closed and managed to scrabble past in spite of locking rear brakes. The American soon realised that fourth place could be his too as Pironi began to slow with fuel vapourisation trouble. For four laps, Andretti would momentarily nose ahead only to have the Ferrari leave the Alfa for dead as the impressive turbo power came into its own on the straight. Both

Labatt
GPA
CERAMICHE
PIEMME
olivetti LONGINES
Agip
LONGINES
olivetti

Gilles Villeneuve and the Ferrari 126C *(left)*.
Photo: Mike Levasheff
Hard work, this Grand Prix racing. Michelob supported more than just the Tyrrell team *(right)*.

Andretti and Cheever eventually got the better of the Ferrari at a left hander where Pironi almost chugged to a standstill.

Tambay, by now, was well and truly into the groove having dealt forceably with Jarier at the hairpin. The Ligier stopped eventually with a down-on-power engine and fuel pump bothers but Tambay went motoring in the manner of an angry young man with a point to prove to the cynics in the pit lane. He came across the stuttering Pironi on lap 58 and almost rammed the Ferrari on the pit straight. Luck, however, was on Patrick's side when a trip up an escape road as he groped for gears amounted to no more than a slightly bent nose wing and the Frenchman went on to set fourth fastest lap of the race. It was a superb performance by any standards and one championship point was too good to be true for the overjoyed Theodore team.

Pironi retired with the engine popping and sprouting flame when the turbocharger overheated while Surer, out with electrical trouble, was the last in a long line of retirements. Reliability paid handsomely as the Williams and Brabham teams proved once again and the top three drivers in the 1980 World Championship trooped off to the press room. Back in the garage, Mario Andretti was delighted to have scored his best place since the 1979 Spanish Grand Prix and you would have been excused for thinking Eddie Cheever had won the race as he poured champagne over his head. The beaming American was delighted to have been so competitive and two points were just reward for the beleagured Tyrrell team.

Down in the scrutineering bay, the owner of 15 Constructors' Points was perplexed to find Reutemann's rear wing two millimetres over the limit. A brief discussion with the scrutineer, Alfa Romeo and Brabham followed and it was agreed that the infringement wasn't worth bothering about. With that, Frank Williams gathered up his brief case and went off to savour a one-two finish which, frankly, he had not expected to earn quite so easily.

In among the armada of motor homes, the race fans continued celebrations as they worked through the Long Beach Grand Prix motto: 'Wear little, drink a lot, see and be seen, party hearty – and phone in sick tomorrow'.

Little, indeed, had changed in Grand Prix racing.

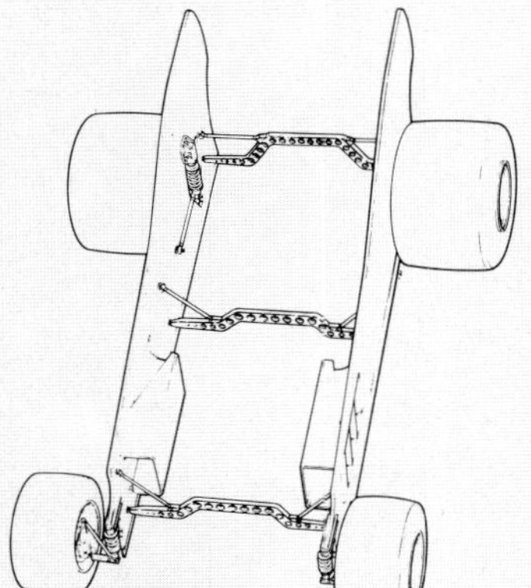

Elio de Angelis in the 88 during practice.

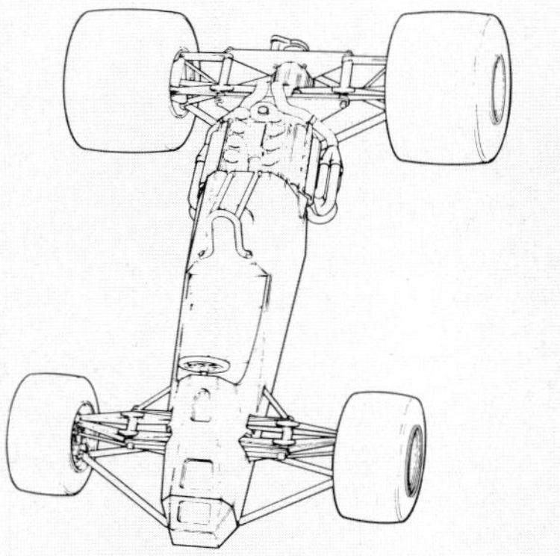

When Colin Chapman held a press conference at London's Heathrow airport to explain why his latest car, the Lotus 88, was legal, it was clear that he did not expect an easy passage at Long Beach a week later.

According to Chapman, the car featured two chassis, each with its own springing system. The primary chassis consisted of the bodywork, sidepods, aerofoils and radiators while riding independently inside that was a secondary chassis composed of the monocoque, fuel tank, engine, gearbox and the front and rear suspension. The outer or primary chassis was suspended on four coil spring/damper units coupled to the bottom of the wheel uprights with the intention of absorbing the aerodynamic loads and yet remain unaffected by the braking, cornering and acceleration handled by the conventional rocker arm/wishbone layout of the inner or secondary chassis.

The car passed scrutineering at Long Beach and de Angelis took part in Friday practice against a background of mounting protests from the majority of teams. At 6 p.m. on Friday, the Stewards issued a statement: 'In the matter of the protest against the Lotus 88, the Stewards of the Meeting, after consideration of the rules and hearing all the parties to the protest decided to uphold the protest. In addition, the times taken (for the Lotus 88) in the qualifying session shall not stand.'

John Bornholdt, Chairman of the Stewards added: "We are dealing with a very innovative car. If the rules were clear it wouldn't have taken so much time to come to a decision."

Chapman appealed immediately and was told that the car could run in the remainder of practice and in the race on the understanding that championship points accrued could be withdrawn if the appeal was not upheld.

So far, the whole business had followed an unfortunate if predictable pattern. That changed when the car was black-flagged during the Saturday morning practice session. Chapman, quick to act on the confusion shown by the race officials, held a press conference.

"We are suffering from a lack of information," he said. "We are still convinced that the car complies to the regulations and we would like to see a written statement as to why it is breaking the rules. The Stewards spent nine hours and upheld the protests without consulting the scrutineer who passed the car in the first place. These days I don't think people are very receptive to innovative ideas but I'd be interested to know precisely on which grounds these protesting teams object to my car. The fact that they haven't specified their objections suggests to me that they're not really sure why they think it's illegal."

When asked to comment later, John Bornholdt said statements on points of illegality were not required by the FISA rules. He added that an error had been made when the car was allowed to practice while under protest. "In searching the rules further, we learned this is not allowed," he said. "Say for instance someone entered a Sherman tank in the event. The tank would be protested and the protest upheld. The tank entrant could appeal and the tank would have to be allowed to compete. The rule was written just for this type of instance."

Colin Chapman tactfully refrained from passing comment on SCCA officials who, presumably, would have accepted a Sherman tank at scrutineering . . . .

Entries and practice times

No.	Driver	Nat	Car	Engine	Entrant	Practice 1	Practice 2
1	Alan Jones	AUS	Saudia-Leyland WILLIAMS FWO7C	Ford Cosworth DFV	Albilad-Williams Racing Team	1m 20·911s	**1m 19·408s**
2	Carlos Reutemann	RA	Saudia-Leyland WILLIAMS FWO7C	Ford Cosworth DFV	Albilad-Williams Racing Team	1m 21·739s	**1m 20·149s**
3	Eddie Cheever	USA	TYRRELL 010	Ford Cosworth DFV	Tyrrell Racing	1m 22·992s	**1m 20·643s**
4	Kevin Cogan	USA	Michelob TYRRELL 010	Ford Cosworth DFV	Tyrrell Racing	1m 25·164s	**1m 22·284s**
5	Nelson Piquet	BR	Parmalat BRABHAM BT49C	Ford Cosworth DFV	Parmalat Racing Team	1m 22·675s	**1m 20·289s**
6	Hector Rebaque	MEX	Parmalat BRABHAM BT49C	Ford Cosworth DFV	Parmalat Racing Team	1m 23·298s	**1m 21·000s**
7	John Watson	GB	Marlboro McLAREN M29F	Ford Cosworth DFV	McLaren International	1m 26·419s	**1m 22·183s**
8	Andrea de Cesaris	I	Marlboro McLAREN M29F	Ford Cosworth DFV	McLaren International	1m 23·728s	**1m 22·028s**
9	Jan Lammers	NL	ATS D4	Ford Cosworth DFV	Team ATS	1m 23·802s	**1m 21·758s**
11	Elio de Angelis	I	Essex LOTUS 81	Ford Cosworth DFV	Team Essex Lotus	1m 22·380s	**1m 20·928s**
12	Nigel Mansell	GB	Essex LOTUS 81	Ford Cosworth DFV	Team Essex Lotus	1m 22·461s	**1m 20·573s**
14	Marc Surer	CH	ENSIGN N180B	Ford Cosworth DFV	Ensign Racing	1m 28·045s	**1m 21·522s**
15	Alain Prost	F	Elf RENAULT RE 20	Renault EF1	Equipe Renault Elf	1m 23·049s	**1m 20·980s**
16	René Arnoux	F	Elf RENAULT RE 20	Renault EF1	Equipe Renault Elf	1m 23·363s	**1m 21·540s**
17	Derek Daly	IRL	Rizla MARCH 811	Ford Cosworth DFV	March Grand Prix	1m 25·017s	**1m 22·356s**
18	Eliseo Salazar	RCH	Rizla MARCH 811	Ford Cosworth DFV	March Grand Prix	1m 26·074s	**1m 24·383s**
20	Keke Rosberg	SF	FITTIPALDI F8C	Ford Cosworth DFV	Fittipaldi Automotive	1m 23·356s	**1m 21·001s**
21	Chico Serra	BR	FITTIPALDI F8C	Ford Cosworth DFV	Fittipaldi Automotive	1m 26·730s	**1m 21·409s**
22	Mario Andretti	USA	Marlboro ALFA ROMEO 179C	Alfa Romeo 1260	Marlboro Team Alfa Romeo	1m 22·020s	**1m 20·476s**
23	Bruno Giacomelli	I	Marlboro ALFA ROMEO 179C	Alfa Romeo 1260	Marlboro Team Alfa Romeo	1m 22·592s	**1m 20·664s**
25	Jean-Pierre Jarier	F	Talbot-Gitanes LIGIER JS17	Matra MS 81	Equipe Talbot Gitanes	1m 21·722s	**1m 20·787s**
26	Jacques Laffite	F	Talbot-Gitanes LIGIER JS17	Matra MS 81	Equipe Talbot Gitanes	1m 23·140s	**1m 20·925s**
27	Gilles Villeneuve	CDN	Fiat FERRARI 126CX	Ferrari 126C	Scuderia Ferrari SpA SEFAC	1m 21·723s	**1m 20·462s**
28	Didier Pironi	F	Fiat FERRARI 126CX	Ferrari 126C	Scuderia Ferrari SpA SEFAC	1m 21·828s	**1m 20·909s**
29	Riccardo Patrese	I	Penthouse-Ragno ARROWS A3	Ford Cosworth DFV	Arrows Racing Team	1m 21·983s	**1m 19·399s**
30	Siegfried Stohr	I	Penthouse-Ragno ARROWS A3	Ford Cosworth DFV	Arrows Racing Team	**1m 23·504s**	–
31	Miguel Angel Guerra	RA	Denim OSELLA FA1B	Ford Cosworth DFV	Osella Squadra Corse	1m 25·190s	**1m 22·673s**
32	Beppe Gabbiani	I	Denim OSELLA FA1B	Ford Cosworth DFV	Osella Squadra Corse	1m 24·032s	**1m 22·213s**
33	Patrick Tambay	F	THEODORE TY 01	Ford Cosworth DFV	Theodore Racing Team	1m 23·373s	**1m 21·298s**
Friday morning and Saturday morning practice sessions not officially recorded						*Fri pm Warm, dry*	*Sat pm Warm, dry*

Starting grid

	29 PATRESE (1m 19·39s) Arrows
1 JONES (1m 19·40s) Williams	
	2 REUTEMANN (1m 20·14s) Williams
5 PIQUET (1m 20·28s) Brabham	
	27 VILLENEUVE (1m 20·46s) Ferrari
22 ANDRETTI (1m 20·47s) Alfa Romeo	
	12 MANSELL (1m 20·57s) Lotus
3 CHEEVER (1m 20·64s) Tyrrell	
	23 GIACOMELLI (1m 20·66s) Alfa Romeo
25 JARIER (1m 20·78s) Talbot-Ligier	
	28 PIRONI (1m 20·90s) Ferrari
26 LAFFITE (1m 20·92s) Talbot-Ligier	
	11 DE ANGELIS (1m 20·92s) Lotus
15 PROST (1m 20·98s) Renault	
	6 REBAQUE (1m 21·00s) Brabham
20 ROSBERG (1m 21·00s) Fittipaldi	
	33 TAMBAY (1m 21·29s) Theodore
21 SERRA (1m 21·40s) Fittipaldi	
	14 SURER (1m 21·52s) Ensign
16 ARNOUX (1m 21·54s) Renault	
	9 LAMMERS (1m 21·75s) ATS
8 DE CESARIS (1m 22·02s) McLaren	
	7 WATSON (1m 22·18s) McLaren
32 GABBIANI (1m 22·21s) Osella	

Did not start:
4 Cogan (Tyrrell), 1m 22·284s, did not qualify
17 Daly (March), 1m 22·356s, did not qualify
31 Guerra (Osella), 1m 22·21s, did not qualify
30 Stohr (Arrows), 1m 23·50s, did not qualify
18 Salazar (March), 1m 24·383s, did not qualify

Past winners

Year	Driver	Nat	Car	Circuit	Distance miles/km	Speed mph/km/h
1975*	Brian Redman	GB	5·0 Lola T332-Chevrolet	Long Beach	101·00/162·54	86·32/138·92
1976	Clay Regazzoni	CH	3·0 Ferrari 312T/76	Long Beach	161·60/260·07	85·57/137·71
1977	Mario Andretti	USA	3·0 JPS/Lotus 78-Ford	Long Beach	161·60/260·07	86·89/139·84
1978	Carlos Reutemann	RA	3·0 Ferrari 312T-3/78	Long Beach	162·61/261·70	87·10/140·17
1979	Gilles Villeneuve	CDN	3·0 Ferrari 312T-4	Long Beach	162·61/261·70	87·81/141·32
1980	Nelson Piquet	BR	3·0 Brabham BT49-Ford	Long Beach	162·61/261·70	88·47/142·38
1981	Alan Jones	AUS	3·0 Williams FWO7C-Ford	Long Beach	162·61/261·70	87·60/140·98

*Formula 5000 Long Beach Grand Prix

Circuit data

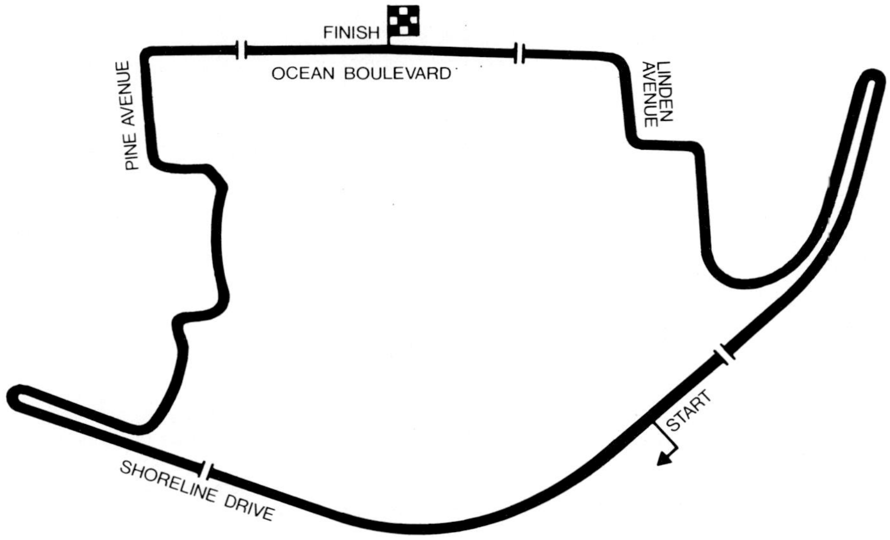

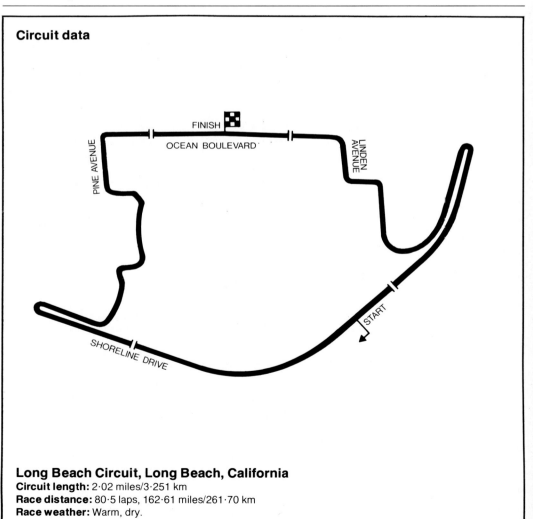

Long Beach Circuit, Long Beach, California
Circuit length: 2·02 miles/3·251 km
Race distance: 80·5 laps, 162·61 miles/261·70 km
Race weather: Warm, dry.

Results and retirements

Place	Driver	Car	Laps	Time and Speed (mph/km/h)/Retirement	
1	Alan Jones	Williams-Cosworth V8	80	1h 50m 41·33s	87·60/140·979
2	Carlos Reutemann	Williams-Cosworth V8	80	1h 50m 50·52s	87·48/140·786
3	Nelson Piquet	Brabham-Cosworth V8	80	1h 51m 16·25s	87·14/140·238
4	Mario Andretti	Alfa Romeo V12	80	1h 51m 30·64s	86·95/139·933
5	Eddie Cheever	Tyrrell-Cosworth V8	80	1h 51m 48·03s	86·73/139·579
6	Patrick Tambay	Theodore-Cosworth V8	79		
7	Chico Serra	Fittipaldi-Cosworth V8	78		
8	René Arnoux	Renault t/c V6	77		
	Marc Surer	Ensign-Cosworth V8	70	Electrics	
	Didier Pironi	Ferrari t/c V6	67	Engine	
	Jean-Pierre Jarier	Talbot-Ligier Matra V12	64	Fuel pump	
	Hector Rebaque	Brabham-Cosworth V8	49	Accident	
	Jacques Laffite	Talbot-Ligier Matra V12	41	Collision with Cheever	
	Bruno Giacomelli	Alfa Romeo V12	41	Collision with Lammers	
	Jan Lammers	ATS-Cosworth V8	41	Collision with Giacomelli	
	Keke Rosberg	Fittipaldi-Cosworth V8	41	Distributor rotor arm	
	Riccardo Patrese	Arrows-Cosworth V8	33	Blocked fuel filter	
	Beppe Gabbiani	Osella-Cosworth V8	26	Accident/broken front suspension	
	Nigel Mansell	Lotus-Cosworth V8	25	Accident	
	Gilles Villeneuve	Ferrari t/c V6	17	Driveshaft	
	John Watson	McLaren-Cosworth V8	16	Engine	
	Elio de Angelis	Lotus-Cosworth V8	13	Accident	
	Alain Prost	Renault t/c V6	0	Hit by de Cesaris	
	Andrea de Cesaris	McLaren-Cosworth V8	0	Hit Prost	

Fastest lap: Jones, on lap 31, 1m 20·901s, 89·887mph/144·659km/h.
Lap record: Nelson Piquet (F1 Brabham BT49-Cosworth DFV), 1m 19·830s, 91·094mph/146·602km/h (1980).

Lap chart

1st	LAP ORDER	1	2	3	4	5	6	7	8	9	10	11	12	13	14	15	16	17	18	19	20	21	22	23	24	25	26	27	28	29	30	31	32	33	34	35	36	37
29	R.Patrese	29	29	29	29	29	29	29	29	29	29	29	29	29	29	29	29	29	29	29	29	29	29	29	29	2	2	2	2	2	2	2	1	1	1	1	1	1
2	C.Reutemann	2	2	2	2	2	2	2	2	2	2	2	2	2	2	2	2	2	2	2	2	2	2	2	2	29	1	1	1	1	1	1	2	2	2	2	2	2
1	A.Jones	1	1	1	1	1	1	1	1	1	1	1	1	1	1	1	1	1	1	1	1	1	1	1	1	1	(29)	5	5	5	5	5	5	5	5	5	5	5
27	G.Villeneuve	27	27	27	28	28	28	28	28	28	28	28	28	28	28	28	28	5	5	5	5	5	5	5	5	5	5	28	28	28	28	28	28	28	28	28	28	28
5	N.Piquet	5	5	5	5	5	5	5	5	5	5	5	5	5	5	5	5	28	28	28	28	28	28	28	28	28	28	3	3	3	3	3	3	3	3	3	3	3
28	D.Pironi	28	28	28	27	27	27	27	27	27	27	27	27	27	27	27	27	27	3	3	3	3	3	3	3	3	3	22	22	22	22	22	26	26	26	26	26	26
3	E.Cheever	3	3	3	3	3	3	3	3	3	3	3	3	3	3	3	3	3	22	22	22	22	22	22	22	22	22	26	26	26	26	26	22	22	22	22	22	22
22	M.Andretti	22	22	22	22	22	22	22	22	22	22	22	22	22	22	22	22	22	26	26	26	26	26	26	26	26	26	20	20	20	20	20	20	23	23	23	23	23
26	J.Laffite	26	26	26	26	26	26	26	26	26	26	26	26	26	26	26	26	26	20	20	20	20	20	20	20	20	20	23	23	23	23	23	23	20	20	20	20	20
11	E.de Angelis	11	11	11	11	11	20	20	20	20	20	20	20	20	20	20	20	20	23	23	23	23	23	23	23	23	23	33	33	33	33	33	33	33	33	33	33	33
23	B.Giacomelli	23	23	23	23	20	11	11	11	11	11	11	11	23	23	23	23	23	25	25	25	25	25	25	25	25	33	25	25	25	25	25	25	25	25	25	25	25
12	N.Mansell	12	20	20	20	23	23	23	23	23	23	23	23	25	25	25	25	25	33	33	33	33	33	33	33	33	25	14	14	14	14	14	14	14	14	14	14	14
20	K.Rosberg	20	12	12	12	12	12	12	12	12	12	25	25	11	33	33	33	33	12	12	12	12	12	12	12	12	14	21	21	21	21	21	21	21	21	21	21	21
25	J-P.Jarier	25	25	25	25	25	25	25	25	25	25	12	12	12	12	12	12	12	21	21	21	21	14	14	14	14	21	9	9	9	9	9	9	9	9	9	9	9
6	H.Rebaque	6	6	6	6	6	33	33	33	33	33	33	33	33	21	21	21	21	14	14	14	14	21	21	21	21	32	29	29	29	29	16	16	16	16	16	16	16
33	P.Tambay	33	33	33	33	33	16	16	16	16	16	16	(16)	21	14	14	14	14	32	32	32	32	32	32	32	32	9	16	16	16	16	29	29	(29)	6	6	6	6
14	M.Surer	14	14	14	14	16	6	6	6	14	21	21	21	14	32	32	32	32	6	6	6	6	6	9	9	9	16	6	6	6	6	6	6	6				
21	C.Serra	21	21	16	16	14	14	14	14	21	14	14	14	32	6	6	6	6	9	9	9	9	9	16	16	16	6											
16	R.Arnoux	16	16	21	21	21	21	21	21	(6)	32	32	32	6	9	9	9	9	16	16	16	16	16	(6)	6	6												
9	J.Lammers	9	9	9	9	7	7	7	32	32	6	6	6	9	16	16	16	16																				
7	J.Watson	7	7	7	7	(9)	32	32	(7)	9	9	9	9	16	7	7	(7)																					
32	B.Gabbiani	32	32	32	32	32	9	9	9	7	7	7	7	7																								

38	39	40	41	42	43	44	45	46	47	48	49	50	51	52	53	54	55	56	57	58	59	60	61	62	63	64	65	66	67	68	69	70	71	72	73	74	75	76	77	78	79	80
1	1	1	1	1	1	1	1	1	1	1	1	1	1	1	1	1	1	1	1	1	1	1	1	1	1	1	1	1	1	1	1	1	1	1	1	1	1	1	1	1	1	1
2	2	2	2	2	2	2	2	2	2	2	2	2	2	2	2	2	2	2	2	2	2	2	2	2	2	2	2	2	2	2	2	2	2	2	2	2	2	2	2	2	2	2
5	5	5	5	5	5	5	5	5	5	5	5	5	5	5	5	5	5	5	5	5	5	5	5	5	5	5	5	5	5	5	5	5	5	5	5	5	5	5	5	5	5	5
28	28	28	28	28	28	28	28	28	28	28	28	28	28	28	28	22	22	22	22	22	22	22	22	22	22	22	22	22	22	22	22	22	22	22	22	22	22	22	22	22	22	22
3	3	3	3	3	3	22	22	22	22	22	22	22	22	22	22	28	3	3	3	3	3	3	3	3	3	3	3	3	3	3	3	3	3	3	3	3	3	3	3	3	3	3
26	26	26	(26)	22	22	3	3	3	3	3	3	3	3	3	3	3	28	28	28	28	28	33	33	33	33	33	33	33	33	33	33	33	33	33	33	33	33	33	33	33	33	
22	22	22	22	33	33	33	33	33	33	33	33	33	33	33	33	33	33	33	33	33	33	28	28	28	28	28	28	28	(28)	14	14	14	21	21	21	21	21	21	21	21		
23	23	23	33	25	25	25	25	25	25	25	25	25	25	25	25	25	25	25	25	25	25	25	25	25	25	25	14	14	14	21	21	21	16	16	16	16	16	16	16			
20	20	33	23	14	14	14	14	14	14	14	14	14	14	14	14	14	14	14	14	14	14	14	14	14	14	14	21	21	21	16	16	16										
33	33	20	25	21	21	21	21	21	21	21	21	21	21	21	21	21	21	21	21	21	21	21	21	21	21	21	16	16	16													
25	25	25	20	16	16	16	16	16	16	16	16	16	16	16	16	16	16	16	16	16	16	16	16	16	16	16																
14	14	14	14	6	6	6	6	6	6	6	6																															
21	21	21	21																																							
9	9	9	(9)																																							
16	16	16	16																																							
6	6	6	6																																							

Fastest laps

Driver	Time	Lap
Alan Jones	1m 20·90s	31
Carlos Reutemann	1m 20·91s	31
Riccardo Patrese	1m 21·42s	14
Patrick Tambay	1m 21·75s	49
Mario Andretti	1m 21·79s	66
Nelson Piquet	1m 21·83s	69
Jacques Laffite	1m 22·08s	33
Didier Pironi	1m 22·23s	26
Eddie Cheever	1m 22·23s	36
Jan Lammers	1m 22·33s	29
Bruno Giacomelli	1m 22·41s	37
René Arnoux	1m 22·54s	34
Gilles Villeneuve	1m 22·54s	15
Hector Rebaque	1m 22·68s	49
Nigel Mansell	1m 22·75s	19
Marc Surer	1m 22·77s	50
Keke Rosberg	1m 22·88s	25
Jean-Pierre Jarier	1m 22·90s	41
Chico Serra	1m 23·09s	19
Elio de Angelis	1m 23·32s	8
John Watson	1m 24·55s	15
Beppe Gabbiani	1m 25·19s	14

Points

WORLD CHAMPIONSHIP OF DRIVERS

1	Alan Jones	9 pts
2	Carlos Reutemann	6
3	Nelson Piquet	4
4	Mario Andretti	3
5	Eddie Cheever	2
6	Patrick Tambay	1

CONSTRUCTORS' CUP

1	Williams	15
2	Brabham	4
3	Alfa Romeo	3
4	Tyrrell	2
5	Theodore	1

Grande Prêmio do Brasil

Carlos Reutemann gets the message.....

Frank Williams was in fine form on March 19. Leyland Vehicles Limited were showing a promotional film in a Mayfair cinema and Frank was on hand to answer questions when it was all over.

The subject of Long Beach and the Lotus 88 was foremost on the agenda followed by a discussion on Alan Jones's successful start to the season. The question of team orders had arisen briefly at Long Beach and Frank was asked to clarify the situation regarding the status of Jones and Carlos Reutemann.

"They have signed the same contracts this year as they did in 1980," said Williams. "Which means that Carlos is subject to team orders if he is leading Alan in a one-two situation and his gap over Alan is less than 'x' seconds. Once Alan was in front in Long Beach we applied team orders and if Carlos had not lost the lead on his own account then we may have had to have signalled Alan through. Now that's very tough on Carlos but they were the conditions that Alan wanted and Carlos agreed to.

"Long Beach was potentially the first instance of having to apply team orders," continued Frank. "I'd like to think that we will be in that situation again but realistically it doesn't happen very often."

It did; 10 days later in Rio de Janeiro. And Frank Williams didn't like the situation very much.

On lap 56 of the rain-soaked Brazilian Grand Prix, Carlos Reutemann led the depleted field onto the pit straight as he continued to display the control and superiority exercised since the race had begun almost two hours earlier. Jones was in second place, over 50 seconds clear of the next man, Riccardo Patrese in the Ragno-Beta Arrows but the Williams pit were not interested in talking about gaps. At least, not interested in talking about gaps over the competition. All that mattered at this stage was that Jones was clearly less than 'x' seconds behind Reutemann and 'JONES – REUT' on Carlos's pit board gave the Argentinian a stark reminder of his contractual obligation.

The signal was repeated again and again but Reutemann pressed on while Jones waited – and waited. The rain had slowed the race to such an extent that it became clear the two hour mark would be reached before 63 laps had been completed. On lap 61 Reutemann was given his orders again – and he responded by setting his fastest lap. At the end of lap 62 the chequered flag was shown and Carlos Reutemann joined Alan Jones at the top of the championship table.

Within minutes, the story had flashed round the world: 'Reutemann disobeys team orders and wins Brazilian Grand Prix'. From that moment on, the rumours and recriminations flowed. Other teams merely wished they had the same problems; Williams, after all, had just scored their fourth consecutive one-two finish.

Patrese finished third while fourth place was taken by Marc Surer after an excellent drive which gave the penniless Ensign team their best result in eight years. Elio de Angelis, forced to use the Essex Lotus 81 after another row over the 88, took fifth place with Jacques Laffite's Talbot-Ligier finishing over 90 seconds behind in sixth place.

Had it not rained, though, the question of a conflict within the Williams camp may not have arisen. The Parmalat Brabham team continued their development work with hydro-pneumatic suspension and Nelson Piquet had taken pole position with ease. An incredible decision to start on dry tyres destroyed Nelson's chances of a home win and the Brazilian slithered into 12th place, two laps behind the race within a race at the head of the field.

ENTRY AND PRACTICE

The second leg of a six week trip brought the teams to the Jacarepaguá track, 30 kms West of Rio de Janeiro and last used for the Brazilian Grand Prix in 1978. That race was won by Carlos Reutemann in a Ferrari and it was the Argentinian driver who set the pace during an unofficial test session on the Wednesday preceding the race. It was an ideal opportunity for teams to continue their suspension development in the quest for a chassis which would conform to the mandatory 6 cm gap between bodywork and track while at a standstill and yet close that gap considerably while on the move.

Williams had abandoned a new system of gas-filled shock absorbers by the time official practice began on Friday and it was a confident Carlos Reutemann, thriving in the heat, who set the fastest time. Jones was not so happy as he tried both cars and struggled to get rid of understeer on the troublesome constant radius curves. Neither driver improved on Saturday and Reutemann found time to wander down to the pit lane and watch the Brabham team. Carlos had flown straight from Long Beach to Brazil where he took a daily run in the heat and the swarthy Argentinian positively revelled in the sultry conditions whereas poor Nelson Piquet found the going tough. None the less, it didn't prevent the local hero from taking pole position.

Nelson's Friday practice had been interrupted by fuel system bothers and the team continued to sort their ingenious suspension. The second stage of springing had been giving the driver a hard ride but by Saturday afternoon Gordon Murray had made headway and, with 20 minutes remaining, Piquet set a time which left the other teams speechless. The hydropneumatic plumbing obviously worked and a glance at the drooping side-pods while the car was on the move merely confirmed what the stop watches had indicated clearly. There was no doubt that the system was legal but suspicions about the gap being restored grew when Piquet's car was jacked up by mechanics before officials could take measurements. Hector Rebaque began practice with the Weismann gearbox but an oil leak meant a change to the Brabham/Hewland box and the Mexican was 11th fastest.

> **MARCH**
> *Mike Hailwood dies after a road accident on March 21.*
>
> *Ford announce plans to return to sports car racing with a new Group 6 car.*

Riccardo Patrese backed up his Long Beach performance with fourth fastest time in spite of damaging his car on kerbing on Friday. A subsequent understeer problem may have been a direct result of that but Siegfried Stohr had few excuses when he crashed his Arrows on Saturday morning. His machine was repaired in time for the Italian to take 21st place on a grid which, surprisingly, featured four DFV-engined cars at the front.

It had been predicted that the turbocharged engines would blow the opposition away on the long straights but Alain Prost in fifth place was the first of the 1.5-litre brigade. Prost had been the fastest Renault-Elf driver throughout practice and he set his time in the spare car on Saturday after losing fourth gear on his regular car the previous day. René Arnoux was very depressed on Friday evening, the little Frenchman seemingly unable to get to grips with the circuit. His plight was made worse on Saturday when he understeered off the circuit and damaged his left-front suspension on a catch-fence pole. René took over Prost's abandoned race car to set eighth fastest time. The Marlboro Alfa Romeo team, by contrast, had a trouble-free practice. Mario Andretti and Bruno Giacomelli started off with different set-ups but Bruno changed to Mario's way of thinking on Saturday and immediately went three-tenths quicker than his team-mate!

"We are 15 kms quicker than the Cosworth cars on the straights but the car is so bad through the corners that it is not doing us much good," said Gilles Villeneuve, summing up the Ferrari team's problems. Both Villeneuve and Didier Pironi used KKK turbos while the Comprex was taken away for further development. The wisdom of the decision was shown when Villeneuve used the same engine throughout practice, working the unit hard on his way to seventh place on the grid. Pironi was 10 places further back after a spin on Saturday damaged the underside of the monocoque and deranged the low-mounted inlet manifold on the V6. Didier was to use the spare car for the remainder of practice and the race.

The Essex Lotus team, of course, were embroiled in the second bout of arguing over the twin-chassis 88, the upshot of which was a return to the elderly 81 for poor de Angelis. Both Elio and Nigel Mansell did their best, the Italian fighting a high speed handling problem, the Englishman struggling with fading brakes and a faulty rev-limiter.

Keke Rosberg began practice in good form with eighth fastest time on Friday but the Fittipaldi team's hopes slipped away the next day when the Finn, unaccountably, could not improve his time. Chico Serra was keen to give a good account of himself in his first home Grand Prix but the loss of fourth gear on Saturday kept the Brazilian at the back of the grid.

Fresh with enthusiasm from their Long Beach success, the Tyrrell team tried a new nose wing on Friday but abandoned that in the hope that Eddie Cheever might continue his good progress on Saturday. It was not to be and a change in pod profile could not rid the team of a problem with the car's balance. Ricardo Zunino brought a handful of cash for the second seat and the Argentinian just managed to scrape onto the back of the grid.

The Marlboro McLaren team had rushed their carbon-fibre MP4 back to Donington immediately

All knees and feet. John Watson untangled himself only to get crossed up in the race when he spun out of fourth place *(below)*.
Marc Surer was the star of the race, setting fastest lap and taking fourth place in the underfinanced Ensign. The Swiss driver charges inside Eddie Cheever's Tyrrell after the American driver had been involved in a start-line shunt *(below left)*.
Didier Pironi and Mauro Forghieri discuss the Ferrari which ran with a KKK turbocharger at Rio. Pironi ended an unhappy weekend when he spun and took off Prost while moving off line to allow the Renault through *(bottom)*.

Riccardo Patrese and the Arrows continued to show good form by finishing a fine third *(right)*. New pit lane profiles. Bernie Ecclestone laid on many side attractions in Brazil *(right, inset)*. Waiting for it to come to the boil. Alan Jones relaxes during practice and looks much happier than he did after the race *(below)*. Pointing out the bad news. Jean-Pierre Jabouille returned to the cockpit for the first time since breaking his leg in the 1980 Canadian Grand Prix. Jabouille was off the pace and stood down in favour of Jean-Pierre Jarier *(bottom)*.

after Long Beach but the English weather put paid to any hopes of lengthy testing. John Watson was rather surprised therefore to find himself so far up the grid with the heavy M29F while Andrea de Cesaris found his level on the tenth row after a series of spins.

While the McLaren team quietly got on with the job, the Talbot-Ligier pit was a scene of confusion throughout practice. Jean-Pierre Jabouille made a welcome return to the cockpit for the first time since his accident in the Canadian Grand Prix the previous year but the lanky Frenchman was off the pace from the start. His right ankle was making life difficult when it came to shifting quickly from throttle to brake and back again but it took the team until Saturday afternoon to make a substitution.

Jean-Pierre Jarier had been standing by and was ready to take over for the final hour of practice. At the end of his fourth lap, Jarier crossed the line sideways and up on the kerb: "I felt the car go sideways so I buried my foot in the throttle – and suddenly there was no power. The linkage had broken." Jarier's time on that lap – broken linkage or not – was good enough to move him onto the back row which was just as well for the Frenchman was unable to do better in Laffite's car which refused to run properly. Jacques was having his problems too. Ligier had fitted extra oil radiators to cope with the heat and smaller nose fins to cope with the constant radius curves but, either way, Laffite could not make the car handle. His chances of improving on Friday's time took a dive when the V12 gave trouble and he switched to the spare chassis.

Ensign simply wished they had the luxury of a spare chassis as they struggled on a tiny budget. Originally, the plan had been to run with financial help from the CanAm and IMSA driver, Ricardo Londono Bridge who drove the Ensign on Wednesday. That proved to be a disastrous affair when, after a few slow laps, the Columbian managed to hit Rosberg's Fittipaldi. To everyone's relief it was discovered that the novice did not have a suitable licence. Marc Surer, fortunately, was on hand and the Swiss, troubled with an engine failure and a leaking oil radiator, did a workmanlike job and took a place ahead of Patrick Tambay in the Theodore. The Frenchman lost time on Saturday while the team fiddled unsuccessfully with different springing and he was unable to produce Friday's form once the car had been converted back to its original settings.

The busy schedule away from home was taking its toll, particularly on the ATS team who had to make do with a patched up chassis for Jan Lammers following his coming together with Giacomelli at Long Beach. The car was never right and the Dutchman's super-human efforts resulted in a couple of spins and a place at the head of the non-qualifiers.

The Denim Osella outfit were in a shambles with their engineer back in Italy and Enzo Osella confined to bed on Saturday. The cars featured new front and rear suspension mountings but the young drivers and mechanics desperately needed leadership and Guerra and Gabbiani failed to qualify. The March team were in an even worse state of disarray when Derek Daly crashed on Friday. The Irishman had been convinced that the front of his car was flexing and, when a bottom left front wishbone pulled out of the monocoque, it confirmed his worst fears. Daly bruised his shins on the steering rack and Robin Herd flew straight back to England, leaving behind an angry and frustrated team. Small wonder then that the lack of confidence and enthusiasm took its toll on Eliseo Salazar who was almost ten seconds off the pace.

RACE

Emerson Fittipaldi delighted the crowd when he completed a few laps in an F8 to acknowledge his retirement. The teams, meanwhile, were looking ahead as they carried out the final preparations and Lotus, in particular, had a busy time as they set to work on Mansell's car after the Englishman had hit the barrier during the warm-up. The gear-box casing had broken, clearly a continuing legacy from the crash at Long Beach, and the Lotus mechanics' speedy work was at the expense of the ATS team who, at one stage, had hoped for a race after all.

The outcome of the race, however, seemed a foregone conclusion when Piquet was a full two seconds quicker than Jones in the warm-up. Dark looks were cast at the Brabham but nothing was said – officially. This was, after all, Bernie Ecclestone's race in more ways than one. The FOCA and Brabham chief had written, produced, directed and, at one stage, starred in the show. There were girls in various stages of undress, dragsters (the mechanical variety) in various stages of tune and, to cap it all, a stunt motorcyclist flew over seven Grand Prix cars including a Brabham with Mr. Ecclestone himself peering anxiously from the cockpit.

A blanket of drizzle and grey cloud showed every intention of staying put for the race and there seemed little doubt that wet tyres were the only way to go. Small wonder, then, that the pit lane looked on in amazement as Piquet opted for slicks. The decision seemed to have been taken by Nelson himself who felt the rain would stop but it was clear that Bernie Ecclestone did not share his driver's optimism.

Pironi and Stohr were of the same opinion as Piquet but they had slightly less to lose as the field churned off the starting grid. Nelson sat with his wheels spinning while, behind the Brabham, chaos reigned as several cars became involved in a pile-up. Villeneuve had made his usual speedy start but Prost was not so fast off the mark and the Ferrari driver bent his nose wing against the back of the Renault. Andretti piled into the back of the Ferrari, flew up into the air and crashed back onto the track. In the subsequent confusion, Rosberg and Cheever collided, Arnoux and Serra came into contact and Stohr thumped the Fittipaldi while Rebaque came away with a damaged nose wing. De Cesaris took one look at the turmoil and moved off the track while Surer did likewise and motored for 200 yards or more along the grass to emerge in ninth place! Others were not so fortunate, Andretti, Arnoux and Serra retiring on the spot and Cheever making a pit stop for repairs and attention to fuel feed problems.

The Williams drivers were blissfully unaware of all this as they sailed into the lead, Reutemann ahead of Jones with Patrese already dropping back and opening a gap on Giacomelli. De Angelis and Rosberg were next while Villeneuve was pressing on in seventh place regardless of his bent nose wing. Prost, none the worse for wear, was followed by Surer who was busy fending off Watson. Laffite was next then de Cesaris, Rebaque, Jarier (another driver to make the most of the early confusion), the slithering Piquet, Mansell, Zunino, Tambay, Pironi and Stohr.

De Angelis moved ahead of Giacomelli on lap four and it was the beginning of the end for the Alfa Romeo driver. An electrical problem during the warm-up had been traced to the battery – or so the team thought – but the trouble returned during the race and it was not until five pit stops later and a new coil that the problem was rectified. By then, Bruno was too far behind to be classified. Rosberg gave chase to de Angelis and Watson followed the Fittipaldi having moved ahead of Surer while Villeneuve called at the pits for a new nose cone. While he was there, the mechanics fitted slicks which, in the event, would have proved useless had Gilles not retired eventually when the turbo gave trouble.

As the track began to dry slightly, Rosberg's hopes faded along with the grip from the front of his Fittipaldi and Watson took fifth place on lap 14, four

CERAMICHE RAGNO
Beta
29

That's done it! Carlos Reutemann takes the chequered flag while Alan Jones gives the Williams team another one-two finish – albeit, not in the planned order *(above)*.
The damp and half-hearted presentation *(right)*.

Williams tried a ride-height control using gas-filled shock absorbers during unofficial testing *(far right)*.

laps after his team-mate had stopped with electrical trouble. Jarier, having a typical charge while he had the chance, had passed Laffite, Prost, Surer and Rosberg and was making inroads on the McLaren. All his work was in vain, however, when a gamble on setting the Ligier up for understeer initially in the hope that it would become neutral later in the race

WHEN THE LOTUS 88 WAS CLEARED BY AN ACCUS appeal court in Atlanta, Georgia on March 19 following its exclusion from the United States Grand Prix (West), it appeared that Colin Chapman's car might stand a better chance of acceptance by the organisers of the Brazilian Grand Prix. Doubts began to grow, however, when FISA made it clear that the court's decisions were applicable 'on American territory only and concern the Long Beach Grand Prix alone'.

The scrutineers passed the car initially but subsequent protests from at least six teams, including Williams and Ferrari, made the officials think again.

Midway through the Friday morning practice session, the Stewards asked to see the car again. They wanted to know if the 88 conformed to the regulation which stated that, with the tyres deflated on one side, the bodywork did not touch the ground. The mechanics duly obliged; the bodywork did not touch the ground. Then the officials pushed the car backwards and forwards; the bodywork did not touch the ground. A grunting official then began to lean heavily on the bodywork – and it touched the ground.

Nothing more was said and, when the car was rolled out to take part in the afternoon session, it was promptly black-flagged and declared illegal – because the bodywork touched the ground!

The whole scenario had been acted out under contrived circumstances and the final insult to the Lotus team was the fact that the majority of the badly organised officials could speak only in Portuguese. The FISA rules stated that the English translation of their regulations was the one which should be used to settle disputes.

A despondent Elio de Angelis waits for his Lotus 81 after the 88 had been excluded from the second race in succession.

failed to pay off on the drying track and Jean-Pierre fell back behind the Ensign. Rebaque made a pit-stop for a new nose and the Mexican was to retire when he fell off the track on lap 22, not long after Stohr's race on slicks had some to an end when he was accidentally punted off by Tambay's sliding Theodore.

The Arrows team's hopes had been pinned on Patrese all along and the Italian, driving with maturity and skill, wisely decided to concentrate on not making any mistakes and aim for a finish in the wet rather than challenge the Williams drivers. Jones held a steady two to three second gap between his team-mate while the remainder of the field appeared to collapse in the spray. On lap 21, Pironi still struggling with slicks, did the gentlemanly thing and moved over when Prost was about to lap him. The Ferrari spun suddenly and collected the hapless Renault in a spectacular accident from which both drivers emerged unscathed.

The rain had returned by lap 30 and Watson was under pressure from an inspired Surer with the Ligiers making the dice a four-some not long after. Watson appeared to have the measure of them all until lap 35 when the McLaren got away from him and he spun down to eighth place. Rosberg was ninth now and Tambay had survived a challenge from Piquet on the dry track but the rain changed all that and Nelson was soon making a mockery of Zunino in the wet-shod Tyrrell. Surer, having claimed fifth place, soon realised fourth could be his as de Angelis struggled with a collapsed shock absorber and a slow puncture. Patrese maintained a steady third place and, with 15 laps to go, attention shifted to the Williams HQ – a green and white brolly protecting Frank at his post by the pit wall.

Reutemann was showing no signs of waving Jones through and Frank Williams ordered the first 'JONES – REUT' signal on lap 56. Reutemann, with a clear track ahead, saw the signal and Jones merely waited for the appropriate gesture from his number two. It never came. The team repeated the signal and Jones, wisely, held station rather than risk a challenge in the treacherous conditions.

The regulations stated that a race should run for either two hours or the prescribed distance (in this case, 63 laps), whichever came first. The two-hour mark was reached when Reutemann was halfway round his 62nd lap and he was duly shown the chequered flag at the end of that lap. Reutemann later claimed he had intended to let Jones through on lap 63 but that theory lost a fair amount of credibility when it was discovered that 'Lole' had been going hell-for-leather and set his fastest lap just before the flag was shown.

Jones, simmering gently and now fully aware that it was every man for himself since contracts obviously meant little to Reutemann, shook hands with Carlos but did not remain on the rostrum. Patrese joined the winner for a rather damp and half-hearted presentation while the Ensign team, by contrast, were cock-a-hoop over Surer's fastest lap and brilliant drive into fourth place. After eight years of struggling, Mo Nunn had scored his best result when he least expected it. Elio de Angelis held on gamely and took fifth place while Jacques Laffite, in difficulties with damp electrics, had dropped behind his team-mate but was waved back into the points by the deferential Jarier, keen to create the right impression.

The Williams drivers, on the other hand, were far too experienced and well established for that kind of behaviour, which, ironically, was one of the main reasons why the Saudia-Leyland Williams had been able to set such an impressive record. Four one-two finishes in a row was a superb achievement regardless of which driver happened to be in front at the time.

Grande Prêmio do Brasil, March 29/statistics

Entries and practice times

No.	Driver	Nat	Car	Engine	Entrant	Practice 1	Practice 2
1	Alan Jones	AUS	Saudia-Leyland WILLIAMS FWO7C	Ford Cosworth DFV	Albilad-Williams Racing Team	**1m 36·337s**	1m 36·690s
2	Carlos Reutemann	RA	Saudia-Leyland WILLIAMS FWO7C	Ford Cosworth DFV	Albilad-Williams Racing Team	**1m 35·390s**	1m 36·000s
3	Eddie Cheever	USA	TYRRELL 010	Ford Cosworth DFV	Tyrrell Racing	**1m 38·160s**	1m 38·521s
4	Ricardo Zunino	RA	TYRRELL 010	Ford Cosworth DFV	Tyrrell Racing	1m 41·036s	**1m 39·798s**
5	Nelson Piquet	BR	Parmalat BRABHAM BT49C	Ford Cosworth DFV	Parmalat Racing Team	1m 35·786s	**1m 35·079s**
6	Hector Rebaque	MEX	Parmalat BRABHAM BT49C	Ford Cosworth DFV	Parmalat Racing Team	1m 38·225s	**1m 37·777s**
7	John Watson	GB	Marlboro McLAREN M29F	Ford Cosworth DFV	McLaren International	1m 40·057s	**1m 38·263s**
8	Andrea de Cesaris	I	Marlboro McLAREN M29F	Ford Cosworth DFV	McLaren International	1m 39·409s	**1m 38·780s**
9	Jan Lammers	NL	ATS D4	Ford Cosworth DFV	Team ATS	1m 40·339s	**1m 39·844s**
11	Elio de Angelis	I	Essex LOTUS 81	Ford Cosworth DFV	Team Essex Lotus	1m 38·352s	**1m 37·734s**
12	Nigel Mansell	GB	Essex LOTUS 81	Ford Cosworth DFV	Team Essex Lotus	1m 38·861s	**1m 38·003s**
14	Marc Surer	CH	ENSIGN N180B	Ford Cosworth DFV	Ensign Racing	1m 39·296s	**1m 38·570s**
15	Alain Prost	F	Elf RENAULT RE 20	Renault EF1	Equipe Renault Elf	1m 37·147s	**1m 36·670s**
16	René Arnoux	F	Elf RENAULT RE 20	Renault EF1	Equipe Renault Elf	1m 38·985s	**1m 37·561s**
17	Derek Daly	IRL	Rizla MARCH 811	Ford Cosworth DFV	March Grand Prix	–	–
18	Eliseo Salazar	RCH	Rizla MARCH 811	Ford Cosworth DFV	March Grand Prix	1m 44·730s	**1m 43·267s**
20	Keke Rosberg	SF	FITTIPALDI F8C	Ford Cosworth DFV	Fittipaldi Automotive	**1m 37·981s**	1m 39·371s
21	Chico Serra	BR	FITTIPALDI F8C	Ford Cosworth DFV	Fittipaldi Automotive	**1m 39·326s**	1m 39·396s
22	Mario Andretti	USA	Marlboro ALFA ROMEO 179C	Alfa Romeo 1260	Marlboro Team Alfa Romeo	1m 37·933s	**1m 37·597s**
23	Bruno Giacomelli	I	Marlboro ALFA ROMEO 179C	Alfa Romeo 1260	Marlboro Team Alfa Romeo	1m 38·682s	**1m 37·283s**
25	Jean-Pierre Jabouille	F	Talbot-Gitanes LIGIER JS17	Matra MS 81	Equipe Talbot Gitanes	**1m 40·306s**	–
25	Jean-Pierre Jarier	F	Talbot-Gitanes LIGIER JS17	Matra MS 81	Equipe Talbot Gitanes	–	**1m 39·398s**
26	Jacques Laffite	F	Talbot-Gitanes LIGIER JS17	Matra MS 81	Equipe Talbot Gitanes	**1m 38·273s**	1m 38·713s
27	Gilles Villeneuve	CDN	Fiat FERRARI 126CK	Ferrari 126C	Scuderia Ferrari SpA SEFAC	1m 37·975s	**1m 37·497s**
28	Didier Pironi	F	Fiat FERRARI 126CK	Ferrari 126C	Scuderia Ferrari SpA SEFAC	1m 39·229s	**1m 38·565s**
29	Riccardo Patrese	I	Ragno-Beta ARROWS A3	Ford Cosworth DFV	Arrows Racing Team	1m 37·231s	**1m 36·667s**
30	Siegfried Stohr	I	Ragno-Beta ARROWS A3	Ford Cosworth DFV	Arrows Racing Team	1m 40·297s	**1m 39·190s**
31	Miguel Angel Guerra	RA	Denim OSELLA FA1B	Ford Cosworth DFV	Osella Squadra Corse	**1m 40·984s**	1m 44·482s
32	Beppe Gabbiani	I	Denim OSELLA FA1B	Ford Cosworth DFV	Osella Squadra Corse	1m 41·954s	**1m 40·709s**
33	Patrick Tambay	F	THEODORE TY 01	Ford Cosworth DFV	Theodore Racing Team	**1m 38·726s**	1m 39·668s
Friday morning and Saturday morning practice sessions not officially recorded						*Fri pm Warm, dry*	*Sat pm Warm, occasional rain*

Starting grid

5 PIQUET (1m 35·079s)
Brabham

2 REUTEMANN (1m 35·390s)
Williams

1 JONES (1m 36·377s)
Williams

29 PATRESE (1m 36·667s)
Arrows

15 PROST (1m 36·670s)
Renault

23 GIACOMELLI (1m 37·283s)
Alfa Romeo

27 VILLENEUVE (1m 37·497s)
Ferrari

16 ARNOUX (1m 37·561s)
Renault

22 ANDRETTI (1m 37·597s)
Alfa Romeo

11 DE ANGELIS (1m 37·734s)
Lotus

6 REBAQUE (1m 37·777s)
Brabham

20 ROSBERG (1m 37·981s)
Fittipaldi

12 MANSELL (1m 38·003s)
Lotus

3 CHEEVER (1m 38·160s)
Tyrrell

7 WATSON (1m 38·263s)
McLaren

26 LAFFITE (1m 38·273s)
Talbot-Ligier

28 PIRONI (1m 38·565s)
Ferrari

14 SURER (1m 38·570s)
Ensign

33 TAMBAY (1m 38·726s)
Theodore

8 DE CESARIS (1m 38·780s)
McLaren

30 STOHR (1m 39·190s)
Arrows

21 SERRA (1m 39·326s)
Fittipaldi

25 JARIER (1m 39·398s)
Talbot-Ligier

4 ZUNINO (1m 39·798s)
Tyrrell

Did not start:
9 Lammers (ATS), 1m 39·844s, did not qualify
25 Jabouille (Talbot-Ligier), 1m 40·306s, withdrew
32 Gabbiani (Osella), 1m 40·709s, did not qualify
31 Guerra (Osella), 1m 40·984s, did not qualify
18 Salazar (March), 1m 43·267s, did not qualify
17 Daly (March), no time recorded, did not qualify

Past winners

Year	Driver	Nat	Car	Circuit	Distance miles/km	Speed mph/km/h
1972*	Carlos Reutemann	RA	3·0 Brabham BT34-Ford	Interlagos	183·01/294·53	112·89/181·68
1973	Emerson Fittipaldi	BR	3·0 JPS/Lotus 72-Ford	Interlagos	197·85/318·42	114·23/183·83
1974	Emerson Fittipaldi	BR	3·0 McLaren M23-Ford	Interlagos	158·28/254·73	112·23/180·62
1975	Carlos Pace	BR	3·0 Brabham BT44B-Ford	Interlagos	197·85/318·42	113·40/182·50
1976	Niki Lauda	A	3·0 Ferrari 312T/76	Interlagos	197·85/318·42	112·76/181·47
1977	Carlos Reutemann	RA	3·0 Ferrari 312T-2/77	Interlagos	197·85/318·42	112·92/181·73
1978	Carlos Reutemann	RA	3·0 Ferrari 312T-2/78	Rio de Janeiro	196·95/316·95	107·43/172·89
1979	Jacques Laffite	F	3·0 Ligier JS11-Ford	Interlagos	197·85/318·42	117·23/188·67
1980	René Arnoux	F	1·5 Renault RS t/c	Interlagos	195·70/314·95	117·40/188·93
1981	Carlos Reutemann	RA	3·0 Williams FWO7C-Ford	Rio de Janeiro	193·82/311·92	96·59/155·45

*Non-championship

Circuit data

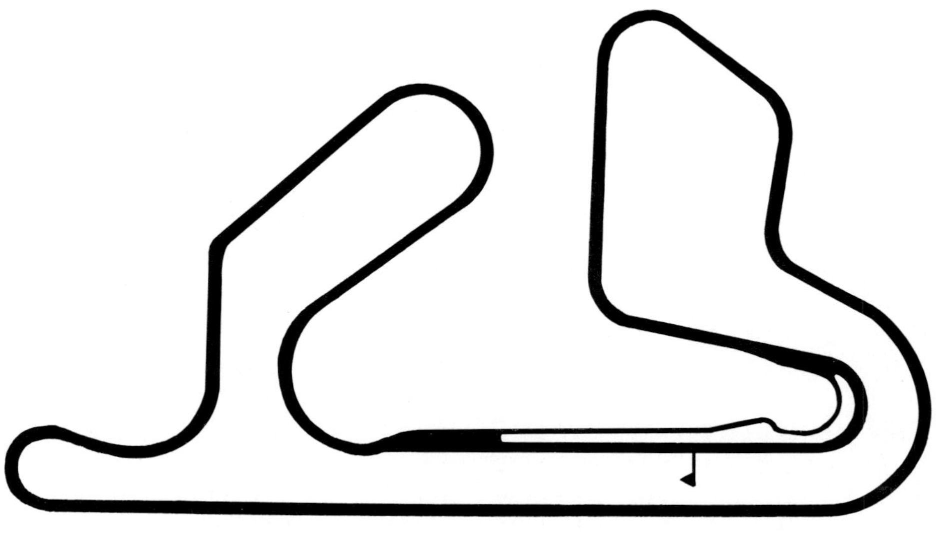

Autodromo Internacional do Rio de Janeiro, Baixada de Jacarepaguá
Circuit length: 3·126 miles/5·031 km
Race distance: 62 laps, 193·82 miles/311·922 km (race scheduled to run for 63 laps but stopped after two hours of racing)
Race weather: Wet.

Results and retirements

Place	Driver	Car	Laps	Time and Speed (mph/km/h)/Retirement
1	Carlos Reutemann	Williams-Cosworth V8	62	2h 00m 23·66s 96·59/155·45
2	Alan Jones	Williams-Cosworth V8	62	2h 00m 28·10s
3	Riccardo Patrese	Arrows-Cosworth V8	62	2h 01m 26·74s
4	Marc Surer	Ensign-Cosworth V8	62	2h 01m 40·69s
5	Elio de Angelis	Lotus-Cosworth V8	62	2h 01m 50·08s
6	Jacques Laffite	Talbot-Ligier Matra V12	62	2h 01m 50·49s
7	Jean-Pierre Jarier	Talbot-Ligier Matra V12	62	2h 01m 53·91s
8	John Watson	McLaren-Cosworth V8	61	
9	Keke Rosberg	Fittipaldi-Cosworth V8	61	
10	Patrick Tambay	Theodore-Cosworth V8	61	
11	Nigel Mansell	Lotus-Cosworth V8	61	
12	Nelson Piquet	Brabham-Cosworth V8	60	
13	Ricardo Zunino	Tyrrell-Cosworth V8	57	
	Eddie Cheever	Tyrrell-Cosworth V8	49	Running, not classified
	Bruno Giacomelli	Alfa Romeo V12	40	Electrics, running, not classified
	Gilles Villeneuve	Ferrari t/c V6	25	Broken turbo wastegate
	Hector Rebaque	Brabham-Cosworth V8	22	Rear suspension damage
	Siegfried Stohr	Arrows-Cosworth V8	20	Collision with Tambay
	Alain Prost	Renault t/c V6	20	Hit by Pironi
	Didier Pironi	Ferrari t/c V6	19	Collision with Prost
	Andrea de Cesaris	McLaren-Cosworth V8	9	Electrics
	Chico Serra	Fittipaldi-Cosworth V8	0	Start-line collision
	René Arnoux	Renault t/c V6	0	Start-line collision
	Mario Andretti	Alfa Romeo V12	0	Start-line collision

Fastest lap: Surer, on lap 36, 1m 54·302s, 98·458mph/158·453km/h.
Lap record: Carlos Reutemann (F1 Ferrari 312T-2), 1m 43·07s, 109·188mph/175·721km/h (1978).

Lap chart

1st LAP ORDER		1	2	3	4	5	6	7	8	9	10	11	12	13	14	15	16	17	18	19	20	21	22	23	24	25	26	27	28
2	C.Reutemann	2	2	2	2	2	2	2	2	2	2	2	2	2	2	2	2	2	2	2	2	2	2	2	2	2	2	2	2
1	A.Jones	1	1	1	1	1	1	1	1	1	1	1	1	1	1	1	1	1	1	1	1	1	1	1	1	1	1	1	1
29	R.Patrese	29	29	29	29	29	29	29	29	29	29	29	29	29	29	29	29	29	29	29	29	29	29	29	29	29	29	29	29
23	B.Giacomelli	23	23	23	11	11	11	11	11	11	11	11	11	11	11	11	11	11	11	11	11	11	11	11	11	11	11	11	11
11	E.de Angelis	11	11	11	23	23	23	20	20	20	20	20	20	20	7	7	7	7	7	7	7	7	7	7	7	7	7	7	7
20	K.Rosberg	20	20	20	20	20	20	27	27	7	7	7	7	7	20	20	25	25	25	25	25	25	25	25	25	25	25	25	25
27	G.Villeneuve	27	27	27	27	27	27	7	7	14	14	14	14	14	14	25	20	20	14	14	14	14	14	14	14	14	14	14	14
15	A.Prost	15	7	7	7	7	7	14	14	27	25	25	25	25	25	14	14	14	20	20	15	26	26	26	26	26	26	26	26
14	M.Surer	14	15	15	14	14	14	15	15	15	15	15	15	15	15	15	15	15	15	15	20	20	20	20	20	20	20	20	20
7	J.Watson	7	14	14	15	15	15	25	25	25	26	26	26	26	26	26	26	26	26	26	26	33	33	33	33	33	33	33	33
26	J.Laffite	26	26	26	26	25	25	26	26	26	(27)	33	33	33	33	33	33	33	33	33	33	12	12	12	12	12	12	12	5
8	A.de Cesaris	8	8	25	25	26	26	(23)	6	6	6	12	12	12	12	12	12	12	12	12	12	5	5	5	5	5	5	5	12
6	H.Rebaque	6	25	8	6	6	6	6	33	33	33	(6)	5	5	5	5	5	5	5	5	5	27	27	(27)	(27)	27	4	4	4
25	J-P.Jarier	25	6	6	8	33	33	33	12	12	12	5	4	4	4	4	4	4	4	4	27	4	4	4	4	4	3	3	3
5	N.Piquet	5	33	33	33	8	8	8	8	(8)	5	4	27	27	27	27	27	27	27	27	30	6	(6)	(3)	3	3	23	23	23
12	N.Mansell	12	12	12	12	12	12	12	5	5	4	27	28	28	28	28	28	28	28	28	4	3	3	23	(23)	23			
4	R.Zunino	4	5	5	5	5	5	5	4	4	28	28	30	30	30	30	30	30	30	30	6	23	23						
33	P.Tambay	33	4	4	4	4	4	4	28	28	30	30	6	6	6	6	6	6	6	6	3								
28	D.Pironi	28	28	28	28	28	28	28	30	30	23	23	(23)	3	3	3	3	3	3	3	23								
30	S.Stohr	30	30	30	30	30	30	30	23	23	3	3	3	23	23	23	23	(23)	23	23									
3	E.Cheever	(3)	3	3	3	3	3	3	3	3																			

29	30	31	32	33	34	35	36	37	38	39	40	41	42	43	44	45	46	47	48	49	50	51	52	53	54	55	56	57	58	59	60	61	62
2	2	2	2	2	2	2	2	2	2	2	2	2	2	2	2	2	2	2	2	2	2	2	2	2	2	2	2	2	2	2	2	2	2
1	1	1	1	1	1	1	1	1	1	1	1	1	1	1	1	1	1	1	1	1	1	1	1	1	1	1	1	1	1	1	1	1	1
29	29	29	29	29	29	29	29	29	29	29	29	29	29	29	29	29	29	29	29	29	29	29	29	29	29	29	29	29	29	29	29	29	29
11	11	11	11	11	11	11	11	11	11	11	11	11	11	11	11	11	11	11	11	14	14	14	14	14	14	14	14	14	14	14	14	14	14
7	7	7	7	7	7	14	14	14	14	14	14	14	14	14	14	14	14	14	14	11	11	11	11	11	11	11	11	11	11	11	11	11	11
14	14	14	14	14	14	26	26	26	26	26	26	26	26	26	26	26	26	25	25	25	25	25	25	25	25	25	25	25	25	25	26	26	26
26	26	26	26	26	26	25	25	25	25	25	25	25	25	25	25	25	25	26	26	26	26	26	26	26	26	26	26	26	26	26	25	25	25
25	25	25	25	25	25	7	7	7	7	7	7	7	7	7	7	7	7	7	7	7	7	7	7	7	7	7	7	7	7	7	7	7	
20	20	20	20	20	20	20	20	20	5	5	5	5	5	5	5	5	5	5	20	20	20	20	20	20	20	20	20	20	20	20	20	20	
33	33	33	33	33	33	33	33	33	20	20	20	20	20	20	20	20	20	20	33	33	33	33	33	33	33	33	33	33	33	33	33	33	
5	5	5	5	5	5	5	5	5	33	33	33	33	33	33	33	33	33	33	5	5	5	12	12	12	12	12	12	12	12	12	12	12	
12	12	12	12	12	12	12	12	12	12	12	12	12	12	12	12	12	12	12	12	12	12	5	5	5	5	5	5	5	5	5	5		
4	4	4	4	4	4	4	4	4	4	4	4	4	4	4	4	4	4	4	4	4	4	4	4	4	4	4	4	4					
3	3	3	3	3	3	3	3	3	3	3	3	3	3	3	3	3	3	3	3	3													
23	(23)	23	23	23	23	23	23	23	23	23	23																						

Fastest laps

Driver	Time	Lap
Marc Surer	1m 54·30s	36
Jacques Laffite	1m 54·50s	37
Nelson Piquet	1m 54·67s	31
Carlos Reutemann	1m 54·78s	61
Alan Jones	1m 55·21s	54
Jean-Pierre Jarier	1m 55·85s	38
Riccardo Patrese	1m 56·10s	9
Elio de Angelis	1m 56·27s	46
Patrick Tambay	1m 56·71s	15
Bruno Giacomelli	1m 56·73s	40
John Watson	1m 56·95s	29
Nigel Mansell	1m 57·12s	10
Alain Prost	1m 57·12s	14
Hector Rebaque	1m 57·27s	14
Keke Rosberg	1m 57·34s	8
Gilles Villeneuve	1m 57·42s	8
Andrea de Cesaris	1m 58·87s	7
Eddie Cheever	1m 59·19s	34
Ricardo Zunino	2m 00·35s	39
Didier Pironi	2m 00·44s	15
Siegfried Stohr	2m 03·42s	12

Points

WORLD CHAMPIONSHIP OF DRIVERS

1 =	Alan Jones	15 pts
1 =	Carlos Reutemann	15
3 =	Nelson Piquet	4
3 =	Riccardo Patrese	4
5 =	Mario Andretti	3
5 =	Marc Surer	3
7 =	Eddie Cheever	2
7 =	Elio de Angelis	2
9 =	Patrick Tambay	1
9 =	Jacques Laffite	1

CONSTRUCTORS' CUP

1	Williams	30
2 =	Brabham	4
2 =	Arrows	4
4 =	Alfa Romeo	3
4 =	Ensign	3
6 =	Tyrrell	2
6 =	Lotus	2
8 =	Theodore	1
8 =	Ligier	1

Gran Premio de la República Argentina

The 80,000 crowd were stunned. It wasn't simply that Carlos Alberto Reutemann had dropped to third place; their hero, more to the point, had been passed by Hector Rebaque and that was more than the Argentinians could stomach. The Brabham had waltzed past the Williams as though it were in a different class – which, in a manner of speaking, it was – and the performance of Rebaque, no more than a gritty journeyman driver by any standards, merely underlined the superiority of Gordon Murray's hydro-pneumatic suspension and heightened the inter-team tension which had been building up throughout the weekend.

Nelson Piquet had taken the lead on lap one, confident that his car was unbeatable, but the Parmalat Brabham team were denied an easy one-two victory when Rebaque saved further embarrassment by retiring with a dead engine halfway through the 53-lap race. Subsequent protests against the Brabham, although rejected, were to cause considerable ill-feeling among the once solid ranks of FOCA.

Reutemann finished second and thus edged into the lead of the championship once more after Alan Jones had to be content with fourth place. The anticipated struggle between the Saudia-Leyland Williams drivers came to nothing when Jones was forced to end a difficult weekend with a down-on-power engine.

The Buenos Aires autodrome should have been Renault territory but the Elf-sponsored team were slightly off the pace and certainly no match for Brabham. Alain Prost started from the front row but realised after five laps that a mysterious vibration would keep him in third place at best while René Arnoux was unable to make any impression on Jones for similar reasons.

The Essex Lotus team received the final insult when the 88 did not even pass scrutineering. Colin Chapman stormed out of the circuit leaving behind a hastily considered press release which gave vent to his pent-up emotions and earned an arbitrary fine from FISA. Elio de Angelis, back in an 81 once more, pulled something out of the weekend with a typically determined drive into sixth place after an incident in the opening laps had dropped him to the back of the field.

The Lotus driver's superb run pushed Riccardo Patrese's Ragno-Beta Arrows out of the points and the Italian, hampered by a front-end vibration, finished ahead of an unhappy Mario Andretti in a Marlboro Alfa Romeo which had a misfire and handled badly. Ferrari, too, were in engine trouble but their problems were minor compared to those of the Talbot-Ligier team who were at a loss to explain why their cars were slow on the straights and would not handle elsewhere. Jean-Pierre Jabouille failed to qualify and Guy Ligier's angry departure from Argentina on Friday merely added further tension to a weekend which the majority of teams were glad to be done with.

ENTRY AND PRACTICE

From the moment Alan Jones set foot in Argentina, he was aware that half the nation, not to mention the frenzied motor racing supporters, knew all about the politics within the Williams team following Reutemann's victory in Brazil. Jones was hassled at customs; pursued by press men, their pencils dripping with his blood; hounded by jeering fans. At the circuit, they seethed behind the fence opposite the Williams pit. Occasionally, Jones would wave in response to cat calls but their fury erupted when he held aloft a pit board saying 'JONES – REUT'. The uniformed police looked uneasy, wishing Jones would stop taunting the locals with what amounted to an attack on their religion.

Then Reutemann arrived and the mood changed. A pit board showing 'REUT – JONES' was the final peace offering; the crowd were delirious and burst into their chant of "Lole...Lole...Lole..." as they reaffirmed their opinion that the Argentine Grand Prix should, at last, belong to Carlos Reutemann. Brabham, however, had other ideas.

Having made such a nonsense of the Brazilian race a fortnight before, Gordon Murray was keen to make the most of his hydro-pneumatic advantage before the others caught up when they returned to Europe. According to the Brabham designer, there were one or two bugs to be ironed out and, once practice began officially on Friday, it was clear that he had overcome problems with the bodywork rising onto soft springs on the slow corners and excessive wheel movement which would allow the bottom of the side-pods to grind away on the track.

It was estimated that Brabham had recovered 80% of the downforce lost by the ban on skirts while the competition were struggling with a mere 50% gain. Such was the team's confidence that Piquet locked up pole after 13 timed laps on Friday and spent the rest of practice running on full tanks. That and almost wiping out AUTOCOURSE's photographer, Nigel Snowdon. Carbon fibre brakes were tried on the spare car at one stage but Piquet left the track at high speed when the pedal went to the floor and he sailed helplessly towards Snowdon. Quick as a flash, our man jumped out of the way as the Brabham hurtled past Snowdon's Nikons. "I tried to turn away but couldn't do anything. I thought I was going to kill him or chop his legs off," said a trembling Piquet who, unfortunately, had not been able to exercise control over his bladder either. Snowdon remained pale and quiet for some time afterwards.

Frank Williams, meanwhile, was whipping up support for a protest against the Brabham on Friday but the complaint was rejected as was a similar protest by Renault and the whole affair merely served to rankle the normally placid Gordon Murray. "I used to respect Patrick Head and Frank Williams," he said. "They admitted our suspension was legal in Brazil and yet they have been trying to muster support for a protest. They're just bad losers. It makes me sick."

So, the Brabham was there to stay, head and shoulders above everyone else at the front of the grid. Hector Rebaque, back to a Hewland gearbox, was sixth fastest in the slower conditions on Saturday and the Mexican found himself in an unaccustomed position on the third row. The pole position battle, if you could call it that, had been between Brabham, Williams and Renault with the turbocharged cars showing their expected speed on the long straight of the Number 15 circuit. Nevertheless, the Frenchmen were rather perplexed to find that they could somehow take the long fifth gear loop without lifting whereas they had to back off while running *with* skirts in 1980. Mind you, they weren't complaining and, after two unhappy races, their confidence was bolstered by a front row time from Alain Prost on his fourth lap on Friday.

René Arnoux's car had been rebuilt around a new monocoque following his shunt in Brazil but the Frenchman simply could not match Prost who appeared to gain tenths of a second by turning into the corners while braking. The team complained of a lack of straightline speed although they appeared unwilling to sacrifice the large amount of rear wing they were running. Generally speaking, though, Jean Sage and Gerard Larrousse were happy with the 100% reliability of their engines due, in part, to the mild April climate in Buenos Aires.

Temperatures were deliberately kept to an artificially low level in the Williams camp following the contretemps in Rio and Reutemann served notice of his intentions by setting a faster time than Jones on Friday. Both drivers had their problems with Reutemann suffering a blown engine towards the end of the first day's practice while Jones complained of a shortage of power from his DFV. Alan had a brand new T-car at his disposal but that was "full of little problems" to be of any assistance when it came to setting a fast time. The reigning World Champion pinned his hopes on Saturday practice but rain in the morning washed the rubber away and made the track slower for the final hour. Undaunted, Jones set the fastest time of the day and it was good enough to ease Reutemann back to fourth place during the final minutes of practice. A superb effort spurred on, no doubt, by the behaviour of the number two Williams driver in Brazil.

Ferrari produced the Comprex supercharger for unofficial practice on Thursday but put it away for good after a belt broke. The team had more serious problems than that, however, when they got through three V6s during the next two days, two of the failures down to Gilles Villeneuve. Again, the handling wasn't quite right as the French Canadian's penchant for returning to the pits covered in grass tended to prove. The red cars were fast in a straight line but the speed through the corners was poor by comparison and Villeneuve did well, therefore, to take seventh fastest time. Pironi had another unhappy practice, opting to use the T-car on Saturday in order to save the engine in his race car for Sunday and the Frenchman had to be satisfied with the sixth row. Rosberg's place alongside Villeneuve may have looked good but Keke was far from happy with the way in which he had to work for such a creditable time on Saturday. "The car doesn't feel very nice at all," he said. "It's very nervous indeed on the fast stuff and I was constantly getting a soft brake pedal. We don't know why." Chico Serra was in similar difficulties and took his Fittipaldi onto the 10th row after breaking his gear lever at one stage!

The Ragno-Beta Arrows team were caught in the

Nelson Piquet used the hydro-pneumatic suspension on his Brabham to good effect and completely cominated the Argentine Grand Prix *(far left)*.
Giving 'em a rev. Alan Jones waves to the Reutemann supporters, restless since the Brazilian Grand Prix *(left)*.

Alain Prost started from the front row but was no match for the Brabhams. Alain finished third but had to give best to Hector Rebaque in the Brabham during the early laps. Riccardo Patrese dropped back with a front end vibration on his Arrows *(below)*.

APRIL:

David Thieme of Essex Motorsport detained by police in Zurich for 14 days after a complaint from a Swiss bank alleging malpractice.

Mike Thackwell breaks ankle as the result of testing accident with Formula 2 Ralt-Honda at Thruxton.

Williams Grand Prix Engineering receive Queen's Award for Export Achievement.

David Thieme: arrested in a haze of confusion.

Thumbs down and a cool response for Jones....
......compared to the reception waiting for Reutemann *(left)*.
Piquet leaves the Williams team in his wake.
The anticipated duel between Jones and Reutemann never happened and the Argentine, easily the best of the rest, took a distant second place behind the Brabham *(right)*.

middle of a row with Jean-Marie Balestre on Friday. The organisers had decided to place a board at the entrance to the pit lane in order to measure the 6cm gap on cars as they came in. During the course of some rather random spot checks, Patrese, Pironi and de Angelis were deemed to be driving illegal cars but the organisers withdrew their claims when it was pointed out that the measuring board was far from level. Enter Jean-Marie Balestre who, supposedly, was present purely as an impartial observer. The FISA president went on television on Friday evening and told the nation that the Arrows was illegal because it had failed the test. Jack Oliver was quick to put pen to press release when he said Balestre had no right to make such an ill-advised statement and added that Arrows would consider suing the Frenchman.

Meanwhile, Patrese got on with the job in his A3 which had been lightened by some 20 kilos. He ran very little wing which didn't help in the twists but his main problem on Saturday was an engine which refused to rev properly. Siegfried Stohr, on the other hand, used more wing but was over 400 revs down on the straight and finished in 19th place. Patrese's time was fractionally faster than Elio de Angelis in the Essex Lotus 81. The team devoted much of their time to the 88 and, when that was turned down flat at scrutineering, they were back to base with the aging 81s. De Angelis could not find a suitable compromise between good handling on the fast curves and grip on the slower corners but tried as hard as ever none the less. Nigel Mansell, apart from having understeer problems, was forced to hold his car in gear after clutch and gearbox problems on Friday and the Birmingham driver did well to take 15th place on the grid.

The McLaren International team came to Argentina in a good frame of mind after encouraging tests with the MP4 in England. John Watson lost a considerable amount of time on Friday when the team chased off in the wrong direction in search of a cure for an understeer problem. This was traced eventually to nothing more than a dud shock absorber and there was disappointment all round when John was unable to improve on his 11th place on Saturday. Andrea de Cesaris's almost desperate efforts in the old M29F saw the little Italian regularly dump loads of grass in the pit lane after adventures on his way to 18th slot on the grid.

Tyrrell, still without a major sponsor, arrived with a modified rear suspension on Eddie Cheever's car but the enthusiastic American was unable to improve his time on Saturday when springing, which turned out to be too soft, spoiled his chances. Ricardo Zunino was relieved to have qualified for his home Grand Prix after engine trouble and a run in the spare car meant little improvement during the final practice. Patrick Tambay, on the other hand, was glad of the chance to improve on Saturday afternoon after problems with the Theodore the previous day and a minor shunt on Saturday morning. A sticking fuel pressure relief valve caused a vapour lock and then he ran out of fuel on Friday. The team were trying a double springing system which worked reasonably well and allowed the cheerful Frenchman to take 14th place after some impressive flat-out motoring during the final hour. Boosted, at least mentally if not financially, by their excellent result in Brazil, the Ensign team had to go carefully with their one remaining DFV. Marc Surer sat out most of the untimed sessions but took 16th place on Friday in spite of understeer through the important right-hander at the end of the straight.

The Marlboro Alfa Romeo team had more than simply understeer to worry about. Neither Mario Andretti nor Bruno Giacomelli could get their engines to pull more than 11,800 revs after a few laps at the normal 12,400rpm and the team were at a loss to explain why. The problem was thought to be related to either a faulty batch of coils or the Magneti Marelli ignition system and it merely compounded difficulties with the handling. The team even produced a 1980 chassis for comparison and Andretti used that on Friday although all the cars were rolling too much in the fast curves and the drivers had to reluctantly accept 17th and 22nd places on the grid.

The Alfa Romeo team's problems were mild by comparison to the Talbot-Ligier team who, coincidentally, used Magneti Marelli ignition and were suffering from down-on-power engines. Guy Ligier had ordered the rapid production of a dual-rate springing system but the team patron stomped back to Paris on Friday when the team were obviously making little headway. The normally sunny Jacques Laffite was very unhappy with a place on the penultimate row while poor Jean-Pierre Jabouille was more upset about the handling than the fact that he had failed to qualify. Joining Zunino on the back row was Jan Lammers in the ATS. That, too, was an unhappy team after the unpredictable Gunter Schmid had shown his displeasure at his team's desire to run a small front wing by picking up the aerofoil and bending it out of recognition. Shortly after the Argentine Grand Prix, several key members were to walk out of the ATS team. The Denim Osella team were unchanged in every respect with Miguel Angel Guerra and Beppe Gabbiani failing to qualify. March, though, had hoped to do something with the stiffer original chassis which had been brought out to Buenos Aires but neither Derek Daly nor Eliseo Salazar were to qualify.

RACE

The crowd were back in force from an early hour on Sunday, waving their own 'REUT – JONES' signals and carrying banners wishing 'Lole' a happy 39th birthday. The warm-up made it clear that a happy result for Carlos would be at the expense of Piquet who comfortably set the fastest time. Jones was even further back when he found his engine to be 600 revs down and the Williams mechanics set to and stripped the fuel system.

Jones's car was ready for the start and he didn't mess about once the lights turned green. The Williams darted to Piquet's left and Alan was first through the right-left flick after a superb start. Piquet, remembering the coming together with Jones under similar circumstances in Montreal the year before, wisely backed off in the knowledge that he could take the lead as and when he pleased.

"It was one of the most memorable starts of my career," Jones said later. "I felt really exhilarated to be in front of the whole field but that only lasted as far as the exit of the sweeping right-hander at the end of the straight. Then I had the sobering experience of watching Nelson's Brabham pass me as if I was parked."

Reutemann was third, to the dismay of the anguished crowd, followed by Patrese with Arnoux, having made a better start than his team-mate, in fifth place. Rebaque was seventh followed by Pironi and Rosberg with Watson running strongly in 10th place. The second McLaren however was trailing round at the back of the field in company with Villeneuve. The Ferrari driver had got out of shape at the fifth gear curve and de Cesaris had spun while avoiding him. The Italian then made matters worse by spinning once more in his desperation to point the McLaren in the right direction. Cheever's race was all too brief when he lost his clutch on the start line and barely managed to complete one lap before posting the first retirement. He was joined a few minutes later by Pironi, Mansell and Rosberg, the Ferrari and Lotus out with engine trouble while the Fittipaldi broke a fuel pump belt.

A roar from the crowd signalled Reutemann's move into second place as Jones discovered his engine was still losing around 500 revs. There was a further shuffling of places when Prost took Rebaque with him as they moved ahead of the Williams while both Arnoux and Patrese eased off with front end vibrations on their cars.

By lap seven, it was obvious that Piquet was in a league of his own when he came through with a 12-second advantage over Reutemann. Prost was still third but he was unable to challenge Reutemann when a tyre vibration caused the Renault to dart dangerously under braking. To make matters worse, Prost had difficulty selecting second gear and he missed three shifts when Rebaque moved ahead on lap 11.

Hector Rebaque pulls off to retire from second place with a broken distributor rotor arm. The Brabham, in any case, looks unlikely to have passed a six centimetre check *(right)*. Jones, with the mandatory six centimetre gap showing clearly, made a storming start but the reigning World Champion had a frustrating race and finished fourth with a down-on-power engine *(below right)*.

The crowd became uneasy when they realised the Mexican was catching their man hand over fist and the ultimate agony and final proof of Brabham's suspension advantage came on lap 15 when Rebaque breezed past Reutemann – on the straight, if you please. Prost held his ground over Jones while Arnoux, holding sixth place after a bird had damaged his nose wing, was coming under pressure from Watson after the Ulsterman had moved ahead of Patrese. Andretti, his Alfa Romeo suffering from a broken exhaust and a misfire, was in eighth place after taking Tambay on lap nine.

There was a fair amount of activity at the back of the field as de Angelis cut through after a spin during the opening laps. The Lotus driver discovered that his car handled well with full tanks and by lap 16 he had caught and passed Villeneuve and was challenging Tambay's 10th place. Stohr, running well despite understeer, was next while Zunino was having no trouble holding off a hard-working Villeneuve, such were Ferrari's handling problems. Surer lost 16th place when a body panel flew off his Ensign and the subsequent overheating contributed towards a blown engine on lap 15. Jacques Laffite finally brought an unhappy weekend to a close four laps later when he stopped his Ligier with a bad vibration and handling which he considered dangerous.

The Brabham team were in no such trouble as their drivers cruised happily at the head of the field. However, any hopes of a one-two finish were dashed on lap 33 when Rebaque parked on the in-field with a broken distributor rotor arm. Reutemann was back in second place. Mayhem in the grandstands once more.

Second place, though, would be his lot as Piquet was over 25 seconds to the good and backing off to such an extent that the team thought he was in trouble! Prost was able to maintain his third place while Jones, in turn, was glad that the hobbled Arnoux was unable to offer any challenge. Watson had been running as quickly as Prost but hopes of taking advantage of the struggling trio were wiped out when he felt a vibration at the rear of the MP4. A quick pit stop revealed nothing and he stopped for good on lap 36 with what turned out to be a damaged crown wheel and pinion. It was an encouraging debut none the less.

Watson's retirement allowed Patrese to take sixth place but, with a few laps remaining, the Arrows driver, struggling with a sticking throttle, lost his championship point to the flying de Angelis. Serra's steady drive came to an end with gearbox trouble, the result, possibly, of Chico being forced to stuff his car into first gear while avoiding the Villeneuve/de Cesaris first lap mêlée. Tambay disappeared when his engine lost its oil and that elevated Andretti and his evil-handling Alfa Romeo while a threat to Stohr's ninth place faded when Giacomelli ran out of fuel with two laps remaining. Villeneuve made a spectacular exit with a huge spin at the fast right-hander and he liberally coated the track with grass before stopping with a broken drive-shaft. Zunino was unable to profit from that after the Tyrrell driver was docked a lap for taking an unauthorised short-cut after overshooting the chicane.

A thwarted spectator showed his disapproval by throwing an orange at Piquet's Brabham during the closing laps but the crowd's disquiet was mild compared to the frustration simmering in the pit lane. Renault lodged a protest more, they said, as a matter of principle than a means of disqualifying Piquet but the protest was rejected. Thus the matter was shelved for the time being but it was clear that Brabham's flag-to-flag victory was the thin end of a wedge which threatened to split FOCA.

As for Reutemann, his mechanics presented him with a bent throttle pedal after the race. That's how hard he was trying; that's how good the Brabhams were.

Following pages:
Laffite and Jabouille confer *(left)*.
Photo: Bernard Asset/A&P
Jacques Laffite and the Talbot-Ligier team play to the grandstand *(below)*.
Photo: Bernard Asset/A&P
Carlos Reutemann *(right)*.
Photo: Nigel Snowdon

FURIOUS THAT HIS LOTUS 88 HAD BEEN BANNED from competition for the third race in succession, Colin Chapman left Buenos Aires before practice started, leaving behind the following strongly worded statement:

For the last four weeks, we have been trying to get the new Essex-Lotus 88 to take part in a Grand Prix, to no avail.

Twice it was accepted by the scrutineers, twice it was turned down by the stewards under pressure of lobbies. The USA national Court of Appeal ruled this new car eligible and gave a firm recommendation it should be allowed to race; it was still forced off the track by protesters and the black flag.

And now we have been turned down again from participating in the Argentine Grand Prix even though the Argentine Automobile Club's technical commission commented on the innovative design it features and the worthiness of its technological advances.

At no time throughout this ordeal has any steward or scrutineer come up with a valid reason for the exclusion consistent with the content and intention of the rule.

It is a particular disappointment for this to have happened at the Argentine Grand Prix which has marked more pleasant points in the history of Team Lotus. It was here, in 1960, that we were welcomed into the band of sportsmen competitors with our first full Formula 1 car, which was as innovative then in its way as the Essex-Lotus 88 is today. It was also here in 1977 that we ran the first ground-effect car ever in motor racing, a principle which every Formula 1 car has since copied.

Throughout these years we have witnessed the changes which have taken place in Grand Prix racing, and unfortunately seen what was fair competition between sportsmen degenerate into power struggles and political manoeuvrings between manipulators and money men attempting to take more out of the sport than they put into it.

We have a responsibility to the public of the Grand Prix and to our drivers and this has stopped us from withdrawing our cars from this event. But for the first time since I started Grand Prix racing, 22 years ago, I shall not be in the Team Lotus pit during a race for this reason. During this period no team has won more races or more championships than we have, nobody has influenced the design of racing cars the way we did through innovations which are already finding their way into everyday motor cars for the benefit of increased safety and energy conservation. And yet we are being put under unbearable pressure by our rival competitors, who are frightened that once again we are setting a trend they may all have to follow.

The matter shall go to its next stage at the FIA Court of Appeal in two weeks' time. We shall defend our case with all the arguments we can muster for the defence of a cause we consider worthy.

When this will be over I shall seriously reconsider with my good friend and sponsor David Thieme of Essex Motorsport whether Grand Prix racing is still what it purports to be: the pinnacle of sport and technological achievement. Unfortunately, this appears to be no longer the case and, if one does not clean it up, Formula 1 will end up in a quagmire of plagiarism, chicanery and petty rule interpretation forced by lobbies manipulated by people for whom the word sport has no meaning.

Colin Chapman
Team Essex Lotus
Buenos Aires
April 10, 1981 9am

PS: When you read this, I shall be on my way to watch the progress of the US Space Shuttle, an achievement of human mankind which will refresh my mind from what I have been subjected to in the last four weeks.

Chapman's statement produced a communiqué from Jean-Marie Balestre which stated that Chapman was in breach of the Concord Agreement and added that his statement had discredited the World Championship. FISA imposed a fine $100,000 on Team Essex Lotus and Balestre's actions prompted a further statement from representatives of 13 Formula 1 teams expressing their concern at the way the President of FISA had handled the Lotus press release – particularly with regard to the fine. It was no surprise when the fine was rescinded 10 days later.

Jean-Marie Balestre, supposedly on hand as a casual observer, could not resist the lure of the microphone in Buenos Aires.

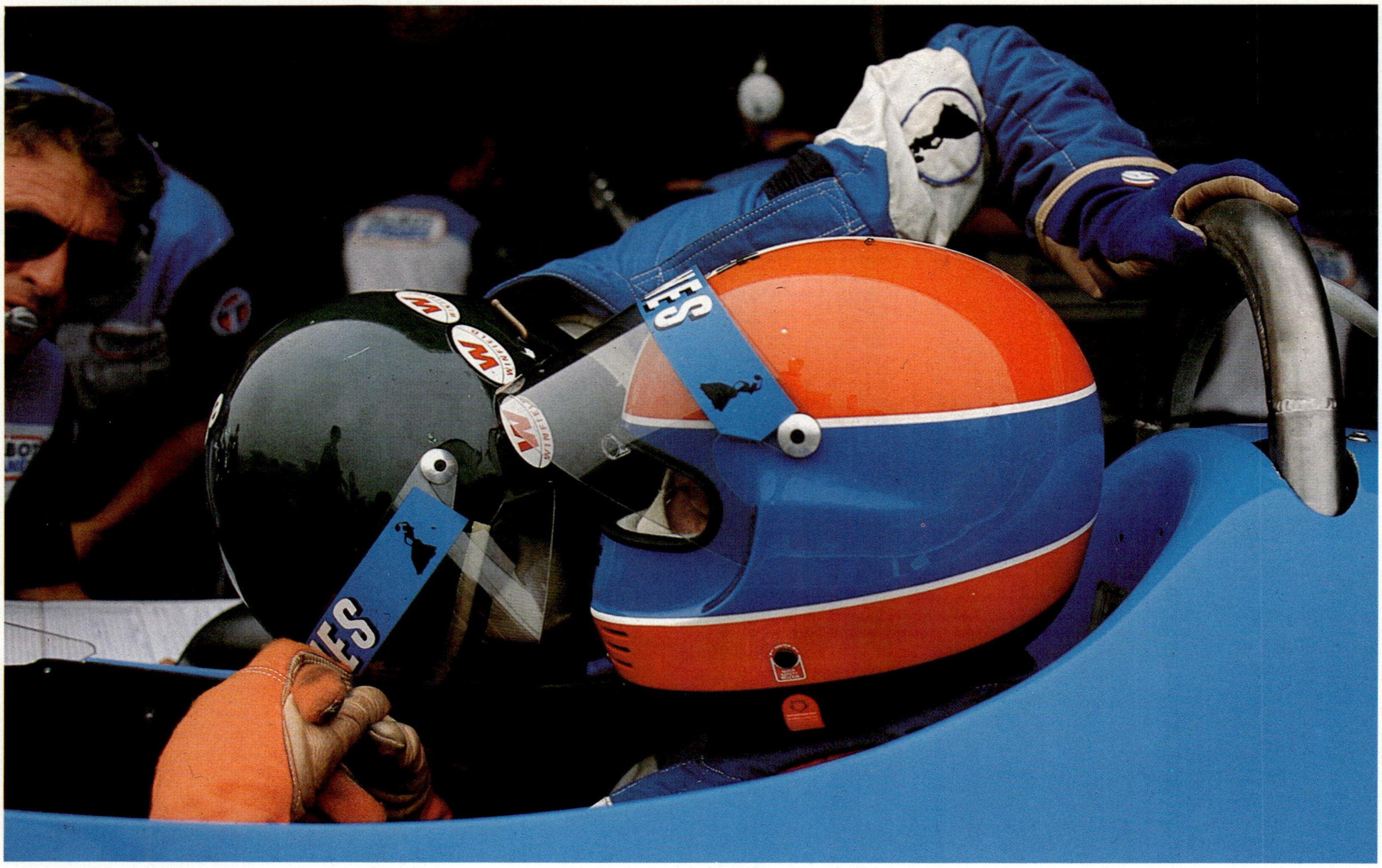

P1 REUT
P2 JONE
JACQUES LAFFITE
NELSON PIQUET

CARLOS REUTEMANN

Gran Premio de la República Argentina, April 12/statistics

Entries and practice times

No.	Driver	Nat	Car	Engine	Entrant	Practice 1	Practice 2
1	Alan Jones	AUS	Saudia-Leyland WILLIAMS FWO7C	Ford Cosworth DFV	Albilad-Williams Racing Team	1m 44·662s	**1m 43·638s**
2	Carlos Reutemann	RA	Saudia-Leyland WILLIAMS FWO7C	Ford Cosworth DFV	Albilad-Williams Racing Team	**1m 43·935s**	1m 44·094s
3	Eddie Cheever	USA	TYRRELL 010	Ford Cosworth DFV	Tyrrell Racing	**1m 45·117s**	1m 45·357s
4	Ricardo Zunino	RA	TYRRELL 010	Ford Cosworth DFV	Tyrrell Racing	**1m 47·464s**	1m 48·143s
5	Nelson Piquet	BR	Parmalat BRABHAM BT49C	Ford Cosworth DFV	Parmalat Racing Team	**1m 42·665s**	1m 44·364s
6	Hector Rebaque	MEX	Parmalat BRABHAM BT49C	Ford Cosworth DFV	Parmalat Racing Team	1m 44·712s	**1m 44·100s**
7	John Watson	GB	Marlboro McLAREN MP4	Ford Cosworth DFV	McLaren International	**1m 45·073s**	1m 45·202s
8	Andrea de Cesaris	I	Marlboro McLAREN M29F	Ford Cosworth DFV	McLaren International	**1m 46·387s**	1m 46·663s
9	Jan Lammers	NL	ATS D4	Ford Cosworth DFV	Team ATS	**1m 47·174s**	1m 47·576s
11	Elio de Angelis	I	Essex LOTUS 81	Ford Cosworth DFV	Team Essex Lotus	1m 45·252s	**1m 45·065s**
12	Nigel Mansell	GB	Essex LOTUS 81	Ford Cosworth DFV	Team Essex Lotus	**1m 45·369s**	1m 45·790s
14	Marc Surer	CH	ENSIGN N180B	Ford Cosworth DFV	Ensign Racing	**1m 45·734s**	1m 46·188s
15	Alain Prost	F	Elf RENAULT RE 20	Renault EF1	Equipe Renault Elf	**1m 42·981s**	1m 43·748s
16	René Arnoux	F	Elf RENAULT RE 20	Renault EF1	Equipe Renault Elf	**1m 43·997s**	1m 44·080s
17	Derek Daly	IRL	Rizla MARCH 811	Ford Cosworth DFV	March Grand Prix	**1m 48·191s**	1m 49·571s
18	Eliseo Salazar	RCH	Rizla MARCH 811	Ford Cosworth DFV	March Grand Prix	–	**1m 51·086s**
20	Keke Rosberg	SF	FITTIPALDI F8C	Ford Cosworth DFV	Fittipaldi Automotive	1m 45·273s	**1m 44·191s**
21	Chico Serra	BR	FITTIPALDI F8C	Ford Cosworth DFV	Fittipaldi Automotive	1m 46·743s	**1m 46·706s**
22	Mario Andretti	USA	Marlboro ALFA ROMEO 179C	Alfa Romeo 1260	Marlboro Team Alfa Romeo	1m 46·329s	**1m 46·059s**
23	Bruno Giacomelli	I	Marlboro ALFA ROMEO 179C	Alfa Romeo 1260	Marlboro Team Alfa Romeo	1m 47·109s	**1m 46·918s**
25	Jean-Pierre Jabouille	F	Talbot-Gitanes LIGIER JS17	Matra MS 81	Equipe Talbot Gitanes	**1m 49·581s**	1m 50·226s
26	Jacques Laffite	F	Talbot-Gitanes LIGIER JS17	Matra MS 81	Equipe Talbot Gitanes	**1m 46·854s**	1m 47·594s
27	Gilles Villeneuve	CDN	Fiat FERRARI 126CK	Ferrari 126C	Scuderia Ferrari SpA SEFAC	1m 44·236s	**1m 44·132s**
28	Didier Pironi	F	Fiat FERRARI 126CK	Ferrari 126C	Scuderia Ferrari SpA SEFAC	**1m 45·108s**	1m 45·599s
29	Riccardo Patrese	I	Ragno-Beta ARROWS A3	Ford Cosworth DFV	Arrows Racing Team	**1m 45·088s**	1m 45·357s
30	Siegfried Stohr	I	Ragno-Beta ARROWS A3	Ford Cosworth DFV	Arrows Racing Team	1m 47·342s	**1m 46·444s**
31	Miguel Angel Guerra	RA	Denim OSELLA FA1B	Ford Cosworth DFV	Osella Squadra Corse	**1m 47·609s**	1m 48·571s
32	Beppe Gabbiani	I	Denim OSELLA FA1B	Ford Cosworth DFV	Osella Squadra Corse	**1m 48·121s**	1m 48·203s
33	Patrick Tambay	F	THEODORE TY 01	Ford Cosworth DFV	Theodore Racing Team	1m 46·872s	**1m 45·297s**

Friday morning and Saturday morning practice sessions not officially recorded

Fri pm
Warm, dry

Sat pm
Warm, dry

Starting grid

15 PROST (1m 42·981s) Renault	5 PIQUET (1m 42·665s) Brabham
2 REUTEMANN (1m 43·935s) Williams	1 JONES (1m 43·638s) Williams
6 REBAQUE (1m 44·100s) Brabham	16 ARNOUX (1m 43·997s) Renault
20 ROSBERG (1m 44·191s) Fittipaldi	27 VILLENEUVE (1m 44·132s) Ferrari
11 DE ANGELIS (1m 45·065s) Lotus	29 PATRESE (1m 45·008s) Arrows
28 PIRONI (1m 45·108s) Ferrari	7 WATSON (1m 45·073s) McLaren
33 TAMBAY (1m 45·297s) Theodore	3 CHEEVER (1m 45·117s) Tyrrell
14 SURER (1m 45·734s) Ensign	12 MANSELL (1m 45·369s) Lotus
8 DE CESARIS (1m 46·387s) McLaren	22 ANDRETTI (1m 46·059s) Alfa Romeo
21 SERRA (1m 46·706s) Fittipaldi	30 STOHR (1m 46·444s) Arrows
23 GIACOMELLI (1m 46·918s) Alfa Romeo	26 LAFFITE (1m 46·854s) Talbot-Ligier
4 ZUNINO (1m 47·464s) Tyrrell	9 LAMMERS (1m 47·174s) ATS

Did not start:
31 Guerra (Osella), 1m 47·609s, did not qualify
32 Gabbiani (Osella), 1m 48·121s, did not qualify
17 Daly (March), 1m 48·191s, did not qualify
25 Jabouille (Talbot-Ligier), 1m 49·581s, did not qualify
18 Salazar (March), 1m 51·086s, did not qualify

Past winners

Year	Driver	Nat	Car	Circuit	Distance miles/km	Speed mph/km/h
1953	Alberto Ascari	I	2·0 Ferrari 500	Buenos Aires No 2	235·81/379·50	78·14/125·75
1954	Juan Manuel Fangio	RA	2·5 Maserati 250 F	Buenos Aires No 2	211·50/340·38	70·14/112·88
1955	Juan Manuel Fangio	RA	2·5 Mercedes-Benz W196	Buenos Aires No 2	235·81/379·50	77·52/124·75
1956	Luigi Musso/ Juan Manuel Fangio	RA	2·5 Lanca-Ferrari D50	Buenos Aires No 2	238·24/383·41	79·39/127·76
1957	Juan Manuel Fangio	RA	2·5 Maserati 250F	Buenos Aires No 2	243·10/391·23	80·62/129·74
1958	Stirling Moss	GB	2·0 Cooper T43-Climax	Buenos Aires No 2	194·48/312·99	83·61/134·56
1960	Bruce McLaren	NZ	2·5 Cooper T51-Climax	Buenos Aires No 2	194·48/312·99	84·66/136·25
1971*	Chris Amon	NZ	3·0 Matra Simca MS 120	Buenos Aires No 9	212·12/341·37	99·18/159·61
1972	Jackie Stewart	GB	3·0 Tyrrell 003-Ford	Buenos Aires No 9	197·49/317·82	100·43/161·63
1973	Emerson Fittipaldi	BR	3·0 JPS/Lotus 72-Ford	Buenos Aires No 9	199·56/321·17	102·95/165·69
1974	Denny Hulme	NZ	3·0 McLaren M23-Ford	Buenos Aires No 15	196·55/316·31	116·72/187·85
1975	Emerson Fittipaldi	BR	3·0 McLaren M23-Ford	Buenos Aires No 15	196·55/316·31	118·60/190·86
1977	Jody Scheckter	ZA	3·0 Wolf WR1-Ford	Buenos Aires No 15	196·55/316·31	117·71/189·44
1978	Mario Andretti	USA	3·0 JPS/Lotus 78-Ford	Buenos Aires No 15	192·84/310·35	119·19/191·82
1979	Jacques Laffite	F	3·0 Ligier JS11-Ford	Buenos Aires No 15	196·55/316·31	122·77/197·59
1980	Alan Jones	AUS	3·0 Williams FW07-Ford	Buenos Aires No 15	196·55/316·31	113·99/183·44
1981	Nelson Piquet	BR	3·0 Brabham BT49C-Ford	Buenos Aires No 15	196·55/316·31	124·66/200·63

*Non-championship

Circuit data

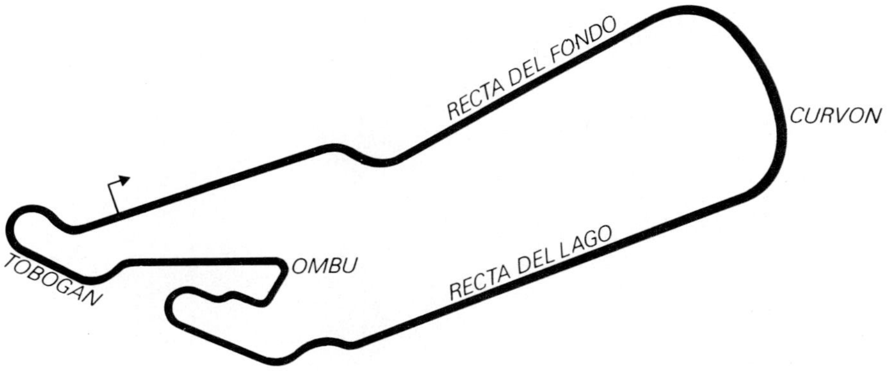

Autodromo Municipal de la Ciudad de Buenos Aires, Circuito No 15
Circuit length: 3·708 miles/5·9682 km
Race distance: 53 laps, 196·548 miles/316·31 km
Race weather: Hot, dry.

Results and retirements

Place	Driver	Car	Laps	Time and Speed (mph/km/h)/Retirement	
1	Nelson Piquet	Brabham-Cosworth V8	53	1 h 34m 32·74s	124·665/200·63
2	Carlos Reutemann	Williams-Cosworth V8	53	1 h 34m 59·35s	
3	Alain Prost	Renault t/c V6	53	1 h 35m 22·72s	
4	Alan Jones	Williams-Cosworth V8	53	1 h 35m 40·62s	
5	René Arnoux	Renault t/c V6	53	1 h 36m 04·59s	
6	Elio de Angelis	Lotus-Cosworth V8	52		
7	Riccardo Patrese	Arrows-Cosworth V8	52		
8	Mario Andretti	Alfa Romeo V12	52		
9	Siegfried Stohr	Arrows-Cosworth V8	52		
10	Bruno Giacomelli	Alfa Romeo V12	51	Out of fuel	
11	Andrea de Cesaris	McLaren-Cosworth V8	51		
12	Jan Lammers	ATS-Cosworth V8	51		
13	Ricardo Zunino	Tyrrell-Cosworth V8	51	Penalised one lap	
	Gilles Villeneuve	Ferrari t/c V6	40	Drive-shaft	
	Patrick Tambay	Theodore-Cosworth V8	36	Engine, lost oil	
	John Watson	McLaren-Cosworth V8	36	Crown-wheel and pinion	
	Hector Rebaque	Brabham-Cosworth V8	32	Distributor rotor arm	
	Chico Serra	Fittipaldi-Cosworth V8	28	Gearbox	
	Jacques Laffite	Talbot-Ligier Matra V12	19	Front-end vibration/handling	
	Marc Surer	Ensign-Cosworth V8	14	Engine	
	Keke Rosberg	Fittipaldi-Cosworth V8	4	Fuel pump belt	
	Nigel Mansell	Lotus-Cosworth V8	3	Engine	
	Didier Pironi	Ferrari t/c V6	3	Engine	
	Eddie Cheever	Tyrrell-Cosworth V8	1	Clutch	

Fastest lap: Piquet, on lap 6, 1m 45·287s, 126·800mph/204·066km/h (record).
Previous lap record: Jacques Laffite (F1 Ligier JS11-Cosworth DFV), 1m 46·91s, 124·875mph/200·97km/h (1979).

Lap chart

1st LAP ORDER		1	2	3	4	5	6	7	8	9	10	11	12	13	14	15	16	17	18	19	20	21	22	23
5	N.Piquet	5	5	5	5	5	5	5	5	5	5	5	5	5	5	5	5	5	5	5	5	5	5	5
1	A.Jones	1	2	2	2	2	2	2	2	2	2	2	2	2	2	6	6	6	6	6	6	6	6	6
2	C.Reutemann	2	1	1	1	15	15	15	15	15	15	6	6	6	6	2	2	2	2	2	2	2	2	2
29	R.Patrese	29	29	15	15	1	6	6	6	6	6	15	15	15	15	15	15	15	15	15	15	15	15	15
16	R.Arnoux	16	15	6	6	6	1	1	1	1	1	1	1	1	1	1	1	1	1	1	1	1	1	1
15	A.Prost	15	6	29	29	29	29	16	16	16	16	16	16	16	16	16	16	16	16	16	16	16	16	16
6	H.Rebaque	6	16	16	16	16	16	29	29	7	7	7	7	7	7	7	7	7	7	7	7	7	7	7
28	D.Pironi	28	28	7	7	7	7	7	7	29	29	29	29	29	29	29	29	29	29	29	29	29	29	29
20	K.Rosberg	20	7	20	33	33	33	33	33	22	22	22	22	22	22	22	22	22	22	22	22	22	22	22
7	J.Watson	7	20	33	22	22	22	22	22	33	33	33	33	33	33	33	33	33	33	33	33	33	33	33
11	E.de Angelis	11	11	22	(20)	30	30	30	30	30	30	30	30	30	30	30	11	11	11	11	11	11	11	11
14	M.Surer	14	14	30	30	4	4	4	4	4	4	4	4	11	11	11	30	30	30	30	30	30	30	30
33	P.Tambay	33	33	4	4	26	26	26	27	27	11	11	11	4	4	4	4	4	4	4	4	4	4	4
30	S.Stohr	30	22	26	26	27	27	27	26	11	27	27	27	27	27	27	27	27	27	27	27	27	27	27
22	M.Andretti	22	30	23	27	23	23	23	23	23	23	23	23	23	23	23	23	23	23	23	23	23	23	23
12	N.Mansell	12	12	27	23	21	21	11	11	26	26	14	14	14	14	26	21	21	21	21	21	21	21	21
26	J.Laffite	26	4	21	21	14	11	14	14	14	14	26	26	26	26	21	26	26	26	8	8	8	8	8
4	R.Zunino	4	26	9	9	11	14	21	21	21	21	21	21	21	21	8	8	8	8	(26)	9	9	9	9
21	C.Serra	21	21	14	14	9	9	9	9	9	9	9	9	(9)	8	9	9	9	9	9				
23	B.Giacomelli	23	23	11	11	8	8	8	8	8	8	8	8	8	9									
9	J.Lammers	9	9	(12)	8																			
27	G.Villeneuve	27	27	(28)																				
8	A.de Cesaris	8	8	8																				
3	E.Cheever	3																						

24	25	26	27	28	29	30	31	32	33	34	35	36	37	38	39	40	41	42	43	44	45	46	47	48	49	50	51	52	53
5	5	5	5	5	5	5	5	5	5	5	5	5	5	5	5	5	5	5	5	5	5	5	5	5	5	5	5	5	5
6	6	6	6	6	6	6	6	6	2	2	2	2	2	2	2	2	2	2	2	2	2	2	2	2	2	2	2	2	2
2	2	2	2	2	2	2	2	2	15	15	15	15	15	15	15	15	15	15	15	15	15	15	15	15	15	15	15	15	15
15	15	15	15	15	15	15	15	15	1	1	1	1	1	1	1	1	1	1	1	1	1	1	1	1	1	1	1	1	1
1	1	1	1	1	1	1	1	1	16	16	16	16	16	16	16	16	16	16	16	16	16	16	16	16	16	16	16	16	16
16	16	16	16	16	16	16	16	16	7	7	29	29	29	29	29	29	29	29	29	29	29	29	11	11	11	11	11	11	
7	7	7	7	7	7	7	7	7	29	29	(7)	11	11	11	11	11	11	11	11	11	11	11	29	29	29	29	29	29	
29	29	29	29	29	29	29	29	29	33	33	11	33	22	22	22	22	22	22	22	22	22	22	22	22	22	22	22	22	
22	22	22	22	22	22	33	33	33	11	11	33	22	30	30	30	30	30	30	30	23	23	23	23	23	23	23	23	30	
33	33	33	33	33	33	22	22	22	22	22	22	30	27	27	27	27	23	23	23	30	30	30	30	30	30	30	30		
11	11	11	11	11	11	11	11	11	30	30	30	27	23	23	23	23	4	4	4	4	4	4	4	4	4	4	4		
30	30	30	30	30	30	30	30	30	4	4	27	23	4	4	4	4	8	8	8	8	8	8	8	8	8	8	8		
4	4	4	4	4	4	4	4	4	27	27	23	4	8	8	8	8	9	9	9	9	9	9	9	9	9	9	9		
27	27	27	27	27	27	27	27	27	23	23	4	8	9	9	9	9													
23	23	23	23	23	23	23	23	23	8	8	8	9																	
21	21	21	21	(21)	8	8	8	8	9	9	9	(7)																	
8	8	8	8	8	9	9	9	9																					
9	9	9	9	9																									

Fastest laps

Driver	Time	Lap
Nelson Piquet	1m 45·28s	6
Carlos Reutemann	1m 46·26s	43
Hector Rebaque	1m 46·35s	8
Alain Prost	1m 46·57s	6
Alan Jones	1m 47·01s	36
René Arnoux	1m 47·18s	33
John Watson	1m 47·34s	31
Elio de Angelis	1m 47·65s	43
Patrick Tambay	1m 47·86s	30
Riccardo Patrese	1m 48·30s	40
Bruno Giacomelli	1m 48·32s	37
Mario Andretti	1m 48·49s	18
Marc Surer	1m 48·77s	4
Siegfried Stohr	1m 48·83s	28
Gilles Villeneuve	1m 48·83s	37
Keke Rosberg	1m 48·92s	3
Ricardo Zunino	1m 49·01s	33
Jan Lammers	1m 49·14s	37
Didier Pironi	1m 49·22s	2
Andrea de Cesaris	1m 49·85s	18
Chico Serra	1m 49·95s	10
Jacques Laffite	1m 50·06s	5
Nigel Mansell	1m 50·88s	2
Eddie Cheever	3m 05·30s	1

Points

WORLD CHAMPIONSHIP OF DRIVERS

1	Carlos Reutemann	21 pts
2	Alan Jones	18
3	Nelson Piquet	13
4 =	Riccardo Patrese	4
4 =	Alain Prost	4
6 =	Mario Andretti	3
6 =	Marc Surer	3
6 =	Elio de Angelis	3
9 =	Eddie Cheever	2
9 =	René Arnoux	2
11 =	Patrick Tambay	1
11 =	Jacques Laffite	1

CONSTRUCTORS' CUP

1	Williams	39
2	Brabham	13
3	Renault	6
4	Arrows	4
5 =	Alfa Romeo	3
5 =	Ensign	3
5 =	Lotus	3
8	Tyrrell	2
9 =	Theodore	1
9 =	Ligier	1

CERAMICHE
PIEMME
Agip
Ferrari
HARIBO

A. Prost

elf
vsd
PROST
GPA
15

saudia
TAG

COGNETEX
Savio
3elle
INFISSI in LEGNO imola
donati
sollevamenti
CARPIGIANI
imeca
GRU IMOLA
Agip
SINT 2000

Gran Premio di San Marino

Gordon Murray stood quietly in the vast Brabham garage at Imola and expressed himself reasonably satisfied. The weekend had started off with bitter feelings over the scrutineers' rigid interpretation of the regulations and a subsequent ruling forced Murray to change the skirt system on the BT49. It was a poor compromise but he did as he was told – and still won the race. That, at least, was cause for satisfaction.

So, too, was the race itself; a busy cut and thrust affair which gave victory to Nelson Piquet after a climb through from ninth place. This time, however, it was not a simple case of the Brabham driver cruising home on the back of a suspension advantage; this time he had to deal with Williams, Arrows and, surprisingly, Ferrari as he worked for his second win in succession and closed the championship gap on Carlos Reutemann.

The Williams driver, brilliant during practice, posed no threat as he struggled through the wet race with a severe tyre vibration. Reutemann finished in third place behind the impressive Arrows of Riccardo Patrese and a mere three seconds ahead of Hector Rebaque, the Mexican giving an aggressive but neat performance.

Apart from the regulations, the main talking point at the San Marino Grand Prix was Ferrari – back in contention and taking their first pole position since the 1979 Monaco Grand Prix. Gilles Villeneuve admitted his shattering lap time was helped by an extra turn or two on the turbo boost control and an early retirement was expected for both cars in the race.

As if to make the most of their advantage while it lasted, Villeneuve and the fast-starting Didier Pironi led the first 14 laps before the French-Canadian stopped for dry tyres. The rain returned just as he left the pits but Pironi was comfortably in command, the superior power making amends for poor handling and pushing him out of reach on the straights.

With 13 laps to go, Piquet made his move and Pironi dropped back to fifth place with a broken skirt and worn tyres. But he finished nevertheless. So, too, did Villeneuve after turning in fastest lap and a scintillating drive into seventh place. Second fastest on the day was John Watson, eventually classified tenth in the McLaren after a silly mistake in the opening laps cost him a place in the points while his team-mate, Andrea de Cesaris, scored his first championship point with sixth place.

Alan Jones lost ground after coming into contact with Reutemann on the opening lap and, of the many incidents which followed, the most serious occurred to Miguel Angel Guerra who was removed to hospital with a broken ankle after crashing his Osella.

Lotus, caught in limbo when the 88 was finally thrown out by a special FIA Court of Appeal, declined to take part in a Grand Prix which saw the arrival of two new drivers and the Toleman team in addition to Pirelli and Avon tyres.

Unfortunately, however, the now familiar bickering and vilification remained.

ENTRY AND PRACTICE

The 1st San Marino Grand Prix was the result of some careful manoeuvring within Italian Motor sport and beyond. With the Italian Grand Prix booked by Monza for September 13, the Imola organisers were keen to cash in on the favourable reception their circuit received while hosting the Grand Prix the previous September. Two Italian Grands Prix in one season were out of the question so the organisers side-stepped the paperwork by calling their race after the nearby independant republic and claiming the event would be in aid of a recent Italian earthquake disaster. The Grand Prix received full approval and nothing more was heard about the earthquake disaster fund as the teams prepared for the beginning of the hectic European season.

The weekend started off on the wrong foot when the scrutineers took a firm hold of the rule book and began to examine the cars in detail. They said no to flexible skirts fitted to cars from Williams, Tyrrell, Brabham, McLaren, ATS, Ensign, Fittipaldi, Alfa Romeo, Arrows, Osella and Theodore. They threw out the little plates which sealed the gap between the end of the side-pods and the rear wheels and they excluded the flexible end-plates on the nose wings.

On the contentious subject of hydro-pneumatic suspensions and the like, the scrutineers, noting that such systems were fitted to Williams, Tyrrell, Brabham, Osella, Fittipaldi and Arrows, added that they were legal – so long as the 6cm gap was maintained. To that end, they stationed Judges of Fact around the track but, in the event, the move proved fruitless when the judges found *all* the cars to be touching the track at some point or other. However, the organisers would check each car in the pit lane – a move guaranteed to cause havoc in the heat of an Italian afternoon.

In the meantime, Renault and Toleman had emerged from scrutineering with flying colours and Alfa Romeo, Ferrari and Osella joined them out on the track on Friday after bringing their cars into line. Several FOCA teams, including Williams, wanted to do likewise but were summoned to a lengthy meeting which kept most of the pit lane inactive throughout the morning. By lunchtime, a compromise with the organisers had been reached. Trick suspensions would stay but flexible skirts were to be replaced by a more rigid variety and, with that, the day's business got under way.

By 4.30 p.m., the teams were ready for an hour of timed practice – and the scrutineers were ready at the end of the pit lane. Brabham and Williams were well placed and Piquet was the first to be checked on the level platform as a queue began to form down the pit lane. One or two drivers were still waiting some 15 minutes later and tempers rose while engines boiled. Brabham and Williams, meanwhile, could not get into their pits and fighting almost broke out when Osella mechanics, urged on by the emotional Gabbiani, felt they were being eased out of the queue. A wonderful thing, sport.

The spectators, having had their fun with that little pantomime, switched their attention to the track as the commentator whipped them to fever pitch with news of Villeneuve's spectacular progress. On his fourth lap, the Ferrari driver had set a remarkable 1m 35.576s and it seemed that a busy modification programme at Maranello was paying off. Gilles was driving a chassis featuring revised front suspension pick-up points and a longer wheelbase. The 15cm

The message from Imola was that Ferrari were back – and finishing races. Villeneuve and Pironi lead the field during the opening laps *(right)*.
Everybody out. Things were mighty still in the garages on Friday morning as FOCA sorted out the scrutineering wrangles *(far right)*.

Previous pages
Gilles Villeneuve and Didier Pironi took turns at leading the first San Marino Grand Prix *(left)*.
Photo: Nigel Snowdon
Alain Prost qualified his Renault on the second row but retired soon after the start with gearbox trouble *(centre)*.
Photo: Nigel Snowdon
Reutemann and Jones: colleagues – but scarcely friends *(top right)*.
Photo: Charles Knight
Jones, his nose-wing showing signs of a brush with Reutemann, leads Arnoux, Watson, Laffite and Rebaque *(bottom right)*.
Photo: Nigel Snowdon

Nelson Piquet won his second Grand Prix in succession after a determined drive through the field. The Brabham driver, shadowed by Tambay one lap in arrears, challenges Pironi for the lead.

spacer between the engine and gearbox altered the weight distribution but did little for the handling and by Saturday Villeneuve was out in the short wheelbase T-car to really set the place alight. Within 10 laps he had taken pole with 1m 34.523s, the result of out and out car control and a judicious tweak of the boost control. Villeneuve parked his car, firm in the knowledge that neither he nor anyone else could do better. Didier Pironi had engine trouble with his car (long wheelbase) and was glad of the opportunity to use the abandoned T-car; it proved to be a wasted effort and the Frenchman had to be satisfied with sixth place.

It was clear from Carlos Reutemann's behaviour on Saturday afternoon that the Williams driver was working up to a fast lap. The Argentinian sat motionless in his car for three or four minutes while the mechanics waited patiently for the signal from the cockpit. Cars roared past the pits; stop watches clicked; commentators gabbled – but still Reutemann remained impassive. Then, the thumb's up; the DFV burst into life and he was away – and straight into the 1m 36s region. Then he reeled off three stunning laps in the low 1m 35s; good enough for the front row – and half a second faster than the next Cosworth driver. That done, Reutemann returned to the pits and went off to change, leaving Alan Jones to thrash angrily round and round in a vain attempt to improve on his Friday time.

Williams had tried their own special ride height control – a 12in steel spring which held the car at 6cms at the appropriate moment. Or, at least, it should have

APRIL:

Niki Lauda discusses test drive with McLaren.

Lotus 88 banned by FIA Court of Appeal.

David Thieme released on bail of £70,000.

Lotus withdraw from San Marino Grand Prix.

Lotus test revised car at Donington.

Patrese heads for second place during the closing stages while Tambay comes under attack from the hard-charging John Watson *(above)*.
"The probem's in there somewhere." Brian Hart and Toleman designer Rory Byrne tackle the mammoth task facing the team on their Grand Prix debut *(right)*.
Michele Alboreto impressed everyone with a neat and tidy Grand Prix debut. His Tyrrell was forced into retirement after an incident with Gabbiani's Osella *(far right)*.
Organised chaos. Officials measure the 6cm gap (ironically, on a pad sponsored by '7 Up') on Pironi's Ferrari at the entrance to the pit lane. Scenes were not so orderly at the opposite end of the pits *(below right)*.
Niki Lauda, back at the races and back in the limelight after rumours of a test drive with McLaren *(opposite page)*.

done. The system was abandoned for Saturday but Jones's afternoon was spoiled by gearbox trouble. He switched to the T-car while the mechanics changed fourth gear in 25 minutes, no less, but his hopes were dashed by traffic during the final minutes and the World Champion had to be content with an unaccustomed place on the fourth row.

Renault had dominated practice for the Italian Grand Prix the previous year and on Friday it seemed that they were poised to do the same when René Arnoux bumped Villeneuve off the over-night pole. His luck changed on Saturday, however, when the V6 refused to run on any more than five cylinders although his Friday time was good enough to keep him on the second row with his team-mate. Prost was in similar trouble after a good showing on Friday. Engine trouble on his race car *and* the T-car meant the sum total of two laps on Saturday and he spent the session keeping an anxious eye on the progress of Nelson Piquet.

Brabham arrived with a revised hydro-pneumatic

system and a separate suspension pull rod allowed adjustments to be made to the springs without upsetting the hydraulics. Gordon Murray's calculations were upset by the ban on flexible skirts and the team were struggling on Friday as they tried to balance the car. Modifications were made overnight and Piquet briefly tried the T-car in standard trim before returning to his race car and taking fifth fastest time towards the end of the session. Hector Rebaque, back in 13th place, lost time on Saturday with a blown engine and the Mexican was unable to improve in the T-car.

John Watson had that confident air about him as he got down to business with two carbon fibre MP4s at his disposal. The second chassis was some 24lbs lighter but progressive double springing proved to be too hard and Watson concentrated on chassis number one on Saturday. The Ulsterman set seventh fastest time near the end of the session and felt he could have gone even faster had he not indulged in a quick spin. Young Andrea de Cesaris was rather peeved when the McLaren management voted him into the old M29F rather than let him loose in an MP4. They wisely felt the pressure to perform well at home might have a detrimental effect on chassis and bodywork and the Italian did well to take a place half-way up the grid.

The delay to proceedings on Friday morning was a source of frustration for the Arrows team, keen to do well in front of their sponsors. Riccardo Patrese's car, built around a fresh monocoque, was running a new Cosworth DFV and repositioned oil, water and fuel pumps meant alterations to the radiators and ancillary plumbing. A special suspension was tried on Friday but did not work satisfactorily and Patrese lost half of Saturday afternoon practice as the team got to grips with metal skirts. Siegfried Stohr added to the work-load when he crashed and damaged the front bulkhead of his car on Saturday morning. Unfortunately, the Italian's time from the previous day was not good enough to keep him in the race.

Ligier had been to the Michelin test track to check out new bodywork and side-pods and they arrived at Imola with their particular version of ride height control. Jacques Laffite had overheating problems throughout but Jean-Pierre Jabouille made the grid with his Friday time after a faulty coil kept him out of the picture on Saturday. Alfa Romeo were very unhappy about the random changes to the regulations. The team felt they had been making progress during testing but their suspension tweaks proved useless without flexible skirts and Mario Andretti and Bruno Giacomelli trashed round and round on Saturday to record almost identical times.

Avon tyres appeared for the first time and were used solely by the Fittipaldi team, Keke Rosberg proving their worth by recording a top ten time on Friday. He slipped down the grid the following day, however, when gearbox problems kept him in the pits for some time and the failure to pass the 6cm test (due possibly to the Avons shrinking when warm) robbed the Finn of a lap some seven-tenths faster than his final grid time. Rosberg became the sole Fittipaldi representative when Chico Serra was restricted to a handful of laps due to various problems including a blown engine on Friday.

Patrick Tambay was in similar trouble when a gearbox fault kept him off the track after a mere five laps on Friday and a fuel system blockage stranded the Theodore out on the circuit the following day. When he did get going finally, the Frenchman set a commendable time in spite of a kerb-hopping moment caused by a broken rear-roll bar. The Tyrrell team, introducing Michele Alboreto and the Imola Ceramica company to Grand Prix racing, had an unsuccessful time with a variable rate suspension system on Eddie Cheever's car despite tests that week at Ferrari's Fiorano track. Alboreto impressed one and all with sensible and smooth laps and the young Italian proved to be quicker than Cheever after Eddie was forced to use the T-car when locking brakes kept his regular machine in the pits.

The Imola race obviously meant a lot to the Osella team and the Italians spent some time testing their suspension variation at Monza. The system was removed for practice but the cars boasted new side-pods and various detailed modifications which trimmed around 30lbs off the weight. Beppe Gabbiani and Miguel Angel Guerra had different ideas about suspension set-ups, the Italian running on soft springs, but, either way, both drivers qualified. So, too, did Marc Surer in the Ensign, the English team's financial plight being such that they were forced to run briefly on an old set of 1980 Goodyears!

Had Lotus been present, then it is a cast iron certainty that neither Eliseo Salazar nor Tommy 'Slim' Borgudd would have made the race. The March team were continuing the unequal struggle with cars which had been strengthened around the front of the monocoque and it was a despondent Derek Daly who failed to make the cut. His frustration was eased slightly when the March mechanics discovered a collapsed rear spring after practice had finished. The ATS team were in turmoil once more after the team manager and one or two key mechanics had walked out leaving the irascible Gunter Schmid to run his own team. Slim Borgudd was drafted in along with backing from the ABBA pop group and the Swede did a respectable job under the circumstances. Poor Jan Lammers, along with new team manager Roger Heavens, was left to make the most of an inefficient hydro-pneumatic suspension system which was finally abandoned on Saturday afternoon. Lammers did his best and there was a tense moment during the closing minutes of practice when Schmid flatly refused to allow Lammers a fresh set of tyres. The Dutchman failed to qualify.

By contrast, the Toleman team cut a professional and impressive image as they quietly made their Grand Prix debut with their turbocharged 4-cylinder Hart engines and Pirelli radial tyres. The 1980 Formula 2 champions were under no illusions whatsoever although the same could not be said for their sponsors, Candy Domestic Appliances, who expected rather more on home territory. The team had a mammoth task before them and their first hurdle was sorting out the intercooling for the single Garrett turbocharger. The intercooling was insufficient for the high boost pressure required and, as a result, the throttle lag was, to quote Brian Henton 'embarrassing'. Derek Warwick had trouble of another sort on Friday when the bodywork caught fire briefly and Henton added to the team's troubles when he inadvertently missed a gear and buzzed his engine. The two Englishmen were hardly surprised when they came bottom of the time sheet.

RACE

Practice had been held under sunny skies but that changed on race morning when rain brought wet tyres rolling into the pit lane for the warm-up. Only Brabham, Ligier and Fittipaldi continued with ride height control systems while the rest went back to standard suspensions in pursuit of a finish. That suddenly seemed a forlorn hope for the Williams team when both drivers reported severe chassis vibrations. A change of tyres did not cure the problem and yet it seemed certain that the wet weather Michelins were disagreeing with the Williams wheel rims. The vibrations continued during the final warm-up lap and Reutemann switched to a fourth set on the line.

On a lighter note, Bernie Ecclestone presented Nelson Piquet with a 'tyre forecaster'; a home-made device which, when turned to 'rain', produced a grooved tyre through a small opening and, similarly, a tiny slick tyre appeared when Piquet turned the dial to 'sun'. Following the Brazilian débâcle, Nelson was taking no chances and kept his wet weather tyres firmly in place although Rosberg, Surer and Tambay gambled on slicks.

On the face of it, Reutemann seemed a certain winner since the Ferraris were not expected to last although the cool conditions were definitely in their favour. The Renaults could upset the balance but, by the time the cars had completed their parade lap, Prost knew he would not be figuring in this race. The Frenchman could not find first gear and he struggled off the line in second as the field surged past.

Villeneuve had been slow to start but soon got into his stride while Pironi, rolling gently into position as the lights turned green, powered through into second place. Jones made an equally brilliant start and was attempting to take third place from Reutemann when he knocked his nose wing askew: "I tried to go on the inside and my team-mate cut me off. But it was fair enough," Jones said later. Reutemann was firmly in command of that battle therefore but the Ferraris were pulling away to the unbridled joy of the crowd.

Jones continued in fourth place before dropping

back and eventually calling at the pits for repairs and a set of slicks. Patrese was next followed by Arnoux, Watson, Laffite and Piquet. Then came Rebaque, the Alfa Romeos, de Cesaris, the two Tyrrells followed by Gabbiani, now the sole-surviving Osella. Poor Guerra's Grand Prix debut lasted half a lap when his car got away from him and he was collected by Salazar. The March continued with a bent nose wing but the Argentinian was removed to hospital with a broken ankle and injured hand. The back of the field consisted of Jabouille, Rosberg (struggling on slicks), Borgudd, Tambay, Surer and Prost – soon to quit his hopeless task.

The other Renault, meanwhile, was featuring in two separate incidents. Watson, perhaps overcome by the excitement of being a leading runner so early in the race, made a complete nonsense on lap five when he rammed the back of Arnoux under braking for the chicane before the pits. His nose cone flew in the air and the McLaren was in the pits a lap later – just as poor Arnoux came under attack from an over-anxious Laffite. The Ligier was damaged beyond immediate repair but Arnoux was able to continue and Piquet made the most of the confusion by slipping into fifth place behind Reutemann.

The Williams driver was in desperate trouble with tyre vibrations which were forcing him to lift off, particularly on the flat-out downhill run. When he ran wide briefly coming into the stadium area, Patrese had seized his chance to make the crowd's joy complete. Rebaque was running strongly and, on lap nine, the Brabham driver proved neatly and conclusively that it was not necessary to clobber Arnoux in order to take sixth place. The Alfas, led by Andretti, were under pressure from de Cesaris who, in turn, had opened a gap over a tight group consisting of Cheever, Alboreto and Gabbiani.

By lap 14, Jabouille had made the first of several pit stops to investigate engine problems and the leaders were lapping Jones and Tambay – the Theodore about to stop for wet tyres. Next time round, Piquet had moved past Reutemann and there was further drama when the leader peeled into the pits. Turbo trouble was diagnosed by the cynics but Villeneuve, noting that the slick-shod Jones was keeping pace, had merely stopped for dry tyres. His timing could not have been more unfortunate. Rain returned just as the Ferrari left the pits and Villeneuve was back to retrieve his wet tyres two laps later. Victory was well and truly lost but the fans were about to be appeased by a memorable drive.

Besides, Pironi was holding a comfortable lead over

Fittipaldi were the first team to use the new Avon crossplies while Toleman brought Pirelli radials into Formula 1 *(left)*.
Slim Borgudd gave a good account of himself after qualifying for his first Grand Prix *(bottom left)*.

Chapman: "I wish I could have taken this decision in better heart."

THE LOTUS 88 WAS BANNED BY AN FIA INTERNATIONAL Court of Appeal in Paris on April 23 despite a well-prepared defence by Colin Chapman, Peter Wright and a team of lawyers.

"I wish I could have taken this decision in better heart," said Chapman. "I wish I could feel that I have had a reasoned discussion with a panel of open-minded persons who were competent to judge on the technicalities involved in the official language of the technical rules of the Concorde Agreement and of motor racing itself.

"And if to be proved wrong, then by logical argument drawn only from the letter and intent of the rules in force, presented in coherent and comprehensive manner.

"So far this has not happened, and when I eventually get a full statement as to the reasons advanced for this bizarre decision, then I may be willing to comment further."

The 88 failed on two counts: the so-called primary chassis did not confirm with the definition in the FIA Yellow Book; the chassis in the Yellow Book is referred to as a body/chassis and therefore the bodywork has to be integral with the chassis. Chapman pointed out that the only definition which counted in Formula 1 was that laid down in the Concorde Agreement.

Commenting on his future plans, Chapman said: "I've got no cars now. Two 88s are built and a third is being built – and I don't know about my sponsor's future." This was a reference to David Thieme, arrested in Zurich on a complaint by Credit Suisse, a leading Swiss bank, alleging malpractice. The Essex Petroleum chief was held for two weeks without charges being laid against him.

At 2.30 p.m. on Tuesday April 28, Colin Chapman announced his decision to withdraw from the San Marino Grand Prix on the grounds that there had been insufficient time to prepare alternate race-worthy cars following the ban on the Lotus 88. It was to be the first Grand Prix not attended by Team Lotus since they began Formula 1 racing in 1958.

Patrese and the Arrows driver was too busy struggling with worn tyres and the constant attention of Piquet to do anything about the Ferrari. The Brabham was through on lap 22 and quickly eating into Pironi's 10-second advantage. Within ten laps, Piquet was climbing all over the Ferrari as Pironi learnt to cope with worn tyres and a broken skirt while skilfully maintaining his lead. The turbo power more than made up for poor handling and Piquet's troubles were compounded by Tambay, running as quickly as the leaders but a lap down. "He was fighting as though he was trying to win the race too," said Piquet. "He made it impossible for me to pass; on top of that, Pironi made no mistakes, none at all. I tried him everywhere and then I had a go going up the hill because I had slightly better traction."

The move worked; Piquet was leading on lap 47. Meanwhile, all sorts of drama had been decimating the field. Rosberg blew an engine and Andretti stopped when his gearbox, having given trouble from the start, finally jammed in third. Giacomelli was left to deal with de Cesaris but the two had a coming-together as the McLaren moved ahead. Cheever was next in line to tackle the Alfa and he, too, had a brush with the Italian. This time the outcome was rather more serious. "I couldn't believe it," said Cheever. "He messed up coming through a corner and we were side by side going up the hill. Then he just turned into me. Just like that. Right across the front of my car. I couldn't believe it." The two cars were parked against the guardrail thus elevating Alboreto into eighth place. That lasted but three laps when the Tyrrell driver, having successfully fended off Gabbiani, was bundled off the track by the impetuous Osella driver as both drivers argued over the same piece of track.

And that, believe it or not, brought Villeneuve into eighth place with a drive which was sheer poetry as he coped with the surging turbo on a greasy track. Time and again the Ferrari would slide into view, Villeneuve setting the fastest lap as he closed remorselessly on Arnoux. By lap 45 he was ahead of the Renault as Arnoux struggled for gears and four laps later he was in front of de Cesaris. It was some consolation for the crowd during the closing laps for Pironi was sliding inexorably down the lap chart. Patrese and then Reutemann had moved ahead and, on lap 58, Rebaque bumped wheels with the Ferrari as he took fourth place. To make matters worse, de Cesaris retook sixth place as Villeneuve struggled with a slipping clutch – but at least the turbos were as healthy as they had been at the start.

Arnoux held on to take eighth place with Surer a worthy ninth after an excellent drive in the Ensign. Watson, all fired up and convinced he could have won had he not goofed, barged past Tambay on the last lap to take tenth place and eleventh was scarcely fair reward for the Theodore driver after an energetic race. Borgudd did all that was asked of him to finish a steady 13th, a lap behind Jones who had made two further pit stops for tyres.

"Who won?" asked the perspiring Australian as he plodded his lonely way through the paddock.

"Piquet."

"What about Carlos?"

"Third."

Silence as Jones totted up his team-mate's seven point advantage.

"What were the other positions?"

"Patrese was second."

"Yeah?"

"Rebaque fourth."

"Rebaque!......Jeez. What about the Ferraris?"

"Led for 46 laps and both finished."

"What, no turbo trouble?"

"No, none."

That said it all.

Gran Premio di San Marino, May 3/statistics

Entries and practice times

No.	Driver	Nat	Car	Engine	Entrant	Practice 1	Practice 2
1	Alan Jones	AUS	Saudia-Leyland WILLIAMS FWO7C	Ford Cosworth DFV	Albilad-Williams Racing Team	**1m 36·280s**	1m 36·317s
2	Carlos Reutemann	RA	Saudia-Leyland WILLIAMS FWO7C	Ford Cosworth DFV	Albilad-Williams Racing Team	1m 35·844s	**1m 35·229s**
3	Eddie Cheever	USA	TYRRELL 010	Ford Cosworth DFV	Tyrrell Racing	1m 38·369s	**1m 38·266s**
4	Michele Alboreto	I	TYRRELL 010	Ford Cosworth DFV	Tyrrell Racing	1m 39·341s	**1m 37·771s**
5	Nelson Piquet	BR	Parmalat BRABHAM BT49C	Ford Cosworth DFV	Parmalat Racing Team	1m 37·417s	**1m 35·733s**
6	Hector Rebaque	MEX	Parmalat BRABHAM BT49C	Ford Cosworth DFV	Parmalat Racing Team	1m 38·822s	**1m 37·264s**
7	John Watson	GB	Marlboro McLAREN MP4	Ford Cosworth DFV	McLaren International	1m 37·639s	**1m 36·241s**
8	Andrea de Cesaris	I	Marlboro McLAREN M29F	Ford Cosworth DFV	McLaren International	1m 38·019s	**1m 37·382s**
9	Jan Lammers	NL	Abba ATS D4	Ford Cosworth DFV	Team ATS	1m 40·872s	**1m 39·419s**
10	Slim Borgudd	S	Abba ATS D4	Ford Cosworth DFV	Team ATS	1m 41·196s	**1m 39·079s**
11	Elio de Angelis	I	Essex LOTUS 81	Ford Cosworth DFV	Team Essex Lotus	Entry withdrawn	
12	Nigel Mansell	GB	Essex LOTUS 81	Ford Cosworth DFV	Team Essex Lotus	Entry withdrawn	
14	Marc Surer	CH	ENSIGN N180B	Ford Cosworth DFV	Ensign Racing	**1m 38·341s**	1m 38·488s
15	Alain Prost	F	Elf RENAULT RE 20	Renault EF1	Equipe Renault Elf	**1m 35·579s**	3m 58·089s
16	René Arnoux	F	Elf RENAULT RE 20	Renault EF1	Equipe Renault Elf	**1m 35·281s**	1m 35·292s
17	Eliseo Salazar	RCH	Rizla MARCH 811	Ford Cosworth DFV	March Grand Prix	1m 39·161s	**1m 38·827s**
18	Derek Daly	IRL	Rizla MARCH 811	Ford Cosworth DFV	March Grand Prix	1m 39·453s	**1m 39·157s**
20	Keke Rosberg	SF	FITTIPALDI F8C	Ford Cosworth DFV	Fittipaldi Automotive	**1m 37·459s**	1m 37·906s
21	Chico Serra	BR	FITTIPALDI F8C	Ford Cosworth DFV	Fittipaldi Automotive	1m 51·453s	**1m 41·114s**
22	Mario Andretti	USA	Marlboro ALFA ROMEO 179C	Alfa Romeo 1260	Marlboro Team Alfa Romeo	1m 37·587s	**1m 36·919s**
23	Bruno Giacomelli	I	Marlboro ALFA ROMEO 179C	Alfa Romeo 1260	Marlboro Team Alfa Romeo	1m 39·372s	**1m 36·776s**
25	Jean-Pierre Jabouille	F	Talbot-Gitanes LIGIER JS17	Matra MS 81	Equipe Talbot Gitanes	**1m 38·140s**	1m 38·702s
26	Jacques Laffite	F	Talbot-Gitanes LIGIER JS17	Matra MS 81	Equipe Talbot Gitanes	1m 38·908s	**1m 36·477s**
27	Gilles Villeneuve	CDN	Fiat FERRARI 126CK	Ferrari 126C	Scuderia Ferrari SpA SEFAC	1m 35·576s	**1m 34·523s**
28	Didier Pironi	F	Fiat FERRARI 126CK	Ferrari 126C	Scuderia Ferrari SpA SEFAC	1m 36·168s	**1m 35·868s**
29	Riccardo Patrese	I	Ragno-Beta ARROWS A3	Ford Cosworth DFV	Arrows Racing Team	1m 37·061s	**1m 36·390s**
30	Siegfried Stohr	I	Ragno-Beta ARROWS A3	Ford Cosworth DFV	Arrows Racing Team	**1m 39·112s**	1m 39·553s
31	Miguel Angel Guerra	RA	Denim OSELLA FA1B	Ford Cosworth DFV	Osella Squadra Corse	1m 39·799s	**1m 38·773s**
32	Beppe Gabbiani	I	Denim OSELLA FA1B	Ford Cosworth DFV	Osella Squadra Corse	1m 39·245s	**1m 38·302s**
33	Patrick Tambay	F	THEODORE TY 01	Ford Cosworth DFV	Theodore Racing Team	1m 39·215s	**1m 37·545s**
35	Brian Henton	GB	Candy TOLEMAN TG 181	Hart 415T	Candy Toleman Motorsport	**1m 49·951s**	–
36	Derek Warwick	GB	Candy TOLEMAN TG 181	Hart 415T	Candy Toleman Motorsport	1m 54·020s	**1m 43·187s**
Friday morning and early afternoon and Saturday morning practice sessions not officially recorded						*Fri pm* *Warm, dry*	*Sat pm* *Warm, dry*

Starting grid

27 VILLENEUVE (1m 34·523s) Ferrari	
	2 REUTEMANN (1m 35·229s) Williams
16 ARNOUX (1m 35·281s) Renault	
	15 PROST (1m 35·579s) Renault
5 PIQUET (1m 35·733s) Brabham	
	28 PIRONI (1m 35·868s) Ferrari
7 WATSON (1m 36·241s) McLaren	
	1 JONES (1m 36·280s) Williams
29 PATRESE (1m 36·390s) Arrows	
	26 LAFFITE (1m 36·477s) Talbot-Ligier
23 GIACOMELLI (1m 36·776s) Alfa Romeo	
	22 ANDRETTI (1m 36·919s) Alfa Romeo
6 REBAQUE (1m 37·264s) Brabham	
	8 DE CESARIS (1m 37·382s) McLaren
20 ROSBERG (1m 37·459s) Fittipaldi	
	33 TAMBAY (1m 37·545s) Theodore
4 ALBORETO (1m 37·771s) Tyrrell	
	25 JABOUILLE (1m 38·140s) Talbot-Ligier
3 CHEEVER (1m 38·266s) Tyrrell	
	32 GABBIANI (1m 38·302s) Osella
14 SURER (1m 38·341s) Ensign	
	31 GUERRA (1m 38·773s) Osella
17 SALAZAR (1m 38·827s) March	
	10 BORGUDD (1m 39·079s) ATS

Did not start:
30 Stohr (Arrows), 1m 39·112s, did not qualify
18 Daly (March), 1m 39·157s, did not qualify
9 Lammers (ATS), 1m 39·419s, did not qualify
21 Serra (Fittipaldi), 1m 41·114s, did not qualify
36 Warwick (Toleman), 1m 43·187s, did not qualify
35 Henton (Toleman), 1m 49·951s, did not qualify

Past winners

Year	Driver	Nat	Car	Circuit	Distance miles/km	Speed mph/km/h
1981	Nelson Piquet	BR	3·0 Brabham BT49C-Ford	Imola	187·90/302·40	101·20/162·87

Circuit data

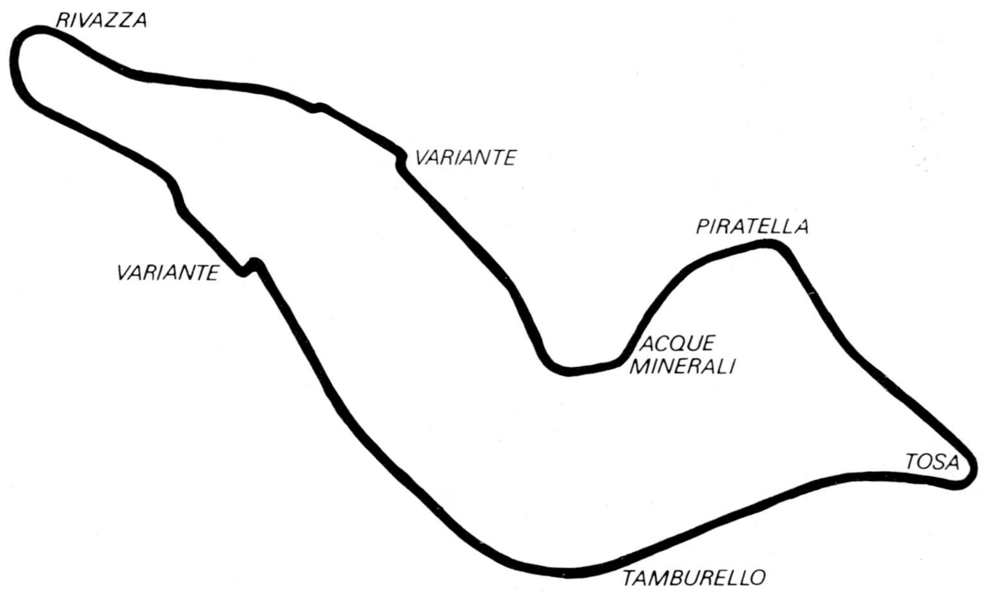

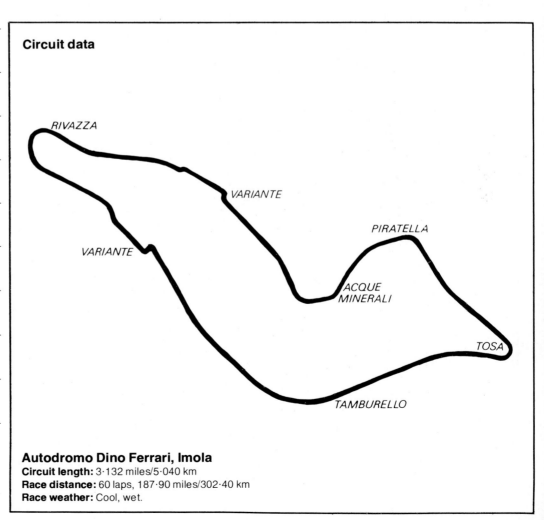

Autodromo Dino Ferrari, Imola
Circuit length: 3·132 miles/5·040 km
Race distance: 60 laps, 187·90 miles/302·40 km
Race weather: Cool, wet.

Results and retirements

Place	Driver	Car	Laps	Time and Speed (mph/km/h)/Retirement	
1	Nelson Piquet	Brabham-Cosworth V8	60	1h 51m 23·97s	101·203/162·87
2	Riccardo Patrese	Arrows-Cosworth V8	60	1h 51m 28·55s	101·134/162·76
3	Carlos Reutemann	Williams-Cosworth V8	60	1h 51m 30·31s	101·109/162·72
4	Hector Rebaque	Brabham-Cosworth V8	60	1h 51m 46·86s	100·861/162·32
5	Didier Pironi	Ferrari t/c V6	60	1h 51m 49·84s	100·817/162·25
6	Andrea de Cesaris	McLaren-Cosworth V8	60	1h 52m 30·58s	100·208/161·27
7	Gilles Villeneuve	Ferrari t/c V6	60	1h 53m 05·94s	99·686/160·43
8	René Arnoux	Renault t/c V6	59		
9	Marc Surer	Ensign-Cosworth V8	59		
10	John Watson	McLaren-Cosworth V8	58		
11	Patrick Tambay	Theodore-Cosworth V8	58		
12	Alan Jones	Williams-Cosworth V8	58		
13	Slim Borgudd	ATS-Cosworth V8	57		
	Jean-Pierre Jabouille	Talbot-Ligier Matra V12	45	Running, not classified	
	Eliseo Salazar	March-Cosworth V8	38	Oil pressure	
	Michele Alboreto	Tyrrell-Cosworth V8	31	Accident with Gabbiani	
	Beppe Gabbiani	Osella-Cosworth V8	31	Accident with Alboreto	
	Bruno Giacomelli	Alfa Romeo V12	28	Accident with Cheever	
	Eddie Cheever	Tyrrell-Cosworth V8	28	Accident with Giacomelli	
	Mario Andretti	Alfa Romeo V12	26	Gearbox	
	Keke Rosberg	Fittipaldi-Cosworth V8	14	Engine	
	Jacques Laffite	Talbot-Ligier Matra V12	7	Accident with Arnoux	
	Alain Prost	Renault t/c V6	3	Gearbox	
	Miguel Angel Guerra	Osella-Cosworth V8	0	Accident	

Fastest lap: Villeneuve, on lap 46, 1m 48·064s, 104·328mph/167·9km/h.
Lap record: Alan Jones (F1 Williams FW07B-Cosworth DFV), 1m 36·089s, 116·399mph/187·326km/h (1980).

Lap chart

1st LAP ORDER	1	2	3	4	5	6	7	8	9	10	11	12	13	14	15	16	17	18	19	20	21	22	23	24	25	26	27
27 G.Villeneuve	27	27	27	27	27	27	27	27	27	27	27	27	27	27	28	28	28	28	28	28	28	28	28	28	28	28	28
28 D.Pironi	28	28	28	28	28	28	28	28	28	28	28	28	28	28	29	29	29	29	29	29	29	5	5	5	5	5	5
2 C.Reutemann	2	2	2	2	2	29	29	29	29	29	29	29	29	29	5	5	5	5	5	5	5	29	29	29	29	29	29
1 A.Jones	1	29	29	29	29	2	2	2	2	2	2	2	2	2	2	2	2	2	2	2	2	2	2	2	2	2	2
29 R.Patrese	29	1	16	16	16	16	5	5	5	5	5	5	5	5	6	6	6	6	6	6	6	6	6	6	6	6	6
16 R.Arnoux	16	16	7	7	26	26	16	16	6	6	6	6	6	6	16	16	16	16	16	16	16	16	16	16	16	16	16
7 J.Watson	7	7	26	26	7	5	6	6	16	16	16	16	16	16	22	22	23	23	23	23	23	23	23	23	23	8	8
26 J.Laffite	26	26	5	5	5	6	22	22	22	22	22	22	22	22	23	23	22	22	8	8	8	8	8	8	8	23	23
5 N.Piquet	5	5	6	6	6	22	23	23	23	23	23	23	23	23	8	8	8	3	3	3	3	3	3	3	3	3	3
6 H.Rebaque	6	6	22	22	22	23	8	8	8	8	8	8	8	8	(27)	3	3	8	22	22	22	22	22	22	22	4	4
22 M.Andretti	22	22	23	23	23	8	(26)	3	3	3	3	3	3	3	3	4	4	4	4	4	4	4	4	4	4	32	32
23 B.Giacomelli	23	23	8	8	8	3	3	4	4	4	4	4	4	4	4	32	32	32	32	32	32	32	32	32	32	(22)	27
4 M.Alboreto	4	8	4	4	4	4	4	32	32	32	32	32	32	32	32	27	17	17	17	17	17	17	27	27	27	27	17
8 A.de Cesaris	8	4	3	3	3	32	32	17	17	17	17	17	17	17	17	17	(27)	27	27	27	27	27	17	17	17	17	(22)
32 B.Gabbiani	32	3	32	32	32	(7)	17	10	10	10	10	10	10	(10)	33	33	33	33	14	14	14	14	14	14	14	14	14
3 E.Cheever	3	32	17	17	17	17	10	20	20	20	20	20	20	20	14	14	7	14	(33)	33	33	33	33	33	33	33	33
20 K.Rosberg	20	17	(1)	10	10	10	20	33	33	33	33	33	33	33	10	7	(14)	(7)	10	7	7	7	7	7	7	7	7
17 E.Salazar	17	25	25	20	20	20	33	14	14	14	14	14	14	14	7	(10)	10	10	7	10	10	10	10	10	10	10	10
25 J-P.Jabouille	25	20	20	25	33	33	14	7	7	7	7	7	7	7	1	(1)	1	(1)	1	1	1	1	1	1	1	1	1
33 P.Tambay	33	10	10	33	14	14	7	(25)	1	1	1	1	1	1	25	25	25	25	(25)	25	25	25	25	25	25	25	25
14 M.Surer	14	15	33	14	(25)	25	25	1	25	25	25	25	(25)	25													
10 S.Borgudd	10	33	14	1	1	1	1																				
15 A.Prost	15	14																									

28	29	30	31	32	33	34	35	36	37	38	39	40	41	42	43	44	45	46	47	48	49	50	51	52	53	54	55	56	57	58	59	60
28	28	28	28	28	28	28	28	28	28	28	28	28	28	28	28	28	28	28	5	5	5	5	5	5	5	5	5	5	5	5	5	5
5	5	5	5	5	5	5	5	5	5	5	5	5	5	5	5	5	5	5	28	28	29	29	29	29	29	29	29	29	29	29	29	29
29	29	29	29	29	29	29	29	29	29	29	29	29	29	29	29	29	29	29	29	29	28	28	28	2	2	2	2	2	2	2	2	2
2	2	2	2	2	2	2	2	2	2	2	2	2	2	2	2	2	2	2	2	2	2	2	2	28	28	28	28	28	28	28	6	6
6	6	6	6	6	6	6	6	6	6	6	6	6	6	6	6	6	6	6	6	6	6	6	6	6	6	6	6	6	6	6	28	28
16	16	8	8	8	8	8	8	8	8	8	8	8	8	8	8	8	8	8	8	8	27	27	27	27	27	27	27	27	27	27	8	8
8	8	16	16	16	16	16	16	16	16	16	16	16	16	16	16	16	27	27	27	27	8	8	8	8	8	8	8	8	8	8	27	27
23	4	4	4	27	27	27	27	27	27	27	27	27	27	27	27	27	16	16	16	16	16	16	16	16	16	16	16	16	16	16	16	
3	32	32	32	17	17	17	17	17	17	17	14	14	14	14	14	14	14	14	14	14	14	14	14	14	14	14	14	14	14	14	14	
4	27	27	27	14	14	14	14	14	14	14	33	33	33	33	33	33	33	33	33	33	33	33	33	33	33	33	33	33	33	7		
32	17	17	17	33	33	33	33	33	33	33	7	7	7	7	7	7	7	7	7	7	7	7	7	7	7	7	7	7	7	33		
27	14	14	14	7	7	7	7	7	7	7	1	1	1	1	1	1	1	1	1	1	1	1	1	1	1	1	1	1	1	1		
17	33	33	33	1	1	1	1	1	1	1	10	10	10	10	10	10	10	10	10	10	10	10	10	10	10	10	10	10	10			
14	7	7	7	10	10	10	10	10	10	10	25	(25)	25	25	25	25	25															
33	10	1	1	25	25	25	25	25	25	(25)																						
7	1	10	10																													
10	10	25	25																													
1	25																															
25																																

Fastest laps

Driver	Time	Lap
Gilles Villeneuve	1m 48·06s	46
John Watson	1m 48·37s	47
Nelson Piquet	1m 48·83s	8
Didier Pironi	1m 49·17s	10
Hector Rebaque	1m 49·18s	45
Riccardo Patrese	1m 49·41s	10
Patrick Tambay	1m 49·56s	48
Alan Jones	1m 49·75s	34
Carlos Reutemann	1m 49·75s	51
René Arnoux	1m 50·10s	14
Marc Surer	1m 50·11s	49
Andrea de Cesaris	1m 50·26s	34
Jacques Laffite	1m 50·34s	6
Eddie Cheever	1m 50·59s	9
Slim Borgudd	1m 50·88s	45
Michele Alboreto	1m 50·95s	9
Beppe Gabbiani	1m 50·98s	15
Mario Andretti	1m 51·11s	13
Bruno Giacomelli	1m 51·23s	10
Jean-Pierre Jabouille	1m 51·49s	33
Eliseo Salazar	1m 51·83s	13
Keke Rosberg	1m 53·86s	14
Alain Prost	1m 57·39s	2

Points

WORLD CHAMPIONSHIP OF DRIVERS

1	Carlos Reutemann	25 pts
2	Nelson Piquet	22
3	Alan Jones	18
4	Riccardo Patrese	10
5	Alain Prost	4
6 =	Mario Andretti	3
6 =	Marc Surer	3
6 =	Elio de Angelis	3
6 =	Hector Rebaque	3
10 =	Eddie Cheever	2
10 =	René Arnoux	2
10 =	Didier Pironi	2
13 =	Patrick Tambay	1
13 =	Jacques Laffite	1
13 =	Andrea de Cesaris	1

CONSTRUCTORS' CUP

1	Williams	43
2	Brabham	25
3	Arrows	10
4	Renault	6
5 =	Alfa Romeo	3
5 =	Ensign	3
5 =	Lotus	3
8 =	Tyrrell	2
8 =	Ferrari	2
10 =	Theodore	1
10 =	Ligier	1
10 =	McLaren	1

Grote Prijs van België

The actual racing had been good – exciting, even – but there were few complaints when the Belgian Grand Prix was brought to a premature halt because of a light shower. Carlos Reutemann, the eventual winner, climbed from his Saudia-Leyland Williams and slumped against the barrier. He was tired. Tired of the protests which had disrupted the start and contributed to what could have been serious injuries to an Arrows mechanic; tired of the rule bashing which saw teams blatantly ignore the regulations; tired of Zolder and its inadequate pit facilities. More than that, however, he was deeply upset by an incident in that crowded pit lane when an Osella mechanic fell between the wheels of Reutemann's car. (The mechanic, Giovanni Amadeo, subsequently died from head injuries on the Monday after the race). Reutemann was completely blameless but he wanted no part of the victory celebration; his funeral face on the rostrum said that.

Jacques Laffite, having given Talbot-Ligier their best result of the season, felt much the same about his second place but Nigel Mansell was understandably elated with third place and his first championship points after a superb drive in the aging Essex Lotus 81. His was one of the few creditable performances in a miserable weekend.

The start had been a shambles following a protest by certain drivers and mechanics and it was hardly surprising when confusion caught Dave Luckett on the grid as he attended to Riccardo Patrese's stalled car. Ironically, the Ragno-Beta Arrows Chief Mechanic was struck by Siegfried Stohr but the officials let the race run while they attempted to rescue Luckett. It was only when Didier Pironi took the law into his own hands that the race was stopped and it was the Ferrari driver who took the lead at the restart.

Climbing into the turbo's glowing exhausts, at least through the corners, were Reutemann, Piquet and Jones and it was a flame-out from the Ferrari which startled Reutemann and allowed the Parmalat Brabham and Jones to move ahead. The leader board changed dramatically as Pironi dropped back; then Piquet crashed after a controversial incident with Jones but the reigning World Champion lost the lead when his Williams jumped out of gear and slammed into the barriers. The water radiator split and Jones was fortunate to escape with no more than a scalded left leg.

Reutemann was left to score his 15th consecutive finish in the points; a remarkable achievement. Laffite and Mansell were next with Gilles Villeneuve giving Ferrari another reliable run and taking fourth place. The remaining points went to Elio de Angelis (Essex Lotus) and Eddie Cheever whose Tyrrell spluttered to a halt just as drizzle and the chequered flag stopped the race. For many, it was a merciful relief as they packed up and hurried away from Zolder after an appalling weekend for Grand Prix racing.

Sad weekend for Carlos. Winning the Belgian Grand Prix was little consolation for Reutemann after the pit-lane accident during practice *(above)*.
The Lotus 81 was quite adequate for Nigel Mansell who scored his first championship points with an excellent third place. Elio de Angelis brought his 81 home in fifth place *(right)*.

ENTRY AND PRACTICE

The rules were clear, or so it seemed, when the Concorde Agreement, drawn up at the beginning of the 1981 season, stated: 'Any device bridging the space between the bodywork and the ground is prohibited. Under no circumstances shall any suspended part of the car be less than 6 cm from the ground with the car in its normal racing trim, the driver on board.... If corrections to the suspension height can be made with the car in motion, the conditions defined above must

MAY:
Brabham continue tests with BMW turbo.
Watkins Glen deleted from 1981 Grand Prix calendar.
Jacky Ickx agrees to return from retirement and drive for Porsche at Le Mans.
Bobby Unser (Penske PC9B) takes pole at Indy at 200.545mph.

be respected with the adjustment at the lowest static position usable in racing.'

Then, a FISA Formula 1 Commission meeting on May 7 brought a further clarification following the problems at Imola: 'To the bottom edge of the mandatory side panels of the bodywork may be attached a piece of single, solid, uniform material of rectangular section.... No ride height adjusting device should allow the car in its lowest position to have a ground clearance of less than 6 centimetres.' That seemed fair enough.

Friday morning at Zolder brought a new slant, however. It was called 'cheating'. And everyone bar a handful of teams were doing it. Quite simply, the teams chose to ignore the final paragraph and proffered the excuse that trick suspensions were legal. What was clearly illegal, however, was the *effect* of those suspension systems when the cars were lowered to less than 6 cms while on the move. Oh, the officials checked the cars religiously as they came into the pit lane and, of course, the teams were ready for that with all manner of systems which brought the cars back to their legal height, but the fact remained that they were anything but legal on the track. They even fitted systems which actually locked the cars in the lower position. This incensed Brabham, the originators of ride height control within the so-called regulations, to such an extent that they fitted a conspicuous red lever to the cockpit of Piquet's car and willed the scrutineers to question it – and hopefully exclude their competitors as a result. But the scrutineers said nothing and cheating became the norm for those who could afford it.

Then there was the question of skirts. The clarification appeared to tie that up nicely – or so Dave Wass thought but the Arrows designer was simmering gently as he surveyed the pit lane on Friday morning.

"It really annoys me," he said. "We agree to do one thing with skirts and then half the buggers produce something else. We've just spent a lot of time and trouble conforming to the new rules and now it looks as though we've been wasting our time."

If Wass was at fault then it was because he hadn't utilised one of the most important tools of a designer's trade in 1981 – a dictionary. The 'clever' designers had fitted rubber skirts and were beating their chests proudly and saying: "Ah, yes. The rules say 'solid' when they really mean 'rigid'. But they haven't said that. You see, rubber is okay because it's solid. Good, eh?" No, pathetic actually. Ligier even fitted hinged skirts but that wasn't quite cricket and the other cheaters asked the Frenchmen if they wouldn't mind bending the rules properly, if you please!

So, once the official business of practice got under way, it was Alan Jones who set the fastest time with a 1m 22.20s – but it wasn't good enough. Or, at least, his car wasn't good enough. As he came to the end of his run, a light on the dash panel told him that his sidepods had not returned to their legal position and, sure enough, the FWO7C failed the 6 cm test. Williams had incorporated a switch on the gear linkage and hurried repairs soon had the angry Australian back on the track but a broken valve ended his chances. The T-car was not fitted with the hydro-mechanical gear and Jones had to be content with sixth place after rain washed out Saturday's practice.

The Williams team may have been frustrated by the incident but at least they knew where they were at fault. Not so fortunate were the March team when the rear corner of Derek Daly's 811 fouled the measuring device. March, of course, were running a car without trick suspension and the officials didn't think to actually inform either Daly or his team of their transgression. Daly had set a 1m 26.71s, good enough for the grid, and you can imagine his alarm when the time was suddenly wiped off the board during the closing minutes of practice. By the time John Macdonald had discovered they were at fault, it was too late and the rain on Saturday sealed their fate. It was ironic when you consider that the March was probably the most legal car on the track. You could slide a box of rule books beneath the lumbering chassis – but it was illegal where it counted most; in the pit lane. The whole business had now gone beyond a joke and it was difficult to take practice seriously from that point on. All of which merely added to the frustration of those attempting to work in the brick bunkers and narrow strip of tarmac which the organisers, in a moment of enthusiasm, referred to as The Pits.

As usual, the place was packed with the World and his wife and the advent of full width nose wings merely added another obstacle for the drivers to circumvent. The shortcomings of the Zolder pit lane were illustrated all too clearly on Friday afternoon when Giovanni Amadeo, a mechanic with the Denim Osella team, slipped off the narrow signalling ledge and fell between the wheels of Carlos Reutemann's Williams as the Argentinian driver edged slowly down the pit lane. The impact threw Amadeo against the pit wall and he was rushed, in a critical condition, to hospital where he succumbed to his injuries three days later. Reutemann, deeply distressed, parked his car and the fact that his previously trouble free day had given him pole position was of little consolation.

The tragic incident brought to a close a day which had had its fair share of trouble, and major bone of contention surrounding the numbers of cars allowed to practice. The Concorde Agreement said that a maximum of 30 cars may be accepted for qualifying and, for the first time, 32 cars and drivers presented themselves at scrutineering. ATS withdrew Jan Lammers to concentrate on Slim Borgudd which left one car too many and the unlucky man was Patrick Tambay. The Agreement said 12 cars from the Manufacturers (two each from Renault, Ferrari, Talbot-Ligier, Alfa Romeo, Osella and Toleman) and 18 from FOCA. As Theodore were 'the last in', they were told to amuse themselves elsewhere which was small consolation for Teddy Yip who had travelled with his elderly Shadows to Kyalami to support FOCA at the beginning of the season. Most people were prepared to allow Tambay in, particularly as he had scored a championship point, but Ferrari said no and insisted that as everyone had accepted and signed the Concorde Agreement, then they should stick to it. The matter was partially resolved on Saturday when Toleman withdrew one car after various engine problems had ruled further participation impracticable for Derek Warwick. Tambay set to his task with vigour on a wet track and had the rain eased a little earlier than it did, then the Theodore would certainly have made the race.

Friday practice, therefore, set the standard and there were few surprises, particularly when it was considered that Zolder was a downforce rather than a horsepower circuit. Piquet joined Reutemann on the front row in spite of an inexplicable shunt in his T-car on Friday afternoon and Hector Rebaque was down the grid after blowing his engine early in the timed session. Ferrari were next and this time it was Didier Pironi who set the pace although the Frenchman was the first to admit that the hydraulic suspension on his car made all the difference. Gilles Villeneuve ran a 126C in standard trim and his practice was disrupted by drive-shaft failures. As was expected, perhaps, the fiery French-Canadian was quickest in the rain on Saturday and his time would have been good enough for the grid!

John Watson was another driver to enjoy the wet conditions which bolstered his confidence further after setting fifth fastest time on Friday. The Marlboro MP4 had an understeer problem and John spun off when his rear brakes locked during the closing minutes of Friday practice but, fortunately, there was little damage. Andrea de Cesaris had to make do with the M29F and he just made the grid after losing time with a broken fuel pump drive. Both Arrows qualified comfortably and it was obvious that the latest suspension worked well when Siegfried Stohr took a place in the middle of the grid while Riccardo Patrese did not take long to set a time good enough for the second row. The Tyrrell team had been busy testing their particular hydraulic suspension at Silverstone and Eddie Cheever took a competitive place on the fourth row even though he was far from happy with the handling. Michele Alboreto started off badly when he ran over Cheever's nose wing in the pit lane and, later in the day, the young Italian received a graphic demonstration from Ken Tyrrell on how to change gear while the mechanics replaced a badly worn dog-ring. Alboreto continued to show good progress, however, and qualified comfortably without any further drama.

The Talbot-Ligier team ran a ride height control operated by engine oil pressure and the suspension system obviously helped give the JS17 excellent grip. Running Campagnolo wheels in preference to the heavier Gotti rims, Laffite finished on the fifth row while Jean-Pierre Jabouille was eight-tenths slower after losing time with gearbox problems on Friday morning. The Essex Lotus team made a welcome return although Elio de Angelis and Nigel Mansell had to make do with the 81s which were heavy and suffered from understeer. Mansell was the quicker of the two drivers thanks to simply concentrating on the job in hand while de Angelis jumped in and out of the spare car on Friday and finally changed his race car to the same set-up as the Englishman on Saturday.

Keke Rosberg was fractionally slower than Mansell and the Finn stuck to Avon tyres while Chico Serra returned to Michelin. The Fittipaldi drivers were persevering with their old F8Cs while the Renault-Elf team, by contrast, wheeled out their new RE 30s for Alain Prost and René Arnoux. Compared to their predecessors, the new cars looked exceptionally trim,

RENÉ ARNOUX FAILED TO QUALIFY AT ZOLDER when rain fell during the final practice session on Saturday afternoon and the Renault driver's day was made complete when he was arrested following an incident while leaving the circuit.

In no mood to sit in a queue of traffic, Arnoux drove up the outside and eased his way in at the exit gate. A marshal did not share René's sporting spirit and made his feelings known by blocking the Renault 5. When ignored, the marshal sat on the bonnet to make his point but Arnoux simply drove off with the third party clinging to the windscreen wipers as they travelled the three mile run to the hotel.

Gerard Larrousse and Jean Sage, who happened to be travelling in the opposite direction, thought their driver was fooling around with a friend as the Renault passed by with its extra passenger sprawled across the bonnet. The marshal was in no mood for joking however and promptly phoned the police while the Grand Prix driver disappeared into the hotel kitchens. There was further confusion when the police arrived in the hotel reception and Alain Prost led them to believe that Jacques Laffite was their man!

Arnoux emerged eventually and was arrested for his troubles, the Frenchman spending Saturday night and most of Sunday as a guest of the Belgian authorities.

particularly in the side-pod area now that the turbos had been tucked out of the way, but the drivers were far from happy with the track behaviour. The team had managed a mere few hours of constructive work from a planned four days of testing and it showed when Arnoux and Prost complained of weaving under braking among other things. Arnoux tried a revised high-revving V6 but a broken distributor belt put an end to that on Friday morning. Swapping to the T-car, René promptly put that in the sand at the first corner and rain the following day reduced the Frenchman to the role of non-qualifier. Prost almost made the weekend a complete disaster for the team when he came within a hair's breadth of collecting the abandoned RE 30 as he fought hard with his spare car on Friday afternoon.

At the other end of the financial scale, Marc Surer did a superb job and qualified on the eighth row in spite of being forced to run an engine which had already seen 750 miles of service. A DFV bolted in for the race had a mere 250 miles and was considered 'fresh' by the enthusiastic Ensign team! The rule changes had an adverse effect on the Marlboro Alfa Romeo team who simply could not get their cars to handle satisfactorily. The team brought four cars with three different ride height control systems but the bemused and frustrated Mario Andretti and Bruno Giacomelli could do no better than occupy the ninth row. Piercarlo Ghinzani was chosen to stand in for the injured Guerra after Giorgio Francia was unable to come up with a suitable licence and the Italian did well to qualify on the back row behind his Osella team-mate Beppe Gabbiani.

Daly became a non-qualifier after the misunderstanding with the scrutineers on Friday and the rain on Saturday and he joined his team-mate, Eliseo Salazar, Arnoux, Slim Borgudd, who had the additional complication of sorting out a new Herve Guilpin designed ATS, Tambay and, finally, the Candy Toleman team of Brian Henton and Derek Warwick. Poor Henton's plight with the new car was made worse by thoughts of his last visit to the Zolder track in 1980 when he set a Formula 2 lap record which would have been good enough for the Grand Prix grid!

RACE

The GPDA had requested a prequalifying session on Saturday morning following the problems with Tambay's Theodore the previous day but the organisers stuck to their guns and practice had continued as usual. Feeling that they had been ignored once again, several drivers chose to make a stand in view of the television cameras minutes before the start of the race. The mechanics, exasperated by the working conditions and angry about the accident to Amadeo, also chose that moment to make a protest. With the warm-up lap completed, the grid area became chaotic as drivers and mechanics milled about while the organisers, perhaps anxious about the live television coverage, continued their countdown to the 3 p.m. start. As soon as the protest had finished, the drivers who had remained in their cars were flagged off immediately to commence what turned out to be their final parade lap. What should have been a slow procession in grid order therefore became nothing more than an irregular jumble of cars confused even further by Piquet who was waved off on another lap.

By the time the Brabham had returned and threaded its way to the front, Reutemann was frantically waving his arms and indicating that his lengthy wait on the grid had caused the water temperature to soar. Villeneuve was the last to arrive and by the time the Ferrari was in place, Patrese had stalled his engine and was waving furiously. It was obvious that many people expected a final parade lap to bring some semblance of order and calm and Mansell was on the point of switching his overheating engine off when the red lights suddenly came on!

On the green, Jones swung round Patrese's Arrows just as Dave Luckett arrived at the back of the stricken car with an air line. Patrese had stopped gesticulating and, with the absence of a yellow flag by the Arrows, the drivers further back on the grid assumed everything to be in order with the Italian. Cheever followed Jones to the left but Mansell, alarmed to find Luckett crouching under the Arrow's rear wing, just scraped through between Patrese and Villeneuve. Stohr, seeing a clear track to his right, swung round Rosberg's Fittipaldi and suddenly the hapless Italian was confronted by his team-mate's car. Stohr hit the brakes but the inevitable crunch shunted Patrese forward and left Luckett sprawled on the track in full view of the television cameras.

That Luckett was not killed out-right was due to the narrow front of Stohr's monocoque taking the full impact against the gearbox of Patrese's car. Luckett, fortunately, had been to one side as he connected the air line to the starter and the Englishman was exceptionally lucky to get away with a broken leg, a broken finger and severe facial lacerations. Beside himself with grief, Stohr stumbled from his car while an ambulance was brought quickly to the scene.

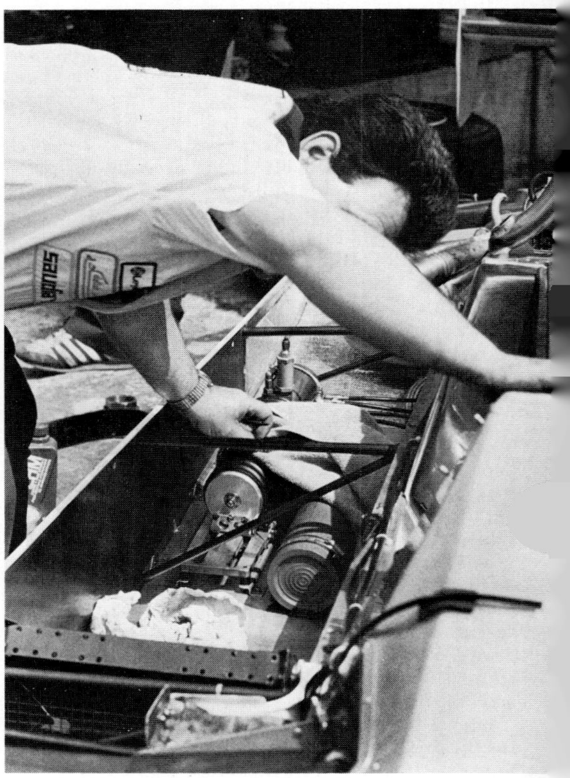

Nigel Mansell makes his way along the absurdly cramped pit lane. The narrow signalling ledge from which the Osella mechanic fell is on the right *(top)*.
Convinced that their hydraulic suspension was within the law while the locking devices which had appeared on rival's cars were not, Brabham deliberately fitted what appeared to be a conspicuous locking control above the gear-lever to draw attention to the cheating *(above)*.
Chief Mechanic Alan Challis puts the covers over the spring linked to the hydro-mechanical ride height control on the Williams *(right)*.

Jacques Laffite revived the hopes of the Talbot-Ligier team by finishing second *(left)*.
"Why can't the Irishman tie his boot laces before he gets in the car?" McLaren mechanics work on John Watson's carbon fibre MP4 which was fifth fastest in practice and held fourth place before dropping back with gearbox trouble *(below)*.
Didier Pironi holds a tenuous lead as the brakes on his Ferrari begin to fade. Piquet and Jones wait their chance *(bottom left)*.

The race, meanwhile, was on and the organisers made no attempt to stop it as Piquet blasted through closely followed by Reutemann and Pironi. Black flags were waved around the circuit but the all-important red flag was not shown to Piquet at the start-and-finish area and the Brazilian kept motoring while Reutemann and the rest began to drop back. Noting that the organisers apparently had no intention of bringing this madness to a halt, Pironi slowed down and stopped to applause from the pits thus leaving the Belgians with no option but to stop their race.

Forty minutes later, the grid reformed minus the Arrows team and, at the restart, Reutemann led the field towards the first corner. Pironi, in a repeat of his manoeuvre in 1980, flew down the inside and the Ferrari led the Williams, Piquet, Watson, Jones, Villeneuve and Laffite at the end of the first lap. Jones took a run at Watson into the first corner and Laffite got the better of Villeneuve while the third turbo-charged car in the race crept into the pits as Prost retired with a broken clutch. Two starts had taken their toll and Renault's miserable weekend was over.

Rosberg was running nicely in eighth place but his luck was out and he retired on lap 10 when the gear lever broke and the Fittipaldi team's interest was to last another 19 laps before Serra stopped with engine trouble. Positions at the front remained static although it was clear that the Ferrari turbo was making up on the straights what the chassis lacked on the corners and the first four cars made a spectacular sight as they ducked and dived in close company. Watson was kept busy by Laffite while, further back, de Angelis shook his fist at Cheever, the Lotus driver desperate to get by as he watched Mansell get away in pursuit of Villeneuve's seventh place.

Pironi remained unflustered by the close attention from behind but Reutemann was becoming increasingly nervous of the flame-throwing, sliding Ferrari and, on lap nine, a particularly desperate moment by Pironi as they swept onto the back straight caused Carlos to lift off fractionally. Piquet and Jones were through in an instant but the Brabham's second place was to be short-lived. Entering *Jochen Rindt Bocht*, Nelson slid wide slightly and Jones was alongside. "He hit my back wheel, but that was no problem," said Piquet. "I let him have the corner because I knew I had plenty of time to get past again. Then he hit my front wheel on the way out of the corner and I went straight off." The Brabham ended up in the catch-fencing and a tearful Piquet stalked back to the pits in a towering rage.

It was ironic that the fatal accident to Giovanni Amadeo in the pit lane should, in part, prompt a protest which, in turn, led to what could have been an appalling accident on the starting grid involving Dave Luckett, Chief Mechanic with Arrows.

Amadeo stumbled into the path of Carlos Reutemann's slow-moving Williams on Friday afternoon, leaving the Argentinian no opportunity to brake and the mechanic suffered severe head injuries as a consequence. Despite attempts to resuscitate him on the way to hospital, it was known on Sunday that he was unlikely to survive and the news increased the mechanics' anger over the impossible working conditions in the cramped pit lane.

When it became known that the drivers had decided to protest about the lack of attention given to their wishes (including a request for a pre-qualifying session at Zolder), the majority of mechanics agreed to make their presence felt on the start line as well. The organisers, on hearing the rumours, issued a statement declaring that the race would start on time regardless of any protests and added that the drivers involved would be reported. As it was, several drivers had been prevailed upon by their team managers to have no part in a protest, no matter how justifiable, during the tense minutes leading up to the start. Others, such as Reutemann, agreed with the cause but felt it was neither the time nor the place to air their grievances.

The cars formed on the grid after their first warm-up lap and, as the start time approached, several drivers including Villeneuve, Pironi, Laffite, Jabouille, Prost, Andretti and Giacomelli, left their cars and walked to the front of the grid where they were joined by mechanics and at least one team manager. The organisers, meanwhile, continued their count-down while Reutemann and Piquet sat patiently on the front row.

As soon as the protest showed signs of finishing, Piquet was ordered to start his car and work his way through the milling throng to commence his final warm-up lap. The start procedure had now been well and truly disrupted and the final parade lap did not take place in the prescribed form of cars circulating in grid formation. Piquet was half-way round his lap while other drivers were still ambling back to their cars and it was at this point that doubt arose over what should happen next.

Piquet added to the confusion by doing a second lap while Reutemann, who had been in position for some minutes, began to wave in desperation as his water temperature soared. By the time Piquet had worked his way to the front of the grid and Villeneuve, the last to arrive, had begun to look for his slot, Patrese was signalling that his engine had stalled.

Regardless of whether the cars were about to do a parade lap in the recognised manner or the race was about to start, the regulations stated clearly that a stalled car could not be attended to until the rest of the field had left the grid. In the event, the organisers decided to start the race and, just as Jones began to move from his position behind Patrese, Luckett hopped over the barrier with an air line. It was easy to understand Luckett's spur of the moment decision as his driver sat helplessly on such a good grid position, nevertheless, he had no right to be on the grid – a point which should have been made forcibly by Alan Rees, the Arrows Team Manager, who was standing by the guardrail.

Equally, it could be argued that the organisers should not have attempted to start the race after the starting procedure had been disrupted – albeit by the irresponsible actions of certain individuals. But, having decided to stick stubbornly to their original plan, the organisers could have avoided the ensuing accident by holding a yellow flag by Patrese's car to warn drivers at the back of the grid.

Clearly, blame could not be apportioned to any one person or group of persons in particular but the events on the starting grid at Zolder left the so-called professional image of Grand Prix racing in tatters. Politics had interfered with the actual racing and the consequences had been disastrous.

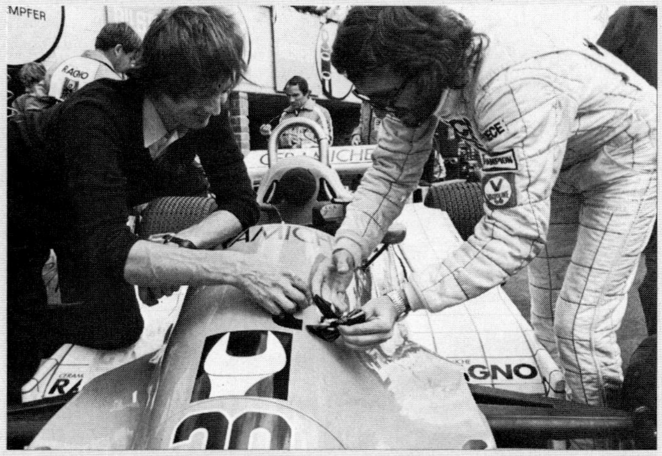

Dave Luckett and Siegfried Stohr during practice.

Patrese signals he is in trouble while the field wait for Villeneuve to arrive on the grid. Alan Rees and a mechanic prepare to lift an air bottle and line onto the track.

Luckett arrives at the back of Patrese's car as the race starts.

Cheever (3) follows Jones around the Arrows, Mansell (12) prepares to squeeze alongside Villeneuve (27) while Stohr begins to move across the track from behind Rosberg's Fittipaldi (20).

Undignified departure for Nelson Piquet after his controversial incident with Jones *(left)*.
A rare practice shot of René Arnoux in the new Renault RE 30 *(below left)*.
'Get the strength of a Williams around you.' Alan Jones escaped with a scalded thigh when his Williams jumped out of gear and crashed heavily while leading *(bottom)*.

By lap 13, the order had changed yet again as Jones and Reutemann moved to the front when Pironi began to lose his brakes. Villeneuve was in trouble too, the Ferrari's suspension leaving the car pointing up at the front and the resulting handling problems kept Gilles very busy as he struggled to stay on the track. Mansell, driving superbly in spite of a heavy cold, was soon on the Ferrari's tail, moving ahead under braking for the back chicane and immediately setting about Watson's fifth place. On the same lap, the McLaren driver lost traction momentarily on the exit of *Jochen Rindt Bocht* and that was enough for Mansell, his adrenalin pumping furiously, to take the place under braking for the following chicane. De Angelis had got past Cheever and the American was demoted further by Rebaque. All three cars were to move up the lap chart, however, as Pironi's brakes became worse but Rebaque was to lose a certain seventh place when he spun off later in the race. Ghinzani also spun off but at least he had an excuse since his rear wing had flown off as the Osella passed the pits on lap 17. The Italian was able to return for repairs just as the lead was about to change hands once again.

Jones had opened a small gap over his team-mate but, on lap 20, the Williams jumped out of gear at the fast right-hander leading onto the back straight. The car slid onto the kerb and ploughed straight into the barrier but Jones was able to walk back to the pits for a treatment to a scalded thigh caused by a burst water radiator. The fact that his injuries were not more serious was a tribute to the strength of the FWO7C monocoque.

Thus, Reutemann inherited a comfortable lead over Laffite who had taken Watson after the Ulsterman had skated off on dirt left by Pironi's wayward Ferrari. Watson dropped back with gearbox trouble to an eventual seventh place while Mansell carefully worked his roll-bar adjustment to trim the handling after the skirts had almost worn away. Compared to the excitement during the opening laps, the race became monotonous although a few spots of rain on lap 50 threatened to liven things up considerably. Alboreto charged into the pits for wet tyres only to be chased back out again by Ken Tyrrell who later informed his young novice that, in future, he would only come in when asked!

The organisers, perhaps anxious to stop the race before another disaster befell them, did not hesitate to show the chequered flag after 55 laps and thus the Belgian Grand Prix was brought to a halt for the second and final time. Two-thirds distance had been covered and full championship points were awarded. Under such circumstances, the finishing order was determined by the order at the end of the previous lap – which was a stroke of good fortune for Eddie Cheever whose car had ground to a halt with engine trouble on lap 55. The Tyrrell team, therefore, came away with one point while de Angelis settled for fifth place after almost climbing over Villeneuve's ill-handling Ferrari. Mansell was scarcely able to register that he had just scored his first four championship points as he passed the chequered flag after a virtually faultless drive. Laffite, troubled by oversteer, was pleased to have scored a decent result for his team, particularly after Jabouille had retired once again, this time with handling and transmission trouble. Pironi took eighth place after beating off occasional attacks from Giacomelli's Alfa Romeo while Andretti struggled home with a misfire and Marc Surer dropped to 11th place with a sick engine after comfortably leading the Alfas at one stage.

The rain had stopped by the time the half-hearted presentation took place but everyone involved with this race was glad of the excuse to be done with Zolder and a dreadful weekend which brought little credit to Grand Prix racing.

Grote Prijs van België, May 17/statistics

Entries and practice times

No.	Driver	Nat	Car	Engine	Entrant	Practice 1	Practice 2
1	Alan Jones	AUS	Saudia-Leyland WILLIAMS FWO7C	Ford Cosworth DFV	Albilad-Williams Racing Team	**1m 23·82s**	1m 27·43s
2	Carlos Reutemann	RA	Saudia-Leyland WILLIAMS FWO7C	Ford Cosworth DFV	Albilad-Williams Racing Team	**1m 22·28s**	1m 36·27s
3	Eddie Cheever	USA	TYRRELL 010	Ford Cosworth DFV	Tyrrell Racing	**1m 24·38s**	1m 31·00s
4	Michele Alboreto	I	TYRRELL 010	Ford Cosworth DFV	Tyrrell Racing	**1m 25·91s**	1m 32·21s
5	Nelson Piquet	BR	Parmalat BRABHAM BT49C	Ford Cosworth DFV	Parmalat Racing Team	**1m 23·13s**	–
6	Hector Rebaque	MEX	Parmalat BRABHAM BT49C	Ford Cosworth DFV	Parmalat Racing Team	**1m 26·52s**	2m 49·14s
7	John Watson	GB	Marlboro McLAREN MP4	Ford Cosworth DFV	McLaren International	**1m 23·73s**	1m 30·92s
8	Andrea de Cesaris	I	Marlboro McLAREN M29F	Ford Cosworth DFV	McLaren International	**1m 26·95s**	1m 30·99s
10	Slim Borgudd	S	Abba ATS HGS 1	Ford Cosworth DFV	Team ATS	**1m 28·98s**	1m 35·79s
11	Elio de Angelis	I	Essex LOTUS 81	Ford Cosworth DFV	Team Essex Lotus	**1m 24·96s**	–
12	Nigel Mansell	GB	Essex LOTUS 81	Ford Cosworth DFV	Team Essex Lotus	**1m 24·44s**	–
14	Marc Surer	CH	ENSIGN N180B	Ford Cosworth DFV	Ensign Racing	**1m 25·19s**	–
15	Alain Prost	F	Elf RENAULT RE 30	Renault EF1	Equipe Renault Elf	**1m 24·63s**	1m 43·35s
16	René Arnoux	F	Elf RENAULT RE 30	Renault EF1	Equipe Renault Elf	**1m 27·93s**	1m 30·71s
17	Eliseo Salazar	RCH	Rizla MARCH 811	Ford Cosworth DFV	March Grand Prix	**1m 28·38s**	1m 35·66s
18	Derek Daly	IRL	Rizla MARCH 811	Ford Cosworth DFV	March Grand Prix	–	–
20	Keke Rosberg	SF	FITTIPALDI F8C	Ford Cosworth DFV	Fittipaldi Automotive	**1m 24·46s**	–
21	Chico Serra	BR	FITTIPALDI F8C	Ford Cosworth DFV	Fittipaldi Automotive	**1m 25·93s**	–
22	Mario Andretti	USA	Marlboro ALFA ROMEO 179C	Alfa Romeo 1260	Marlboro Team Alfa Romeo	**1m 25·56s**	1m 32·17s
23	Bruno Giacomelli	I	Marlboro ALFA ROMEO 179C	Alfa Romeo 1260	Marlboro Team Alfa Romeo	**1m 25·31s**	1m 37·77s
25	Jean-Pierre Jabouille	F	Talbot-Gitanes LIGIER JS17	Matra MS 81	Equipe Talbot Gitanes	**1m 25·28s**	1m 38·87s
26	Jacques Laffite	F	Talbot-Gitanes LIGIER JS17	Matra MS 81	Equipe Talbot Gitanes	**1m 24·41s**	1m 44·07s
27	Gilles Villeneuve	CDN	Fiat FERRARI 126CK	Ferrari 126C	Scuderia Ferrari SpA SEFAC	**1m 23·94s**	1m 27·33s
28	Didier Pironi	F	Fiat FERRARI 126CK	Ferrari 126C	Scuderia Ferrari SpA SEFAC	**1m 23·47s**	1m 36·76s
29	Riccardo Patrese	I	Ragno-Beta ARROWS A3	Ford Cosworth DFV	Arrows Racing Team	**1m 23·67s**	1m 38·28s
30	Siegfried Stohr	I	Ragno-Beta ARROWS A3	Ford Cosworth DFV	Arrows Racing Team	**1m 24·66s**	–
31	Piercarlo Ghinzani	I	Denim OSELLA FA1B	Ford Cosworth DFV	Osella Squadra Corse	**1m 27·48s**	–
32	Beppe Gabbiani	I	Denim OSELLA FA1B	Ford Cosworth DFV	Osella Squadra Corse	**1m 26·69s**	–
33	Patrick Tambay	F	THEODORE TY 01	Ford Cosworth DFV	Theodore Racing Team	–	**1m 32·47s**
35	Brian Henton	GB	Candy TOLEMAN TG 181	Hart 415 T	Candy Toleman Motorsport	**1m 36·37s**	1m 42·95s
36	Derek Warwick	GB	Candy TOLEMAN TG 181	Hart 415 T	Candy Toleman Motorsport	**1m 35·97s**	–
Friday morning and Saturday morning practice sessions not officially recorded						*Fri pm Warm, dry*	*Sat pm Warm, wet*

Starting grid

2 REUTEMANN (1m 22·28s) Williams	
	5 PIQUET (1m 23·13s) Brabham
28 PIRONI (1m 23·47s) Ferrari	
	*29 PATRESE (1m 23·67s) Arrows
7 WATSON (1m 23·73s) McLaren	
	1 JONES (1m 23·82s) Williams
27 VILLENEUVE (1m 23·94s) Ferrari	
	3 CHEEVER (1m 24·38s) Tyrrell
26 LAFFITE (1m 24·41s) Talbot-Ligier	
	12 MANSELL (1m 24·44s) Lotus
20 ROSBERG (1m 24·46s) Fittipaldi	
	15 PROST (1m 24·63s) Renault
*30 STOHR (1m 24·66s) Arrows	
	11 DE ANGELIS (1m 24·96s) Lotus
14 SURER (1m 25·19s) Ensign	
	25 JABOUILLE (1m 25·28s) Talbot-Ligier
23 GIACOMELLI (1m 25·31s) Alfa Romeo	
	22 ANDRETTI (1m 25·56s) Alfa Romeo
4 ALBORETO (1m 25·91s) Tyrrell	
	21 SERRA (1m 25·93s) Fittipaldi
6 REBAQUE (1m 26·52s) Brabham	
	32 GABBIANI (1m 26·69s) Osella
8 DE CESARIS (1m 26·95s) McLaren	
	31 GHINZANI (1m 27·48s) Osella

*Did not take part in restart

Did not start:
16 Arnoux (Renault), 1m 27·93s, did not qualify
17 Salazar (March), 1m 28·38s, did not qualify
9 Borgudd (ATS), 1m 28·98s, did not qualify
33 Tambay (Theodore), 1m 32·47s, restricted practice, did not qualify
36 Warwick (Toleman), 1m 35·97s, did not qualify
35 Henton (Toleman), 1m 36·37s, did not qualify
18 Daly (March), time disallowed, did not qualify

Past winners

Year	Driver	Nat	Car	Circuit	Distance miles/km	Speed mph/km/h
1925	Antonio Ascari	I	2·0 Alfa Romeo P2 s/c	Francorchamps	501·63/807·29	74·44/119·80
1930	Louis Chiron	F	2·0 Bugatti T35C s/c	Francorchamps	371·58/598·00	72·12/116·08
1931	"W. Williams"/ Caberto Conelli	GB I	2·3 Bugatti T51 s/c	Francorchamps	820·46/1320·40	82·05/132·04
1933	Tazio Nuvolari	I	3·0 Maserati 8CM s/c	Francorchamps	369·59/594·80	89·27/143·66
1934	René Drefus	F	3·3 Bugatti T59 s/c	Francorchamps	369·59/594·80	89·95/139·94
1935	Rudi Caracciola	D	4·0 Mercedes-Benz W25 s/c	Francorchamps	314·15/505·57	97·91/157·57
1937	Rudolf Hasse	D	6·0 Auto Union C-Type s/c	Francorchamps	314·15/505·57	104·11/167·56
1939	Hermann Lang	D	3·0 Mercedes-Benz W163 s/c	Francorchamps	314·15/505·57	94·43/151·97
1946	Eugene Chaboud	F	3·5 Delahaye	Brussels	73·10/117·64	64·73/104·18
1947	Jean-Pierre Wimille	B	1·5 Alfa Romeo 158 s/c	Francorchamps	315·34/507·49	95·32/153·40
1949	Louis Rosier	F	4·5 Lago-Talbot	Francorchamps	315·34/507·49	96·99/156·09
1950	Juan Manuel Fangio	RA	1·5 Alfa Romeo 158 s/c	Francorchamps	307·08/494·20	110·04/177·09
1951	Giuseppe Farina	I	1·5 Alfa Romeo 159 s/c	Francorchamps	315·85/508·31	114·32/183·99
1952	Alberto Ascari	I	2·0 Ferrari 500	Francorchamps	315·85/508·31	103·13/165·96
1953	Alberto Ascari	I	2·0 Ferrari 500	Francorchamps	315·85/508·31	112·47/181·00
1954	Juan Manuel Fangio	RA	2·5 Maserati 250F	Francorchamps	315·85/508·31	115·06/185·17
1955	Juan Manuel Fangio	RA	2·5 Mercedes-Benz W196	Francorchamps	315·85/508·31	118·83/191·24
1956	Peter Collins	GB	2·5 Lancia-Ferrari D50	Francorchamps	315·85/508·31	118·44/190·61
1958	Tony Brooks	GB	2·5 Vanwall	Francorchamps	210·27/338·40	129·92/209·09
1960	Jack Brabham	AUS	2·5 Cooper T53-Climax	Francorchamps	315·41/507·60	133·63/215·06
1961	Phil Hill	USA	1·5 Ferrari Dino 156	Francorchamps	262·84/423·00	128·15/206·24
1962	Jim Clark	GB	1·5 Lotus 25-Climax	Francorchamps	280·36/451·19	131·90/212·27
1963	Jim Clark	GB	1·5 Lotus 25-Climax	Francorchamps	280·36/451·19	114·10/183·63
1964	Jim Clark	GB	1·5 Lotus 25-Climax	Francorchamps	280·36/451·19	132·79/213·71
1965	Jim Clark	GB	1·5 Lotus 33-Climax	Francorchamps	280·36/451·19	117·16/188·55
1966	John Surtees	GB	3·0 Ferrari 312/66	Francorchamps	245·32/394·80	113·93/183·36
1967	Dan Gurney	USA	3·0 Eagle T1G-Gurney-Weslake	Francorchamps	245·32/394·80	145·99/234·95
1968	Bruce McLaren	NZ	3·0 McLaren M7A-Ford	Francorchamps	245·32/394·80	147·14/236·80
1970	Pedro Rodriguez	MEX	3·0 BRM P153	Francorchamps	245·32/394·80	149·97/241·36
1972	Emerson Fittipaldi	BR	3·0 JPS/Lotus 72-Ford	Nivelles-Baulers	196·69/316·54	113·35/182·42
1973	Jackie Stewart	GB	3·0 Tyrrell 006-Ford	Zolder	183·55/295·39	107·74/173·38
1974	Emerson Fittipaldi	BR	3·0 McLaren M23-Ford	Nivelles-Baulers	196·69/316·54	113·10/182·02
1975	Niki Lauda	A	3·0 Ferrari 312T/75	Zolder	185·38/298·34	107·05/172·28
1976	Niki Lauda	A	3·0 Ferrari 312T/76	Zolder	185·38/298·34	108·11/173·98
1977	Gunnar Nilsson	S	3·0 JPS/Lotus 78-Ford	Zolder	185·38/298·34	96·64/155·53
1978	Mario Andretti	USA	3·0 JPS/Lotus 79-Ford	Zolder	185·38/298·34	111·38/179·24
1979	Jody Scheckter	ZA	3·0 Ferrari 312T-4	Zolder	185·38/298·34	111·24/179·02
1980	Didier Pironi	F	3·0 Ligier JS11/15-Ford	Zolder	190·66/306·86	115·82/186·40
1981	Carlos Reutemann	RA	3·0 Williams FW07C-Ford	Zolder	143·01/230·15	112·12/180·44

Circuit data

Omloop Terlamen Zolder, near Hasselt
Circuit length: 2·648 miles/4·262 km
Race distance: 54 laps, 143·007 miles/230·148 km
Race weather: Dry, warm, then wet

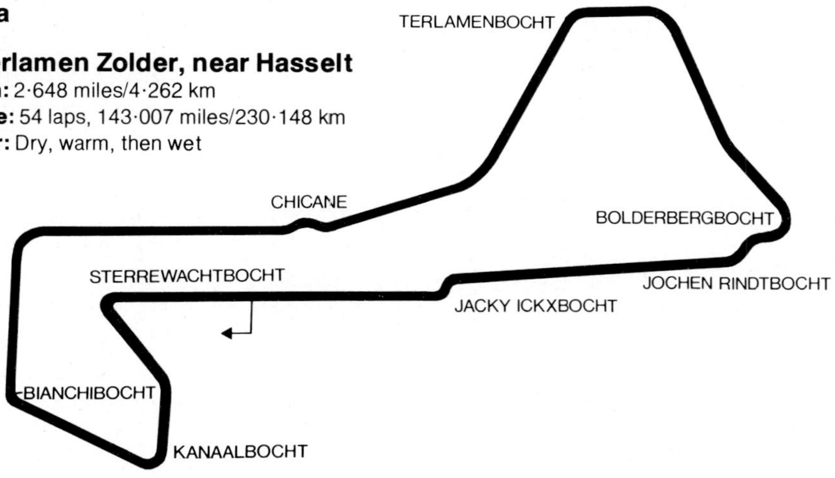

For many, the return to Spa-Francorchamps could not come soon enough.

Results and retirements

Place	Driver	Car	Laps	Time and Speed (mph/km/h)/Retirement	
1	Carlos Reutemann	Williams-Cosworth V8	54	1h 16m 31·61s	112·123/180·445
1	Jaques Laffite	Talbot-Ligier Matra V12	54	1h 17m 07·67s	111·249/179·039
3	Nigel Mansell	Lotus-Cosworth V8	54	1h 17m 15·30s	111·066/178·744
4	Gilles Villeneuve	Ferrari t/c V6	54	1h 17m 19·25s	110·972/178·592
5	Elio de Angelis	Lotus-Cosworth V8	54	1h 17m 20·81s	110·934/178·532
6	Eddie Cheever	Tyrrell-Cosworth V8	54	1h 17m 24·12s	110·856/178·405
7	John Watson	McLaren-Cosworth V8	54	1h 17m 33·27s	110·637/178·054
8	Didier Pironi	Ferrari t/c V6	54	1h 18m 03·65s	109·920/176·899
9	Bruno Giacomelli	Alfa Romeo V12	54	1h 18m 07·19s	109·836/176·765
10	Mario Andretti	Alfa Romeo V12	53		
11	Marc Surer	Ensign-Cosworth V8	52		
12	Michele Alboreto	Tyrrell-Cosworth V8	52		
13	Piercarlo Ghinzani	Osella-Cosworth V8	50		
	Hector Rebaque	Brabham-Cosworth V8	39	Accident	
	Jean-Pierre Jabouille	Talbot-Ligier Matra V12	35	Transmission	
	Chico Serra	Fittipaldi-Cosworth V8	29	Engine	
	Beppe Gabbiani	Osella-Cosworth V8	22	Engine	
	Alan Jones	Williams-Cosworth V8	19	Accident	
	Andrea de Cesaris	McLaren-Cosworth V8	11	Gearbox	
	Nelson Piquet	Brabham-Cosworth V8	10	Accident/collision with Jones	
	Keke Rosberg	Fittipaldi-Cosworth V8	10	Broken gear-lever	
	Alain Prost	Renault t/c V6	2	Clutch	

Fastest lap: Reutemann, on lap 37, 1m 23·30s, 114·451mph/184·192km/h.
Lap record: Jacques Laffite (F1 Ligier JS11/15-Cosworth DFV), 1m 20·88s, 117·876mph/189·703km/h (1980).

Did not take part in restart

Driver	Car	Laps	Retirement
Siegfried Stohr	Arrows-Cosworth V8	0	Accident with Patrese
Riccardo Patrese	Arrows-Cosworth V8	0	Hit by Stohr

Lap chart

1st LAP ORDER	1	2	3	4	5	6	7	8	9	10	11	12	13	14	15	16	17	18	19	20	21	22	23	24
28 D.Pironi	28	28	28	28	28	28	28	28	28	28	28	28	1	1	1	1	1	1	1	2	2	2	2	2
2 C.Reutemann	2	2	2	2	2	2	2	2	2	5	1	1	2	2	2	2	2	2	2	26	26	26	26	26
5 N.Piquet	5	5	5	5	5	5	5	5	5	1	2	2	26	26	26	26	26	26	26	12	12	12	12	12
7 J.Watson	7	1	1	1	1	1	1	1	1	2	26	26	28	28	28	28	28	28	28	7	7	7	7	7
1 A.Jones	1	7	7	7	7	7	7	7	7	7	7	7	7	7	7	7	7	12	12	27	27	27	27	27
27 G.Villeneuve	27	26	26	26	26	26	26	26	26	26	27	27	27	27	27	27	27	7	7	11	11	11	11	11
26 J.Laffite	26	27	27	27	27	27	27	27	27	27	12	12	12	12	12	12	12	27	27	28	28	28	28	28
20 K.Rosberg	20	20	20	20	12	12	12	12	12	12	11	11	11	11	11	11	11	11	11	6	6	6	6	6
12 N.Mansell	12	12	12	12	20	20	20	20	20	11	3	3	6	6	6	6	6	6	6	3	3	3	3	3
3 E.Cheever	3	3	3	3	3	3	3	11	11	3	6	6	3	3	3	3	3	3	3	14	14	14	14	14
11 E.de Angelis	11	11	11	11	11	11	11	3	3	6	14	14	14	14	14	14	14	14	14	23	23	23	23	23
14 M.Surer	14	14	14	14	14	14	14	6	6	14	22	23	23	23	23	23	23	23	23	22	22	22	22	22
25 J-P.Jabouille	25	25	25	25	25	25	25	14	14	22	23	22	22	22	22	22	22	22	22	32	32	32	21	21
22 M.Andretti	22	22	22	22	22	6	6	25	22	23	21	21	21	21	21	21	21	21	21	21	21	21	4	4
21 C.Serra	21	21	23	23	6	22	22	22	23	21	32	32	32	32	32	32	32	32	32	4	4	4	31	31
23 B.Giacomelli	23	23	6	6	23	23	23	23	21	32	4	4	4	4	4	4	4	4	4	31	31	31	25	25
6 H.Rebaque	6	6	21	21	21	21	21	21	32	4	31	31	31	31	31	31	31	31	31	25	25	25		
32 B.Gabbiani	32	32	32	32	32	32	32	32	4	31	25	25	25	25	25	25	25	25	25					
4 M.Alboreto	4	4	4	4	4	4	4	4	31	20	8													
8 A.de Cesaris	8	8	8	8	8	8	8	8	8	8														
31 P.Ghinzani	31	31	31	31	31	31	31	31	25	25														
15 A.Prost	15	15																						

25	26	27	28	29	30	31	32	33	34	35	36	37	38	39	40	41	42	43	44	45	46	47	48	49	50	51	52	53	54
2	2	2	2	2	2	2	2	2	2	2	2	2	2	2	2	2	2	2	2	2	2	2	2	2	2	2	2	2	2
26	26	26	26	26	26	26	26	26	26	26	26	26	26	26	26	26	26	26	26	26	26	26	26	26	26	26	26	26	26
12	12	12	12	12	12	12	12	12	12	12	12	12	12	12	12	12	12	12	12	12	12	12	12	12	12	12	12	12	12
7	7	7	7	7	7	7	7	7	7	7	7	7	7	7	7	7	7	7	7	7	7	7	27	27	27	27	27	27	27
27	27	27	27	27	27	27	27	27	27	27	27	27	27	27	27	27	27	27	27	27	27	27	7	11	11	11	11	11	11
11	11	11	11	11	11	11	11	11	11	11	11	11	11	11	11	11	11	11	11	11	11	11	11	7	3	3	3	3	3
28	28	28	28	3	3	3	3	3	3	6	6	6	6	6	3	3	3	3	3	3	3	3	3	3	7	7	7	7	7
6	6	6	6	6	6	6	6	6	6	3	3	3	3	3	28	28	28	28	28	28	28	28	28	28	28	28	28	28	28
3	3	3	3	28	28	28	28	28	28	28	28	28	28	28	23	23	23	23	23	23	23	23	23	23	23	23	23	23	23
14	14	14	14	14	14	14	14	14	14	14	23	23	23	23	14	14	22	22	22	22	22	22	22	22	22	22	22	22	
23	23	23	23	23	23	23	23	23	23	23	14	14	14	14	22	22	14	14	14	14	14	14	14	14	14	14	14		
22	22	22	22	22	22	22	22	22	22	22	22	22	22	22	4	4	4	4	4	4	4	4	4	4	4	4	4		
21	21	21	4	4	4	4	4	4	4	4	4	4	4	4	31	31	31	31	31	31	31	31	31	31	31				
4	4	4	31	31	31	31	31	31	31	31	31	31	31	31															
31	31	31	25	25	25	25	25	25	25	25																			
25	25	25	21	21																									

Fastest laps

Driver	Time	Lap
Carlos Reutemann	1m 23·30s	37
Alan Jones	1m 23·40s	18
Jacques Laffite	1m 23·65s	34
Hector Rebaque	1m 23·74s	34
Eddie Cheever	1m 24·21s	34
John Watson	1m 24·36s	46
Nigel Mansell	1m 24·43s	46
Elio de Angelis	1m 24·50s	35
Gilles Villeneuve	1m 24·65s	40
Bruno Giacomelli	1m 24·73s	37
Nelson Piquet	1m 24·75s	7
Didier Pironi	1m 24·82s	7
Marc Surer	1m 25·23s	30
Jean-Pierre Jabouille	1m 25·25s	32
Mario Andretti	1m 25·82s	29
Keke Rosberg	1m 25·95s	8
Piercarlo Ghinzani	1m 26·58s	17
Michele Alboreto	1m 26·71s	17
Beppe Gabbiani	1m 26·85s	16
Chico Serra	1m 26·89s	16
Andrea de Cesaris	1m 27·00s	5
Alain Prost	1m 41·44s	1

Points

WORLD CHAMPIONSHIP OF DRIVERS

1	Carlos Reutemann	34 pts
2	Nelson Piquet	22
3	Alan Jones	18
4	Riccardo Patrese	10
5	Jacques Laffite	7
6	Elio de Angelis	5
7 =	Alain Prost	4
7 =	Nigel Mansell	4
9 =	Mario Andretti	3
9 =	Marc Surer	3
9 =	Hector Rebaque	3
9 =	Gilles Villeneuve	3
9 =	Eddie Cheever	3
14 =	René Arnoux	2
14 =	Didier Pironi	2
16 =	Patrick Tambay	1
16 =	Andrea de Cesaris	1

CONSTRUCTORS' CUP

1	Williams	52 pts
2	Brabham	25
3	Arrows	10
4	Lotus	9
5	Ligier	7
6	Renault	6
7	Ferrari	5
8 =	Alfa Romeo	3
8 =	Ensign	3
8 =	Tyrrell	3
11 =	Theodore	1
11 =	McLaren	1

Grand Prix de Monaco

The Contenders: Nelson Piquet, who led from pole in his Brabham until pressured into a mistake by Alan Jones, the Williams driver then leading for 19 laps before an engine misfire forced him to make way for Gilles Villeneuve's Ferrari with four laps remaining *(below)*. Alan Jones drove an inspired race in the Saudia-sponsored Williams at Monte Carlo but the reigning World Champion was robbed of victory during the closing laps *(right)*.
Photo: David Winter

It's Saturday evening, around 7.30 p.m., and a policeman has stopped a moped rider at the top of the hill near Casino Square. The motorcyclist, it seems, had wanted to slip through the square regardless of the road being closed to traffic but, at Grand Prix weekend, there are no exceptions. None at all.

The officer, checking credentials and filing a summons, is implacable. The rider, wearing a blue bomber jacket and jeans and carrying a red and white helmet, stares straight ahead. The conversation goes something like this:

"Name?"

"Piquet."

"Spell."

"P-I-Q-U-E-T."

"Address?"

"Brazil. B-R-A-Z-I-L."

If the policeman has any idea just who he has stopped, it certainly doesn't show as he goes on to check the rented bike's papers. The tax is out of date. More form filling. The constable is clearly not a motor racing fan and probably on duty against his will. After some 20 minutes the rider replaces his helmet and goes on his way at an angry 20mph. Earlier in the day, he had passed the same spot at a furious 150mph only, on that occasion, he had defended pole position and earned nothing but applause.

One way or another, though, it was to be an unhappy weekend for Nelson Piquet. He had taken pole position on Thursday but his performance in the Parmalat Brabham, over one second faster than the next man, had caused a ripple or two along the pit lane. Some said Brabham had used a special lightweight car; others merely supported Piquet's belief that the BT49C was as perfect as the bumps would allow and he had found a couple of clear laps. Nelson, for his part, was too busy telling anyone who would listen just how angry he was with Alan Jones after their barging match in the Belgian Grand Prix two weeks previously. Jones was crazy and he, Piquet, would have him off one day when Jones was still running and he had made a pit stop.

They were words Piquet probably regretted when, during the race, he came under heavy pressure from the Saudia-Leyland Williams driver. Piquet may have held sway during practice but the race was a different matter as Jones darted and weaved in the Brabham's mirrors. Nelson became rattled and eventually threw the race away with a serious misjudgement which put him into the barrier while lapping a back-marker.

Jones took command after a typically cool and intelligent drive which had seen the Australian patiently work his way up the leader board in spite of suffering considerable pain from his left thigh scalded at Zolder a fortnight before. Gilles Villeneuve was now some 30 seconds in arrears in a comfortable second place and it would have been understandable if the Ferrari driver had cruised to a safe six points. Conservative motoring held no interest to Villeneuve and he pressed on in the same spectacular style which had earned a position on the front row of the grid. His perseverance paid when, on lap 66, Jones began to slow with an engine misfire. He had enough lee-way for a quick pit stop but a cure could not be found and Villeneuve passed the stuttering Williams to give Ferrari their first win with the turbocharged V6.

Jacques Laffite took third place in the Talbot-Ligier Gitanes, the only other driver to complete 76 laps. Didier Pironi finished fourth from a poor grid position after two incident-packed days of practice with his Ferrari. Eddie Cheever (Tyrrell) took fifth place followed by Marc Surer after another determined drive in the Ensign. Patrick Tambay, his Theodore stuck in third gear for the last 30 laps, was the final finisher in a typical Monaco race of attrition.

The race itself was in doubt after fire had broken out in the kitchens of the Loews Hotel which straddles the track. Water poured through the tunnel roof and the drivers agreed to race on the understanding that there would be no overtaking in the tunnel area. Their exemplary behaviour on this occasion made a welcome contrast to the acrimony surrounding the Belgian Grand Prix.

It was at Zolder that Nigel Mansell began to establish himself as more than just a competent driver and the Englishman astounded the establishment with a brilliant practice performance at Monaco. From the second row of the grid, the Lotus driver held a comfortable third place until sidelined by a rear suspension failure. The most important retirement, however, was that of Carlos Reutemann, the championship leader, who brought an unprecedented run of 15 consecutive finishes in the points to an end when he stopped with gearbox trouble.

MAY:

- *Danny Ongais crashes Interscope while leading Indy 500.*
- *Herbert Müller killed while driving Porsche 908/3 in Nürburgring 1000kms.*
- *Mario Andretti (Wildcat Mk8) wins Indy 500 after Bobby Unser (Penske PC9B) is penalised one lap for overtaking under yellow flag.*
- *Marlboro and Renault express concern over the state of Grand Prix racing.*
- *David Thieme sues Credit Suisse for £100m.*
- *Gilles Villeneuve and Didier Pironi re-sign with Ferrari.*
- *Alain Ferté (Martini-Alfa Romeo Mk34) wins Monaco Formula 3 race.*

ENTRY AND PRACTICE

Practice opened dramatically at 8 a.m. on Thursday with an hour of prequalifying for nine drivers: Henton and Warwick (Candy-Toleman); Daly and Salazar (March); Borgudd (ATS); Gabbiani and Ghinzani (Denim-Osella); Surer (Ensign) and Tambay (Theodore). This was a hectic affair with little time for niceties such as chassis tuning or tyre changing. The organisers, in their wisdom, had hosed down the track which meant the times tumbled throughout the session. It was clear from the start that Salazar and Borgudd were out of the running and the slim overnight bags brought to Monaco by members of the Toleman team indicated that they did not expect a lengthy stay in the Principality!

Daly, Tambay and Surer hacked away at the lap times but the Irishman's luck was out when a drive-shaft broke with 15 minutes to go. During the closing minutes, the Osellas bettered his time and the frustrated Daly was a non-starter for the sixth race in succession while Tambay posted the fastest time at 1m 30.492s.

By the end of the first untimed session, Nelson Piquet had reduced that by almost three seconds – a fair indication of what the Brabham driver was about to do when the stop-watches were running officially in the afternoon. The time he eventually recorded, however, left the pit lane reeling. After a mere 10 laps, Piquet recorded a 1m 25.710s, a full second faster than the next driver and good enough to keep pole on Saturday. "I did it on two successive laps," said Piquet.

GITANES
FLY saudia
TAG
Techniques d'Avant Garde
saudia
TAG
1
SIYANCO
SIYANCO

Tired but happy. Villeneuve on the victory rostrum where Prince Rainier and Princess Grace were notable by their absence *(right)*. Lotus bounced back with the 87 and a brilliant practice performance from Nigel Mansell. The Englishman started from the second row but retired with a rear suspension failure *(centre)*. Mario Andretti gives some thought to Andrea de Cesaris's behaviour on the opening lap after the McLaren driver (number 8) had collided with the American's Alfa Romeo *(below left & far right)*.

"I got a good clear run so there was no problem. The car was fine..."

Jacques Laffite had other opinions which he expressed quite freely in *L'Equipe* the following day: "He (Piquet) has two cars, one ultra-light which he only uses in practice, and then his race car which is of normal weight. A normal Brabham is already on the weight limit. Good for them. But the practice car has carbon-fibre brake discs which save 12 kilos, and I'm told that the car also has a tiny fuel tank, much lighter than the normal one. The car should be weighed as soon as Piquet stops, before the mechanics can touch it. But no, no one will do anything because it is a Brabham, owned by Ecclestone, and no one can touch him. Everyone is frightened of him."

There were indeed two cars for Nelson, one of which did not reappear in the pit lane on Saturday or Sunday but Gordon Murray emphatically denied the allegations made by Laffite. Having set their time, Brabham spent Saturday trying to find the best compromise after problems raised during full tank tests. Inbetween all that, Hector Rebaque shunted his car on Thursday and broke a drive-shaft on Saturday which meant he was a non-qualifier.

If Piquet was not out to improve his time on Saturday then it left the way clear for brilliant performances from Gilles Villeneuve and Nigel Mansell as they scratched closer and closer to pole – and the guard-rails. Villeneuve astounded everyone by setting second fastest time on Thursday in a car which was not supposed to suit the street circuit but his driving on Saturday was simply out of this world. The Ferrari team had installed different camshafts and valve springs to help extract suitable torque characteristics and, in addition, they ran two separate hydro-pneumatic suspension systems to the front and rear of the cars. A lot of thought was given to finding the correct gearing which meant a busy time for first gear – not to mention the driver. Didier Pironi, so much in command while driving a Ligier at Monaco in 1980, had a fraught weekend, hitting the barrier no less than three times and forcing the team to bring a fourth chassis from Italy. Villeneuve complained that his car was jumping all over the road (discovered later to have been caused by a faulty shock absorber) but he extracted every ounce of boost, every last reserve of his driving skill as he chucked the car around the town on Saturday afternoon.

During those desperate closing laps, Gilles had time to notice that he was being followed by Nigel Mansell – and the Lotus driver was keeping in touch. Lotus had brought along two 87s – 'conventional' models based around the carbon fibre/kevlar monocoques used on the 88 and some 60 lbs lighter than the 81. The one major problem was chronic understeer, Mansell's gloved hands shaking visibly as he turned into the corners, yet the Englishman urged the car round the track in a clean and most impressive manner. On one occasion he tapped the barrier at the swimming pool but no damage was done – except, perhaps, to Elio de Angelis's pride! Elio had other problems, particularly on Saturday afternoon when he lost 30 minutes while waiting for a gear ratio and ride height change to be made. Sixth fastest time after just nine laps was a first class effort therefore. On the 12th lap he stopped by the swimming pool and one or two uncharitable voices suggested it was because his ride-height control had failed and he thus avoided the test at the end of the pit lane – and a possible scrubbing of his times.

Carlos Reutemann did fail the 6cm test (conducted with help from a laiser beam) when a side-pod mounting broke on Thursday afternoon and he lost 4th fastest time as a result. In no mood to take that sort of thing after he had driven his heart out, Reutemann abandoned his car on the 'flat spot' and left the harassed officials to sort out the ensuing traffic jam! The Williams had not been turning in satisfactorily and Reutemann said he could only manage one or two quick laps at a time as the bumps and physical pounding from the stiff suspension were literally taking his breath away. Nevertheless, he managed to record fourth fastest time while Alan Jones had to be content with seventh place. Jones was still troubled by burns on his left thigh, the result of a split radiator in the Belgian Grand Prix shunt, and he lost considerable time when his new chassis developed fuel system bothers on Saturday afternoon. He was unable to make any improvement in the spare car.

The Ragno-Beta Arrows team fitted softer springs in a bid to increase traction and stop the A3 from bouncing all over the road but Riccardo Patrese had further problems when the steering broke. Using a hydro-pneumatic suspension linked to engine revs, the Italian was able to maintain his good form with fifth fastest time while Siegfried Stohr did well to qualify 14th after his dismal showing on the Long Beach street circuit. Once Jacques Laffite had his say in print, he left his mark on the track by using gearing which allowed maximum use of his rev-range. Jacques was eighth fastest but his Talbot-Ligier team-mate, Jean-Pierre Jabouille, failed to qualify after a practice ruined by breakdowns out on the circuit; a dead engine and electrical problems on Saturday, for example. On Saturday, therefore, he had no time to sort the car satisfactorily.

Members of the Toleman team watched with interest as their Renault-Elf counterparts struggled through a busy practice with their RE 30s. René Arnoux had gear-linkage problems and then his V6 lost power, forcing him to use the spare. He was back in the T-car on Saturday afternoon after he had inexplicably touched the wall at the entrance to the swimming pool chicane and cannoned into the

Joann Villeneuve looks rather anxious as Gilles takes a racing line around the harbour front *(left)*.
Overleaf:
Jacques Laffite carried Talbot's colours into a consistent third place.
Photo: Nigel Snowdon

barriers as a result. Prost had gearbox trouble on Thursday but, as the T-car was already in use, he had to wait until Saturday to set ninth fastest time in his repaired race car. The bumpy surface was too much for John Watson and he switched his Marlboro MP4 back to standard suspension. The Ulsterman said his car appeared to be "loosing out everywhere" and a change to what should have been superior tyres was ruined by traffic on Saturday. Andrea de Cesaris, having a run in an MP4 for the first time, stuck with the trick suspension and ended up fractionally slower than Watson in spite of bending a rocker arm on Saturday afternoon.

Apart from Piquet, Mario Andretti was the only driver not to improve on Saturday. The Marlboro Alfa Romeo team continued to experiment with different side-pod profiles and wings but the handling left a lot to be desired and Andretti's problems were compounded by a return of the old gear selection problems. Bruno Giacomelli was even further back after his car caught fire on Saturday, much to the amusement of the *poseurs* on the balconies around Casino Square. The Tyrrell team just scraped in when Michele Alboreto became the final qualifier and Eddie Cheever managed one quick lap "otherwise I would have been a spectator for sure". Patrick Tambay, having a second Theodore chassis at his disposal, continued his impressive progress in spite of minor gear selection problems and Marc Surer made the grid after finding a full second during the final fifteen minutes. Considering the Ensign team could scarcely afford a new roll bar and a shunt would have spelt financial disaster, Surer's was a particularly impressive effort.

With the news that Harvey Postlethwaite was to leave Fittipaldi, it was hardly surprising that morale was low when both Keke Rosberg and Chico Serra failed to qualify. The team switched from Avon back to Michelin but it made no difference whatsoever and both drivers bent steering arms in their efforts to make the race. They were joined by the Osella team, both drivers spinning on Saturday and, surprisingly, it was Ghinzani who set the fastest time.

RACE

Race morning and the sun shone on the Italians streaming across the border, lured, no doubt, by a Ferrari on the front row. Villeneuve did not share their optimism after the warm-up when he realised his skirts were wearing badly on full tanks. The Williams mechanics had worked until 3.30 a.m. as they thoroughly checked the fuel system on Jones's new car and Alan rewarded their efforts by setting fastest time during the warm-up. More to the point, however, he was some 1.2 seconds faster than Piquet so an absorbing race was obviously in store.

With a comparatively late start of 3.30 p.m., drivers retreated to the calm of their motor homes while a rather sparse crowd (by Monaco standards at least) eyed the topless sunbathers bobbing about in the harbour. Suddenly, the tranquil scene was interrupted by sirens as fire engines and ambulances sped towards the Loews Hotel where a fire in the kitchen was causing havoc. The appliances parked by the service entrance in the tunnel and it was not long before water was cascading through the roof and onto the track. With the fire under control, the residents returned to their *Pâté de Fois Gras* but, down in the tunnel, there was growing consternation as the water continued to seep through. There was every chance that the race might not be run and Bernie Ecclestone, along with GPDA President, Jody Scheckter, were called in to assess the situation.

There was a dry line, about a car's width, running round the outside lane of the tunnel and it was agreed that the race would be run under a yellow flag from *Portier* to the chicane. Thus, almost one hour late, the drivers left the pits for two warm-up laps before gathering on the grid to receive final instructions. The drivers, of course, were equally mindful of the *Ste Devote* and the first corner shambles the previous year when Daly overtook several cars by the unconventional means of two-and-a-half cartwheels through the air.

Piquet made a clean start followed by Villeneuve and the rest in orderly fashion through *Ste Devote*. All 20 cars left the corner in one piece – but not before de Cesaris had touched Prost on the way out and damaged the McLaren as a result. The Italian, partly out of control, ran up the hill with Prost alongside on his right – and Watson nudging his way through on the left. Andretti, meanwhile, was watching from a respectful distance, fully aware that an accident was about to happen and, before he knew it, the McLaren number 8 was turning right to trap the Alfa Romeo against the barrier. Andretti couldn't believe his eyes as the McLaren ripped off his left-front wheel and sent the pair of them into retirement. Cheever, caught behind this mêlée, squeezed left as did Pironi but Surer ran over some debris and made a pit stop to have the Ensign checked over.

Piquet looked completely in command as he pulled away from Villeneuve with Mansell holding a comfortable third place and thinking about ways of moving ahead of the Ferrari. Reutemann had Jones sitting on his gearbox while Patrese was not much further behind, followed by de Angelis, Laffite, Prost,

26
26
MICHELIN
LIGIER

J.LAFFITE
TALBOT
MATRA
GITANES
FACOM
SKF
Valeo

Beginning of the end for Carlos. The Williams driver makes his way to the pits after touching Mansell's Lotus on lap 14. Reutemann was to return for good with gearbox trouble on lap 34 *(right)*.
The lead changes hands for the last time as Villeneuve forges ahead of Jones's ailing Williams *(below right)*.

Carlos Reutemann's unprecedented run of 15 consecutive finishes in the top six point-scoring positions came to an end at Monaco when the Saudia-Leyland Williams driver retired with gearbox trouble. Reutemann began his run in the 1980 Belgian Grand Prix where he finished third and he went on to score 81 points, or an average of 5.4 points per race. His average during the first five races in 1981 was 6.8 points, a remarkable record and a tribute to the Argentinian's consistent driving as well as the immaculate preparation by the Williams team.

Arnoux, Watson, Tambay, Cheever, Stohr (soon to retire with a misfire caused by a faulty distributor), Giacomelli, Pironi and Alboreto.

Surer was able to rejoin and, on lap 11, the Ensign driver, going as hard as he could, unwittingly let Piquet get away as he held up the close gaggle of cars led by the turbo Ferrari. On lap 14, Mansell hesitated slightly at the exit from Station Hairpin and Reutemann, too close to take avoiding action, bent his front wing against the back of the Lotus and headed for the pits. One lap later and Mansell was also in the pit lane after feeling the rear of his Lotus become skittish. A tyre change confirmed that the problem was more serious than that and the Englishman was back one lap later to retire with a broken top link mounting point. At the time, it seemed obvious to connect the two events but Lotus said the joint had broken through fatigue while Reutemann commented that he had seen Mansell touch the barrier in the tunnel. Either way, the field was down to 16 runners as Reutemann resumed in last place.

At the other end of the race, Piquet had opened a six second gap while Jones, carefully biding his time, began to close on Villeneuve. By lap 18 he was looking for a way past and Villeneuve, realising it would be futile to block a faster car for over 50 laps, left Jones just enough room as the Williams moved ahead under braking for *Mirabeau*.

Besides, Gilles's brakes were giving out and Patrese was soon in third place although a sensible drive by the Italian was to end on lap 30 when the gearbox pinion on the Arrows failed after a mere 200 miles of service. That put Villeneuve back to third but fourth place for Elio de Angelis was to be short-lived when the Lotus ground to a smoky halt on the harbour front. Elio had left his oily mark around the track as Arnoux was ready to testify after he had spun off at Station Hairpin and ended a tenacious drive in the old Renault. Laffite, driving consistently if not quickly, moved into fourth place with Watson fifth, Prost, struggling with a bent monocoque after the incident on lap one, in sixth place ahead of Tambay and Pironi, the Ferrari driver having got past Giacomelli after being rudely blocked during the opening laps. Alboreto was the only driver to remain unlapped after Cheever lost ground when punted into a spin by Pironi at *Mirabeau*.

Surer was driving with gay abandon in last place but, unfortunately, the Ensign driver was once again to fall foul of the leaders as he tried to make way on the cramped circuit. Jones had set to work on Piquet and relentlessly cut an eight second gap by a fraction here, a fraction there, moving ever closer to the white Brabham. On lap 40, Jones was right behind Piquet as the Brazilian became snared momentarily behind Surer and Monaco watched spellbound as battle commenced.

Lap 43 and Piquet got out of shape as he turned into the swimming pool chicane. You could almost hear Jones chuckle as he watched the Brabham driver gather his car up and press on. Clearly, Piquet was rattled and, no doubt, regretting his earlier remarks as

Didier Pironi had a fraught weekend, shunting three times during practice but finishing fourth after a steady drive from the back of the grid *(below)*.
A fire in the Loews Hotel and the subsequent flooding of the track delayed the start and caused drivers to race under a yellow flag in the tunnel area *(bottom)*.

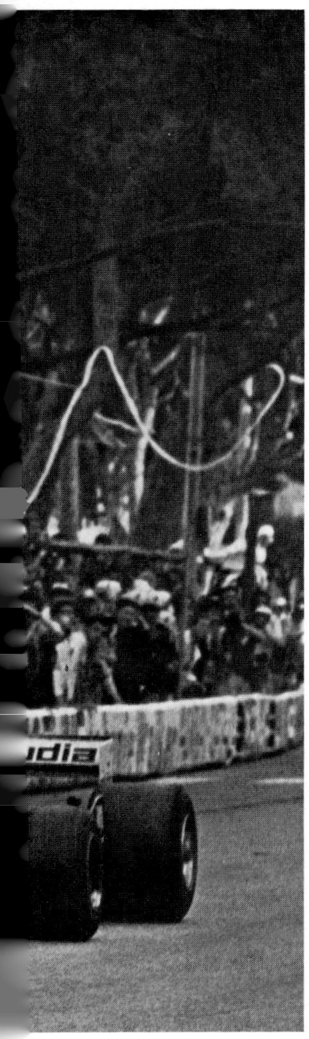

the Williams darted and weaved in his mirrors. At least two more errors brought a ragged and almost desperate edge to Nelson's driving – but he kept in front; it was, after all, Monaco and, barring any major errors, in front he would stay. Jones made a lunge at *Ste Devote* on lap 45 and then dropped back into the cooler air to reconsider his position. The plan, he decided, was to come back in a rush and thoroughly unsettle Piquet but, in the event, that was to prove unnecessary.

On the 54th lap, Piquet came across Cheever and Tambay at *Tabac* and, in his desperation to get by, Nelson made an appalling error of judgement as he tried to squeeze through on the inside as the Theodore turned into the corner. The Brabham's front wheels locked on the dust and sent Piquet straight across the track to thump the barrier on the exit. A disgruntled Nelson hauled himself from the cockpit and walked back to the pits where he made his views known to the Theodore team.

His retirement was to be the last in a long line of casualties. Almost unnoticed, Reutemann had made his first retirement in 15 races when he stopped with gearbox trouble while a broken valve spelt the end for Alain Prost. Michele Alboreto, who had driven with exceptional smoothness and good sense, looked set to score a point when he threw it all away with a spin at *Ste Devote*. That in itself had been harmless enough for he kept the DFV running and was about to continue when Giacomelli appeared on the scene and promptly drove into the front of the Tyrrell. Both retired on the spot. Watson, holding a steady fifth place, rolled to a halt three laps later after his engine had consumed all its oil for no apparent reason. With 12 laps to go, that left seven runners and the order seemed more or less settled as Jones conserved a massive 30-second advantage over Villeneuve. Alan, however, had his doubts as he felt a sickening hesitation every now and then. Thinking he might be running low on fuel and craftily calculating he had enough time for a quick pit-stop, he darted into the pits on lap 67, took on two-and-a-half gallons and rejoined just under six seconds ahead of Villeneuve. His calculations had been correct; his diagnosis had not.

parmalat
5

Gilles Villeneuve
SMEG
LONGINES
7
MAGNETI
MARELLI

After dominating practice, Nelson Piquet's Brabham looked certain to win until forced into a mistake by Alan Jones in the Williams *(far left)*.
Photo: Charles Knight

Nigel Mansell was the sensation of practice and qualified on the second row first time out in the Lotus 87 *(left)*.
Photo: Charles Knight

Gilles Villeneuve won his first European Grand Prix and gave the turbocharged Ferrari an unexpected victory at Monaco *(bottom left)*.
Photo: Diana Burnett

Imola Ceramics continued to support Alboreto's Tyrrell as well as providing glamour on the quayside *(left)*.

Sign of the times. Grandstand seats, normally sold out by the beginning of practice, were available on race morning *(below)*.

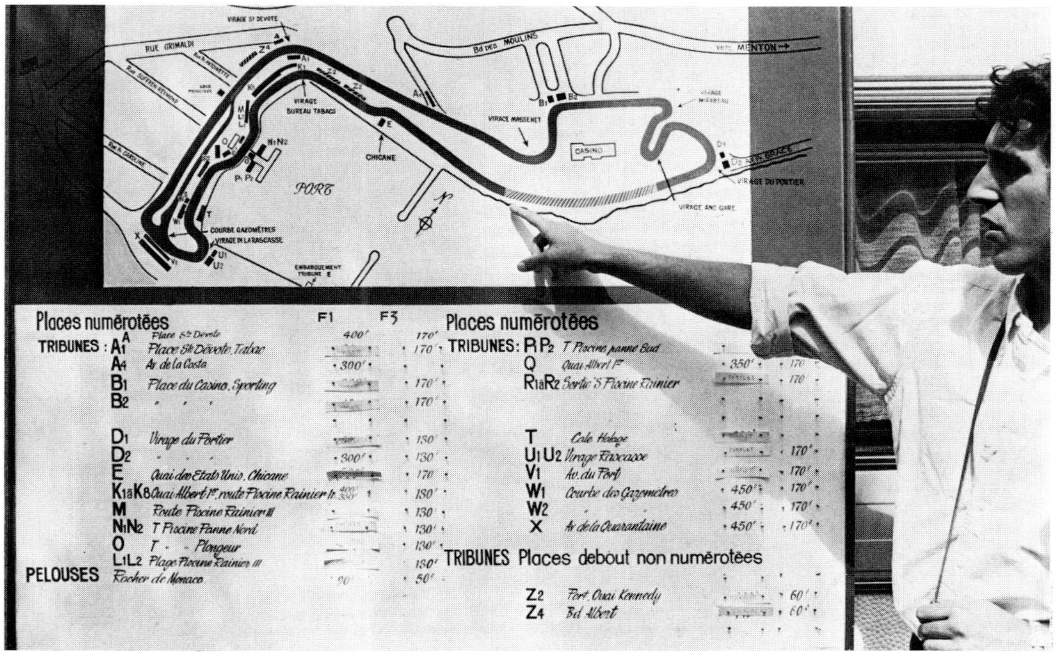

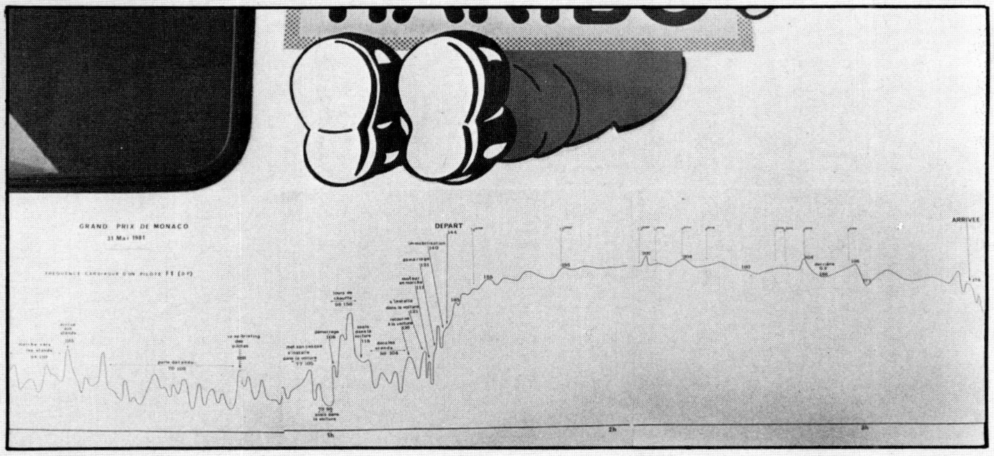

YOU'D BE SURPRISED AT WHAT GOES ON UNDER A driver's overalls! Take Didier Pironi, surely one of the calmest individuals in the pit lane, as an example. During race day at Monaco, his heart beat was monitored and the results showed that the phlegmatic Ferrari driver registered between 144 and 207 – for one hour, 55 minutes and 3.9 seconds. The survey, carried out by Dr. Jean-Paul Richalet and Dr. Catherine Bertrand of the *Université Paris Val-de-Marne*, revealed clearly the emotions and stress involved in a racing driver's world.

Arrival in the pits produced 125, a particularly high reading attributable to the unique atmosphere of Monaco, no doubt. His pulse varied between 70 and 102 while chatting; a drivers' briefing produced 108 followed by 105 while preparing to climb into the car. Then, perhaps the most revealing reading of all; a sudden plunge to 73 as Pironi sat in the cockpit, earplugs and helmet in place, and shut himself off from the surrounding ballyhoo.

Starting the engine brought a leap to 108 followed by a peak of 156 during the warm-up. A generally high level during the start preambles climbed to 144 at the green light. Compared to what followed, 144 was a low reading but it should be borne in mind that Pironi was in 17th place on the grid, a rather more relaxing place than pole. Once into battle however, the heart rate jumped to 165 and reached a peak of 207 while battling with Eddie Cheever. A gradual fall to 178 during a lonely drive to the finish but Dr. Richalet reported that it took several minutes out of the cockpit before the rate fell below 170.

A consistently high reading throughout the race came as no surprise to the doctors but the chart illustrated clearly the strain placed on a driver who, in spite of the lack of pure physical effort (compared to running or skiing, say), worked in stress conditions compounded by high cockpit temperatures and a physical buffeting from G-forces. The stiff suspension and the streets of Monaco also played their part although an unmarked high while Pironi was chatting in the pit lane was attributed to more natural causes. Apparently, Pironi was embraced with considerable enthusiasm by a well-built admirer – which all goes to prove that racing drivers are human after all.

Climbing the hill towards Casino, he felt the hesitation once more and Jones could merely wish and hope. Villeneuve, meanwhile, had been pressing on in his usual manner and frantic waving from the tribunes told him something was amiss. "I could see the people were happy," he said afterwards. "So I knew for sure that maybe Jones was in trouble. Then I see his car ahead of me and I think he has had a spin." (It was not until after the race that Villeneuve learned about the pit stop.)

Sensing a whiff of victory, Gilles pushed his cumbersome Ferrari to the very limit and the gap closed relentlessly from 6s to 4.2s to 3.5s to 2s. If the crowd were happy before then they became hysterical as the Ferrari surged past the spluttering Williams at the end of lap 72, Jones giving Gilles just enough room as they approached *Ste Devote*. Jones had enough of an advantage over Laffite to at least earn six points after a brilliant drive while Pironi, one lap behind, picked up a surprise three points with Cheever a further lap in arrears, finishing in fifth place. Another gritty drive from Marc Surer brought Ensign a valuable point while Tambay, stuck in third gear since lap 50 or thereabouts, was the final finisher.

The marshals waved their flags, the stands erupted, ships and boats sounded their sirens and hooters as Villeneuve trickled round on his slowing down lap. The little man looked exhausted as they plonked a Michelin cap on his head and sent him on his way to receive his trophy. Twenty minutes later in the press room, perspiration continued to trickle down his face as he talked about this most unexpected victory:

"I tell you, my car, it was very hard to drive with the suspension so stiff it was like a go-kart. I bumped my head all the time on the roll-over bar and now I ache all over. It was one of the most tiring races of my life – but I am very, very happy with this win. My brakes were finished and we lost a big advantage when water in the tunnel took away the fastest part of the circuit for the Ferrari. When the brakes started to go, I had to be very brutal with my car, particularly the gearbox, but it lasted okay. I am very lucky today."

Not so lucky were Jones and the Williams team as they pondered over the engine misfire. You could say, too, that Nelson Piquet had been unfortunate – but then it hadn't been his weekend in many respects.

Grand Prix de Monaco, May 31/statistics

Entries and practice times

No.	Driver	Nat	Car	Engine	Entrant	Practice 1	Practice 2
1	Alan Jones	AUS	Saudia-Leyland WILLIAMS FWO7C	Ford Cosworth DFV	Albilad-Williams Racing Team	1m 26·938s	**1m 26·538s**
2	Carlos Reutemann	RA	Saudia-Leyland WILLIAMS FWO7C	Ford Cosworth DFV	Albilad-Williams Racing Team	1m 27·643s	**1m 26·010s**
3	Eddie Cheever	USA	TYRRELL 010	Ford Cosworth DFV	Tyrrell Racing	1m 29·282s	**1m 27·594s**
4	Michele Alboreto	I	TYRRELL 010	Ford Cosworth DFV	Tyrrell Racing	1m 30·699s	**1m 28·358s**
5	Nelson Piquet	BR	Parmalat BRABHAM BT49C	Ford Cosworth DFV	Parmalat Racing Team	**1m 25·710s**	1m 28·667s
6	Hector Rebaque	MEX	Parmalat BRABHAM BT49C	Ford Cosworth DFV	Parmalat Racing Team	**1m 29·188s**	1m 29·256s
7	John Watson	GB	Marlboro McLAREN MP4	Ford Cosworth DFV	McLaren International	1m 28·137s	**1m 27·058s**
8	Andrea de Cesaris	I	Marlboro McLAREN MP4	Ford Cosworth DFV	McLaren International	1m 28·966s	**1m 27·122s**
10	Slim Borgudd	S	Abba ATS D4	Ford Cosworth DFV	Team ATS	Failed to pre-qualify	
11	Elio de Angelis	I	Essex LOTUS 87	Ford Cosworth DFV	Team Essex Lotus	1m 28·381s	**1m 26·259s**
12	Nigel Mansell	GB	Essex LOTUS 87	Ford Cosworth DFV	Team Essex Lotus	1m 27·174s	**1m 25·815s**
14	Marc Surer	CH	ENSIGN N180B	Ford Cosworth DFV	Ensign Racing	1m 29·611s	**1m 28·339s**
15	Alain Prost	F	Elf RENAULT RE 30	Renault EF1	Equipe Renault Elf	1m 27·623s	**1m 26·953s**
16	René Arnoux	F	Elf RENAULT RE 30	Renault EF1	Equipe Renault Elf	1m 28·613s	**1m 27·513s**
17	Eliseo Salazar	RCH	Rizla MARCH 811	Ford Cosworth DFV	March Grand Prix	Failed to pre-qualify	
18	Derek Daly	IRL	Rizla MARCH 811	Ford Cosworth DFV	March Grand Prix	Failed to pre-qualify	
20	Keke Rosberg	SF	FITTIPALDI F8C	Ford Cosworth DFV	Fittipaldi Automotive	1m 29·924s	**1m 28·436s**
21	Chico Serra	BR	FITTIPALDI F8C	Ford Cosworth DFV	Fittipaldi Automotive	1m 32·109s	**1m 29·434s**
22	Mario Andretti	USA	Marlboro ALFA ROMEO 179C	Alfa Romeo 1260	Marlboro Team Alfa Romeo	**1m 27·512s**	1m 28·162s
23	Bruno Giacomelli	I	Marlboro ALFA ROMEO 179C	Alfa Romeo 1260	Marlboro Team Alfa Romeo	1m 28·335s	**1m 28·323s**
25	Jean-Pierre Jabouille	F	Talbot-Gitanes LIGIER JS17	Matra MS 81	Equipe Talbot Gitanes	1m 29·752s	**1m 28·841s**
26	Jacques Laffite	F	Talbot-Gitanes LIGIER JS17	Matra MS 81	Equipe Talbot Gitanes	1m 27·468s	**1m 26·704s**
27	Gilles Villeneuve	CDN	Fiat FERRARI 126CK	Ferrari 126C	Scuderia Ferrari SpA SEFAC	1m 26·891s	**1m 25·788s**
28	Didier Pironi	F	Fiat FERRARI 126CK	Ferrari 126C	Scuderia Ferrari SpA SEFAC	1m 29·150s	**1m 28·266s**
29	Riccardo Patrese	I	Ragno-Beta ARROWS A3	Ford Cosworth DFV	Arrows Racing Team	1m 27·447s	**1m 26·040s**
30	Siegfried Stohr	I	Ragno-Beta ARROWS A3	Ford Cosworth DFV	Arrows Racing Team	1m 29·789s	**1m 27·564s**
31	Beppe Gabbiani	I	Denim OSELLA FA1B	Ford Cosworth DFV	Osella Squadra Corse	1m 30·963s	**1m 29·795s**
32	Piercarlo Ghinzani	I	Denim OSELLA FA1B	Ford Cosworth DFV	Osella Squadra Corse	–	**1m 29·649s**
33	Patrick Tambay	F	THEODORE TY 01	Ford Cosworth DFV	Theodore Racing Team	1m 28·897s	**1m 27·939s**
35	Brian Henton	GB	Candy TOLEMAN TG 181	Hart 415 T	Candy Toleman Motorsport	Failed to pre-qualify	
36	Derek Warwick	GB	Candy TOLEMAN TG 181	Hart 415 T	Candy Toleman Motorsport	Failed to pre-qualify	
Thursday morning and Saturday morning practice sessions not officially recorded						*Thur pm Warm, dry*	*Sat pm Warm, dry*

Starting grid

	5 PIQUET (1m 25·710s) Brabham
27 VILLENEUVE (1m 25·788s) Ferrari	
	12 MANSELL (1m 25·815s) Lotus
2 REUTEMANN (1m 26·010s) Williams	
	29 PATRESE (1m 26·040s) Arrows
11 DE ANGELIS (1m 26·259s) Lotus	
	1 JONES (1m 26·538s) Williams
26 LAFFITE (1m 26·704s) Talbot-Ligier	
	15 PROST (1m 26·953s) Renault
7 WATSON (1m 27·058s) McLaren	
	8 DE CESARIS (1m 27·122s) McLaren
22 ANDRETTI (1m 27·512s) Alfa Romeo	
	16 ARNOUX (1m 27·513s) Renault
30 STOHR (1m 27·564s) Arrows	
	3 CHEEVER (1m 27·594s) Tyrrell
33 TAMBAY (1m 27·939s) Theodore	
	28 PIRONI (1m 28·266s) Ferrari
23 GIACOMELLI (1m 28·323s) Alfa Romeo	
	14 SURER (1m 28·339s) Ensign
4 ALBORETO (1m 28·358s) Tyrrell	

Did not start:
20 Rosberg (Fittipaldi), 1m 28·436s, did not qualify
25 Jabouille (Talbot-Ligier), 1m 28·841s, did not qualify
6 Rebaque (Brabham), 1m 29·188s, did not qualify
21 Serra (Fittipaldi), 1m 29·434s, did not qualify
32 Ghinzani (Osella), 1m 29·649s, did not qualify
31 Gabbiani (Osella), 1m 29·795s, did not qualify
10 Borgudd (ATS), 1m 33·285s, failed to pre-qualify
18 Daly (March), 1m 33·800s, failed to pre-qualify
17 Salazar (March), 1m 35·249s, failed to pre-qualify
35 Henton (Toleman), 1m 37·528s, failed to pre-qualify
36 Warwick (Toleman), 1m 41·966s, failed to pre-qualify

Past winners

Year	Driver	Nat	Car	Circuit	Distance miles/km	Speed mph/km/h
1929	"W. Williams"	GB	2·3 Bugatti T35B s/c	Monte Carlo	197·60/318·01	49·83/80·19
1930	René Dreyfus	F	2·3 Bugatti T35B s/c	Monte Carlo	197·60/318·01	53·63/86·32
1931	Louis Chiron	F	2·3 Bugatti T52 s/c	Monte Carlo	197·60/318·01	54·10/87·06
1932	Tazio Nuvolari	I	2·3 Alfa Romeo Monza s/c	Monte Carlo	197·60/318·01	55·81/89·82
1933	Achille Varzi	I	2·3 Bugati T51 s/c	Monte Carlo	197·60/318·01	57·05/91·81
1934	Guy Moll	DZ	2·9 Alfa Romeo P3 s/c	Monte Carlo	197·60/318·01	56·05/90·20
1935	Luigi Fagioli	I	4·0 Mercedes-Benz W25 s/c	Monte Carlo	197·60/318·01	58·16/93·61
1936	Rudi Caracciola	D	4·7 Mercedes-Benz W25 s/c	Monte Carlo	197·60/318·01	51·69/83·20
1937	Manfred von Brauchitsch	D	5·7 Mercedes-Benz W125 s/c	Monte Carlo	197·60/318·01	63·26/101·82
1948	Giuseppe Farina	I	1·5 Maserati 4CLT s/c	Monte Carlo	197·60/318·01	59·74/96·15
1950	Juan Manuel Fangio	RA	1·5 Alfa Romeo 158 s/c	Monte Carlo	197·60/318·01	61·33/98·70
1952*	Vittorio Marzotto	I	2·7 Ferrari 225MM	Monte Carlo	195·42/314·50	58·20/93·66
1955	Maurice Trintignant	F	2·5 Ferrari 625	Monte Carlo	195·42/314·50	65·81/105·91
1956	Stirling Moss	GB	2·5 Maserati 250F	Monte Carlo	195·42/314·50	64·94/104·51
1957	Juan Manuel Fangio	RA	2·5 Maserati 250F	Monte Carlo	205·19/330·22	64·72/104·16
1958	Maurice Trintignant	F	2·0 Cooper T45-Climax	Monte Carlo	195·42/314·50	67·99/109·41
1959	Jack Brabham	AUS	2·5 Cooper T51-Climax	Monte Carlo	195·42/314·50	66·71/107·36
1960	Stirling Moss	GB	2·5 Lotus 18-Climax	Monte Carlo	195·42/314·50	67·48/108·60
1961	Stirling Moss	GB	1·5 Lotus 18-Climax	Monte Carlo	195·42/314·50	70·70/113·79
1962	Bruce McLaren	NZ	1·5 Cooper T60-Climax	Monte Carlo	195·42/314·50	70·46/113·40
1963	Graham Hill	GB	1·5 BRM P57	Monte Carlo	195·42/314·50	72·43/116·56
1964	Graham Hill	GB	1·5 BRM P261	Monte Carlo	195·42/314·50	72·64/116·91
1965	Graham Hill	GB	1·5 BRM P261	Monte Carlo	195·42/314·50	74·34/119·64
1966	Jackie Stewart	GB	1·9 BRM P261	Monte Carlo	195·42/314·50	76·51/123·14
1967	Denny Hulme	NZ	3·0 Brabham BT20-Repco	Monte Carlo	195·42/314·50	75·90/122·14
1968	Graham Hill	GB	3·0 Lotus 49B-Ford	Monte Carlo	156·34/251·60	77·82/125·24
1969	Graham Hill	GB	3·0 Lotus 49B-Ford	Monte Carlo	156·34/251·60	80·18/129·04
1970	Jochen Rindt	A	3·0 Lotus 49C-Ford	Monte Carlo	156·34/251·60	81·85/131·72
1971	Jackie Stewart	GB	3·0 Tyrrell 003-Ford	Monte Carlo	156·34/251·60	83·49/134·36
1972	Jean-Pierre Beltoise	F	3·0 BRM P160B	Monte Carlo	156·34/251·60	63·85/102·75
1973	Jackie Stewart	GB	3·0 Tyrrell 006-Ford	Monte Carlo	158·87/255·68	80·96/130·29
1974	Ronnie Peterson	S	3·0 JPS/Lotus 72-Ford	Monte Carlo	158·87/255·68	80·74/129·94
1975	Niki Lauda	A	3·0 Ferrari 312T/75	Monte Carlo	152·76/245·84	75·53/121·55
1976	Niki Lauda	A	3·0 Ferrari 312T-2/76	Monte Carlo	160·52/258·34	80·36/129·32
1977	Jody Scheckter	ZA	3·0 Wolf WR1-Ford	Monte Carlo	156·41/251·71	79·61/128·12
1978	Patrick Depailler	F	3·0 Tyrrell 008-Ford	Monte Carlo	154·35/248·40	80·36/129·33
1979	Jody Scheckter	ZA	3·0 Ferrari 312T-4	Monte Carlo	156·41/251·71	81·34/130·90
1980	Carlos Reutemann	RA	3·0 Williams FW07B-Ford	Monte Carlo	156·41/251·71	81·20/130·68
1981	Gilles Villeneuve	CDN	1·5 Ferrari 126CK	Monte Carlo	156·41/251·71	82·04/132·03

*Non-championship (sports cars)

Circuit data

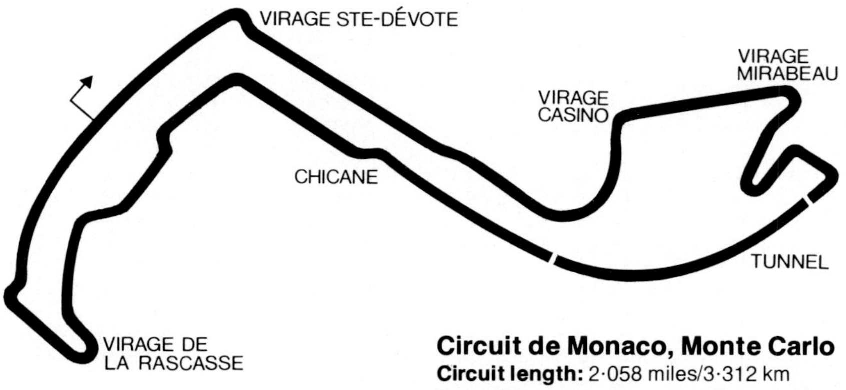

Circuit de Monaco, Monte Carlo
Circuit length: 2·058 miles/3·312 km
Race distance: 76 laps, 156·406 miles/251·712 km
Race weather: Warm, dry.

Results and retirements

Place	Driver	Car	Laps	Time and Speed (mph/km/h)/Retirement	
1	Gilles Villeneuve	Ferrari t/c V6	76	1h 54m 23·38s	82·039/132·03
2	Alan Jones	Williams-Cosworth V8	76	1h 55m 03·29s	81·567/131·27
3	Jacques Laffite	Talbot-Ligier Matra V12	76	1h 55m 52·62s	80·983/130·33
4	Didier Pironi	Ferrari t/c V6	75		
5	Eddie Cheever	Tyrrell-Cosworth V8	74		
6	Marc Surer	Ensign-Cosworth V8	74		
7	Patrick Tambay	Theodore-Cosworth V8	72		
	Nelson Piquet	Brabham-Cosworth V8	53	Accident	
	John Watson	McLaren-Cosworth V8	53	Engine	
	Michele Alboreto	Tyrrell-Cosworth V8	50	Spun; accident with Giacomelli	
	Bruno Giacomelli	Alfa Romeo V12	50	Accident with Alboreto	
	Alain Prost	Renault t/c V6	45	Engine	
	Carlos Reutemann	Williams-Cosworth V8	34	Gearbox	
	René Arnoux	Renault t/c V6	32	Accident	
	Elio de Angelis	Lotus-Cosworth V8	32	Engine	
	Riccardo Patrese	Arrows-Cosworth V8	29	Gearbox	
	Nigel Mansell	Lotus-Cosworth V8	16	Rear suspension	
	Siegfried Stohr	Arrows-Cosworth V8	15	Electrical misfire	
	Andrea de Cesaris	McLaren-Cosworth V8	0	Collision with Prost	
	Mario Andretti	Alfa Romeo V12	0	Hit by de Cesaris	

Fastest lap: Jones, on lap 48, 1m 27·470s, 84·699mph/136·311km/h.
Lap record: Riccardo Patrese (F1 Arrows A3-Cosworth DFV), 1m 26·058s, 86·089mph/138·548km/h (1980).

Lap chart

1st LAP ORDER		1	2	3	4	5	6	7	8	9	10	11	12	13	14	15	16	17	18	19	20	21	22	23	24	25	26	27	28	29	30	31	32	33	34	35
5	N.Piquet	5	5	5	5	5	5	5	5	5	5	5	5	5	5	5	5	5	5	5	5	5	5	5	5	5	5	5	5	5	5	5	5	5	5	5
27	G.Villeneuve	27	27	27	27	27	27	27	27	27	27	27	27	27	27	27	27	27	27	27	1	1	1	1	1	1	1	1	1	1	1	1	1	1	1	1
12	N.Mansell	12	12	12	12	12	12	12	12	12	12	12	12	12	12	1	1	1	1	1	27	27	27	27	27	29	29	29	29	29	27	27	27	27	27	27
2	C.Reutemann	2	2	2	2	2	2	2	2	2	2	2	2	2	1	29	29	29	29	29	29	29	29	29	29	27	27	27	27	27	11	11	11	26	26	26
1	A.Jones	1	1	1	1	1	1	1	1	1	1	1	1	1	29	11	11	11	11	11	11	11	11	11	11	11	11	11	11	11	26	26	26	7	7	7
29	R.Patrese	29	29	29	29	29	29	29	29	29	29	29	29	29	11	12	26	26	26	26	26	26	26	26	26	26	26	26	26	26	16	16	16	15	15	15
11	E.de Angelis	11	11	11	11	11	11	11	11	11	11	11	11	11	26	26	16	16	16	16	16	16	16	16	16	16	16	16	16	16	15	15	7	33	33	33
26	J.Laffite	26	26	26	26	26	26	26	26	26	26	26	26	26	16	16	15	15	15	15	15	15	15	15	15	15	15	15	15	15	7	7	15	3	28	28
15	A.Prost	15	15	15	15	15	15	15	15	15	15	16	16	16	15	15	7	7	7	7	7	7	7	7	7	7	7	7	7	7	33	33	33	28	23	23
16	R.Arnoux	16	16	16	16	16	16	16	16	16	16	15	15	15	7	7	33	33	33	33	33	33	33	33	33	33	33	33	33	33	3	3	3	23	4	4
7	J.Watson	7	7	7	7	7	7	7	7	7	7	7	7	7	33	33	3	3	3	3	3	3	3	3	3	3	3	3	3	3	28	28	28	4	3	3
33	P.Tambay	33	33	33	33	33	33	33	33	33	33	33	33	33	3	3	23	23	23	23	23	23	23	23	23	23	28	28	28	28	23	23	23	2	14	14
3	E.Cheever	3	3	3	3	3	3	3	3	3	3	3	3	3	23	23	28	28	28	28	28	28	28	28	28	28	23	23	23	23	4	4	4	14	2	
30	S.Stohr	30	30	30	30	30	30	30	30	30	23	23	23	23	28	28	4	4	4	4	4	4	4	4	4	4	4	4	4	4	2	2	2			
23	B.Giacomelli	23	23	23	23	23	23	23	23	23	28	28	28	28	4	4	12	14	14	14	14	14	14	14	14	14	14	14	14	2	14	14	14			
28	D.Pironi	28	28	28	28	28	28	28	28	28	4	4	4	4	2	14	14	2	2	2	2	2	2	2	2	2	2	2	2	14						
4	M.Alboreto	4	4	4	4	4	4	4	4	4	30	14	14	14	14	2	2																			
14	M.Surer	14	14	14	14	14	14	14	14	14	14	30	30	30	30	30																				

36	37	38	39	40	41	42	43	44	45	46	47	48	49	50	51	52	53	54	55	56	57	58	59	60	61	62	63	64	65	66	67	68	69	70	71	72	73	74	75	76
5	5	5	5	5	5	5	5	5	5	5	5	5	5	5	5	5	5	1	1	1	1	1	1	1	1	1	1	1	1	1	1	1	1	1	1	1	27	27	27	27
1	1	1	1	1	1	1	1	1	1	1	1	1	1	1	1	1	1	27	27	27	27	27	27	27	27	27	27	27	27	27	27	27	27	27	27	27	1	1	1	1
27	27	27	27	27	27	27	27	27	27	27	27	27	27	27	27	27	27	26	26	26	26	26	26	26	26	26	26	26	26	26	26	26	26	26	26	26	26	26	26	26
26	26	26	26	26	26	26	26	26	26	26	26	26	26	26	26	26	26	28	28	28	28	28	28	28	28	28	28	28	28	28	28	28	28	28	28	28	28	28	28	
7	7	7	7	7	7	7	7	7	7	7	7	7	7	7	7	7	7	3	3	3	3	3	3	3	3	3	3	3	3	3	3	3	3	3	3	3	3	3		
15	15	15	15	15	15	15	15	15	15	33	4	28	28	28	28	28	28	33	33	14	14	14	14	14	14	14	14	14	14	14	14	14	14	14	14	14	14	14		
33	33	33	33	33	33	33	33	33	33	28	28	4	4	4	33	3	3	14	14	33	33	33	33	33	33	33	33	33	33	33	33	33	33	33	33	33				
28	28	28	28	28	28	28	28	28	28	4	33	23	23	23	3	33	33																							
23	23	23	23	23	23	4	4	4	4	23	23	33	33	33	14	14	14																							
4	4	4	4	4	4	23	23	23	23	3	3	3	3	3																										
3	3	3	3	3	3	3	3	3	3	14	14	14	14	14																										
14	14	14	14	14	14	14	14	14	14																															

Fastest laps

Driver	Time	Lap
Alan Jones	1m 27·47s	48
Nelson Piquet	1m 28·04s	47
Carlos Reutemann	1m 28·76s	30
Gilles Villeneuve	1m 29·00s	71
Riccardo Patrese	1m 29·01s	23
John Watson	1m 29·23s	44
Jacques Laffite	1m 29·40s	43
Elio de Angelis	1m 29·52s	29
Nigel Mansell	1m 29·52s	7
Didier Pironi	1m 29·61s	51
René Arnoux	1m 29·74s	26
Bruno Giacomelli	1m 29·82s	50
Alain Prost	1m 29·90s	25
Michele Alboreto	1m 30·36s	48
Eddie Cheever	1m 30·55s	44
Marc Surer	1m 30·77s	45
Patrick Tambay	1m 30·92s	12
Siegfried Stohr	1m 31·72s	8

Points

WORLD CHAMPIONSHIP OF DRIVERS

1	Carlos Reutemann	34 pts
2	Alan Jones	24
3	Nelson Piquet	22
4	Gilles Villeneuve	12
5	Jacques Laffite	11
6	Riccardo Patrese	10
7=	Didier Pironi	5
7=	Eddie Cheever	5
7=	Elio de Angelis	5
10=	Marc Surer	4
10=	Alain Prost	4
10=	Nigel Mansell	4
13=	Mario Andretti	3
13=	Hector Rebaque	3
15	René Arnoux	2
16=	Patrick Tambay	1
16=	Andrea de Cesaris	1

CONSTRUCTORS' CUP

1	Williams	58
2	Brabham	25
3	Ferrari	17
4	Ligier	11
5	Arrows	10
6	Lotus	9
7	Renault	6
8	Tyrrell	5
9	Ensign	4
10	Alfa Romeo	3
11=	Theodore	1
11=	McLaren	1

Gran Premio de España

'Number Two forms the queue,
Yah-boo to Number Two.'

So says an old rhyme which was illustrated perfectly during the memorable closing laps of the Spanish Grand Prix. Five cars, covered by less than two seconds, crossed the line after 80 laps run in searing heat around the tortuous Jarama circuit.

At the front, Gilles Villeneuve hanging on grimly to a lead which, in theory at least, he had no right to hold. The turbo power was his ace card, the evil handling of the Ferrari his joker, and he played them both to a stunning degree.

Expecting to enjoy five, maybe ten laps near the front, Villeneuve made another brilliant start and held second place by the end of lap one. He could do nothing about the leader, Alan Jones, as the Saudia-Leyland Williams driver opened an unassailable lead before making an uncharacteristic mistake and flying off the track.

Jones was not the only driver to play into Villeneuve's hands. Jacques Laffite had taken an easy pole in the vastly improved Talbot-Ligier Matra but his advantage was ruined by a creeping clutch on the start line. Dabbing the brake pedal as the lights flicked green, Jacques was pushed back to 11th and so began a storming drive into second place by lap 62. Villeneuve was soon hauled in but, if catching the Ferrari had been easy, getting past was impossible.

Clumsy through the many tight corners, the turbo stroked away on the straight and the slow pace pulled Watson, having his best race in the Marlboro McLaren MP4, and Carlos Reutemann, holding his Williams in third gear, to the front. Elio de Angelis, in the newly painted John Player Special Lotus 87 latched on to the train and thus Laffite's challenge for the lead became a careful defence of second place. Number Two had formed the queue.

De Angelis, the only driver with nothing to lose, made several lunges at Reutemann; the rest prudently held their ground lest they fell to fifth place at the drop of a wheel or a fumbled gearchange. The track was so dirty off line that their only hope was a mistake by Villeneuve. He made one or two – but recovered in the most astonishing manner to win a race on sheer tenacity coupled with out-and-out car control.

Nigel Mansell, driving one of the toughest races of his short but rapidly improving career, finished sixth. Jones recovered to take fastest lap and seventh place – and that was one reason why the top of the World Championship remained virtually unchanged. The other reason was that Nelson Piquet went off at the same corner as Jones and ended a below par weekend for the Parmalat Brabham team. Reutemann, therefore, added three points to his lead; Jones and Piquet remained stationary while Villeneuve closed to within one point of the Brabham driver after leading the queue across the line.

Others who could just as easily have been involved in the scramble were Alain Prost, running third at one stage in the Renault-Elf, and Mario Andretti, showing excellent form in the Marlboro Alfa Romeo before coming emboiled in a dispute with Piquet.

ENTRY AND PRACTICE

This was Talbot's weekend in more ways than one. A tasteful blue motif wrapped around the Spanish Automobile Club crest signified that the *XXVII Gran Premio de España* was sponsored by Talbot. Michael Turner posters around Madrid illustrated the two French cars leading the field and, after practice at least, that was 50 per cent correct. For the third year in succession, Jacques Laffite was on pole at Jarama.

Ligier had been busy. Solid, constructive tests at Dijon had improved small details such as skirts and aerodynamic tweaks and the immaculate handling put Jacques in a league of his own. Straight line speed was still not up to scratch although the rev limit was raised to 12,800rpm. Practice had not been that straight-forward, however. A new car for Laffite presented oversteer and bottoming on Friday and the engine would not rev thanks to a minor electrical problem. All that was cured the following day and the little Frenchman bounced back to prominence after 30

Against all odds – for the second race in succession. An exhausted Gilles Villeneuve after a splendid and unexpected victory for Ferrari. *(left).*
Villeneuve, running alongside Reutemann (2), makes his mark from the start. Laffite, who started from pole, has already fallen behind Prost's Renault (15) while Pironi makes a superb charge on the extreme left. *(below left).*
This was how they ran for the final 20 laps; Villeneuve holding off Laffite followed by Watson, Reutemann and de Angelis. *(main picture).*

minutes of practice. Laffite's promise, unhappily, accentuated Jean-Pierre Jabouille's despair. A non-qualifier at Monaco, Jabouille made the grid at Jarama but he was almost three seconds slower than his team-mate; the new chassis used by Laffite was not *that* good.

The bulky profile of Patrick Head, festooned with intercoms and cables, was prominent in the Williams pit once more following his visit to Indy with the Longhorn team. Judging by the performance of Alan Jones and Carlos Reutemann, second and third on the grid, Patrick was probably glad to be back after an unhappy few weeks at the Brickyard. The reigning World Champion was on sparkling form despite losing two engines during the weekend. The second blow-up occurred on Saturday morning and the subsequent engine change meant Jones lost 15 minutes of practice – just the sort of thing to fire the Australian into a handy, aggressive mood. Once onto the track, Jones reeled off 16 laps, recording his time on the 13th and beating Reutemann by three-tenths. Laffite was a further three-tenths ahead but Jones seemed neither surprised nor worried about the performance of the Ligier. Reutemann's practice had been reasonably trouble-free apart from clutch trouble on Friday which forced him to use the T-car normally reserved for Jones.

The grid had a new look about it when John Watson parked the red and white Marlboro McLaren MP4 on the second row. The team were continuing their steady development work, running new skirts and adding scoops to duct air around the rear suspension. Watson had a valve spring break on Saturday morning and he lost 30 minutes in the afternoon session as a result. Undaunted, John climbed into the immaculate machine and set his time on his second flying lap! Andrea de Cesaris set his time on his third lap but his practice was not as simple as that. A broken steering arm sent the Italian into the sand on Friday and then he spun off on his fourth lap on Saturday and damaged the car. Had he not done so, de Cesaris might have been higher than 14th on the grid.

René Arnoux was another driver to have a

Villeneuve had to deal with repeated attacks from Reutemann. . . *(below right)*.
. . . before fending off an equally determined Laffite. *(right)*.

JUNE:

Harvey Postlethwaite leaves Fittipaldi and joins Ferrari.

Kenny Acheson breaks right leg while disputing lead in Pau Formula 2 race.

John Player return to sponsor Lotus.

Williams change name from 'Albilad' to 'TAG' Williams Team.

Alistair Caldwell leaves Brabham Formula 1 team.

Jacky Ickx wins Le Mans for fifth time. His Porsche 936 co-driven by Derek Bell.

RAC Technical Commission declare revised Lotus 88B legal.

Jean-Louis Lafosse killed at Le Mans.

Jean-Pierre Jabouille announces retirement from Formula 1.

Goodyear announce return to Formula 1.

disastrous weekend. A new chassis proved troublesome on Friday while, on Saturday, Arnoux managed a total of four laps after turbo compressor trouble on the race car *and* the T-car. Alain Prost, by contrast, was much happier after two trouble-free days and a place on row three. His only complaint was a sore neck, the aftermath of a heavy shunt during testing at Dijon where he wrote off RE 31. The Marlboro Alfa Romeo team had carried out their testing at Jarama and Mario Andretti and Bruno Giacomelli approached practice in a confident frame of mind. As so often happens, however, cars which had been well balanced during testing suddenly lacked grip during the heat of official practice but Bruno at least was reasonably happy with his place on the third row, his best position since Brazil.

Splitting the Alfa Romeos was a struggling Gilles Villeneuve, in dire handling trouble with the Ferrari 126CK. Unable to take any of the quick corners flat-out, Gilles had driven on the limit to make the most of fresh tyres which gave the chassis its optimum performance for no more than four laps. Didier Pironi was three rows in arrears after suffering three separate bearing seal failures on the turbo. Didier's progress around the circuit was marked by swirling clouds of blue smoke which, at one stage, caused a pursuing Jacques Laffite to come to a standstill and wave his arms in despair. The relatively poor performance by the Ferraris was expected perhaps but it was something of a shock to find Nelson Piquet on the fifth row. The Brabham had been handling inconsistently from the start; good on slow corners, poor on the fast curves one minute, followed by a complete reversal the next. For once, Gordon Murray was unable to come up with an answer for Saturday and Hector Rebaque underlined the problem by taking a place alongside Arnoux on the ninth row.

The Lotus team, resplendent in their new John Player Special black and gold livery, came to Jarama brimfull of confidence after their splendid showing in Monaco. From the word go, however, practice was fraught with minor difficulties such as the wide front wings for Nigel Mansell's 87 being delayed in Customs until Saturday. The front track had been widened but the cars were lacking in downforce and Mansell prudently stopped his car when he felt the engine begin to tighten after setting sixth fastest time on Friday. Mansell's time was beaten by de Angelis and it was good enough to put the Italian on row five after he lost time on Saturday with an off-course excursion while fiddling with the brake-balance bar. Joining Mansell on the next row was Riccardo Patrese in the Ragno-Beta Arrows, the Italian struggling to find traction out of the slow corners. Siegfried Stohr was in

Mario Andretti was running as high as fourth in the Alfa Romeo before having a disagreement with Nelson Piquet's Brabham at the end of the pit straight. *(below left)*.

more serious trouble after tangling with Slim Borgudd at the end of the main straight on Friday afternoon but the number two Arrows scraped into the back row the following day. Chico Serra was another driver to tangle wheels during practice, the Brazilian having a dusty excursion at the same corner with Eliseo Salazar in the Ensign. Serra complained of gear selection problems while Keke Rosberg spent practice trying to sort the handling, a task made more difficult since Harvey Postlethwaite's departure to Ferrari. Nonetheless, both Fittipaldis qualified, which was an achievement in itself following the debacle at Monaco.

Of the rest, Patrick Tambay continued to look extremely confident in the Theodore, qualifying on row eight, four places ahead of Eddie Cheever in the Tyrrell. The cars from Ripley were beginning to look much the worse for wear and a lack of sponsorship and Michele Alboreto failed to make the grid. By contrast, Derek Daly and the Guinness Rizla March team were on the up-and-up now that Adrian Reynard had joined Gordon Coppuck on the design team. The trio worked well together and a combination of revised pods and Daly's irrepressible enthusiasm saw the black car qualify for the first time in a World Championship Grand Prix. March had entered just one car now that Eliseo Salazar had taken his much-needed finance to Ensign and the man from Chile took the last place on the grid after having the unenviable task of sorting a new hydro-pneumatic suspension on a car which he had never driven before.

Neither Beppe Gabbiani nor Giorgio Francia were able to qualify their Denim Osellas which featured revised nose wings and side-pods. Gabbiani's chances received a set-back on Saturday when he damaged a chassis after a wheel flew off and he was forced to use Francia's car. Slim Borgudd, apart from his alarming incident with Stohr, had an altogether unhappy weekend, the ATS team becoming victims of a clumsy piece of political manoeuvring by the Spanish organisers. 30 cars had been entered as per the Concorde Agreement but Emileo de Villota rocked the boat when he turned up with his Williams FW07. The organisers, keen to bolster the entry with a local man, eased ATS out because their team manager had been late arriving due to delays at London Heathrow. The ATS, said the organisers, had arrived too late for scrutineering and de Villota took part in the practice session on Friday morning. All that changed, however, when, during the lunch break, a press release appeared and stated that if de Villota took part, the terms of the Concorde Agreement would be contravened and the race would not count for the World Championship. That made the matter perfectly clear to the organisers, particularly in the light of the fiasco at Jarama 12 months previously. De Villota was out; Borgudd and the ATS were in.

The Candy Toleman team continued their busy programme of development which included a new turbo installation on top of the engine and revised intercooling. Brian Henton showed even more enthusiasm than usual and recorded times in the 1m 18s bracket on his best tyres before the Spaniards interrupted practice as was their wont given the slightest excuse. Derek Warwick also managed to look more competitive inbetween the usual mechanical trails and tribulations, the most serious of which was a split intercooler.

RACE

On Sunday, the Spaniards voted with their feet and stayed away from Jarama. It was difficult to judge whether it was due to de Villota's bitter outburst in the local press, a lack of enthusiasm for Grand Prix racing and its unhappy image or, quite simply, the stifling heat. Either way, the attendance figures gave fair warning to those who seemed destined to destroy

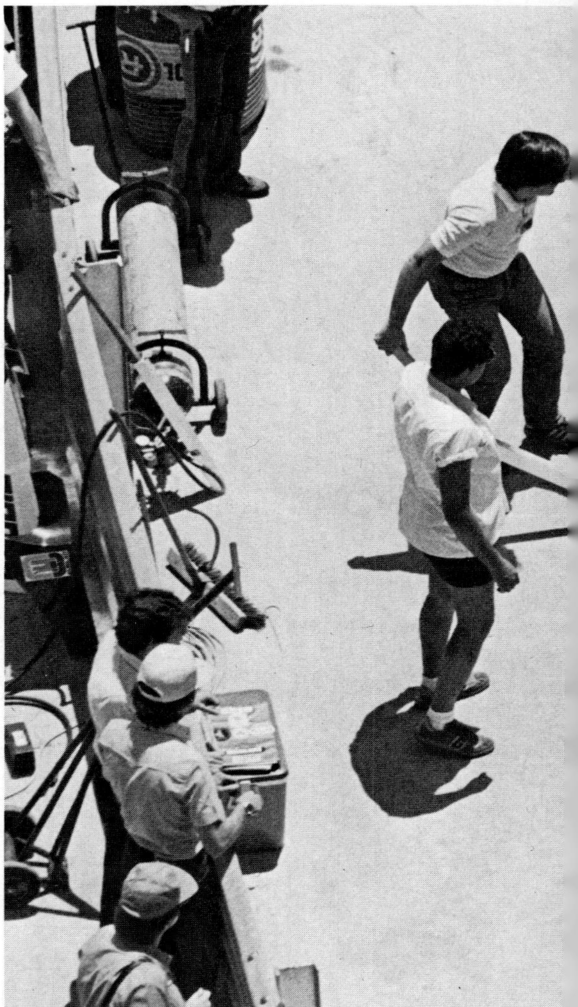

Black is back. Lotus appeared in their new John Player Special livery – and finished fifth and sixth. The 6cm gap on Nigel Mansell's 87 is checked during practice. *(right)*. Nelson Piquet's expression sums up a dismal weekend for Brabham. *(below right)*.

Jean-Pierre Jabouille announced his retirement soon after the Spanish Grand Prix. The Talbot-Ligier driver never recovered fully from leg injuries received when he crashed his Renault during the 1980 Canadian Grand Prix and his return to the cockpit in 1981 was marked by brave but disappointing performances.

Jabouille, more of an engineer than a driver of outstanding natural ability, was the driving force behind Renault's involvement in Formula 1. Indeed, the French marque played a major part in Jabouille's motor racing career which began with an R8 Gordini in 1966.

Born in Paris in October 1942, Jabouille interupted his career as an interior designer to begin a long association with racing cars. By 1967 he was racing a Matra in Formula 3, winning at Reims and finishing second in the French Championship. Asked to join the Alpine Formula 3 team in 1969, Jabouille drove alongside Patrick Depailler before moving into Formula 2 and 2-litre sports cars.

Combining his engineering talents with driving skill, Jean-Pierre won the 1976 European Formula 2 Championship in an Elf 2 designed and developed himself. Jabouille made his Grand Prix début with Tyrrell in 1975 at Paul Ricard and, shortly afterwards, work began on the Renault Formula 1 project. Inbetween sports car races for Renault, Jabouille developed the turbocharged car and made the team's Grand Prix début at Silverstone in 1977.

Jabouille went on to win six pole positions but, without doubt, his finest hour was at Dijon in 1979 when he won the French Grand Prix convinvingly although his most tenacious drive, perhaps, was in Austria the following year when he nursed his RE 23 across the line to a splendid victory.

His technical skills were such that the new Talbot-Ligier regime signed Jabouille with an eye to using his experience on future turbocharged projects. A purposeful future at the wheel was cut short at Montreal when a broken wishbone sent his Renault into the crash-barrier and Jean-Pierre broke his right leg.

Talbot-Ligier kept faith and the lanky Frenchman with the Danny Kaye looks worked hard at his recovery. Sadly, it was not to be, the injuries refusing to heal properly and the quiet, unassuming Jabouille was left with no option but to accept a role outside the cockpit.

Formula 1 with petty wrangling.

The drivers had other things on their minds as they set off on the 30 minute warm-up, Jacques Laffite setting the standard with 1m 16.313s. Jones was next but a hurried consultation Frank Williams and Patrick Head indicated that all was not well. Jones's throttle had jammed open long enough to send the Williams perilously close to the guardrail and Wayne Eckersley, recently returned to work from hospital where he had received treatment for a back injury, got down to business. In addition, a brake bleed nipple on the front-left calliper had been cross-threaded and the part was changed.

Nelson Piquet had been unable to make much of an improvement and the Brazilian wandered across the pit lane to study the times displayed on a monitor. He was fifth fastest behind Reutemann and Prost. The Renault driver was much happier, his car handling better than it had been all weekend and Alain's major concern was the installation of a supply of water to his helmet. Jarama may have lacked charm and character but it was one of the most physically demanding circuits on the calendar and, as the 4 p.m. start drew nearer, temperatures approached the 100° mark.

From the moment Laffite took his place on pole, he felt the clutch creeping. The Ligier began to edge forward and, as Jacques dabbed the brake pedal, the lights turned green. Jones, determined to lead into the first corner, had no opposition therefore and Reutemann followed his team leader. Slotting into third place, and bending Prost's nose wing along the way, was none other than Gilles Villeneuve, the Ferrari driver enjoying another of his lightning starts. His car would be good on full tanks and Gilles intended to make the most of it. Hanging on to the Williams duo, Gilles entered the pit straight on the limit and took Reutemann by surprise under braking for the first corner. Andretti was next followed by Prost (his nose wing bent but still attached), Watson, Giacomelli, Piquet, Pironi (moving ahead of Patrese and damaging the Ferrari nose wing in the process), Laffite (slow off the line and boxed in at the first corner as he allowed his clutch to cool), de Angelis, Rosberg, Arnoux, de Cesaris (after banging wheels mercilessly with Rebaque), Daly (soon to stop with a sticking throttle), Mansell, Cheever, Jabouille, Salazar, Stohr, Serra and, finally, Tambay who stopped at the pits for a new nose cone.

Jones was in command, no question about that as he pulled away at over a second a lap. The rest of the field held station except for Pironi who took Giacomelli on lap two. De Cesaris had another incident on lap 10 and spun into retirement while the progress of Laffite held everyone's attention. Dealing with Patrese, he moved into 10th place and made short work of Pironi. Watson was next but the resolute Ulsterman was hanging on in spite of Laffite's frenzied efforts to get by. It became a battle for sixth place with a dramatic change at the front of the field on lap 14.

With the race seemingly in his pocket, Jones unaccountably locked his brakes going into *Virage Ascari* and ploughed onto the sandy run-off area. No harm had been done – mechanically, at least – and, by the time Alan had been push-started, he was back in 16th place. Villeneuve, against all odds, was leading the race. But that, surely, would not last.

Reutemann, a couple of lengths behind, was in trouble, his Williams jumping out of third gear but the Argentinian closed on the Ferrari and had a couple of attempts at getting by. Prost, driving superbly regardless of his handling problems, had taken Andretti and was pulling away while the Alfa Romeo was coming under pressure from Piquet with Laffite climbing all over Watson just a few yards further back.

Lap 20, and Pironi understeered off the track before calling at his pit for a new nose and tyres, followed one lap later by Patrese with imminent engine failure. Thus de Angelis assumed eighth place, his team-mate challenging Giacomelli for ninth. Jones was soon into 10th place although further progress was limited by gear selection problems while Rebaque had no trouble keeping ahead of Arnoux as the Frenchman struggled with a poor engine.

Dust flew at the first corner on lap 25 when Piquet had a run down the inside of Andretti. The move didn't come off, the cars touched and ran wide as Watson and Laffite took their chance and gained two places. The Alfa and the Brabham continued although Nelson's race was to end 19 laps later when he flew off the road again, this time at the spot where Jones had misjudged his braking. The result for Piquet was more terminal, however, and he walked back to the pits to wait his chance to apologise to a furious Andretti.

By now, the leader board had changed yet again, Prost having been caught out by his inconsistent handling and spun off on lap 29. Reutemann was continuing to make stabs at Villeneuve; Laffite was unable to do anything about Watson while de Angelis and Mansell were running solidly in fifth and sixth places. Jones was even further back in seventh place ahead of Andretti, Arnoux and Giacomelli. Rosberg had been lapped and Serra was closing on his team leader after Rabaque had stopped with gearbox trouble. Jabouille had been in and out of the pits for tyres and the Ligier driver, along with Salazar, was about to change the running order at the front of the field.

On lap 49, the leaders came across the second Ligier and, whether by accident or design, Laffite emerged in front of Watson and set off in pursuit of Villeneuve and Reutemann. By lap 56, he had caught the leaders and their slow pace allowed Watson to join the train. Then, on lap 62, the quartet closed on Salazar as the Ensign driver left *Esses de Bugatti*. Villeneuve moved ahead but, going through the fast right-hander onto the straight, Salazar surprised Reutemann by taking his line and the Williams driver was trapped on the left-hand side of the track. In an instant, Laffite and Watson were second and third.

De Angelis had come into the reckoning but, more

(below, from top to bottom).
Better – but not quite good enough. Derek Warwick gives some thought to the new location for the Garrett turbocharger and compressor on the Toleman.
"No, no. Not the car; your tea – how d'you like it? One lump or two?" Mo Nunn makes Eliseo Salazar feel at home after the Chilean driver had moved his money from March to Ensign.
Not again! Andrea de Cesaris spun his McLaren into retirement.
Adrian Reynard joined the March design team and helped move Derek Daly onto the grid.

important, we had a fresh attack on Villeneuve. His days at the front had to be numbered. For the next 18 laps the tenacious French-Canadian kept his cool by using his V6 turbo power to good advantage on the straight while his frustrated pursuers climbed all over the Ferrari in the corners. Round and round they went; Ferrari, Ligier, McLaren, Williams and Lotus. Occasionally Jacques would run alongside at the exit of a corner but now he had to think about Watson – and Reutemann – and de Angelis. One mistake and second place would become fifth; six points would reduce to two in the twinkling of an eye. Villeneuve, of course, relied on the circumspect behaviour of his rivals as the chequered flag drew closer although, de Angelis, with nothing to lose, kept up a constant attack on Reutemann. Round and round; red leading blue leading red and white leading green and white leading black – in the space of two seconds – for lap after lap. The tension was unbearable.

Into the final two miles and Laffite made a couple of attempts to get by but, in the end, all four drivers had to give best to a truly remarkable performance from Villeneuve. "It wasn't a race, it was a show," said Reutemann, fourth, but still leading the championship. "We were lapping in the 1m 21s. It was very slow; ridiculous – but there was nothing you could do. One time, Gilles went right across the white line on the edge of the track – all four wheels – but he come back. I don't know how – but he come back. It's a fantastic victory for him – but he know we have no chance."

The first three drivers sat sweating on the podium while waiting for King Juan Carlos to arrive. Villeneuve, drained but bemused, talked to Laffite, the man who had worked so hard all weekend and had to accept second best at the end of a gruelling race. Watson, for his part, was simply delighted to be on the podium for the first time since January 1979. It had been a long wait and was a sign of even better things to come.

Gran Premio de España, June 21/statistics

Entries and practice times

No.	Driver	Nat	Car	Engine	Entrant	Practice 1	Practice 2
1	Alan Jones	AUS	Saudia-Leyland WILLIAMS FW07C	Ford Cosworth DFV	TAG Williams Team	1m 14·424s	**1m 14·024s**
2	Carlos Reutemann	RA	Saudia-Leyland WILLIAMS FW07C	Ford Cosworth DFV	TAG Williams Team	1m 14·808s	**1m 14·342s**
3	Eddie Cheever	USA	TYRRELL 010	Ford Cosworth DFV	Tyrrell Racing	1m 17·459s	**1m 16·641s**
4	Michele Alboreto	I	TYRRELL 010	Ford Cosworth DFV	Tyrrell Racing	1m 18·859s	**1m 17·943s**
5	Nelson Piquet	BR	Parmalat BRABHAM BT49C	Ford Cosworth DFV	Parmalat Racing Team	1m 16·861s	**1m 15·355s**
6	Hector Rebaque	MEX	Parmalat BRABHAM BT49C	Ford Cosworth DFV	Parmalat Racing Team	1m 16·722s	**1m 16·527s**
7	John Watson	GB	Marlboro McLAREN MP4	Ford Cosworth DFV	McLaren International	1m 15·094s	**1m 14·657s**
8	Andrea de Cesaris	I	Marlboro McLAREN MP4	Ford Cosworth DFV	McLaren International	1m 16·119s	**1m 15·850s**
9	Slim Borgudd	S	Abba ATS HGS 1	Ford Cosworth DFV	Team ATS	1m 20·028s	**1m 18·263s**
11	Elio de Angelis	I	John Player Special LOTUS 87	Ford Cosworth DFV	John Player Team Lotus	**1m 15·399s**	1m 15·449s
12	Nigel Mansell	GB	John Player Special LOTUS 87	Ford Cosworth DFV	John Player Team Lotus	1m 16·226s	**1m 15·562s**
14	Eliseo Salazar	RCH	ENSIGN N180B	Ford Cosworth DFV	Ensign Racing	1m 18·769s	**1m 17·822s**
15	Alain Prost	F	Elf RENAULT RE 30	Renault EF1	Equipe Renault Elf	1m 14·980s	**1m 14·669s**
16	René Arnoux	F	Elf RENAULT RE 30	Renault EF1	Equipe Renault Elf	1m 17·132s	**1m 16·406s**
17	Derek Daly	IRL	Rizla MARCH 811	Ford Cosworth DFV	March Grand Prix	1m 17·416s	**1m 16·979s**
20	Keke Rosberg	SF	FITTIPALDI F8C	Ford Cosworth DFV	Fittipaldi Automotive	1m 16·040s	**1m 15·924s**
21	Chico Serra	BR	FITTIPALDI F8C	Ford Cosworth DFV	Fittipaldi Automotive	1m 18·705s	**1m 16·782s**
22	Mario Andretti	USA	Marlboro ALFA ROMEO 179C	Alfa Romeo 1260	Marlboro Team Alfa Romeo	1m 15·576s	**1m 15·159s**
23	Bruno Giacomelli	I	Marlboro ALFA ROMEO 179C	Alfa Romeo 1260	Marlboro Team Alfa Romeo	1m 16·807s	**1m 14·897s**
25	Jean-Pierre Jabouille	F	Talbot-Gitanes LIGIER JS17	Matra MS 81	Equipe Talbot Gitanes	**1m 16·559s**	1m 16·794s
26	Jacques Laffite	F	Talbot-Gitanes LIGIER JS17	Matra MS 81	Equipe Talbot Gitanes	1m 14·822s	**1m 13·754s**
27	Gilles Villeneuve	CDN	Fiat FERRARI 126CK	Ferrari 126C	Scuderia Ferrari SpA SEFAC	1m 16·548s	**1m 14·987s**
28	Didier Pironi	F	Fiat FERRARI 126CK	Ferrari 126C	Scuderia Ferrari SpA SEFAC	1m 16·522s	**1m 15·715s**
29	Riccardo Patrese	I	Ragno-Beta ARROWS A3	Ford Cosworth DFV	Arrows Racing Team	1m 16·038s	**1m 15·627s**
30	Siegfried Stohr	I	Ragno-Beta ARROWS A3	Ford Cosworth DFV	Arrows Racing Team	1m 18·331s	**1m 17·294s**
31	Beppe Gabbiani	I	Denim OSELLA FA1B	Ford Cosworth DFV	Osella Squadra Corse	–	**1m 18·169s**
32	Giorgio Francia	I	Denim OSELLA FA1B	Ford Cosworth DFV	Osella Squadra Corse	**1m 19·586s**	8m 22·382s
33	Patrick Tambay	F	THEODORE TY 01	Ford Cosworth DFV	Theodore Racing Team	1m 17·347s	**1m 16·355s**
35	Brian Henton	GB	Candy TOLEMAN TG 181	Hart 415T	Candy Toleman Motorsport	1m 19·815s	**1m 18·340s**
36	Derek Warwick	GB	Candy TOLEMAN TG 181	Hart 415T	Candy Toleman Motorsport	1m 20·342s	**1m 18·872s**
37	Emileo de Villota	E	WILLIAMS FW07	Ford Cosworth DFV	Equipo Banco Occidental	Entry withdrawn	

Friday morning and Saturday morning practice sessions not officially recorded — *Fri pm Hot, dry* — *Sat pm Hot, dry*

Starting grid

	26 LAFFITE (1m 13·754s) Talbot-Ligier
1 JONES (1m 14·024s) Williams	
	2 REUTEMANN (1m 14·342s) Williams
7 WATSON (1m 14·657s) McLaren	
	15 PROST (1m 14·669s) Renault
23 GIACOMELLI (1m 14·897s) Alfa Romeo	
	27 VILLENEUVE (1m 14·987s) Ferrari
22 ANDRETTI (1m 15·159s) Alfa Romeo	
	5 PIQUET (1m 15·355s) Brabham
11 DE ANGELIS (1m 15·399s) Lotus	
	12 MANSELL (1m 15·562s) Lotus
29 PATRESE (1m 15·627s) Arrows	
	28 PIRONI (1m 15·715s) Ferrari
8 DE CESARIS (1m 15·850s) McLaren	
	20 ROSBERG (1m 15·924s) Fittipaldi
33 TAMBAY (1m 16·355s) Theodore	
	16 ARNOUX (1m 16·406s) Renault
6 REBAQUE (1m 16·527s) Brabham	
	25 JABOUILLE (1m 16·559s) Talbot-Ligier
3 CHEEVER (1m 16·641s) Tyrrell	
	21 SERRA (1m 16·782s) Fittipaldi
17 DALY (1m 16·979s) March	
	30 STOHR (1m 17·294s) Arrows
14 SALAZAR (1m 17·822s) Ensign	

Did not start:
4 Alboreto (Tyrrell), 1m 17·943s, did not qualify
31 Gabbiani (Osella), 1m 18·169s, did not qualify
9 Borgudd (ATS), 1m 18·263s, did not qualify
35 Henton (Toleman), 1m 18·340s, did not qualify
36 Warwick (Toleman), 1m 18·872s, did not qualify
32 Francia (Osella), 1m 19·586s, did not qualify
37 De Villota (Williams), entry withdrawn

Past winners

Year	Driver	Nat	Car	Circuit	Distance miles/km	Speed mph/km/h
1913	Carlos de Salamanca	E	7·4 Rolls-Royce	Guadarrama	191·00/307·38	54·00/ 86·90
1923	Albert Divo	F	2·0 Sunbeam	Sitges-Terramar	248·00/399·12	96·91/155·96
1926	Meo Costantini	I	2·0 Bugatti T35	San Sebastian	420·00/675·92	76·88/123·73
1927	Robert Benoist	F	1·5 Delage s/c	San Sebastian	429·91/691·87	80·52/129·58
1928	Louis Chiron	F	2·0 Bugatti T35C s/c	San Sebastian	161·00/259·10	78·92/127·01
1929	Louis Chiron	F	2·0 Bugatti T35C s/c	San Sebastian	–	72·40/116·52
1930	Achille Varzi	I	2·5 Maserati 8C s/c	San Sebastian	302·23/486·40	86·82/139·72
1933	Louis Chiron	F	2·6 Alfa Romeo P3 s/c	San Sebastian	302·23/486·40	83·32/134·09
1934	Luigi Fagioli	I	3·7 Mercedez-Benz W25 s/c	San Sebastian	302·23/486·40	91·13/146·66
1935	Rudi Caracciola	D	4·0 Mercedez-Benz W25 s/c	San Sebastian	302·23/486·40	101·92/164·02
1951	Juan Manuel Fangio	RA	1·5 Alfa Romeo 159M s/c	Pedralbes	274·72/442·12	98·79/158·99
1954	Mike Hawthorn	GB	2·5 Ferrari 553	Pedralbes	313·97/505·28	97·05/156·19
1967*	Jim Clark	GB	3·0 Lotus 49-Ford	Jarama	126·92/204·26	83·59/134·53
1968	Graham Hill	GB	3·0 Lotus 49-Ford	Jarama	190·38/306·39	84·41/135·84
1969	Jackie Stewart	GB	3·0 Matra MS80-Ford	Montjuich	211·95/341·10	92·91/149·52
1970	Jackie Stewart	GB	3·0 March 701B-Ford	Jarama	190·38/306·39	87·22/140·36
1971	Jackie Stewart	GB	3·0 Tyrrell 003-Ford	Montjuich	176·62/284·24	97·19/156·41
1972	Emerson Fittipaldi	BR	3·0 JPS/Lotus 72-Ford	Jarama	190·38/306·39	92·35/148·63
1973	Emerson Fittipaldi	BR	3·0 JPS/Lotus 72-Ford	Montjuich	176·62/284·24	97·86/157·49
1974	Niki Lauda	A	3·0 Ferrari 312B-3/74	Jarama	177·69/285·96	88·48/142·40
1975	Jochen Mass	D	3·0 McLaren M23-Ford	Montjuich	68·31/109·93	95·54/153·76
1976	James Hunt	GB	3·0 McLaren M23-Ford	Jarama	158·65/255·32	93·01/149·69
1977	Mario Andretti	USA	3·0 JPS/Lotus 78-Ford	Jarama	158·65/255·32	91·79/147·73
1978	Mario Andretti	USA	3·0 JPS/Lotus 79-Ford	Jarama	158·65/255·32	93·52/150·51
1979	Patrick Depailler	F	3·0 Ligier JS11-Ford	Jarama	158·65/255·32	95·97/154·45
1980	Alan Jones	AUS	3·0 Williams FW07B-Ford	Jarama	164·64/264·96	95·69/154·00
1981	Gilles Villeneuve	CDN	1·5 Ferrari 126CK	Jarama	164·64/264·96	92·68/149·16

*Non-championship since 1950

Circuit data

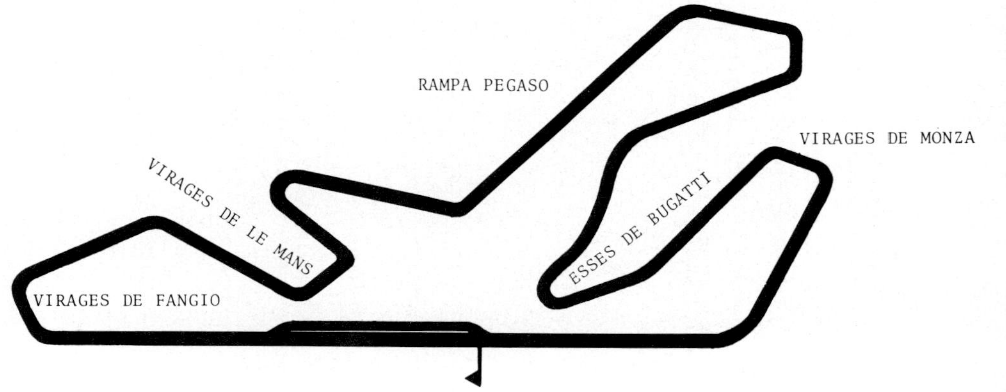

Circuito Permanente del Jarama, near Madrid

Circuit length: 2·058 miles/3·312 km
Race distance: 80 laps, 164·64 miles/264·96 km
Race weather: Hot, dry.

Results and retirements

Place	Driver	Car	Laps	Time and Speed (mph/km/h)/Retirement
1	Gilles Villeneuve	Ferrari t/c V6	80	1h 46m 35·01s 92·682/149·56
2	Jacques Laffite	Talbot-Ligier Matra V12	80	1h 46m 35·23s
3	John Watson	McLaren-Cosworth V8	80	1h 46m 35·59s
4	Carlos Reutemann	Williams-Cosworth V8	80	1h 46m 36·02s
5	Elio de Angelis	Lotus-Cosworth V8	80	1h 46m 36·25s
6	Nigel Mansell	Lotus-Cosworth V8	80	1h 47m 03·59s
7	Alan Jones	Williams-Cosworth V8	80	1h 47m 31·59s
8	Mario Andretti	Alfa Romeo V12	80	1h 47m 35·81s
9	René Arnoux	Renault t/c V6	80	1h 47m 42·09s
10	Bruno Giacomelli	Alfa Romeo V12	80	1h 47m 48·66s
11	Chico Serra	Fittipaldi-Cosworth V8	79	
12	Keke Rosberg	Fittipaldi-Cosworth V8	78	
13	Patrick Tambay	Theodore-Cosworth V8	78	
14	Eliseo Salazar	Ensign-Cosworth V8	77	
15	Didier Pironi	Ferrari t/c V6	76	
16	Derek Daly	March-Cosworth V8	75	
	Eddie Cheever	Tyrrell-Cosworth V8	61	Running, not classified
	Jean-Pierre Jabouille	Talbot-Ligier Matra V12	52	Brakes
	Hector Rebaque	Brabham-Cosworth V8	46	Gearbox
	Nelson Piquet	Brabham-Cosworth V8	43	Accident
	Siegfried Stohr	Arrows-Cosworth V8	43	Engine
	Alain Prost	Renault t/c V6	28	Accident
	Riccardo Patrese	Arrows-Cosworth V8	21	Engine
	Andrea de Cesaris	McLaren-Cosworth V8	9	Accident

Fastest lap: Jones, on lap 5, 1m 17·818s, 95·207mph/153·22km/h.
Lap record: Alan Jones (F1 Williams FWO7B-Cosworth DFV), 1m 15·467s, 98·173mph/157·994km/h (1980).

Lap chart

1st LAP ORDER		1	2	3	4	5	6	7	8	9	10	11	12	13	14	15	16	17	18	19	20	21	22	23	24	25	26	27	28	29	30	31	32	33	34	35	36	37
1	A.Jones	1	1	1	1	1	1	1	1	1	1	1	1	1	27	27	27	27	27	27	27	27	27	27	27	27	27	27	27	27	27	27	27	27	27	27	27	27
2	C.Reutemann	2	27	27	27	27	27	27	27	27	27	27	27	27	2	2	2	2	2	2	2	2	2	2	2	2	2	2	2	2	2	2	2	2	2	2	2	2
27	G.Villeneuve	27	2	2	2	2	2	2	2	2	2	2	2	2	15	15	15	15	15	15	15	15	15	15	15	15	15	15	15	7	7	7	7	7	7	7	7	7
22	M.Andretti	22	22	22	22	22	22	22	22	22	22	22	22	22	22	22	22	22	22	22	22	22	22	22	22	7	7	7	7	26	26	26	26	26	26	26	26	26
15	A.Prost	15	15	15	15	15	15	15	15	15	15	15	15	15	5	5	5	5	5	5	5	5	5	5	5	26	26	26	26	5	5	5	5	5	5	5	5	5
7	J.Watson	7	7	7	7	7	7	7	5	5	5	5	5	5	7	7	7	7	7	7	7	7	7	7	7	5	5	5	5	11	11	11	11	11	11	11	11	11
23	B.Giacomelli	23	5	5	5	5	5	5	7	7	7	7	7	7	26	26	26	26	26	26	26	26	26	26	26	22	22	22	11	22	22	22	12	12	12	12	12	12
5	N.Piquet	5	28	28	28	28	28	28	28	28	28	26	26	26	28	28	28	28	28	28	11	11	11	11	11	11	11	11	22	12	12	12	22	22	22	1	1	1
29	R.Patrese	29	23	23	23	23	23	23	26	26	26	28	28	28	23	23	11	11	11	11	23	23	23	12	12	12	12	12	12	1	1	1	1	1	1	22	22	22
28	D.Pironi	28	29	29	29	29	26	26	23	23	23	23	23	23	11	11	29	29	29	29	12	12	12	23	23	23	23	23	1	23	23	23	23	23	23	23	23	23
26	J.Laffite	26	26	26	26	26	29	11	11	11	11	11	11	11	29	29	23	23	23	23	29	6	6	1	1	1	1	1	23	6	6	6	16	16	16	16	16	16
11	E.de Angelis	11	11	11	11	11	11	29	29	29	29	29	29	29	20	20	12	12	12	12	20	1	1	6	6	6	6	6	6	16	16	16	6	6	6	6	6	6
20	K.Rosberg	20	20	20	20	20	20	20	20	20	20	20	20	20	16	12	20	20	20	20	6	20	16	16	16	16	16	16	16	20	20	20	20	20	20	20	20	20
16	R.Arnoux	16	16	16	16	16	16	16	16	16	16	16	16	16	16	16	16	16	16	6	1	16	20	20	20	20	20	20	20	21	21	21	21	21	21	21	21	21
8	A.de Cesaris	8	8	8	8	8	8	6	6	6	6	12	12	12	6	6	6	6	6	16	16	(29)	21	21	21	21	21	21	21	30	30	30	30	30	30	14	14	14
6	H.Rebaque	6	6	6	6	6	6	8	8	8	12	6	6	6	1	1	1	11	1	1	(28)	21	30	30	30	30	30	30	30	14	14	14	14	14	14	25	25	25
17	D.Daly	17	12	12	12	12	12	12	12	12	3	3	3	25	(25)	30	30	30	30	30	30	30	14	14	14	14	14	14	14	33	25	25	25	25	25	33	33	33
12	N.Mansell	12	3	3	3	3	3	3	3	3	25	25	25	(3)	30	21	21	21	21	21	21	14	33	33	33	33	33	33	33	25	33	33	33	33	33	(30)	17	17
3	E.Cheever	3	25	25	25	25	25	25	25	25	30	30	30	30	21	14	14	14	14	14	14	33	25	25	25	25	25	25	25	17	17	17	17	17	17	17	28	28
25	J-P.Jabouille	25	14	30	30	30	30	30	30	30	21	21	21	21	14	33	33	33	33	33	33	25	17	17	17	17	17	17	17	28	28	28	28	28	28	28	30	30
14	E.Salazar	14	30	14	14	21	21	21	21	21	14	14	14	14	33	25	25	25	25	25	25	17	28	28	28	28	28	28	28	3	3	3	3	3	3	3	3	3
30	S.Stohr	30	21	21	21	14	14	14	14	14	33	33	33	33	17	17	17	17	17	17	17	28	3	3	3	3	3	3	3									
21	C.Serra	21	(17)	17	(17)	33	33	33	33	33	17	17	17	17	3	3	3	3	3	3	3	3																
33	P.Tambay	(33)	33	33	33	17	17	17	17	17																												

38	39	40	41	42	43	44	45	46	47	48	49	50	51	52	53	54	55	56	57	58	59	60	61	62	63	64	65	66	67	68	69	70	71	72	73	74	75	76	77	78	79	80
27	27	27	27	27	27	27	27	27	27	27	27	27	27	27	27	27	27	27	27	27	27	27	27	27	27	27	27	27	27	27	27	27	27	27	27	27	27	27	27	27	27	27
2	2	2	2	2	2	2	2	2	2	2	2	2	2	2	2	2	2	2	2	2	2	2	2	26	26	26	26	26	26	26	26	26	26	26	26	26	26	26	26	26	26	26
7	7	7	7	7	7	7	7	7	7	7	26	26	26	26	26	26	26	26	26	26	26	26	26	7	7	7	7	7	7	7	7	7	7	7	7	7	7	7	7	7	7	7
26	26	26	26	26	26	26	26	26	26	26	7	7	7	7	7	7	7	7	7	7	7	7	7	2	2	2	2	2	2	2	2	2	2	2	2	2	2	2	2	2	2	2
5	5	5	5	5	5	11	11	11	11	11	11	11	11	11	11	11	11	11	11	11	11	11	11	11	11	11	11	11	11	11	11	11	11	11	11	11	11	11	11	11	11	11
11	11	11	11	11	11	12	12	12	12	12	12	12	12	12	12	12	12	12	12	12	12	12	12	12	12	12	12	12	12	12	12	12	12	12	12	12	12	12	12	12	12	12
12	12	12	12	12	12	1	1	1	1	1	1	1	1	1	1	1	1	1	1	1	1	1	1	1	1	1	1	1	1	1	1	1	1	1	1	1	1	1	1	1	1	1
1	1	1	1	1	1	22	22	22	22	22	22	22	22	22	22	22	22	22	22	22	22	22	22	22	22	22	22	22	22	22	22	22	22	22	22	22	22	22	22	22	22	22
22	22	22	22	22	22	16	16	16	16	16	16	16	16	16	16	16	16	16	16	16	16	16	16	16	16	16	16	16	16	16	16	16	16	16	16	16	16	16	16	16	16	16
23	16	16	16	16	16	23	23	23	23	23	23	23	23	23	23	23	23	23	23	23	23	23	23	23	23	23	23	23	23	23	23	23	23	23	23	23	23	23	23	23	23	23
16	23	23	23	23	23	6	20	20	20	20	20	20	20	20	20	20	20	20	20	20	20	20	20	20	20	20	20	20	20	20	20	20	20	20	21	21	21	21	21	21	21	
6	6	6	6	6	6	20	(6)	21	21	21	21	21	21	21	21	21	21	21	21	21	21	21	21	21	21	21	21	21	21	21	21	21	21	21	20	20	20	20	20	20		
20	20	20	20	20	20	21	21	25	(25)	33	33	33	33	33	33	33	33	33	33	33	33	33	33	33	33	33	33	33	33	33	33	33	33	33	33	33	33	33	33	33		
21	21	21	21	21	21	25	25	33	33	14	14	14	14	14	14	14	14	14	14	14	14	14	14	14	14	14	14	14	14	14	14	14	14	14	14	14	14	14	14			
14	25	25	25	25	25	33	33	14	14	17	17	17	17	17	17	17	28	28	28	28	28	28	28	28	28	28	28	28	28	28	28	28	28	28	28	28	28	28				
25	14	14	14	14	33	14	14	(6)	17	28	28	28	28	28	28	28	17	17	17	17	17	17	17	17	17	17	17	17	17	17	17	17	17	17	17	17	17	17				
33	33	33	33	33	14	17	17	17	28	25	25	25	25	(25)	3	3	3	3	3	3	3	3	3																			
17	17	17	17	17	17	28	28	28	3	3	3	3	3	3																												
28	28	28	28	28	28	3	3	3																																		
30	30	30	30	30	(30)																																					
3	3	3	3	3	3																																					

Fastest laps

Driver	Time	Lap
Alan Jones	1m 17·81s	5
Patrick Tambay	1m 18·22s	21
Gilles Villeneuve	1m 18·43s	6
Carlos Reutemann	1m 18·47s	6
Jacques Laffite	1m 18·50s	9
Didier Pironi	1m 18·69s	4
Elio de Angelis	1m 18·72s	65
Alain Prost	1m 18·81s	24
Nelson Piquet	1m 18·92s	5
John Watson	1m 18·95s	48
Nigel Mansell	1m 19·00s	18
Mario Andretti	1m 19·07s	5
Riccardo Patrese	1m 19·39s	9
Jean-Pierre Jabouille	1m 19·43s	25
René Arnoux	1m 19·56s	38
Bruno Giacomelli	1m 19·58s	6
Hector Rebaque	1m 19·76s	17
Andrea de Cesaris	1m 19·95s	9
Keke Rosberg	1m 20·01s	5
Eddie Cheever	1m 20·02s	44
Chico Serra	1m 20·09s	61
Derek Daly	1m 20·11s	8
Siegfried Stohr	1m 20·68s	38
Eliseo Salazar	1m 22·20s	66

Points

WORLD CHAMPIONSHIP OF DRIVERS

1	Carlos Reutemann	37 pts
2	Alan Jones	24
3	Nelson Piquet	22
4	Gilles Villeneuve	21
5	Jacques Laffite	17
6	Riccardo Patrese	10
7	Elio de Angelis	7
8 =	Nigel Mansell	5
8 =	Didier Pironi	5
8 =	Eddie Cheever	5
11 =	Marc Surer	4
11 =	Alain Prost	4
11 =	John Watson	4
14 =	Mario Andretti	3
14 =	Hector Rebaque	3
16	René Arnoux	2
17 =	Patrick Tambay	1
17 =	Andrea de Cesaris	1

CONSTRUCTORS' CUP

1	Williams	61
2	Ferrari	26
3	Brabham	25
4	Ligier	17
5	Lotus	12
6	Arrows	10
7	Renault	6
8 =	McLaren	5
8 =	Tyrrell	5
10	Ensign	4
11	Alfa Romeo	3
12	Theodore	1

Grand Prix de France

The rain had stopped but Nelson Piquet wasn't happy about returning to his car. Neither, for that matter, were Alain Prost and John Watson. The first three drivers to cross the line when the French Grand Prix had been halted by a cloudburst did not want to complete the remaining 22 laps for entirely different reasons: Piquet, because he knew the Renault-Elf team would fit sticky Michelins to Prost's car, turn up the boost and send their man out with the perfect setup for the final sprint; Watson, because he had done so well to hold second place in the Marlboro McLaren. He would have soft Michelins too but now his concentration and rhythm had been broken. And Prost, the man both Piquet and Watson feared? He didn't want to go racing because his Renault had lost fourth gear. The mechanics hadn't time to find the fault during the 45 minute break and the Frenchman could see his well-worked third place sliding away.

On the warm-up lap, however, Prost tried fourth – and it worked. He tried again; it worked perfectly. Never mind why, it simply worked and, from the moment the lights went green, the Frenchman was gone. Running the race as he pleased, Prost kept Watson at bay to score his first Grand Prix win not far from his home at St. Etienne. Watson was delighted to finish second but, alas, poor Piquet. Robbed by freak circumstances and left behind on his Goodyears, the Brazilian managed no better than fifth on the road and third on aggregate.

It was a result which reflected unfairly on Goodyear, back in Grand Prix racing for the first time since their withdrawal at the end of 1980. Servicing Brabham and Williams, Goodyear had revived the tyre war and panicked Michelin into producing softer qualifying tyres. Goodyear, conservative in their choice of rubber, had been beaten during practice but their race tyres on Piquet's Parmalat Brabham had been perfect. Nelson had simply dominated the first 58 laps in spite of worries about a sticking throttle. Then came the rain and the Grand Prix was stopped on lap 59; one more lap and the race would have passed three-quarters distance – the point of no return.

Technically, the race had ended as the leaders crossed the line at the end of lap 58 and, in the event, the partisan crowd got their remaining 22 laps and a popular victory. Completing their day was René Arnoux in fourth place after the Renault had taken a stunning pole position. Didier Pironi was classified fifth but his effervescent team-mate, Gilles Villeneuve, failed to score points on this occasion when his Ferrari stopped with electrical trouble in the first part. Elio de Angelis finished sixth ahead of Nigel Mansell after a spirited dice in part two between the John Player Team Lotus pair.

Carlos Reutemann struggled gamely into fourth place in part one with a blistered front tyre but his chances of scoring points were ruined by a chronic misfire during the final 22 laps. Similarly, Alan Jones, caught out by a chaotic start when the lights failed to function properly, lost time in the pits with a damaged steering tie rod. If circumstances had caught Piquet on the wrong rubber then spare a thought for his team-mate, Hector Rebaque, who drove splendidly during the first 58 laps and sliced through the field only to have his hard work slide away in the second part with a spin. At least he received the Walter Wolf Trophy for 'Fighting Spirit' whereas Piquet could merely stand dejectedly on the rostrum and wonder why another victory had slipped though his fingers for the third race in succession.

ENTRY AND PRACTICE

It was with considerable enthusiasm that the Grand Prix fraternity returned to Dijon-Prenois after a trip the previous year to the bland Paul Ricard facility on the South coast. Dijon held many attractions, not the least of which was a dauntingly quick but chicane-free circuit for the drivers and an abundant supply of well-rounded Beaujolais for the more bibulous members of the press corps.

Renault were particularly keen to return to the scene of their first Grand Prix victory in 1979 on a circuit which suited the characteristics of the turbo. Even the weather played its part during practice by creating overcast and cool conditions which were ideal for the V6 but it was with some alarm that Alain Prost found he could not match the times set during lengthy test sessions three weeks previously. Where the RE 30 had been good on slow and medium speed corners, now it understeered and practice was spent trying to dial the trouble out. Running a single pillar rear wing and extended side-pods, the Renaults were very quick through the plunging downhill right-hander and had plenty of power to push them up the rise and along the pit straight. Some speed traps indicated the yellow and white cars were touching 200mph on the straight – which may have been a trifle optimistic – but, whatever the speed, the Renaults were quick where it mattered most. Prost was third fastest despite a down-on-power engine and poor handling (discovered on Saturday night to have been caused by incorrect springing at the rear) but René Arnoux was in no such trouble and celebrated his 33rd birthday on Saturday by setting a stunning time for pole position. Of course, there were the usual mutterings about 'turned up boost' and 'special tyres' but the fact remained that Arnoux's time was one second under Jabouille's pole in 1979.

Two years before that, John Watson had dominated the race and here he was, back on the front row once more. John was to be found in the Marlboro motor home after practice – but not for a debrief. There, the Ulsterman crouched on the floor, backed by a gallery of tennis freaks to watch the Borg v McEnroe final at Wimbledon. At least it took Wattie's mind off practice – and his disapointment at not taking pole. Make no mistake, this was not a swaggering boast from Watson. He genuinely believed he could do it; that was the measure of the McLaren's superiority and its driver's soaring confidence. Having set fastest time on Friday, Watson said the MP4 felt superb through the fast corners – and that's where it counted most. The slow corners still weren't right but Watson's impressively steady line and a constant engine note through *Courbe de Pouas* and onto the straight left no doubt about the quality of the car. Even Andrea de Cesaris seemed able to do remarkable deeds with his MP4, the Italian appearing on a variety of lines, soon corrected by a deft flick of the wheel and a forgiving chassis with bags of downforce and grip. His time was all the more commendable when it was considered he was forced to use Watson's discarded qualifiers.

McLaren, like Renault, were running on soft Michelins but the return of Goodyear meant Williams and Brabham had to rethink and adapt. As a result, both Carlos Reutemann and Alan Jones were unable to tackle the fast corners with the same aplomb, their softest 'D' Goodyears being rock hard compared to the French rubber. It was clear that a tyre war was imminent as Michelin supplied their contracted teams (Renault, Ferrari, Talbot-Ligier and Alfa Romeo) plus McLaren and, for this race, Lotus, with one set each of special practice rubber. As for the rest, they could purchase hard Michelin tyres – a state of affairs which did not please Arrows for example, the pole-sitter at Long Beach qualifying 18th while Siegfried Stohr failed to make the race. Avon supplied March, Ensign and Theodore.

"Give us a kiss and I'll let you win". René Arnoux (left) celebrated his 33rd birthday with pole position but it was Alain Prost who won the next day *(below)*.
Alain Prost races to his first Grand Prix victory under the menacing clouds which played a major part in the race *(right)*.
Alas, poor Piquet. The expression on Nelson's face says it all *(inset, right)*.

So, it was hardly surprising when the Renaults, split by Watson, occupied the front of the grid but perhaps the most significant performance came from Nelson Piquet who set fourth fastest time on what amounted to race rubber. That was a superb effort by both Nelson and Gordon Murray who carefully adapted the BT49C to suit the crossplies. After recording more laps than anyone else during practice, Piquet remarked that the Goodyears were more forgiving on the limit and the team were confident of a good showing in the race. Williams were not so happy, Jones and Reutemann reporting the FW07Cs to be unpredictable due possibly to excessive skirt wear among other things. Jones spent more time in his T-car and opted to run it in the race while Reutemann persevered in the hope that a consistent drive would earn valuable points in the race.

Ahead of Reutemann on the grid was Jacques Laffite, his Talbot-Ligier not handling as well as he would have liked on the fast corners – a fact

JUNE:
FISA declare Lotus 88B illegal.
Las Vegas Grand Prix confirmed for October.
FISA fines drivers involved in Belgian Grand Prix start line protest.
Patrick Tambay chosen to replace Jabouille at Talbot-Ligier; Marc Surer to drive Theodore.
Final approval given to the construction of a new 2·8-mile circuit at the Nürburgring.

elf
15
RENAULT
MICHELIN
Marlboro

underlined by Patrick Tambay, the man who replaced Jean-Pierre Jabouille much to the annoyance of Jean-Pierre Jarier who felt he had merited the drive. Resplendent in his sparkling Gitanes overalls, Tambay looked extremely happy with his new role and acute understeer scarcely seemed to bother the amiable Frenchman as he flung the JS17 into lurid drifts through *Courbe de Pouas*.

Nigel Mansell had begun to familiarise himself with Dijon-Prenois the day before practice by walking and then cycling round the track. Mansell then expressed his approval by setting the quickest time on a damp track on Friday morning. Once conditions were back to normal, however, the Lotus 87 continued to display its tendency to understeer in the dry and Mansell's problems were not helped by a fire breaking out when a fuel line worked loose. Pulling up at a marshals' post, the man with the extinguisher doused the 87 from stem to stern and Mansell lost 20 minutes of timed practice while the mess was cleaned up. Elio de Angelis was also out of action while waiting for an engine change on Saturday and the Italian eventually managed to split Reutemann and Jones.

Mansell took 12th spot behind Bruno Giacomelli with Mario Andretti parking his similar 1980 model Marlboro Alfa Romeo on the fifth row ahead of Gilles Villeneuve. Quite how the Ferrari driver managed his time was a mystery to one and all. The 126CK was a handful – even on the straights where fearful porpoising made Villeneuve feel the car was about to flip any minute. Through *Courbe de Pouas* though, the French Canadian achieved his speed by sheer bravado and astonishing reflexes; nothing more. On one occasion the tail flicked out of line, Villeneuve cranking on opposite lock and keeping his right foot firmly on the power. The car, teetering on the edge of disaster, continued in this manner for over 100 yards before straightening out and the driver's efforts were all the more remarkable in the light of an accident at the same spot earlier in the day. The same thing happened – but the car did not respond and Villeneuve ploughed into the waiting catch-fencing. Writing off the two left-hand corners, Villeneuve calmly returned to the pits with no more than a blood blister on his cheek to show for a moment which would have subsequently required a long lie in a shaded room for we mortals.

Pironi, three-tenths slower than Mansell, set his time on Friday during a weekend fraught with electrical problems and a broken turbo. Hector Rebaque, hampered by an oil leak on his clutch, was next followed by Tambay and Keke Rosberg. The Finn only managed 11 laps on Saturday afternoon after popping in and out of the pits with a broken fuel pump and hydraulic ride height problems. His time was a fine effort considering the financial problems inflicted on the team which still lacked a major sponsor. Chico Serra added to the bills by blowing an engine on Saturday afternoon but the Brazilian got down to business in the spare car and eased into the race during the closing minutes of practice.

In fact, Serra's heroic efforts knocked Siegfried Stohr into the non-qualifiers' section, a move which did not help the mood of the Ragno-Beta Arrows team. Left to struggle with 'wooden' Michelins, Riccardo Patrese was unable to make any headway with Dave Wass's new rear suspension and slim-line gearbox casing. If anything, the suspension, designed to improve air flow, worked too well and Patrese was left to sort out vicious understeer. Eddie Cheever was next, running what he hoped would be his last race in the 010 Tyrrell and the American just beat Derek Daly into 20th place, the Irishman expressing himself reasonably satisfied with the Avons mounted on his Guinness Rizla March. Adrian Reynard and Gordon Coppuck had adapted the March reasonably well to the switch from Michelin radials to Avon crossplies but Theodore were not so well off. The wider Avons induced massive oversteer and required a completely different set-up which was not settled until race morning. Marc Surer, Tambay's replacement, lost time when his car failed the ludicrous 6cm test on Friday but he qualified ahead of his previous employers, Ensign. Salazar, feeling more at home, was in 22nd place ahead of Michele Alboreto in the 2nd Tyrrell and, of course, Serra's Fittipaldi.

With eight minutes of practice remaining, Brian Henton and the Candy Toleman team looked as though they would have a race at last. The continuing development had been such that Henton failed by four-hundredths of a second after a typical two days loaded with problems. Henton's first complaint was one of his own making after eating suspect food on Thursday night. He was back to his usual chirpy self on Saturday but poor Derek Warwick looked less than pleased with himself after crunching his own car during the slowing down lap at the end of the morning session. The car was not repaired in time and the Englishman was stuck at the bottom of the time sheet

John Watson drove superbly, starting from the front row in the McLaren MP4 and challenging Prost throughout.

Key to their success. Renault mechanics dry the sticky Michelins on Prost's car prior to the restart.

THE RULES STATED THAT IF A RACE WAS STOPPED after two laps, but before three-quarters distance, then the event would be run in two parts, the result being decided on aggregate times. Consequently, when the French Grand Prix was stopped during lap 59 – just before three-quarters distance – spectators were left with a confusing mathematical equation as the drivers raced the final 22 laps.

Occasionally, circumstances dictate that a race must be stopped and, obviously, there has to be legislation of some kind. Whether the French Grand Prix should have been stopped is open to question however.

The downpour was indeed sudden and violent but the tricky situation was exacerbated by drivers remaining on slicks – fearful that the race might be stopped while they were changing tyres in the pits. It was indicative of an increasing tendency by race organisers to stop races at the slightest excuse – the Belgian Grand Prix being a prime example. Drivers had come to expect the race to be stopped as a matter of course and the few laps run on slicks presented appalling dangers which, it was felt, could have been overcome by means other than the use of the red flag.

When the cars did stop, the outcome of the race was changed entirely by the use of soft Michelins by Renault and McLaren for the remaining 22 laps – an entirely legal but unsatisfactory state of affairs which could have been solved by the use of a parc ferme.

Nelson Piquet walked away with the first 58 laps but could do no better than take fifth place on 'hard' tyres behind Didier Pironi at the restart *(right)*.
Hector Rebaque tangles with Pironi during an otherwise impressive race for the Brabham driver *(below)*.

behind Beppe Gabbiani (the sole Denim Osella representative) and Slim Borgudd in the ATS.

RACE

After the variables thrown up by the Michelin qualifiers during practice, it was all eyes to the lap times during the warm-up on Sunday morning. Reutemann, Piquet and Jones were the quickest and Goodyear were to the fore where it mattered most; Michelin and Renault, one second off the pace, were struggling to find a decent race tyre. An interesting race was in prospect although the field was reduced by one when Serra shunted his Fittipaldi and the spare was not considered race-worthy.

The start was reduced to a free-for-all. The lights had gone from red to green but an electrical fault flicked them back to red and, finally, to green once more. Arnoux was about to go when he saw the second red – and hesitated. Other drivers did the same but Prost and Piquet put the hammer down at the first hint of green. Cars went every whichway. The Brabham led the charge into the first corner with Prost, mindful of his previous first lap experiences, giving way to Watson. De Cesaris was next, battling it out with Laffite, the Ligier driver backing off and allowing Villeneuve to make the most of another demon start and charge down the inside. Reutemann was next followed by Andretti and a furious Arnoux, the pole position man running ahead of Pironi who had careered through from the middle of the grid.

With the first corner offering plenty of run-off area and the best opportunity for overtaking, the scenes at the end of the straight during the opening laps were hectic to say the least. Prost took Watson on lap two, Villeneuve moved ahead of de Cesaris (a brave move, that) while Arnoux dealt with Andretti, Laffite and de Cesaris on successive laps. By lap eight he had passed Villeneuve and the field began to settle down. Missing were Salazar (out on lap 6 with a broken rear rocker arm) and Jones, who was in the pits for a replacement steering tie-rod. The Williams driver had been held up badly at the start and somewhere along the way he damaged the steering after hitting Andretti, the result being a lengthy pit stop at the end of lap 3. Jones was to return to the pits later for front tyres and another quick stop, when he thought the wheels were loose, ensured that the reigning World Champion was well and truly out of the reckoning.

Reutemann, on the other hand, moved through to fourth place by lap six, leaving Villeneuve to fend off de Cesaris and Laffite. By lap 10, Piquet appeared to be in command although the Brabham driver had been driving with his hand poised over the 'kill switch' ever since his throttle cable began to stick at an early stage. Prost was in trouble, too, the Frenchman unable to select fourth gear while Watson was busy keeping an eye on Reutemann – who, in turn, was anxiously watching a growing blister on his left front tyre! Further back, Daly, struggling with understeer after hitting the nose of his March against Rebaque's Brabham at the start, was leading Cheever and Alboreto before calling at the pits when the throttle stuck open.

Piquet was about to lap Rosberg when the Fittipaldi retired with rear wheel steering thanks to a broken bolt in a rear crossmember but, by lap 20, the leaders had begun to hit the thick of the back markers. Choosing their moments carefully in relation to their various mechanical problems, Piquet and Prost worked their way through but, by lap 40, trouble was in store as Nelson came across a frantic battle for sixth place.

Villeneuve, desperately fighting his Ferrari, was leading Rebaque (who had moved through from 15th place in an exceptionally aggressive manner), Laffite, de Angelis and de Cesaris, the Lotus driver having slipped past the McLaren on lap 37. In the middle of this mob was Jones, running some three laps behind. Piquet began his daunting task by taking de Cesaris on lap 42 and, at that moment, Villeneuve relieved the situation somewhat by parking his Ferrari with a dead engine and joining Dave Wass as a spectator at the first corner. Wass was appalled by the handling of the Arrows as Patrese struggled to keep ahead of Cheever. By contrast, the Theodore was one of the most impressive through the long right-hander at the end of the straight, Surer putting the power down early and running round the outside of Giacomelli with ease although the Swiss driver's progress was limited by the loss of second gear.

Piquet was past his team-mate by lap 49 but Jones stuck rigidly to Nelson's tail. Prost, still struggling without fourth gear, was not having an easy passage in second place and Watson began to close on the Renault. Reutemann, now nursing his tyre and provoking oversteer, had dropped back towards Arnoux and an exciting few laps were in store when rain began to fall and de Cesaris dived into the pits to have a wheel nut tightened. The track became slippery in parts and Jones rode Piquet even harder as the Brazilian waited to see whether the race would be stopped. Suddenly, on lap 59, there was no question about it as the heavens opened. The red flag was shown, the race was stopped and sodden drivers returned to the pits to see what would happen next.

The dark clouds disappeared as quickly as they had arrived and it was announced that the final 22 laps

would be run, the drivers restarting in the order they had crossed the line at the end of lap 58. The activity in the pits was frantic. Damp drivers paced around as the adrenalin continued to flow, some walking to the pit wall and inspecting the rapidly drying track. There was no question that slicks would be the order of the day and Michelin, weighing up the odds, rolled out qualifying tyres, not necessarily the softest, but ones suitable for the short sprint. Prost's mechanics, meanwhile, had taken apart the gearbox but with the start just 20 minutes away, there was no time for remedial action and a gloomy Prost did not relish the thought of losing his hard-worked second place. Watson was annoyed about losing his rhythm and concentration while Piquet, having worked so hard, knew Goodyear had no answer to the soft Michelins.

The lights worked perfectly as the 19 cars left the grid, Prost barrelling into the first corner ahead of Watson – just. The Ulsterman, really fired up now, actually took the lead – just. Running wide on a damp patch, John slid onto a kerb and Prost was back in charge. The Renault had finished 'part one' 6·79 seconds behind Piquet but it was immediately apparent that the Brabham was no match under the conditions as Nelson held fourth place before slipping behind Pironi. Laffite was an immediate retirement with damaged front suspension after banging wheels with Reutemann and the Williams began to drop back dramatically with a violent misfire similar to Jones's problem at Monaco. Prost began to edge away from the hard-charging Watson; Arnoux held a lonely third place while Pironi kept a frustrated Piquet in fifth place and out of the hunt. De Cesaris was next after the most amazing piece of overtaking at the end of lap 55. Struggling along with violent understeer in eighth place came Bruno Giacomelli and the Alfa Romeo driver ran wide at the first corner causing the closely following Andretti to lift off and take a tighter line on the inside. Through the *middle*, however, came de Cesaris, flat out and bouncing off Andretti's car as he avoided Giacomelli. The Italian eventually got ahead of the startled Andretti while de Angelis and Mansell fought tooth and nail for ninth place on the road. De Angelis was not prepared to give an inch after a dispute over the allocation of the single set of soft Michelins made available to Lotus. Chapman had split the set between his two drivers and answered de Angelis's assertion that he, the number one, should have all four tyres by saying that number one drivers should turn up for the test sessions when asked – a blunt reference to the Italian's absence from a recent session at Silverstone.

Rebaque had spun his Brabham during a moment of over-enthusiasm on the opening lap and was struggling to keep ahead of a busy battle between Cheever and Surer. In many cases, however, the final few laps were purely academic. At the front, though, it was clear that Prost was going to win his first Grand Prix and the Frenchman crossed the line over two seconds ahead of Watson – and 22 seconds ahead of Piquet in fifth place.

On the rostrum, Prost and Watson, former team-mates who had seen hard times in 1980, congratulated one another while a doleful Piquet peered out from under his Goodyear cap and thought about a certain nine points – given two more laps.

Marc Surer replaced Tambay in the Theodore and gave another superb performance.

Patrick Tambay, resplendent in his new overalls, tries out the Talbot-Ligier cockpit.

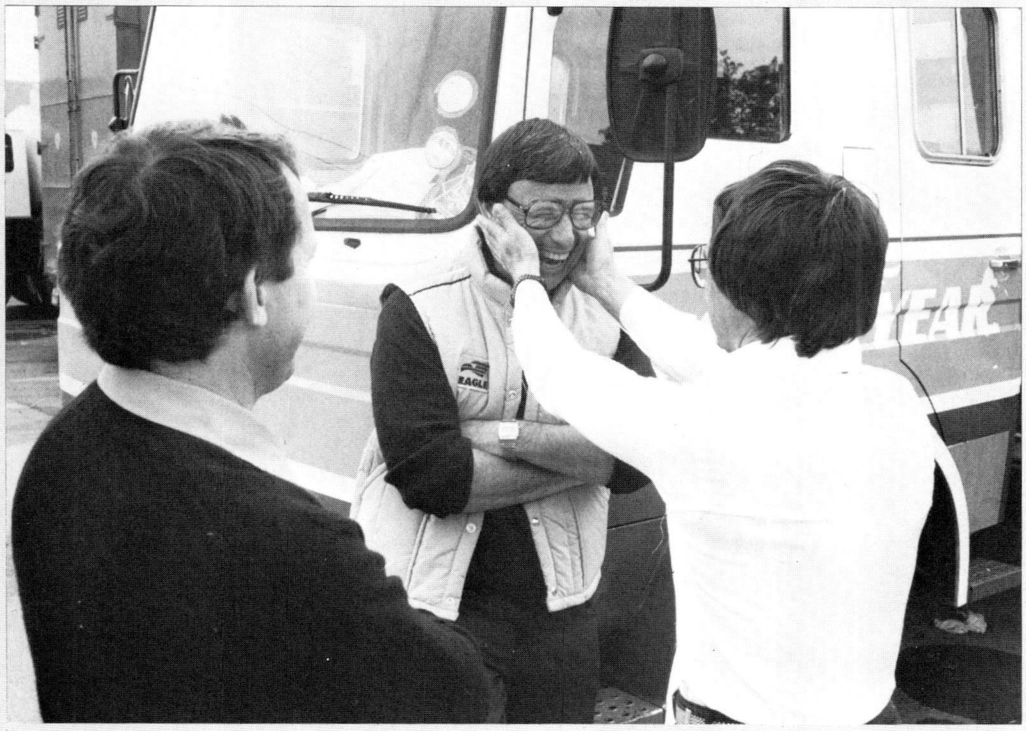

"Good to have you back". Bernie Ecclestone jokes with Leo Mehl of Goodyear. Jackie Oliver, forced to run his Arrows on hard Michelins, was not so amused.

IT WAS IRONIC THAT GOODYEAR SHOULD RETURN TO Formula 1 at Dijon, the circuit where they were beaten soundly by Michelin during their last confrontation there in 1979. The decision to return was made a matter of weeks before the French Grand Prix and gave the American company just enough time to collect the tyres used during test sessions at Paul Ricard in November 1980 and ship them back to France.

"It literally was a last minute decision", said Leo Mehl, Director of Racing for Goodyear. "We haven't done a thing since the Ricard test and now we are out of touch with ground effects without skirts. We have only had a brief test session at Silverstone to help us".

Goodyear, supplying Brabham and Williams, chose conservatively and their compounds, although perfect for the race, were no match to the soft practice rubber produced by Michelin.

The results at Dijon, showing Michelin first and second, did not do Goodyear justice in an event ruled by freak circumstances and Michelin qualifiers during the final 22 laps. The regrettable practice of using qualifying tyres, banned in 1980, had returned although Goodyear were adamant that they wished to avoid qualifiers if at all possible.

MICHELIN
FACOM
de Carbon
15
europcar
REN

PROST
LONGINES
ULT elf
FERODO
RENAULT
elf
elf

Grand Prix de France, July 5/statistics

Entries and practice times

No.	Driver	Nat	Car	Engine	Entrant	Practice 1	Practice 2
1	Alan Jones	AUS	Saudia-Leyland WILLIAMS FWO7C	Ford Cosworth DFV	TAG Williams Team	1m 09·28s	**1m 07·53s**
2	Carlos Reutemann	RA	Saudia-Leyland WILLIAMS FWO7C	Ford Cosworth DFV	TAG Williams Team	1m 08·83s	**1m 07·42s**
3	Eddie Cheever	USA	TYRRELL 010	Ford Cosworth DFV	Tyrrell Racing	1m 11·50s	**1m 09·88s**
4	Michele Alboreto	I	TYRRELL 010	Ford Cosworth DFV	Tyrrell Racing	1m 12·37s	**1m 10·64s**
5	Nelson Piquet	BR	Parmalat BRABHAM BT49C	Ford Cosworth DFV	Parmalat Racing Team	1m 09·21s	**1m 06·91s**
6	Hector Rebaque	MEX	Parmalat BRABHAM BT49C	Ford Cosworth DFV	Parmalat Racing Team	1m 09·69s	**1m 08·21s**
7	John Watson	GB	Marlboro McLAREN MP4	Ford Cosworth DFV	McLaren International	1m 07·05s	**1m 06·36s**
8	Andrea de Cesaris	I	Marlboro McLAREN MP4	Ford Cosworth DFV	McLaren International	1m 08·83s	**1m 07·03s**
9	Slim Borgudd	S	Abba ATS HGS 1	Ford Cosworth DFV	Team ATS	1m 14·62s	**1m 12·20s**
11	Elio de Angelis	I	John Player Special LOTUS 87	Ford Cosworth DFV	John Player Team Lotus	1m 08·40s	**1m 07·52s**
12	Nigel Mansell	GB	John Player Special LOTUS 87	Ford Cosworth DFV	John Player Team Lotus	1m 09·06s	**1m 07·72s**
14	Eliseo Salazar	RCH	ENSIGN N180B	Ford Cosworth DFV	Ensign Racing	1m 15·59s	**1m 10·50s**
15	Alain Prost	F	Elf RENAULT RE 30	Renault EF1	Equipe Renault Elf	1m 07·57s	**1m 06·36s**
16	René Arnoux	F	Elf RENAULT RE 30	Renault EF1	Equipe Renault Elf	1m 07·09s	**1m 05·95s**
17	Derek Daly	IRL	Rizla MARCH 811	Ford Cosworth DFV	March Grand Prix	1m 12·10s	**1m 09·94s**
20	Keke Rosberg	SF	FITTIPALDI F8C	Ford Cosworth DFV	Fittipaldi Automotive	1m 10·13s	**1m 09·35s**
21	Chico Serra	BR	FITTIPALDI F8C	Ford Cosworth DFV	Fittipaldi Automotive	1m 13·60s	**1m 10·86s**
22	Mario Andretti	USA	Marlboro ALFA ROMEO 179B	Alfa Romeo 1260	Marlboro Team Alfa Romeo	1m 10·09s	**1m 07·56s**
23	Bruno Giacomelli	I	Marlboro ALFA ROMEO 179B	Alfa Romeo 1260	Marlboro Team Alfa Romeo	1m 09·81s	**1m 07·63s**
25	Patrick Tambay	F	Talbot-Gitanes LIGIER JS17	Matra MS 81	Equipe Talbot Gitanes	1m 09·51s	**1m 08·47s**
26	Jacques Laffite	F	Talbot-Gitanes LIGIER JS17	Matra MS 81	Equipe Talbot Gitanes	1m 08·71s	**1m 07·09s**
27	Gilles Villeneuve	CDN	Fiat FERRARI 126CK	Ferrari 126C	Scuderia Ferrari SpA SEFAC	**1m 07·60s**	1m 07·68s
28	Didier Pironi	F	Fiat FERRARI 126CK	Ferrari 126C	Scuderia Ferrari SpA SEFAC	**1m 08·09s**	1m 08·27s
29	Riccardo Patrese	I	Ragno-Beta ARROWS A3	Ford Cosworth DFV	Arrows Racing Team	**1m 09·37s**	1m 10·14s
30	Siegfried Stohr	I	Ragno-Beta ARROWS A3	Ford Cosworth DFV	Arrows Racing Team	1m 13·13s	**1m 11·24s**
31	Beppe Gabbiani	I	Denim OSELLA FA1B	Ford Cosworth DFV	Osella Squadra Corse	**1m 12·24s**	1m 36·20s
33	Marc Surer	CH	THEODORE TY 01	Ford Cosworth DFV	Theodore Racing Team	1m 19·46s	**1m 10·21s**
35	Brian Henton	GB	Candy TOLEMAN TG 181	Hart 415T	Candy Toleman Motorsport	1m 29·13s	**1m 11·28s**
36	Derek Warwick	GB	Candy TOLEMAN TG 181	Hart 415T	Candy Toleman Motorsport	**1m 13·65s**	–

Thursday morning and Friday morning practice sessions not officially recorded

	Thur pm	*Fri pm*
	Cool, dry then wet	*Cool, dry*

Starting grid

7 WATSON (1m 06·36s) McLaren	16 ARNOUX (1m 05·95s) Renault
5 PIQUET (1m 06·91s) Brabham	15 PROST (1m 06·36s) Renault
26 LAFFITE (1m 07·09s) Talbot-Ligier	8 DE CESARIS (1m 07·03s) McLaren
11 DE ANGELIS (1m 07·52s) Lotus	2 REUTEMANN (1m 07·42s) Williams
22 ANDRETTI (1m 07·56s) Alfa Romeo	1 JONES (1m 07·53s) Williams
23 GIACOMELLI (1m 07·63s) Alfa Romeo	27 VILLENEUVE (1m 07·60s) Ferrari
28 PIRONI (1m 08·09s) Ferrari	12 MANSELL (1m 07·72s) Lotus
25 TAMBAY (1m 08·47s) Talbot-Ligier	6 REBAQUE (1m 08·21s) Brabham
29 PATRESE (1m 09·37s) Arrows	20 ROSBERG (1m 09·35s) Fittipaldi
17 DALY (1m 09·94s) Tyrrell	3 CHEEVER (1m 09·88s) Tyrrell
14 SALAZAR (1m 10·50s) Ensign	33 SURER (1m 10·21s) Theodore
*21 SERRA (1m 10·86s) Fittipaldi	4 ALBORETO (1m 10·64s) Tyrrell

Did not start:
30 Stohr (Arrows), 1m 11·24s, did not qualify
35 Henton (Toleman), 1m 11·28s, did not qualify
9 Borgudd (ATS), 1m 12·20s, did not qualify
31 Gabbiani (Osella), 1m 12·24s, did not qualify
36 Warwick (Toleman), 1m 13·65s, did not qualify
*21 Serra (Fittipaldi), 1m 10·86s, crashed during warm-up.

Previous pages:
Double top. Alain Prost scored his first Grand Prix victory and the first of the season for the Renault-Elf team after a well-judged performance at Dijon.
Photos: David Winter and Agence Vandystadt

Past winners

Year	Driver	Nat	Car	Circuit	Distance miles/km	Speed mph/km/h
1906	Frenc Szisz	H	13·0 Renault	Circuit de la Sarthe	769·35/1238·16	62·88/101·20
1907	Felice Nazzaro	I	15·3 Fiat	Circuit de la Seine-Inférieure	478·38/ 769·88	70·61/113·64
1908	Christian Lautenschlager	D	12·8 Mercedes	Circuit de la Seine-Inférieure	478·38/ 769·88	69·05/111·13
1912	Georges Boillot	F	7·6 Peugeot	Circuit de la Seine-Inférieure	956·76/1539·76	68·51/110·26
1913	Georges Boillot	F	5·7 Peugeot	Circuit de Picardie	569·80/ 917·01	72·12/116·06
1914	Christian Lautenschlager	D	4·5 Mercedes	Circuit de Lyon	467·66/ 752·62	65·56/105·52
1921	Jimmy Murphy	USA	3·0 Duesenberg	Circuit de la Sarthe	321·78/ 517·86	78·11/125·70
1922	Felice Nazzaro	I	2·0 Fiat 804	Strasbourg	498·84/ 802·80	79·33/127·67
1923	Henry Segrave	GB	2·0 Sunbeam	Tours	496·51/ 799·05	75·36/121·27
1924	Giuseppe Campari	I	2·0 Alfa Romeo P2 s/c	Circuit de Lyon	503·36/ 810·08	70·97/114·21
1925	Robert Benoist/ Albert Divo	F F	2·0 Delage s/c	Montlhéry	621·37/1000·00	69·73/112·21
1926	Jules Goux	F	1·5 Bugatti T39A s/c	Miramas	310·69/ 500·00	68·16/109·69
1927	Robert Benoist	F	1·5 Delage s/c	Montlhéry	382·82/ 600·00	78·30/126·01
1928	"Williams"	GB	2·3 Bugatti T35C s/c	Comminges	163·42/ 263·00	66·39/106·85
1929	"Williams"	GB	2·3 Bugatti T35B s/c	Circuit de la Sarthe	376·13/ 605·32	82·66/133·03
1930	Phillippe Etancelin	F	2·3 Bugatti T35B s/c	Pau	245·99/ 395·88	90·37/145·45
1931	Louis Chiron/ Achille Varzi	F I	2·3 Bugatti T51 s/c	Montlhéry	782·20/1258·83	78·22/125·88
1932	Tazio Nuvolari	I	2·7 Alfa Romeo P3 s/c	Reims-Gueux	461·58/ 742·84	92·32/148·57
1933	Giuseppe Campari	I	3·0 Maserati 8C s/c	Montlhéry	310·69/ 500·00	81·49/131·14
1934	Louis Chiron	F	2·9 Alfa Romeo P3 s/c	Montlhéry	310·69/ 500·00	85·05/136·88
1935	Rudi Caracciola	D	4·0 Mercedes-Benz W25 s/c	Montlhéry	310·69/ 500·00	77·40/124·57
1936	Jean-Pierre Wimille/ Raymond Sommer	F F	3·3 Bugatti T35S	Montlhéry	621·37/1000·00	77·85/125·29
1937	Louis Chiron	F	4·0 Talbot	Montlhéry	310·69/ 500·00	82·47/132·73
1938	Manfred von Brauchitsch	D	3·0 Mercedes-Benz W154 s/c	Reims-Gueux	310·78/ 500·16	101·13/162·76
1939	Hermann Müller	D	3·0 Auto Union D-type s/c	Reims-Gueux	247·66/ 398·57	105·25/169·38
1947	Louis Chiron	F	4·5 Lago-Talbot	Lyon-Parilly	317·09/ 510·30	78·08/125·66
1948	Jean-Pierre Wimille	F	1·5 Alfa Romeo 158 s/c	Reims-Gueux	310·81/ 500·20	102·96/165·70
1949	Charles Pozzi	F	2·5 Delahaye	Comminges	314·41/ 506·00	88·14/141·84
1950	Juan Manuel Fangio	RA	1·5 Alfa Romeo 158 s/c	Reims-Gueux	310·81/ 500·20	104·84/168·72
1951	Luigi Fagioli/ Juan Manuel Fangio	I RA	1·5 Alfa Romeo 159 s/c	Reims-Gueux	373·94/ 601·80	110·97/178·59
1952	Alberto Ascari	I	2·0 Ferrari 500	Rouen-les-Essarts	240·39/ 386·88	80·13/128·96
1953	Mike Hawthorn	GB	2·0 Ferrari 500	Reims	314·56/ 506·23	113·64/182·89
1954	Juan Manuel Fangio	RA	2·5 Mercedes-Benz W196	Reims	314·64/ 506·36	115·97/186·64
1956	Peter Collins	GB	2·5 Lancia-Ferrari D50	Reims	314·64/ 506·36	122·29/196·80
1957	Juan Manuel Fangio	RA	2·5 Maserati 250F	Rouen-les-Essarts	313·01/ 503·74	100·02/160·96
1958	Mike Hawthorn	GB	2·4 Ferrari Dino 246	Reims	257·90/ 415·05	125·45/201·90
1959	Tony Brooks	GB	2·4 Ferrari Dino 246	Reims	257·90/ 415·05	127·43/205·08
1960	Jack Brabham	AUS	2·5 Cooper T53-Climax	Reims	257·90/ 415·05	131·80/212·11
1961	Giancarlo Baghetti	I	1·5 Ferrari Dino 156	Reims	268·22/ 431·66	119·85/192·87
1962	Dan Gurney	USA	1·5 Porsche 804	Rouen-les-Essarts	219·51/ 353·27	101·84/163·89
1963	Jim Clark	GB	1·5 Lotus 25-Climax	Reims	273·37/ 439·95	125·31/201·67
1964	Dan Gurney	USA	1·5 Brabham BT7-Climax	Rouen-les-Essarts	231·71/ 372·90	108·77/175·04
1965	Jim Clark	GB	1·5 Lotus 25-Climax	Clermont-Ferrand	200·21/ 322·21	89·22/143·58
1966	Jack Brabham	AUS	3·0 Brabham BT19-Repco	Reims	247·58/ 398·44	136·90/220·32
1967	Jack Brabham	AUS	3·0 Brabham BT24-Repco	Bugatti au Mans	219·82/ 353·77	98·90/159·16
1968	Jacky Ickx	B	3·0 Ferrari 312/66	Rouen-les-Essarts	243·90/ 392·52	100·45/161·66
1969	Jackie Stewart	GB	2·0 Matra MS80-Ford	Clermont-Ferrand	190·20/ 306·10	97·71/157·25
1970	Jochen Rindt	A	3·0 Lotus 72-Ford	Clermont-Ferrand	190·20/ 306·10	98·42/158·39
1971	Jackie Stewart	GB	3·0 Tyrrell 003-Ford	Paul Ricard	198·56/ 319·55	111·66/179·70
1972	Jackie Stewart	GB	3·0 Tyrrell 003-Ford	Clermont-Ferrand	190·20/ 306·10	101·56/163·44
1973	Ronnie Peterson	S	3·0 JPS/Lotus 72-Ford	Paul Ricard	194·95/ 313·74	115·12/185·26
1974	Ronnie Peterson	S	3·0 JPS/Lotus 72-Ford	Dijon-Prenois	163·49/ 263·11	119·75/192·72
1975	Niki Lauda	A	3·0 Ferrari 312T/75	Paul Ricard	194·95/ 313·74	116·60/187·65
1976	James Hunt	GB	3·0 McLaren M23-Ford	Paul Ricard	194·95/ 313·74	115·84/186·42
1977	Mario Andretti	USA	3·0 JPS/Lotus 78-Ford	Dijon-Prenois	188·90/ 304·00	113·72/183·01
1978	Mario Andretti	USA	3·0 JPS/Lotus 79-Ford	Paul Ricard	194·95/ 313·74	118·31/190·40
1979	Jean-Pierre Jabouille	F	1·5 Renault RS t/c	Dijon-Prenois	188·88/ 304·00	118·88/191·32
1980	Alan Jones	AUS	3·0 Williams FW07B-Ford	Paul Ricard	194·95/ 313·74	126·15/203·02
1981	Alain Prost	F	1·5 Renault RE t/c	Dijon-Prenois	188·88/ 304·00	118·30/190·39

Note Grand Prix de l'Automobile Club de France results 1906-1967

Circuit data

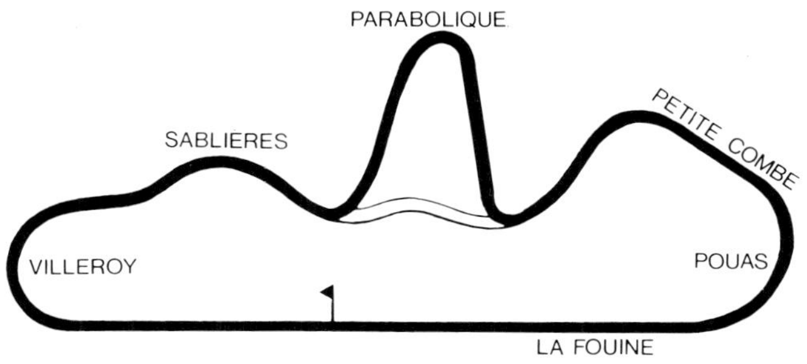

Circuit de Dijon-Prenois, near Dijon

Circuit length: 2·361 miles/3·800 km
Race distance: 80 laps, 188·88 miles/304·00 km
Race weather: Cool dry. Race stopped during cloudburst; restarted on drying track

Results and retirements

(Combined from times in two races; one over 58 laps, one over 22 laps)

Place	*Driver*	*Car*	*Laps*	*Time and Speed (mph/km/h)/Retirement*	
1	Alain Prost	Renault t/c V6	80	1h 35m 48·13s	118·304/190·392
2	John Watson	McLaren-Cosworth V8	80	1h 35m 50·42s	118·257/190·317
3	Nelson Piquet	Brabham-Cosworth V8	80	1h 36m 12·35s	117·807/189·593
4	René Arnoux	Renault t/c V6	80	1h 36m 30·43s	117·440/189·002
5	Didier Pironi	Ferrari t/c V6	79		
6	Elio de Angelis	Lotus-Cosworth V8	79		
7	Nigel Mansell	Lotus-Cosworth V8	79		
8	Mario Andretti	Alfa Romeo V12	79		
9	Hector Rebaque	Brabham-Cosworth V8	78		
10	Carlos Reutemann	Williams-Cosworth V8	78		
11	Andrea de Cesaris	McLaren-Cosworth V8	78		
12	Marc Surer	Theodore-Cosworth V8	78		
13	Eddie Cheever	Tyrrell-Cosworth V8	77		
14	Riccardo Patrese	Arrows-Cosworth V8	77		
15	Bruno Giacomelli	Alfa Romeo V12	77		
16	Michele Alboreto	Tyrrell-Cosworth V8	77		
17	Alan Jones	Williams-Cosworth V8	76		
	Jacques Laffite	Talbot-Ligier Matra V12	57	Damaged front suspension	
	Derek Daly	March-Cosworth V8	55	Engine	
	Gilles Villeneuve	Ferrari t/c V6	41	Electrics	
	Patrick Tambay	Theodore-Cosworth V8	30	Rear wheel bearing	
	Keke Rosberg	Fittipaldi-Cosworth V8	11	Broken rear cross-member	
	Eliseo Salazar	Ensign-Cosworth V8	6	Rear suspension	
	Chico Serra	Fittipaldi-Cosworth V8	0	Crashed on warm-up; did not start	

Fastest lap: Prost, on lap 64, 1m 09·14s, 122·944mph/197·859km/h (record).
Previous lap record: René Arnoux (F1 Renault RS t/c V6), 1m 09·16s, 122·908mph/197·802km/h (1979).

Lap chart

1st LAP ORDER		1	2	3	4	5	6	7	8	9	10	11	12	13	14	15	16	17	18	19	20	21	22	23	24	25	26	27	28	29	30	31	32	33	34	35	36	37
5	N,Piquet	5	5	5	5	5	5	5	5	5	5	5	5	5	5	5	5	5	5	5	5	5	5	5	5	5	5	5	5	5	5	5	5	5	5	5	5	5
7	J.Watson	7	7	15	15	15	15	15	15	15	15	15	15	15	15	15	15	15	15	15	15	15	15	15	15	15	15	15	15	15	15	15	15	15	15	15	15	15
15	A.Prost	15	15	7	7	7	7	7	7	7	7	7	7	7	7	7	7	7	7	7	7	7	7	7	7	7	7	7	7	7	7	7	7	7	7	7	7	7
8	A.de Cesaris	8	8	27	27	27	2	2	2	2	2	2	2	2	2	2	2	2	2	2	2	2	2	2	2	2	2	2	2	2	2	2	2	16	16	16	16	16
27	G.Villeneuve	27	27	8	2	2	27	27	16	16	16	16	16	16	16	16	16	16	16	16	16	16	16	16	16	16	16	16	16	16	16	16	16	2	2	2	2	2
26	J.Laffite	26	2	2	16	16	16	16	27	2	27	27	27	27	27	27	27	27	27	27	27	27	27	27	27	27	27	27	27	27	27	27	27	27	27	27	27	27
22	M.Andretti	22	26	16	8	8	8	8	8	8	8	8	8	8	8	8	26	26	26	26	26	26	26	26	26	26	26	26	26	26	6	6	6	6	6	6	6	6
2	C.Reutemann	2	16	26	26	26	26	26	26	26	26	26	26	26	26	26	8	8	8	8	8	8	8	8	8	8	8	8	8	6	26	26	26	26	26	26	26	26
16	R.Arnoux	16	22	28	28	28	28	28	28	28	28	28	28	28	28	28	28	28	28	28	28	6	6	6	6	6	6	6	6	8	8	8	8	8	8	8	8	11
28	D.Pironi	28	28	22	22	11	11	11	11	11	11	11	11	11	11	11	6	6	6	6	6	11	11	11	11	11	11	11	11	11	11	11	11	11	11	11	11	8
1	A.Jones	1	1	11	11	22	22	22	22	22	22	6	6	6	6	6	11	11	11	11	11	28	28	28	28	28	28	28	28	28	28	28	28	28	28	28	28	28
11	E.de Angelis	11	11	12	12	12	12	12	12	12	6	22	22	22	22	22	22	22	22	22	22	12	12	12	12	12	12	12	12	12	12	12	12	12	12	12	12	12
12	N.Mansell	12	12	23	23	23	23	6	6	6	12	12	12	12	12	12	12	12	12	12	12	22	22	22	22	22	22	22	22	22	22	22	22	22	22	22	22	22
23	B.Giacomelli	23	23	6	25	25	6	23	23	23	23	23	23	23	23	23	23	23	23	23	23	23	23	23	25	25	25	25	25	23	23	23	23	23	23	23	23	23
25	P.Tambay	25	25	25	6	6	25	25	25	25	25	25	33	33	33	33	25	25	25	25	25	25	25	25	23	23	23	23	23	29	29	29	29	29	29	29	29	33
6	H.Rebaque	6	6	17	17	17	33	33	33	33	33	33	25	25	25	25	29	29	29	29	29	29	29	29	29	29	29	29	29	33	33	33	33	33	33	33	33	29
20	K.Rosberg	20	20	29	29	33	17	29	29	29	29	29	29	29	29	29	33	33	33	33	33	33	33	33	33	33	33	33	33	(25)	3	3	3	3	3	3	3	3
29	R.Patrese	29	29	33	33	29	29	17	17	17	17	17	17	17	17	17	17	17	17	17	17	17	17	17	17	3	3	3	3	3	4	4	4	4	4	4	4	4
17	D.Daly	17	17	20	4	14	14	3	3	3	3	3	3	3	3	3	3	3	3	3	3	3	3	3	3	(17)	4	4	4	4	25	(25)	1	1	1	1	1	1
33	M.Surer	33	33	14	20	20	3	4	4	4	4	4	4	4	4	4	4	4	4	4	4	4	4	4	4	4	1	1	1	1	1	1	17	17	17	17	17	17
3	E.Cheever	3	3	3	3	3	20	20	20	20	20	(20)	1	1	1	1	1	(1)	(1)	1	1	1	1	1	1	1	17	17	17	17	17	17						
14	E.Salazar	14	14	(4)	4	4	4	(14)	1	1	1	1																										
4	M.Alboreto	4	4	(1)	1	1	1	1																														

38	39	40	41	42	43	44	45	46	47	48	49	50	51	52	53	54	55	56	57	58	59	60	61	62	63	64	65	66	67	68	69	70	71	72	73	74	75	76	77	78	79	80
5	5	5	5	5	5	5	5	5	5	5	5	5	5	5	5	5	5	5	5	5	15	15	15	15	15	15	15	15	15	15	15	15	15	15	15	15	15	15	15	15	15	15
15	15	15	15	15	15	15	15	15	15	15	15	15	15	15	15	15	15	15	15	15	7	7	7	7	7	7	7	7	7	7	7	7	7	7	7	7	7	7	7	7	7	7
7	7	7	7	7	7	7	7	7	7	7	7	7	7	7	7	7	7	7	7	7	16	16	16	16	16	16	16	16	16	16	16	16	16	16	16	16	16	16	16	16	16	16
16	16	16	16	16	16	16	2	2	2	2	2	2	2	2	2	2	2	2	2	2	5	5	5	5	5	5	5	5	5	5	5	5	5	5	5	5	2	28	28	28	28	28
2	2	2	2	2	2	2	16	16	16	16	16	16	16	16	16	16	16	16	16	16	2	2	2	2	2	2	2	2	2	2	2	2	2	2	2	2	28	5	5	5	5	5
27	27	27	27	6	6	6	6	6	6	6	6	6	6	6	6	6	6	6	6		28	28	28	28	28	28	28	28	28	28	28	28	28	28	28	28	5	8	8	8	8	8
6	6	6	6	26	26	26	26	26	26	26	26	26	26	26	26	26	26	26	26		12	12	12	12	12	12	12	8	8	8	8	8	8	8	8	8	8	22	22	22	22	22
26	26	26	26	11	11	11	8	8	8	8	8	8	8	8	8	8	8	11	11		23	23	23	22	22	8	8	22	22	22	22	22	22	22	22	22	22	2	12	12	12	12
11	11	11	11	8	8	8	11	11	11	11	11	11	11	11	11	11	11	28	28		11	22	22	8	8	22	22	12	12	12	12	12	12	12	12	12	12	12	11	11	11	11
8	8	8	8	28	28	28	28	28	28	28	28	28	28	28	28	28	28	12	12		22	11	11	11	11	11	11	11	11	11	11	11	11	11	11	11	11	11	2	2		
28	28	28	28	12	12	12	12	12	12	12	12	12	12	12	12	12	12	8	22		29	8	8	23	23	29	29	3	3	3	3	3	3	6	6	6	6	6	6	6		
12	12	12	12	22	22	22	22	22	22	22	22	22	22	22	22	22	22	22	33		8	29	29	29	29	3	3	33	33	33	33	33	6	3	3	3	3	3	3	3		
22	22	22	22	23	23	23	23	23	33	33	33	33	33	33	33	33	33	33	23		33	33	33	33	33	33	33	6	6	6	6	6	33	33	33	33	33	33	33	33		
23	23	23	23	33	33	33	33	33	23	23	23	23	23	23	23	23	23	23	8		3	3	3	3	3	6	6	29	29	29	29	29	29	29	29	29	29	29	29	29		
33	33	33	33	29	29	29	29	29	29	29	29	29	29	29	29	29	29	29	29		4	4	6	6	6	23	23	4	4	4	4	4	4	4	4	4	4	4	4	4		
29	29	29	29	3	3	3	3	3	3	3	3	3	3	3	3	3	3	3	3		(26)	6	4	4	4	4	4	23	23	23	23	23	23	23	23	23	23	23	23	23		
3	3	3	3	4	4	4	4	4	4	4	4	4	4	4	4	4	4	4	4		6	1	1	1	1	1	1	1	1	1	1	1	1	1	1	1	1	1	1	1		
4	4	4	4	1	1	1	1	1	1	1	1	1	1	1	1	1					1	17	17	17	17	17	17															
1	1	1	1	17	17	17	17	17	17	17	17	17	17								17																					
17	17	17	17																																							

Fastest laps

Driver	*Time*	*Lap*
Alain Prost	1m 09·14s	64
Nelson Piquet	1m 09·29s	66
John Watson	1m 09·30s	66
René Arnoux	1m 09·32s	67
Alan Jones	1m 09·85s	69
Andrea de Cesaris	1m 09·97s	67
Mario Andretti	1m 09·97s	69
Didier Pironi	1m 10·30s	65
Hector Rebaque	1m 10·75s	74
Carlos Reutemann	1m 10·76s	6
Elio de Angelis	1m 10·99s	68
Nigel Mansell	1m 11·13s	74
Eddie Cheever	1m 12·21s	71
Marc Surer	1m 12·24s	72
Jacques Laffite	1m 12·39s	44
Gilles Villeneuve	1m 12·58s	4
Riccardo Patrese	1m 30·19s	8
Patrick Tambay	1m 13·37s	28
Bruno Giacomelli	1m 13·55s	10
Derek Daly	1m 13·93s	28
Michele Alboreto	1m 14·15s	68
Eliseo Salazar	1m 14·30s	6
Keke Rosberg	1m 15·01s	5

Points

WORLD CHAMPIONSHIP OF DRIVERS

1	Carlos Reutemann	37 pts
2	Nelson Piquet	26
3	Alan Jones	24
4	Gilles Villeneuve	21
5	Jacques Laffite	17
6	Alain Prost	13
7 =	John Watson	10
7 =	Riccardo Patrese	10
9	Elio de Angelis	8
10	Didier Pironi	7
11 =	Nigel Mansell	5
11 =	Eddie Cheever	5
11 =	René Arnoux	5
14	Marc Surer	4
15 =	Mario Andretti	3
15 =	Hector Rebaque	3
17 =	Patrick Tambay	1
17 =	Andrea de Cesaris	1

CONSTRUCTORS' CUP

1	Williams	61
2	Brabham	29
3	Ferrari	28
4	Renault	18
5	Ligier	17
6	Lotus	13
7	McLaren	11
8	Arrows	10
9	Tyrrell	5
10	Ensign	4
11	Alfa Romeo	3
12	Theodore	1

UNIPART

Marlboro F3
Mobil
7

MICHELIN
TALBOT
GITANES
elf
Marlboro
British Grand Prix

Previous pages: Winning Way: John Watson lines up for a successful weekend for Unipart and McLaren in the Marlboro British Grand Prix *(main picture)*.
Photo: David Winter
John Watson and Andrea de Cesaris started from the third row *(above right)*.
Photo: Bruce Grant-Braham
"Unaccustomed as I am . . ." John Watson handles the Moët at Silverstone *(below right)*.
Photo: Diana Burnett

Watson looks for a way past Arnoux's stricken Renault.

Alain Prost retires his Renault.

Marlboro British Grand Prix

John Watson, driving a Marlboro sponsored car, was leading the Marlboro British Grand Prix in front of an ecstatic 80,000 crowd. Eight laps to go; could he possibly score his second Grand Prix win in such a fairytale manner? Knowing 'Wattie's' luck during the preceding 115 Grands Prix, the chances had to be slim. Something had to go wrong. Indeed, one way or another, things hadn't gone right since the French Grand Prix on July 5.

His Volkswagen Golf GTI had been broken into; he was hounded constantly by the hungry media; his McLaren MP4 was not quite as he would have liked – there was nothing particularly wrong, it just wasn't quite right – and then, to cap it all, the security man at the helicopter pad did not recognise poor John on race morning and refused to let the only UK driver in the Grand Prix through the gate without a ticket.

All the bad omens were wiped out on lap four. That was when Gilles Villeneuve, struggling to keep his ill-handling Ferrari in fifth place, spun at the Woodcote chicane in a cloud of tyre smoke which engulfed the pursuing Alan Jones, Watson and Andrea de Cesaris. Jones hit Villeneuve while de Cesaris ran into the catch-fencing. Watson, his brakes locked, ploughed through the smoke – and emerged unscathed. Given his usual luck, it would have been Watson cursing gently in the fencing while the others continued on their way.

Having dropped to 10th place, Watson's chances of victory appeared to be at an end as the Renault-Elf team of Alain Prost and René Arnoux extended their lead with ease. Nelson Piquet, their closest challenger, crashed his Parmalat Brabham heavily when a front tyre failed on the approach to Becketts on lap 12. Five laps later, Prost stopped at the pits with the first hint of trouble for the French team and his car was wheeled away with a burnt-out valve. Watson had worked his way into second place and for 30 dreary laps, stalemate existed as Arnoux held a steady 25-second gap over the McLaren which, in turn, was a comfortable 30 seconds ahead of Carlos Reutemann in his Saudia-Leyland Williams. The result appeared to be a foregone conclusion.

Then, a change in the Renault V6 drone on lap 50 heralded another engine failure and Watson closed the gap. Arnoux went slower and slower; Watson crept closer and closer; the crowd became more and more voluable. By lap 61, the deed was done. Would Watson finish? Would his luck hold this time? It did – and John Watson came home to a stunning reception.

Almost unnoticed, Carlos Reutemann took second place and extended his championship lead further. Jacques Laffite finished third after Riccardo Patrese lost the place when his engine failed – the same fate which befell Didier Pironi earlier in the race after starting his Ferrari from the second row. Mario Andretti would have been fourth but for a broken throttle linkage on his Marlboro Alfa Romeo and his retirement with eight laps to go gave Eddie Cheever three points. That at least was some consolation for the Tyrrell team after the American had crashed their new car heavily during practice.

The retirement rate had been exceptionally high, a fact underlined by fifth place for Hector Rebaque in spite of two pit stops by the Brabham driver. Slim Borgudd scored his first championship point after a steady drive in the ATS while Derek Daly finished seventh after a storming drive in the March following an early pit stop.

Borgudd had to be helped from his car after a broken foot rest had made his left leg numb. Watson, for his part, felt numb all over on a day when he had achieved a cherished ambition in front of an emotional audience.

JULY:

- *Derek Bell and Manfred Winkelhock test Ford C100 sports prototype.*
- *Lancia Monte Carlos finish 1 – 2 at Watkins Glen and clinch 1981 World Endurance Championship.*
- *Lotus join Brabham and McLaren on Goodyear tyres.*
- *Jean-Pierre Jarier joins Osella.*
- *Alan Jones re-signs with Williams for fifth successive season in 1982.*
- *Gerard Ducarouge leaves Talbot-Ligier.*
- *Alfa Romeo launch turbo V8.*

ENTRY AND PRACTICE

Silverstone, that most British of circuits, was trimmed and polished, ready to hold what promised to be an intriguing race at the half-way point in the season. This should have been a race free from hassle but trouble was brewing as teams unpacked their transporters on Wednesday. Controversy surrounded the contents of the black truck from Hethel, the RAC scrutineers having passed Colin Chapman's so-called revised versions of the Lotus 88. By 8 p.m. protests from Ferrari, Talbot-Ligier and Alfa Romeo had been laid at the RAC's door and it was clear that the weekend would be far from plain sailing for the Stewards of the meeting.

The Lotus 88Bs, featuring no more than minor revisions, were wheeled out on Thursday morning and it was apparent that Elio de Angelis and Nigel Mansell did not share their boss's enthusiasm for the twin-chassis machine. By Thursday evening, Jean-Marie Balestre had made FISA's presence felt by ruling the 88B to be illegal and the RAC were left with no option but to agree. Thus, the Lotus mechanics had to face a 12-hour conversion job on Mansell's car while an 87 was brought from Hethel for de Angelis. The outcome of Chapman's intransigence, fostered in part by the RAC's refusal to see the inevitable, led to an agonising weekend for Nigel Mansell. Faced with a car that had not run on Goodyears – the American tyre company adding Lotus to their fold from this race – Mansell had little hope of making headway and the Englishman suffered the horror of failing to qualify for the British Grand Prix at Silverstone, a stone's throw from his home town.

Life at the front of the grid turned out to be much as expected as the Renaults took their places on the front row. Although the *Régie* had not been seen at Silverstone since the Grand Prix in 1979, the Frenchmen were well prepared after extensive wind tunnel work and tests at Hockenheim. The RE 30s, running single pillar rear wings, took a while to set up satisfactorily but Arnoux and Prost dominated both timed sessions none the less. René had problems balancing his car due to excessive skirt wear and Gilles Villeneuve made his modifications to the Renault when he clipped the left front suspension just as Arnoux was leaving the pit lane. Prost blew an engine on Friday afternoon but was able to sprint back to the pits and record a time in the spare car which was fractionally slower than Arnoux.

Renault, of course, had been enjoying the benefit of soft Michelins which made Nelson Piquet's time in the Goodyear-shod Brabham all the more praiseworthy. Brabham knew Silverstone well, having spent many hours pounding round the Northamptonshire track and Gordon Murray spent Thursday making fine adjustments. The result was a car which handled superbly and gave Piquet immense confidence as he flung the BT49C through the corners at an astonishing rate. He even found time to run the BMW turbo BT50 for the first time in public on Thursday morning. Having used their quota of tyres on Friday afternoon, and having extracted the maximum out of the BT49C, Brabham wheeled the turbo out once more in order to gain some sort of performance yardstick during the heat of an official practice session. The result was a very creditable 1m 12.6s and evil oversteer indicated that the time was the result of a prodigious turn of speed along the straights, the BT50 bursting through the speed traps at 192mph, about 15mph faster than the Cosworth.

Ferrari, said some pundits, would be long gone on the straights at Silverstone but the pundits conveniently forgot about the fast corners linking the straights. The 126 chassis continued to be a handful and even a much modified car made little difference. The 'B' update of chassis 051 had revised front suspension and a fully enclosed foot well section, both drivers trying the car during practice; Pironi, after blowing an engine on Thursday morning, and Villeneuve on Thursday afternoon. Gilles recommended minor modifications on Thursday night to cure porpoising and he concentrated on the car the next day although his chances were ruined by a poor engine. Pironi, thanks to a do-or-die effort on Friday afternoon, hauled himself onto the second row after a typically brave performance.

After encouraging times during pre-race testing at Silverstone and a front row grid position at Dijon, John Watson and the Marlboro McLaren team had high hopes of taking their first pole position of the season. The MP4 remained virtually unchanged but Watson was struggling – perhaps too hard – throughout practice. Commenting that the MP4 was "not bad – but not as good as I would have expected for no apparent reason", John just managed to squeeze into fifth place towards the end of a practice session spent rushing in and out of the pits. His time was a scant one-hundredth of a second faster than de Cesaris who showed a remarkably clean bill of health on a circuit he knew and liked.

It was somewhat galling, therefore, for Alan Jones to be in seventh place with a car which lacked downforce and traction out of the corners. The reigning World Champion was one of four drivers not to improve his time on Friday afternoon when a broken valve put paid to his chances. Carlos Reutemann, back in ninth position, was hindered by the dreaded misfire which was beginning to become more than simply a niggling complaint. Both drivers spent practice juggling around with 13ins and 15ins wheels at the front while Brabham persevered with 13ins. The Ragno Beta Arrows team were studying tyres and rims sizes as well after tests at Donington with Pirelli. Although there was a considerable weight penalty to be had from using the radials, Riccardo Patrese expressed himself very pleased with the balance of his car and the team concentrated on sifting through the selection of rubber available. Riccardo eventually set 10th fastest time and brought Pirelli back to a Grand Prix for the first time since 1958. Initially there was doubt about Siegfried Stohr being the recipient of the Italian rubber but the number two received his fair share although, in the event, he was still a second and a half slower than his team leader.

The Marlboro Alfa Romeo team had been busy since the French Grand Prix putting the finishing touches to a new chassis. Giorgio Francia completed the initial shakedown at the Balocco test track before the car was loaded up and rushed to Silverstone in time for Thursday's practice. Mario Andretti spent some time at the wheel of the new car which was 5cms lower and incorporated revised rear suspension. Deciding that the 179E needed more development, Mario switched to his usual car and set 11th fastest time, just under a tenth of a second faster than Bruno Giacomelli. Hector Rebaque was next having lost time trying 15ins wheels, the Mexican qualifying in 13th place on his last lap of practice. The Talbot-Ligier Matra team lost ground on Thursday when a spate of rear wheel bearing failures meant Jacques Laffite and Patrick Tambay were forced to share the wide-track spare chassis. Revised parts were flown from France

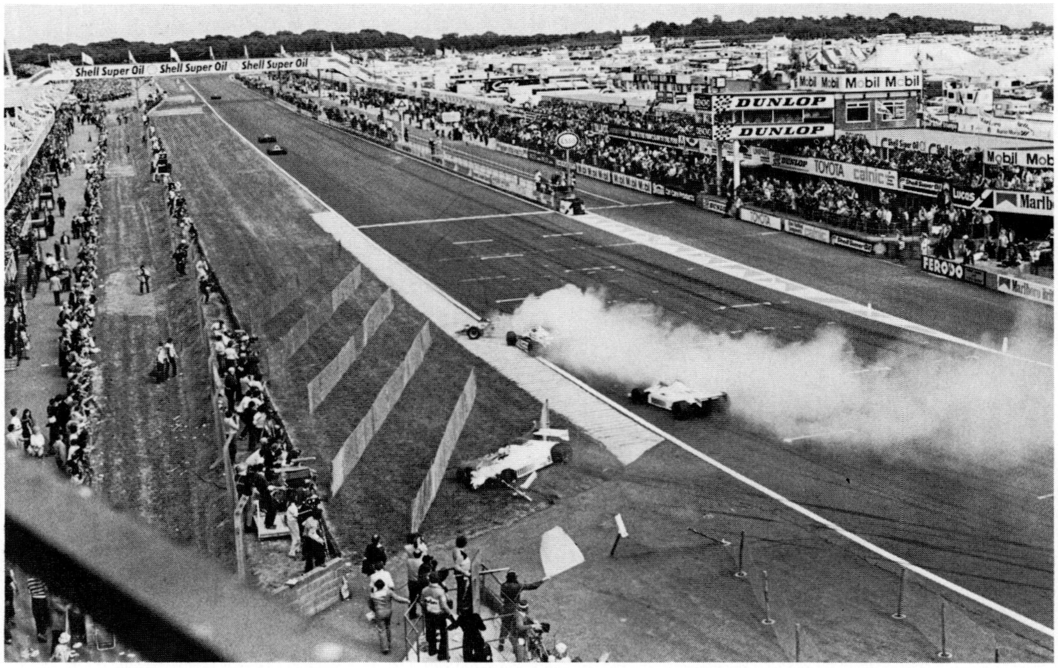

Villeneuve finishes his spin in front of Jones while Watson brakes hard and hopes for the best. De Cesaris spins into the catch-fencing in the foreground *(right)*.
Brabham ran their turbo BMW during practice for the first time *(below)*.
"But the scoreboard says you're in fifth place . . ." Gilles Villeneuve vacates his wrecked Ferrari after a vain attempt to return to the pits *(bottom)*.

on Friday morning but the JS17 chassis, apart from understeering, lacked the necessary straight-line speed for Silverstone.

The Fittipaldi team simply lacked cash as they battled on without a major sponsor. As a result, the F8Cs were much as before, Keke Rosberg struggling gamely with steering which tended to stiffen at places like the fifth gear Abbey Curve but the plucky Finn managed to carry his car into 16th spot on the grid. Chico Serra failed to make the race after his car failed to pass the 6cm test at a critical point, just 15 minutes before the end of practice on Friday. The Brazilian had just made the most of his best tyres, such as they were, and his times were duly disallowed at that point.

A brand new chassis for Derek Daly put the Irishman in 12th place on Thursday but the March team were unable to improve the following day and Daly slipped to 17th slot. The new car, 12 inches shorter and 58 lbs lighter, was run with angled skirts which set out to cure understeer but brought on a dreadful bout of porpoising in return. Favouring the former to the latter, the skirts were changed for race day and the team, the quickest on Avon tyres, were confident of a good result.

Plodding manfully on without a major sponsor, Ken Tyrrell took the gamble of building a new car in the hope of scoring results and attracting the necessary backing. The white 011 completed around 200 miles at Donington in the hands of Eddie Cheever before appearing at Silverstone and the American expressed himself to be cautiously optimistic. "I've had to learn how to drive it," he explained. "The chassis is so stiff, it means you have to be very careful. I nearly lost it a couple of times." And, to prove the point in a dramatic fashion on Thursday afternoon, Cheever clipped a kerb at the chicane and the Tyrrell shot across the track and charged head-long into the catch-fencing. The front was beyond immediate repair but it was apparent that the driver safety cell, complying with the regulations due to come into force in 1982, had done its job extremely well. Cheever was able to walk back to the pits and prepare to carry on in the 010 spare chassis. Michele Alboreto, meanwhile, had been using Cheever's previous race chassis and the Italian managed to qualify on Friday by using a supply of old Goodyear tyres Tyrrell had kept since the test sessions at Paul Ricard the previous November. Cheever, two tenths slower, managed to scrape onto the back row.

Jean-Pierre Jarier, present at the French Grand Prix two weeks previously, had been telling anyone who would listen just how upset he was at Talbot's decision to overlook him in favour of Tambay. Jarier added that he would only accept top line drives – but his competitive instincts got the better of him and he accepted an offer from the Denim-Osella team to drive their car at Silverstone. Jean-Pierre had tested the Osella at Ricard and he qualified two seconds faster than Beppe Gabbiani. The Italian was rather put out by the whole affair, particularly when the one set of soft Michelins available were entrusted to Jarier. Gabbiani finished an unhappy two days at the bottom of the time sheet. Alistair Caldwell's arrival in the ATS team began to bear fruit immediately, Slim Borgudd qualifying for the first time since Imola. De Angelis managed to make the race thanks to one superhuman lap in the spooky 87 and he took a place on the penultimate row ahead of Cheever and Marc Surer in the Theodore, the Swiss driver experiencing difficulty with his Avon tyres on a new and stiffer chassis. And that was just one of his problems. Transferring to the older car, Surer could not get the chassis to handle either so he jumped back in the new car – and the engine blew. Back in the old car once again and a shock absorber fell apart while a return to the new chassis brought a broken skirt and, eventually, one lap which was good enough for the grid.

". . . and then I dreamt you stuffed the car at Becketts and Bernie asked me to take your place . . ." Jan Lammers was mentioned as a replacement for Piquet but Nelson's injuries were not serious *(below right)*.
Piquet's Brabham slams into the sleepers after his left front tyre had failed on the approach to Becketts *(bottom)*.

Once again, Brian Henton seemed poised to put the Candy Toleman on the grid and, once again, trouble was in store during the crucial moments of practice. Henton had just completed a lap in the 1m 16s bracket on Thursday afternoon and he was in the process of finishing an even quicker lap when the Toleman failed to negotiate the chicane: "the car turned in, took the right hander but just didn't want to know about the left hander. I just don't know what happened," explained a bemused Henton. The result was a steaming heap of scrap from which Henton was lucky to escape with no more than a scalded thigh. Driving the cobbled up spare the following day, Henton was waiting to take the 6cm check in the pit lane when the prototype exhaust manifold on the car caught fire and ended any chances of qualifying. Derek Warwick felt he was making progress with his chassis but a blown exhaust gasket meant he could only manage 10 laps on Friday afternoon. The Ensign team had fitted revised rear uprights set into the rear wheels and Eliseo Salazar had qualified the MN180B on Thursday only to be bumped off the grid by Surer the next day.

RACE

A 30,000 crowd to watch practice on Friday indicated a torrid time in the Northamptonshire lanes on race day. Such fears for the motorist and hopes for the race organisers were well-founded as queues began to form at an early hour. The more experienced and practical members of the 80,000 spectators had camped overnight and Saturday at Silverstone dawned to the unique aroma of eggs and bacon.

Fleet Street had played its part in attracting the crowds and, on Saturday morning, the papers were broadcasting details of the Lotus fiasco and describing Nigel Mansell as the innocent victim of political humbug. As far as Nigel was concerned, he was a spectator and that's all there was to it. Indeed, Mansell was one of the few people in the paddock actually looking forward to Hockenheim.

John Watson had his thoughts firmly fixed on Silverstone as he flew in by helicopter. He had a job to do this day – as did a security man at the gate who failed to recognise the Ulsterman. Watson had no ticket and felt he really shouldn't have to part with £9 to gain admission. Eventually, the matter was resolved and Watson joined his team in time for the warm-up. The McLaren team had become apprehensive about de Cesaris; two days and not a single shunt. Andrea, as if on cue, obliged by spinning off at Stowe but, luckily, what should have been a major accident amounted to no more than superficial bodywork damage. The only activity of note was in the other Marlboro pit where the Alfa Romeo mechanics began a speedy engine change on Andretti's car. It was a hurried move which would cost them dearly.

Nelson Piquet had been fastest during the warm-up although an element of uncertainty was added by Gordon Murray's decision to race carbon fibre discs for the first time. René Arnoux had been second quickest which was encouraging for Renault, particularly as Bernard Hannon, their Managing Director, was present. Down in the Williams camp there had been concern about tyres. Reutemann had found his 13ins fronts, particularly the left, overheating and a sudden switch to 15ins saw Carlos squeeze in three warm-up laps as the cars left the pits for the last time. When he did arrive on the grid, Reutemann was soon out of his car and making adjustments to cure oversteer. That done, the cars set off on their final parade lap, the yellow and white Renaults leading the burbling, darting field as tyres were brought to a reasonable temperature.

Piquet positioned himself for a run at the front row but both Renaults made surprisingly good starts. Rather than a white car nudging through, however, it was the red Ferrari of Didier Pironi moving among his countrymen followed by Villeneuve who, as ever, seemed to have a telepathic link with the starter and was ahead of Piquet and Arnoux by the time they reached Stowe.

Funnelling through Woodcote at the end of lap one, Prost had begun to pull away while Villeneuve was clearly impatient to get by his team-mate. An unsuccessful lunge by Gilles at Club saw Arnoux steal third place and the move was watched by Siegfried Stohr, a spectator on the banking after having a moment with Rebaque. The field was reduced even further as Alboreto crawled into the pits, his clutch having fried on the line, and Daly appeared to be another retirement as he rushed towards the March pit at the end of lap two. His gear linkage had worked loose but hasty repairs had the Irishman on his way for a hard charging drive, exactly one lap in arrears.

After three laps, Prost had pulled out a lead of five seconds while Arnoux moved into second place as Villeneuve dropped to fifth spot. His tenure there was destined to last one more lap.

Coming through the chicane, Gilles clipped a kerb which launched the Ferrari briefly before the rock hard suspension took over and bounced Villeneuve broadside in front of the pack. Jones, confronted by swirling tyre smoke, had no option but to disappear into the catch-fencing with the Ferrari while Watson locked his brakes and simply hoped for the best as he ploughed into the mire. De Cesaris, who had been right on Watson's gearbox, was unsighted initially and the Italian pulled left to avoid ramming his team-mate and rushed headlong into the fencing. Watson, meanwhile, emerged unscathed, selected first gear and left the three unhappy drivers to sort themselves out. Villeneuve, adopting the theory that if it moves then it is worth continuing, limped as far as Stowe with the tattered remains of his car. At least he was out of earshot as de Cesaris and Jones expressed their understandable frustration.

That incident cost Watson several places, Reutemann, Andretti, Giacomelli, Tambay and Laffite having moved ahead. The McLaren driver was soon into his stride, quickly taking the Ligiers before moving ahead of Andretti on lap 12 and dispensing with Reutemann in a positive manner at the chicane one lap later. It was an impressive performance from the Ulsterman as he closed his mind to nasty scenes at Becketts following a massive shunt involving Piquet.

The Brabham driver appeared to be the only person capable of keeping pace with the fleeing Renaults but, exiting Maggots on lap 12, Piquet's left front tyre literally fell apart and flicked the Brabham towards the sleepers at high speed. Piquet, miraculously, escaped with no more than severe bruising to his left foot and he lay on the bank while waiting for an ambulance to arrive.

So, by lap 13, Watson was in fourth place and Pironi handed the McLaren driver third spot when the Ferrari engine expired in a cloud of blue smoke. Giacomelli had disappeared with gearbox trouble and Tambay was the next to go with ignition trouble leaving 15 runners with 52 laps remaining. Piquet's accident had left the Renaults in a league of their own but their chances were reduced by half when Prost peeled into the pit lane at the end of lap 17. Alain had driven with extreme care from as early as lap five, avoiding kerbs and using fifth instead of fourth gear at Club corner. But his caution was to no avail. The V6 had begun to misfire and tighten and the pit stop revealed the worst – valve trouble of some description and instant retirement. Would Arnoux encounter the same problem?

It certainly didn't seem that way as he droned round, 25 seconds ahead of Watson and countering the McLaren driver's every attempt to close the gap with insolent ease. Reutemann was not far behind with Andretti a lonely fourth and de Angelis closing on Patrese's fifth place. The Italian's storming drive had not gone unnoticed – particularly by the Observer at Becketts where Elio passed Laffite under the yellow flag and almost collected the ambulance carrying Piquet to the medical centre. The black flag was shown and it took de Angelis several laps to come in for a lecture in the pit lane. When he did eventually stop, de Angelis reacted angrily to the dressing down from Robert Langford by climbing out of his car, arms waving, and stalking off down the pit lane. Rather than continue – as he had every right to do – the impetuous Italian assumed he had been disqualified and a baffled Colin Chapman ended a miserable weekend by expressing his views on television before learning the whole story.

At least the incident gave the cameras a useful diversion from what had become a rather boring race. Arnoux was keeping Watson at arm's length; Reutemann could make no impression on the McLaren and Andretti was even further behind in fourth place. Patrese appeared to be the only driver making any progress at all, his Arrows handling well during its first race on Pirellis and, on lap 38, he moved ahead of the Alfa Romeo at the chicane. At the end of the following lap, Rebaque pulled in for fresh rubber and the Mexican was back ten laps later for another front left tyre. The Renault mechanics caused a minor stir by standing in readiness with new tyres but René Arnoux appeared to be in no bother whatsoever. On lap 50 he set his fastest lap but, almost immediately, the Renault began to sound off song. The McLaren team began to give Watson the gap and the Ulsterman soon realised Arnoux was in trouble. So, too, did the crowd.

Amid unparalleled scenes of delight, Watson sliced two and sometimes three seconds a lap off the leader. By lap 55, the gap was 10.3 seconds; by lap 59, it was 2.5 seconds. Almost unnoticed in the mayhem, Mario Andretti free-wheeled out of the chicane and parked his Alfa Romeo by the end of the pit wall, the V12 healthy but the throttle assembly useless after a split-pin had gone missing.

The field, decimated during the first six laps, had been whittled further when a rear wishbone pickup point broke on Rosberg's Fittipaldi. As far as the spectators were concerned, they had eyes for one man only and on lap 61, he was looking for a way past the Renault at Copse. Determined if nothing else, Arnoux held his ground but the hapless Frenchman could merely watch Watson slip through under braking for Becketts. The place erupted. Now all Wattie had to do was finish – a difficult task in view of his track record on occasions such as this. Not daring to take in the furious waving from the enclosures, John stared straight ahead as he kept off the kerbs and conserved his revs.

For Arnoux, there would not even be a championship point to show for his 43 laps in the lead. With four laps to go, the turbo cried enough and he rolled to a halt, the victim of another valve failure. Engine failures, suspension failures, punctures, fuel shortages, careless back markers. Those thoughts ran through Watson's mind as he started his last lap but the MP4 was to run as sweetly as ever during the final 2.9 miles.

Reutemann was a distant second but the winner of six more points none the less while Eddie Cheever, driving forcefully in the old chassis, chased Jacques Laffite across the line to give the beleagured Tyrrell team some consolation. In spite of his pit stops, Hector Rebaque was fifth and Slim Borgudd took his first championship point after a steady drive in spite of a stray piece of metal fouling the pedals on his ATS. Daly never gave up and lapped as quickly as Laffite on his way to seventh place while Jarier took eighth after an early pit stop to adjust the rear wing on his Osella. Apart from the bitterly disappointed Renault team, there were resigned faces in the Arrows and Theodore camps after Patrese had stopped with engine failure and Marc Surer ran out of fuel after an excellent dice with Cheever.

Such tales of woe scattered around the circuit merely heightened Watson's awareness of his own good fortune. Scarcely able to believe it, John gingerly raised his right arm as he crossed the line. He'd seen the chequered flag, yes. But was it *really* for him? The emotional scenes which followed left him in no doubt that it was. Forget the hassle of the preceding two weeks; forget the misunderstanding at the helicopter pad; forget the element of luck. John Watson had won the British Grand Prix. And there was a new Jaguar XJS from Unipart to help him forget about the vandalised Volkswagen.

THE LOTUS 88, THOUGHT TO HAVE BEEN BANNED for once and for all by FISA in April, was back in the limelight at Silverstone. Colin Chapman, never a man to take these things lying down, had presented a revised version to the RAC in June. The revisions amounted to no more than new positions for the gearbox oil radiator and the windscreen. More important, perhaps, was a change in the terminology. Instead of having two 'chassis', the Lotus 88B had two 'sprung structures' and the RAC Motor Sports Association interpreted the cars as being legal.

'The Scrutineers of the British Grand Prix, the RAC Technical Commission, have unanimously decided that the new Lotus 88B racing car does not breach the Formula 1 Technical Regulations. That means, assuming identical are presented to the scrutineers at Silverstone, that unless the decision of the scrutineers is successfully changed before the Stewards of the Meeting, the Lotus 88B will be competitively raced.'

The predictable reaction from Paris was swift. Jean-Marie Balestre pointed out that the Lotus 88 – and all derivatives of the 88 – were in breach of the regulations. Furthermore, any organisation accepting an illegal car for its event would breach the Concorde Agreement and thereby strip the race of its World Championship status.

The RAC, in another lengthy statement, confirmed their belief that the Lotus 88B should be allowed to race and added that they had every right to go against the will of the FISA without jeopardising the World Championship status of the British Grand Prix. The FOCA teams, apparently, agreed not to protest the revised version of the Lotus although the possible actions of the 'grandee' constructors were predictable if unspoken.

Taking the RAC at their word and putting all his fragile eggs in one delicate basket, Chapman initiated a production programme for the three 88Bs (two of them based on the 87s) for Silverstone. On Wednesday afternoon, the cars were duly presented at scrutineering – and passed. In the evening, Ferrari, Alfa Romeo and Talbot-Ligier filed protests.

On Thursday morning, de Angelis and Mansell were allowed to practise in the meantime; the Stewards discussed the protests and Jean-Marie Balestre issued a statement which was presented to the Clerk of the Course *after* practice had started. FISA said the 88Bs did not comply with the Formula 1 Technical Regulations and charged the RACMSA with upholding this decision.

The Stewards discussed the FISA statement and came to the conclusion that as the International Sporting Code gave FISA the direct authority to inflict a penalty, they had no option but to exclude the 88Bs from the British Grand Prix and declare the times set during the timed practice on Thursday afternoon to be null and void.

The RACMSA, believing they had supreme power over their own Grand Prix, had interpreted the Lotus 88B to be legal and supported Chapman accordingly. The FIA, however, through its representative, FISA, proved it could overrule any decision made by the organisers – all of which lost Nigel Mansell a place on the grid and left Chapman with the job of converting his cars to 87 specification overnight. An 87 was brought from Hethel for de Angelis and the Italian qualified with one heroic lap while Mansell, who had qualified on Thursday in the 88B, was left to struggle unsuccessfully with a hastily converted and rebuilt 87. The latest saga in the history of the Lotus 88 showed a surprising lack of foresight by both Colin Chapman and the RACMSA.

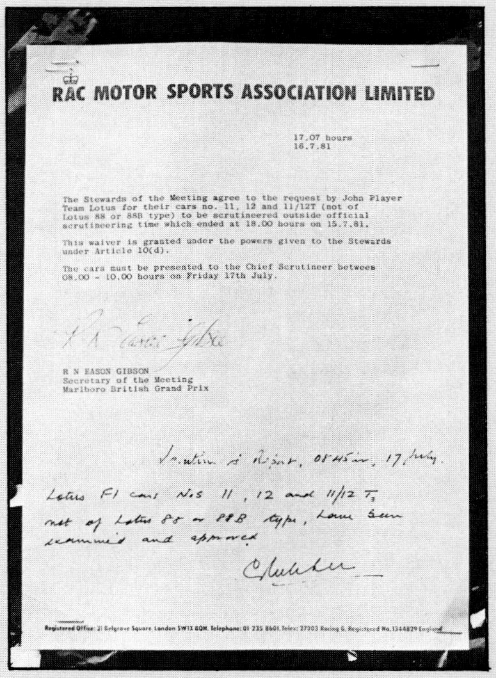
RAC MOTOR SPORTS ASSOCIATION LIMITED

17.07 hours
16.7.81

The Stewards of the Meeting agree to the request by John Player Team Lotus for their cars no. 11, 12 and 11/12T (not of Lotus 88 or 88B type) to be scrutineered outside official scrutineering time which ended at 18.00 hours on 15.7.81.

This waiver is granted under the powers given to the Stewards under Article 10(d).

The cars must be presented to the Chief Scrutineer betwees 08.00 - 10.00 hours on Friday 17th July.

R N EASON GIBSON
Secretary of the Meeting
Marlboro British Grand Prix

Lotus F1 cars No.s 11, 12 and 11/12 T, not of Lotus 88 or 88B type, have been examined and approved

Registered Office: 31 Belgrave Square, London SW1X 8QH. Telephone: 01-235 8601. Telex: 27203 Racing G. Registered No. 1344829 England

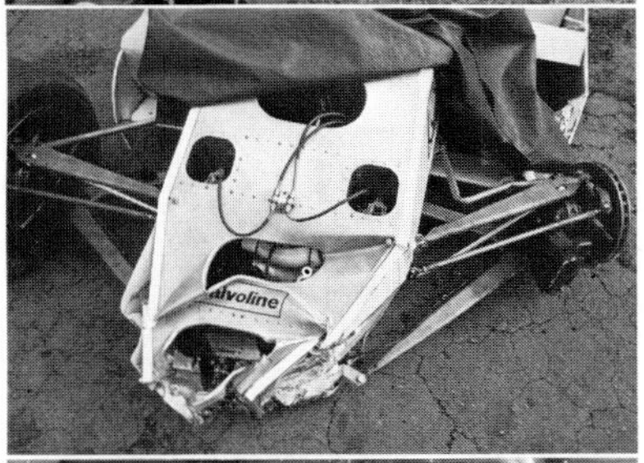

The end. Watson takes the flag to a tumultuous reception *(top)*.
A busy weekend for the mechanics. Piquet's Brabham; Stohr's Arrows; Cheever's new Tyrrell and the charred remains of Henton's engine cover on the Toleman *(above)*.
Running on Pirellis for the first time, Riccardo Patrese was certain to take fourth place when his engine blew with four laps remaining. Siegfried Stohr (foreground) crashed on the first lap *(above left)*.
Slim Borgudd scored his first championship point in the ATS while Jean-Pierre Jarier, driving for Osella, was the eighth and final finisher *(left)*.

Marlboro British Grand Prix, July 18/statistics

Entries and practice times

No.	Driver	Nat	Car	Engine	Entrant	Practice 1	Practice 2
1	Alan Jones	AUS	Saudia-Leyland WILLIAMS FW07C	Ford Cosworth DFV	TAG Williams Team	**1m 12·998s**	1m 13·250s
2	Carlos Reutemann	RA	Saudia-Leyland WILLIAMS FW07C	Ford Cosworth DFV	TAG Williams Team	1m 13·467s	**1m 13·371s**
3	Eddie Cheever	USA	TYRRELL 010	Ford Cosworth DFV	Tyrrell Racing	1m 16·381s	**1m 16·099s**
4	Michele Alboreto	I	TYRRELL 010	Ford Cosworth DFV	Tyrrell Racing	1m 16·446s	**1m 15·850s**
5	Nelson Piquet	BR	Parmalat BRABHAM BT49C	Ford Cosworth DFV	Parmalat Racing Team	1m 12·328s	**1m 11·952s**
5	Nelson Piquet	BR	Parmalat BRABHAM BT50	BMW M12/13	Parmalat Racing Team	–	1m 12·600s
6	Hector Rebaque	MEX	Parmalat BRABHAM BT49C	Ford Cosworth DFV	Parmalat Racing Team	1m 14·594s	**1m 14·542s**
7	John Watson	GB	Marlboro McLAREN MP4	Ford Cosworth DFV	McLaren International	1m 13·370s	**1m 12·712s**
8	Andrea de Cesaris	I	Marlboro McLAREN MP4	Ford Cosworth DFV	McLaren International	1m 13·976s	**1m 12·728s**
9	Slim Borgudd	S	Abba ATS HGS 1	Ford Cosworth DFV	Team ATS	1m 16·758s	**1m 15·959s**
11	Elio de Angelis	I	John Player Special LOTUS 88B	Ford Cosworth DFV	John Player Team Lotus	*1m 16·029s	–
11	Elio de Angelis	I	John Player Special LOTUS 87	Ford Cosworth DFV	John Player Team Lotus	–	**1m 15·971s**
12	Nigel Mansell	GB	John Player Special LOTUS 88B	Ford Cosworth DFV	John Player Team Lotus	*1m 15·992s	–
12	Nigel Mansell	GB	John Player Special LOTUS 87	Ford Cosworth DFV	John Player Team Lotus	–	**1m 16·432s**
14	Eliseo Salazar	RCH	ENSIGN N180B	Ford Cosworth DFV	Ensign Racing	1m 17·053s	**1m 16·694s**
15	Alain Prost	F	Elf RENAULT RE 30	Renault EF1	Equipe Renault Elf	1m 12·237s	**1m 11·046s**
16	René Arnoux	F	Elf RENAULT RE 30	Renault EF1	Equipe Renault Elf	1m 12·158s	**1m 11·000s**
17	Derek Daly	IRL	Rizla MARCH 811	Ford Cosworth DFV	March Grand Prix	**1m 15·189s**	1m 15·303s
20	Keke Rosberg	SF	FITTIPALDI F8C	Ford Cosworth DFV	Fittipaldi Automotive	1m 16·695s	**1m 15·165s**
21	Chico Serra	BR	FITTIPALDI F8C	Ford Cosworth DFV	Fittipaldi Automotive	1m 18·173s	**1m 16·360s**
22	Mario Andretti	USA	Marlboro ALFA ROMEO 179C	Alfa Romeo 1260	Marlboro Team Alfa Romeo	1m 14·440s	**1m 13·928s**
23	Bruno Giacomelli	I	Marlboro ALFA ROMEO 179C	Alfa Romeo 1260	Marlboro Team Alfa Romeo	**1m 14·119s**	1m 14·442s
25	Patrick Tambay	F	Talbot-Gitanes LIGIER JS17	Matra MS 81	Equipe Talbot Gitanes	1m 15·656s	**1m 14·976s**
26	Jacques Laffite	F	Talbot-Gitanes LIGIER JS17	Matra MS 81	Equipe Talbot Gitanes	1m 15·313s	**1m 14·798s**
27	Gilles Villeneuve	CDN	Fiat FERRARI 126CK	Ferrari 126C	Scuderia Ferrari SpA SEFAC	1m 14·182s	**1m 13·311s**
28	Didier Pironi	F	Fiat FERRARI 126CK	Ferrari 126C	Scuderia Ferrari SpA SEFAC	1m 14·070s	**1m 12·644s**
29	Riccardo Patrese	I	Ragno-Beta ARROWS A3	Ford Cosworth DFV	Arrows Racing Team	1m 15·217s	**1m 13·762s**
30	Siegfried Stohr	I	Ragno-Beta ARROWS A3	Ford Cosworth DFV	Arrows Racing Team	1m 17·229s	**1m 15·304s**
31	Beppe Gabbiani	I	Denim OSELLA FA1B	Ford Cosworth DFV	Osella Squadra Corse	1m 20·377s	**1m 17·784s**
32	Jean-Pierre Jarier	F	Denim OSELLA FA1B	Ford Cosworth DFV	Osella Squadra Corse	1m 15·943s	**1m 15·898s**
33	Marc Surer	CH	THEODORE TY 01	Ford Cosworth DFV	Theodore Racing Team	1m 17·124s	**1m 16·155s**
35	Brian Henton	GB	Candy TOLEMAN TG 181	Hart 415T	Candy Toleman Motorsport	**1m 16·388s**	1m 19·602s
36	Derek Warwick	GB	Candy TOLEMAN TG 181	Hart 415T	Candy Toleman Motorsport	1m 17·998s	**1m 16·891s**

* Time disallowed

Thursday morning and Friday morning practice sessions not officially recorded

Thur pm — *Warm, dry* | *Fri pm* — *Warm, dry*

Starting grid

	16 ARNOUX (1m 11·000s) Renault
15 PROST (1m 11·046s) Renault	
	5 PIQUET (1m 11·952s) Brabham
28 PIRONI (1m 12·644s) Ferrari	
	7 WATSON (1m 12·712s) McLaren
8 DE CESARIS (1m 12·728s) McLaren	
	1 JONES (1m 12·998s) Williams
27 VILLENEUVE (1m 13·311s) Ferrari	
	2 REUTEMANN (1m 13·371s) Williams
29 PATRESE (1m 13·762s) Arrows	
	22 ANDRETTI (1m 13·928s) Alfa Romeo
23 GIACOMELLI (1m 14·119s) Alfa Romeo	
	6 REBAQUE (1m 14·542s) Brabham
26 LAFFITE (1m 14·798s) Talbot-Ligier	
	25 TAMBAY (1m 14·976s) Talbot-Ligier
20 ROSBERG (1m 15·165s) Fittipaldi	
	17 DALY (1m 15·189s) March
30 STOHR (1m 15·304s) Arrows	
	4 ALBORETO (1m 15·850s) Tyrrell
32 JARIER (1m 15·898s) Osella	
	9 BORGUDD (1m 15·959s) ATS
11 DE ANGELIS (1m 15·971s) Lotus	
	3 CHEEVER (1m 16·099s) Tyrrell
33 SURER (1m 16·155s) Theodore	

Did not start:
21 Serra (Fittipaldi), 1m 16·360s, did not qualify
35 Henton (Toleman), 1m 16·388s, did not qualify
12 Mansell (Lotus), 1m 16·432s, did not qualify
14 Salazar (Ensign), 1m 16·694s, did not qualify
36 Warwick (Toleman), 1m 16·891s, did not qualify
31 Gabbiani (Osella), 1m 17·784s, did not qualify

Past winners

Year	Driver	Nat	Car	Circuit	Distance miles/km	Speed mph/km/h
1926	Robert Sénéchal/	F				
	Louis Wagner	F	1·5 Delage s/c	Brooklands	287·76/463·10	71·61/115·24
1927	Robert Benoist	F	1·5 Delage s/c	Brooklands	327·00/526·25	85·59/137·74
1935*	Richard Schuttleworth	GB	2·9 Alfa Romeo P3 s/c	Donington	318·88/513·18	63·97/102·95
1936*	Hans Reusch/	CH				
	Dick Seaman	GB	3·8 Alfa Romeo 8C s/c	Donington	306·12/492·65	69·23/111·41
1937*	Bernd Rosemeyer	D	6·1 Auto Union C-type s/c	Donington	250·00/402·34	82·86/133·35
1938*	Tazio Nuvolari	I	3·0 Auto Union D-type s/c	Donington	250·00/402·34	80·49/129·54
1948†	Luigi Villoresi	I	1·5 Maserati 4CLT/48 s/c	Silverstone	238·55/383·91	72·27/116·31
1949	Emmanuel de Graffenried	CH	1·5 Maserati 4CLT/48 s/c	Silverstone	300·00/482·80	77·31/124·41
1950	Giuseppe Farina	I	1·5 Alfa Romeo 158 s/c	Silverstone	202·20/325·41	90·96/146·38
1951	Froilán González	RA	4·5 Ferrari 375	Silverstone	259·97/418·38	96·11/154·67
1952	Alberto Ascari	I	2·0 Ferrari 500	Silverstone	248·80/400·40	90·92/146·32
1953	Alberto Ascari	I	2·0 Ferrari 500	Silverstone	263·43/423·95	92·97/149·62
1954	Froilán González	RA	2·5 Ferrari 625	Silverstone	263·43/423·95	89·69/144·34
1955	Stirling Moss	GB	2·5 Mercedes-Benz W196	Aintree	270·00/434·52	86·47/139·16
1956	Juan Manuel Fangio	RA	2·5 Lancia-Ferrari D50	Silverstone	295·63/475·77	98·65/158·76
1957	Tony Brooks/	GB				
	Stirling Moss	GB	2·5 Vanwall	Aintree	270·00/434·52	86·80/139·69
1958	Peter Collins	GB	2·4 Ferrari Dino 246	Silverstone	219·53/353·30	102·05/164·23
1959	Jack Brabham	AUS	2·5 Cooper T51-Climax	Aintree	225·00/362·10	98·88/159·13
1960	Jack Brabham	AUS	2·5 Cooper T53-Climax	Silverstone	225·00/362·10	108·69/174·92
1961	Wolfgang von Trips	D	1·5 Ferrari Dino 156	Aintree	225·00/362·10	83·91/135·04
1962	Jim Clark	GB	1·5 Lotus 25-Climax	Aintree	225·00/362·10	92·25/148·46
1963	Jim Clark	GB	1·5 Lotus 25-Climax	Silverstone	240·00/386·25	107·75/173·41
1964	Jim Clark	GB	1·5 Lotus 25-Climax	Brands Hatch	212·00/341·18	94·14/151·50
1965	Jim Clark	GB	1·5 Lotus 33-Climax	Silverstone	240·00/386·25	112·02/180·28
1966	Jack Brabham	AUS	3·0 Brabham BT19-Repco	Brands Hatch	212·00/341·18	95·48/153·66
1967	Jim Clark	GB	3·0 Lotus 49-Ford	Silverstone	240·00/386·25	117·64/189·32
1968	Jo Siffert	CH	3·0 Lotus 49B-Ford	Brands Hatch	212·00/341·18	104·83/168·71
1969	Jackie Stewart	GB	3·0 Matra MS80-Ford	Silverstone	245·87/395·69	127·25/204·79
1970	Jochen Rindt	A	3·0 Lotus 72-Ford	Brands Hatch	212·00/341·18	108·69/174·92
1971	Jackie Stewart	GB	3·0 Tyrrell 003-Ford	Silverstone	199·04/320·32	130·48/209·99
1972	Emerson Fittipaldi	BR	3·0 JPS/Lotus 72-Ford	Brands Hatch	201·40/324·12	112·06/180·34
1973	Peter Revson	USA	3·0 McLaren M23-Ford	Silverstone	196·11/315·61	131·75/212·03
1974	Jody Scheckter	ZA	3·0 Tyrrell 007-Ford	Brands Hatch	198·75/319·86	115·74/186·26
1975	Emerson Fittipaldi	BR	3·0 McLaren M23-Ford	Silverstone	164·19/264·24	120·02/193·15
1976	Niki Lauda	A	3·0 Ferrari 312T-2/76	Brands Hatch	198·63/319·67	114·24/183·85
1977	James Hunt	GB	3·0 McLaren M26-Ford	Silverstone	199·38/320·88	130·36/209·79
1978	Carlos Reutemann	RA	3·0 Ferrari 312T-3/78	Brands Hatch	198·63/319·67	116·61/187·66
1979	Clay Regazzoni	CH	3·0 Williams FW07-Ford	Silverstone	199·38/320·88	138·80/223·37
1980	Alan Jones	AUS	3·0 Williams FW07B-Ford	Brands Hatch	198·63/319·67	125·69/202·28
1981	John Watson	GB	3·0 McLaren MP4-Ford	Silverstone	199·38/320·88	137·64/221·51

* Donington (English) Grand Prix † RAC Grand Prix

A disastrous weekend for Lotus. Nigel Mansell and his wife Rosanne contemplate the remains of an 88B *(right)*.

Circuit data

Silverstone Grand Prix Circuit, near Towcester, Northamptonshire

Circuit length: 2·932 m les/4·719 km

Race distance: 68 laps, 199·38 miles/320·88 km

Race weather: Warm, dry

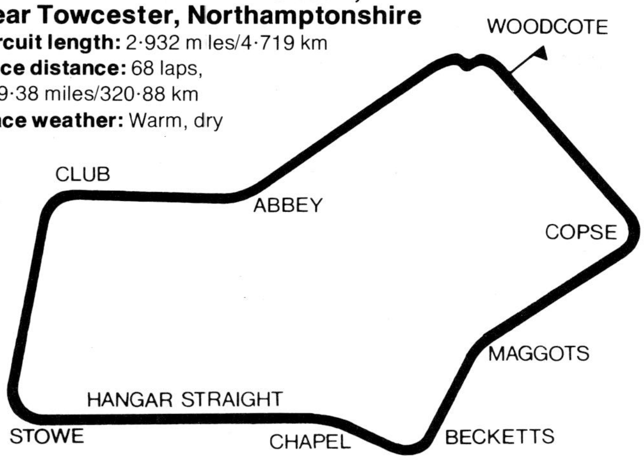

Results and retirements

Place	Driver	Car	Laps	Time and Speed (mph/km/h)/Retirement	
1	John Watson	McLaren-Cosworth V8	68	1h 26m 54·80s	137·64/221·509
2	Carlos Reutemann	Williams-Cosworth V8	68	1h 27m 35·45s	136·57/219·900
3	Jacques Laffite	Talbot-Ligier Matra V12	67		
4	Eddie Cheever	Tyrrell-Cosworth V8	67		
5	Hector Rebaque	Brabham-Cosworth V8	67		
6	Slim Borgudd	ATS-Cosworth V8	67		
7	Derek Daly	March-Cosworth V8	66		
8	Jean-Pierre Jarier	Osella-Cosworth V8	65		
9	René Arnoux	Renault t/c V6	64	Engine	
10	Riccardo Patrese	Arrows-Cosworth V8	64	Engine	
11	Marc Surer	Theodore-Cosworth V8	61	Fuel pressure	
	Mario Andretti	Alfa Romeo V12	59	Throttle linkage	
	Keke Rosberg	Fittipaldi-Cosworth V8	56	Rear suspension	
	Elio de Angelis	Lotus-Cosworth V8	25	Black-flagged; did not continue	
	Alain Prost	Renault t/c V6	17	Engine	
	Patrick Tambay	Talbot-Ligier Matra V12	15	Ignition	
	Didier Pironi	Ferrari t/c V6	13	Engine	
	Nelson Piquet	Brabham-Cosworth V8	11	Accident/tyre failure	
	Bruno Giacomelli	Alfa Romeo V12	5	Gearbox	
	Gilles Villeneuve	Ferrari t/c V6	4	Accident	
	Alan Jones	Williams-Cosworth V8	3	Accident with Villeneuve	
	Andrea de Cesaris	McLaren-Cosworth V8	3	Accident with Villeneuve	
	Michele Alboreto	Tyrrell-Cosworth V8	0	Clutch	
	Siegfried Stohr	Arrows-Cosworth V8	0	Accident	

Fastest lap: Arnoux, on lap 50, 1m 15·067s, 140·61mph/226·289km/h.
Lap record: Clay Regazzoni (F1 Williams FWO7-Cosworth DFV), 1m 14·40s, 141·87mph/228·32km/h (1979).

Lap chart

1st	LAP ORDER	1	2	3	4	5	6	7	8	9	10	11	12	13	14	15	16	17	18	19	20	21	22	23	24	25	26	27	28	29	30	31
15	A.Prost	15	15	15	15	15	15	15	15	15	15	15	15	15	15	15	15	16	16	16	16	16	16	16	16	16	16	16	16	16	16	16
28	D.Pironi	28	28	16	16	16	16	16	16	16	16	16	16	16	16	16	16	(15)	7	7	7	7	7	7	7	7	7	7	7	7	7	7
27	G.Villeneuve	27	16	28	28	5	5	5	5	5	5	5	28	28	7	7	7	7	2	2	2	2	2	2	2	2	2	2	2	2	2	2
16	R.Arnoux	16	27	5	5	28	28	28	28	28	28	28	2	7	2	2	2	2	22	22	22	22	22	22	22	22	22	22	22	22	22	22
5	N.Piquet	5	5	27	2	2	2	2	2	2	2	2	7	2	22	22	22	22	29	29	29	29	29	29	29	29	29	29	29	29	29	29
1	A.Jones	1	1	1	22	22	22	22	22	22	22	22	22	22	26	29	29	29	26	11	11	11	11	11	11	6	6	6	6	6	6	6
7	J.Watson	7	7	7	23	23	7	7	7	7	7	7	26	26	29	26	26	26	11	6	6	6	6	6	6	26	26	26	26	26	26	26
8	A.de Cesaris	8	8	8	25	25	25	25	25	25	26	26	29	29	6	6	11	11	6	26	26	26	26	26	26	(11)	3	3	3	3	3	3
2	C.Reutemann	2	2	2	26	7	26	26	26	26	25	29	6	6	11	11	6	6	3	3	3	3	3	3	3	3	33	33	33	33	33	33
22	M.Andretti	22	22	22	7	26	29	29	6	6	29	6	11	11	3	3	3	3	20	33	33	33	33	33	33	33	9	9	9	9	9	9
23	B.Giacomelli	23	23	23	29	29	6	6	29	29	6	11	20	20	20	20	20	20	33	9	9	9	9	9	9	9	20	20	20	20	20	20
25	P.Tambay	25	25	25	20	6	20	11	11	11	11	20	3	3	9	9	9	9	9	20	32	20	20	20	20	20	17	17	17	17	17	17
26	J.Laffite	26	26	26	6	20	11	20	20	20	20	3	9	9	32	32	32	32	32	32	20	(32)	17	17	17	17	32	32	32	32	32	32
20	K.Rosberg	20	20	29	11	11	3	3	3	3	3	9	32	32	33	33	33	32	17	17	17	17	32	32	32	32						
29	R.Patrese	29	29	20	3	3	9	9	9	9	9	32	33	33	17	17	17	17														
17	D.Daly	17	6	6	32	9	32	32	32	32	32	(25)	17	17	25	(25)																
6	H.Rebaque	6	11	11	9	32	33	33	33	33	33	33	(25)	25																		
32	J-P.Jarier	32	3	3	33	33	17	17	17	17	17	17																				
3	E.Cheever	3	32	32	27	17																										
11	E.de Angelis	11	9	9	17																											
9	S.Borgudd	9	33	33																												
33	M.Surer	33	(17)	17																												

32	33	34	35	36	37	38	39	40	41	42	43	44	45	46	47	48	49	50	51	52	53	54	55	56	57	58	59	60	61	62	63	64	65	66	67	68
16	16	16	16	16	16	16	16	16	16	16	16	16	16	16	16	16	16	16	16	16	16	16	16	16	16	16	16	16	7	7	7	7	7	7	7	7
7	7	7	7	7	7	7	7	7	7	7	7	7	7	7	7	7	7	7	7	7	7	7	7	7	7	7	7	7	16	16	16	16	2	2	2	2
2	2	2	2	2	2	2	2	2	2	2	2	2	2	2	2	2	2	2	2	2	2	2	2	2	2	2	2	2	2	2	2	2	26	26	26	
22	22	22	22	22	22	29	29	29	29	29	29	29	29	29	29	29	29	29	29	29	29	29	29	29	29	29	29	29	29	29	29	29	3	3	3	
29	29	29	29	29	29	22	22	22	22	22	22	22	22	22	22	22	22	22	22	22	22	22	22	22	22	22	22	26	26	26	26	26	6	6	6	
6	6	6	6	6	6	6	(6)	26	26	26	26	26	26	26	26	26	26	26	26	26	26	26	26	26	26	26	26	3	3	3	3	3	9	9	9	
26	26	26	26	26	26	26	26	3	3	3	3	3	3	3	3	3	3	3	3	3	3	3	3	3	3	3	3	33	33	6	6	6	17	17		
3	3	3	3	3	3	3	3	33	33	33	33	33	33	33	33	33	33	33	33	33	33	33	33	33	33	33	33	9	6	9	9	9	32			
33	33	33	33	33	33	33	33	6	6	6	6	6	6	6	6	6	(6)	9	9	9	9	9	9	9	9	9	9	6	9	17	17	17				
9	9	9	9	9	9	9	9	9	9	9	9	9	9	9	9	9	9	6	6	6	6	6	6	6	6	6	6	17	17	32	32	32				
20	20	20	20	20	20	20	20	20	20	20	20	20	20	20	20	20	20	20	20	20	20	20	20	17	17	17	17	32	32							
17	17	17	17	17	17	17	17	17	17	17	17	17	17	17	17	17	17	17	17	17	17	17	17	32	32	32	32									
32	32	32	32	32	32	32	32	32	32	32	32	32	32	32	32	32	32	32	32	32	32	32	32	(20)												

Fastest laps

Driver	Time	Lap
René Arnoux	1m 15·06s	50
Alain Prost	1m 15·19s	4
John Watson	1m 15·32s	59
Nelson Piquet	1m 15·33s	10
Hector Rebaque	1m 15·84s	58
Carlos Reutemann	1m 15·89s	52
Riccardo Patrese	1m 16·11s	45
Derek Daly	1m 16·51s	46
Andrea de Cesaris	1m 16·88s	3
Jacques Laffite	1m 17·03s	62
Marc Surer	1m 17·07s	45
Elio de Angelis	1m 17·12s	23
Mario Andretti	1m 17·16s	27
Eddie Cheever	1m 17·18s	48
Alan Jones	1m 17·20s	3
Didier Pironi	1m 17·44s	4
Slim Borgudd	1m 17·44s	55
Jean-Pierre Jarier	1m 17·64s	45
Gilles Villeneuve	1m 17·70s	3
Bruno Giacomelli	1m 17·79s	3
Patrick Tambay	1m 18·23s	7
Keke Rosberg	1m 18·40s	51
Michele Alboreto	2m 49·45s	1

Points

WORLD CHAMPIONSHIP OF DRIVERS

1	Carlos Reutemann	43 pts
2	Nelson Piquet	26
3	Alan Jones	24
4=	Gilles Villeneuve	21
4=	Jacques Laffite	21
6	John Watson	19
7	Alain Prost	13
8	Riccardo Patrese	10
9=	Eddie Cheever	8
9=	Elio de Angelis	8
11	Didier Pironi	7
12=	Nigel Mansell	5
12=	René Arnoux	5
12=	Hector Rebaque	5
15	Marc Surer	4
16	Mario Andretti	3
17=	Patrick Tambay	1
17=	Andrea de Cesaris	1
17=	Slim Borgudd	1

CONSTRUCTORS' CUP

1	Williams	67
2	Brabham	31
3	Ferrari	28
4	Ligier	21
5	McLaren	20
6	Renault	18
7	Lotus	13
8	Arrows	10
9	Tyrrell	8
10	Ensign	4
11	Alfa Romeo	3
12=	Theodore	1
12=	ATS	1

Grosser Preis von Deutschland

The line between winning and losing was marked by a wire fence at the back of the Hockenheim victory enclosure. On the one side, Nelson Piquet spraying champagne after his third win of the season; on the other, Alan Jones and Carlos Reutemann waiting silently in the queue of hire cars about to leave the paddock.

For Piquet and the Parmalat Brabham team it had been a race of perseverance rewarded by an opportune win. For the Saudia-Leyland Williams equipe, the day had been a complete disaster.

Initially, the race had followed form and developed into a battle between the Renault-Elf team and Williams. Alain Prost led from pole and it was Jones who challenged the turbo throughout, taking the lead at the halfway mark with one of the most incisive manoeuvres seen all season.

Jones's lead lasted for 18 laps until the misfire, which lost the Australian the Monaco Grand Prix, returned to force the Williams into the pits. Reutemann had experienced the same misfire during the morning warm-up but an engine failure in the spare car put the championship leader into retirement while holding an impressive fourth place.

Piquet's race had not been easy, the Brabham driver having ruined a skirt after running over debris in the early stages. Nelson however, was there when it mattered most and with seven laps to go, he passed Prost whose Renault had refused to rev properly throughout the race.

Joining Piquet and Prost on the rostrum was a bemused Jacques Laffite, the Talbot-Ligier driver having earned the place through reliability more than anything else. Hector Rebaque, on the other hand, produced an aggressive charge from his customary position near the back of the grid and finished fourth ahead of Eddie Cheever in the new Tyrrell 011. An unhappy sixth was John Watson, complaining bitterly about the rough ride in the spare Marlboro McLaren MP4 which he had been forced to use at the last minute.

Watson's performance demonstrated the rapidly changing fortunes in Grand Prix racing. The Silverstone winner had been fortunate two weeks previously and, equally, Piquet had taken his opportunity at Hockenheim. That was little consolation to Jones or Reutemann and Patrick Head's tight-lipped expression as he marched down the line of hire cars indicated that the buck stopped at his drawing board. With five races to run and just eight points between Reutemann and Piquet, the situation was indeed critical.

ENTRY AND PRACTICE

Shortly after the British Grand Prix, the Formula 1 designers put their heads together and everyone – including Mauro Forghieri of Ferrari – agreed to do away with the hydraulic ride height control equipment and reduce the weight limit by an equivalent amount. Thus the silly, not to say highly dangerous, go-kart suspensions would be avoided and the designers' motion was put before the teams. Everyone agreed – except Marco Piccinini of Ferrari who pointed out that Ferrari did not invent the suspension systems and he (i.e. Enzo Ferrari) could not see why the weight limit fixed in the Concorde Agreement should be changed. So, cast iron suspension systems and the farcical six centimetre test remained in force at Hockenheim.

As far as the drivers were concerned, their main worry was getting through the fifth gear *Ostkurve* in one piece. "We're hardly going through there any slower than we were with sliding skirts and yet it's a hell of a lot more dangerous," said Alan Jones when comparing his 1981 car with the previous year. "You don't get the consistent downforce with these cars. They hit a bump, come off the ground a bit and your downforce is gone."

For all that, however, Jones was the fastest driver through the corner which said a lot for his determination to get on with the job regardless of the circumstances. Williams had been busy with three days of testing in England and the result was considerable aerodynamic improvements which helped the drivers get the best from their Goodyear cross-plys. The full-width front wing had been replaced by two smaller wings either side of the nose cone; there were new side-pod wing profiles and two 'ears' on the engine cover fed air directly to the DFV. In addition, Jones had a new chassis designated 16D which, in fact, was not a new design but simply a chassis built for the proposed experimental six-wheeler but brought into service following Jones's shunt at Silverstone.

Quickest in all the untimed sessions, Jones set his time on Friday afternoon and concentrated on running-in race tyres when his engine was down on power during the final session. Williams had been running a revised Cosworth engine designed to give more mid-range power at the expense of top end power although the advantage was thought to be minimal. Both Jones and Carlos Reutemann used 15ins fronts throughout practice and, at the end of the day, it was the Argentinian who set the faster time with a superb effort on Saturday afternoon. A crack in his usual car's oil tank on Friday meant Reutemann was 10th fastest in the spare chassi but, the following day, he set a time on his second lap which was beaten only by Alain Prost in the Renault.

The French team, of course, were enjoying their now traditional advantage at Hockenheim – a reserve of horsepower allowing both Prost and René Arnoux to run huge amounts of rear wing compared to their normally aspirated rivals. Prost reported problems turning into the chicanes but otherwise the cars were perfect and required no more than a 'confidence lift' at the *Ostkurve* when running Michelin qualifiers. It was thanks to the limited life of the qualifiers (no more than two laps) that Prost completed a mere six laps on Saturday afternoon. That was indicative of the practice session which lacked excitement due to the reappearance of soft qualifying tyres and the 'two sets per car per timed session' limit set in the Concorde Agreement. Renault had traced their Silverstone problems to a heat build-up around valves which were not seated properly and they were confident that the trouble would not reappear. The RE 30s carried extensions to the side-pods at the rear and both cars were to start from the front row after Arnoux, who had set the fastest time on Friday, was beaten by his team-mate on Saturday.

With the Williams team occupying the second row, that left Didier Pironi and Nelson Piquet to share row three with times set during the first timed session. Ferrari had three cars available as usual, the spare running revised rear suspension which Villeneuve did not rate too highly after a brief try-out during untimed practice. Pironi blew an engine on Friday morning while Villeneuve did likewise on Saturday afternoon and brought to an end a practice spent trying to coax an appalling chassis through the stadium.

After examining photographs of Nelson Piquet's shunt at Silverstone, it was surprising to see the Brazilian turn up at Hockenheim without a scratch. The same could not be said for his car and Brabham had built a fresh machine which was generally stiffer and featured carbon fibre in the side-pods. Happy that the tyre problem had been caused by a production fault rather than the use of the smaller 13ins front wheels, Brabham spent Friday trying both 15ins and 13ins before settling on the smaller fronts for Saturday. Unfortunately, a leaking hydro-pneumatic system meant Piquet was unable to match his earlier time while Hector Rebaque simply made no impression either day and took 16th place on the grid.

Jacques Laffite seemed rather surprised to find himself in seventh place, the Talbot-Ligier driver saying his Matra V12 was well-suited to the straights while the handling in the stadium was superb. The team did not appear to suffering as a result of the sudden departure of Gerard Ducarouge and it was apparent that Jean-Pierre Jabouille was assuming the

It may have been an opportune win but Piquet drove a tenacious race none the less *(above left)*.
"If only . . ." Carlos Reutemann reflects ruefully on championship points lost in a cloud of smoke *(left)*.
Early battle as Jones and Piquet chase Prost. The Brabham has yet to break a skirt but the front wing shows signs of contact with Arnoux's Renault during the opening lap *(above)*.
The end of lap one and Reutemann shows he means business by hanging on to Prost's Renault *(right)*.

AUGUST:
Alfa Romeo test turbo V8.
BMW produce 500th Formula 2 M12 engine.
Basil Tye resigns from FISA Safety Commission.
Mauro Baldi wins European Formula 3 Championship.

role of team manager with ease in spite of Guy Ligier's insistence that *he* was overseeing the team. The race cars had a wider track front and rear but Patrick Tambay was a couple of places further back after a recurrence of the wheel bearing problem experienced at Silverstone.

The old adage that a win lasts no more than about ten minutes after a race has finished was proved by the rather glum faces in the Marlboro McLaren team. With Silverstone now just a happy piece of history, John Watson was perplexed to find that his MP4 was not at home on the bumps at Hockenheim. A switch to the T-car brought some improvement but Watson lost 20 minutes and his last set of tyres when his engine blew out on the circuit after eight laps. The McLaren was one of the quickest through the stadium but, according to Watson, that was cancelled by unbelievable bouncing on the straights. Andrea de Cesaris moved onto the fifth row with his team leader after a quick lap on Saturday although the Italian did manage a spin at one of the chicanes before the session was over. Indeed, the chicanes seemed to be causing more problems than the rest of the circuit put together as Mario Andretti discovered throughout practice. The Marlboro Alfa Romeo was reasonable through the stadium and the V12 was giving enough horsepower elsewhere – but the chicanes were two corners rather than a fast swerve. With Bruno Giacomelli back in 19th position, the Alfa Romeo team were having an unhappy weekend made worse by the fact that Saturday August 1 was the first anniversary of Patrick Depailler's fatal accident at the *Ostkurve*.

The Ragno Beta Arrows team continued to spend most of their time sifting through the variety of Pirelli tyres available. They were unable to reach a satisfactory conclusion, Riccardo Patrese reporting that his car, complete with revised hydraulic suspension was well balanced but the tyres were giving poor traction. Siegfried Stohr was the final qualifier after setting his time on race tyres on Friday. After the fiasco at Silverstone, John Player Team Lotus presented a more sensible picture as Elio de Angelis and Nigel Mansell went out to practise in their 87s while Colin Chapman forgot about his Lotus 88 hobby horse for the time being. Both drivers were reasonably quick through the stadium but, once again, the chicanes were troublesome, Mansell reporting oversteer on the way out and vibration under braking on the way into the stadium. Both drivers ran 15ins fronts despite a lack of testing with the taller tyres and a heavy steering as a result. Time was lost running a 'D' compound which Goodyear had reckoned to be a qualifying tyre but Lotus, in common with Williams and Brabham, claimed the tyre to be nothing of the sort. Mansell finished practice one-tenth of a second slower than de Angelis which was a good effort considering the Englishman had run the same engine throughout.

Obviously on form and keen to please, Jean-Pierre Jarier thrashed round and round in the Denim Osella to set an impressive time on Friday afternoon – a time which was good enough to put the Frenchman on the ninth row in spite of a broken rear wing mounting. The Tyrrell team switched to Avons and Eddie Cheever began to make progress with the new Tyrrell although the major problem was lack of traction and understeer at the *Ostkurve*, Michele Alboreto, struggling with the aging 010, failed to qualify during his unparalleled 43 laps of practice. Slim Borgudd completed 38 laps in the ATS and the Swede did well to qualify after losing time with a broken rear bulkhead on Friday and a DFV which sprayed oil everywhere on Saturday. Derek Daly and the Guinness March team had an eventful few days one way or another. Practice got off to a bad start when two gearbox failures meant a total of three laps on Friday morning. In the afternoon, Daly became confused by the officials at the measuring pad who could not agree on the legality of his March at the 6cm test. Understandably upset by their vacillation, Daly gave the officials a touch of wheelspin as he left the pad – and was fined £100 for his trouble. Rain on Saturday morning meant further setting up was limited although the Irishman was consistently quick in the damp conditions. In the afternoon, however, he made the grid even if he was unable to make the most of a tow offered by Watson. Daly was 21st, two-tenths ahead of Marc Surer's Theodore and Eliseo Salazar who lost time with the wrong springing on Friday but set his time with well worn tyres in the final session.

The saddest scene of all was in the Fittipaldi pit where neither driver managed to qualify. Keke Rosberg, eighth fastest in the same car in 1980,

Sunday sponsor. Essex stickers were uncovered for race day only *(right)*.
(Right, from top to bottom:)
Among the many improvements to the Williams was an air box for the Ford-Cosworth DFV.
Brabham fitted gauges to check temperatures on the carbon fibre disc brakes fitted to Piquet's spare car.
The World Champion's overalls get an airing along with lucky tee-shirt and underpants.

complained of weaving on the approach to fast corners and a recalcitrant second gear while Chico Serra was the slowest of all. The Candy Toleman team's future looked much brighter with the introduction of a new Hart engine featuring an integral block and head. Brian Henton qualified on Friday but a seized turbo early on Saturday put paid to his chances. Derek Warwick had a reasonable chassis, particularly in the stadium, but annual holidays in Italy meant there weren't enough soft Pirellis just when the Englishman needed them most.

RACE

Although the morning warm-up was but thirty minutes long, it provided enough problems to fill a normal practice session. Villeneuve trailed into the pit lane with his rear wing missing; Watson stopped out on the circuit and had a black box replaced; Jarier was towed in for an engine change and Reutemann, one of the fastest on full tanks, came in with ten minutes remaining to report a misfire. The engine was changed in time for the start but the team were in something of a dilemma. Would the misfire suddenly reappear – just like it had done in Monaco, France and England? Reutemann had completed a few laps in the spare car and it was much slower, the engine being down-on-power and the side pods being of the earlier and less effective configuration. Playing safe, Reutemann opted for the spare while, down in the Lotus pit, Peter Collins, the team manager, peeled off black tape on the side pods to reveal the Essex stickers after David Thieme and Colin Chapman had come to some form of agreement following certain financial uncertainties between the two. Nigel Mansell, however, was more concerned about a tummy bug which had kept him up half the night but at least he was consoled by a competitive time during the warm-up. Renault settled on a tyre for the race while, in the interests of reliability, the rev limit was set at 10,800rpm compared to the 11,400rpm used during practice.

With Prost choosing the cleaner line on the left of the track, it was he who led the field into the first corner with Reutemann, obviously in a very determined mood, charging through to take second place ahead of Pironi. Jones was trapped behind Arnoux while Laffite attempted to run round the outside of the Williams. Going into the *Ostkurve*, Piquet challenged Arnoux and the Brabham's left front nose wing inadvertantly slashed Arnoux's right rear tyre. Arnoux slowed immediately while Piquet dropped behind Jones and Laffite as they entered the stadium for the first time. The French didn't know which way to look; one Renault leading the field, the other at the back. Poor Arnoux hobbled into the pits, his tyre in shreds, while Prost and Reutemann began to pull away from the rest. Pironi's run near the front had been short-lived, the Frenchman pulling off with a blown engine while his team-mate, back in sixth place, began to hold up Tambay, Andretti, Watson and de Cesaris. The Ulsterman, forced to use his original race car after the preferred chassis was found to be using too much oil on race morning, was having a very unhappy ride as the car bounced unmercifully on the straights and John had his work cut out just keeping his feet on the pedals. He began a quick slide down the lap chart and any hope of salvation for McLaren was lost when de Cesaris spun off and could not restart while attempting to take seventh place from Tambay. The Italian said he was alongside the Ligier as they went through the *Sachskurve* but Tambay banged wheels with the McLaren and de Cesaris's engine died when he lifted off. Tambay did not agree with that version of the story needless to say. Salazar had called at his pit to have a leaking brake calliper seen to and a speedy replacement job by the Ensign mechanics had the Chilean on his way for an impressive slog some five laps in arrears.

Going into the second chicane on lap five, Jones took second place from Reutemann as the Argentinian felt the power of his DFV begin to dwindle. Within three laps, Jones was on Prost's gearbox – and staying with him. Indeed, Jones was the faster driver through the *Ostkurve* and the Renault, supposedly at a power advantage, was not getting away on the straights. Although the engine sounded healthy, Prost was well aware that he had a major problem. The revs had been restricted alright – to 10,400rpm rather than 10,800rpm. As a result, he had the power but couldn't use it. At least it made for exciting racing – particularly on lap 10. Coming into the *Sachskurve*, Jones dived for the inside and to all intents and purposes had the line –

More points for Hector Rebaque after a storming drive from his customary position in the rear quarter of the grid *(above left)*. There were many startling figures in the paddock *(left)*.

and the lead. Prost, however, was not about to give up just like that and the Frenchman rode the corner out alongside the Williams before planting his right foot firmly on the throttle. He may have been short on top end power but he had torque and traction and he was about to use them both. Taking a slight advantage, Prost edged ahead fractionally and aimed for the left-right flick and the right-hander which followed. Holding his ground, Prost lined up for the right-hander and Jones had no alternative but to back off. The crowd voiced their approval. More was to follow.

Settling back into second place once more, Jones began to keep an eye out for the fast approaching Piquet who had worked his way ahead of Laffite and then Reutemann. Part of the damaged nose wing had blocked the Brabham's oil cooler but, fortunately, the debris blew off just as Nelson was about to stop at the pits. Tambay was next and coming under increasing pressure from Rebaque who had sliced through the field in an impressive manner. Patrese was eighth followed closely by Cheever with Andretti dropping back into tenth place. Behind the Alfa Romeo came what could best be described as an unruly mob as de Angelis, Daly and Mansell climbed over each other as they tried to get ahead of Villeneuve. On one occasion they passed the pits three abreast and all four cars then made a nonsense of the following right-hander. Going into the next chicane, Daly and Mansell touched, the result being a bent wheel rim on the March. Daly made a quick stop but his race was to last four more laps, a tie rod finally breaking as a result of the tussle with Mansell. The Lotus driver, having smashed his nose cone against Villeneuve's Ferrari, had charged into the pits but, from the speed he evacuated his car, it was clear that something rather more serious was amiss. Ripping off his overalls, Mansell shouted for water to be applied to his body after petrol had sloshed into the cockpit. It was a familiar feeling for the agonised Englishman, a badly seated fuel cap having caused exactly the same problem in Austria the previous year.

Villeneuve had stopped for fresh tyres which left the way clear for de Angelis to close on Andretti, the Lotus taking tenth place on lap 14. Rebaque had moved into sixth place in spite of a poor clutch while Patrese was closing on Tambay, the Italian taking seventh spot just before the Ligier retired with wheel bearing failure.

Up at the front, Reutemann was back in third place after Piquet had slowed when a stray piece of metal had ripped the left skirt on the Brabham. Nelson took a few laps to settle into the style required by too much understeer but at least he was free to do so as the Brabham was well clear of Laffite running in a lonely fifth place.

Approaching the half-way mark, the leaders began to haul in Arnoux as they powered through the *Ostkurve* and it was clear that the Renault drivers would make the most of the situation if they could. When René didn't give way on the approach to the stadium, it became obvious that he intended to let Prost by just before the *Sachskurve* and thus keep Jones at bay until the pit straight at the earliest. Approaching the braking area for the *Sachskurve*, Arnoux kept to the left while Prost duly took his line on the right. Neither driver, however, bargained for the wily Jones, the Australian leaving his braking to the last possible moment and darting *between* the startled Renault drivers to take the corner. It was a brilliantly incisive move which brought the packed grandstands to their feet once more and Jones rammed the point home by immediately pulling away while Arnoux beat his helmet in frustration.

Four laps later and Piquet was into his stride and catching Reutemann who, in turn was, pressing Prost. The Argentinian's race, however, was almost run and going through the *Ostkurve* he felt his engine begin to tighten. By the time he reached the second chicane, the deed was done, smoke poring from every oriface on the Williams as a dejected Reutemann kissed vital championship points goodbye. Piquet spared the leader of the championship no sympathy as he closed on Prost and the pattern of the race began to change dramatically as Jones's engine was heard to misfire.

Fine drizzle, which had been in the air since the early laps, began to intensify and Jones signalled to his pit in the hope that the race would be stopped. With ten laps remaining, Piquet moved into second place and closed rapidly on the Williams, taking the lead on lap 39. Jones slipped to third place before diving into the pits where the mechanics descended on the car – but to no avail. The spark box was changed, wires checked, but, as Jones accelerated away minus engine cover, it was obvious that the elusive misfire was still present. The

Alan Jones took the lead with a brilliant manoeuvre – only to lose it with a recurrence of the misfire which cost him the Monaco Grand Prix *(above right)*.
Eddie Cheever's first race in the Tyrrell 011 brought championship points for fifth place *(right)*.

gamble had not paid off and a place in the top six had been sacrificed for an eventual 11th position.

Piquet carefully reeled off the remaining few laps to score an opportune but none the less worthy win after a difficult race. Prost was reasonably satisfied with second place although the Frenchman felt, perhaps justifiably, that the rev-limiter problem had cost him the race. Jacques Laffite was rather surprised to be on the rostrum but gratefully accepted the four points and third place in the championship. The Ligier had picked up an excessive amount of rubber on the front tyres and, apart from the resulting understeer, his race had been trouble-free if rather quiet. Hector Rebaque gave Brabham three more points towards the Constructors' Championship and Eddie Cheever finished in the points once more after an impressive run in the new Tyrrell. Watson, one lap down, at least took one point at the end of an extremely uncomfortable ride, de Angelis was seventh after Patrese had retired with a blown engine while Jarier deserved more than eighth place after a competitive run in the Osella. Ninth was Andretti and Villeneuve, working hard to the end in his oversteering Ferrari, took tenth place away from Jones on the last lap. Stohr was next and Arnoux worked his way into 13th place with Surer classified 14th in spite of going off on the very last corner when the front suspension broke on the Theodore. Giacomelli was the final driver to be classified but spare a thought for Eliseo Salazar who drove superbly after his pit stop and took sixth fastest lap for his trouble.

Piquet's drive was not without merit. He had gambled on using 13ins fronts, survived two potentially disastrous incidents – and finished first. But it was easy to understand Jones's frustration as he flung his briefcase into the boot of his Mercedes-Benz. He had been the undoubted star of this race and was worthy of the nine points which should have put him into second place in the championship. Indeed, but for that dreaded misfire, he might have been *leading* the championship.

"We got what we deserved," said Frank Williams. "We didn't have bad luck today. We had two cars that let our drivers down." A fact which Carlos Reutemann was well aware of as he watched a smiling Nelson Piquet leave the rostrum on the other side of the fence.

Denis Jenkinson, special contributor to this edition of Autocourse, discusses the present day Grand Prix scene with Frank Gardner (left), a visitor to Hockenheim *(above)*.
Sign of the times. The unsponsored Tyrrell team, minus a motor home, hold a debrief behind the pits *(left)*.

Entries and practice times

No.	Driver	Nat	Car	Engine	Entrant	Practice 1	Practice 2
1	Alan Jones	AUS	Saudia-Leyland WILLIAMS FWO7C	Ford Cosworth DFV	TAG Williams Team	**1m 48·49s**	1m 49·38s
2	Carlos Reutemann	RA	Saudia-Leyland WILLIAMS FWO7C	Ford Cosworth DFV	TAG Williams Team	1m 50·20s	**1m 48·43s**
3	Eddie Cheever	USA	TYRRELL 011	Ford Cosworth DFV	Tyrrell Racing	**1m 52·19s**	1m 52·44s
4	Michele Alboreto	I	TYRRELL 010	Ford Cosworth DFV	Tyrrell Racing	**1m 53·69s**	1m 54·19s
5	Nelson Piquet	BR	Parmalat BRABHAM BT49C	Ford Cosworth DFV	Parmalat Racing Team	**1m 49·03s**	1m 49·26s
6	Hector Rebaque	MEX	Parmalat BRABHAM BT49C	Ford Cosworth DFV	Parmalat Racing Team	**1m 51·17s**	1m 51·49s
7	John Watson	GB	Marlboro McLAREN MP4	Ford Cosworth DFV	McLaren International	**1m 49·52s**	1m 50·36s
8	Andrea de Cesaris	I	Marlboro McLAREN MP4	Ford Cosworth DFV	McLaren International	1m 50·07s	**1m 49·58s**
9	Slim Borgudd	S	Abba ATS HGS 1	Ford Cosworth DFV	Team ATS	**1m 52·54s**	1m 54·14s
11	Elio de Angelis	I	John Player Special LOTUS 87	Ford Cosworth DFV	John Player Team Lotus	1m 52·36s	**1m 50·74s**
12	Nigel Mansell	GB	John Player Special LOTUS 87	Ford Cosworth DFV	John Player Team Lotus	1m 51·98s	**1m 50·86s**
14	Eliseo Salazar	RCH	ENSIGN N180B	Ford Cosworth DFV	Ensign Racing	1m 55·58s	**1m 53·16s**
15	Alain Prost	F	Elf RENAULT RE 30	Renault EF1	Equipe Renault Elf	1m 48·09s	**1m 47·50s**
16	René Arnoux	F	Elf RENAULT RE 30	Renault EF1	Equipe Renault Elf	**1m 47·96s**	1m 48·08s
17	Derek Daly	IRL	Rizla MARCH 811	Ford Cosworth DFV	March Grand Prix	1m 55·80s	**1m 52·65s**
20	Keke Rosberg	SF	FITTIPALDI F8C	Ford Cosworth DFV	Fittipaldi Automotive	**1m 53·28s**	1m 53·38s
21	Chico Serra	BR	FITTIPALDI F8C	Ford Cosworth DFV	Fittipaldi Automotive	1m 55·22s	**1m 54·89s**
22	Mario Andretti	USA	Marlboro ALFA ROMEO 179C	Alfa Romeo 1260	Marlboro Team Alfa Romeo	**1m 50·64s**	1m 50·73s
23	Bruno Giacomelli	I	Marlboro ALFA ROMEO 179C	Alfa Romeo 1260	Marlboro Team Alfa Romeo	**1m 52·21s**	1m 52·59s
25	Patrick Tambay	F	Talbot-Gitanes LIGIER JS17	Matra MS 81	Equipe Talbot Gitanes	1m 50·27s	**1m 49·28s**
26	Jacques Laffite	F	Talbot-Gitanes LIGIER JS17	Matra MS 81	Equipe Talbot Gitanes	**1m 50·00s**	1m 50·61s
27	Gilles Villeneuve	CDN	Fiat FERRARI 126CK	Ferrari 126C	Scuderia Ferrari SpA SEFAC	**1m 49·44s**	1m 50·24s
28	Didier Pironi	F	Fiat FERRARI 126CK	Ferrari 126C	Scuderia Ferrari SpA SEFAC	**1m 49·00s**	1m 49·97s
29	Riccardo Patrese	I	Ragno-Beta ARROWS A3	Ford Cosworth DFV	Arrows Racing Team	1m 50·68s	**1m 50·65s**
30	Siegfried Stohr	I	Ragno-Beta ARROWS A3	Ford Cosworth DFV	Arrows Racing Team	**1m 53·19s**	1m 53·33s
31	Beppe Gabbiani	I	Denim OSELLA FA1B	Ford Cosworth DFV	Osella Squadra Corse	1m 55·53s	**1m 53·39s**
32	Jean-Pierre Jarier	F	Denim OSELLA FA1B	Ford Cosworth DFV	Osella Squadra Corse	**1m 52·19s**	1m 52·95s
33	Marc Surer	CH	THEODORE TY 01	Ford Cosworth DFV	Theodore Racing Team	**1m 52·85s**	1m 53·50s
35	Brian Henton	GB	Candy TOLEMAN TG 181	Hart 415T	Candy Toleman Motorsport	**1m 53·31s**	1m 54·77s
36	Derek Warwick	GB	Candy TOLEMAN TG 181	Hart 415T	Candy Toleman Motorsport	1m 54·59s	**1m 53·58s**
Friday morning and Saturday morning practice sessions not officially recorded						*Fri pm Warm, dry*	*Sat pm Warm, dry*

Starting grid

15 PROST (1m 47·50s) Renault	
	16 ARNOUX (1m 47·96s) Renault
2 REUTEMANN (1m 48·43s) Williams	
	1 JONES (1m 48·49s) Williams
28 PIRONI (1m 49·00s) Ferrari	
	5 PIQUET (1m 49·03s) Brabham
26 LAFFITE (1m 49·28s) Talbot-Ligier	
	27 VILLENEUVE (1m 49·44s) Ferrari
7 WATSON (1m 49·52s) McLaren	
	8 DE CESARIS (1m 49·58s) McLaren
25 TAMBAY (1m 50·00s) Talbot-Ligier	
	22 ANDRETTI (1m 50·64s) Alfa Romeo
29 PATRESE (1m 50·65s) Arrows	
	11 DE ANGELIS (1m 50·74s) Lotus
12 MANSELL (1m 50·86s) Lotus	
	6 REBAQUE (1m 51·17s) Brabham
32 JARIER (1m 52·19s) Osella	
	3 CHEEVER (1m 52·19s) Tyrrell
23 GIACOMELLI (1m 52·21s) Alfa Romeo	
	9 BORGUDD (1m 52·54s) ATS
17 DALY (1m 52·65s) March	
	33 SURER (1m 52·85s) Theodore
14 SALAZAR (1m 53·16s) Ensign	
	30 STOHR (1m 53·19s) Arrows

Did not start:
20 Rosberg (Fittipaldi), 1m 53·28s, did not qualify
35 Henton (Toleman), 1m 53·31s, did not qualify
31 Gabbiani (Osella), 1m 53·39s, did not qualify
36 Warwick (Toleman), 1m 53·58s, did not qualify
4 Alboreto (Tyrrell), 1m 53·69s, did not qualify
21 Serra (Fittipaldi), 1m 54·89s, did not qualify

Past winners

Year	Driver	Nat	Car	Circuit	Distance miles/km	Speed mph/km/h
1926	Rudi Caracciola	D	2·0 Mercedes s/c	Avus	243·70/392·20	83·95/135·10
1927	Otto Merz	D	6·8 Mercedes-Benz S s/c	Nürburgring Full	316·13/508·77	63·31/101·88
1928	Rudi Caracciola/ Christian Werner	D D	7·0 Mercedes-Benz SS s/c	Nürburgring Full	316·13/508·77	64·43/103·69
1929	Louis Chiron	F	2·0 Bugatti T35C s/c	Nürburgring Full	316·13/508·77	66·30/106·70
1931	Rudi Caracciola	D	7·0 Mercedes-Benz SSKL s/c	Nürburgring North	311·82/501·82	67·26/108·24
1932	Rudi Caracciola	D	2·6 Alfa Romeo P3 s/c	Nürburgring North	354·34/570·25	73·98/119·06
1934	Hans Stuck	D	4·4 Auto Union A-type s/c	Nürburgring North	354·34/570·25	76·38/122·92
1935	Tazio Nuvolari	I	3·2 Alfa Romeo P3 s/c	Nürburgring North	311·82/501·82	75·24/121·09
1936	Bernd Rosemeyer	D	6·0 Auto Union C-type s/c	Nürburgring North	311·82/501·82	81·82/131·68
1937	Rudi Caracciola	D	5·5 Mercedes-Benz W125 s/c	Nürburgring North	311·82/501·82	82·78/133·23
1938	Dick Seaman	GB	3·0 Mercedes-Benz W154 s/c	Nürburgring North	311·82/501·82	80·72/129·91
1939	Rudi Caracciola	D	3·0 Mercedes-Benz W163 s/c	Nürburgring North	311·82/501·82	75·23/121·07
1950*	Alberto Ascari	I	2·0 Ferrari 166	Nürburgring North	266·78/364·96	77·75/125·13
1951	Alberto Ascari	I	4·5 Ferrari 375	Nürburgring North	283·47/456·20	83·76/134·80
1952	Alberto Ascari	I	2·0 Ferrari 500	Nürburgring North	255·12/410·58	82·20/132·29
1953	Giuseppe Farina	I	2·0 Ferrari 500	Nürburgring North	255·12/410·58	83·91/135·04
1954	Juan Manuel Fangio	RA	2·5 Mercedes-Benz W196	Nürburgring North	311·82/501·82	82·87/133·37
1956	Juan Manuel Fangio	RA	2·5 Lancia-Ferrari D50	Nürburgring North	311·82/501·82	85·45/137·52
1957	Juan Manuel Fangio	RA	2·5 Maserati 250F	Nürburgring North	311·82/501·82	88·82/142·94
1958	Tony Brooks	GB	2·5 Vanwall	Nürburgring North	212·60/342·15	90·31/145·34
1959	Tony Brooks	GB	2·4 Ferrari Dino 256	Avus	309·44/498·00	145·35/230·70
1960*	Jo Bonnier	S	1·5 Porsche 718	Nürburgring South	154·04/247·90	80·23/129·12
1961	Stirling Moss	GB	1·5 Lotus 18/21-Climax	Nürburgring North	212·60/342·15	92·30/148·54
1962	Graham Hill	GB	1·5 BRM P57	Nürburgring North	212·60/342·15	80·35/129·31
1963	John Surtees	GB	1·5 Ferrari 156	Nürburgring North	212·60/342·15	95·83/154·22
1964	John Surtees	GB	1·5 Ferrari 158	Nürburgring North	212·60/342·15	96·58/155·43
1965	Jim Clark	GB	1·5 Lotus 33-Climax	Nürburgring North	212·60/342·15	96·76/160·55
1966	Jack Brabham	AUS	3·0 Brabham BT19-Repco	Nürburgring North	212·60/342·15	86·75/139·61
1967	Denny Hulme	NZ	3·0 Brabham BT24-Repco	Nürburgring North	212·60/342·15	101·41/163·20
1968	Jackie Stewart	GB	3·0 Matra MS10-Ford	Nürburgring North	198·65/319·69	85·71/137·94
1969	Jacky Ickx	B	3·0 Brabham BT26A-Ford	Nürburgring North	198·65/319·69	108·43/174·50
1970	Jochen Rindt	A	3·0 Lotus 72-Ford	Hockenheim	210·92/339·44	124·07/199·67
1971	Jackie Stewart	GB	3·0 Tyrrell 003-Ford	Nürburgring North	170·27/274·02	114·45/184·19
1972	Jacky Ickx	B	3·0 Ferrari 312B-2/72	Nürburgring North	198·65/319·69	116·62/187·68
1973	Jackie Stewart	GB	3·0 Tyrrell 006-Ford	Nürburgring North	198·65/319·69	116·79/187·95
1974	Clay Regazzoni	CH	3·0 Ferrari 312B-3/74	Nürburgring North	198·65/319·69	117·33/188·82
1975	Carlos Reutemann	RA	3·0 Brabham BT44B-Ford	Nürburgring North	198·65/319·69	117·73/189·47
1976	James Hunt	GB	3·0 McLaren M23-Ford	Nürburgring North	198·65/319·69	117·18/188·59
1977	Niki Lauda	A	3·0 Ferrari 312T-2/77	Hockenheim	198·27/319·08	129·57/208·53
1978	Mario Andretti	USA	3·0 JPS Lotus 79-Ford	Hockenheim	189·83/305·51	129·41/208·26
1979	Alan Jones	AUS	3·0 Williams FW07-Ford	Hockenheim	189·83/305·51	134·27/216·09
1980	Jacques Laffite	F	3·0 Ligier JS11/15-Ford	Hockenheim	189·83/305·51	137·22/220·83
1981	Nelson Piquet	BR	3·0 Brabham BT49C-Ford	Hockenheim	189·83/305·51	132·53/213·29

* Non-championship (Formula 2)

Circuit data

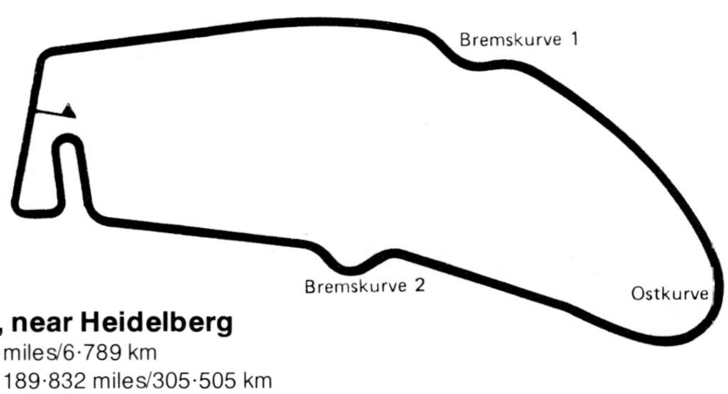

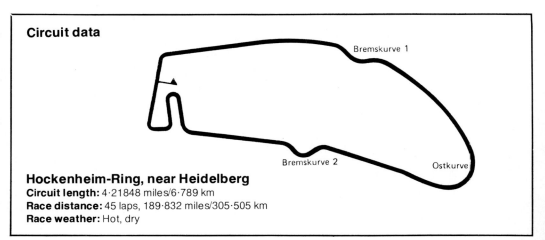

Hockenheim-Ring, near Heidelberg

Circuit length: 4·21848 miles/6·789 km
Race distance: 45 laps, 189·832 miles/305·505 km
Race weather: Hot, dry

Results and retirements

Place	Driver	Car	Laps	Time and Speed (mph/km/h)/Retirement	
1	Nelson Piquet	Brabham-Cosworth V8	45	1h 25m 55·60s	132·534/213·294
2	Alain Prost	Renault t/c V6	45	1h 26m 07·12s	132·239/212·818
3	Jacques Laffite	Talbot-Ligier Matra V12	45	1h 27m 00·20s	130·894/210·654
4	Hector Rebaque	Brabham-Cosworth V8	45	1h 27m 35·29s	130·020/209·247
5	Eddie Cheever	Tyrrell-Cosworth V8	45	1h 27m 46·12s	129·753/208·817
6	John Watson	McLaren-Cosworth V8	44		
7	Elio de Angelis	Lotus-Cosworth V8	44		
8	Jean-Pierre Jarier	Osella-Cosworth V8	44		
9	Mario Andretti	Alfa Romeo V12	44		
10	Gilles Villeneuve	Ferrari t/c V6	44		
11	Alan Jones	Williams-Cosworth V8	44		
12	Siegfried Stohr	Arrows-Cosworth V8	44		
13	René Arnoux	Renault t/c V6	44		
14	Marc Surer	Theodore-Cosworth V8	43		
15	Bruno Giacomelli	Alfa Romeo V12	43		
	Eliseo Salazar	Ensign-Cosworth V8	39	Running, not classified	
	Slim Borgudd	ATS-Cosworth V8	35	Engine	
	Carlos Reutemann	Williams-Cosworth V8	27	Engine	
	Riccardo Patrese	Arrows-Cosworth V8	27	Engine	
	Patrick Tambay	Talbot-Ligier Matra V12	27	Rear wheel bearing	
	Derek Daly	March-Cosworth V8	15	Steering tie rod	
	Nigel Mansell	Lotus-Cosworth V8	12	Fuel leak	
	Andrea de Cesaris	McLaren-Cosworth V8	4	Spun off	
	Didier Pironi	Ferrari t/c V6	1	Engine	

Fastest lap: Jones, on lap 4, 1m 52·42s, 135·068mph/217·371km/h.
Lap record: Alan Jones (F1 Williams FWO7B-Cosworth DFV), 1m 48·49s, 139·960mph/225·245km/h (1980).

Lap chart

1st LAP ORDER		1	2	3	4	5	6	7	8	9	10	11	12	13	14	15	16	17	18	19	20	21	22	23
15	A.Prost	15	15	15	15	15	15	15	15	15	15	15	15	15	15	15	15	15	15	15	15	1	1	1
2	C.Reutemann	2	2	2	2	1	1	1	1	1	1	1	1	1	1	1	1	1	1	1	1	15	15	15
28	D.Pironi	28	1	1	1	2	2	2	2	5	5	5	5	5	5	2	2	2	2	2	2	2	2	2
1	A.Jones	1	26	5	5	5	5	5	5	2	2	2	2	2	2	5	5	5	5	5	5	5	5	5
26	J.Laffite	26	5	26	26	26	26	26	26	26	26	26	26	26	26	26	26	26	26	26	26	26	26	26
5	N.Piquet	5	27	27	27	27	27	27	25	25	25	25	6	6	6	6	6	6	6	6	6	6	6	6
27	G.Villeneuve	27	25	25	25	25	25	25	27	6	6	6	25	25	25	25	25	25	25	29	29	29	3	3
22	M.Andretti	22	22	8	8	29	29	29	6	29	29	29	29	29	29	29	29	29	29	25	3	3	25	25
25	P.Tambay	25	8	22	22	22	6	6	29	3	3	3	3	3	3	3	3	3	3	3	25	25	29	29
7	J.Watson	7	7	29	29	6	22	22	22	22	22	22	22	22	11	11	11	11	11	11	11	11	11	11
8	A.de Cesaris	8	29	11	11	23	11	11	11	27	11	11	11	11	22	22	22	22	22	22	22	22	22	22
11	E.de Angelis	11	11	6	6	11	23	3	3	11	27	27	32	32	32	32	32	32	32	32	32	32	32	32
29	R.Patrese	29	6	23	23	3	3	17	17	17	17	12	27	23	7	7	7	7	7	7	7	7	7	7
6	H.Rebaque	6	23	3	3	17	17	12	12	12	12	32	23	7	23	23	23	23	30	30	30	30	30	30
23	B.Giacomelli	23	3	7	17	12	12	23	23	7	23	7	7	30	30	30	30	30	9	9	9	9	9	9
3	E.Cheever	3	17	17	7	7	7	7	7	23	7	23	30	9	9	9	9	9	23	27	27	27	27	27
17	D.Daly	17	33	33	12	33	32	32	32	32	32	30	9	27	27	27	27	27	27	16	16	16	16	16
12	N.Mansell	12	14	12	33	32	33	33	33	30	30	9	12	16	16	16	16	16	16	33	33	33	33	33
33	M.Surer	33	32	14	32	30	30	30	30	9	9	16	16	33	33	33	33	33	33	23	23	23	23	23
14	E.Salazar	14	12	32	30	9	9	9	9	33	16	17	33	17	17	17	14	14	14	14	14	14	14	14
32	J-P.Jarier	32	30	30	9	16	16	16	16	16	33	33	17	14	14	14								
30	S.Stohr	30	9	9	14	14	14	14	14	14	14	14	14											
9	S.Borgudd	9	16	16	16																			
16	R.Arnoux	16																						

1st LAP ORDER		24	25	26	27	28	29	30	31	32	33	34	35	36	37	38	39	40	41	42	43	44	45
15	A.Prost	1	1	1	1	1	1	1	1	1	1	1	1	1	1	1	5	5	5	5	5	5	5
2	C.Reutemann	15	15	15	15	15	15	15	15	15	15	15	15	15	5	5	15	15	15	15	15	15	15
28	D.Pironi	2	2	2	5	5	5	5	5	5	5	5	5	5	15	15	1	1	1	26	26	26	26
1	A.Jones	5	5	5	2	26	26	26	26	26	26	26	26	26	26	26	26	26	26	1	6	6	6
26	J.Laffite	26	26	26	26	6	6	6	6	6	6	6	6	6	6	6	6	6	6	6	3	3	3
5	N.Piquet	6	6	6	6	3	3	3	3	3	3	3	3	3	3	3	3	3	3	3	7	7	
27	G.Villeneuve	3	3	3	3	11	11	11	11	11	11	11	11	11	11	7	7	7	7	7	11	11	
22	M.Andretti	25	29	29	29	22	22	22	22	22	22	22	7	7	7	11	11	11	11	11	32	32	
25	P.Tambay	29	25	25	25	32	32	32	32	32	32	32	32	32	32	32	32	32	32	32	1	22	
7	J.Watson	11	11	11	11	7	7	7	7	7	7	7	22	22	22	22	22	22	22	22	22	27	
8	A.de Cesaris	22	22	22	22	30	30	30	30	30	27	27	27	27	27	27	27	27	27	27	27	1	
11	E.de Angelis	32	32	32	32	27	27	27	27	27	30	30	30	30	30	30	30	30	30	30	30	30	
29	R.Patrese	7	7	7	7	9	9	9	16	16	16	16	16	16	16	16	16	16	16	16	16	16	
6	H.Rebaque	30	30	30	30	16	16	16	9	33	33	33	33	33	33	33	33	33	33	33	33		
23	B.Giacomelli	9	9	9	27	33	33	33	33	23	23	23	23	23	23	23	23	23	23	23	23		
3	E.Cheever	27	27	27	9	23	23	23	23	9	9	9	9	14	14	14	14	14					
17	D.Daly	16	16	16	16	14	14	14	14	14	14	14	14										
12	N.Mansell	33	33	33	33																		
33	M.Surer	23	23	23	23																		
14	E.Salazar	14	14	14	14																		
32	J-P.Jarier																						
30	S.Stohr																						
9	S.Borgudd																						
16	R.Arnoux																						

Points

WORLD CHAMPIONSHIP OF DRIVERS

1	Carlos Reutemann	43 pts
2	Nelson Piquet	35
3	Jacques Laffite	25
4	Alan Jones	24
5	Gilles Villeneuve	21
6	John Watson	20
7	Alain Prost	19
8 =	Riccardo Patrese	10
8 =	Eddie Cheever	10
10 =	Elio de Angelis	8
10 =	Hector Rebaque	8
12	Didier Pironi	7
13 =	Nigel Mansell	5
13 =	René Arnoux	5
15	Marc Surer	4
16	Mario Andretti	3
17 =	Patrick Tambay	1
17 =	Andrea de Cesaris	1
17 =	Slim Borgudd	1

CONSTRUCTORS' CUP

1	Williams	67
2	Brabham	43
3	Ferrari	28
4	Ligier	25
5	Renault	24
6	McLaren	21
7	Lotus	13
8 =	Arrows	10
8 =	Tyrrell	10
10	Ensign	4
11	Alfa Romeo	3
12 =	Theodore	1
12 =	ATS	1

Fastest laps

Driver	Time	Lap
Alan Jones	1m 52·42s	4
Nelson Piquet	1m 52·60s	7
Alain Prost	1m 53·51s	4
Carlos Reutemann	1m 53·69s	3
Hector Rebaque	1m 54·47s	13
Eliseo Salazar	1m 54·61s	4
Riccardo Patrese	1m 54·84s	20
Jacques Laffite	1m 54·96s	13
Eddie Cheever	1m 55·25s	10
Patrick Tambay	1m 55·31s	17
Nigel Mansell	1m 55·55s	8
Bruno Giacomelli	1m 55·56s	4
John Watson	1m 55·56s	42
Andrea de Cesaris	1m 55·82s	4
Elio de Angelis	1m 55·98s	8
Derek Daly	1m 56·15s	5
René Arnoux	1m 56·20s	3
Mario Andretti	1m 56·21s	5
Gilles Villeneuve	1m 56·26s	16
Jean-Pierre Jarier	1m 56·61s	42
Siegfried Stohr	1m 56·70s	7
Slim Borgudd	1m 56·74s	7
Marc Surer	1m 56·89s	16
Didier Pironi	2m 01·67s	1

Grosser Preis von Österreich

The end of a majestic circuit? Rumours were rife that the Austrian Grand Prix at the Österreichring *(above)* was no longer a financial proposition.

Considering the turmoil which had surrounded the Talbot-Ligier team since the start of the season, Jacques Laffite and Guy Ligier were in a relaxed frame of mind when they arrived in Austria. Booking into their hotel in the village of Obdach, a French watering hole since the Matra sports car days, the team were greeted by the local band. Ligier took up the bass drum, Patrick Tambay clanged the cymbals while Laffite played the fool with the conductor's baton. The team may have undergone political change, switched engines, swapped drivers and, more recently, fired their team manager, but it scarcely showed in Austria. Laffite may have racked up points due to reliability and consistency – but he was third in the championship none the less.

On Sunday afternoon, he consolidated that position with his first win of the season. And this was a victory which was thoroughly deserved for, on August 16, Laffite and the Talbot-Ligier team were in a league of their own. Success was due in part to Jean-Pierre Jabouille, the man who had been a minor embarrassment in the cockpit but who more than fulfilled his role as team manager/engineer in the pit lane. During Michelin tyre tests at Zandvoort, Jabouille had earmarked a compound which, to his experienced eye, would be suitable for the Österreichring. Few agreed with his choice but Jabouille persisted and, during the final stages of the 53-lap race, Laffite reaped the rewards of the softer compound as he snatched the lead from René Arnoux.

True to form, the Renault-Elf team had buttoned up the front of the grid and, to underline the turbo advantage 2000 feet above sea level, Gilles Villeneuve was third fastest ahead of Laffite. The Ferrari led briefly before brake trouble intervened and what appeared to be a Renault monopoly began to crumble when Alain Prost crashed out of the lead with front suspension failure. Arnoux, fighting understeer on his hard Michelins, was overhauled by Laffite while the Brabham and Williams teams struggled in their wake. Nelson Piquet took third place and closed the gap on Carlos Reutemann to six points after the Saudia-Leyland Williams driver could do no better than finish fifth behind Alan Jones.

At least the Williams team had scored points after their disaster in Germany but a broken spring platform on Jones's car gave some indication of the punishment handed out by the stiff suspensions pounding over the Austrian bumps. John Watson struggled into sixth place in his Marlboro McLaren to score points for the fifth race in succession.

In spite of glorious weather, it had been a difficult race for everyone bar the winner. Laffite had driven magnificently and, to complete his day, set fastest lap and closed to within 11 points of Reutemann. Cause indeed for Guy Ligier to beat his Talbot drum into the small hours of Monday morning.

AUGUST:

Gerard Ducarouge joins Alfa Romeo.

Basil Tye to stand for Presidency of FISA in October elections.

ENTRY AND PRACTICE

Grinding along the three-hour drive from Vienna to the unspoilt but basic hinterland of Knittelfeld, it was easy to be persuaded that the Grand Prix calendar could manage without the Österreichring. The truck-infested, single-lane route was lightened briefly by a spirited dash up the Semmering Pass but, otherwise, the journey seemed without end. There was time to consider the strengthening rumours that this would be the last Grand Prix for the Österreichring, in use for a mere decade.

Heavy taxes on gate money; low attendances; crippling inflation; no Austrian drivers; poor Ferrari performances. These were said to be the nails in the coffin for the traditional circuits of the Seventies while, on the other side of the Atlantic, the Big Buck, TV-orientated track of the Eighties was being conceived – in a Las Vegas car park, no less.

Then there was the rain. When the dark clouds gathered in Styria, they had a habit of unleashing their fury in a wicked fashion and turning the circuit into a

JACQUES LAFFITE

quagmire in minutes. In 1981, however, the sun shone brilliantly. The Österreichring was bathed in all its natural splendour and you couldn't help but marvel at the surroundings and the challenge of this magnificent circuit. After the concrete of Hockenheim, it was another world.

There were handicaps, of course. The pit lane was absurdly cramped and the silly cars with their silly suspensions gave the drivers a dreadful time on the high speed bumps. But the sun shone and the heat made little difference to the turbos. The altitude out-weighed that disadvantage and the Renault team set the fastest times with nonchalant ease. Friday was generally accepted as being the faster of the two days yet both Alain Prost and René Arnoux went out during the final hour on Saturday and improved their times within a handful of laps. The Renaults ran plenty of rear wing and, apart from a touch of understeer, there were few complaints. As it was, Prost was spending his spare time dashing to the phone, awaiting news of the arrival of his first child. The pit crew had a special signal ready just in case, but it was never used. Arnoux, fastest on both days, took his second Austrian pole in succession but, as the beady-eyed Frenchman reminded us, it was the seventh Grand Prix pole of his career – and he had yet to win from that position....

Gilles Villeneuve, on the other hand, had won a Grand Prix from his first pole position (1979 U.S. Grand Prix West) although the Ferrari driver did not expect to repeat the performance this weekend. True, Villeneuve had made the most of his turbocharged advantage and taken a magnificent third place on the grid but tyres and the ease with which his rivals could overtake would probably conspire against him in the race. Ferrari had been continuing with their half-hearted attempts to make the chassis reasonable and, for this race, a new rear end was fitted to the proposed race cars. The suspension was held together by a single dural plate instead of a magnesium alloy casting but the drivers reported little improvement. Didier Pironi crashed on Friday morning and lost time in the afternoon while waiting for his car to be repaired. Villeneuve, meanwhile, set his time on his sixth lap – just before an engine failure next time round. Pironi improved on Saturday and took eighth place.

Jacques Laffite made sure Michelin dominated the front two rows by setting his time immediately after a pit stop for fresh qualifiers on Saturday afternoon. Modifications to the Matra engine allowed the drivers to rev to 13,000rpm but the Talbot-Ligier's main advantage lay in its handling, Laffite taking the *Boschkurve* with a precision lacked by all but the Renaults. According to rival teams, Ligier's stability was due in no small part to skirts made of two materials at the point of contact with the track. This was strictly forbidden according to a Gentleman's Agreement but, as a FISA representative pointed out, it was no more than an agreement between the teams. FISA were powerless – not that they would have done anything if their handling of the 6cm fiasco was anything to go by – and, as a result, Ligier continued to use their composite skirts. Patrick Tambay was down in 17th place thanks to understeer on a car which had different roll bars and springs from those used on Laffite's chassis – all of which added up to a two-second gap between the drivers.

Following their disasters at Hockenheim, Williams had engaged in serious testing at Silverstone in a bid to get to the bottom of the misfire problem which had bedevilled the team since Monaco. The answer seemed to lie in the fuel system and Patrick Head was quietly confident that he had the problem licked. Indeed, there was scarcely a missed beat to be heard although Carlos Reutemann had a terminal misfire of sorts on Saturday morning when his DFV dropped a valve and set off a chain reaction which finished with a con-rod punching its way through the block! The irony was that this was the engine Carlos should have used in Germany had he not been forced to switch to the spare car. Clearly, Carlos's race card at Hockenheim was marked 'DNF' regardless of which car he used! Reutemann was the fastest Williams driver with a lap of 1m 34.531s on Friday. Alan Jones, however, did a 1m 33.670s on Saturday morning with the aid of new low profile fronts from Goodyear and you can imagine the Australian's chagrin when it was discovered that there was but one set available. The reigning World Champion was not well pleased and had to settle for his Friday time set in the spare car.

Brabham stuck with 13ins fronts as usual, the smaller tyre presenting surprisingly few problems on the left front through the fast right-hand curves. Hector Rebaque kept the mechanics busy from the

Jacques Laffite, running a perfect tyre compound chosen by Jean-Pierre Jabouille, closes in on pole position man, René Arnoux *(right)*.
End of lap one and Prost challenges Villeneuve while Arnoux, Pironi and the eventual winner, Laffite, follow. Note the black marks left on the bumps by the flexible skirts *(below)*.
Laffite sprays the Giacobazzi while Niki Lauda interviews the loser for Austrian television *(bottom)*.
The leader of the band. Guy Ligier beats his drum while Patrick Tambay joins in on the cymbals *(bottom right)*.

Following pages:
René Arnoux took another pole position and finished second *(below)*.
(photo: Nigel Snowdon)
Jacques Laffite and the Talbot-Ligier team won their first Grand Prix of the season in Austria *(left)*.
(photo: Nigel Snowdon)
Attractive support for ATS......*(right)*.
(photo: Charles Knight)

Showing her credentials... *(below)*.
Prost lost the lead when the front suspension on his Renault broke *(below left)*.

word go when a momentary aberration while braking for the *Hella Licht* chicane on Friday morning sent the Mexican into the side of Tambay's Ligier. Rebaque used the spare car while the mechanics began repairs to the left-front corner but Hector had to hand the spare over to Piquet in the afternoon when Nelson's engine blew just after he had set his best time. Rebaque had his own car back in time for the final session and he set a 1m 36.150s, good enough for 15th place on the grid.

There was a certain amount of political horse-play going on in the John Player Team Lotus pit. Apart from another episode of the 'Now You See Them – Now You Don't' game with the Essex stickers, Colin Chapman was busy enticing Elio de Angelis to remain with the team for 1982. As ever, though, Chapman's methods were highly specialised. De Angelis arrived on Friday morning to find the spare car decked out with Nigel Mansell's number but the Italian got on with his job and put in more laps than anyone else during the timed session in the afternoon to become the fastest Lotus driver. Perhaps Chapman's logic was not so confused after all. What was apparent, however, was the evil handling of the 87s over the bumps. Mansell may have been the slower driver but it was not through the want of trying, the Englishman keeping his right foot firmly on the throttle as the car bucked and weaved through the corners. Part of his problem was traced to faulty shock absorbers and he spent some time in the spare car trying different springs on Saturday while de Angelis caused minor damage with a spin at *Hella Licht*.

Splitting the black and gold cars was Riccardo Patrese in the orange and white Ragno-Beta Arrows, the Italian running smoothly throughout practice and making the most of his limited supply of qualifying tyres. The same could not be said for Siegfried Stohr who appeared ill at ease and scratched onto the back row on Saturday afternoon. Before practice began, John Watson explained that understeer was the least desirable vice to have on this fast circuit. You had to be able to turn in accurately and get the power down efficiently but, unfortunately, the Marlboro McLaren MP4 was unable to provide Watson with the perfect set-up. In addition, there appeared to be excessive downforce, the Ulsterman complaining that the revs dropped away when he changed into fifth. He was disappointed therefore to be in 12th place but John's problems were minor compared to those of his team-mate. Andrea de Cesaris had been six-tenths

TALBOT

NAULT elf
elf
16
MICHELIN

ATS
FORMULA ONE

Nelson Piquet finished a steady third and closed the championship gap on Carlos Reutemann. The Brabham driver laps Eliseo Salazar who drove impressively before retiring his Ensign with engine failure.

slower than Watson on Friday but the young Italian's withering reputation received another crushing blow when he spun off on his first lap of practice on Saturday afternoon. De Cesaris lost control coming through the left-hand *Sebring* curve, the McLaren bouncing high in the air before spinning across the grass in a welter of fibre-glass and wings. Somehow, the monocoque remained intact and the long-suffering mechanics began repairs in time for the race.

There had been strong rumours that the Marlboro Alfa Romeo team might run Goodyear tyres in Austria following conclusive back-to-back tests at Balocco. In the public air of the Österreichring paddock, however, it was made plain that Alfa Romeo and Michelin would continue their association to appease, it was thought, the healthy contract between the two in terms of supplying Alfa Romeo road cars leaving the factory. Whatever the political wire-pulling, Mario Andretti was unhappy with the decision, saying that the engine was good but the grip was not as it should be in spite of new rear suspension and carbon-fibre side wings.

One driver quite happy with Michelin was Jean-Pierre Jarier, the Frenchman receiving full treatment from the tyre company and putting his Denim Osella in the middle of the grid. Beppe Gabbiani lost a left-front wheel before it was discovered that the rim was fouling the upright and the Italian was the slowest of all after just nine laps of practice. Derek Daly was the fastest – and the most spectacular – Avon runner. Approaching the *Boschkurve* on Saturday morning, a bolt in the rear suspension failed and sent the Guinness March into a high-speed spin. Fortunately, Daly did not hit anything and he was raring to go once the timed session began in the afternoon. After setting a time good enough for 19th place on the grid, Daly was trying to improve further when the right-rear tyre exploded at the same flat-out-in-fifth kink. The March lurched violently in all directions but, somehow, Daly managed to gather it up before reaching the *Boschkurve*. Carlos Reutemann had been following the March and the Argentinian, fearing a massive accident, slowed down and then motored slowly past the crippled car, shaking his head in disbelief.

With the so-called Avon qualifiers making little difference to lap times, Mo Nunn and the Ensign time spent most of practice dialling in a decent race set-up on their N180B. Eliseo Salazar, full of enthusiasm after his storming drive at Hockenheim, completed more laps than anyone else and took a creditable position on the tenth row. The ATS team stiffened the chassis on the HGS 1 and added a new nose profile with side wings, Slim Borgudd taking 21st place in a car which appeared to handle the bumps better than most.

Life down in the Tyrrell pit was rather confused. Michele Alboreto was running the old 010 model on Avons as usual but, somehow, a deal had been done whereby Eddie Cheever and the new 011 were kitted out with Goodyears. There had been no time for testing and Cheever soon discovered that the car couldn't cope with the 15ins fronts. Complaining of a complete lack of grip, Cheever switched to the spare 010 on Saturday – only to stop soon after with a water leak. Alboreto, meanwhile, had stopped out on the circuit with distributor trouble and the car was towed in during a break while officials chased an errant deer off the track. It took the mechanics a few minutes to trace and rectify the problem by which time it was too late to put Eddie in his young team-mate's car. To make matters worse, it had been Alboreto who finally bumped Cheever into the non-qualifier's section!

The Theodore team were down to just one car after Marc Surer's last lap shunt at Hockenheim. The Swiss had damaged a rib in the incident and the injury was aggravated when he crashed on Saturday morning and tore off the front suspension. The mechanics worked miracles and had the car ready for the final session but their hard work was cancelled by an engine failure after three laps. Fortunately, Surer's Friday time was good enough to keep him in the race. Brian Henton accepted a job as commentator with Simon Taylor on BBC radio when the Candy-Toleman driver failed to qualify once again. A test session at Zandvoort had not been particularly fruitful and the team came to Austria without their best engines which were being rebuilt in Brian Hart's workshop. Derek Warwick's car featured a revised radiator system and a nose-mounted oil cooler which brought the temperatures down and allowed higher boost pressures. Warwick failed to make the race by five-hundredths of a second which was disappointing considering there were only 28 cars going for 24 places. The absentees were the Fittipaldi team, financial problems and a shortage of engines obliging Keke Rosberg and Chico Serra to miss this race.

RACE

When Renault began to practice tyre changes on race morning, it was obvious that the question of wear might be crucial during the 53-lap race. Furthermore, the warm-up had painted an entirely different picture to that of official practice, Piquet setting the fastest time ahead of Watson, Jones and Reutemann. Then there was the question of the Brabham's 13ins fronts lasting. Would the taller fronts used by Williams be the better bet? Would the soft Michelin advised by

Jabouille for Laffite outlast them all? And, to cap it all, the weather forecast had mentioned rain – and now dark clouds were gathering above the surrounding hills. The Ferrari mechanics were too busy to notice that as they changed a turbo on Villeneuve's car and, similarly, the Osella team were hard at work on Jarier's car as they reluctantly replaced a blown DFV with a well-worn unit. The Talbot-Ligier crew were switching Matra V12s on Tambay's car while, outside their garage, Jody Scheckter rehearsed his lines and slipped into his black CBS blazer before stepping in front of the waiting cameras. Across the track, in one of the little wooden boxes arranged along the back of the grandstand, Niki Lauda began similar duties for Austrian television.

Shortly before three o'clock, 23 cars had formed on the grid while the 24th, Marc Surer's Theodore, was towed into the pit lane with a broken distributor. As the red lights glowed, cars crept forward with the single exception of Villeneuve, the Ferrari remaining motionless until the red lights dimmed. Then the French-Canadian shot forward and made for the gap between Arnoux and the pit wall. For a fleeting moment it seemed that the Renault driver would ease the Ferrari out but René held station while Villeneuve kept coming on the inside. Side by side they went up the hill to the *Hella Licht* with Villeneuve taking the corner and the lead. Clearly, the Ferrari driver meant to make the most of the limited life of his Michelins. At the end of the first lap, Villeneuve was still in front closely followed by Prost, Arnoux, Pironi (from the fourth row!), Laffite, Reutemann, Piquet and Jones – who had missed a gear at the start.

Ferrari had fitted extra hard brake pads to Villeneuve's car in the interests of reliability but they contributed little to slowing the car down as Gilles reached *Hella Licht* for the second time. The Ferrari refused to turn into the corner, slithered down the escape road and dropped to sixth place. Reutemann arrived on the outside of Laffite and he, too, went straight across the kerbs and resumed in eighth place. All this dust and confusion allowed the Renaults to pull away while Pironi, gamely holding on to third place thanks to shattering acceleration away from the corners, came under pressure from Laffite, Piquet, Jones and Reutemann.

Daly had been the first visitor to the pits after a plug had oiled on the grid and it took two further stops to sort the problem out. The Theodore mechanics, meanwhile, had repaired Surer's car and he charged out of the pit lane as the leaders completed their fourth lap. His race was to be short-lived, however, the rotor arm giving a repeat performance within a few yards of the pit exit and leaving the hard-working team with no reward after a hectic weekend. Lap six saw Andretti charge into the pits for fresh Michelins all round while Rebaque coasted in with what he thought was an engine on the point of failure. A quick check revealed everything to be in order and the Mexican was sent on his way.

The Renaults, by now, had opened a 13-second gap over the hard-pressed Pironi who was now under attack from Piquet. The Brabham driver had taken Laffite on the run up the hill to *Hella Licht* but, no sooner had he completed the move, Piquet suddenly realised the mistake he had made. Throughout practice, Piquet had avoided the right-hand side of the track where a particularly nasty bump was causing rear wheels to jump into the air but, in the heat of the moment on lap 6, Nelson had bounced heavily as he ran alongside Laffite and ripped a skirt in the process. Within a couple of laps, understeer had set in and Piquet dropped back to fifth place.

The Renaults continued to extend their lead but stop-watches began clicking on lap nine as Laffite, Piquet and Jones all managed to pass Pironi's lumbering Ferrari. Villeneuve had slipped down the field, the result of his inefficient brakes and skirts which had been damaged during his cross-country manoeuvres at *Hella Licht*. On lap 12, the brakes proved to be no match for the driver's enthusiasm and the Ferrari ploughed into the guard rail at the *Boschkurve* before ricocheting across the track. The car was severely damaged but Villeneuve was able to return to the paddock where he changed before flying off in his helicopter. Before he left, however, Gilles hovered over the *Boschkurve* and watched Laffite begin to close on Arnoux.

By lap 20, the gap had closed to nine seconds with Piquet hanging on in fourth place. Jones had dropped back as he coped with erratic handling thanks to a broken rear spring platform while Reutemann, in sixth place, knew from the start that he should have chosen a softer compound, his hard 'A' tyres giving no grip whatsoever. Nigel Mansell had opted for the more suitable 'B' compound and the Lotus driver had produced a superb performance, taking Giacomelli, Villeneuve, Pironi and Patrese on his way to seventh place. Unfortunately, that was as far as he would get, an engine failure stranding him out on the circuit on lap 24. His retirement allowed Watson to take the place and the McLaren driver moved into the points when the leader retired suddenly at the start of lap 27.

Approaching *Hella Licht*, the front-left rocker arm broke and Prost slithered to a dusty halt along the escape road. Arnoux narrowly missed his team-mate

GOODYEAR
saudia
Canon
CHAMPION
Marlboro
WORLD CHAMPIONSHIP TEAM
Marlboro
WORLD CHAMPIONSHIP TEAM
WILLIAMS
GRAND PRIX
ENGINEERING
BOSS
AKAI AKAI
AKAI AKAI
ALAN
JONES
agv
Akai's Okay OK.

AJ's OK. Alan Jones carried Akai's colours into fourth place in Austria *(left)*.
Photo: David Winter
"Queue up .... queue up ...." Pironi, having wrestled with his Ferrari through the *Hella Licht* chicane, leaves a frustrated Watson, Patrese and de Angelis as he uses the turbo power to accelerate away *(below)*.
"These your new Guccis, Nelson?" Bernie Ecclestone tries Piquet's ski boots for size *(bottom)*.

and the situation had become critical for there, a mere five seconds away, was Jacques Laffite in the Talbot-Ligier. To make matters worse, René's race tyres, for some obscure reason, were provoking excessive understeer and losing the Frenchman around a second a lap. Laffite warmed to his task and cut the gap further in spite of a massive understeering moment at the *Boschkurve* on lap 32. Piquet was a lonely third, the two Williams drivers couldn't wait for this race to finish while Watson consolidated his sixth place. Behind the Ulsterman, however, there was a race of unequalled ferocity as de Angelis and Patrese fumed behind Pironi's slithering Ferrari. Mansell, Watson and others had proved it was possible to pass the Ferrari but the Italians were too hell-bent on beating each other to see sense. Time and again they would squabble amongst themselves and trip over each other as they attempted to scramble past the Ferrari. On one occasion, de Angelis actually got alongside Pironi and almost climbed out of his cockpit in a senseless display of fist waving. Next time round and Pironi was back in front again! Mixed in with this lot was Derek Daly, his engine running sweetly at last, while catching them hand over fist was Eliseo Salazar, driving superbly in the Ensign. On lap 36, Pironi could hold out no longer and began to fall back while Patrese's efforts proved to be in vain when his engine failed thanks to a blocked oil filter. Salazar barely had time to make the most of Patrese's problem when he, too, stopped with a blown engine caused, in this instance, by the fire extinguisher blocking the oil cooler.

The field had been disintegrating rapidly. Tambay, having stopped with faulty hydraulics, retired eventually with engine failure. Stohr had a similar problem; Rebaque stopped with a broken clutch while Giacomelli made the most spectacular exit of all, his Alfa Romeo bursting into flames at the entrance to the pit lane. The fire was caused by a faulty distributor which retarded the ignition and caused the engine to overheat. As a result, the titanium exhausts caught fire and the shower of white sparks set the engine cover alight! Prior to that, Giacomelli had been dicing with Slim Borgudd in the ATS but the Swede was destined to stop with transmission trouble. Similarly, Michele Alboreto had been running with the Alfa Romeo, the Tyrrell driver inadvertantly taking second gear as he tried to dive inside at the *Boschkurve*. The gearbox responded to that sort of treatment by eventually jamming in fourth gear and the engine, in turn, cried enough by dropping a valve on lap 40.

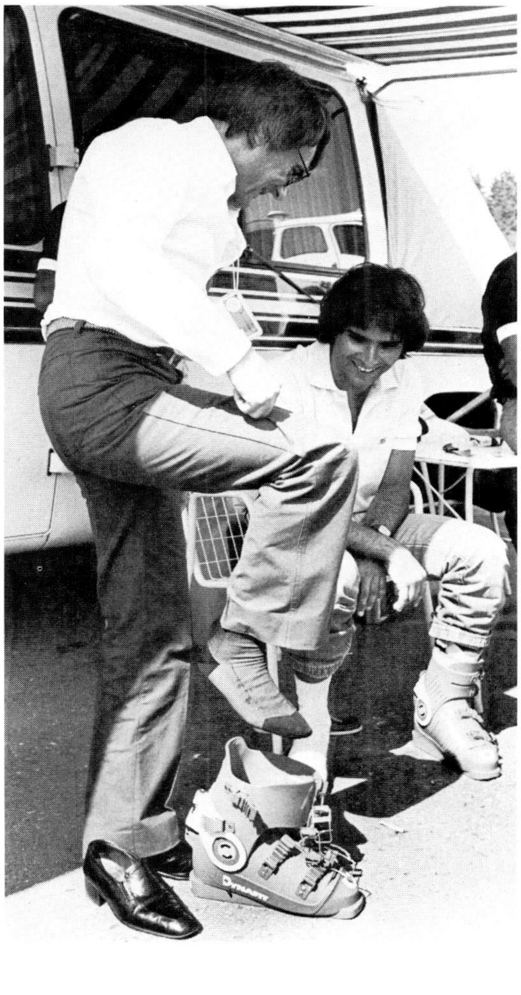

Ten laps earlier, Laffite had been looking for a way past Arnoux. Jacques tried the inside at *Hella Licht* but was forced to drop back and he lost further ground when Andrea de Ceasaris let the Renault through but forced Laffite to run wide at the *Boschkurve*. Jacques was soon on the attack, however, and as the leaders came across the de Angelis/Patrese/Pironi/Salazar quartet, Laffite made his move at the *Texaco Schikane* and took the lead. Arnoux didn't give up that easily but Laffite responded to the brief challenge by setting the fastest lap and gradually easing open a five second gap. Apart from a blinking oil pressure light, Laffite had no problems, the Ligier running perfectly on Jabouille's hand-picked Michelins and crossing the line to give the Talbot team their first victory of the season. Arnoux was a disappointed second while Piquet was pleased with third place considering his problems. Jones worked hard for fourth but fifth place for Reutemann meant the championship lead had narrowed further, Piquet now just six points in arrears. Watson took sixth place in spite of a cracked exhaust pipe, de Angelis was next with de Cesaris taking a subdued but much needed finish in eighth place ahead of Pironi, Jarier and Daly.

Guy Ligier embraced Jabouille in recognition of the role Jean-Pierre had played in this victory. Laffite, for his part, beamed happily as he was whisked away to a radio interview. There was much to say. Not only had he driven superbly, he had taken nine more points. Instead of being merely a fortunate third in the championship, Laffite was talking in terms of taking the title. That's how important his win had been.

Grosser Preis von Österreich, August 16/statistics

Entries and practice times

No.	Driver	Nat	Car	Engine	Entrant	Practice 1	Practice 2
1	Alan Jones	AUS	Saudia-Leyland WILLIAMS FW07C	Ford Cosworth DFV	TAG Williams Team	**1m 34·654s**	1m 34·999s
2	Carlos Reutemann	RA	Saudia-Leyland WILLIAMS FW07C	Ford Cosworth DFV	TAG Williams Team	**1m 34·531s**	1m 35·633s
3	Eddie Cheever	USA	TYRRELL 011	Ford Cosworth DFV	Tyrrell Racing	**1m 38·583s**	1m 39·351s
4	Michele Alboreto	I	TYRRELL 010	Ford Cosworth DFV	Tyrrell Racing	1m 39·674s	**1m 38·084s**
5	Nelson Piquet	BR	Parmalat BRABHAM BT49C	Ford Cosworth DFV	Parmalat Racing Team	**1m 34·871s**	1m 35·519s
6	Hector Rebaque	MEX	Parmalat BRABHAM BT49C	Ford Cosworth DFV	Parmalat Racing Team	1m 36·511s	**1m 36·150s**
7	John Watson	GB	Marlboro McLAREN MP4	Ford Cosworth DFV	McLaren International	1m 36·007s	**1m 35·977s**
8	Andrea de Cesaris	I	Marlboro McLAREN MP4	Ford Cosworth DFV	McLaren International	**1m 36·657s**	–
9	Slim Borgudd	S	Abba ATS HGS 1	Ford Cosworth DFV	Team ATS	1m 38·529s	**1m 37·709s**
11	Elio de Angelis	I	John Player Special LOTUS 87	Ford Cosworth DFV	John Player Team Lotus	**1m 35·294s**	1m 35·858s
12	Nigel Mansell	GB	John Player Special LOTUS 87	Ford Cosworth DFV	John Player Team Lotus	1m 36·688s	**1m 35·569s**
14	Eliseo Salazar	RCH	ENSIGN N180B	Ford Cosworth DFV	Ensign Racing	1m 38·273s	**1m 37·631s**
15	Alain Prost	F	Elf RENAULT RE 30	Renault EF1	Equipe Renault Elf	1m 32·798s	**1m 32·321s**
16	René Arnoux	F	Elf RENAULT RE 30	Renault EF1	Equipe Renault Elf	1m 32·682s	**1m 32·018s**
17	Derek Daly	IRL	Rizla MARCH 811	Ford Cosworth DFV	March Grand Prix	1m 37·777s	**1m 37·230s**
20	Keke Rosberg	SF	FITTIPALDI F8C	Ford Cosworth DFV	Fittipaldi Automotive	Entry withdrawn	
21	Chico Serra	BR	FITTIPALDI F8C	Ford Cosworth DFV	Fittipaldi Automotive	Entry withdrawn	
22	Mario Andretti	USA	Marlboro ALFA ROMEO 179C	Alfa Romeo 1260	Marlboro Team Alfa Romeo	1m 36·560s	**1m 36·079s**
23	Bruno Giacomelli	I	Marlboro ALFA ROMEO 179C	Alfa Romeo 1260	Marlboro Team Alfa Romeo	1m 37·637s	**1m 36·216s**
25	Patrick Tambay	F	Talbot-Gitanes LIGIER JS17	Matra MS 81	Equipe Talbot Gitanes	**1m 36·233s**	1m 36·443s
26	Jacques Laffite	F	Talbot-Gitanes LIGIER JS17	Matra MS 81	Equipe Talbot Gitanes	1m 35·002s	**1m 34·398s**
27	Gilles Villeneuve	CDN	Fiat FERRARI 126CK	Ferrari 126C	Scuderia Ferrari SpA SEFAC	**1m 33·334s**	1m 35·150s
28	Didier Pironi	F	Fiat FERRARI 126CK	Ferrari 126C	Scuderia Ferrari SpA SEFAC	1m 35·346s	**1m 35·037s**
29	Riccardo Patrese	I	Ragno-Beta ARROWS A3	Ford Cosworth DFV	Arrows Racing Team	1m 35·912s	**1m 35·442s**
30	Siegfried Stohr	I	Ragno-Beta ARROWS A3	Ford Cosworth DFV	Arrows Racing Team	1m 38·616s	**1m 38·546s**
31	Beppe Gabbiani	I	Denim OSELLA FA1B	Ford Cosworth DFV	Osella Squadra Corse	**1m 41·198s**	1m 46·079s
32	Jean-Pierre Jarier	F	Denim OSELLA FA1B	Ford Cosworth DFV	Osella Squadra Corse	1m 38·004s	**1m 36·117s**
33	Marc Surer	CH	THEODORE TY 01	Ford Cosworth DFV	Theodore Racing Team	**1m 38·522s**	1m 44·262s
35	Brian Henton	GB	Candy TOLEMAN TG 181	Hart 415T	Candy Toleman Motorsport	1m 39·987s	**1m 38·691s**
36	Derek Warwick	GB	Candy TOLEMAN TG 181	Hart 415T	Candy Toleman Motorsport	1m 40·391s	**1m 38·593s**
Friday morning and Saturday morning practice sessions not officially recorded						*Fri pm Hot, dry*	*Sat pm Hot, dry*

Starting grid

	16 ARNOUX (1m 32·018s) Renault
15 PROST (1m 32·321s) Renault	
	27 VILLENEUVE (1m 33·334s) Ferrari
26 LAFFITE (1m 34·398s) Talbot-Ligier	
	2 REUTEMANN (1m 34·531s) Williams
1 JONES (1m 34·654s) Williams	
	5 PIQUET (1m 34·871s) Brabham
28 PIRONI (1m 35·037s) Ferrari	
	11 DE ANGELIS (1m 35·294s) Lotus
29 PATRESE (1m 35·442s) Arrows	
	12 MANSELL (1m 35·569s) Lotus
7 WATSON (1m 35·977s) McLaren	
	22 ANDRETTI (1m 36·079s) Alfa Romeo
32 JARIER (1m 36·117s) Osella	
	6 REBAQUE (1m 36·150s) Brabham
23 GIACOMELLI (1m 36·216s) Alfa Romeo	
	25 TAMBAY (1m 36·233s) Talbot-Ligier
8 DE CESARIS (1m 36·657s) McLaren	
	17 DALY (1m 37·230s) March
14 SALAZAR (1m 37·631s) Ensign	
	9 BORGUDD (1m 37·709s) ATS
4 ALBORETO (1m 38·084s) Tyrrell	
	33 SURER (1m 38·522s) Theodore
30 STOHR (1m 38·546s) Arrows	

Did not start:
3 Cheever (Tyrrell), 1m 38·583s, did not qualify
36 Warwick (Toleman), 1m 38·593s, did not qualify
35 Henton (Toleman), 1m 38·691s, did not qualify
31 Gabbiani (Osella), 1m 41·198s, did not qualify

Past winners

Year	Driver	Nat	Car	Circuit	Distance miles/km	Speed mph/km/h
1963*	Jack Brabham	AUS	1·5 Brabham BT7-Climax	Zeltweg	159·07/ 256·00	96·34/115·04
1964	Lorenzo Bandini	I	1·5 Ferrari 156	Zeltweg	208·78/ 336·00	99·20/159·65
1965†	Jochen Rindt	A	3·3 Ferrari 250LM	Zeltweg	198·84/ 320·00	97·13/156·32
1966†	Gerhard Mitter/ Hans Herrmann	D D	2·0 Porsche 906	Zeltweg	312·18/ 502·40	99·68/160·42
1967†	Paul Hawkins	AUS	4·7 Ford GT40	Zeltweg	312·18/ 502·40	95·29/153·35
1968†	Jo Siffert	CH	3·0 Porsche 908/02 Spyder	Zeltweg	312·18/ 502·40	106·86/171·97
1969†	Jo Siffert/ Kurt Ahrens	CH D	4·5 Porsche 917	Österreichring	624·40/1004·87	115·78/186·33
1970	Jacky Ickx	B	3·0 Ferrari 312B-1/70	Österreichring	220·38/ 354·67	129·27/208·04
1971	Jo Siffert	CH	3·0 BRM P160	Österreichring	198·34/ 319·20	131·64/211·85
1972	Emerson Fittipaldi	BR	3·0 JPS/Lotus 72-Ford	Österreichring	198·34/ 319·20	133·29/214·51
1973	Ronnie Peterson	S	3·0 JPS/Lotus 72-Ford	Österreichring	198·34/ 319·20	133·99/215·64
1974	Carlos Reutemann	RA	3·0 Brabham BT44-Ford	Österreichring	198·34/ 319·20	134·09/215·80
1975	Vittorio Brambilla	I	3·0 March 751-Ford	Österreichring	106·12/ 170·78	110·30/177·51
1976	John Watson	GB	3·0 Penske PC4-Ford	Österreichring	198·29/ 319·11	132·00/212·41
1977	Alan Jones	AUS	3·0 Shadow DN8-Ford	Österreichring	199·39/ 320·89	122·98/197·91
1978	Ronnie Peterson	S	3·0 JPS/Lotus 79-Ford	Österreichring	199·39/ 320·89	118·03/189·95
1979	Alan Jones	AUS	3·0 Williams FW07-Ford	Österreichring	199·39/ 320·89	136·52/219·71
1980	Jean-Pierre Jabouille	F	1·5 Renault RS t/c	Österreichring	199·39/ 320·89	138·69/223·20
1981	Jacques Laffite	F	3·0 Ligier JS17-Matra	Österreichring	195·70/ 314·95	134·03/215·70

* Non-championship (Formula 1)
† Sports car race

Circuit data

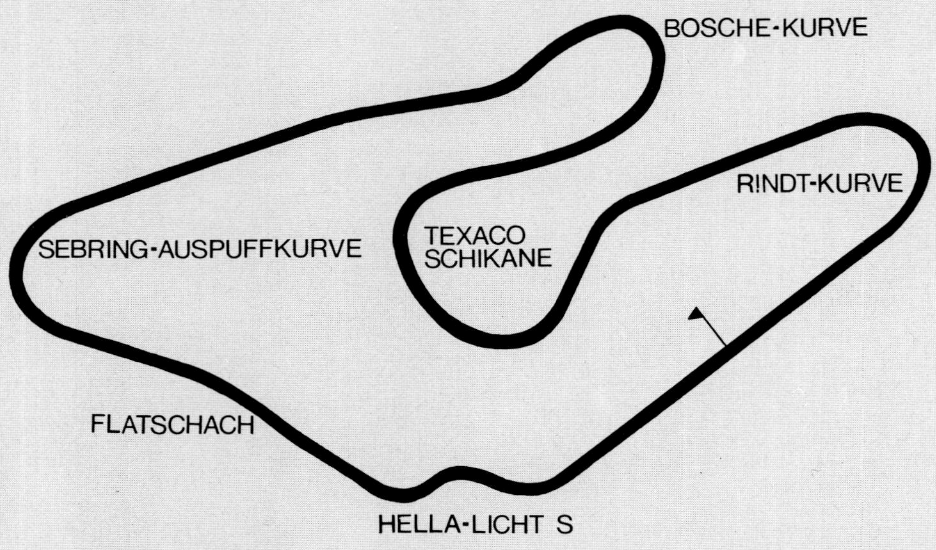

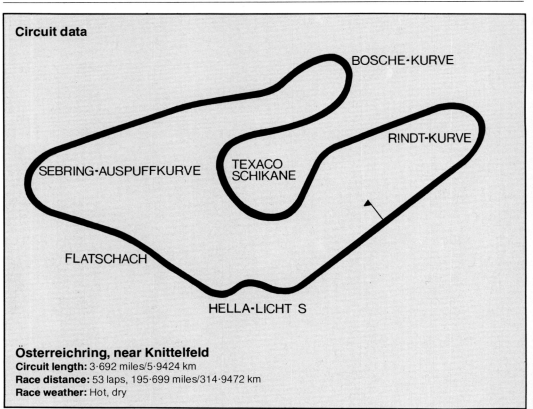

Österreichring, near Knittelfeld
Circuit length: 3·692 miles/5·9424 km
Race distance: 53 laps, 195·699 miles/314·9472 km
Race weather: Hot, dry

Ferrari fitted a single dural plate to the rear suspension in an unsuccessful attempt to improve the handling.

Results and retirements

Place	Driver	Car	Laps	Time and Speed (mph/km/h)/Retirement	
1	Jacques Laffite	Talbot-Ligier Matra V12	53	1h 27m 36·47s	134·028/215·698
2	René Arnoux	Renault t/c V6	53	1h 27m 41·64s	133·896/215·486
3	Nelson Piquet	Brabham-Cosworth V8	53	1h 27m 43·81s	133·841/215·397
4	Alan Jones	Williams-Cosworth V8	53	1h 27m 48·51s	133·722/215·205
5	Carlos Reutemann	Williams-Cosworth V8	53	1h 28m 08·32s	133·221/214·399
6	John Watson	McLaren-Cosworth V8	53	1h 29m 07·61s	131·744/212·022
7	Elio de Angelis	Lotus-Cosworth V8	52		
8	Andrea de Cesaris	McLaren-Cosworth V8	52		
9	Didier Pironi	Ferrari t/c V6	52		
10	Jean-Pierre Jarier	Osella-Cosworth V8	51		
11	Derek Daly	March-Cosworth V8	47		
	Mario Andretti	Alfa Romeo V12	46	Engine	
	Slim Borgudd	ATS-Cosworth V8	44	Brakes	
	Riccardo Patrese	Arrows-Cosworth V8	43	Engine	
	Eliseo Salazar	Ensign-Cosworth V8	43	Engine	
	Michele Alboreto	Tyrrell-Cosworth V8	40	Engine	
	Bruno Giacomelli	Alfa Romeo V12	35	Engine fire	
	Hector Rebaque	Brabham-Cosworth V8	31	Clutch	
	Siegfried Stohr	Arrows-Cosworth V8	27	Spun; could not restart	
	Alain Prost	Renault t/c V6	26	Front suspension	
	Patrick Tambay	Talbot-Ligier Matra V12	26	Engine	
	Nigel Mansell	Lotus-Cosworth V8	23	Engine	
	Gilles Villeneuve	Ferrari t/c V6	11	Accident	
	Marc Surer	Theodore-Cosworth V8	0	Distributor	

Fastest lap: Laffite, on lap 47, 1m 37·62s, 136·168mph/219·142km/h.
Lap record: René Arnoux (F1 Renault RE-t/c V6), 1m 32·53s, 143·659mph/231·197km/h (1980).

Lap chart

1st LAP ORDER		1	2	3	4	5	6	7	8	9	10	11	12	13	14	15	16	17	18	19	20	21	22	23
27	G.Villeneuve	27	15	15	15	15	15	15	15	15	15	15	15	15	15	15	15	15	15	15	15	15	15	15
15	A.Prost	15	16	16	16	16	16	16	16	16	16	16	16	16	16	16	16	16	16	16	16	16	16	16
16	R.Arnoux	16	28	28	28	28	28	28	28	26	26	26	26	26	26	26	26	26	26	26	26	26	26	26
28	D.Pironi	28	26	26	26	26	5	5	26	5	5	5	5	5	5	5	5	5	5	5	5	5	5	5
26	J.Laffite	26	5	5	5	5	26	26	5	1	1	1	1	1	1	1	1	1	1	1	1	1	1	1
2	C.Reutemann	2	27	27	1	1	1	1	1	28	2	2	2	2	2	2	2	2	2	2	2	2	2	2
5	N.Piquet	5	1	1	2	2	2	2	2	2	28	28	28	28	28	28	28	12	12	12	12	12	12	12
1	A.Jones	1	2	2	27	27	29	29	29	29	29	29	29	12	12	12	12	28	28	28	28	28	28	28
22	M.Andretti	22	22	29	29	29	27	27	27	12	12	12	12	29	29	29	7	7	29	7	7	7	7	7
6	H.Rebaque	6	29	22	22	12	12	12	12	27	27	27	7	7	7	7	29	29	7	29	29	29	29	29
29	R.Patrese	29	12	12	12	7	7	7	7	7	7	7	25	11	11	11	11	11	11	11	11	11	11	11
12	N.Mansell	12	6	7	7	6	23	23	25	25	25	25	11	25	25	14	14	14	14	14	14	14	14	14
7	J.Watson	7	7	6	6	22	25	25	23	11	11	11	14	14	14	25	23	23	23	23	4	4	8	8
11	E.de Angelis	11	23	23	23	23	11	11	11	14	14	14	23	23	23	23	4	4	4	4	8	8	23	23
23	B.Giacomelli	23	25	25	25	25	14	14	14	23	23	23	4	4	4	4	8	8	8	8	23	23	9	9
25	P.Tambay	25	11	11	11	11	4	4	4	4	4	4	9	9	8	8	9	9	9	9	9	9	4	4
4	M.Alboreto	4	14	14	14	14	32	32	32	9	9	9	8	8	9	9	25	32	32	32	32	32	32	32
14	E.Salazar	14	4	4	4	4	9	9	9	8	8	8	32	32	32	32	32	30	30	30	30	30	30	30
32	J-P.Jarier	32	32	32	32	32	8	8	8	32	32	32	30	30	30	30	30	22	22	22	22	22	22	22
8	A.de Cesaris	8	8	8	8	8	6	30	30	30	30	30	22	22	22	22	22	6	6	6	6	6	6	6
9	S.Borgudd	9	9	9	9	9	22	22	22	22	22	22	6	6	6	6	6	25	25	25	25	25	25	25
30	S.Stohr	30	30	30	30	30	30	6	6	6	6	6	17	17	17	17	17	17	17	17	17	17	17	17
17	D.Daly	17	17	17	17	17	17	17	17	17	17	17												

24	25	26	27	28	29	30	31	32	33	34	35	36	37	38	39	40	41	42	43	44	45	46	47	48	49	50	51	52	53
15	15	15	16	16	16	16	16	16	16	16	16	16	16	16	26	26	26	26	26	26	26	26	26	26	26	26	26	26	26
16	16	16	26	26	26	26	26	26	26	26	26	26	26	26	16	16	16	16	16	16	16	16	16	16	16	16	16	16	16
26	26	26	5	5	5	5	5	5	5	5	5	5	5	5	5	5	5	5	5	5	5	5	5	5	5	5	5	5	5
5	5	5	1	1	1	1	1	1	1	1	1	1	1	1	1	1	1	1	1	1	1	1	1	1	1	1	1	1	1
1	1	1	2	2	2	2	2	2	2	2	2	2	2	2	2	2	2	2	2	2	2	2	2	2	2	2	2	2	2
2	2	2	7	7	7	7	7	7	7	7	7	7	7	7	7	7	7	7	7	7	7	7	7	7	7	7	7	7	7
7	7	7	28	28	28	28	28	28	11	28	28	11	11	11	11	11	11	11	11	11	11	11	11	11	11	11	11	11	
28	28	28	11	11	29	11	11	11	28	11	11	28	29	29	29	29	29	29	29	8	8	8	8	8	8	8	8	8	
29	11	11	29	29	11	29	29	29	29	29	29	29	28	28	14	14	8	14	14	28	28	28	28	28	28	28	28	28	
11	29	29	14	14	14	14	14	14	14	14	14	14	14	14	8	8	14	8	8	9	22	22	32	32	32	32	32		
14	14	14	8	8	8	8	8	8	8	8	8	8	8	8	28	28	28	28	28	22	32	32	17						
8	8	8	23	23	23	23	23	23	23	23	9	9	9	9	9	9	9	9	9	32	17	17							
23	23	23	9	9	9	9	9	9	9	9	4	4	4	4	4	4	22	22	22	17									
9	9	9	4	4	4	4	4	4	4	4	32	32	32	32	32	32	32	32	32										
4	4	4	32	32	32	32	32	32	32	32	22	22	22	22	22	22	17	17	17										
32	32	32	22	22	22	22	22	22	22	22	17	17	17	17	17	17													
30	30	30	30	6	6	6	6	17	17	17																			
22	22	22	6	17	17	17	17																						
6	6	6	17																										
25	25	25																											
17	17	17																											

Fastest laps

Driver	Time	Lap
Jacques Laffite	1m 37·62s	47
Alan Jones	1m 37·66s	51
Nelson Piquet	1m 38·00s	52
René Arnoux	1m 38·24s	36
Alain Prost	1m 38·41s	4
John Watson	1m 38·65s	42
Carlos Reutemann	1m 38·69s	29
Riccardo Patrese	1m 38·85s	38
Nigel Mansell	1m 39·36s	21
Elio de Angelis	1m 39·37s	40
Andrea de Cesaris	1m 39·71s	52
Derek Daly	1m 40·18s	40
Eliseo Salazar	1m 40·42s	41
Hector Rebaque	1m 40·47s	25
Didier Pironi	1m 40·66s	4
Patrick Tambay	1m 40·82s	11
Slim Borgudd	1m 40·88s	42
Gilles Villeneuve	1m 41·05s	3
Mario Andretti	1m 41·32s	8
Michele Alboreto	1m 41·32s	21
Bruno Giacomelli	1m 41·36s	33
Jean-Pierre Jarier	1m 42·46s	6
Siegfried Stohr	1m 42·80s	18

Points

WORLD CHAMPIONSHIP OF DRIVERS

1	Carlos Reutemann	45 pts
2	Nelson Piquet	39
3	Jacques Laffite	34
4	Alan Jones	27
5 =	John Watson	21
5 =	Gilles Villeneuve	21
7	Alain Prost	19
8	René Arnoux	11
9 =	Riccardo Patrese	10
9 =	Eddie Cheever	10
11 =	Elio de Angelis	8
11 =	Hector Rebaque	8
13	Didier Pironi	7
14	Nigel Mansell	5
15	Marc Surer	4
16	Mario Andretti	3
17 =	Patrick Tambay	1
17 =	Andrea de Cesaris	1
17 =	Slim Borgudd	1

CONSTRUCTORS' CUP

1	Williams	72
2	Brabham	47
3	Ligier	34
4	Renault	30
5	Ferrari	28
6	McLaren	22
7	Lotus	13
8 =	Arrows	10
8 =	Tyrrell	10
10	Ensign	4
11	Alfa Romeo	3
12 =	Theodore	1
12 =	ATS	1

Grote Prijs van Nederland

On Sunday night in Zandvoort, the champagne flew. So, too, did the bread rolls and the crockery in the Bouwes Hotel; the Renault-Elf team were celebrating at last. Indeed, the mechanics had been in high spirits all day. Breaking camp on race morning, they had smothered Bruno Giacomelli's road car in an awning after the unsuspecting Italian had blown his horn once too often while edging through the paddock.

Their mood had been optimistic because, once again, both turbos were on the front row. Mind you, that had happened before – three times to be precise – but, by Sunday night, the team had every reason to celebrate. Alain Prost had scored a superb win after a mature and confident drive while under pressure from Alan Jones. The Saudia-Leyland Williams driver had produced another stunning performance and actually snatched the lead for a couple of hundred yards during the height of a clean but thrusting battle with the Renault.

Jones's tyres were no match for his blistering pace and he eventually dropped back and gave best to Nelson Piquet during the closing laps. Nelson was in tyre trouble too but the Parmalat Brabham driver had raced accordingly and his second place moved him into a shared lead of the World Championship after Carlos Reutemann had crashed out of the race. Disputing fourth place with Jacques Laffite, an over-anxious Reutemann tried an impossible move and wiped out both cars to give the championship a dramatic turn in every sense.

Hector Rebaque finished an excellent fourth for the third time, Elio de Angelis was fifth after his now customary battle with Riccardo Patrese and Eliseo Salazar scored his first World Championship point after an aggressive drive into sixth place in the Ensign.

Apart from the Prost/Jones battle, the race held little interest thanks to a list of retirements which opened within the first few hundred yards. Gilles Villeneuve, having made his usual speedy start, was trapped between two cars and the Ferrari spun through the air. Fortunately, the consequences were not serious and, equally, Mario Andretti was lucky to escape with minor bruising when his Alfa Romeo crashed heavily after a front tyre had blown during the closing laps.

Andretti had held high hopes for this race but his chances were dashed on the first lap when Reutemann ran over his nose wing. Mario had qualified on the fourth row alongside John Watson but the Ulsterman's luck was not much better, his Marlboro McLaren stopping with a dead engine while in an easy fourth place.

That was the sort of misfortune which normally befell Alain Prost but, for once, the Frenchman had a perfect day. His wife had presented him with their first child, a boy, earlier in the week and, apart from winning his second Grand Prix, Dad had secured his family's immediate future by re-signing with Renault for 1982.

ENTRY AND PRACTICE

It was no surprise to find the Renaults on the front row simply because they had been on pole in Holland for the past two years. This time, however, it was Alain Prost who set the fastest time and prevented René Arnoux from scoring a hat-trick of pole positions at Zandvoort. Prost had a new car at his disposal, one which was built specifically with hydro-pneumatic suspension in mind, and Alain set his time on Saturday after altering the set-up to favour more rear and less front wing.

Arnoux, obviously recovered from a period of self-doubt at the beginning of the season, enjoyed the superb handling on the fast sections and headed the time sheet on Friday. He had been bothered by a misfire during the morning but, on Saturday, his only complaint was traffic as he tried to beat his team-mate's time. Thus, Renault had dominated practice but, this time, their rivals were snapping at their heels.

The difference was that the yellow and white cars cruised round Zandvoort with ease while the rest bucked and bounced across the bumps. It was a vivid demonstration of the senseless state of the technical

Alain Prost scored Renault's second win of the season.

How to do it: Prost and Jones waged a superb battle during the early laps, the Renault and Williams running side-by-side through *Tarzan* on two occasions. Jones slides on the loose and Prost retakes the lead after losing it briefly at the end of lap 18.
How not to do it: Jacques Laffite fought hard to hold his fourth place and Reutemann's attempt to overtake ended in disaster.

regulations and Jean-Marie Balestre's pathetic attempts to police them. Worse still, the lap speeds (on which Balestre hinged his arguments for banning skirts) were only fractionally slower than in 1980.

One of the most outspoken opponents of the farce masquerading as a professional sport was Alan Jones. The reigning World Champion was making serious noises about quitting for no other reason than the solid state of the suspensions and the subsequent bruising and battering dealt out to the hapless drivers. Nonetheless, Jones was hacking it with the best of them when it came to doing *his* job properly and he qualified on the second row alongside Nelson Piquet. To be honest, the front row was being ignored when it came to talking in terms of the championship. The battle, at this stage, was between Parmalat Brabham and Saudia-Leyland Williams with Talbot-Ligier in with a chance after Austria.

Piquet and Jones were two-hundredths of a second apart and while Reutemann may have been the championship leader, everyone, including Nelson, knew that Jones was anxious to win another race after his season of problems. Piquet spent practice making use of both cars available, setting his race chassis up on full tanks on Saturday morning and then hopping into the spare (minus front wings) and taking third fastest time of the day. Practice on Friday had been hampered by a poor engine which let go with ten minutes remaining but, otherwise, the team had few complaints. Hector Rebaque was back in his usual spot, driving his usual car after major monocoque repairs following his practice shunt in Austria.

While Brabham stuck with 13ins front wheels, Williams were on 15ins but running new low profile Goodyears. Jones was reasonably happy, his only problem being a blown engine in the T-car while setting up on full tanks. Carlos Reutemann had a new chassis for Zandvoort but the handling was not to his liking on Friday. Despite suffering from a stiff neck, Carlos was able to improve on Saturday but his time was not good enough to get him onto the second row with Nelson.

A chorus of trumpets and plenty of shouting from the main grandstand indicated that the Talbot-Ligier victory in Austria had the full approval of a vociferous knot of French fans. What's more, they obviously expected a repeat performance, Jacques Laffite's every move out of the cockpit prompting another volley from across the track. Jacques, for his part, was happy enough as he explained that perhaps he could do with more top end power but otherwise – '*parfait*'. It was noticeable throughout practice that Jacques was able to take a tight line entering *Tarzan*, braking late and pivoting the JS17 around the apex before powering away towards *Gerlachbocht*. Patrick Tambay had his chassis updated and stiffened but an engine failure meant few laps in his race car on Friday. Then the car caught fire briefly and he was forced to use the spare chassis while a misfire the following day kept him in the middle of the grid.

In the light of Gerard Ducarouge's dismissal from the Ligier team just after Silverstone, it must have given the Frenchman great delight to find his new employer, Alfa Romeo, parked behind Laffite on the grid. Mario Andretti was in no doubt as to why he was enjoying his most competitive practice since Long Beach: "We've been testing a revised car at Monza and the thing's been transformed. New side-pods, different front suspension geometry, things like that." Ducarouge was obviously making his presence felt and Andretti responded on the track. In fact, he didn't need to resort to qualifiers on Saturday although his practice was spoiled by a side-pod working loose and making the car unstable in the corners. Bruno Giacomelli did not have the benefit of the revised bits and pieces and the Italian had to be satisfied with 14th place.

John Watson made it two Marlboro cars on row four although he was far from happy with his McLaren. The MP4 was continuing to give the Ulsterman a rough ride and the nose could be seen to be bouncing under braking for *Tarzan*. The turning in capabilities of the car were causing concern but at least the chassis was handling well on the fast curves. John was sixth fastest on Friday but failed to improve the following day and slipped to eighth place. Any problems 'Wattie' may have had were minor compared to those of Andrea de Cesaris who suffered from a recurrence of his usual trouble – crashing. Having spun off every conceivable way during the season, Andrea did a proper job this time and damaged the monocoque by bouncing it into the tyre barrier at the end of the straight. Until then, de Cesaris had been doing a reasonable job although it was noticeable that the Italian was braking very late at *Tarzan*. On Saturday, he excelled himself and shot straight across the corner when his brake pedal went hard. That was Andrea's version although observers at the corner reported the McLaren to be accompanied by blue smoke from locked front tyres. Either way, the team had had enough for the time being and it was decided not to entrust de Cesaris with the spare car and his race car was shipped back to England without delay.

The side-pods on the John Player Lotus 87s were revised inwardly while the outer surfaces continued to show signs of petty wrangling and general bad taste as the Essex stickers disappeared (for practice at least) under yards of black tape. Elio de Angelis and Nigel Mansell had other problems as they hustled the cars over the bumps, de Angelis taking a worthy ninth place while poor Mansell was caught in a catalogue of minor disasters. There was a misfire on Friday and a switch to the T-car produced a soft brake pedal. More time was lost with an engine change but the abiding problem was handling, traced eventually to a roll bar which had flipped to over-centre to give understeer followed by oversteer when power was applied. Mansell had a busy time making 17th position.

The Ragno Beta Arrows team had been busy testing at Donington but the stiff springs found suitable in Derbyshire were of no use by the sea in Holland. Riccardo Patrese was in his usual position on the grid as was Siegfried Stohr, some two seconds behind. Once again, the Ferraris were in dire handling trouble over the bumps but now they had no straight line speed either which explained their lowly positions on the grid. Didier Pironi was slightly better off in spite of a terrifying shunt at the fast right-hand *Scheivlak* corner. According to Didier, the car just bounced clean off the track before ploughing through a catch-fence. Pironi was unhurt and resorted to the T-car for the rest of the day. He was back in the spare chassis on Saturday when a rotor bearing broke on the turbo but his race car was ready for the afternoon session. Villeneuve, by comparison, had no major problems apart from a decent turn of speed onto the straight and his characteristic sideways efforts were worth nothing more than 16th place.

Jean-Pierre Jarier qualified comfortably in the

AUGUST:

Jacques Villeneuve tests Arrows at Donington.

Riccardo Patrese signs for Brabham.

Alain Prost and René Arnoux re-sign for Renault.

Plans to revive British Formula 1 series announced.

Denim Osella while Beppe Gabbiani crashed on Friday having already damaged one chassis during testing at Monza. Derek Daly had two Guinness March cars on hand although he preferred the race chassis to the wide-track spare. He was forced to use the T-car on Friday, however, when problems with the hydro-pneumatic suspension intervened. Then, on Saturday, a valve spring broke after just seven laps in the race car but at least his time was good enough for 19th place. The Tyrrell team had been busy finishing a second 011 for Michele Alboreto but he didn't get far before metering unit trouble caused the Italian to return to his old car. Alboreto's practice was halted once more with engine trouble in the 010 chassis and when he finally did get motoring in the new car, he missed the cut by six-hundredths of a second. He was in luck, however, for the withdrawal of de Cesaris left a gap on the grid. Eddie Cheever was on Goodyears once again although he could do no better than take 21st place with a car which was handling badly and continually locking the left front brake.

Marc Surer had to work hard in the Theodore as he battled with the Ensign of Eliseo Salazar and Slim Borgudd's ATS for a place on the grid. Not so fortunate were the Fittipaldi team who made a return after missing the Austrian Grand Prix. The white cars were well polished but both drivers suffered misfires and, once again, Keke Rosberg and Chico Serra were free to go home on Saturday night. The Candy Toleman team were in good shape with their 'monobloc' engine after Brian Henton had qualified in 22nd place on Friday with a new chassis which was some 20 kilos lighter. Just as the team were poised to qualify and perhaps improve the next day, a jubilee clip worked loose and cut the drive-belt to the valve-gear. As a result, there were some expensive noises as the pistons came into contact with valves and Brian Hart was understandably put out after all the hard work lavished on the engine. Henton was back in the 'old nail' spare car while Derek Warwick was left struggling with his usual car on Saturday and, sadly, both failed to qualify for the ninth race in succession.

RACE

Tyres dominated conversations as drivers prepared for the morning warm-up. Alain Prost had spent over an hour the previous day locked in discussion with his engineer, Michel Tetu, Pierre Dupasquiet of Michelin and Gerard Larrousse. They talked about compounds, about wear, about grip. Prost wanted to run the softest tyre available but he was concerned about the wear rate during tests on Saturday morning. Eventually it was agreed that he would run a soft compound on the inside and he duly tried this combination on Sunday morning. At the back of his mind, however, Prost had a feeling that soft tyres all round would last given the correct treatment from the cockpit and he eventually got his way. Down at the Williams pit, Jones and Reutemann found the hard Goodyears to be over a second slower and they joined Piquet in choosing the softer 'C' compound. As usual, the warm-up had shown these three to be the quickest on full tanks with Prost in fourth place ahead of Watson and de Angelis. Much would depend on the start.

This time, however, Arnoux made a good start and kept pace with Prost as they aimed for *Tarzan* and the two were out of reach as they hit the braking area. Had he been in the front quarter of the grid, the chances were that Gilles Villeneuve would have been muscling through given his usual jet-propelled start. Unfortunately, he was back on row eight and confronted by drivers not so well-versed in his starting procedures. Gilles was quick off the mark but so, too, was Giacomelli who darted from right to left as he made the most of the space vacated by de Cesaris. Closing

The Fittipaldi team, still lacking a major sponsor, missed the Austrian Grand Prix but Keke Rosberg (20) and Chico Serra had little hope of qualifying in Holland.

All dressed up with nowhere to go. Andrea de Cesaris had to sit the race out after crashing his McLaren during practice *(below)*.
Jarier qualified his Osella comfortably but retired with gearbox trouble. Jean-Pierre talks to Enzo Osella (left) and team manager Gianfranco Palazzoli – better known as former sportscar driver 'Pal Joe' *(bottom)*.

rapidly on Tambay, Bruno began to edge towards Patrese on his right, blissfully unaware that Villeneuve was coming through the middle at a different sort of speed. In an instant, the Ferrari was launched into the air and a series of spins, Gilles bouncing back onto the track and careering to a halt in a cloud of dust on the left-hand side of the track. Miraculously, no-one else was involved.

The Renaults, meanwhile, were through *Tarzan* followed by Jones, Piquet and Laffite with Andretti running alongside Reutemann as they approached *Gerlachbocht*. Mario, realising he could sit it out with the Williams, preferred to let Carlos through and on his way towards championship points – and the Argentinian promptly repaid Andretti by running over his nose wing. Further round the lap, Pironi and Tambay tangled, the incident retiring the Talbot-Ligier with broken front suspension while the Ferrari driver limped back to the pits to have his rear suspension attended to. Once repairs had been carried out, Pironi did one more lap before calling it a day, the handling being even worse than usual.

Prost had opened a gap over his team-mate as they crossed the line at the end of lap one but Jones was climbing all over Arnoux with Piquet and Laffite darting every which-way as they barrelled into *Tarzan* in a flurry of blipping throttles and frenzied braking. Lap three and Jones was still looking for a way past. Coming onto the straight, Alan whipped out from behind Arnoux and edged ahead as they passed the pits to take the place under braking. Clearly, Arnoux was unable to respond in the usual turbocharged way, the Renault driver beginning to feel the effects of a down-on-power engine and hard tyres. A couple of laps later and Piquet had demoted the Renault with Laffite doing likewise on lap seven. Andretti, furious but determined to keep going, had to give best to Watson on lap three but when de Angelis moved ahead, Mario realised he was fighting a losing battle and called in the pits on lap nine. It took four minutes to remove the battered nose wing and with it went Andretti's hopes of a good result, the American rejoining at the back of the field.

Nigel Mansell's race was short-lived after an electrical problem stopped the Lotus out on the circuit. Derek Daly was the next to go when a sandwich plate sheared due, it was thought, to the loads transmitted by the rock hard suspension.

That left 19 runners headed by Prost with Jones gradually closing the gap as the Renault driver eased off slightly to preserve his tyres. Piquet, oversteering excessively on his soft tyres, applied caution and dropped back while Laffite was beginning to come under pressure from Reutemann. Arnoux was still struggling along in sixth place and blocking an increasingly impatient Watson, the Ulsterman eventually taking the place on lap 12 with a brilliant manoeuvre round the outside of the Renault at *Tarzan*. As Watson did not hold the Frenchman in particularly high regard, he was delighted with the outcome of such a clean and precise move. Patrese was next, having got the better of de Angelis after another cut and thrust deal with his fellow countryman but the Arrows driver's run was destined to last until the end of lap 17 when he crept into the pits with broken suspension, a legacy of his incident with Villeneuve at the start. That left de Angelis to deal with a hard-charging Rebaque, the gritty little Mexican getting the better of the Lotus driver after one or two hairy moments under braking.

By now, Jones had closed on Prost and once or twice he had a look at the inside down at *Tarzan*. Then he had a go around the outside, the two running wheel to wheel, Prost edging Jones onto the dust and causing the Williams to slide briefly before falling back into place. There was no question of banging wheels or

Prost kept his cool under pressure and won from pole.

dubious tactics from over-anxious drivers. Where Jones had found a professional sparring partner in Villeneuve in 1979 and Pironi a year later, now he was enjoying the gamesmanship of a rapidly improving Alain Prost. Further proof of that came on lap 18.

Battling at the back of the field were Stohr, Salazar, Alboreto and Borgudd and the leaders began to move among this quartet at the exit from *Panoramabocht*. Going through '*Bos Uit*', Prost missed a gear and Jones was in the lead. Sensing that this was the opportunity he had been waiting for, Jones put the hammer down. Alboreto was ahead; the Williams would enjoy a nice tow from the Tyrrell just in time to slip ahead before *Tarzan*; Prost would have his work cut out to keep in touch. Everything went according to plan, Jones sling-shotting past Alboreto as they approached *Tarzan*. Drafting past *Jones*, however, came Renault number 15, Prost attacking immediately with a confident move which startled Jones and saw the two sit side by side through the corner. The lead was in dispute until the exit where the turbo came on song and pushed Alain back into a lead he was never to lose again. Impressive stuff.

That, more or less, was the end of Jones's challenge. At the 30 lap mark, his fuel load had decreased to such an extent that the ride height had altered and thus affected the car's ground effect. The net result was more sliding and more wear on tyres which Jones had taken to their limit during the early laps. Prost, by contrast, had taken things easy at the beginning and his Michelins were in perfect shape.

Carlos Reutemann had adopted the same policy and he was soon keen to move ahead of Laffite and get after Piquet. Jacques, by virtue of his tight entry to the corners, was not an easy man to pass as Reutemann discovered on lap 15 when he tried to move inside at the Marlboro chicane. By lap 18, he was pushing the Ligier once more and the Williams made the faster exit onto the straight. Going past the pits, it was obvious that he was not close enough to challenge yet Carlos kept aiming for the inside. Jacques took the same line he had used for the preceding 18 laps – and Carlos kept coming. Jacques braked late and aimed for his usual tight apex – and Carlos kept coming. The Williams kicked up dirt on the inside of the corner before crashing into the side of the Ligier and launching it briefly into the air. Laffite spun into the catch-fencing while Reutemann limped round the corner, his left-front wheel askew. Both drivers were out of the race and, in Laffite's case, possibly the championship.

With the field thinning out rapidly – Giacomelli crashed with suspension failure on lap 20 and Arnoux spun off two laps later – attention switched to the back of the field where Eliseo Salazar was having a superb run in the Ensign. Having dealt with the two Tyrrells, he set after Surer, the Chilean driver spurred on by the fact that Marc was a particular favourite of Mo Nunn. Having caught the Theodore, Salazar didn't mess about and passed Surer by running down the inside with four wheels on the grass! Salazar's progress was such that he began to close on Jones as the Williams driver struggled with tyres which were offering no grip whatsoever. Eliseo, a newcomer with a sense of protocol, was in something of a predicament: "I was embarrassed. He was running very slow but I thought 'No, I can't pass him. He is the World Champion!'" While he deliberated, Alboreto moved back into what had become sixth place and thus dispelled any charitable thoughts Mo Nunn may have held for his driver! Championship points were vital to a team such as Ensign but Mo need not have worried for Salazar was back in sixth place after the Tyrrell blew an engine on its last lap.

Up at the front, John Watson had lost fourth place when his McLaren stopped with an electrical short

Gerard Ducarouge's arrival at Alfa Romeo helped put Mario Andretti on the fourth row but his race was foiled by a damaged nose wing during the early laps. Elio de Angelis waits his chance to move ahead and take an eventual fifth place *(below and right)*.
Nelson Piquet moves ahead of Jones to take second place and joint leadership of the World Championship with Reutemann *(bottom)*.

Following pages:
"Watch out for Jones coming through on the inside......
Photo: Bernard Asset/A&P
...... at Tarzan."
Photo: David Winter
Alain Prost drove a mature race at Zandvoort.
Photo: Nigel Snowdon

between a high-tension lead and a water pipe. Four laps earlier, Cheever had crashed at the chicane while under pressure from Salazar, the American reporting later that his suspension had broken. The final and most potentially serious retirement occurred to Andretti on his 63rd lap. The Alfa Romeo driver, nursing a badly worn front-left tyre, had been running at the back of the field but the Michelin suddenly let go on a fast right-hander and the Alfa canoned into the guardrail, tearing off the left-hand side-pod as it did so. Andretti was trapped for a few minutes and was lucky to escape with nothing more than a shaking and a bruised leg.

Another driver in tyre trouble was Alan Jones, the Williams struggling home with a left-rear which was down to the canvas. Piquet, too, was nursing his tyres but prudent behaviour during the early laps paid off when he moved ahead of Jones with four laps remaining and scored six vital championship points. Nelson had equalled Reutemann's score thus ensuring that there would be everything to play for during the final three races.

Rebaque took a worthy fourth place ahead of de Angelis while a delighted Salazar made something of a historical landmark by scoring the first championship point for Chile. Stohr was seventh while Surer wobbled home with the handling of his Theodore made unpredictable by broken bolts between the engine and the bellhousing! Alboreto was classified ninth and Borgudd was tenth after a pit stop to replace a punctured front tyre.

At long last, Prost had made his mark with a performance which had been on the cards since the start of the season. Whereas he had won under unusual circumstances in France, this victory had been earned by a faultless drive and a cool head under pressure.

THE 'SILLY SEASON' WAS IN FULL SWING AT ZANDVOORT. Listed below are the predictions bouncing around the pages of the specialist press in late August. As you can see, the title 'Silly Season' is apt....
Riccardo Patrese (Arrows) reported to have turned down an offer from Alfa Romeo but signs for Brabham – Elio de Angelis (Lotus), Eddie Cheever (Tyrrell) and Jean-Pierre Jarier (Osella) mentioned as likely replacement for Patrese – Marc Surer (Theodore), Derek Warwick (Toleman) and Jacques Villeneuve (Formula Atlantic) rumoured for number two Arrows seat – Nelson Piquet (Brabham) to join McLaren – Mario Andretti (Alfa Romeo) receives offers from Brabham and McLaren – Tyrrell to run Jan Lammers – Gilles Villeneuve (Ferrari) holding talks with Williams – Keke Rosberg (Fittipaldi) to replace Andrea de Cesaris at McLaren – Elio de Angelis talks to Alfa Romeo – Carlos Reutemann (Williams) approached by Talbot-Ligier – Eddie Cheever to use TAG connections for Williams seat – Niki Lauda considering test drive in McLaren and offer from Brabham – Mario Andretti to give up Formula 1 and concentrate on CART racing.

TALBOT
25 GITANES
Marlboro
TALBOT
Marlboro
TALBOT
G TANES
FLY saudia
parmala
5
saudia
TAG
1

ALAIN PROST

Entries and practice times

No.	Driver	Nat	Car	Engine	Entrant	Practice 1	Practice 2
1	Alan Jones	AUS	Saudia-Leyland WILLIAMS FW07C	Ford Cosworth DFV	TAG Williams Team	**1m 18·672s**	1m 19·133s
2	Carlos Reutemann	RA	Saudia-Leyland WILLIAMS FW07C	Ford Cosworth DFV	TAG Williams Team	1m 19·067s	**1m 18·844s**
3	Eddie Cheever	USA	TYRRELL 011	Ford Cosworth DFV	Tyrrell Racing	1m 21·849s	**1m 21·698s**
4	Michele Alboreto	I	TYRRELL 011	Ford Cosworth DFV	Tyrrell Racing	1m 25·976s	**1m 22·030s**
5	Nelson Piquet	BR	Parmalat BRABHAM BT49C	Ford Cosworth DFV	Parmalat Racing Team	1m 19·236s	**1m 18·652s**
6	Hector Rebaque	MEX	Parmalat BRABHAM BT49C	Ford Cosworth DFV	Parmalat Racing Team	**1m 20·547s**	1m 20·872s
7	John Watson	GB	Marlboro McLAREN MP4	Ford Cosworth DFV	McLaren International	**1m 19·312s**	1m 19·651s
8	Andrea de Cesaris	I	Marlboro McLAREN MP4	Ford Cosworth DFV	McLaren International	1m 20·651s	**1m 20·377s**
9	Slim Borgudd	S	Abba ATS HGS 1	Ford Cosworth DFV	Team ATS	**1m 21·760s**	1m 22·302s
11	Elio de Angelis	I	John Player Special LOTUS 87	Ford Cosworth DFV	John Player Team Lotus	1m 21·662s	**1m 19·738s**
12	Nigel Mansell	GB	John Player Special LOTUS 87	Ford Cosworth DFV	John Player Team Lotus	1m 21·106s	**1m 20·663s**
14	Eliseo Salazar	RCH	ENSIGN N180B	Ford Cosworth DFV	Ensign Racing	1m 22·382s	**1m 22·024s**
15	Alain Prost	F	Elf RENAULT RE 30	Renault EF1	Equipe Renault Elf	1m 18·279s	**1m 18·176s**
16	René Arnoux	F	Elf RENAULT RE 30	Renault EF1	Equipe Renault Elf	**1m 18·255s**	1m 18·301s
17	Derek Daly	IRL	Rizla MARCH 811	Ford Cosworth DFV	March Grand Prix	1m 22·274s	**1m 21·391s**
20	Keke Rosberg	SF	FITTIPALDI F8C	Ford Cosworth DFV	Fittipaldi Automotive	**1m 23·518s**	6m 09·795s
21	Chico Serra	BR	FITTIPALDI F8C	Ford Cosworth DFV	Fittipaldi Automotive	1m 23·677s	**1m 23·613s**
22	Mario Andretti	USA	Marlboro ALFA ROMEO 179C	Alfa Romeo 1260	Marlboro Team Alfa Romeo	1m 19·896s	**1m 19·040s**
23	Bruno Giacomelli	I	Marlboro ALFA ROMEO 179C	Alfa Romeo 1260	Marlboro Team Alfa Romeo	**1m 20·384s**	1m 20·495s
25	Patrick Tambay	F	Talbot-Gitanes LIGIER JS17	Matra MS 81	Equipe Talbot Gitanes	1m 20·802s	**1m 19·979s**
26	Jacques Laffite	F	Talbot-Gitanes LIGIER JS17	Matra MS 81	Equipe Talbot Gitanes	1m 19·386s	**1m 19·018s**
27	Gilles Villeneuve	CDN	Fiat FERRARI 126CK	Ferrari 126C	Scuderia Ferrari SpA SEFAC	1m 21·049s	**1m 20·595s**
28	Didier Pironi	F	Fiat FERRARI 126CK	Ferrari 126C	Scuderia Ferrari SpA SEFAC	1m 21·293s	**1m 20·248s**
29	Riccardo Patrese	I	Ragno-Beta ARROWS A3	Ford Cosworth DFV	Arrows Racing Team	1m 21·010s	**1m 19·864s**
30	Siegfried Stohr	I	Ragno-Beta ARROWS A3	Ford Cosworth DFV	Arrows Racing Team	**1m 21·568s**	1m 21·713s
31	Beppe Gabbiani	I	Denim OSELLA FA1B	Ford Cosworth DFV	Osella Squadra Corse	–	**1m 23·898s**
32	Jean-Pierre Jarier	F	Denim OSELLA FA1B	Ford Cosworth DFV	Osella Squadra Corse	**1m 21·086s**	1m 21·294s
33	Marc Surer	CH	THEODORE TY 01	Ford Cosworth DFV	Theodore Racing Team	1m 22·389s	**1m 21·454s**
35	Brian Henton	GB	Candy TOLEMAN TG 181	Hart 415T	Candy Toleman Motorsport	**1m 22·226s**	1m 24·167s
36	Derek Warwick	GB	Candy TOLEMAN TG 181	Hart 415T	Candy Toleman Motorsport	1m 25·104s	**1m 24·028s**
Friday morning and Saturday morning practice sessions not officially recorded						*Fri pm Warm, dry*	*Sat pm Warm, dry*

Starting grid

15 PROST (1m 18·176s) Renault	16 ARNOUX (1m 18·255s) Renault
5 PIQUET (1m 18·652s) Brabham	1 JONES (1m 18·672s) Williams
2 REUTEMANN (1m 18·844s) Williams	26 LAFFITE (1m 19·018s) Talbot-Ligier
22 ANDRETTI (1m 19·040s) Alfa Romeo	7 WATSON (1m 19·312s) McLaren
11 DE ANGELIS (1m 19·738s) Lotus	29 PATRESE (1m 19·864s) Arrows
25 TAMBAY (1m 19·979s) Talbot-Ligier	28 PIRONI (1m 20·248s) Ferrari
	23 GIACOMELLI (1m 20·384s) Alfa Romeo
6 REBAQUE (1m 20·547s) Brabham	27 VILLENEUVE (1m 20·595s) Ferrari
12 MANSELL (1m 20·663s) Lotus	32 JARIER (1m 21·086s) Osella
17 DALY (1m 21·391s) March	33 SURER (1m 21·454s) Theodore
30 STOHR (1m 21·568s) Arrows	3 CHEEVER (1m 21·698s) Tyrrell
9 BORGUDD (1m 21·760s) ATS	14 SALAZAR (1m 22·024s) Ensign
* 4 ALBORETO (1m 22·030s) Tyrrell	

Did not start:
8 De Cesaris (McLaren), 1m 20·377s, withdrawn
35 Henton (Toleman), 1m 22·226s, did not qualify
20 Rosberg (Fittipaldi), 1m 23·518s, did not qualify
21 Serra (Fittipaldi), 1m 23·613s, did not qualify
31 Gabbiani (Osella), 1m 23·898s, did not qualify
36 Warwick (Toleman), 1m 24·028s, did not qualify
** Alboreto did not qualify but allowed to start in place of de Cesaris*

Past winners

Year	Driver	Nat	Car	Circuit	Distance miles/km	Speed mph/km/h
1949*	Luigi Villoresi	I	1·5 Ferrari 125 GP s/c	Zandvoort	104·22/167·72	77·09/124·06
1950*	Louis Rosier	F	4·5 Lago-Talbot	Zandvoort	234·49/377·37	76·63/123·32
1951*	Louis Rosier	F	4·5 Lago-Talbot	Zandvoort	234·49/377·37	78·45/126·26
1952	Alberto Ascari	I	2·0 Ferrari 500	Zandvoort	234·49/377·37	81·13/130·53
1953	Alberto Ascari	I	2·0 Ferrari 500	Zandvoort	234·49/377·37	81·05/130·43
1955	Juan Manuel Fangio	RA	2·5 Mercedes-Benz W196	Zandvoort	260·54/419·30	89·65/144·27
1958	Stirling Moss	GB	2·5 Vanwall	Zandvoort	195·41/314·48	93·93/151·17
1959	Jo Bonnier	S	2·5 BRM P25	Zandvoort	195·41/314·48	93·46/150·42
1960	Jack Brabham	AUS	2·5 Cooper T53 Climax	Zandvoort	195·41/314·48	96·27/154·93
1961	Wolfgang von Trips	D	1·5 Ferrari Dino 156	Zandvoort	195·41/314·48	96·23/154·83
1962	Graham Hill	GB	1·5 BRM P57	Zandvoort	208·43/335·44	95·44/153·60
1963	Jim Clark	GB	1·5 Lotus 25-Climax	Zandvoort	208·43/355·44	97·53/156·96
1964	Jim Clark	GB	1·5 Lotus 25-Climax	Zandvoort	208·43/335·44	98·02/157·74
1965	Jim Clark	GB	1·5 Lotus 33-Climax	Zandvoort	208·43/335·44	100·87/162·33
1966	Jack Brabham	AUS	3·0 Brabham BT19-Repco	Zandvoort	234·49/377·37	100·10/161·11
1967	Jim Clark	GB	3·0 Lotus 49-Ford	Zandvoort	234·49/377·37	104·45/168·09
1968	Jackie Stewart	GB	3·0 Matra MS10-Ford	Zandvoort	234·49/377·37	84·66/136·25
1969	Jackie Stewart	GB	3·0 Matra MS80-Ford	Zandvoort	234·49/377·37	111·04/178·71
1970	Jochen Rindt	A	3·0 Lotus 72-Ford	Zandvoort	208·43/335·44	112·96/181·78
1971	Jacky Ickx	B	3·0 Ferrari 312B-2/71	Zandvoort	182·38/293·51	94·06/151·38
1973	Jackie Stewart	GB	3·0 Tyrrell 006-Ford	Zandvoort	189·07/304·27	114·35/184·02
1974	Niki Lauda	A	3·0 Ferrari 312B-3/74	Zandvoort	196·94/316·95	114·72/184·62
1975	James Hunt	GB	3·0 Hesketh 308-Ford	Zandvoort	196·94/316·95	100·48/177·80
1976	James Hunt	GB	3·0 McLaren M23-Ford	Zandvoort	196·94/316·95	112·68/181·35
1977	Niki Lauda	A	3·0 Ferrari 312T-2/77	Zandvoort	196·94/316·95	116·12/186·87
1978	Mario Andretti	USA	3·0 JPS/Lotus 79-Ford	Zandvoort	196·94/316·95	116·92/188·16
1979	Alan Jones	AUS	3·0 Williams FW07-Ford	Zandvoort	196·94/316·95	116·62/187·67
1980	Nelson Piquet	BR	3·0 Brabham BT49-Ford	Zandvoort	190·23/306·14	116·19/186·99
1981	Alain Prost	F	1·5 Renault RE t/c	Zandvoort	190·23/306·14	113·71/183·00

* Non-championship

Circuit data

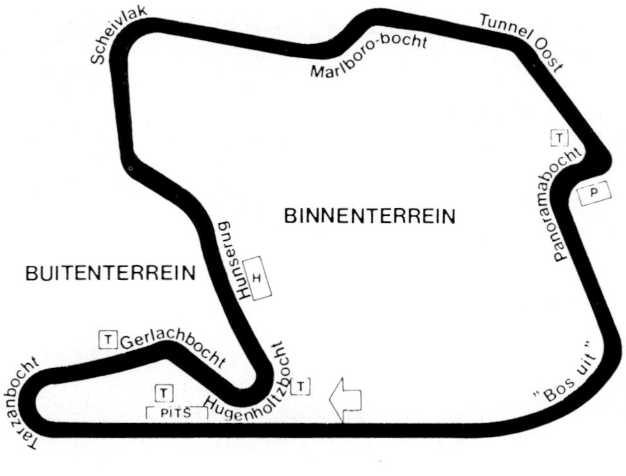

Circuit van Zandvoort, near Haarlem
Circuit length: 2·642 miles/4·252 km
Race distance: 72 laps, 190·228 miles/306·144 km
Race weather: Warm, dry

Results and retirements

Place	Driver	Car	Laps	Time and Speed (mph/km/h)/Retirement	
1	Alain Prost	Renault t/c V6	72	1h 40m 22·43s	113·712/183·002
2	Nelson Piquet	Brabham-Cosworth V8	72	1h 40m 30·67s	113·557/182·752
3	Alan Jones	Williams-Cosworth V8	72	1h 40m 57·93s	113·046/181·930
4	Hector Rebaque	Brabham-Cosworth V8	71		
5	Elio de Angelis	Lotus-Cosworth V8	71		
6	Eliseo Salazar	Ensign-Cosworth V8	70		
7	Siegfried Stohr	Arrows-Cosworth V8	69		
8	Marc Surer	Theodore-Cosworth V8	69		
9	Michele Alboreto	Tyrrell-Cosworth V8	68	Engine	
10	Slim Borgudd	ATS-Cosworth V8	68		
	Mario Andretti	Alfa Romeo V12	62	Accident/tyre failure	
	John Watson	McLaren-Cosworth V8	50	Electrics	
	Eddie Cheever	Tyrrell-Cosworth V8	46	Accident/broken suspension	
	Jean-Pierre Jarier	Osella-Cosworth V8	29	Gearbox	
	René Arnoux	Renault t/c V6	21	Accident	
	Bruno Giacomelli	Alfa Romeo V12	19	Accident	
	Jacques Laffite	Talbot-Ligier V12	18	Accident with Reutemann	
	Carlos Reutemann	Williams-Cosworth V8	18	Accident with Laffite	
	Riccardo Patrese	Arrows-Cosworth V8	16	Broken suspension	
	Derek Daly	March-Cosworth V8	5	Broken suspension	
	Didier Pironi	Ferrari t/c V6	4	Accident damage	
	Nigel Mansell	Lotus-Cosworth V8	1	Electrics	
	Patrick Tambay	Talbot-Ligier V12	0	Accident with Pironi	
	Gilles Villeneuve	Ferrari t/c V12	0	Accident with Giacomelli and Patrese	

Fastest lap: Jones, on lap 15, 1m 21·83s, 116·234mph/187·061km/h.
Lap record: René Arnoux (F1 Renault RE-t/c V6), 1m 19·35s, 119·867mph/192·907km/h (1980).

Lap chart

1st LAP ORDER		1	2	3	4	5	6	7	8	9	10	11	12	13	14	15	16	17	18	19	20	21	22	23	24	25	26	27	28	29	30	31	32	33
15	A.Prost	15	15	15	15	15	15	15	15	15	15	15	15	15	15	15	15	15	15	15	15	15	15	1	15	15	15	15	15	15	15	15	15	15
16	R.Arnoux	16	16	1	1	1	1	1	1	1	1	1	1	1	1	1	1	1	1	1	1	1	1	16	1	1	1	1	1	1	1	1	1	1
1	A.Jones	1	1	16	16	5	5	5	5	5	5	5	5	5	5	5	5	5	5	5	5	5	5	5	5	5	5	5	5	5	5	5	5	5
5	N.Piquet	5	5	5	5	16	16	26	26	26	26	26	26	26	26	26	26	26	26	7	7	7	7	7	7	7	7	7	7	7	7	7	7	7
26	J.Laffite	26	26	26	26	26	26	16	16	2	2	2	2	2	2	2	2	2	2	16	16	16	6	6	6	6	6	6	6	6	6	6	6	6
2	C.Reutemann	2	2	2	2	2	2	2	2	16	16	16	16	7	7	7	7	7	7	6	6	6	11	11	11	11	11	11	11	11	11	11	11	11
22	M.Andretti	22	22	7	7	7	7	7	7	7	7	7	7	16	16	16	16	16	16	11	11	11	32	32	32	32	32	32	32	33	33	33	33	33
7	J.Watson	7	7	22	22	22	22	22	11	11	11	29	29	29	11	11	11	6	6	23	32	32	33	33	33	33	33	33	33	3	3	3	3	3
11	E.de Angelis	11	11	11	11	11	11	11	22	29	29	11	11	11	6	6	6	11	11	32	33	33	3	3	3	3	3	3	3	4	4	4	4	14
29	R.Patrese	29	29	29	29	29	29	29	29	23	23	6	6	6	29	29	23	23	23	33	3	3	4	4	4	4	4	4	4	14	14	14	14	4
23	B.Giacomelli	23	23	23	23	23	23	23	23	6	6	23	23	23	23	23	32	32	32	3	4	4	9	9	9	14	14	14	14	30	30	30	30	30
6	H.Rebaque	6	6	6	6	6	6	6	6	22	32	32	32	32	32	32	33	33	33	30	14	9	14	14	14	9	9	9	9	9	9	9	9	9
17	D.Daly	17	17	17	17	32	32	32	32	32	33	33	33	33	33	33	3	3	3	14	9	14	30	30	30	30	30	30	30	32	22	22	22	22
32	J-P.Jarier	32	32	32	32	33	33	33	33	33	3	3	3	3	3	3	30	30	30	4	30	30	22	22	22	22	22	22	22	22				
12	N.Mansell	12	33	33	33	3	3	3	3	3	14	14	14	14	14	30	14	14	14	9	22	22												
33	M.Surer	33	3	3	3	14	14	14	14	14	4	30	30	30	30	14	4	4	4	22														
3	E.Cheever	3	14	14	14	30	4	4	4	4	30	4	4	4	4	4	9	9	9															
30	S.Stohr	30	30	30	30	4	30	30	30	30	9	9	9	9	9	9	29	22	22															
14	E.Salazar	14	4	4	4	9	9	9	9	9	22	22	22	22	22	22	22																	
4	M.Alboreto	4	9	9	9	17																												
9	S.Borgudd	9	28	28	28																													
28	D.Pironi	28																																

34	35	36	37	38	39	40	41	42	43	44	45	46	47	48	49	50	51	52	53	54	55	56	57	58	59	60	61	62	63	64	65	66	67	68	69	70	71	72
15	15	15	15	15	15	15	15	15	15	15	15	15	15	15	15	15	15	15	15	15	15	15	15	15	15	15	15	15	15	15	15	15	15	15	15	15	15	15
1	1	1	1	1	1	1	1	1	1	1	1	1	1	1	1	1	1	1	1	1	1	1	1	1	1	1	1	1	1	1	1	1	1	1	5	5	5	5
5	5	5	5	5	5	5	5	5	5	5	5	5	5	5	5	5	5	5	5	5	5	5	5	5	5	5	5	5	5	5	5	5	5	5	1	1	1	1
7	7	7	7	7	7	7	7	7	7	7	7	7	7	7	7	7	6	6	6	6	6	6	6	6	6	6	6	6	6	6	6	6	6	6	6	6	6	
6	6	6	6	6	6	6	6	6	6	6	6	6	6	6	6	6	11	11	11	11	11	11	11	11	11	11	11	11	11	11	11	11	11	11	11	11	11	
11	11	11	11	11	11	11	11	11	11	11	11	11	11	11	11	11	33	33	33	33	33	14	14	14	14	14	14	14	14	14	14	14	14	14	14	14		
33	33	33	33	33	33	33	33	33	33	33	33	33	33	33	33	33	14	14	14	14	14	33	33	33	33	33	33	4	4	4	4	4	4	14	30			
3	3	3	3	3	3	3	3	3	3	3	3	3	14	14	14	14	4	4	4	4	4	4	4	4	4	4	4	33	33	33	33	33	33	30	33			
14	14	14	14	14	14	14	14	14	14	14	14	14	4	4	4	4	30	30	30	30	30	30	30	30	30	30	30	30	30	30	30	30	30	33				
4	4	4	4	4	4	4	4	4	4	4	4	4	30	9	30	30	9	9	9	9	9	9	9	9	9	9	9	9	9	9	9	9	9	9				
30	30	30	30	30	30	30	30	30	30	30	30	30	9	30	9	9	22	22	22	22	22	22	22	22	22	22	22	22										
9	9	9	9	9	9	9	9	9	9	9	9	9	22	22	22	22																						
22	22	22	22	22	22	22	22	22	22	22	22	22																										

Fastest laps

Driver	Time	Lap
Alan Jones	1m 21·83s	15
Nelson Piquet	1m 22·04s	12
Alain Prost	1m 22·06s	13
Carlos Reutemann	1m 22·10s	16
Jacques Laffite	1m 22·32s	15
John Watson	1m 22·64s	8
Bruno Giacomelli	1m 22·66s	4
René Arnoux	1m 22·82s	8
Marc Surer	1m 23·17s	4
Riccardo Patrese	1m 23·26s	4
Hector Rebaque	1m 23·53s	4
Mario Andretti	1m 23·61s	14
Elio de Angelis	1m 23·90s	13
Jean-Pierre Jarier	1m 23·95s	4
Eliseo Salazar	1m 24·18s	4
Eddie Cheever	1m 24·54s	4
Siegfried Stohr	1m 24·87s	53
Derek Daly	1m 24·98s	2
Slim Borgudd	1m 25·04s	53
Michele Alboreto	1m 25·06s	6
Didier Pironi	1m 26·09s	3
Nigel Mansell	1m 37·80s	1

Points

WORLD CHAMPIONSHIP OF DRIVERS

1 =	Carlos Reutemann	45 pts
1 =	Nelson Piquet	45
3	Jacques Laffite	34
4	Alan Jones	31
5	Alain Prost	28
6 =	John Watson	21
6 =	Gilles Villeneuve	21
8 =	René Arnoux	11
8 =	Hector Rebaque	11
10 =	Riccardo Patrese	10
10 =	Eddie Cheever	10
10 =	Elio de Angelis	10
13	Didier Pironi	7
14	Nigel Mansell	5
15	Marc Surer	4
16	Mario Andretti	3
17 =	Patrick Tambay	1
17 =	Andrea de Cesaris	1
17 =	Slim Borgudd	1
17 =	Eliseo Salazar	1

CONSTRUCTORS' CUP

1	Williams	76
2	Brabham	56
3	Renault	39
4	Ligier	34
5	Ferrari	28
6	McLaren	22
7	Lotus	15
8 =	Arrows	10
8 =	Tyrrell	10
10	Ensign	5
11	Alfa Romeo	3
12 =	Theodore	1
12 =	ATS	1

FLY sa
GOODYEAR

udia
saudia
Avant Garde
TAG
1
GOODYEAR
GOODYEAR

Gran Premio d'Italia

They were at their work by 8 a.m. Well, it wasn't work exactly. More a vocation; a natural urge that can scarcely be supressed. When it comes to motor racing at Monza, the Italian fan has no equal in terms of natural guile and raw enthusiasm. You don't like paying the prices? Then you climb the wall, burrow under the fence, cut the wire or simply argue your way in. And they were at their work from an early hour.

Five miles away, in the Hotel Fossati, Alain Prost was thinking about breakfast and the race to follow. He wasn't on pole – he wasn't even on the front row thanks to a practice frought with minor problems and a rare mistake. After winning at Zandvoort, second place at Monza would be unacceptable.

Prost did hold second place briefly as he surged through from the second row and took a lead he was never to lose. The Renault-Elf driver, having changed his suspension set-up, had a perfect race in far from perfect conditions. A local shower soaked a section of the track and caught out René Arnoux who started the race from his fourth pole position of the season.

Alongside him on the front row had been Carlos Reutemann after a positively brilliant practice lap and the Argentinian driver carefully worked out the perfect set-up for a dry race. His plans were foiled by the rain and, as the Saudia-Leyland Williams slithered helplessly to eighth place, it seemed his championship lead would be lost for the first time since Brazil.

A drying track helped pull him back to fourth place but Nelson Piquet seemed secure in third spot – until the last lap when he suffered the appalling agony of a blown engine. The Parmalat Brabham driver was classified sixth behind Elio de Angelis's John Player Lotus and Didier Pironi's Ferrari which had dropped back after an early charge.

Alan Jones, racing with a broken finger, drove exceptionally well in a car more suited to the slippery conditions and moved through the field to take a strong second place. Other notable performances in the wet came from Patrick Tambay, the Talbot-Ligier holding fourth place before puncturing a tyre, and Bruno Giacomelli who battled into third position before his Marlboro Alfa Romeo encountered gearbox trouble.

There were several incidents, the most serious occurring to John Watson as he chased Pironi for sixth place. Exiting fron the second Lesmo, Watson allowed his McLaren to ride over the kerb, the car then spinning across the track and clouting the guardrail backwards. The impact ripped the engine and gearbox off and sent them bouncing onto the track while Watson stepped from the intact monocoque section of the car. An accident of horrifying proportions which, judging by Watson's unruffled expression, looked worse from outside the cockpit than it did from within!

Motoring through the rain and the wreckage came ten survivors with Brian Henton, the final finisher, receiving well-earned applause for not only qualifying a Candy-Toleman for the first time but also bringing the turbo across the line after a difficult race.

Prost, on the other hand, said it had never been easier. Now he was joint third in the championship with Alan Jones but Reutemann had eased three points clear of Piquet. Five drivers may have had a mathematical chance of winning the title but, at this stage, the fight was between the two South Americans. And, sadly for the Tifosi, neither driver was in a Ferrari.

ENTRY AND PRACTICE

René Arnoux made the mistake of casually complaining about his steering wheel; it was too slippery, his gloves wouldn't grip the leather. As the Frenchman sauntered into the pit lane on Friday morning, the mechanics could hardly stifle their giggles. Parked out on the pit road was 'Néné's' RE 33 – complete with a fluffy steering wheel cover. René stood, hands on hips, and laughed, flicking his eyes at each mechanic in turn before wandering off in search of Jean Sage. Doubtless the mischievious Team Manager was at the bottom of this.

Previous pages:
Despite a broken finger, Alan Jones provided a superb spectacle at Monza.
Photo: Nigel Snowdon

A broken finger didn't deter Alan Jones from finishing second *(left)*.
Alain Prost made up for not making the front row of the grid by taking the lead at the 1st chicane *(main picture)*.

Arnoux remained in good form throughout practice, his car giving no trouble as he glided to his fourth pole position of the season. As ever, the Renault appeared to cruise over the bumps and it wasn't until the commentator read out the times that you were staggered by the turbo's speed. Arnoux set the fastest time in both sessions while Alain Prost spent practice sorting out a variety of problems. The hydropneumatic suspension refused to work properly, the nose taking a couple of laps to settle into the lower position. Then the skirts were wearing excessively and the brakes were spongy. On Saturday, Alain was ready to go for pole on his final set of qualifiers. Completing his first flying lap, he came across the slow-moving de Cesaris and rather foolishly decided to pass the McLaren on the right. Andrea began to head towards the pits leaving Prost with no option but to attack the cones marking the edge of the track at that point. Prost's nose wing received a hefty thump and cut its way into a tyre thus ending his practice. Nevertheless Prost, second fastest on Friday, had improved enough to take third place on the grid and it would have been a Renault front row had it not been for a brilliant performance by Carlos Reutemann.

The disaster at Zandvoort was forgotten as

Jacques Laffite appeared to lose any chance of making a bid for the championship when a rear tyre failed and sent the Talbot-Ligier into the sand at the first chicane *(right)*.
They were at their work from an early hour... *(below)*.
Juan Manuel Fangio gave an impressive demonstration in the Lancia D50 *(bottom)*.

Reutemann and Laffite chatted at dinner on Friday evening. Indeed, it was becoming a standing joke; Zolder in 1978, Jarama in 1980 and then it was Carlos's turn again at Zandvoort. No matter, that was history and both drivers were looking forward to Monza – particularly Reutemann who was in a confident mood having completed over 900 miles of testing at the circuit. Fastest during the unofficial session on Friday morning, Carlos was the closest Renault challenger in the afternoon but, on Saturday, he really made his mark with a typically superb one-off lap. After that, he simply spent the remaining 30 minutes bedding in brakes, confident that no one bar Renault could approach his time. Not even Alan Jones.

The reigning World Champion blew an engine on Saturday afternoon but, apart from that, he had problems of his own making. Poking through his right-hand driving glove were two heavily bandaged fingers, the little one having been broken in what Jones described as "an altercation with some black gentlemen in Chiswick High Road". The Marlboro News Service said he had been defending himself against an attack by muggers but Jones offered the more honest suggestion that his driving tactics may have caused the other motorist to become annoyed and nudge the bumper of his Mazda RX7. Jones had words with the driver but questioned the wisdom of that decision when two passengers emerged and a fracas ensued on the pavement. Apparently Jones broke his finger against someone's jaw! Alan was ninth fastest which was a creditable time considering he had to brake early and carefully move his hand from steering wheel to gear lever in order to avoid bashing the protruding fingers. Furthermore, he was unable to pitch the car into the corners and cancel the understeer provoked by running without nose wings as the team searched for straight-line speed.

On Friday, Jacques Laffite was down in 11th place, a fraction slower than Patrick Tambay. The next day, it was a rueful Tambay who stood in the pit lane and observed that perhaps he had gone too fast on Friday: "now they change my car, just like that," he said with a resigned shrug as he prepared to climb into Laffite's Talbot-Ligier. This was a stiffer chassis yet, strangely, Tambay was unable to improve his time while Laffite knocked over a second off and moved onto the second row alongside Prost. Jacques knew what he was doing after all!

The championship needle match was between Reutemann and Piquet, both drivers level on 45 points. There was no contest throughout practice, particularly after Carlos's effort on Saturday afternoon, and Nelson had to make do with his Friday time after an alarming incident during the final session. Out for a quick lap in a T-car specially prepared for practice, Nelson pumped the brakes on the approach to the *Ascari* chicane. Nothing happened. Hitting the middle pedal again, Piquet suddenly had too much braking as the rears locked and sent the Brabham into the sand. The team were amazed to discover that a stone had found its way through the brake-duct before jamming between the calliper and the wheel – whereupon it cut through the rim like a knife through butter! Fortunately, there was little damage to either the driver or the car. The net result was sixth fastest time for Piquet while Hector Rebaque would have improved on row seven had he not run low on fuel during his last lap on qualifiers.

Practice was barely 45 minutes old when officials brought proceedings to a halt. Someone had gone off at the first chicane. Almost instinctively, eyes turned to the Marlboro McLaren pit and, sure enough, car

Nelson Piquet was set to take the lead of the World Championship until the last lap when an engine failure cost him third place *(below)*. Lucky to finish third, a frustrated Carlos Reutemann walks back after his plans had been upset by a shower of rain *(bottom)*.

SEPTEMBER:

Geoff Lees wins European Formula 2 Championship for Ralt-Honda.

Leyland Vehicles announce withdrawal from Formula 1 sponsorship in 1982.

Niki Lauda tests Marlboro McLaren MP4 at Donington.

Australia announces plans to run a Grand Prix on a new circuit near Melbourne.

Brian Redman wins Camel IMSA GT Championship in Lola-Chevrolet T600.

number eight had not returned. Andrea had done it again. Eventually, the red and white MP4 came in on the back of a truck and the tight-lipped mechanics gathered round to find the left rear corner ripped right off, drive-shaft and all. De Cesaris was obliged to sit out the rest of Friday practice and watch Watson set sixth fastest time. John spent most of the day alternating between his usual car and the spare which featured a wider front track and new front uprights. Having found what he hoped would be the ideal set-up for Saturday, Watson then had a frustrating final session when his car stopped out on the track with an electrical problem. Rushing back to the pits, John found that the spare car would not fire up due to fuel vapourisation. Eventually he did get going and improved enough to take a place on the fourth row.

Monza meant Ferrari, of course, but Maranello produced little to suggest that they were likely to improve on their recent poor performances. As ever, the red transporter was the last to arrive, the 'home' team being ushered into the paddock in the pouring rain early on Thursday evening. The mechanics were kept busy throughout as they tended to the four cars available to Villeneuve and Pironi and it was the latter who got through more than his fair share of chassis. Halfway through the first timed session, Didier inexplicably crashed at the exit of the 150mph second *Lesmo*. The car, he said, simply lost all grip at the front and understeered off before virtually destroying the left-hand side. The impact jarred one of Pironi's ribs but the Frenchman was soon in his spare car and improving his time. He continued with his T-car on Saturday only to have an engine fail within the first few minutes of timed practice. Mauro Forghieri then put Didier into Villeneuve's spare – and a few minutes later, the French-Canadian was trundling into the pits with his engine on the way out. He was not amused to find himself with an unused set of qualifying tyres and no car to put them on. Indeed, that effectively robbed the final session of any excitement for Villeneuve had been intent on improving on his Friday time. As it was, he had to be content with ninth place behind Pironi while the crowd were far from happy, having seen their hero for no more than a handful of laps.

The Alfa Romeos, having shown such good form at Zandvoort, were in trouble with the chicanes at Monza. It was much the same as Hockenheim, the cars refusing to change direction smoothly but Bruno Giacomelli used his home advantage to pip Andretti by half-a-second during the final session. Splitting the red and white cars were the John Player Team Lotus drivers, Nigel Mansell just failing to beat Elio de Angelis on Saturday. The mechanics spent Thursday night building a new chassis for Mansell while, on Friday, de Angelis experimented with 13ins fronts and the low profile 15ins fronts. It was Mansell's first visit to Monza and he had the added handicap of a tired engine on Friday. A water radiator punctured on Saturday morning but a fresh engine helped him improve in the afternoon in spite of understeer and a car which continued to be a handful on the bumps.

Tyrrell fitted revised front and rear suspension which lengthened the wheelbase on Cheever's 011 chassis, Eddie taking 17th place after improving considerably on Saturday, while Michele Alboreto, fresh from his first Formula 2 victory, faced the stiff reality of Grand Prix racing from a place on the penultimate row of the grid. The Denim Osella team gained valuable publicity by unveiling their new car at Monza. Jean-Pierre Jarier had been allowed to complete a few shake-down laps in the car at Fiorano where he found the FA1C to be a considerable improvement but obviously in need of much development. Nevertheless, Jarier qualified but Beppe Gabbiani failed once again. Taking what had become a habitual 19th place, Derek Daly qualified the Guinness-Rizla March in spite of fuel starvation problems on Saturday. The Irishman was reasonably pleased with his time but the same could not be said for Riccardo Patrese, languishing in 20th place in the Ragno-Beta Arrows. Poor tyres and extra weight from the mandatory skirt mountings were said to be the problem but whatever the cause, it was not the place to be for an Italian driver nor a team sponsored by Italian companies. Patrese was barely half-a-second faster than Slim Borgudd in the ATS, the Swede sharing row 11 with Alboreto.

Sharing the back row, however, was none other than Brian Henton in the Candy-Toleman, the British team fortuitously qualifying for the first time on the door-step of their Monza-based sponsor. Running the Hart Monobloc engine, Henton had shown promise throughout although practice on Friday was curtailed by a split intercooler. Fingers were crossed on Saturday and Brian's lap of 1m 38.012s was greeted with champagne when he made his triumphant return to the pit lane. It was as though he had won the race! In all the euphoria, it was easy to overlook the feelings of poor Derek Warwick, a non-qualifier once again in spite of his usual 100% effort out on the track. His Monobloc engine did not arrive until Friday evening but practice the following day was ruined by a shortage of revs and the usual popping and banging from the engine. The Toleman team's pleasure was tinged slightly by a protest from Theodore, the first non-qualifiers. Once again, skirts were the point of contention, Theodore arguing that they had spent time and money making their skirt mounting system conform to the agreed regulations. Toleman, meanwhile, had not been able to convert their system. Hence the protest. It was unfortunate this had to arise when it was considered Toleman withdrew one of their cars at Zolder, a move which allowed Theodore to practice their car. Clearly, a firm hand by FISA would not have allowed the matter to arise in the first place.

The final qualifier was Eliseo Salazar in the Ensign with a time of 1m 38.053s. The Chilean driver's time did not appear to match his hard work out on the track and of more consequence, perhaps, was a time of 1m 37.9s set on race tyres on Saturday morning. Siegfried Stohr, having his last outing with the Arrows team, failed to qualify although the Italian was one of the first to congratulate the Toleman team. Fittipaldi were present once again but neither Keke Rosberg nor Chico Serra were able to put the beleagured team into the race.

RACE

Faces in the Toleman pit paled visibly when Henton disappeared during the warm-up. Fortunately, he had slipped harmlessly into the sand and would make the start although the chances of the turbo finishing the race seemed remote. Ferrari were in trouble again when Pironi lost another engine, a similar fate befalling ATS while Mario Andretti complained of a misfire. Otherwise, the warm-up provided few dramas and the main preoccupation was choosing the right tyres for the relatively cool conditions.

With the race not starting until 3.30 p.m., the rather sparse crowd (by Monza standards) was entertained by none other than Juan Manuel Fangio at the wheel of an Alfa Romeo 159 similar to the model with which he won his first World Championship 30 years previously. Having cut one or two impressive laps Fangio, wearing his familiar brown helmet, switched to a Lancia D50 and pushed the rumbling V8 around Monza at a startling speed for a man of 70. Fangio was just a lad compared to Luigi Villoresi, however, and the grey-haired Italian then climbed aboard the Lancia and shot off at an astonishing rate. Both men obviously relished the moment and one was tempted to speculate whether Carlos Reutemann and Nelson Piquet would be performing similar deeds at Las Vegas in 30 years time...

For the time being, both drivers were concentrating on the 1981 championship, Reutemann giving his race set-up a lot of thought and coming to the line without nose wings, but with a small rear wing and a 'B' compound tyre on the left rear. Jones, figuring it might rain, ran the softer 'C' compounds all round and opted to fit nose wings. It was a gamble but one worth taking for a driver with little to lose. Prost, almost in desperation, had asked to have Arnoux's settings transferred to his car and René's hard work paid off. The car was transformed and Alain pulled up on the grid in a confident frame of mind.

All eyes were on Villeneuve but it was his team-mate

At last! Brian Henton not only qualified the Toleman-Hart but also managed to finish in spite of a broken rev-counter and a misfire.

who made a brilliant start, spearing through the fourth row before passing Jones and taking Laffite under braking for the first chicane. By the time Pironi had reached *Lesmo*, he had dealt with Arnoux and Reutemann and was in second place behind Prost. Of the two Renault drivers Alain, as usual, had made the better start, moving ahead of Arnoux before the first chicane. René was under attack all the way round the opening lap and Reutemann pushed the Renault down to fourth place by running neatly round the outside at *Curvetta Sud*.

Down at the back of the grid, there had been drama during the parade lap as Rebaque's engine began to die. The Brabham crept into the pit lane registering zero fuel pressure and a quick check pinpointed the electrical system as the culprit. The engine was fired up again and Hector left the pit lane only to have the engine stop for good out on the circuit. A loose wire in the spark box was later discovered to have been the cause. Similarly, Michele Alboreto failed to take the start from the grid when he pulled into the Tyrrell pit with an electrical problem but the Italian was able to lap consistently once the trouble had been sorted out.

By the end of lap two, Jacques Laffite had taken Jones and Piquet for fifth place with Villeneuve's Ferrari following suit. The spectator enclosures buzzed with anticipation but their excitement was to be short-lived, the Ferrari grinding to a smokey halt with a blown turbo. Then, complete despondency set in when Pironi's second place came under threat from Arnoux, the Renault driver having woken up and retaken Reutemann. René was into his stride and by lap five he made it a Renault one-two at the front although Prost, by now, was long gone. Laffite had continued to make good progress but he was no sooner into third place when a deflating left-rear tyre quickly dropped the Ligier down the field before blowing completely and depositing Jacques in the sand at the first chicane. Down at the back of the field and about to be lapped, Brian Henton and his Toleman plugged gamely on. Surely they would retire soon?

On lap 10, Prost came by the pits with his finger pointing skywards. Rain had begun to fall on parts of the circuit as Slim Borgudd was to testify after spinning off when suddenly confronted with a wet piece of road at *Curvetta Sud*. Eddie Cheever was the next to go and René Arnoux then spun off while trying to take avoiding action. While the Renault was stuck in the sand, the Tyrrell remained, unscathed, on the track. Unfortunately, Cheever had burnt out his clutch at the start and the American was therefore unable to get going.

The rain, heavy enough at certain points to cause plumes of spray, kept away from the pit area although lap charts began to give an indication of how the drivers were coping with the tricky conditions. Down went Reutemann, his Williams useless without wings and soft tyres all round, up came Jones as he made the most of plenty of downforce and 'C' compounds all round and, behind him in third place came Bruno Giacomelli, driving superbly through the field. Piquet was next but soon gave way to Tambay as the Talbot-Ligier moved forward on soft compounds. Pironi was next followed by Watson with Reutemann losing ground fast and about to be overtaken by Andretti under the most bizarre circumstances.

Powering through the second *Lesmo* at over 150mph in pursuit of Pironi, John Watson allowed his McLaren to ride the kerb at the exit. The stiff suspension then took control and flicked the car sideways before spinning the hapless Watson backwards into the barrier on the opposite side of the track. The guardrails opened momentarily, snaring a rear corner of the MP4 and ripping the engine clean off the monocoque. There was an immediate ball of orange flame as the fuel lines to the engine caused a flash fire before sealing themselves and preventing what could have been a holocaust. Unharmed and unaware of the severity of the impact – until he saw his engine and gearbox on the opposite side of the track – Watson simply threw off his belts, climbed from the monocoque section of the car and walked away. About to make a similar trek back to the pits was Michele Alboreto who had nudged the guardrail while trying to avoid the spinning rear quarters of the McLaren. Reutemann was next on the scene and managed to pick his way through on the grass while Andretti, who had more choice in the matter, stayed on the track and moved into what had suddenly become seventh place.

Alfa Romeo were, at long last, looking good. But their joy was to last three more laps before Giacomelli dived into the pits to investigate a gearbox jammed in fifth. Having lost a lap, the Italian rejoined only to return to the pits with a recurrence of the problem. All was not lost, however, for Andretti was now fifth after Tambay had ended an excellent run with a puncture caused by debris from Watson's wreckage. Italian interest was see-sawing rapidly as Patrese parked his Arrows with a stripped fifth gear and Chilean hopes, after a healthy boost at Zandvoort, took a dive when Salazar retired after a tyre failure while the Ensign was in the middle of *Curvetta Sud*. Eliseo survived the moment to tell the tale with relish. Nigel Mansell ended an unhappy race when his handling became impossible after his skirts had worn away during the early, full tank laps but de Angelis had worked his way through to seventh place after having given best to Daly on lap 18. The March driver had shown typically agressive race form as he made the most of running without nose wings and the subsequent straight-line speed. A possible position in the points was lost with severe gearbox problems caused by an inadequate oil-feed. And Henton kept going.

With the track beginning to dry, Prost was able to maintain a 20-second gap over Jones. Piquet was a comfortable third but Reutemann was back in the groove once more and he took fourth place from Pironi as the Frenchman struggled with loose bodywork and pain from his injured rib. Any chance Andretti may have had of capitalising on Pironi's problems was cut short by a broken flywheel coupling on lap 42 and his retirement allowed de Angelis to move into the points with de Cesaris following in a subdued but sensible seventh place. Giacomelli was next while Jean-Pierre Jarier put in a gallant drive in the Osella after being involved in a serious road

Alain Prost scored an easy win for Renault *(left)*.
Jean-Pierre Jarier qualified the new Osella *(below left)*.
Sort that lot out! The remains of Pironi's Ferrari after a practice shunt *(bottom left)*.
Is nothing sacred? Thieves broke into Gilles Villeneuve's helicopter – twice *(below)*.

accident the previous evening. A 13-year-old boy had been killed and, although Jean-Pierre was entirely blameless, the effects of the incident remained with the Frenchman. And Henton kept going.

During the closing laps, Prost eased his pace as Jones became hobbled by a broken valve spring. Reutemann really put the hammer down now and closed the gap on Piquet to 4.3 seconds on the penultimate lap but the Brazilian driver looked set to lead the championship as he sailed past the pits to start his last lap. The white Brabham was not seen again.

Piquet was horrified to see the oil light flash as he braked for the first chicane and, almost immediately, the engine blew in a depressing cloud of blue smoke. Pulling to the side, Nelson sat motionless in the car for a few minutes, unable to take in such a cruel blow.

Reutemann, de Angelis and Pironi flashed by while de Cesaris, who should have been next, went off with a puncture. Thus, Piquet managed to rake one point from the ashes of his despair.

And Henton? Despite a broken rev-counter and a misfiring engine, the Toleman driver crossed the line to make history of sorts. The turbo had finished its first race which was more than could be said for either Renault or Ferrari and the Toleman team broke out the champagne with some justification.

At the far end of the pits, Prost sprayed champagne from the rostrum and talked about a victory which could not have been easier. His car had been perfect and, on this occasion, Jones had been unable to challenge in spite of another press-on performance. Third place on the rostrum remained vacant as Reutemann made for the Williams motor home to vent his feelings about the weather and the hard rear tyre he had been forced to run. In the motor home next door, poor Piquet was scarcely consoled by a single point instead of four.

In a nearby field, Gilles Villeneuve was just as annoyed to discover that his helicopter had been broken into and the radio equipment stolen. While attending a power boat race at Lake Como a week before, thieves had smashed a window on the same chopper and removed his briefcase. Villeneuve had spent the week reorganising his passport, credit cards and air tickets. Then he had retired his Ferrari from the Italian Grand Prix after an unhappy two days of practice. And now this.

A couple of hours later in a local restaurant, the Renault team held a victory dinner while, outside, someone was breaking into a mechanic's car and pinching the presents he had bought for his family. They also forced their way into a Fiat 132 rented by journalist Eoin Young and stole his briefcase as well as the typewriter and valuable notes belong to the Editor of *Autocourse*.

They were at their work until a late hour on September 13.

Gran Premio d'Italia, September 13/statistics

Entries and practice times

No.	Driver	Nat	Car	Engine	Entrant	Practice 1	Practice 2
1	Alan Jones	AUS	Saudia-Leyland WILLIAMS FWO7C	Ford Cosworth DFV	TAG Williams Team	1m 35·983s	**1m 35·359s**
2	Carlos Reutemann	RA	Saudia-Leyland WILLIAMS FWO7C	Ford Cosworth DFV	TAG Williams Team	1m 35·153s	**1m 34·140s**
3	Eddie Cheever	USA	TYRRELL 011	Ford Cosworth DFV	Tyrrell Racing	1m 38·736s	**1m 37·160s**
4	Michele Alboreto	I	TYRRELL 011	Ford Cosworth DFV	Tyrrell Racing	1m 38·411s	**1m 37·912s**
5	Nelson Piquet	BR	Parmalat BRABHAM BT49C	Ford Cosworth DFV	Parmalat Racing Team	**1m 35·449s**	1m 35·484s
6	Hector Rebaque	MEX	Parmalat BRABHAM BT49C	Ford Cosworth DFV	Parmalat Racing Team	1m 37·131s	**1m 36·472s**
7	John Watson	GB	Marlboro McLAREN MP4	Ford Cosworth DFV	McLaren International	1m 35·795s	**1m 35·557s**
8	Andrea de Cesaris	I	Marlboro McLAREN MP4	Ford Cosworth DFV	McLaren International	–	**1m 37·019s**
9	Slim Borgudd	S	Abba ATS HGS 1	Ford Cosworth DFV	Team ATS	1m 39·106s	**1m 37·807s**
11	Elio de Angelis	I	John Player Special LOTUS 87	Ford Cosworth DFV	John Player Team Lotus	**1m 36·158s**	1m 36·309s
12	Nigel Mansell	GB	John Player Special LOTUS 87	Ford Cosworth DFV	John Player Team Lotus	1m 38·100s	**1m 36·210s**
14	Eliseo Salazar	RCH	ENSIGN N180B	Ford Cosworth DFV	Ensign Racing	1m 39·033s	**1m 38·053s**
15	Alain Prost	F	Elf RENAULT RE 30	Renault EF1	Equipe Renault Elf	1m 34·492s	**1m 34·374s**
16	René Arnoux	F	Elf RENAULT RE 30	Renault EF1	Equipe Renault Elf	1m 34·042s	**1m 33·467s**
17	Derek Daly	IRL	Rizla MARCH 811	Ford Cosworth DFV	March Grand Prix	1m 38·852s	**1m 37·303s**
20	Keke Rosberg	SF	FITTIPALDI F8C	Ford Cosworth DFV	Fittipaldi Automotive	1m 42·229s	**1m 40·345s**
21	Chico Serra	BR	FITTIPALDI F8C	Ford Cosworth DFV	Fittipaldi Automotive	1m 41·185s	**1m 40·437s**
22	Mario Andretti	USA	Marlboro ALFA ROMEO 179C	Alfa Romeo 1260	Marlboro Team Alfa Romeo	1m 37·166s	**1m 36·296s**
23	Bruno Giacomelli	I	Marlboro ALFA ROMEO 179C	Alfa Romeo 1260	Marlboro Team Alfa Romeo	1m 38·617s	**1m 35·946s**
25	Patrick Tambay	F	Talbot-Gitanes LIGIER JS17	Matra MS 81	Equipe Talbot Gitanes	**1m 36·515s**	1m 36·545s
26	Jacques Laffite	F	Talbot-Gitanes LIGIER JS17	Matra MS 81	Equipe Talbot Gitanes	1m 36·529s	**1m 35·062s**
27	Gilles Villeneuve	CDN	Fiat FERRARI 126CK	Ferrari 126C	Scuderia Ferrari SpA SEFAC	**1m 35·627s**	1m 55·012s
28	Didier Pironi	F	Fiat FERRARI 126CK	Ferrari 126C	Scuderia Ferrari SpA SEFAC	1m 35·977s	**1m 35·596s**
29	Riccardo Patrese	I	Ragno-Beta ARROWS A3	Ford Cosworth DFV	Arrows Racing Team	**1m 37·355s**	1m 37·552s
30	Siegfried Stohr	I	Ragno-Beta ARROWS A3	Ford Cosworth DFV	Arrows Racing Team	**1m 39·713s**	1m 39·776s
31	Beppe Gabbiani	I	Denim OSELLA FA1B	Ford Cosworth DFV	Osella Squadra Corse	1m 40·930s	**1m 38·474s**
32	Jean-Pierre Jarier	F	Denim OSELLA FA1C	Ford Cosworth DFV	Osella Squadra Corse	1m 38·167s	**1m 37·264s**
33	Marc Surer	CH	THEODORE TY 01	Ford Cosworth DFV	Theodore Racing Team	1m 38·778s	**1m 38·114s**
35	Brian Henton	GB	Candy TOLEMAN TG 181	Hart 415T	Candy Toleman Motorsport	1m 41·369s	**1m 38·012s**
36	Derek Warwick	GB	Candy TOLEMAN TG 181	Hart 415T	Candy Toleman Motorsport	1m 39·936s	**1m 39·279s**

Friday morning and Saturday morning practice sessions not officially recorded	*Fri pm* *Warm, dry*	*Sat pm* *Warm, dry*

Starting grid

16 ARNOUX (1m 33·467s) Renault	2 REUTEMANN (1m 34·140s) Williams
15 PROST (1m 34·374s) Renault	26 LAFFITE (1m 35·062s) Talbot-Ligier
1 JONES (1m 35·359s) Williams	5 PIQUET (1m 35·449s) Brabham
7 WATSON (1m 35·557s) McLaren	28 PIRONI (1m 35·596s) Ferrari
27 VILLENEUVE (1m 35·627s) Ferrari	23 GIACOMELLI (1m 35·946s) Alfa Romeo
11 DE ANGELIS (1m 36·158s) Lotus	12 MANSELL (1m 36·210s) Lotus
22 ANDRETTI (1m 36·296s) Alfa Romeo	6 REBAQUE (1m 36·472s) Brabham
25 TAMBAY (1m 36·515s) Talbot-Ligier	8 DE CESARIS (1m 37·019s) McLaren
3 CHEEVER (1m 37·160s) Tyrrell	32 JARIER (1m 37·264s) Osella
17 DALY (1m 37·303s) March	29 PATRESE (1m 37·355s) Arrows
9 BORGUDD (1m 37·807s) ATS	4 ALBORETO (1m 37·912s) Tyrrell
35 HENTON (1m 38·012s) Toleman	14 SALAZAR (1m 38·053s) Ensign

Did not start:
33 Surer (Theodore), 1m 38·114s, did not qualify
31 Gabbiani (Osella), 1m 38·474s, did not qualify
36 Warwick (Toleman), 1m 39·279s, did not qualify
30 Stohr (Arrows), 1m 39·713s, did not qualify
20 Rosberg (Fittipaldi), 1m 40·345s, did not qualify
21 Serra (Fittipaldi), 1m 40·437s, did not qualify

Past winners

Year	Driver	Nat	Car	Circuit	Distance miles/km	Speed mph/km/h
1921	Jules Goux	F	3·0 Ballot	Brescia	322·49/ 519·00	89·94/144·74
1922	Pietro Bordini	I	2·0 Fiat 804	Monza	497·10/ 800·00	86·90/139·85
1923	Carlo Salamano	I	2·0 Fiat 805 s/c	Monza	497·10/ 800·00	91·03/146·50
1924	Antonio Ascari	I	2·0 Alfa Romeo P2 s/c	Monza	497·10/ 800·00	98·79/158·99
1925	Gastone Brilli-Peri	I	2·0 Alfa Romeo P2 s/c	Monza	497·10/ 800·00	94·82/152·60
1926	Lotus Charavel	F	1·5 Bugatti T39A s/c	Monza	372·82/ 600·00	85·88/138·20
1927	Robert Benoist	F	1·5 Delage s/c	Monza	310·69/ 500·00	89·66/144·30
1928	Louis Chiron	F	2·0 Bugatti T35C s/c	Monza	372·82/ 600·00	99·36/159·90
1931	Giuseppe Campari/ Tazio Nuvolari	I	2·3 Alfa Romeo Monza s/c	Monza	967·94/1557·75	96·79/155·78
1932	Tazio Nuvolari/ Giuseppe Campari	I	2·7 Alfa Romeo ZP3 s/c	Monza	520·46/ 837·61	104·09/167·52
1933	Luigi Fagioli	I	2·7 Alfa Romeo P3 s/c	Monza	310·69/ 500·00	108·58/174·74
1934	Rudi Caracciola/ Luigi Fagioli	D I	2·4 Mercedes-Benz W25 s/c	Monza	310·66/ 499·96	65·35/105·18
1935	Hans Stuck	D	5·0 Auto Union B-type s/c	Monza	312·53/ 502·97	85·18/137·08
1936	Bernd Rosemeyer	D	6·0 Auto Union C-type s/c	Monza	313·17/ 504·00	84·10/135·35
1937	Rudi Caracciola	D	5·7 Mercedes-Benz W125 s/c	Leghorn	223·18/ 359·18	81·59/131·31
1938	Tazio Nuvolari	I	3·0 Auto Union D-type s/c	Monza	260·71/ 419·58	96·76/155·73
1947	Carlo Felice Trossi	I	1·5 Alfa Romeo 158 s/c	Milan Park	214·37/ 345·00	70·34/113·19
1948	Jean-Pierre Wimille	F	1·5 Alfa Romeo 158 s/c	Turin	223·69/ 360·00	70·38/113·26
1949	Alberto Ascari	I	1·5 Ferrari 125 s/c	Monza	313·17/ 504·00	105·04/169·04
1950	Giuseppe Farina	I	1·5 Alfa Romeo 158 s/c	Monza	313·17/ 504·00	109·70/176·54
1951	Alberto Ascari	I	4·5 Ferrari 375	Monza	313·17/ 504·00	115·52/185·92
1952	Alberto Ascari	I	2·0 Ferrari 500	Monza	313·17/ 504·00	110·04/177·09
1953	Juan Manuel Fangio	RA	2·0 Maserati A6SSG	Monza	313·17/ 504·00	110·68/178·13
1954	Juan Manuel Fangio	RA	2·5 Mercedes-Benz W196	Monza	313·17/ 504·00	111·98/180·22
1955	Juan Manuel Fangio	RA	2·0 Mercedes-Benz W196	Monza	310·69/ 500·00	128·49/206·79
1956	Stirling Moss	GB	2·5 Maserati 250F	Monza	310·69/ 500·00	129·73/208·79
1957	Stirling Moss	GB	2·5 Vanwall	Monza	310·84/ 500·25	129·73/208·79
1958	Tony Brooks	GB	2·5 Vanwall	Monza	250·10/ 402·50	121·21/195·08
1959	Stirling Moss	GB	2·5 Cooper T45-Climax	Monza	257·25/ 414·00	124·38/200·18
1960	Phil Hill	USA	2·4 Ferrari Dino 246	Monza	310·69/ 500·00	132·06/212·53
1961	Phil Hill	USA	1·5 Ferrari Dino 156	Monza	267·19/ 430·00	130·11/209·39
1962	Graham Hill	GB	1·5 BRM P57	Monza	307·27/ 494·50	123·62/198·94
1963	Jim Clark	GB	1·5 Lotus 25-Climax	Monza	302·27/ 494·50	127·74/205·58
1964	John Surtees	GB	1·5 Ferrari 158	Monza	278·68/ 448·50	127·77/205·63
1965	Jackie Stewart	GB	1·5 BRM P261	Monza	271·54/ 437·00	130·46/209·96
1966	Ludovico Scarfiotti	I	3·0 Ferrari 312/66	Monza	242·96/ 391·00	135·92/218·75
1967	John Surtees	GB	3·9 Honda RA300	Monza	242·96/ 391·00	140·50/226·12
1968	Denny Hulme	NZ	3·0 McLaren M7A-Ford	Monza	242·96/ 391·00	145·41/234·02
1969	Jackie Stewart	GB	3·0 Matra MS80-Ford	Monza	242·96/ 391·00	146·97/236·52
1970	Clay Regazzoni	CH	3·0 Ferrari 312B-1/70	Monza	242·96/ 391·00	147·08/236·67
1971	Peter Gethin	GB	3·0 BRM P160	Monza	196·51/ 316·25	150·75/242·62
1972	Emerson Fittipaldi	BR	3·0 JPS/Lotus 72-Ford	Monza	197·36/ 317·63	131·61/211·81
1973	Ronnie Peterson	S	3·0 JPS/Lotus 72-Ford	Monza	197·36/ 317·63	132·63/213·45
1974	Ronnie Peterson	S	3·0 JPS/Lotus 72-Ford	Monza	186·76/ 300·56	135·10/217·42
1975	Clay Regazzoni	CH	3·0 Ferrari 312T/75	Monza	186·76/ 300·56	135·48/218·03
1976	Ronnie Peterson	S	3·0 March 761-Ford	Monza	187·41/ 301·60	124·12/199·75
1977	Mario Andretti	USA	3·0 JPS/Lotus 78-Ford	Monza	187·41/ 301·60	128·01/206·02
1978	Niki Lauda	A	3·0 Brabham BT46-Alfa Romeo	Monza	144·16/ 232·00	128·95/207·53
1979	Jody Scheckter	ZA	3·0 Ferrari 312T-4	Monza	180·20/ 290·00	131·85/212·18
1980	Nelson Piquet	BR	3·0 Brabham BT49-Ford	Imola	186·41/ 300·00	113·98/183·44
1981	Alain Prost	F	1·5 Renault RE t/c	Monza	187·40/ 301·60	129·87/209·00

Circuit data

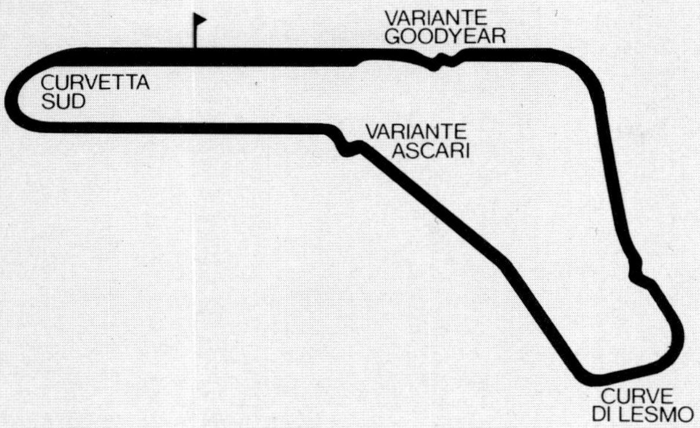

Autodromo Nazionale di Monza, near Milan
Circuit length: 3·6039 miles/5·80 km
Race distance: 52 laps, 187·403 miles/301·600 km
Race weather: Warm, occasional showers

Results and retirements

Place	Driver	Car	Laps	Time and Speed (mph/km/h)/Retirement	
1	Alain Prost	Renault t/c V6	52	1h 26m 33·897s	129·866/209·00
2	Alan Jones	Williams-Cosworth V8	52	1h 26m 56·072s	
3	Carlos Reutemann	Williams-Cosworth V8	52	1h 27m 24·484s	
4	Elio de Angelis	Lotus-Cosworth V8	52	1h 28m 06·799s	
5	Didier Pironi	Ferrari t/c V6	52	1h 28m 08·419s	
6	Nelson Piquet	Brabham-Cosworth V8	51	Engine	
7	Andrea de Cesaris	McLaren-Cosworth V8	51	Accident/tyre failure	
8	Bruno Giacomelli	Alfa Romeo V12	50		
9	Jean-Pierre Jarier	Osella-Cosworth V8	50		
10	Brian Henton	Toleman-Hart t/c Straight 4	49		
	Mario Andretti	Alfa Romeo V12	41	Engine flywheel coupling	
	Derek Daly	March-Cosworth V8	37	Gearbox	
	Patrick Tambay	Talbot-Ligier V12	22	Puncture	
	Nigel Mansell	Lotus-Cosworth V8	21	Handling	
	John Watson	McLaren-Cosworth V8	19	Accident	
	Riccardo Patrese	Arrows-Cosworth V8	19	Gearbox	
	Michele Alboreto	Tyrrell-Cosworth V8	16	Accident	
	Eliseo Salazar	Ensign-Cosworth V8	13	Tyre failure	
	René Arnoux	Renault t/c V6	12	Accident	
	Eddie Cheever	Tyrrell-Cosworth V8	11	Spun off	
	Jacques Laffite	Talbot-Ligier V12	11	Puncture	
	Slim Borgudd	ATS-Cosworth V8	10	Spun off	
	Gilles Villeneuve	Ferrari t/c V6	6	Turbo	
	Hector Rebaque	Brabham-Cosworth V8	0	Electrics	

Fastest lap: Reutemann, on lap 48, 1m 37·528s, 133·030mph/214·092km/h.
Lap record: Clay Regazzoni (F1 Williams FW07-Cosworth DFV), 1m 35·600s, 135·713mph/218·408km/h (1979).

Lap chart

1st LAP ORDER		1	2	3	4	5	6	7	8	9	10	11	12	13	14	15	16	17	18	19	20	21	22	23
15	A.Prost	15	15	15	15	15	15	15	15	15	15	15	15	15	15	15	15	15	15	15	15	15	15	15
28	D.Pironi	28	28	28	28	16	16	16	16	16	16	16	16	1	1	1	1	1	1	1	1	1	1	1
2	C.Reutemann	2	2	2	16	28	26	26	2	2	2	2	1	2	2	2	23	23	23	23	23	23	23	23
16	R.Arnoux	16	16	16	2	26	28	2	26	28	1	1	2	5	5	23	5	5	5	25	25	25	25	5
5	N Piquet	5	26	26	26	2	2	28	28	26	5	5	5	28	23	5	28	25	25	5	28	28	5	28
1	A.Jones	1	1	27	27	27	23	1	1	1	28	28	28	23	28	28	25	28	28	28	5	5	28	22
26	J.Laffite	26	27	1	23	23	1	5	5	5	23	23	23	7	7	25	7	7	7	7	22	22	22	2
27	G Villereuve	27	5	23	1	1	5	23	23	23	26	7	7	25	25	7	2	2	2	2	2	2	2	8
23	B.Giacomelli	23	23	5	5	5	7	7	7	7	7	17	17	8	8	8	8	8	8	22	8	8	8	11
11	E.de Angelis	11	11	7	7	7	17	17	17	17	17	26	25	22	22	22	22	22	22	8	17	17	17	17
7	J.Watson	7	7	11	11	11	11	11	11	11	11	25	8	11	29	29	11	11	17	17	11	11	11	32
12	N Mansell	12	12	12	12	17	12	8	8	8	25	11	22	17	11	11	17	17	11	11	12	32	32	35
22	M.Andretti	22	17	17	17	12	8	22	22	25	8	8	11	29	17	17	29	29	12	12	32	35	35	
8	A de Cesaris	8	25	8	8	8	22	25	25	22	22	22	29	12	12	12	12	12	29	29	35	12		
17	D.Daly	17	8	22	22	22	25	12	12	12	29	29	14	14	32	32	32	32	32	32				
25	P Tambay	25	22	25	25	25	29	29	29	29	14	14	12	32	35	35	35	35	35	35				
32	J-P Jarier	32	29	29	29	29	14	14	14	14	12	3	32	35	4	4	4							
29	R.Patrese	29	32	32	32	14	32	9	3	3	3	12	35	4										
14	E Salazar	14	14	14	14	32	9	32	9	9	9	32	4											
9	S.Borgudd	9	9	9	9	9	3	3	32	32	32	35												
35	B.Henton	35	35	35	3	3	35	35	35	35	35	4												
3.	E.Cheever	3	3	3	35	35	27	4	4	4	4													
4.	M.Alboreto	4	4	4	4	4	4																	

24	25	26	27	28	29	30	31	32	33	34	35	36	37	38	39	40	41	42	43	44	45	46	47	48	49	50	51	52
15	15	15	15	15	15	15	15	15	15	15	15	15	15	15	15	15	15	15	15	15	15	15	15	15	15	15	15	15
1	1	1	1	1	1	1	1	1	1	1	1	1	1	1	1	1	1	1	1	1	1	1	1	1	1	1	1	1
23	23	5	5	5	5	5	5	5	5	5	5	5	5	5	5	5	5	5	5	5	5	5	5	5	5	5	5	2
5	5	28	28	28	28	28	28	28	28	28	28	28	28	2	2	2	2	2	2	2	2	2	2	2	2	2	2	11
28	28	22	22	22	22	22	22	22	2	2	2	2	2	28	28	28	28	28	28	11	11	11	11	11	11	11	11	28
22	22	2	2	2	2	2	2	2	22	22	22	22	22	22	22	22	11	11	11	28	28	28	28	28	28	28	28	
2	2	8	8	8	8	8	8	8	11	11	11	11	11	11	11	11	8	8	8	8	8	8	8	8	8	8	8	
8	8	23	11	11	11	11	11	11	8	8	8	8	8	8	8	8	22	23	23	23	23	23	23	23	23	23		
11	11	11	17	17	17	17	17	17	17	17	17	17	23	23	23	23	23	32	32	32	32	32	32	32	32	32		
17	17	17	23	23	23	32	32	32	32	32	32	32	32	32	32	32	32	35	35	35	35	35	35	35	35			
32	32	32	32	32	32	23	23	23	23	23	23	23	17	35	35	35	35											
35	35	35	35	35	35	35	35	35	35	35	35	35	35															

Fastest laps

Driver	Time	Lap
Carlos Reutemann	1m 37·528s	48
Alan Jones	1m 37·536s	47
Nelson Piquet	1m 37·598s	45
Alain Prost	1m 37·702s	9
René Arnoux	1m 37·886s	8
Bruno Giacomelli	1m 37·893s	48
Elio de Angelis	1m 38·498s	31
Jacques Laffite	1m 38·532s	5
Patrick Tambay	1m 38·575s	9
Gilles Villeneuve	1m 38·814s	3
Derek Daly	1m 39·139s	8
John Watson	1m 39·366s	8
Andrea de Cesaris	1m 39·481s	32
Mario Andretti	1m 39·585s	30
Didier Pironi	1m 39·652s	9
Eliseo Salazar	1m 40·131s	7
Eddie Cheever	1m 40·165s	7
Nigel Mansell	1m 40·257s	4
Michele Alboreto	1m 40·628s	7
Riccardo Patrese	1m 40·845s	7
Slim Borgudd	1m 41·117s	4
Brian Henton	1m 41·825s	3
Jean-Pierre Jarier	1m 41·835s	3
Hector Rebaque	4m 28·329s	2

Points

WORLD CHAMPIONSHIP OF DRIVERS

1	Carlos Reutemann	49 pts
2	Nelson Piquet	46
3 =	Alain Prost	37
3 =	Alan Jones	37
5	Jacques Laffite	34
6 =	John Watson	21
6 =	Gilles Villeneuve	21
8	Elio de Angelis	13
9 =	René Arnoux	11
9 =	Hector Rebaque	11
11 =	Riccardo Patrese	10
11 =	Eddie Cheever	10
13	Didier Pironi	9
14	Nigel Mansell	5
15	Marc Surer	4
16	Mario Andretti	3
17 =	Patrick Tambay	1
17 =	Andrea de Cesaris	1
17 =	Slim Borgudd	1
17 =	Eliseo Salazar	1

CONSTRUCTORS' CUP

1	Williams	86
2	Brabham	57
3	Renault	48
4	Ligier	34
5	Ferrari	30
6	McLaren	22
7	Lotus	18
8 =	Arrows	10
8 =	Tyrrell	10
10	Ensign	5
11	Alfa Romeo	3
12 =	Theodore	1
12 =	ATS	1

Grand Prix Labatt du Canada

"I didn't like racing today. The rain; it was impossible to see," said Laffite.

"The worst race conditions I've ever driven in," criticised Watson.

"It wasn't too bad," contradicted Villeneuve. "You can race in any conditions – even snow – so long as you have the right equipment. There's always some kind of speed you can do – even if it's only ten miles an hour . . ."

In fact, Jacques Laffite averaged an astonishing 85mph on his way to victory in the most appalling conditions and, under the circumstances, there was no question that he had the right equipment – Michelin wet weather tyres. Laffite gave the Talbot-Ligier team their second win of the season and revitalised his championship challenge at the eleventh hour with a superb drive around the water-logged Ile Notre Dame at Montreal.

The tricky conditions allowed John Watson to exploit his Michelins, not to mention a delicate touch, as he set fastest lap on his way to second place in the Marlboro McLaren. Watson drove with exceptional smoothness but the same could not be said for Gilles Villeneuve who, as ever, raced his way into a spectacular third place. Rain was the only salvation for the local hero, his Ferrari handling as badly as ever during practice but Gilles grabbed his opportunity as he slithered and bumped his way up the field. A battered nose wing made little difference – not even when it wrapped itself around the Ferrari cockpit after a particularly heavy brush with another competitor. The wing flew off eventually and the Ferrari danced into the most incredible angles as Villeneuve brought the car home against all odds.

Bruno Giacomelli scored points for the first time in the season by bringing his Marlboro Alfa Romeo into an impressive fourth place after starting from the eighth row of the grid. Indeed, such was the superiority of Michelin's wet weather rubber that the first four cars were equipped with the French radials and all four started from the middle of the grid. Conversely, Goodyear had completely dominated practice in the dry but their wet patterns were to spell disaster for Carlos Reutemann and Nelson Piquet, leaders of the championship.

Both men were eyeball-to-eyeball on the front row with Jones and his third place partner in the championship, Alain Prost, on row two – all four drivers ready for what should have been a superb showdown. The rain on Sunday changed all that.

Jones took an immediate lead and splashed off into the distance, determined to win the championship for a second time in spite of announcing his impending retirement a week before Montreal. Conditions became worse and Jones spun off, allowing Prost to take over at the front before the Renault dropped back with locking brakes. Laffite, having picked his way through the field, then moved into a lead he was never to lose and nine points brought him within striking distance of Nelson Piquet who eventually finished fifth. The Parmalat Brabham driver earned his two points after a difficult drive but Carlos Reutemann simply lost interest with a car which proved impossible to drive, the Saudia-Leyland Williams finishing in a forlorn tenth place, three laps behind the leader.

Andrea de Cesaris, having kept out of trouble all weekend, threw away sixth place near the end and his retirement gave the point to Elio de Angelis. The number two John Player Lotus of Nigel Mansell unwittingly caused the retirement of Prost when the two came into contact as the Renault tried to lap the slick-shod Lotus. Thus, Prost's slim championship chances were eliminated after an impressive practice and a steady race.

Running with equal skill in the wet was Derek Daly whose Guinness-Rizla March started from its customary place on the tenth row of the grid but the Irishman was soon into seventh position before brake trouble intervened. The March was classified eighth behind the Alfa Romeo of Mario Andretti when the race was brought to a halt at the two hour mark.

It was possible that Reutemann could have tied up the championship or extended his three point lead over Piquet. Reutemann had, after all, dominated the Brazilian Grand Prix in similar conditions but now, with one race remaining, the gap had shrunk to one point and, worst still, Jacques Laffite was in with a chance as Williams and Brabham paid the price for a mid-season switch from Michelin to Goodyear.

ENTRY AND PRACTICE

Constructed in 1978, the *Ile Notre Dame* circuit may have been tight and rather tedious but it was considered to be one of the smoothest tracks on the calendar – until the advent of the crazy cars of 1981 that is. Suddenly the drivers were finding bumps they never knew about and the worst section by far came just after the pits. Here, a right-left-right esses was taken in fifth gear with a nasty bump to unsettle the cars at the first apex. Once again, the stupidity of the rules governing Grand Prix racing in 1981 was demonstrated to an alarming degree as the cars leaped the across the track, the drivers hanging on and hoping. To make matters worse, the series of bends was surrounded by concrete walls, the approach and line being completely blind as a result. Taking these corners flat required total commitment from the drivers and their progress was simply awe-inspiring. And slightly crazy.

One of the smoothest (if you could call it that) was Nelson Piquet, enjoying a new chassis but setting a pole position time in the spare Brabham towards the end of Friday practice. Piquet set out to improve on that the next day but the Brazilian was thwarted by his first set of qualifiers being out of balance and heavy traffic while running on his last set. It was during his final lap that Piquet was blocked by René Arnoux, the Renault driver apparently giving Nelson a 'brake test' just before the first right-hander. Having blistered one of his rear tyres, Piquet came in and asked to have one of Rebaque's right rears fitted so that he could get back

The glamour of Grand Prix racing . . . Alan Jones still nursing a broken finger, puts his name to the French edition of Autocourse 1980-81 *(right)*.

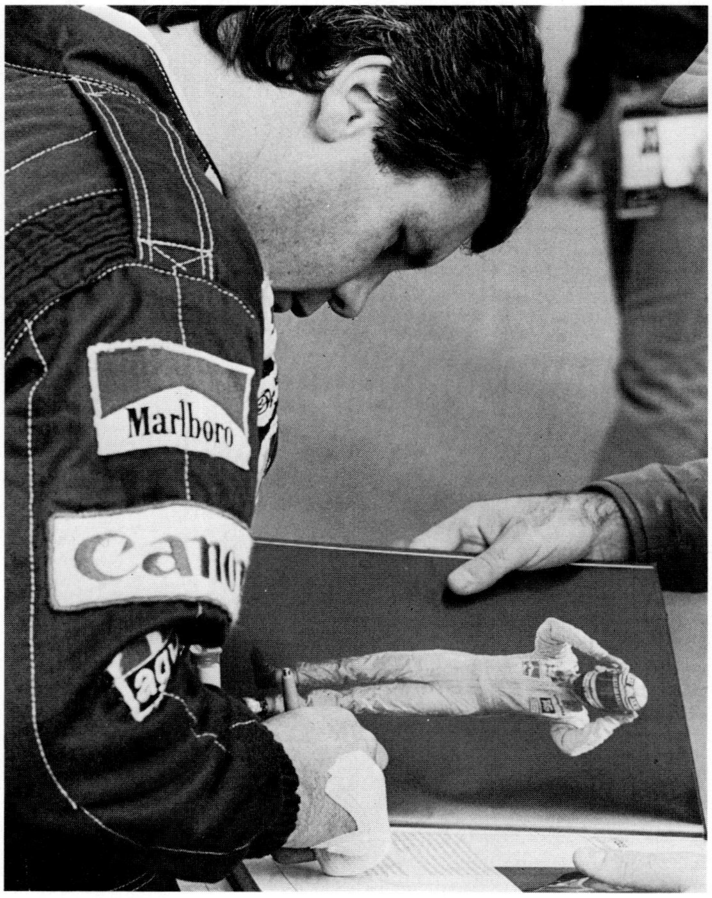

out there and deal with the rude Renault. It was a move which infringed the regulations governing the use of eight tyres per car per session but Piquet, knowing his Friday time had earned pole, felt he had nothing to lose.

Carlos Reutemann, of course, knew nothing about the game of cat and mouse taking place out on the circuit and he raised the alarm when he saw Piquet return with '6' (Rebaque's number) stamped on the right rear. Piquet was not about to explain to the Stewards just what he had been up to and the Brabham team accepted the official scrubbing of their times during the latter part of the session. The were 'cheating' in a manner of speaking but no-one, except the local press and the organisers, was particularly bothered although there was a long delay in issuing the times while the *brouhaha* was sorted out.

The official grid eventually showed Piquet to be fractionally quicker than Carlos Reutemann, the principal championship contenders setting the pace in true story-book fashion. Williams had four cars present and they tried water-cooled brakes during practice but, at the end of the day, Reutemann turned in a superb practice effort on his first set of qualifiers on Saturday and kept Alan Jones back on row two. The Australian was the centre of attention after his surprise announcement the previous week that he would be retiring from Formula 1 at the end of the season. Would he continue to drive with his customary fire and vigour? That was answered by a hard-working practice in spite of pain from the broken finger which had required re-setting earlier in the week. Jones was unable to improve on his Friday best when the Williams jumped out of gear and gave brake trouble during the final session. None the less, the carefree Jones was poised behind the jittery front row, ready to capitalise on any mistakes and make the most of his slim chance of winning the championship.

Alain Prost was in the same frame of mind after a remarkable practice effort which put the Renault driver alongside Jones on the second row. The turbos were not supposed to go well on this tight circuit but a busy session at the Michelin test track in France had obviously paid off. So, too, had the appearance of black carbon-fibre wings which along with lighter side-pods, brought the overall weight down to competitive proportions although a new fuel injection system was not so successful. The weather during practice remained surprisingly mild but generating a workable temperature in the Michelins continued to be a problem at this track. Renault, making the most of their healthy horsepower, cranked on more rear wing and overcame the problem that way, Prost setting his time on Saturday afternoon. René Arnoux was further back and said his final efforts were hampered by traffic – a veiled reference to Piquet, no doubt.

The Renaults, as ever, had appeared to cruise over the bumps while the John Player Team Lotus drivers continued to terrify observers, particularly at the first right-hander. Nigel Mansell was exceptionally brave, his right foot remaining firmly planted on the throttle while the car jumped its erratic course through the corner. Mansell had an unhappy time with various teething troubles including a misfire on the new chassis and a rear brake-line coming adrift during the first session but he got down to business on Saturday afternoon and put the 87 on the third row alongside Hector Rebaque's Brabham. Elio de Angelis was a couple of tenths slower than Mansell and lost any hope of improving when his top rocker arm broke on the rear suspension while he was rushing along the back leg of the circuit in fifth gear. The Lotus spun wildly but, fortunately, missed the barriers and Elio brought the car back with the left-front wheel pawing the air! If understeer had been a minor problem before, it was diabolical now!

The teams had but a few days to sort themselves out after Monza before the cars were loaded up at Heathrow airport. Not only had the Marlboro McLaren team finished off a new car for John Watson to replace the one shunted in Italy, they had found time to run Niki Lauda in a test session at Donington. 'The Rat' had reeled off several laps and was not far off times set by John Watson but that scarcely seemed to bother the Ulsterman as he set about practice in Montreal. The new car lacked the dreaded bounce inherent in the spare chassis and, on Saturday morning, Watson really went motoring as he powered the MP4 through the chicanes in an aggressive and purposeful manner. John was the quickest during the untimed session but he was unable to match that time in the afternoon when the track became slippery towards the end. Whereas the earlier time would have put him on the third row, his official lap of 1m 30.566s placed Watson on row five alongside Jaques Laffite. Andrea de Cesaris, meanwhile, had covered 28 laps of official practice without – whisper it – crashing and the Italian marked his first anniversary in Formula 1 by qualifying in the middle of the grid.

SEPTEMBER:

Clay Regazzoni loses claim against Long Beach Grand Prix Association.

Bob Garretson wins World Endurance Drivers' Championship.

Niki Lauda announces intention to return to Formula 1 in 1982.

Alain Prost comes under pressure from John Watson. The Renault driver lost any hope of challenging for the Championship when he became involved in an incident with Nigel Mansell and lost fourth place *(above)*. Jacques Laffite made the most of his Michelins to give a superb display and move into contention for the Championship *(left)*.

APART FROM THE BATTLE FOR THE 1981 TITLE, WORLD Champions past and present were under discussion at Montreal. Alan Jones surprised everyone – including Frank Williams – with his sudden decision to stop Grand Prix racing at the end of the season. While Jones was making his reasons official in London on September 18, the newspapers were carrying details of Niki Lauda's test drive in a Marlboro McLaren MP4 at Donington.

Rumours of the Austrian's impending return to Grand Prix racing had been rife for some time and his drive in the MP4 showed that Lauda had lost none of his skill since his abrupt departure from Brabham and Formula 1 in September 1979.

At the wheel of an unfamiliar car on a circuit he knew little about, Lauda lapped a few tenths slower than John Watson. Wearing his familiar helmet with Parmalat and Marlboro identification, Lauda completed over 60 laps. Although tired after his first experience with stiff suspensions, Lauda felt a desire to return to racing but, when he made an official announcement to that effect two weeks later, the motivation behind his decision was questioned.

Lauda brushed aside reports that he was making a return simply to earn a vast retainer (reported to be between 2.5 and 3 million dollars) and pay off

Keeping the Matra V12 stoked up through the slow corners turned out to be the major problem for the Talbot-Ligier drivers. Jacques Laffite had the benefit of a large rear wing to encourage reasonable tyre temperatures but Patrick Tambay had no such assistance and, apart from experiencing trouble with the hydro-pneumatic suspension, the Frenchman was fouled by traffic on the few laps the car was running perfectly. The Ferrari drivers would have been happy with a car which was perfect for just one lap! As it was, the 126 chassis seemed to be worse than ever and the staunch *Quebecois* supporters were disappointed to find their man in eleventh place alongside his team-mate. Both Gilles Villeneuve and Didier Pironi had their moments; Gilles when he lost control at the fast flick after the pits and Didier when he had a brake problem to add to previous troubles with the electrics and fuel feed. "The trouble is," explained Villeneuve to the local press, "these cars have no suspension movement and my car moves six or seven feet to the left when it goes over the bumps at the right-hander after the pits. The cars just keeps bouncing and that makes it hard to line up for the left-hander which follows and if you get that wrong then there is another right-hander waiting for you. All this is very fast – fifth gear – and its very dangerous. I was lucky. I got up on a kerb on the way through and just bent bits on the car here and there. But we could see someone lose it in a big way . . ." Exit the local press thoroughly baffled by the state of the art in Formula 1, the pinnacle of International auto racing . . .

As far as Eddie Cheever was concerned, the pinnacle of Formula 1 would be achieved a lot easier if he could work his way into the Williams seat about to be vacated by Alan Jones. Cheever's name occurred more than any other when it came to discussing the list of likely candidates and the American was more than anxious to do something useful in the Tyrrell this weekend. A modest performance on Friday was helped by a switch to the rear suspension tried by Alboreto at Monza and the following day Eddie was 14th quickest although he claimed he could have improved further had he not been delayed by de Angelis limping home with his damaged Lotus. Michele Alboreto, meanwhile, quietly got on with his job and put the Avon-shod 011 on the penultimate row. There was little to chose between the Marlboro Alfa Romeo drivers as they set times within a fraction of each other to occupy the eighth row. Speculation continued over Andretti's future in Formula 1 and he was hardly encouraged by a car which remained mediocre in spite of two days of practice spent trying various side-pods and suspension settings.

The Ragno-Beta Arrows pit became the centre of attention as Jacques Villeneuve attempted to qualify a Grand Prix car for the first time. While the French-Canadian may have mastered Formula Atlantic, he found the current breed of Formula 1 car to be a different animal entirely. Jacques never looked at home in the A3 as he worked hard simply trying to keep the car pointing in a straight line and his efforts were not helped by a continual overheating problem. He had a few moments, of course, but his biggest *faux pas* was to inadvertently carve up brother Gilles during practice on Friday! Jacques was no stranger to the circuit and his skill was not in question but his failure to qualify gave some indication of the competitiveness of Formula 1. His performance was put into perspective when Riccardo Patrese could do no better than take 18th place on the grid, the Italian being handicapped more than ever by the heavy Pirelli radials.

After failing to qualify at Monza, Marc Surer did well to set the fastest Avon time and take 19th place in the Theodore. Derek Daly was next thanks to turning in more laps than anyone else during the final session. It took an effort like that to qualify the Guinness-Rizla March after Friday's practice which, according to Daly, was a complete disaster, the car's handling being unpredictable and dangerous. A thorough head to head discussion with Adrian Reynard brought the 811 into reasonable shape on Saturday. Slim Borgudd put his ATS alongside Alboreto after losing time with electrical trouble while Jean-Pierre Jarier and Eliseo Salazar shared the back row. The Denim-Osella had a fuel feed problem, traced eventually to the pick-up in the tank and that left Jarier with little time to sort out the rear suspension. Salazar and the Ensign team had starred in the local paper the previous Wednesday ("because we were the only ones working when the photographer came round the garages!") and the Chilean driver qualified quite comfortably after an engine change on Saturday.

"You tell Frank that I say you should have the drive . . ." Eddie Cheever and his wife Rita discuss the rumours concerning Alan Jones's replacement at Williams *(above)*. John Watson showed all his skill and experience with a fine drive into second place *(right)*.

outstanding personal taxes plus debts incurred by his air charter company.

Brabham and McLaren were mentioned as the most likely candidates for Lauda's services with Marlboro's links with the latter perhaps settling the issue. If so, then Lauda was likely to renew a driving partnership with John Watson and Niki was not slow in firing off one or two acid comments about 'Wattie's' performance with the car. "It's a pity Niki didn't go fast enough to find out what the car was really like," retorted John at the beginning of a friendly needle match which promised to keep both drivers on their toes.

Lauda and Watson: friends and rivals.

The hard-pressed Fittipaldi team made the trip to North America but the cars looked appalling through the right-hander after the pits. Neither Keke Rosberg nor Chico Serra could think about taking the corner flat, the cars jumping out of line at the slightest undulation. It was hardly surprising when the frustrated drivers failed to qualify. The Candy-Toleman team had one problem after another and were unable to make the most of reasonable conditions for the Hart turbo. Henton spun on Friday and then part of a spark plug helicoil fell into the Monobloc and, later, the fuel filler cap fell into the tank! Derek Warwick wiped off the oil cooler at the front of his car with a spin on Friday so, all in all, the drivers had little time to think about sorting the chassis for the tricky circuit. Slowest of all was Beppe Gabbiani in the old Osella, the Italian managing only six laps on Saturday afternoon after an engine change.

RACE

By 11.25 a.m. the teams had made the trek from the garages to the pits and were preparing for the morning warm-up. Engines were fired up, drivers pulled on their helmets and gloves; seat belts were made ready. Gradually the pace began to slow; engines were switched off one by one; drivers wriggled out of their cockpits; ear plugs were put away. Gossip and rumour became the order of the day. It soon became clear that an insurance problem of some sort was delaying proceedings and curiosity changed to concern as the minutes became hours. There were television schedules to meet; planes to catch. And then there were the puzzled spectators who had parted with their money a long time before and were waiting patiently for some action as lunch time came and went. Needless to say, they were kept in total ignorance.

An insurance waiver was the root of the trouble and it took Bernie Ecclestone a couple of hours of hard talking to break the deadlock. Finally he emerged with a revised version of the document and once the teams had signed (some under protest) the way was clear for sport to continue. The time table had been shot to pieces and it was announced that a short warm-up would take place with the race starting one hour later than planned. Then, to make matters worse, it started to rain – very hard.

Air hammers chattered up and down the pit lane as wet weather tyres were fitted and, one by one the cars ventured out onto the track. The blustery conditions continued to whip up the black clouds and, as the rain intensified, it became obvious that the drainage on the track was not all that it should have been. De Cesaris, Patrese, Cheever, Jones, Rebaque, Tambay and Laffite all had brief excursions but otherwise the drivers managed to return in one piece and complain about the appalling conditions. No matter, the race would run as planned and the lap times indicated problems for the front row as the Michelin-shod cars, led by Pironi, set the pace.

After a short delay, the cars were waved out to take their places on the grid. Reutemann was clearly perplexed by the conditions as he climbed from his car, vaulted the pit rail and set off for another lap – this time in his spare car which was fitted with machine patterned Goodyears. Carlos found the 'Gatorback' pattern produced understeer as he splashed his way round the track and, as he pulled up alongside his race car, Reutemann opted to run that chassis fitted with the 'Gatorbacks' on the rear and the hand cut grooves on the front. Either way, the question of which Goodyear to use was purely academic – something the World Championship leader obviously realised as he sat in the cockpit and shook his head in despair. Carlos Reutemann had lost this race before it had started.

As for the rest, they pulled their safety straps an extra notch or two, raised their visors and prepared for the worst. In conditions such as this, the only place to be was at the front – a thought which had obviously occurred to Alan Jones as he streaked through the murk, banging wheels with Reutemann as he went, and took the lead. Reutemann actually led the race for a few yards or so but the Argentinian was soon swallowed by the churning pack on the run down to the far end of the circuit. Everyone scrabbled through the bottom corner safely but the inevitable happened on the back leg of the track. And it was poor René Arnoux who came off the worst; 1981 could not end quickly enough for the hapless Frenchman. Braking for a chicane, the Renault became caught in a pincer movement by the two Ferraris as Villeneuve came barrelling through; Pironi spun but Arnoux was pushed onto the grass before bouncing along the

Alan Jones led briefly before spinning off, his wet weather Goodyears being no match for the streaming conditions.

A damaged nose wing scarcely seemed to bother Gilles Villeneuve. The wing eventually wrapped itself around the cockpit before blowing off; Villeneuve carried on regardless and finished third. The Ferrari driver laps the Tyrrell of Michele Alboreto.

Armco and into retirement.

At the end of the lap, Jones had pulled away from Piquet who led Prost, de Angelis, Reutemann, Laffite, Mansell and Villeneuve. Pironi was in 21st place; a superb drive was in store. On lap two, Patrick Tambay slithered off only to return and spin off for good not long afterwards. Reutemann had dropped to 10th place while Jones appeared to be making the most of a driving line. All that changed, however, when the rain returned with a vengeance on lap six and Jones slowed as his shallow-grooved Goodyears attempted to cope with the deep pools of water. The Australian eventually went off when his front brakes locked and positions at the front began to change rapidly. Piquet held the lead briefly before Prost took over with Jacques Laffite moving the Brabham into third spot a few yards later. Then, going past the pits, Villeneuve hurled through the spray and moved his Ferrari into third place while poor Piquet came under attack from Watson. Mario Andretti, meanwhile, had a moment or two on the grass, Patrese hit the wall and damaged his nose wing before retiring with impossible handling, Salazar spun off and Reutemann slipped to 18th place.

By lap 10, Prost, Laffite and Villeneuve were running nose to tail, Watson had pulled out five seconds on Piquet while Pironi's stunning car control had helped the Ferrari driver into sixth place. The two Lotuses were next followed by Daly who was making impressive progress in the March, taking Mansell in lap 11 and de Angelis five laps later.

Prost gave in eventually to Laffite's relentless pressure and Villeneuve pushed the Renault into third place in lap 15. Watson closed on his former team-mate and Prost was in fourth place two laps later while Pironi caught and passed Piquet for fifth place on lap 19. Jones spun once more before stopping for tyres but the Williams driver called it a day just as Pironi's splendid run came to an end with engine trouble. Rebaque had been in and out of the pits inbetween spins and the Mexican had a hand in Jean-Pierre Jarier's retirement when the two collided on lap 26.

By now there were 17 saturated runners remaining led comfortably by Laffite as he continued to set the fastest laps while pulling away from the spectacular Villeneuve. The Ferrari driver was hampered by an engine misfire which allowed Watson to close the gap and, on lap 27, there was further excitement as Laffite indulged in a quick spin. No harm was done and the Talbot-Ligier was able to resume with over 11 seconds in hand over Villeneuve. Prost was in a lonely fourth place, Piquet continued to do a superb job on his Goodyears in fifth spot while Giacomelli had romped ahead of Daly and taken sixth place. De Cesaris, driving with great caution, had nevertheless taken eighth place ahead of de Angelis and Andretti. The Alfa Romeo driver was about to be lapped but it took five laps for an agitated Laffite to move ahead by which time Villeneuve and Watson had closed the gap slightly. The McLaren driver could hear the misfire from the Ferrari V6 and knew he would be able to get by sooner or later. Sure enough, Watson was able to choose his moment on lap 38 but Laffite responded to this news on his pit board by setting the fastest lap and opening the gap even further.

Villeneuve now held a 21 second advantage over Prost but that was reduced considerably when the Ferrari driver came into contact with de Angelis's Lotus at the hairpin. Both cars spun, Gilles continuing with a tattered nose wing which did not appear to impede his progress one bit! De Angelis eventually got going again without losing too much ground but his team-mate was experiencing handling problems with his car. A subsequent pit stop saw Mansell have slicks fitted which only made matters worse, the Lotus spinning off almost immediately. Marshals pushed the car back onto the track and somewhere along the line, the rear wing took on a distinct list to Port. Creeping back to the pits, Mansell was unaware of the fast approaching Prost as he took his line for the hairpin. Similarly, Prost was caught out by the very early braking point used by Mansell and, as the Lotus moved across the track, Prost locked his rear brakes, promptly spinning the Renault into the back of Mansell. Both drivers retired on the spot, Prost extremely vexed that his slim championship hopes should have been frittered away on such a silly accident.

By now, 14 cars were left, Rebaque having crashed for good and Borgudd having sustained minor damage when he nudged a tyre barrier. The next retirement, regrettably, was Andrea de Cesaris, the Italian having produced a sensible drive when he needed it most but he threw it all away with a rash manoeuvre which almost wiped out Piquet and the leader in one hit! With a secure championship point under his belt, de Cesaris became over-excited when he came across Piquet as the Brabham slithered along in fifth place. A desperate stab at out-braking Piquet

The Autumn leaves fall as Bruno Giacomelli steers his way into fourth place and his first Championship points of the season.

The appalling conditions equalised chassis performance to a certain extent and Derek Daly moved his March into seventh place before the rear brakes gave trouble.

saw the McLaren driver slide into the back of the Brabham and spin off while, behind them both, Laffite just managed to take avoiding action. Piquet gathered his car up with a swift touch of opposite lock, Laffite heaved a sigh of relief while de Cesaris was on the point of tears as he tried unsuccessfully to restart his car.

Laffite lapped Piquet without difficulty while Watson set the fastest lap of the race towards the end of a beautiful drive. Villeneuve, by contrast, was having all manner of excitement as the bent nose wing wrapped itself around the cockpit. Gilles peering round the aerofoil and charging along at undiminished speed. The question of black-flagging the Ferrari was resolved when the wing eventually flew off although Villeneuve said later that he had no intention of stopping as he would not have been able to see the black flag had it been shown! So, during the final ten minutes, Gilles entertained the crowds with remarkable antics as he drove sideways to a well-deserved third place. Bruno Giacomelli salvaged three points from a disappointing season and Piquet thoroughly deserved his two points after a tenacious drive on next to useless Goodyears. De Angelis was sixth ahead of Andretti and Daly who had been forced to ease his impressive pace when the back brakes on the March began to fail. Surer was next while Reutemann came home in a miserable 10th place, no less than three laps behind the leaders. Michele Alboreto was the final finisher, his team-mate having stopped with a blown engine after a difficult drive on Goodyears.

There was probably a lot of foot shuffling in Akron on Monday morning. Goodyear may have won the qualifying battle but defeat on Sunday afternoon hurt more than most and now Jacques Laffite had thrown his Michelin hat back in the championship ring. Had it remained dry though . . .

Jacques Villeneuve (left) joined Riccardo Patrese at Arrows but failed to qualify.

Grand Prix Labatt du Canada, September 27/statistics

Entries and practice times

No.	*Driver*	*Nat*	*Car*	*Engine*	*Entrant*	*Practice 1*	*Practice 2*
1	Alan Jones	AUS	Saudia-Leyland WILLIAMS FWO7C	Ford Cosworth DFV	TAG Williams Team	**1m 29·728s**	1m 29·781s
2	Carlos Reutemann	RA	Saudia-Leyland WILLIAMS FWO7C	Ford Cosworth DFV	TAG Williams Team	1m 29·601s	**1m 29·359s**
3	Eddie Cheever	USA	TYRRELL 011	Ford Cosworth DFV	Tyrrell Racing	1m 32·652s	**1m 31·547s**
4	Michele Alboreto	I	TYRRELL 011	Ford Cosworth DFV	Tyrrell Racing	1m 34·245s	**1m 32·709s**
5	Nelson Piquet	BR	Parmalat BRABHAM BT49C	Ford Cosworth DFV	Parmalat Racing Team	**1m 29·211s**	1m 29·537s
6	Hector Rebaque	MEX	Parmalat BRABHAM BT49C	Ford Cosworth DFV	Parmalat Racing Team	1m 31·545s	**1m 30·182s**
7	John Watson	GB	Marlboro McLAREN MP4	Ford Cosworth DFV	McLaren International	1m 31·617s	**1m 30·566s**
8	Andrea de Cesaris	I	Marlboro McLAREN MP4	Ford Cosworth DFV	McLaren International	1m 32·281s	**1m 31·507s**
9	Slim Borgudd	S	Abba ATS HGS 1	Ford Cosworth DFV	Team ATS	1m 34·002s	**1m 32·652s**
11	Elio de Angelis	I	John Player Special LOTUS 87	Ford Cosworth DFV	John Player Team Lotus	1m 31·212s	**1m 30·231s**
12	Nigel Mansell	GB	John Player Special LOTUS 87	Ford Cosworth DFV	John Player Team Lotus	1m 32·233s	**1m 29·997s**
14	Eliseo Salazar	RCH	ENSIGN N180B	Ford Cosworth DFV	Ensign Racing	1m 36·016s	**1m 33·848s**
15	Alain Prost	F	Elf RENAULT RE 30	Renault EF1	Equipe Renault Elf	1m 31·629s	**1m 29·908s**
16	René Arnoux	F	Elf RENAULT RE 30	Renault EF1	Equipe Renault Elf	1m 34·151s	**1m 30·232s**
17	Derek Daly	IRL	Rizla MARCH 811	Ford Cosworth DFV	March Grand Prix	1m 35·552s	**1m 32·305s**
20	Keke Rosberg	SF	FITTIPALDI F8C	Ford Cosworth DFV	Fittipaldi Automotive	1m 34·634s	**1m 34·310s**
21	Chico Serra	BR	FITTIPALDI F8C	Ford Cosworth DFV	Fittipaldi Automotive	1m 36·937s	**1m 36·546s**
22	Mario Andretti	USA	Marlboro ALFA ROMEO 179C	Alfa Romeo 1260	Marlboro Team Alfa Romeo	1m 32·648s	**1m 31·740s**
23	Bruno Giacomelli	I	Marlboro ALFA ROMEO 179C	Alfa Romeo 1260	Marlboro Team Alfa Romeo	1m 34·995s	**1m 31·600s**
25	Patrick Tambay	F	Talbot-Gitanes LIGIER JS17	Matra MS 81	Equipe Talbot Gitanes	**1m 31·747s**	1m 31·817s
26	Jacques Laffite	F	Talbot-Gitanes LIGIER JS17	Matra MS 81	Equipe Talbot Gitanes	1m 31·593s	**1m 30·705s**
27	Gilles Villeneuve	CDN	Fiat FERRARI 126CK	Ferrari 126C	Scuderia Ferrari SpA SEFAC	1m 32·077s	**1m 31·115s**
28	Didier Pironi	F	Fiat FERRARI 126CK	Ferrari 126C	Scuderia Ferrari SpA SEFAC	1m 31·976s	**1m 31·350s**
29	Riccardo Patrese	I	Ragno-Beta ARROWS A3	Ford Cosworth DFV	Arrows Racing Team	**1m 31·969s**	1m 32·277s
30	Jacques Villeneuve	CDN	Ragno-Beta ARROWS A3	Ford Cosworth DFV	Arrows Racing Team	**1m 36·720s**	1m 38·308s
31	Beppe Gabbiani	I	Denim OSELLA FA1B	Ford Cosworth DFV	Osella Squadra Corse	**1m 37·493s**	1m 55·307s
32	Jean-Pierre Jarier	F	Denim OSELLA FA1C	Ford Cosworth DFV	Osella Squadra Corse	**1m 33·432s**	1m 33·643s
33	Marc Surer	CH	THEODORE TY 01	Ford Cosworth DFV	Theodore Racing Team	1m 34·424s	**1m 32·253s**
35	Brian Henton	GB	Candy TOLEMAN TG 181	Hart 415T	Candy Toleman Motorsport	1m 40·505s	**1m 36·648s**
36	Derek Warwick	GB	Candy TOLEMAN TG 181	Hart 415T	Candy Toleman Motorsport	**1m 36·999s**	1m 37·256s

Friday morning and Saturday morning practice sessions not officially recorded — *Fri pm Warm, dry* — *Sat pm Warm, dry*

Starting grid

5 PIQUET (1m 29·211s)
Brabham

2 REUTEMANN (1m 29·359s)
Williams

1 JONES (1m 29·728s)
Williams

15 PROST (1m 29·908s)
Renault

12 MANSELL (1m 29·997s)
Lotus

6 REBAQUE (1m 30·182s)
Brabham

11 DE ANGELIS (1m 30·231s)
Lotus

16 ARNOUX (1m 30·232s)
Renault

7 WATSON (1m 30·566s)
McLaren

26 LAFFITE (1m 30·705s)
Talbot-Ligier

27 VILLENEUVE (1m 31·115s)
Ferrari

28 PIRONI (1m 31·350s)
Ferrari

8 DE CESARIS (1m 31·507s)
McLaren

3 CHEEVER (1m 31·547s)
Tyrrell

23 GIACOMELLI (1m 31·600s)
Alfa Romeo

22 ANDRETTI (1m 31·740s)
Alfa Romeo

25 TAMBAY (1m 31·747s)
Talbot-Ligier

29 PATRESE (1m 31·969s)
Arrows

33 SURER (1m 32·253s)
Theodore

17 DALY (1m 32·305s)
March

9 BORGUDD (1m 32·652s)
ATS

4 ALBORETO (1m 32·709s)
Tyrrell

32 JARIER (1m 33·432s)
Osella

14 SALAZAR (1m 33·848s)
Ensign

Did not start:
20 Rosberg (Fittipaldi), 1m 34·310s, did not qualify
21 Serra (Fittipaldi), 1m 36·546s, did not qualify
35 Henton (Toleman), 1m 36·648s, did not qualify
30 Villeneuve (Arrows), 1m 36·720s, did not qualify
36 Warwick (Toleman), 1m 36·999s, did not qualify
31 Gabbiani (Osella), 1m 37·493s, did not qualify

Past winners

Year	*Driver*	*Nat*	*Car*	*Circuit*	*Distance miles/km*	*Speed mph/km/h*
1961*	Pete Ryan	CDN	2·5 Lotus 19-Climax	Mosport Park	245·90/395·74	88·38/142·23
1962*	Masten Gregory	USA	2·5 Lotus 19-Climax	Mosport Park	245·90/395·74	88·52/142·46
1963*	Pedro Rodriguez	MEX	3·0 Ferrari 250P	Mosport Park	245·90/395·74	91·55/147·34
1964*	Pedro Rodriguez	MEX	4·0 Ferrari 330P	Mosport Park	245·90/395·74	94·36/151·86
1965*	Jim Hall	USA	5·4 Chaparral 2B-Chevrolet	Mosport Park	245·90/395·74	93·78/150·92
1966*	Mark Donohue	USA	6·0 Lola T70 Mk 2-Chevrolet	Mosport Park	209·02/336·38	101·87/163·94
1967	Jack Brabham	AUS	3·0 Brabham BT24-Repco	Mosport Park	221·31/356·16	82·99/133·56
1968	Denny Hulme	NZ	3·0 McLaren M7A-Ford	St Jovite	238·50/383·83	97·22/156·47
1969	Jacky Ickx	B	3·0 Brabham BT26A-Ford	Mosport Park	221·31/356·16	111·19/179·93
1970	Jacky Ickx	B	3·0 Ferrari 312B/70	St Jovite	238·50/383·83	101·27/162·98
1971	Jackie Stewart	GB	3·0 Tyrrell 003-Ford	Mosport Park	157·38/253·27	81·96/131·90
1972	Jackie Stewart	GB	3·0 Tyrrell 005-Ford	Mosport Park	196·72/316·59	114·28/183·92
1973	Peter Revson	USA	3·0 McLaren M23-Ford	Mosport Park	196·72/316·59	99·13/159·53
1974	Emerson Fittipaldi	BR	3·0 McLaren M23-Ford	Mosport Park	196·72/316·59	117·52/189·13
1976	James Hunt	GB	3·0 McLaren M23-Ford	Mosport Park	196·72/316·59	117·84/189·65
1977	Jody Scheckter	ZA	3·0 Wolf WR1-Ford	Mosport Park	196·72/316·59	118·03/189·95
1978	Gilles Villeneuve	CDN	3·0 Ferrari 312T-3/78	Ile Notre-Dame	195·72/314·98	99·67/160·40
1979	Alan Jones	AUS	3·0 Williams FW07-Ford	Ile Notre-Dame	197·28/317·52	105·35/169·54
1980	Alan Jones	AUS	3·0 Williams FW07B-Ford	Ile Notre-Dame	191·82/308·70	110·00/177·03
1981	Jacques Laffite	F	3·0 Ligier JS17-Matra	Ile Notre-Dame	172·62/277·83	85·31/137·29

* *Non-championship (sports cars)*

Circuit data

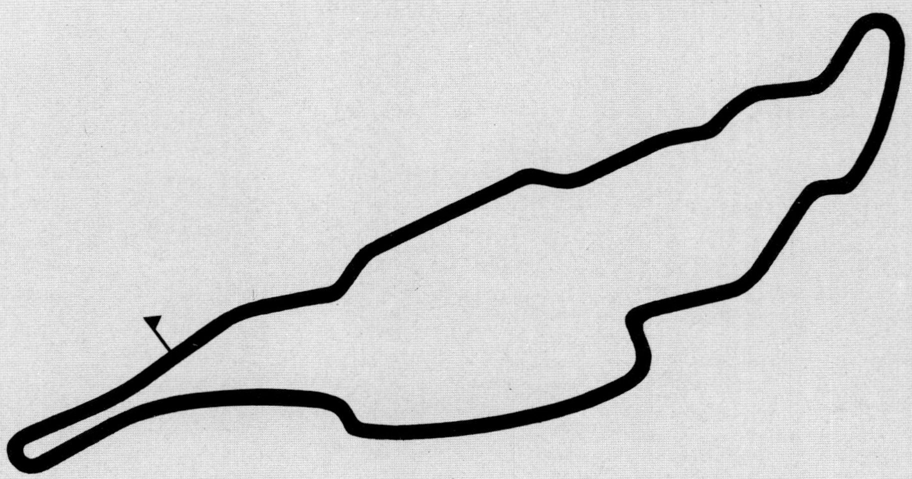

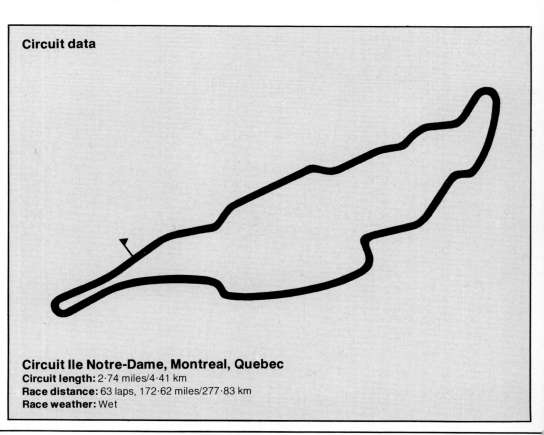

Circuit Ile Notre-Dame, Montreal, Quebec

Circuit length: 2·74 miles/4·41 km
Race distance: 63 laps, 172·62 miles/277·83 km
Race weather: Wet

Results and retirements

Place	Driver	Car	Laps	*Time and Speed (mph/km/h)/Retirement*	
1	Jacques Laffite	Talbot-Ligier V12	63	2h 01m 25·205s	85·308/137·289
2	John Watson	McLaren-Cosworth V8	63	2h 01m 31·438s	85·235/137·173
3	Gilles Villeneuve	Ferrari t/c V6	63	2h 03m 15·480s	84·036/135·243
4	Bruno Giacomelli	Alfa Romeo V12	62		
5	Nelson Piquet	Brabham-Cosworth V8	62		
6	Elio de Angelis	Lotus-Cosworth V8	62		
7	Mario Andretti	Alfa Romeo V12	62		
8	Derek Daly	March-Cosworth V8	61		
9	Marc Surer	Theodore-Cosworth V8	61		
10	Carlos Reutemann	Williams-Cosworth V8	60		
11	Michele Alboreto	Tyrrell-Cosworth V8	59		
12	Eddie Cheever	Tyrrell-Cosworth V8	56	Engine	
	Andrea de Cesaris	McLaren-Cosworth V8	51	Spun off	
	Alain Prost	Renault t/c V6	48	Accident with Mansell	
	Nigel Mansell	Lotus-Cosworth V8	45	Accident with Prost	
	Slim Borgudd	ATS-Cosworth V8	39	Spun off	
	Hector Rebaque	Brabham-Cosworth V8	35	Spun off	
	Jean-Pierre Jarier	Osella-Cosworth V8	26	Accident with Rebaque	
	Didier Pironi	Ferrari t/c V6	24	Engine	
	Alan Jones	Williams-Cosworth V8	24	Handling	
	Eliseo Salazar	Ensign-Cosworth V8	8	Spun off	
	Patrick Tambay	Talbot-Ligier V12	6	Spun off	
	Riccardo Patrese	Arrows-Cosworth V8	6	Spun off	
	René Arnoux	Renault t/c V6	0	Accident	

Fastest lap: Watson, on lap 43, 1m 49·475s, 90·11mph/145·019km/h.
Lap record: Didier Pironi (F1 Ligier JS11/15-Cosworth DFV), 1m 28·769s, 113·397mph/182·496km/h (1980).

Lap chart

1st LAP ORDER		1	2	3	4	5	6	7	8	9	10	11	12	13	14	15	16	17	18	19	20	21	22	23	24	25	26	27	28
1	A.Jones	1	1	1	1	1	1	15	15	15	15	15	15	26	26	26	26	26	26	26	26	26	26	26	26	26	26	26	26
5	N.Piquet	5	5	5	5	5	5	26	26	26	26	26	26	15	15	27	27	27	27	27	27	27	27	27	27	27	27	27	27
15	A.Prost	15	15	15	15	15	15	27	27	27	27	27	27	27	27	15	15	7	7	7	7	7	7	7	7	7	7	7	7
11	E.de Angelis	11	11	11	11	26	26	5	7	7	7	7	7	7	7	7	7	15	15	15	15	15	28	28	28	15	15	15	15
2	C.Reutemann	2	26	26	26	11	27	7	5	5	5	5	5	5	5	5	5	5	5	28	28	28	15	15	15	5	5	5	5
26	J.Laffite	26	12	12	27	27	11	11	11	11	28	28	28	28	28	28	28	28	28	5	5	5	5	5	5	23	23	23	23
12	N.Mansell	12	27	27	12	7	7	1	12	12	11	11	11	11	11	11	17	17	17	17	17	17	17	23	23	17	17	17	17
25	P.Tambay	25	7	7	7	12	12	22	22	28	12	17	17	17	17	17	11	11	23	23	23	23	23	17	17	11	8	8	8
7	J.Watson	7	22	22	22	22	22	12	28	17	17	12	12	23	23	23	23	23	11	11	11	11	11	11	11	8	11	11	11
27	G.Villeneuve	27	2	17	17	17	17	17	17	23	23	23	23	12	12	8	8	8	8	8	8	8	8	8	8	32	32	22	22
8	A.de Cesaris	8	17	8	8	8	8	28	8	8	8	8	8	8	8	12	32	32	32	32	32	32	32	32	32	22	22	12	12
22	M.Andretti	22	8	2	28	28	28	8	23	22	22	22	32	32	32	32	22	22	22	22	22	22	22	22	22	12	12	33	33
23	B.Giacomelli	23	6	6	23	23	23	23	1	32	32	32	22	22	22	22	12	12	12	12	12	12	12	12	12	33	33	3	3
17	D.Daly	17	23	28	6	25	25	32	32	1	3	3	3	3	3	3	3	3	3	3	3	3	3	33	33	3	3	9	9
6	H.Rebaque	6	33	23	25	6	6	6	6	3	33	33	33	33	33	33	33	33	33	33	33	33	33	3	3	9	9	2	2
33	M.Surer	33	28	33	33	2	32	3	3	33	2	2	2	2	2	2	2	9	9	9	9	9	9	9	9	2	2	4	4
3	E.Cheever	3	3	25	2	32	4	2	33	2	9	9	9	9	9	9	9	2	2	2	2	2	2	2	2	4	4	6	6
32	J-P.Jarier	32	32	3	3	3	3	33	2	9	1	1	1	1	1	1	1	1	1	4	4	4	4	4	4	6	6		
14	E.Salazar	14	25	32	32	9	2	9	9	6	4	4	4	4	4	4	4	4	4	1	1	1	1	1	1				
4	M.Alboreto	4	4	4	9	4	9	14	14	4	6	6	6	6	6	6	6	6	6	6	6	6	6	6	6				
28	D.Pironi	28	9	9	4	33	33	4	4																				
9	S.Borgudd	9	14	14	14	14	14																						
29	R.Patrese	29	29	29	29	29	29																						

29	30	31	32	33	34	35	36	37	38	39	40	41	42	43	44	45	46	47	48	49	50	51	52	53	54	55	56	57	58	59	60	61	62	63
26	26	26	26	26	26	26	26	26	26	26	26	26	26	26	26	26	26	26	26	26	26	26	26	26	26	26	26	26	26	26	26	26	26	26
27	27	27	27	27	27	27	27	27	7	7	7	7	7	7	7	7	7	7	7	7	7	7	7	7	7	7	7	7	7	7	7	7	7	7
7	7	7	7	7	7	7	7	7	27	27	27	27	27	27	27	27	27	27	27	27	27	27	27	27	27	27	27	27	27	27	27	27	27	27
15	15	15	15	15	15	15	15	15	15	15	15	15	15	15	15	15	15	15	15	23	23	23	23	23	23	23	23	23	23	23	23	23	23	
5	5	5	5	5	5	5	23	23	23	23	23	23	23	23	23	23	23	23	23	5	5	5	5	5	5	5	5	5	5	5	5	5	5	
23	23	23	23	23	23	23	5	5	5	5	5	5	5	5	5	5	5	5	5	8	8	8	11	11	11	11	11	11	11	11	11	11	11	
17	17	17	8	8	8	8	8	8	8	8	8	8	8	8	8	8	8	8	8	11	11	11	22	22	22	22	22	22	22	22	22	22	22	
8	8	8	17	17	17	17	17	17	17	17	17	17	17	11	11	11	11	11	11	22	22	22	17	17	17	17	17	17	17	17	17	17		
11	11	11	11	11	11	11	11	11	11	11	11	11	11	17	22	22	22	22	22	17	17	17	33	33	33	33	33	33	33	33	33	33		
22	22	22	22	22	22	22	22	22	22	22	22	22	22	22	17	17	17	17	17	33	33	33	3	3	3	3	3	2	2	2	2			
12	12	33	33	33	33	33	33	33	33	33	33	33	33	33	33	33	33	33	33	3	3	3	2	2	2	2	2	4	4	4				
33	33	3	3	3	3	3	3	3	3	3	3	3	3	3	3	3	3	3	3	2	2	2	4	4	4	4	4							
3	3	12	12	12	12	12	12	12	12	12	12	12	12	12	12	12	2	2	2	4	4	4												
9	9	9	9	9	9	9	9	9	9	9	9	2	2	2	2	2	4	4	4															
2	2	2	2	2	2	2	2	2	2	2	2	4	4	4	4	4																		
4	4	4	4	4	4	4	4	4	4	4	4																							
6	6	6	6	6	6	6																												

Fastest laps

Driver	*Time*	*Lap*
John Watson	1m 49·475s	43
Jacques Laffite	1m 49·765s	46
Carlos Reutemann	1m 50·309s	39
Andrea de Cesaris	1m 50·762s	46
Marc Surer	1m 51·020s	40
Alain Prost	1m 51·197s	48
Bruno Giacomelli	1m 51·490s	55
Nelson Piquet	1m 51·849s	45
Elio de Angelis	1m 51·927s	47
Gilles Villeneuve	1m 52·087s	47
Mario Andretti	1m 52·580s	61
Eddie Cheever	1m 53·994s	42
Slim Borgudd	1m 54·794s	38
Derek Daly	1m 54·946s	41
Hector Rebaque	1m 55·172s	33
Jean-Pierre Jarier	1m 55·949s	26
Michele Alboreto	1m 55·977s	52
Didier Pironi	1m 56·285s	24
Alan Jones	1m 56·624s	5
Nigel Mansell	1m 56·718s	37
Patrick Tambay	1m 59·888s	4
Eliseo Salazar	2m 03·264s	4
Riccardo Patrese	2m 07·558s	3

Points

WORLD CHAMPIONSHIP OF DRIVERS

1	Carlos Reutemann	49 pts
2	Nelson Piquet	48
3	Jacques Laffite	43
4 =	Alan Jones	37
4 =	Alain Prost	37
6	John Watson	27
7	Gilles Villeneuve	25
8	Elio de Angelis	14
9 =	René Arnoux	11
9 =	Hector Rebaque	11
11 =	Riccardo Patrese	10
11 =	Eddie Cheever	10
13	Didier Pironi	9
14	Nigel Mansell	5
15	Marc Surer	4
16 =	Mario Andretti	3
16 =	Bruno Giacomelli	3
18 =	Patrick Tambay	1
18 =	Andrea de Cesaris	1
18 =	Slim Borgudd	1
18 =	Eliseo Salazar	1

CONSTRUCTORS' CUP

1	Williams	86
2	Brabham	59
3	Renault	48
4	Ligier	43
5	Ferrari	34
6	McLaren	28
7	Lotus	19
8 =	Arrows	10
8 =	Tyrrell	10
10	Alfa Romeo	6
11	Ensign	5
12 =	Theodore	1
12 =	ATS	1

Caesars Palace Grand Prix

Charlie Whiting stood on the rear wall of the pit lane, watching intently to his left, waiting for the familiar red and white hooped helmet to appear for the 75th and final time. The Brabham chief mechanic knew his man was flagging, the lolling helmet telling the tale of neck muscles punished mercilessly by the fast left-hand corners of the Caesars Palace circuit. Nelson Piquet was fifth, Carlos Reutemann was back in eighth place and the two points would be sufficient to give the Brazilian his first World Championship.

On the other hand, John Watson and Jacques Laffite were closing rapidly and the Parmalat Brabham team would come away with nothing if Piquet was overtaken during the final two miles of the 15-race championship. After 3,000 miles of racing around the world, there was one lap remaining. Just one. Could Nelson hang on? The crew chief, living up to his name, went deathly pale.

Next door, the Saudia Leyland Williams team gave a practised cheer as Alan Jones took the flag after a stunning performance to round off his career – for the time being at least – with a flag-to-flag victory. Alain Prost was next, another forceful and impressive drive from the Renault-Elf driver, followed by an on-form Bruno Giacomelli in the Marlboro Alfa Romeo. Then came Nigel Mansell after an intelligent race in the John Player Special Lotus. But where was Nelson?

He had dropped even further behind – and the McLaren and the Ligier were only a couple of seconds adrift. Steering more by automatic reaction than anything else, Piquet rounded the corner and pointed his Brabham towards the flag. Laffite, having overtaken Watson at the last corner, gave chase but the Brabham made it. The grandstand behind the pits, full of Brazilians in green and yellow tee-shirts, erupted; Whiting, taught with emotion, ran across the pit lane and embraced his team; Hector Rebaque climbed onto the pit wall and smothered Bernie Ecclestone in kisses!

A few yards away from the pandemonium, Neil Oatley stood alone as he ticked off Carlos Reutemann's last lap before staring silently at his clip-board; a year's work down the pan. Removing his head-phones and putting away his pencil, the Williams engineer looked to the right, his misery compounded by the Brabham team clambering over the wall to receive Piquet. The car trickled to a halt and, for several minutes, the new World Champion lay slumped in the cockpit, every last ounce of adrenalin and energy drained from his body. Jones, by contrast, looked reasonably fresh as he received the laurels of victory in the first Caesars Palace Grand Prix.

Apart from the see-sawing battle for the championship (Laffite having worked his way into second place before stopping for tyres) the race and surroundings were unmemorable if unusual. The facilities and the track were of a reasonably high standard but, as our American Editor pointed out, the event was no more than a gambler's side-show.

And on this occasion, Piquet had taken the Jackpot, Jones had cashed in his chips with a flourish while Reutemann, the man who rarely gambled, had lost heavily.

ENTRY AND PRACTICE

On the Monday before the race, Carlos Reutemann stretched out on a sun-lounger by the Caesars Palace pool. Dressed in shorts and tee-shirt, the leader of the World Championship looked lean and relaxed. He had arrived early to unwind and get to grips with this new venue on the calendar. Forgetting the jingling, tinsel backdrop, this was another circuit just the same but, on Saturday, the championship would be decided for once and for all.

Earlier, Reutemann had donned his peacock blue Tacchini track suit and walked past the shower rooms, through the car park which would soon become the CanAm paddock and out towards the rows of 3ft high concrete walls zig-zagging across the flat piece of land bounded by Flamingo Road, Las Vegas Boulevard and the marzipan-like Caesars Palace hotel.

The organisers, with guidance from Chris Pook and his Long Beach team, had done a surprisingly good job. The track was wide, the surface smooth and local taxi drivers had been called in to season the tarmac. The corners were not too tight; first gear would not be necessary after all; the back section could be taken flat even though the designers did not plan it that way. So, contrary to predictions, there would be overtaking and average speeds might just be higher than the predicted 85mph. On top of that, temperatures were in the mid-70s. Maybe this place wasn't so bad after all.

Gradually the drivers filtered into the hotel, relative unknowns in this strange world of the one-armed bandit and chattering roulette wheel. Spectators seemed to be few and far between, adding weight to stories that the $50-250 seats were moving slowly. Generally speaking, the locals had no idea what was about to hit them although the television stations, inbetween dreadful adverts and outlandish quiz shows, were giving the event ample coverage.

It was hardly surprising, therefore, that pedestrians in Las Vegas Boulevard were taken aback at 10.45 a.m. on Wednesday morning as Derek Daly made history by leading the cars onto the circuit. Nine minutes later, Andrea de Cesaris made his mark by having the first spin, the McLaren mechanics catching sight of his rotating helmet and roll-over bar on a piece of track some six or seven concrete walls away!

Initial reports were favourable. The track was fast although the stiff suspensions were seeking out previously invisible bumps and the prevailing left-hand bends (the cars running in an unaccustomed anti-clockwise direction) would play havoc with neck muscles. Stamina, it seemed, would play a vital part and with that in mind, Carlos Alberto Reutemann had the edge on the comparatively frail Nelson Piquet and the slender Jacques Laffite.

As though sensing his advantage, Reutemann went about his business in a positive, confident frame of mind and slayed the opposition on Thursday with one of those brilliant laps which leave you gaping in admiration. Then, when he casually mentioned he had lost time on oil while doing it, the championship seemed certain to go back to Argentina for the first time since 1957.

Williams had four cars available, Reutemann making use of his spare on Friday after a misjudgement while lapping Nelson Piquet. The Williams rode over the Brabham's rear wheel and flew briefly into the air before crashing onto the track and bending the suspension pick-up points. Nevertheless, his time

OCTOBER:

Basil Tye loses FISA Presidential Election to Jean-Marie Balestre.

Jonathan Palmer (Ralt-Toyota) wins Marlboro British Formula 3 Championship.

Plans for Detroit Grand Prix postponed to 1983.

Jan Corsmit appointed President of FISA Safety Committee.

Bobby Unser confirmed as winner of Indy 500 by USAC committee of enquiry.

Richard Noble (Thrust II) fails to beat Land Speed Record at Utah.

Eppie Wietzes (Chevrolet Corvette) wins CAC Chemicals TransAm Championship.

Eddie Cheever signs for Talbot-Ligier.

James Hunt turns down £2.6 million offer to return to Formula 1.

Phillippe Etancelin dies.

Geoff Brabham (VDS-Chevrolet) wins CanAm Championship.

The Brabham team tried harnessing Nelson Piquet's helmet to help protect his neck muscles during practice. By the end of the race he was completely exhausted – but World Champion nevertheless *(left)*.
Jones's head rolls as he corners the Williams on his way to a superb victory *(below)*.
Most of the Michelin runners were forced to make pit stops, Pironi setting fastest lap and Prost cutting back through the field to take an excellent second place *(bottom)*.

from Thursday stood although Alan Jones made a superb effort during the closing minutes and pushed Piquet off the front row. Those who had backed the reigning World Champion at 8–1 in the local betting office smiled quietly. Like I said, the locals were at sea when it came to talking about 'them noisy race cars'.

Piquet's odds were 2–1 and seemed rather short in the light of a troubled practice for the Brabham driver. His car was well suited to the circuit but the same could not be said for Nelson who suffered from nausia on Wednesday and a stiff neck on Thursday. To make matters worse, he was over a second slower than Reutemann after failing to make the most of his qualifiers when the red flag brought practice to a halt for the 'umpteenth time. There was always Friday, of course, but Piquet woke up to find his back bruised after a session with the masseur the previous day; sitting in the car would be difficult, let alone driving it at speed. Nevertheless, Piquet went to work for 11 laps and put himself on the second row although progress was halted by gear selection problems on the spare car (which also featured water-cooled brakes).

What of the third championship contender, Jacques Laffite? Well, the normally sunny Frenchman was rather tense even though he had nothing to lose. His mood and confidence were not helped when Patrick Tambay was quicker in both practice sessions and Jacques indulged in some rather fruitless chassis swapping in a desperate effort to save face. His main complaint was lack of grip and an engine pick-up problem and he opted to start from his sixth row position in Tambay's car. Patrick, by now, was accepting the whole business with a resigned shrug since he had been informed by Guy Ligier that his services would not be required in 1982. Ligier had signed Eddie Cheever in a surprise move which did not gain full approval from either Talbot or Gitanes and it was a curious decision to make at a time when the team should have been concentrating on 1981 rather than 1982 . . .

On paper, the Las Vegas track seemed the sort of place where the Ferraris might go well but no-one seriously expected Gilles Villeneuve to record third fastest time. The 2,200ft altitude may have helped the turbo but the bumps, particularly those at the apex of the left-hander before the pits made the 126C even more unstable than usual although they did contribute to Gilles tweaking his car into the most extraordinary angles. Of the two Ferrari drivers, once again it was Didier Pironi who had more than his fair share of trouble during practice, first of all with the handling and skirts followed by a blown turbo and fuel injection bothers with the spare chassis. As a result, Didier had to settle for 18th place with his Thursday time.

To emphasise the turbo's suitability to the medium and reasonably fast corners, Alain Prost set fifth fastest time in the Renault – and that was a result of his Thursday time after a series of problems during the final session. Gear selection bothers meant he was able to use only one set of qualifiers although his problems were minimal compared to those of René Arnoux. A new chassis had been flown in from France to replace the one damaged at Montreal but René was forced to use the T-car after an oil leak caused a turbo fire on Thursday. Then he was back in the spare car the following day after crashing and damaging the rear corner of his race car and thereby losing the benefit of the special weight-saving carbon-fibre front and rear wings.

John Watson looked upon Las Vegas with a jaundiced eye when the air conditioning in his hotel room aggravated a nasty head cold. Wattie found himself to be a liability out on the track and called it a day before he had an accident. He did well to set sixth fastest time during the final session although, initially, there was a misunderstanding about unmarked qualifying tyres. Andrea de Cesaris managed to keep his car away from the walls throughout practice and took 14th place on the grid for what appeared to be his last race for Marlboro McLaren. Joining Tambay, having his last race for Talbot-Ligier, on row four was the Marlboro Alfa Romeo of Bruno Giacomelli. Gerard Ducarouge was continuing to make his presence felt, the cars turning in and generally handling better than before although Mario Andretti, 10th fastest was unable to make the most of the improvements. Rumoured to be having his last Formula 1 race, Andretti was disappointed to find a fuel pick-up problem meant he had to run with a minimum of 20 gallons on board throughout the final practice session.

Splitting the Alfa Romeos was Nigel Mansell who, like Andretti, was unable to make the most of a car which went reasonably well on this circuit. Sixth fastest on Thursday, Nigel had to use the spare chassis during the final session after an ignition problem had halted his race car during the morning. Repairs were carried out in time for the afternoon session but somewhere along the line, the engine had lost power and Mansell slipped to ninth place. Elio de Angelis was a couple of rows behind having lost time with a broken front anti-roll bar on Thursday. Pirellis had produced a new tyre which Arrows designer Dave Wass reckoned to be worth a second per lap and Riccardo Patrese took a place in the middle of the grid as a result. Jacques Villeneuve, making his second attempt to qualify for a Grand Prix, looked ill-at-ease once again and he spent much of final practice driving the T-car which appeared to handle even more precariously than his race chassis. That particular car had stopped early in the session with an electrical problem and marshals left the abandoned Arrows right on the line at the exit of a corner. Gilles Villeneuve won the prize for coming closest to the car without actually hitting it. Brother Jacques, meanwhile, failed to qualify.

Hector Rebaque was back in 16th place, his most dramatic moment being a brake failure in the T-car. Avon produced a qualifying tyre which was good for about one lap, Michele Alboreto making the best use of the rubber with an impressive effort in the Tyrrell. Eddie Cheever was the centre of attention after the unexpected press release concerning his future with Talbot-Ligier but the American did nothing during practice to prove that he had been chosen on pure merit and he qualified in 19th place on Goodyears. Against impossible odds, the pennyless Fittipaldi team made the trip and Keke Rosberg's perseverance with an appalling chassis was rewarded with 20th place on the grid. The team were given one set of the improved Pirellis and these were entrusted to Chico Serra, the Brazilian novice ending a miserable season by spinning during the final session and failing to qualify for the sixth race in succession. The Denim Osella team were plagued with poor oil pressure on Jean-Pierre Jarier's FA1C at the start of both practice sessions but, when the problem was rectified, the Frenchman had further delays with worn skirts and a down-on-power engine. Beppe Gabbiani complained once again that his team-mate was receiving all the attention and didn't run in the final session. He failed to qualify by a comfortable margin.

Having worked solidly all season without complaining, Derek Warwick received just reward by qualifying for the first time in the Candy Toleman-Hart. The Englishman didn't spin once and used the same engine throughout, setting his time on Friday with a particularly spectacular lap. Brian Henton, on the other hand, spun on his first set of qualifiers on Friday and relegation to the T-car meant his chances of qualifying were slim. Judging by the lack of grip on the Theodore, Marc Surer would be hard pushed to make the race but the Swiss earned full marks and a place on the back row for his sideways efforts. Eliseo Salazar was the final qualifier, the Ensign, sponsored by Budweiser, showing a marked tendency to bounce into oversteer at an alarming rate on the bumps. Slim Borgudd crashed his ATS on Friday morning and failed to qualify the spare care while Derek Daly was totally perplexed by his lack of speed when it mattered most. The Guinness-Rizla March had recorded a time worth about 20th place during the untimed session on Friday but the Irishman was unable to match it later in the day.

RACE

As they waited on the grid, you could sense what the outcome would be. Nelson Piquet looked small and frail as he sat strapped in the Brabham, his right shoulder hunched uncomfortably against a white support pad stuck to the cockpit side. Gordon Murray perched on the left-front wishbone, his long legs tucked around the side-pod as he made light conversation. They talked about the weather; joked about the water supply which bubbled through a perspex pipe to the front of Nelson's helmet; checked the helmet support bar was positioned properly. Bernie Ecclestone was strangely inactive; the mechanics stood quietly by, their work done.

A couple of feet away, Alan Jones was out of his car and chatting easily with Innes Ireland and Stirling Moss. Rolling his ear-plugs between thumb and forefinger, the Australian looked completely relaxed as he cast an eye towards pole position and made a mental note that Reutemann appeared to be fussing once again.

Carlos had remained in his car for the drivers' briefing and now sat with his helmet in his lap but white balaclava still in place as he told Frank Williams about a sudden handling problem; understeer on right-handers. The car had been fine during the

Jones stamps his superiority on the first Caesars Palace Grand Prix by taking the lead into the first corner. Villeneuve slots into second place and Prost runs round the outside of the pole position man, Carlos Reutemann *(left)*.

Nigel Mansell produced a typically determined drive and finished fourth *(below left)*.

USUALLY, YOU GET PLENTY OF WARNING. THE TIMED practice has been under way for 20 minutes or so and he comes by, cruising gently, quite often with his visor raised. He'll repeat the procedure for a lap or two, rehearsing his lines, choosing a break in the traffic, then – wham – the Williams paints a different picture entirely next time round.

Reutemann arrives visibly quicker than either he or anyone else has gone before. If there's a white line, he'll place a front wheel inside it at the apex; if there's a wall, he'll shave it but not touch it. Braking will be late but not rushed; the turn in, razor sharp but not violent; the exit, fast but economical. And always, the shining helmet will be erect, no matter what. No slouching, sawing or sliding. Just incredible speed and grace that makes you wait in hot anticipation for the next lap.

But the next lap doesn't come. By now he's cruising back to the pits and rivals are staring at the lap time in disbelief. Here's what they saw on Thursday afternoon in Las Vegas:

1m 20.371s
1m 35.592s
1m 19.444s
1m 31.005s
1m 23.615s
1m 20.494s
IN
1m 19.354s
1m 35.187s
1m 17.821s
2m 03.541s
1m 25.141s
IN

Regrettably, a brilliant practice lap isn't everything . . .

Bruno Giacomelli holds fourth place ahead of Laffite and Watson. Piquet, coming under pressure from Andretti, decides it's time to challenge Reutemann *(below)*.
Jacques Laffite, the third contender for the championship, seen here in the spare Talbot-Ligier, lost time switching cars during practice but drove an aggressive race *(below centre)*.
After a season of frustration, Derek Warwick qualified his Toleman for the first time *(bottom)*.

morning warm-up but, with the top bodywork removed, a quick check revealed nothing amiss. Williams discussed tyre pressure with Patrick Head and the mechanics. Everything was in order. What could it be? Everyone stood around helplessly; Reutemann stared vacantly at his helmet; Jones continued to chat with enthusiasm; Villeneuve sheltered from the sun under an umbrella and thought about the importance of another good start; Piquet lapsed into silence.

Clerk of the Course, Bob Swenson, had made it clear that any driver failing to take up his starting position in the allocated box marked on the track would be subject to exclusion. As the cars rolled to a halt, Villeneuve was too preoccupied with slotting through the gap in the middle of the front row to notice that he was parked to the left of his designated position. As the lights turned green (or, in Villeneuve's case, as the red lights went out) the Ferrari shot forward but was no match for Alan Jones who took the initiative as the field went through the right-hand curve and aimed for the first left-hander. By the time they were on the brakes, Villeneuve had tucked in behind Jones and Prost was running round the outside of Reutemann.

During the course of the next two miles, Alan Jones turned on a withering display as he stood the car on its ear and pulled out a two-second gap. Villeneuve was holding second place ahead of the Renault but Bruno Giacomelli had pushed Reutemann into fifth place. Watson was next closely followed by Laffite (another good start), Piquet and Mansell. The field was already one short when Jean-Pierre Jarier failed to get off the line with a broken drive-shaft and there were two more retirements in as many minutes. Elio de Angelis pitted at the end of lap two to investigate impossible handling but got no further when the team discovered a water leak on the Lotus. Andrea de Cesaris, holding twelfth place, locked wheels with Patrick Tambay while attempting to pass the Ligier. Both cars spun and continued although Tambay then had a horrific accident when his car ploughed off the track at the exit of a fast left-hander and smashed into a wall of tyres and concrete. The front section of the Ligier, wheels and pedal box included, were ripped clean off but Patrick was fortunate to receive no more than heavy bruising to one ankle.

By the end of lap two, Jones was five seconds in front of Villeneuve who was under pressure from Prost, the Renault moving ahead with a neat piece of outbraking on the following lap. Giacomelli had pulled away from Reutemann but the Williams was to slip two more places as Watson and Laffite hammered past on lap three. No matter, Carlos's championship was safe so long as Piquet remained in eighth place. Laffite, of course, had everything to go for and he turned on an aggressive display as he passed Watson and set off in pursuit of Giacomelli's fourth place.

Prost put everything he had into closing the gap on Jones but by lap five the Frenchman realised he was in tyre trouble as his Michelins began to pick up rubber from the track, the resulting imbalance causing a worrying vibration. Jones, therefore, was able to hold a six second advantage as the field began to settle down for the long, tiring slog on a hot afternoon.

Salazar dashed into the pits to discover that his rear brake line was leaking and René Arnoux was the next visitor, his engine misfiring due to a broken spark-plug which proved impossible to repair. Cheever stopped with a blown engine and de Cesaris made his way into the pits to change tyres, Pironi doing likewise a few laps later. His team-mate, meanwhile, was leading a tight gaggle of cars although it would be fair to say that the Ferrari wasn't exactly holding them up. Giacomelli was unable to get close enough to have a stab at third place and, besides, the Alfa Romeo driver was being shadowed by Laffite and Watson.

As far as the championship was concerned, Reutemann had the upper hand even though he was in seventh place, but, on lap 16, Piquet was on his tail and looking for a way past. The Brabham, in turn, was coming under pressure from Andretti and, on lap 17, Nelson decided it was time to have a go: "He made it easy for me. He braked early and it was easy to pass, no problem." For a few laps the championship position remained unchanged but, on lap 23, the situation began to alter dramatically.

The organisers had decided to carry out their threat by disqualifying Villeneuve but the matter was resolved when the Ferrari stopped out on the circuit. Thus, Laffite was into third place (four points) and, at the same time, Piquet took Watson and moved into sixth place (one point). That became fifth place (two points) a couple of laps later when Giacomelli spun down the field and, by lap 33, Nelson was third after Prost stopped for fresh tyres. Laffite, of course, was second by now and the permuations seemed endless as Reutemann came under pressure from Nigel Mansell and dropped back to sixth place!

The Lotus driver was running a canny race. Realising tyre wear would be critical during the early, full-tank laps, he waited until 25 laps had passed before making his move. Spurred on by a rapidly advancing Patrese, Mansell closed on the leading group and made up a place when Watson made his stop for tyres on lap 29. Prost, meanwhile, had confused the situation further by rejoining quickly and moving ahead of Reutemann into fifth place. While all this was going on, Surer had stopped with broken rear suspension, Rebaque had spun off and then retired while Andretti, running strongly in fourth place at one stage, was extremely disappointed to have been forced to stop with broken rear suspension when the car was running well. De Cesaris was back in the pits, complaining about his handling, and it was only then that the mechanics were able to discover a bent steering arm, the result of his incident with Tambay.

At the half-way stage, Jones was stroking along with a 40-second advantage over Laffite who, in turn was 11 seconds clear of Piquet. Prost was closing fast, however, his car handling perfectly as the fuel load lightened and by lap 48 he had passed both Piquet and Laffite although he had little chance of catching the Williams. Laffite's Michelins, by now, were next to useless and the Frenchman slipped to fifth place before deciding to stop. That effectively knocked Jacques out of the championship equation and, as the race entered the final 20 laps, it appeared that

An unfortunate coincidence even though most of the teams had a fair amount of rebuilding after Montreal . . .

Reutemann had the race carefully worked out after all and was about to cruise to the title.

Giacomelli was reaping the benefit of his hard Michelins and had moved back to third place while Piquet appeared to be fading fast as he fell to fifth place. Reutemann, however, seemed to go slower than ever and he offered no resistance whatsoever as Watson and Laffite raced back up the lap chart and pushed the Williams into eighth place. Alboreto was ninth but destined to retire with a blown engine after a steady race while Derek Warwick reduced the field further when an oil leak onto his rear brakes had caused him to overtax the gearbox. None the less, the Toleman driver had not disgraced himself during his first race in over a year. Pironi, having stopped to check skirt damage, set the fastest lap on a new set of tyres while second fastest lap went to none other than Andrea de Cesaris who really went motoring after his delay in the pits. Keke Rosberg, unfamiliar in Laffite's spare helmet, kept going in spite of heavy steering caused by running wider front tyres than usual and Riccardo Patrese rejoined a long way behind the Fittipaldi after a pit stop.

Jones continued on his way, having humiliated Reutemann further by lapping the Argentinian in front of the pits. As he started his final ten laps, Jones's helmet was rolling around the cockpit as he deliberately chose not to overtax his neck muscles. Nevertheless, it was an alarming sight as the Williams came round the corner before the pits, its driver staring at the sky under acceleration! Prost was in a comfortable second place and Giacomelli was still charging along for all he was worth ahead of Mansell. The Lotus driver was turning in a superb performance considering he had pinched a nerve in his left thigh, his clutch was slipping and his engine was down to 10,000rpm because of a broken valve spring. The Englishman was as strong as an ox, however, and his stamina was never in doubt. Nelson Piquet was a different case entirely as he staggered through the final laps under threat from the advancing Watson and Laffite. If the Brabham was demoted to seventh, the championship would go to Reutemann who was holding a very uninspiring eighth place.

Nelson made it to the flag but had the race been one lap longer, Laffite, who had taken Watson at the last corner after a misunderstanding between the McLaren driver and his pit, would have passed the Brabham. It was also equally certain that another two miles would have finished Piquet completely.

When car number five rolled to a halt by the pit wall, the mechanics found their man had been sick in his helmet and was on the point of passing out. Surrounded by chanting fans and prying pressmen, Nelson was revived slowly and lifted from his car. It took over 15 minutes before the new World Champion was able to walk to the rostrum and join the celebrations. There, a remarkably fresh Alan Jones drank a cool beer after a drive which had outclassed the entire field. His performance had been such that the championship battle between Piquet and Reutemann had been shown in its true perspective. Nelson may have won the title but, beyond any shadow of doubt, Alan Jones had proved once again that he was the best *racing* driver of 1981.

As for Reutemann, the Argentinian climbed sadly from his car, mentioned something about handling and gearbox problems to Frank Williams and disappeared to his hotel room. Having led the championship since April; having left Silverstone with a 17 point advantage in July, it seemed inconceivable that Carlos could have lost the championship. But he had. By one point.

Another lap, and Neil Oatley would have been drinking champagne. Another lap and Charlie Whiting would still be standing on the pit wall.

"Listen, listen . . . I'll get Gordon to put the engine in the front and we'll run the thing on five-inch Engleberts . . . Now will you come back?"

FLEET STREET REPORTERS HAD JUST CHECKED INTO their hotels after long flights to Las Vegas when they were called from their beds to follow up juicy but unlikely stories concerning the return of James Hunt and Jackie Stewart to Formula 1.

Hunt was reported to have been offered £2.6m by the Brabham team on behalf of an unnamed sponsor. Stewart, as ever, went one better, his offer reputedly being in the region of £3m.

Fleet Street went berserk while Hunt and Stewart wrung the publicity dry with evasive statements full of mutual admiration.

"It looks like James may be coming back," said Jackie. "The sort of offer I have had is very difficult to turn down. If all three of us (Lauda, Hunt and Stewart) came back it would be the greatest thing on earth for motor racing. The offer to James doesn't surprise me, the sponsors are looking for big names. I am not saying who made the offer to me, but I will be thinking about it long and hard."

"It's great news," said James of Jackie's offer. "I can't think of anything better than racing against him. But we both have an awful lot of thinking to do. I don't need the money and when I retired it was for reasons of self-preservation and that reason doesn't change.

"Anyway, what do you do with the money? I am not being big-headed. I lead a very modest life and when I retired I was well enough off. I agree with Jackie that it would be the best thing in the world for motor racing if we came back and were in top condition.

"I would certainly have no worries in that direction. It is true that motor racing needs big names. I will make my decision known to Brabham in Las Vegas."

James duly appeared on television and announced that he would reluctantly have to turn down the offer while Peter Hunt, no doubt, was busy gathering his brother's press clippings . . .

That story finished, rumours that the 1980 World Champion may not be retiring after all gathered strength. And, at the end of the day, Nelson Piquet said he would carry number 1 on his Brabham while poor Carlos Reutemann simply wished that he could be a World Champion . . .

Caesars Palace Grand Prix, October 17/statistics

Entries and practice times

No.	Driver	Nat	Car	Engine	Entrant	Practice 1	Practice 2
1	Alan Jones	AUS	Saudia-Leyland WILLIAMS FWO7C	Ford Cosworth DFV	TAG Williams Team	1m 18·236s	**1m 17·995s**
2	Carlos Reutemann	RA	Saudia-Leyland WILLIAMS FWO7C	Ford Cosworth DFV	TAG Williams Team	**1m 17·821s**	1m 18·343s
3	Eddie Cheever	USA	TYRRELL 011	Ford Cosworth DFV	Tyrrell Racing	1m 21·116s	**1m 20·475s**
4	Michele Alboreto	I	TYRRELL 011	Ford Cosworth DFV	Tyrrell Racing	1m 21·964s	**1m 19·774s**
5	Nelson Piquet	BR	Parmalat BRABHAM BT49C	Ford Cosworth DFV	Parmalat Racing Team	1m 18·954s	**1m 18·161s**
6	Hector Rebaque	MEX	Parmalat BRABHAM BT49C	Ford Cosworth DFV	Parmalat Racing Team	1m 20·555s	**1m 19·571s**
7	John Watson	GB	Marlboro McLAREN MP4	Ford Cosworth DFV	McLaren International	1m 19·975s	**1m 18·617s**
8	Andrea de Cesaris	I	Marlboro McLAREN MP4	Ford Cosworth DFV	McLaren International	1m 19·338s	**1m 19·217s**
9	Slim Borgudd	S	Abba ATS HGS 1	Ford Cosworth DFV	Team ATS	**1m 21·665s**	1m 21·731s
11	Elio de Angelis	I	John Player Special LOTUS 87	Ford Cosworth DFV	John Player Team Lotus	1m 20·337s	**1m 19·562s**
12	Nigel Mansell	GB	John Player Special LOTUS 87	Ford Cosworth DFV	John Player Team Lotus	**1m 19·044s**	1m 19·623s
14	Eliseo Salazar	RCH	ENSIGN N180B	Ford Cosworth DFV	Ensign Racing	1m 22·616s	**1m 21·629s**
15	Alain Prost	F	Elf RENAULT RE 30	Renault EF1	Equipe Renault Elf	**1m 18·433s**	1m 18·760s
16	René Arnoux	F	Elf RENAULT RE 30	Renault EF1	Equipe Renault Elf	1m 19·966s	**1m 19·197s**
17	Derek Daly	IRL	Rizla MARCH 811	Ford Cosworth DFV	March Grand Prix	1m 21·846s	**1m 21·824s**
20	Keke Rosberg	SF	FITTIPALDI F8C	Ford Cosworth DFV	Fittipaldi Automotive	1m 21·299s	**1m 20·729s**
21	Chico Serra	BR	FITTIPALDI F8C	Ford Cosworth DFV	Fittipaldi Automotive	1m 22·612s	**1m 21·672s**
22	Mario Andretti	USA	Marlboro ALFA ROMEO 179C	Alfa Romeo 1260	Marlboro Team Alfa Romeo	1m 19·594s	**1m 19·068s**
23	Bruno Giacomelli	I	Marlboro ALFA ROMEO 179C	Alfa Romeo 1260	Marlboro Team Alfa Romeo	1m 20·570s	**1m 18·792s**
25	Patrick Tambay	F	Talbot-Gitanes LIGIER JS17	Matra MS 81	Equipe Talbot Gitanes	1m 19·874s	**1m 18·681s**
26	Jacques Laffite	F	Talbot-Gitanes LIGIER JS17	Matra MS 81	Equipe Talbot Gitanes	1m 19·878s	**1m 19·167s**
27	Gilles Villeneuve	CDN	Fiat FERRARI 126CK	Ferrari 126C	Scuderia Ferrari SpA SEFAC	1m 18·457s	**1m 18·060s**
28	Didier Pironi	F	Fiat FERRARI 126CK	Ferrari 126C	Scuderia Ferrari SpA SEFAC	**1m 19·899s**	1m 21·347s
29	Riccardo Patrese	I	Ragno-Beta ARROWS A3	Ford Cosworth DFV	Arrows Racing Team	1m 20·132s	**1m 19·152s**
30	Jacques Villeneuve	CDN	Ragno-Beta ARROWS A3	Ford Cosworth DFV	Arrows Racing Team	1m 22·977s	**1m 22·822s**
31	Beppe Gabbiani	I	Denim OSELLA FA1B	Ford Cosworth DFV	Osella Squadra Corse	**1m 26·634s**	—
32	Jean-Pierre Jarier	F	Denim OSELLA FA1C	Ford Cosworth DFV	Osella Squadra Corse	—	**1m 20·781s**
33	Marc Surer	CH	THEODORE TY 01	Ford Cosworth DFV	Theodore Racing Team	1m 21·889s	**1m 21·430s**
35	Brian Henton	GB	Candy TOLEMAN TG 181	Hart 415T	Candy Toleman Motorsport	1m 23·857s	**1m 22·960s**
36	Derek Warwick	GB	Candy TOLEMAN TG 181	Hart 415T	Candy Toleman Motorsport	1m 22·491s	**1m 21·294s**
Thursday morning and Friday morning practice sessions not officially recorded						*Thur pm Cool, dry*	*Fri pm Hot, dry*

Starting grid

	2 REUTEMANN (1m 17·821s) Williams
2 JONES (1m 17·995s) Williams	
	27 VILLENEUVE (1m 18·060s) Ferrari
5 PIQUET (1m 18·161s) Brabham	
	15 PROST (1m 18·433s) Renault
7 WATSON (1m 18·617s) McLaren	
	25 TAMBAY (1m 18·681s) Talbot-Ligier
23 GIACOMELLI (1m 18·792s) Alfa Romeo	
	12 MANSELL (1m 19·044s) Lotus
22 ANDRETTI (1m 19·068s) Alfa Romeo	
	29 PATRESE (1m 19·152s) Arrows
26 LAFFITE (1m 19·167s) Talbot-Ligier	
	16 ARNOUX (1m 19·197s) Renault
8 DE CESARIS (1m 19·217s) McLaren	
	11 DE ANGELIS (1m 19·562s) Lotus
6 REBAQUE (1m 19·571s) Brabham	
	4 ALBORETO (1m 19·774s) Tyrrell
28 PIRONI (1m 19·899s) Ferrari	
	3 CHEEVER (1m 20·475s) Tyrrell
20 ROSBERG (1m 20·729s) Fittipaldi	
	32 JARIER (1m 20·781s) Osella
36 WARWICK (1m 21·294s) Toleman	
	33 SURER (1m 21·430s) Theodore
14 SALAZAR (1m 21·629s) Ensign	

Did not start:
9 Borgudd (ATS), 1m 21·665s, did not qualify
26 Serra (Fittipaldi), 1m 21·672s, did not qualify
17 Daly (March), 1m 21·824s, did not qualify
30 Villeneuve (Arrows), 1m 22·822s, did not qualify
35 Henton (Toleman), 1m 22·960s, did not qualify
31 Gabbiani (Osella), 1m 26·634s, did not qualify

Past winners

Year	Driver	Nat	Car	Circuit	Distance miles/km	Speed mph/km/h
1981	Alan Jones	AUS	3·0 Williams FWO7C-Ford	Caesars Palace	170·1/273·75	97·9/157·55

Circuit data

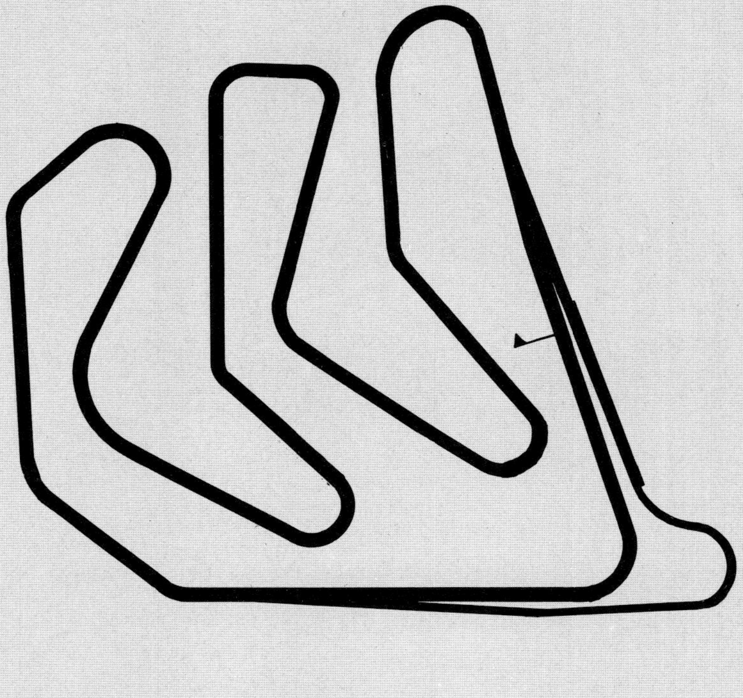

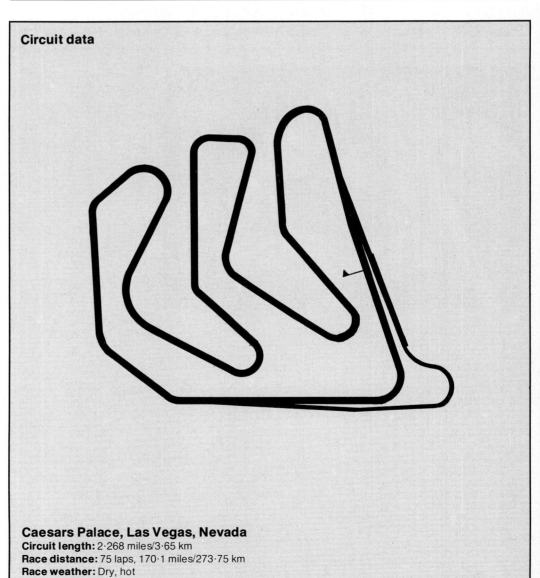

Caesars Palace, Las Vegas, Nevada
Circuit length: 2·268 miles/3·65 km
Race distance: 75 laps, 170·1 miles/273·75 km
Race weather: Dry, hot

Results and retirements

Place	Driver	Car	Laps	Time and Speed (mph/km/h)/Retirement	
1	Alan Jones	Williams-Cosworth V8	75	1h 44m 09·077s	97·9/157·554
2	Alain Prost	Renault t/c V6	75	1h 44m 29·125s	97·6/157·071
3	Bruno Giacomelli	Alfa Romeo V12	75	1h 44m 29·505s	97·6/157·071
4	Nigel Mansell	Lotus-Cosworth V8	75	1h 44m 56·550s	97·2/156·428
5	Nelson Piquet	Brabham-Cosworth V8	75	1h 45m 25·515s	96·8/155·784
6	Jacques Laffite	Talbot-Ligier Matra V12	75	1h 45m 27·252s	96·7/155·623
7	John Watson	McLaren-Cosworth V8	75	1h 45m 27·574s	96·7/155·623
8	Carlos Reutemann	Williams-Cosworth V8	74		
9	Didier Pironi	Ferrari t/c V6	73		
10	Keke Rosberg	Fittipaldi-Cosworth V8	73		
11	Riccardo Patrese	Arrows-Cosworth V8	71		
12	Andrea de Cesaris	McLaren-Cosworth V8	69		
	Michele Alboreto	Tyrrell-Cosworth V8	67	Running, not classified	
	Eliseo Salazar	Ensign-Cosworth V8	61	Running, not classified	
	Derek Warwick	Toleman t/c Straight 4	43	Gearbox	
	Mario Andretti	Alfa Romeo V12	29	Rear suspension	
	Hector Rebaque	Brabham-Cosworth V8	20	Spun off	
	Marc Surer	Theodore-Cosworth V8	19	Rear suspension	
	Eddie Cheever	Tyrrell-Cosworth V8	10	Engine	
	René Arnoux	Renault t/c V6	10	Electrics	
	Patrick Tambay	Talbot-Ligier Matra V12	2	Accident	
	Elio de Angelis	Lotus-Cosworth V8	2	Water leak	
	Jean-Pierre Jarier	Osella-Cosworth V8	0	Transmission	
	Gilles Villeneuve	Ferrari t/c V6	–	Disqualified	

Fastest lap: Pironi, on lap 49, 1m 20·156s, 101·861mph/163·929km/h (record).
Previous lap record: Teo Fabi (CanAm March 817-Chevrolet), 1m 24·105s, 97·078mph/156·234km/h (1981).

Lap chart

1st LAP ORDER		1	2	3	4	5	6	7	8	9	10	11	12	13	14	15	16	17	18	19	20	21	22	23	24	25	26	27	28	29	30	31	32	33	34
1	A.Jones	1	1	1	1	1	1	1	1	1	1	1	1	1	1	1	1	1	1	1	1	1	1	1	1	1	1	1	1	1	1	1	1	1	1
27	G.Villeneuve	27	27	15	15	15	15	15	15	15	15	15	15	15	15	15	15	15	15	15	15	15	15	15	15	15	15	15	15	15	15	15	(15)	26	26
15	A.Prost	15	15	27	27	27	27	27	27	27	27	27	27	27	27	27	27	27	27	27	27	27	27	26	26	26	26	26	26	26	26	26	26	5	5
23	B.Giacomelli	23	23	23	23	23	23	23	23	23	23	23	23	23	23	23	23	23	23	23	23	23	23	23	23	23	23	22	22	22	5	5	5	12	12
2	C.Reutemann	2	7	7	26	26	26	26	26	26	26	26	26	26	26	26	26	26	26	26	26	26	26	22	22	22	22	5	5	5	2	2	12	2	2
7	J.Watson	7	2	26	7	7	7	7	7	7	7	7	7	7	7	7	7	7	7	7	7	7	5	5	5	5	5	7	7	2	12	12	2	15	15
26	J.Laffite	26	26	2	2	2	2	2	2	2	2	2	2	2	2	2	2	5	5	5	5	5	7	7	7	7	7	2	2	12	23	23	23	23	23
5	N.Piquet	5	5	5	5	5	5	5	5	5	5	5	5	5	5	5	2	22	22	22	22	22	22	2	2	2	2	12	12	(7)	29	29	4	7	7
12	N.Mansell	12	12	12	22	22	22	22	22	22	22	22	22	22	22	22	22	2	2	2	2	2	2	12	12	12	12	29	29	29	4	4	7	4	4
25	P.Tambay	25	22	22	12	16	16	16	16	16	8	12	12	12	12	12	12	12	12	12	12	12	12	29	29	29	29	23	23	23	7	7	(29)	20	20
22	M.Andretti	22	25	16	16	8	8	8	8	8	12	29	29	29	29	29	29	29	29	29	29	29	29	4	4	4	4	4	4	4	20	20	20	29	29
8	A.de Cesaris	8	15	8	8	12	12	12	12	12	29	6	6	6	6	6	6	6	6	6	4	4	4	8	8	8	(8)	20	20	20	28	28	28	28	28
16	R.Arnoux	16	3	3	3	3	28	28	28	28	28	28	28	28	28	28	4	4	4	4	8	8	8	20	20	20	20	28	28	28	36	36	36	36	36
6	H.Rebaque	6	3	28	28	28	29	29	29	29	6	4	4	4	4	4	(28)	20	20	8	20	20	20	36	28	28	28	36	36	36	8	8	8	8	8
3	E.Cheever	3	29	29	29	29	3	3	3	6	3	20	20	20	20	20	20	8	8	20	36	36	36	28	36	36	36	8	8	8	14	14	14	14	14
29	R.Patrese	29	5	6	6	6	6	6	6	3	4	36	36	36	36	8	8	36	36	36	(6)	28	28	14	14	14	14	14	14	14					
11	E.de Angelis	11	28	20	20	20	20	20	4	4	20	33	33	33	8	36	36	33	28	28	28	14	14												
28	D.Pironi	28	20	4	4	4	4	4	20	20	(16)	(8)	8	8	33	33	33	(28)	(33)	(33)	14														
20	K.Rosberg	20	36	36	36	36	36	36	36	36	36	14	14	14	14	(14)	14	14	14	14															
36	D.Warwick	36	4	33	33	33	33	33	33	33	33																								
14	E.Salazar	14	33	14	14	14	(14)	14	14	14	14																								
4	M.Alboreto	4	14																																
33	M.Surer	33	(11)																																

35	36	37	38	39	40	41	42	43	44	45	46	47	48	49	50	51	52	53	54	55	56	57	58	59	60	61	62	63	64	65	66	67	68	69	70	71	72	73	74	75
1	1	1	1	1	1	1	1	1	1	1	1	1	1	1	1	1	1	1	1	1	1	1	1	1	1	1	1	1	1	1	1	1	1	1	1	1	1	1	1	1
26	26	26	26	26	26	26	26	26	26	26	15	15	15	15	15	15	15	15	15	15	15	15	15	15	15	15	15	15	15	15	15	15	15	15	15	15	15	15	15	15
5	5	5	5	5	5	5	5	5	5	5	26	26	26	26	5	5	12	12	12	12	12	12	23	23	23	23	23	23	23	23	23	23	23	23	23	23	23	23	23	23
12	15	15	15	15	15	15	15	15	15	15	5	5	5	5	26	12	5	5	23	23	23	23	12	12	12	12	12	12	12	12	12	12	12	12	12	12	12	12	12	12
15	12	12	12	12	12	12	12	12	12	12	12	12	12	12	12	26	23	23	5	5	5	5	5	5	5	5	5	5	5	5	5	5	5	5	5	5	5	5	5	5
2	2	2	2	2	2	2	2	2	2	2	23	23	23	23	23	23	(26)	2	2	2	2	2	2	7	7	7	7	7	7	7	7	7	7	7	7	7	7	7	7	26
23	23	23	23	23	23	23	23	23	23	23	2	2	2	2	2	2	2	7	7	7	7	7	7	2	2	2	2	2	2	2	2	2	2	26	26	26	26	26	26	7
7	7	7	7	7	7	7	7	7	7	7	7	7	7	7	7	7	7	26	26	26	26	26	26	26	26	26	26	26	26	26	26	26	26	2	2	2	2	2	2	
4	4	4	4	4	4	4	4	4	4	4	4	4	4	4	4	4	4	4	4	4	4	4	4	4	4	4	4	4	4	4	4	(4)	20	20	20	20	20	20		
20	20	20	20	20	20	20	20	20	20	20	20	20	20	20	20	20	20	20	20	20	20	20	20	20	20	20	20	20	20	20	20	20	28	28	28	28	28			
29	29	29	29	29	29	29	29	29	29	29	29	29	29	29	29	29	29	29	29	29	(29)	28	28	28	28	28	28	28	28	28	28	28	29	29	29	29				
28	28	28	28	28	28	28	28	28	28	(28)	28	28	28	28	28	28	28	28	28	28	28	29	29	29	29	29	29	29	29	29	29	29	8	8						
36	36	36	36	36	36	36	36	8	8	8	8	8	8	8	8	8	8	8	8	8	8	8	8	8	8	8	8	8	8	8	8	8								
8	8	8	8	8	8	8	8	14	14	14	14	14	14	14	14	14	14	14	14	14	14	14	14	14	14	14	14													
14	14	14	14	14	14	14	14																																	

Fastest laps

Driver	Time	Lap
Didier Pironi	1m 20·156s	49
Andrea de Cesaris	1m 20·302s	29
John Watson	1m 21·178s	32
Alain Prost	1m 21·249s	41
Jacques Laffite	1m 21·337s	73
Alan Jones	1m 21·642s	14
Bruno Giacomelli	1m 21·748s	54
Mario Andretti	1m 21·883s	28
Riccardo Patrese	1m 21·969s	49
Nigel Mansell	1m 22·477s	65
Nelson Piquet	1m 22·679s	31
Carlos Reutemann	1m 22·916s	11
Hector Rebaque	1m 23·012s	19
Michele Alboreto	1m 23·231s	25
René Arnoux	1m 23·473s	5
Keke Rosberg	1m 24·370s	15
Eliseo Salazar	1m 24·606s	50
Eddie Cheever	1m 24·619s	8
Derek Warwick	1m 25·104s	36
Marc Surer	1m 26·133s	12
Patrick Tambay	3m 02·696s	2
Elio de Angelis	3m 22·696s	2

Points

WORLD CHAMPIONSHIP OF DRIVERS

1	Nelson Piquet	50 pts
2	Carlos Reutemann	49
3	Alan Jones	46
4	Jacques Laffite	44
5	Alain Prost	43
6	John Watson	27
7	Gilles Villeneuve	25
8	Elio de Angelis	14
9 =	René Arnoux	11
9 =	Hector Rebaque	11
11 =	Riccardo Patrese	10
11 =	Eddie Cheever	10
13	Didier Pironi	9
14	Nigel Mansell	8
15	Bruno Giacomelli	7
16	Marc Surer	4
17	Mario Andretti	3
18 =	Patrick Tambay	1
18 =	Andrea de Cesaris	1
18 =	Slim Borgudd	1
18 =	Eliseo Salazar	1

CONSTRUCTORS' CUP

1	Williams	95
2	Brabham	61
3	Renault	54
4	Ligier	44
5	Ferrari	34
6	McLaren	28
7	Lotus	22
8 =	Arrows	10
8 =	Tyrrell	10
8 =	Alfa Romeo	10
11	Ensign	5
12 =	Theodore	1
12 =	ATS	1

Nashua Grand Prix of South Africa, Kyalami, February 7

The gamble that paid off. FOCA ran their own race, with skirts, at Kyalami to open the Formula 1 season. Nelson Piquet was fastest in both practice sessions and led comfortably in the wet conditions at the start. The track dried out quickly and the Brabham driver had to give best to Carlos Reutemann. Starting on slicks, Reutemann was never lower than eighth in the treacherous conditions and moved into the lead just before half distance. John Watson showed well in the rain, as did Nigel Mansell, but it was Elio de Angelis who took a spectacular third place after running on slicks throughout.

Entries and practice times

No.	Driver	Nat	Car	Engine	Entrant	Practice 1	Practice 2
1	Alan Jones	AUS	Saudia-Leyland WILLIAMS FWO7B	Ford Cosworth V8	Albilad-Williams Racing Team	1m 13·78s	**1m 13·28s**
2	Carlos Reutemann	RA	Saudia-Leyland WILLIAMS FWO7B	Ford Cosworth V8	Albilad-Williams Racing Team	**1m 12·98s**	–
3	Eddie Cheever	I	TYRRELL 010	Ford Cosworth V8	Tyrrell Racing	**1m 14·95s**	1m 15·32s
4	Desiré Wilson	ZA	Deutz TYRRELL 010	Ford Cosworth V8	Tyrrell Racing	**1m 15·56s**	1m 16·22s
5	Nelson Piquet	BR	Parmalat BRABHAM BT49	Ford Cosworth V8	Parmalat Racing Team	1m 12·94s	**1m 12·78s**
6	Ricardo Zunino	RA	Parmalat BRABHAM BT49	Ford Cosworth V8	Parmalat Racing Team	1m 14·71s	**1m 14·35s**
7	John Watson	GB	Marlboro McLAREN M29	Ford Cosworth V8	McLaren International	**1m 15·25s**	1m 15·85s
8	Andrea de Cesaris	I	Marlboro McLAREN M29	Ford Cosworth V8	McLaren International	1m 14·91s	**1m 14·39s**
9	Jan Lammers	NL	ATS D4	Ford Cosworth V8	Team ATS	1m 14·93s	**1m 14·85s**
11	Elio de Angelis	I	Essex LOTUS 81	Ford Cosworth V8	Team Essex Lotus	1m 14·00s	**1m 13·47s**
12	Nigel Mansell	GB	Essex LOTUS 81	Ford Cosworth V8	Team Essex Lotus	**1m 14·38s**	1m 14·48s
14	Marc Surer	CH	ENSIGN N180B	Ford Cosworth V8	Ensign Racing	1m 15·63s	**1m 15·18s**
17	Derek Daly	IRL	MARCH 811	Ford Cosworth V8	March Grand Prix	**1m 16·80s**	–
18	Eliseo Salazar	RCH	MARCH 811	Ford Cosworth V8	March Grand Prix	–	–
20	Keke Rosberg	SF	FITTIPALDI F8C	Ford Cosworth V8	Fittipaldi Automotive	1m 14·45s	**1m 13·29s**
21	Chico Serra	BR	FITTIPALDI F8	Ford Cosworth V8	Fittipaldi Automotive	**1m 15·06s**	–
29	Riccardo Patrese	I	Ragno-Beta ARROWS A3	Ford Cosworth V8	Arrows Racing Team	1m 15·03s	**1m 14·07s**
30	Siegfried Stohr	I	Ragno-Beta ARROWS A3	Ford Cosworth V8	Arrows Racing Team	1m 16·16s	**1m 14·93s**
33	Geoff Lees	GB	THEODORE TR2	Ford Cosworth V8	Theodore Racing Team	1m 17·39s	**1m 17·08s**
Thursday morning and Friday morning practice sessions not officially recorded						*Thur pm Hot, dry*	*Fri pm Cool, dry then wet*

Starting grid

5 PIQUET (1m 12·78s)
Brabham

2 REUTEMANN (1m 12·98s)
Williams

1 JONES (1m 13·28s)
Williams

20 ROSBERG (1m 13·29s)
Fittipaldi

11 DE ANGELIS (1m 13·47s)
Lotus

29 PATRESE (1m 14·07s)
Arrows

6 ZUNINO (1m 14·35s)
Brabham

12 MANSELL (1m 14·38s)
Lotus

8 DE CESARIS (1m 14·39s)
McLaren

9 LAMMERS (1m 14·85s)
ATS

30 STOHR (1m 14·93s)
Arrows

3 CHEEVER (1m 14·95s)
Tyrrell

21 SERRA (1m 15·06s)
Fittipaldi

14 SURER (1m 15·18s)
Ensign

7 WATSON (1m 15·25s)
McLaren

4 WILSON (1m 15·56s)
Tyrrell

17 DALY (1m 16·80s)
March

33 LEES (1m 17·08s)
Theodore

18 SALAZAR (no time recorded)
March

Results and retirements

Place	Driver	Car	Laps	Time and Speed (mph/km/h)/Retirement	
1	Carlos Reutemann	Williams-Cosworth V8	77	1h 44m 54·03s	112.31/180.75
2	Nelson Piquet	Brabham-Cosworth V8	77	1h 45m 14·17s	
3	Elio de Angelis	Lotus-Cosworth V8	77	1h 46m 00·27s	
4	Keke Rosberg	Fittipaldi-Cosworth V8	76		
5	John Watson	McLaren-Cosworth V8	76		
6	Riccardo Patrese	Arrows-Cosworth V8	76		
7	Eddie Cheever	Tyrrell-Cosworth V8	76		
8	Ricardo Zunino	Brabham-Cosworth V8	75		
9	Chico Serra	Fittipaldi-Cosworth V8	75		
10	Nigel Mansell	Lotus-Cosworth V8	74		
11	Derek Daly	March-Cosworth V8	74		
	Alan Jones	Williams-Cosworth V8	62	Damaged skirt	
	Marc Surer	Ensign-Cosworth V8	58	Loose battery	
	Andrea de Cesaris	McLaren-Cosworth V8	54	Spun off	
	Desiré Wilson	Tyrrell-Cosworth V8	52	Spun off	
	Eliseo Salazar	March-Cosworth V8	32	Gearbox	
	Jan Lammers	ATS-Cosworth V8	17	Brakes	
	Siegfried Stohr	Arrows-Cosworth V8	12	Engine/valve	
	Geoff Lees	Theodore-Cosworth V8	11	Accident	

Fastest lap: Reutemann, on lap 72, 1m 13·61s, 124.71mph/200.70km/h.
Lap record: René Arnoux (F1 Renault t/c V6), 1m 13·15s, 125·49mph/201·96km/h (1980).

Fastest laps

Driver	Time	Lap
Carlos Reutemann	1m 13·61s	72
Nelson Piquet	1m 13·89s	67
Ricardo Zunino	1m 14·54s	74
Nigel Mansell	1m 14·67s	73
Elio de Angelis	1m 14·73s	59
Keke Rosberg	1m 14·89s	55
Alan Jones	1m 15·00s	53
Riccardo Patrese	1m 15·19s	69
Chico Serra	1m 15·34s	64
John Watson	1m 15·44s	70
Marc Surer	1m 16·14s	57
Eddie Cheever	1m 16·20s	60
Andrea de Cesaris	1m 16·20s	51
Desiré Wilson	1m 17·18s	48
Derek Daly	1m 17·84s	71

Past winners

Year	Driver	Nat	Car	Circuit	Distance miles/km	Speed mph/km/h
1934	Whitney Straight	GB	2·9 Maserati 8CM s/c	Prince George	91·20/146·77	95·68/153·98
1936	'Mario' Massacurati	I	2·0 Bugatti T35B s/c	Prince George	198·54/319·52	87·43/140·70
1937	Pat Fairfield	ZA	1·0 ERA A-type s/c	Prince George	198·54/319·52	89·17/143·50
1938	Buller Meyer	ZA	1·5 Riley	Prince George	198·54/319·52	86·53/139·26
1939	Luigi Villoresi	I	1·5 Maserati 4CM	Prince George	198·54/319·52	99·67/160·40
1960*	Paul Frère	B	1·5 Cooper T45-Climax	East London	145·80/234·64	84·88/136·60
1960*	Stirling Moss	GB	1·5 Porsche 718	East London	194·40/312·86	89·24/143·62
1961*	Jim Clark	GB	1·5 Lotus 21-Climax	East London	194·40/312·86	92·20/148·38
1962	Graham Hill	GB	1·5 BRM P57	East London	199·26/320·68	93·57/150·59
1963	Jim Clark	GB	1·5 Lotus 25-Climax	East London	206·55/332·41	95·10/153·05
1965	Jim Clark	GB	1·5 Lotus 25-Climax	East London	206·55/332·41	97·97/157·68
1966*	Mike Spence	GB	2·0 Lotus 33-Climax	East London	145·80/234·64	97·75/157·31
1967	Pedro Rodriguez	MEX	3·0 Cooper T81-Maserati	Kyalami	203·52/327·53	97·09/156·25
1968	Jim Clark	GB	3·0 Lotus 49-Ford	Kyalami	204·00/328·31	107·42/172·88
1969	Jackie Stewart	GB	3·0 Matra MS10-Ford	Kyalami	204·00/328·31	110·62/178·03
1970	Jack Brabham	AUS	3·0 Brabham BT33-Ford	Kyalami	204·00/328·31	111·70/179·76
1971	Mario Andretti	USA	3·0 Ferrari 312B-1/71	Kyalami	201·45/324·20	112·36/180·83
1972	Denny Hulme	NZ	3·0 McLaren M19A-Ford	Kyalami	201·41/324·20	114·23/183·83
1973	Jackie Stewart	GB	3·0 Tyrrell 006-Ford	Kyalami	201·45/324·20	117·14/188·52
1974	Carlos Reutemann	RA	3·0 Brabham BT44-Ford	Kyalami	198·90/320·10	116·22/187·04
1975	Jody Scheckter	ZA	3·0 Tyrrell 007-Ford	Kyalami	198·90/320·10	115·55/185·96
1976	Niki Lauda	A	3·0 Ferrari 312T/76	Kyalami	198·90/320·10	116·65/187·73
1977	Niki Lauda	A	3·0 Ferrari 312T-2/77	Kyalami	198·90/320·10	116·59/187·63
1978	Ronnie Peterson	S	3·0 JPS/Lotus 78-Ford	Kyalami	198·90/320·10	116·70/187·81
1979	Gilles Villeneuve	CDN	3·0 Ferrari 312T-4	Kyalami	198·90/320·10	117·19/188·60
1980	René Arnoux	F	1·5 Renault RE t/c	Kyalami	198·90/320·10	123·19/198·25
1981*	Carlos Reutemann	RA	3·0 Williams FWO7B-Ford	Kyalami	196·35/315·99	112·31/180·75

*Non-championship

Circuit data
Kyalami Grand Prix Circuit, Johannesburg

Circuit length: 2·55 miles/4·104 km
Race distance: 77 laps, 196·35 miles/315·99 km
Race weather: Warm, wet then dry.

Bitter-sweet season for Lees and Ralt-Honda

by Ian Phillips, Formula 2 Correspondent, *Autosport*

Corrado Fabi took a mature win at Mugello in his March-BMW.

A bookmaker would not have given very long odds on the outcome of this year's European Formula 2 championship before it began. The Ralt-Honda team had clearly shown its hand at the conclusion of the 1980 season and the prospect was of a succession of professional one-two victories, the interest being solely which driver would be *allowed* to win.

How wrong one can be!

The statistics reveal that eight drivers, five chassis, three engines and two tyre manufacturers shared the victory spoils. It was not, as is often the case in such an open year, a battle for supremacy among the mediocre. It was a clean contest at the highest level of skill and engineering conducted in the pleasant atmosphere which epitomises Formula 2.

Ron Tauranac and Honda last combined in the 1-litre Formula 2 of the mid-sixties. After one exploratory year they wiped the board in 1966. They joined forces again in 1980 to explore the scene. Their final probe of the year indicated that gold was within striking distance, when at Hockenheim their two cars did everything but win. With six months to prepare for the strike, the writing on the wall became increasingly indelible as the team took shape.

The ample Honda budget gave Tauranac a free choice of drivers and he picked 30-year-old Geoff Lees and 19-year-old Mike Thackwell. Neither had to bring money, indeed both were paid. It was an enviable position and a good choice.

Honda took the 80 degree V6 iron block engine back to Japan for a development and refinement programme which would, hopefully, result in increased performance but, more importantly at this stage, allow a full consummation of its marriage to Tauranac's aerodynamically refined Ralt chassis. The contrasting backgrounds of the two major elements did not match the generics required by the modern ground effects racing car. The industrious Japanese complied with Tauranac's requests and supplied 20 of their engines to the team with a claimed 10% power advantage over the 315bhp best BMWs and Harts.

Over the winter one element unforseeably changed: tyres. Goodyear withdrew leaving Pirelli, whose radials had won the championship for Toleman the year before, to fill the void. A few teams opted to go with M&H but the leading runners all went with the Italian firm. Bad weather reduced pre-season testing opportunities and come the first race at a wet and blustery Silverstone it became obvious that the Pirelli radials were no simple bolt-on option. Thackwell, just a day before his 20th birthday, and without the experience to be prejudicial about the set-up of the car, displayed brilliant form all weekend and cleaned up despite a team which was all at sea.

A week later at Hockenheim the New Zealander, despite a practice accident, looked all set to lead home a Ralt-Honda 1-2. Then it went wrong. Thackwell began to run out of fuel and Lees, having started on marginal tyres, spun away victory. In unofficial practice at a ridiculously bumpy Thruxton, Thackwell had one of motor racing's biggest impact accidents. Unconscious for three days and with a broken left leg, he left the next three races to Lees. The quietly spoken Midlander, having made his debut for the team at the final 1980 race and then taken the gamble to forsake the money of CanAm and the lure of Formula 1 to concentrate on Formula 2, was not a happy man at this stage. It was just not the car he had expected. The handling on the Pirelli radials destroyed his confidence and the narrow power band and poor pick-up of the engine just compounded his problems and he began to make uncharacteristic mistakes.

Following a lead set by the March team, Tauranac switched to Japanese Bridgestone radials at Thruxton. A hard working two man engineering team had watched, listened, measured and photographed every aspect of Formula 2 tyre technology in the first two rounds in preparation for their European debut. Their product proved itself immediately on the vice-less March-BMW chassis. The Ralt-Honda team had other bugs to iron out still but the Bridgestones immediately gave Lees his confidence back. At least the car felt safe. Thackwell's two chassis bending accidents had kept the team busy with repairs between

Geoff Lees gambled by stepping back into Formula 2 but three wins with his Ralt-Honda gave the English driver a well deserved championship.
Photo: Rodger Calvert

Of the many newcomers, Roberto Guerrero (Maurer-BMW) ranked among the best. The Columbian won at Thruxton *(below)*. Thierry Boutsen scored two wirs in the works March-BMW, victory at the Nürburgring being his most impressive *(bottom)*.

races and it was not until after the fifth race that they afforded themselves the luxury of a test day away from the spotlight which, by this time, was shining embarrassingly strongly.

That day appeared to make all the difference. At Mugello, venue of the test, Lees led initially and finished a good second. The tide had undoubtedly turned. At Pau he became winner number seven in what he rated as his hardest drive. He would have won at Enna but for the overweight car (almost 100lbs over the limit) overheating an adventurous choice of soft compound Bridgestones to self-destruct proportions. The message was loud and clear; the combination had clicked. Unchallenged wins at Spa and Donington put Lees in the lead of the championship and second place at Misano wrapped it up. The second half of Lees' season was as sweet as the first was bitter and his clean, commanding performances, making full use of the equipment at his disposal, made him a worthy winner of the championship.

Thackwell made his comeback at Mugello and it was questionable if he was really fit. Nevertheless he scored points in his first two comeback races and in the third was on the front row. From there on though, his season went downhill as he found it difficult to string together clean laps and he never showed the form which everyone knew he was capable of. The accident and rapid comeback probably took more out of him than he was prepared to admit.

With no more than a detailed update on their 802 chassis, the well-known 4-cylinder BMW engine and two drivers, Thierry Boutsen and Corrado Fabi, fresh out of European F3, March Racing were, for once, the underdogs. But the management of John Wickham and Gordon Coppuck had done their winter homework well. At Silverstone the young cubs qualified second and third. Fabi, the youngest man in the series, finishing third. "Beginner's Luck" thought everyone at Hockenheim a week later as the team had a horrid weekend. But it wasn't. The Belgian Boutsen switched to Bridgestones at Thruxton and took the first of five pole positions and two wins; Nürburgring, by an incredible 62 secs, and Enna. Fabi, who stayed faithful to Pirelli throughout, joined his team-mate on the front row three times and scored a very mature win at Mugello. He wasn't as consistent as his team mate, who challenged Lees for the championship up to the penultimate round, but both of them showed exciting potential and are certain stars of the future.

With everyone having to use Pirellis at the start of the season, it looked certain that the reigning champions Toleman would have an early advantage with their previous year's experience. The works team was entrusted to the Silverstone based Docking-Spitzley team with the powerful but woefully under-budgeted Stefan Johansson and Kenny Acheson as drivers. Johansson scored the season's most spectacular win at Hockenheim when he silenced 80,000 partisan Germans by overtaking Manfred Winkelhock at the penultimate corner on the last lap. Both drivers finished in the points at Nürburgring and Johansson finished a good second at Vallelunga as one of Pirellis favoured runners of the weekend. Acheson, who had outqualified his team mate in three of the first four races, was not looked after by Pirelli and was subjected to a confidence shattering uncompetitive period. He and the team overcame it all at Pau when he put his car on the front row but disaster followed as he had an enormous accident while attempting to wrestle the lead. The resultant badly broken right leg put him out until the last race.

With Acheson out and Pirelli moving further and further away from the stiff sidewall tyres required by the Toleman, Johansson and the team went through a torrid patch which not even the Swede's extraordinary *racing* ability could lift them from. However it all came back at the last race when Johansson won in devastating style on home ground and Acheson, debuting the new Avon tyres, took a marvellous, and brave, third. Johansson's third place in the championship was just reward for the best race driver of the year while Acheson surely did enough to illustrate that he's got what it takes.

The German Maurer-BMW team often promised to carry all before them but somehow their results were not commensurate with their potential. Both the experienced Eje Elgh and newcomer Roberto Guerrero won a race apiece but, mainly due to Pirelli's mid-season disinterest, were able to do no more than contest the lesser points placings. The Gustav Brunner-designed chassis was the neatest and cleanest of all and the reliability, in particular Elgh's, was excellent. In a year of many impressive newcomers, Guerrero ranked among the best although on occasions he tended to overdrive.

The Italian Minardi team, in their second year as constructors, broke their duck before a home crowd at Misano when Michele Alboreto drove a storming race to become winner number eight. Sometimes criticised for being overly aggressive, there is no doubting that this young man is a racer in the Johansson class.

Of those that didn't win races, Ricardo Paletti threatened to early on in the Onyx March and Huub Rothengatter in the second half of the year in a similar private March. Richard Dallest rarely looked like giving the French AGS outfit further success despite occasional flashes of competitiveness. As the year wore on Johnny Cecotto looked increasingly likely to make the grade on four wheels as he got to grips with the Markus Hotz March. The Toleman was never a good customer car even though Jim Crawford and Jo Gartner did their utmost on limited resources.

All in all, a supremely competitive year and with all the major teams continuing in 1982 and being joined by a second Honda powered team, the prospects are extremely healthy.

Doctor's dilemma

by David Tremayne, Formula 3 Correspondent, *Motoring News*

Raul Boesel showed excellent form in his Ralt RT3 during the Brazilian's first season of Formula 3 *(right)*.
A superb win in the rain at Silverstone for Jonathan Palmer and his Ralt RT3 was a fitting prelude to a successful season for the Sussex doctor *(below)*.
Photo: Bruce Grant-Braham

1981 may well be looked back on as a vintage year of Formula 3 racing. With Vandervell's withdrawal, Marlboro eagerly stepped forward to sponsor the UK national series and the tobacco giant's offer of Formula 1 test drives to the top three points scorers acted as a major incentive to the young lions and ensured healthy grids, particularly in the early races.

Throughout the season the quality of competition remained at a very high level and the category pushed several new names into the limelight. However, just when it seemed that Dr Jonathan Palmer had clinched the Marlboro series a major controversy concerning the width of the bodywork on his car put his title (which he had apparently put beyond the reach of his rivals in the 17th round) in jeopardy. At the time of going to press, Palmer faces disqualification from the 18th round results and imposition of an 18 point penalty although a typically aggressive performance in the penultimate round assured him of the title.

The controversy came as a sad footnote to what had been an enjoyable season's racing, in which Ron Tauranac's Ralt RT3 design had the upper hand. Indeed, 1981 was the Year of the Ralt in the Marlboro series. If doubts over the RT3's superiority persisted during the winter layoff they were swiftly dispelled as the Weybridge wing-car dominated the first five races. There was a brief hiatus as March took the sixth, but from then on the Ralts had it all their own way. The message was simple: if you were serious about winning you needed a Ralt RT3. By mid-season March's challenge was weakened further as more Ralts appeared, while Argo, which began the year with high hopes for its full ground effect JM8, was in even worse trouble. Delays in building the car arose and then a series of inconclusive test sessions masked inherent chassis stiffness. By the season opener, number one driver Thierry Tassin found the JM8 off the pace; by the fourth race he had abandoned ship to drive a Ralt for Neil Trundle's team. From then on Argo struggled, but never relaxed its efforts to get back on terms. Hopefully, an all-new JM10 should restore the Norfolk company's fortunes in 1982.

Stefan Johansson stole the 1980 championship in the closing stages and during the winter his Ralt was acquired by young Sussex doctor and Formula Ford driver Jonathan Palmer. From the outset he was fast in testing but when he won the opening race at Silverstone his rivals were quick to point to his well sorted car. When he won his fourth consecutive race at Mallory however, that excuse had become rather tired and people began to look at Palmer anew. Quite simply, he proved the most outstanding driver of the year. With a blend of talent, dedication and determination and the backing of the West Surrey Engineering team headed by Dick Bennetts, he maintained his early season advantage and even when he wasn't winning, Palmer was finishing in the points. With a further three wins, he had apparently sewn up the title by the 17th round at Oulton Park (he won). However, at the 18th round his car was found to have illegally wide rear bodywork (fitted for this race only) and the threat of an 18 point penalty could have put his points tally within reach of Tassin and Boesel. Naturally, his team lodged an appeal against exclusion but at the time of going to press no decision had been reached. With speed and cunning, allied to the ability to sort a car, Palmer represents a major British hope for future GP honours.

Following the switch from Argo to Ralt, Tassin became Palmer's strongest rival. In his second season of Formula 3, the Belgian put in some splendid performances and proved particularly canny at setting his car's aerodynamics to best advantage on the faster tracks such as Silverstone and Thruxton. Without doubt the false start to his year lost him valuable opportunities but with Trundle he wanted for nothing, the team even trying a pneumatic Formula 1-style suspension system and a John Judd development VW engine in place of the regular 2-litre Toyota.

But for Palmer, Rookie of the Year would surely have been former FF pilot Raul Boesel. The Brazilian put himself in Murray Taylor's capable hands and the two established a rapport that saw Raul put in several fine performances, particularly on wet surfaces, and take his first Formula 3 win at Silverstone in early July.

Another Brazilian to make his mark was fellow FF graduate Roberto Moreno who joined the Barron Racing Team at the seventh round. Barron had originally been set up to run Glenn Bosch but when he was injured in a road accident Dutchman Michael Bleekemolen was drafted in. He proved competent but not outstanding for a man with Grand Prix experience, but once Moreno took over the team began to run near the front. Using Bridgestone tyres (and therefore running in the Euro class and ineligible for Marlboro points), Moreno beat Mauro Baldi in the

Mauro Baldi (March 813-Alfa Romeo) won the European Championship. The Italian leads Mike White whose similar car was outclassed by the Ralts in the British series *(below left)*. A switch from Argo to Ralt put Thierry Tassin back in contention for the Championship *(left)*.

combined European/Marlboro series confrontation at Silverstone in June, went on to win the Marlboro round supporting the British GP, and then took victory at Mallory Park. But a major controversy blew up when a routine post-GP fuel check by the RAC found the petrol used at the meeting by Moreno to be of illegally high octane rating. He was thus stripped of his win and trophies and forfeited a further 18 points. From then on Barron's fortunes slumped until Oulton Park in September, but with a Lotus testing contract in his pocket and similar talent to Boesel, Moreno is destined to go a long way in racing. If they stay in Formula 3 in 1982, both Brazilians will pose formidable threats.

Much was expected of South African Mike White, driver of the Autowindscreens-backed works March 813 Alfa Romeo. But after a couple of strong opening races and a fine win at Thruxton in May, he began a hapless slide down the grids as more Ralts were sold. With Formula 1, Formula 2, CanAm and CART racing programmes in hand, March let development of the 813 (iteself a development of the previous year's 803B) lag and even White's skill could not reduce the deficit. Apart from his Thruxton win he had to be satisfied with a runaway victory in the European round at Donington Park. He surely deserved better.

From a patriotic viewpoint a heartening aspect of the 1981 series was the marked resurgence of British talent, so sorely needed in Grands Prix. Apart from Palmer, other Brits to show promise were David Leslie, James Weaver and Dave Scott. Both Leslie and Weaver found their seasons dogged by financial problems and neither competed in every round. Leslie began the year in the Hope Scott RT3, sat out a few races when that team ran out of money, and then raced Eddie Jordan's Ralt with backing from the Racing for Britain scheme, which also helped Palmer. Weaver scored a fabulous win over Palmer at Snetterton in May, driving a Tiga Ralt, but when his sponsor Eurosports pulled out he made only sporadic appearances – a cruel waste of talent.

Nineteen-year-old Scott began his year quietly, learning the ropes in an old Argo JM6 run by Mario Andretti's former chief mechanic Glenn Waters, then switched to a Ralt to put in pole position winning performances that culminated in a very good win at Silverstone in August. With age and a mature outlook on his side, he will be a strong championship contender in 1982.

In the European series, where tyre choice is not restricted, Mauro Baldi proved the dominant driver, winning race after race in his Euroracing March 813 Alfa. On Michelin rubber the engine/chassis combination that afforded White little pleasure worked well, and Baldi exploited its full potential to clinch the title. With professionally run Ralts thin on the ground, Martini's Mk34 model provided strong opposition in the hands of drivers such as Monaco winner Alain Ferté and Philippe Alliot, but only on tighter tracks where its lack of downforce was less of a disadvantage. In Oscar Larrauri, Argentinian Formula 3 fans found a hero to cheer as he drove his Goodyear and then Avon-shod March with considerable panache to humble some of the favoured Michelin runners on more than one occasion.

As a breeding ground for future Grand Prix drivers Formula 3 lived up to its purpose and reputation in 1981, nurturing new talent. However, the problems at the 18th Marlboro round created a very sour note on which to end the year. The controversy came at a televised round when the formula needed all the good publicity it could get to attract finance for 1982.

On the positive side, several of the principal teams met towards the end of the year to discuss methods of improving the organisation and promotion of what is clearly a basically sound formula.

Porsche perfection gives Ickx a record win

The story of the 1981 Le Mans began on March 5, 1980. That day, after vigorous lobbying by the 'privateer' American Championship teams, USAC abruptly changed its engine regulations, reducing the turbo boost pressure allowed to full-race six-cylinder power units. The only team planning to race a six-cylinder was Porsche, whose newly developed 2.65-litre turbo – then being track-tested – was rendered obsolete overnight by the extraordinary USAC ruling. Porsche's perplexed competitions boss, Manfred Jantke, flew immediately to Indianapolis to try to persuade USAC to change its mind. His journey was in vain. Still puzzled after an acrimonious meeting, Jantke emerged and was taken to one side by Roger Penske, one of the leaders of the breakaway CART group of private owners. Seeing Jantke's failure to understand, Penske said in his ear, "Look at it this way, Manfred. We're not interested in racing against factory teams . . ."

There are two ironies here. First, the Porsche engine is essentially a stock-block, still based on the 911 road car unit albeit with full-race heads. Second, at the heart of Porsche's entry to a new arena – Indycar racing – was the decision to withdraw from endurance racing, and that decision was made because of Porsche's judgement that it was undesirable to compete against their own customers, the private owner . . .

Jantke returned to Stuttgart, to order that his ten race-ready Indy engines should be put on the shelf. The power plant was eligible for no other racing category: its development seemed to have been nothing more than an expensive design exercise. The Porsche competitions department concentrated its effort towards the development of its new Group B car, the 924 Carrera.

Angered and frustrated by officialdom in the USA, Jantke had a piece of stunningly good news a year later from officialdom in Europe. Concerned about the prospect of dwindling entries in the final year of its current endurance racing formula, the FIA decided to set the scene for the 1982 Group C by allowing engines of over 3 litres to compete in Group 6. Subjected to the FIA turbo equivalency factor of 1.4:1, the Porsche Indy motor had a theoretical capacity of 3.7 litres. Designed to produce well over 700bhp for Indy, it could be adapted to run on petrol instead of methanol, and converted into an outstanding long-distance engine. In short – it was the ideal power plant for Le Mans.

Jantke hurriedly instigated a feasibility study. He could run the 936 chassis which had won Le Mans in 1976-77, in 2.1-litre form, if he recovered one of the two spaceframe cars from the back of a workshop and the other from its stand in the Porsche Museum. To cope with the extra power of the Indy engine, the cars could be fitted with the very strong four-speed gearbox used on the old CanAm 917/30. The British Dunlop company confirmed that they would assist in the project.

Jantke's two Group 6 entries were among the last to be made before the Le Mans closing date set be the ACO. There was no time properly to test the cars – although Porsche completed a 31-hour simulation on a rolling road – but the package was so very impressive that it persuaded Jacky Ickx ("Only a fool will never change his mind") out of retirement once more, and he asked to be joined in Jantke's lead entry by Derek Bell, his co-winner in 1975. Ickx drove the car briefly at the Porsche private test facility at Weissach, but Bell never cast eyes on it until he arrived at Le Mans in time for scrutineering.

"The first two laps I took gently through the kink," said Bell, "but on the third I took it absolutely flat, so good was the car. And I had never been that quickly round Le Mans before. It was just like sitting in a very fast armchair." At this point, not even its drivers were fully aware that the Indy-engined Porsche 936 was arguably the most effective Le Mans car ever conceived. The team had a very late sponsorship offer from Jules (a Christian Dior brand of men's perfume), and they were certainly backing the right horse for the course. During qualifying, the car shot the Mulsanne Straight speed trap at 236mph, and the beam at the Dunlop Curve after the pits at 172. Although retaining the old bodywork (save for a new rear wing), it achieved these speeds with an extraordinary stability. And there was nothing at Le Mans to touch it during qualifying. As the 55 cars lined up for the rolling start at 3 p.m. on June 14 (an hour earlier than usual because of French national elections), the factory Porsches of Ickx/Bell and Jochen Mass/Hurley Haywood/Vern Schuppan were at their head. And Porsche had a 1-2-3, thanks to the effort of Reinhold Jöst and his 936 replica, the car built last year for Ickx to drive, this year co-driven by Dale Whittington and Klaus Niedzwiedz.

Winners in 1980, the locally based Rondeau team wilted under the pressure of a full factory attack by Porsche. Rondeau fielded five of the latest C-spec M379 cars, two in GTP and three in Group 6, two of the latter being fitted with the latest 3.3-litre Ford-Cosworth DFL endurance racing engine and capable of just under 210mph. Also away from the front-running pace were the purposeful little Le Mans coupes built at Thorigny, near Paris, by Gérard Weltier and Michel Meunier although, this time, the WM team had formal works backing from Peugeot. The increasingly sports-minded French motor man-

A superb effort by John Cooper, Dudley Wood and Claude Bourgoignie brought this British-based Porsche 935 home in fourth place *(above)*.
The unique atmosphere of Le Mans *(top right)*. Photo: Nigel Snowdon
236mph on the Mulsanne Straight and a faultless run with Derek Bell in the Porsche 936/81 brought Jacky Ickx a record fifth win at Le Mans *(right)*. Photo: David Winter

Jules
PORSCHE
11
Shell
DUNLOP
Shell BOSCH BILSTEIN

The Martini-sponsored Lancias scored maximum points at Le Mans by winning the 2-litre category.
Photo: Nigel Snowdon

ufacturer supplied WM with new engines, still based on the unlikely 'PRV' 2.7-litre V6, but with twin-cam four-valve cylinder heads and twin turbos, producing about 520bhp, the same as the normally aspirated DFL. That's 100bhp less than the works Porsches . . .

Although, as usual, there was a smattering of Porsche 935s among the fastest qualifiers, two interesting cars were notably absent from the top of the list. Proving that ground-effect is not the answer to everything in motor racing, the semi-works Ultramar/Banco Occidental DFL-engined Lola T600 was lucky to see 190mph on the 3½-mile straight, even with an inordinately high top gear. And the Kremer brothers' Porsche 917K-81, a brand new replica of perhaps the most popular Le Mans car of all time, found its 580bhp flat-12 engine starved of air by its rear cowl, hitting only 180mph.

Through eight hours of qualifying and 24 hours of racing, it never once rained at Le Mans and, if the weather had been hot on the practice days, it was stifling during the great event itself, especially on the Sunday. In front of a 200,000 crowd (well up on recent years), it was Ickx who made the first mark in the race, cutting across the bows of a charging Henri Pescarolo in the Rondeau team's 3.3-litre 'hare' to lead the first lap.

Ironically, Jantke's works team not only had first place, but also last. It was a curious feature of this Le Mans that, if the winning Porsche had no problems of any kind, its sister car took over its share. Mass was the first pit-caller, a spark plug broken. Worse was to come.

Soon, however, Porsche had an oddball 1-2-3, for Jöst established his 908-80 in second place and American Ted Field the latest development Kremer Porsche 935 in third. Through the first routine pitstops, both these cars briefly led the race, as did the Rondeaus of Pescarolo/Patrick Tambay and Jean Ragnotti/Jean-Louis Lafosse. By the fourth hour, however, Ickx and Bell had pushed the Jules Porsche so far ahead that they could refuel, each stop taking two minutes, without losing the advantage.

The field had already been diminished, and tragically. Formula 2 ace Thierry Boutsen, lining up his 215mph Group C WM for the Mulsanne kink, instantaneously became a helpless passenger as something broke on the front of the coupe. The little projectile dug into the road surface and shot into the right-hand barrier, shedding debris which killed a marshal and injured two others. Like a pinball, the WM cannoned off both barriers, right-left-right-left, before coming to rest, its driver badly shocked but unhurt.

This happened after an hour of racing, and brought out the ACO's three Mercedes course cars, picking up three separate groups of line-astern racers as the wreckage was cleared. An hour later, they were back. Lafosse, accelerating through about 160mph down Mulsanne, had also abruptly lost control. Still no one knows what happened, but the Rondeau hit the right-hand barrier a sickening blow which literally tore the car to pieces, killing its poor driver instantly, and injuring two more marshals.

There was no evidence of a mechanical failure and, although distressed by the tragedy, the Rondeau team under its British manager Keith Greene, decided to continue.

There was no prospect, however, of catching that immaculately driven Porsche. Rondeau's hopes took another, if less cruel, turn for the worse when both the Group 6 cars were delayed by fuel pump failures, caused by an installation omission of cooling ducts which led to the pumps, sited next to the DFL's exhausts, overheating and then seizing. The Jean-Pierre Jaussaud/Jean Rondeau car lost 90 minutes, the Pescarolo/Tambay entry two hours. Later, they were both retired anyway, the former with a chassis failure and the latter with a recurrence of the fuel pump problem which stranded the unlucky Pesca – still awaiting his fourth Le Mans win – out in the country. Only the two GTP Rondeau cars now remained.

Neither was losing Boutsen's car the end of WM's troubles. The race's live TV camera car, driven by an alarmed Roger Dorchy, arrived at Mulsanne Corner on fire. It was quickly extinguished by the marshals' but the car was too badly damaged to continue. A little later, the other Group C WM, Jean-Daniel Raulet at the wheel, collided with Beppe Gabbiani's works Martini-Lancia under braking for Mulsanne, both cars out on the spot in an incident which brought the course cars into action for a third time. In all, 50 minutes of the race were run 'under the yellow', the only reason the winning Porsche failed to improve on the distance record of 3134 miles.

The second 936-81 took seven hours to establish itself back in second place, helped by the demise of the Ted Field K3 with piston failure, and of the Jöst 908-80 which lost a wheel, Dale Whittington smiting the barrier. For the next nine hours, the Group 6 Porsches led the race in tandem, about four laps apart, driving through a balmy night towards what looked to be a major one-two triumph. Jantke had now slowed their pace, but the white cars were still leaving the two GTP Rondeaus far behind.

At around 6 a.m., though, Schuppan brought in his 936 with a broken clutch, and the backup crew suffered another delay (over an hour) while it was replaced, rejoining in 12th place. Four hours later, it had once more come up behind the Porsche-Rondeau-Rondeau phalanx to lie fourth, with every prospect of restoring the status quo thanks to some purposeful driving. But then Schuppan (is he jinxed?) was stranded out near the Porsche Curve with the fuel injection on full-rich. Talked through a bodge-up repair on the two-way radio to the pits, the Australian spent 45 minutes tinkering with the injection before he could get the car back home for proper repairs, which cost another 42 minutes. Finally, a lowly 12th place, 42 laps behind their untroubled team-mates, was their reward for a difficult race.

Unusually for Le Mans, Sunday morning and early afternoon were largely devoid of close racing even for the lower places. Disbelieving the mechanical perfection (there is no other word) of an outstanding motor car, Bell finished the race a massive 14 laps in the lead, to faint from heat exhaustion amid the emotional scenes with Ickx on the rostrum. Once again, Rondeau won GTP, with second place for veteran Jacky Haran and F3 hotshoes Jean-Louis Schlesser (nephew of Jo) and Phillippe Streiff. Five more laps down, Gordon Spice repeated his result of 1980, co-driving this time with François Migault, the second surviving GTP Rondeau delayed by a mid-race misfire.

Five more laps down, there was the Group 5 class winner. The British Charles Ivey Racing team did not have an entry ten days before the race, but took over the slot of a sponsorless Claude Bourgoignie, who joined John Cooper and Dudley Wood in Ivey's Travel Cruiser Porsche 935 K3. They wound up shaming the organisers, who had turned the car down, by claiming a very fine fourth overall, as well as bringing in the maximum World Championship points for Porsche.

The only cloud on Jantke's horizon was that Lancia, leading the Makes series by a scant 2½ points after the Nürburgring, also landed a maximum at Le Mans. Unashamedly running both his Montecarlos and his drivers on very low boost, and virtually unopposed in 2-litre Group 5, Cesare Fiorio lost one car in the Gabbiani/Raulet accident and another with head gasket failure, but two of the 1.4-litre turbocars finished. Eddie Cheever claimed eighth overall with Michele Alboreto and Carlo Facetti, while the semi-works car driven by Giorgio Pianta/Giorgio Schon/ Martino Finotto, came home 15th.

Between the two Group 5 protagonists, we did have a chase in the last hours of Le Mans. All weekend, the Ferrari Boxers in the IMSA GTX category had shown once again that they are in their element at the Sarthe, a match for the Porsches on Mulsanne with a 200mph top speed. And as the marathon drew towards its end, there was a struggle between a Ferrari and a Porsche for fifth overall – and the class win.

The 512 BB was driven by veterans Jean-Claude Andruet and Claude Ballot-Lena, and entered by the French Ferrari importer Charles Pozzi. The 935 was the Daytona 24 hours winning K3 of Cooke-Woods racing, who had already suffered the disappointment of failing to qualify its exciting, but unfinished, Porsche-engined Lola T600. Ralph Kent-Cooke and Bob Garretson, joined by the race's only lady driver, the experienced Anny-Charlotte Verney, had had a less reliable run than the clockwork Pozzi Ferrari and, despite some spirited driving towards the end, failed to catch it by a lap.

Seventh overall, after a reasonably reliable if lacklustre run, was another works Porsche entry, this the so-called '944 LM' GTP car with its experimental 2½-litre turbo engine, driven by Jurgen Barth and Walter Rohrl. Its sister car, similarly bodied but with the latest 2-litre version of the 924 Carrera GTR engine, was 11th for Manfred Schurti/Andy Rouse, finishing the race on only three cylinders.

Behind the American entered, Belgian driven Rennod Racing Ferrari, and the Vegla Porsche 935, Bob Atkin's Coca Cola Porsche should have finished in that 11th place, but was hit by vicious misfortune. On the very last lap, would you believe, when some of the cars had already taken the chequered flag, a big short-circuit behind the dash stranded an understandably tearful Paul Miller out on Mulsanne.

Another American, Charles Mendez, was driving the sole surviving WM, surviving a wishbone breaking in the middle of the Indianapolis left-hander and less frightening delays to finish 13th with Denis Morin.

All manner of things went wrong with the DFL powered Lola T600, but somehow it finished, 15th of the 20 survivors from a field of 55. The Kremer Porsche 917 showed little evidence of a higher top speed than in qualifying before it was eliminated during the seventh hour when Xavier Lapeyre put it backwards into the barriers.

Although one of the four Group 5 BMW M1 cars did finish, the race was a disappointment for Dieter Stappert's motorsport division, which had looked in good shape with its two works-blessed, Peter Sauber built spaceframe M1s. Helmut Henzler crashed the GS Tuning car shared with Hans Stuck and Jean-Pierre Jarier, while the Sauber/Würth entry lost its engine much later on, sidelining Marc Surer/Dieter Quester/David Deacon. The British entered EMKA Group 5 car, driven by David Hobbs/Eddie Jordan/ Steve O'Rourke, also lost its engine, only two hours away from the finish.

Also among the retirements were the cars making up almost the entire over 2-litre Group 6 class, namely two De Cadenets, the Japanese Dome, the Ibec and the Swiss ACR, and also both the semi-works, RX-7 based Mazda 253i rotary cars. Broken fuel injection put paid to Preston Henn's ex-Fitzpatrick 935, which had been the fastest qualifier in IMSA GTX.

How shall we remember this 49th Le Mans? For two fatalities, for the blistering heat, for the big crowd which heralded the best field for many years. For the decimation of the Rondeaus and WMs. For the accidents on Mulsanne. Most of all, for five times winner Jacky Ickx at last exceeding the record he shared with Olivier Gendebien, and for the perfection of the Porsche which he drove.

MARTINI RACING
65
MARTINI
PIRELLI
VS
MARTINI
MARTINI RACING
67
MARTINI
PIRELLI
VS
VS
PIRELLI
MARTINI LANCIA

Nineteen eighty-one was an interim year for World series endurance racing, signifying the end of the old FIA Groups 5 and 6, and pending the arrival of the new Groups C and B. FISA reformed its official World Endurance Championships along the lines which we will see in 1982, restricting the Makes series to only six races (Daytona, Monza, Silverstone, Nürburgring, Le Mans, Watkins Glen), and administering a separate Drivers championship. This comprised the same six 'classics' and nine other events (Sebring, Mugello, Riverside, Enna, Daytona again, Spa, Mosport, Elkhart Lake, Brands Hatch).

The second race at Daytona and the 24-hour event at Spa were restricted to touring cars only, but all the other counters were thrown open to all manner of sports-racing cars. Points could be scored in the Drivers series in any one of a dozen classes, but only Group 5 type cars (IMSA GTX machines were grouped in over 2-litre Group 5) were eligible to score points towards the Makes title. Cars in all classes were permitted to carry only 120 litres of fuel, a sign of FISA's preoccupation with the fuel economy concept which has led to the Americans opting out of World endurance racing in 1982.

WORLD ENDURANCE CHAMPIONSHIP OF MAKES

As in 1980, Lancia fielded the only proper factory team in the series, and had virtually nil opposition in 2-litre Group 5. Run by Cesare Fiorio out of Turin, the team was sponsored by Martini and conducted its short programme in close cooperation with Pirelli. Lancia's equipment was a further development of the mid-engined Montecarlo, powered by an improved version of the familiar transverse, single-turbo four-cylinder engine of 1.4 litres, probably now producing around 430bhp. On paper, it was an impressive package, enhanced by the quality of the factory drivers. They included Riccardo Patrese, Eddie Cheever, Michele Alboreto, Piercarlo Ghinzani, Andrea de Cesaris and Henri Pescarolo.

The cars, however, turned out to be woefully unreliable. With only six events on the Makes schedule, and the privately entered, 700bhp Porsche 935s also almost unopposed in the other points-scoring class, Fiorio could not afford to make even one slip, but he made several. It was incredibly fortunate that he got away with it.

At Daytona, one of the factory cars broke its engine during the night, and the other was delayed by electrical bothers, struggling home 18th. The 24 Hours was won by one of the army of Porsche 935s which abound on both sides of the Atlantic, driven by Brian Redman/Bobby Rahal/Bob Garretson.

Luckily for Lancia – sure that their fearsome new Ferrari 308 GTB twin-turbo would not last, Carlo Facetti and Martino Finotto had taken the precaution of qualifying their 1980 model Lancia. When the Ferrari did break, they switched to the Jolly Club entered Montecarlo and, with Emanuele Pirro, won the class in seventh place overall.

Porsche 20: Lancia 20

On to home ground at Monza, and a constantly wet 1000km, Lancia's strength was boosted by the entry of the Jolly Club team's 1981 Montecarlo, a car with works support and sponsorship by Lubrifilm. The factory team itself again fielded two cars, but one of them was fitted with an oversize 1.8-litre power unit with which Fiorio hoped to deprive Porsche of points in the over 2-litre class. After only nine laps, it failed. The 1.4-litre Martini car led the race overall until its fuel pump broke. The Jolly Club car lost its gearbox. The race was won by the Porsche of the German Weralit team, driven by Edgar Dören/Jurgen Lässig.

Luckily for Lancia – an Italian club racer called Germano Nataloni had been sold one of the old 1979 team cars. Now scruffily prepared and off the pace, it had been entered for a one-off International outing, and somehow it survived to win the class, seventh overall.

Porsche 40: Lancia 40

At Silverstone, Fiorio ran one of his cars not with the too-new 1.8 engine, but with one of the slightly oversize turbo 1.4 units which had done the trick for the team in 1980, by twice winning the over 2-litre class. To the alarm of Cheever, this car lost a wheel just after a routine pit stop. The 1.4 Martini car had been eliminated in an early accident. The 6 Hours was won by the Vegla Porsche of Harald Grohs/Walter Rohrl/ Dieter Schornstein.

Luckily for Lancia – although chaotically managed, the Lubrifilm entry, crewed by Beppe Gabbiani/ Giorgio Pianta/Giorgio Schon, secured a third class win by finishing seventh overall.

Porsche 60: Lancia 60

The Makes series had reached its halfway point, and the marque Lancia still tied with Porsche, even though the factory team had yet to win its class....

The team's strength was further increased at the Nürburgring by the inclusion of the German 'sprint' championship Montecarlo usually run by GS Tuning. This and one of the Martini cars were fitted with 1.8 engines, for Fiorio knew that he still had to take an over 2-litre maximum away from Porsche. Neither car managed to pull this off, but at last the team did achieve a maximum in the smaller class. The Pescarolo/de Cesaris entry was running tenth overall when the 1000km was stopped before half-distance, following a dreadful accident which claimed the life of the popular Swiss veteran, Herbert Müller, in a Porsche 908/3.

Luckily for Lancia (and especially so) – when the red flag was shown, the teams were engaged in a series of routine pit stops, which gave a false picture of the race positions. Yet to stop, and in the lead at the time, was the spaceframe Group 5 BMW M1 newly built for GS Tuning by Peter Sauber. Driven by Nelson Piquet/ Hans Stuck, the BASF sponsored BMW was declared the winner, and Porsche had dropped that maximum. Half points were awarded for the shortened event.

Porsche 67½: Lancia 70

All Fiorio had to do now was to maintain that lead. The troublesome 1.8 engine project was abandoned, along with the development of twin-turbo versions of both the 1.4 and the 1.8. Fiorio went to Le Mans with a three-car works attack, his well proven 1.4 engines screwed down to low boost pressure, and his drivers instructed to finish at all cost to overall race positions. One went out five hours after the start in an accident, another fell victim to head gasket failure five hours before the end. But the Cheever/Alboreto/Facetti Martini entry claimed eighth overall and the class maximum, while the Jolly Club Lancia also finished. The British entered Charles Ivey Racing Porsche of John Cooper/Dudley Wood/Claude Bourgoignie was fourth in the 24 Hours, taking another maximum score for the German marque.

Porsche 87½: Lancia 90

Only Watkins Glen remained and, for some time, with the New York facility in severe financial difficulties, Fiorio may have hoped that the event would be cancelled, the title already his. When the 6 Hours was confirmed, however, Lancia took to the USA the same line-up of no-nonsense 1.4-litre entries. Although one of them was retired with accident damage, Fiorio pulled off such a spectacular success that the failures earlier in the season were forgotten. The US-entered IMSA GTX Porsches were decimated by an extraordinary series of engine and tyre failures, and Patrese/Alboreto and Pescarolo/de Cesaris came through to score a resounding one-two. Bob Garretson's Porsche, co-driven on this occasion by Indycar aces Rick Mears and Johnny Rutherford, was third, scoring the last ever World Championship points for the classic 935.

But Lancia had clinched the crown by the narrowest of margins.

Porsche 107½: Lancia 110

And the World Championship of Makes had been decided by that twist of fate of the Nürburgring.

WORLD ENDURANCE CHAMPIONSHIP OF DRIVERS

This FIA series was given more publicity and prestige in 1981 and, having been of interest in the past mainly in the USA, it gained more general recognition. Nevertheless, the 15-race title chase included seven events in north America, and, with more drivers travelling east across the Atlantic to race than there were going west, it was no surprise when the crown was claimed by an American.

This was wealthy West Coast businessman Bob Garretson, who started out his season by winning at Daytona, his Kremer-Porsche 935–K3 run in association with Cooke-Woods Racing. Garretson prepared the Cooke-Woods race cars in his own shop in California, but split with the team after Le Mans. Thereafter, he ran his own Style Auto sponsored Porsche with a variety of co-drivers, and showed that commitment and financial investment will win the Drivers championship, and the $50,000 that goes with it.

Garretson contested nine of the 15 races, eight of them with the Porsche, the touring car race at Daytona in July with a Mazda RX–3. A fourth at Riverside, sixth at Le Mans and third at the Glen were his only good placings after the win at Daytona in January, until he came on strong at the end of the series with a fourth at Elkhart Lake and a second place finish at Brands Hatch, which clinched the title in the final round.

A worthy runner-up was the spectacular German, Harald Grohs, who drove a five-race European programme with the Vegla Porsche, and four races in north America with the Andial Meister team's similar, but older 935. Grohs achieved three race victories, for Dieter Schornstein's Vegla team at Silverstone, and for Howard Meister's Andial operation at Mosport and Elkhart Lake. In contrast to Garretson – whose relative lack of pace was overcome by co-drivers like Brian Redman, Bobby Rahal, Rick Mears and Johnny Rutherford – Grohs tended to be let down by his co-driver in the Sekurit-backed Vegla entry (its owner), although he had a rapid partner Stateside in Rolf Stommelen.

Another European to take in nine Drivers rounds was Edgar Dören, also from Germany, who did the first part of the season with the Weralit team's Porsche 935–K3, took in singleton races with a Porsche 934 and an Audi 80, and finished his year with three rides in Preston Henn's K3. Dören's only win came at Monza in the Wera car.

Bobby Rahal, the very fast American, managed ten races by driving Porsches for both Garretson and Bob Akin, but won only in the Daytona 24 Hours. Akin himself, driving his Coca Cola Porsche 935–K3 plus an AMX Spirit and a Ford Capri in the touring car races at Daytona and Spa, did a grand total of 11 events, a figure matched only by Derek Bell, who competed in six different cars.

Apart from the Porsche 936–81 with which he won Le Mans, the English long-distance ace aimed for the Drivers title in Steve O'Rourke's EMKA BMW M1, two different Porsche 935s, a Porsche 934 and a BMW 530. The Le Mans victory, two second places (both with the BMW, a modified Procar) and a third were virtually all he had to show for his globe-trotting.

Others to do well in the Drivers series, despite not contesting as many rounds as these main protagonists, included Italians Giorgio Francia and Lella Lombardi, who won at Mugello with the fleet works Osella-BMW 2-litre Group 6 car. The Osella's low fuel consumption made it into a competitive proposition under the latest fuel limitation rules.

Guy Edwards and Emilio de Villota also featured strongly with the GRID team's semi-works Lola T600, one of the new-generation ground-effects sports-prototypes of the type which will be contesting Group C. Fitted with one of the new Ford-financed Ford-Cosworth DFL long-distance engines, of 3.3 litres, the massive Ultramar/Banco Occidental Lola won a very poorly supported race at Enna and ended the season on a high note for the future with a second victory, at Brands Hatch. Across the Atlantic, Brian Redman achieved two second place finishes in Drivers rounds with Cooke-Woods Racing's Chevrolet engined Lola T600, the car with which he defeated the Porsche 935 teams to win the Camel IMSA GT Championship.

The works Porsche 936 and Rondeau sports-prototypes competed only at Le Mans in 1981, but further evidence that endurance racing may at last have turned the corner came in the last round in England, where the Ford Motor Company made the debut of the new Len Bailey designed Ford C100. This Group C type machine, fitted with a 3.9 DFL power plant, qualified on pole position and led the race until halted by a gearbox failure. Hard evidence of Ford's commitment to long-distance racing did much to boost the confidence of the teams, who ended a hotch-potch 1981 season with the prospect of a 1982 World Championship of Makes contested by factory teams from Ford, Lancia, Ferrari, Porsche, Mazda, Peugeot and possibly BMW, and smaller works programmes from specialist constructors like Lola, March, Mirage and Sauber.

That is a very healthy prospect – even without the big American races and teams.

Quentin Spurring

See Results Section for final championship placings.

Danny Ongais crashed the Interscope 002 while giving the car its debut at Indy.

Following America's yellow-brick road

With Formula 1 taking its recent step down the golden pathway of gamblers' sideshows as it moves from the streets and parking lots of Long Beach to the back lot of Caesar's Palace and, possibly, on to the streets of downtown Detroit, you might have guessed that Grand Prix racing's American media binge successfully overshadowed the many native forms of American motorsport in 1981. For Messrs. Ecclestone, Balestre and others, the SCCA included, the sudden and unprecedented growth of Formula 1 in the USA was undoubtedly a Good Thing. For the SCCA it brought relief from a long-running battle against a poor balance sheet and it also helped the club's political strength, at the expense of the NASCAR-IMSA-USAC coalition. The political waters frothed more mightily than ever......

Light years away from that world, the thousands of journeymen race car drivers and builders in America continued to drive their rigs across the vast interstate highway system of the country racing week after week, night after night, on the eight hundred and more bullrings between the North Atlantic and Pacific Oceans. It was business-as-usual there in the heartland as the racers battled not only one against the other but also the familiar headaches of ever-rising costs and ever-threatened rule changes.

Aside from those occupational hazards the grass roots business of automobile racing continued to roll along happily as ever in North America. At the national level, in fact, things looked particularly healthy as the American auto manufacturers took more and more active interest in many phases of the sport, more sponsors spread themselves around the business than ever and the boom in cable TV resulted in a sharp increase in television coverage of the sport.

Both of the USA's leading series seemed to be in the middle of a new boom as NASCAR's Grand National championship and CART's Indy Car World Series were blessed with deeper and stronger fields than ever. NASCAR coped fairly well with a switch to slightly smaller cars while CART established itself as a sound organisation that was beginning to move almost as fast as Bernie!

CART STEPS AHEAD

On the Indy car front the political wars of the past two years began to fade as CART emerged with a well-promoted, extensively-televised series that paid more than double the prize money than the USAC Championship of three years ago. CART also staged a wild but very successful 500-miler at Roger Penske's own Michigan International Speedway in mid-summer and at the end of August they were at Riverside for a 500km road race which was backed by the *Los Angeles Times* and otherwise replaced the woebegone California 500 which had died the previous winter along with the Ontario Motor Speedway. Spectator attendances at CART races returned to figures not seen in more than ten years while the depth and quality of the fields underwent a dramatic transformation.

By the end of the season a brace of very experienced teams from other series were beginning to make announcements that they were turning to CART and Indy car racing in 1982. Four-time CanAm Champion team boss Carl Haas and three-time Formula Atlantic Champion Doug Shierson were among the entrants to make the switch while former Atlantic ace Kevin Cogan became the most sought-after newcomer to the CART ranks. The road race portion of the CART schedule also began to solidify with news that the three road races of 1980 and '81 would be expanded to six in 1982.

The championship was won for the second time by Rick Mears who bounced back from facial burns received in a pit fire at the Indy 500 to score a series of wins and wrap-up the title at Michigan in September. With team-mate Bobby Unser often setting the pace in another Penske PC9B and Bill Alsup running strongly enough in a third works Penske entry to take third in the championship, the Penske team were as strong as ever.

In late August the news broke that the 48-year-old Unser would be leaving Penske at the end of the year to go into semi-retirement as manager, test driver and occasional team-mate to wealthy young Mexican Josele Garza. That meant Mears would become the undis-

48
GOODYEAR

NORTON
SIMPSON
GOODYEAR
SIMPSON

GOULD

GOULD
THE
GOULD
CHARGE
KRACO
MEARS
GOODYEAR
AB DICK
NORTON
MONROE
GOULD
KRACO

Previous pages:
Despite suffering facial burns at the Indy 500, Rick Mears won the CART Championship for the second time in a Penske *(main picture)*.
The unique 'stock-block' Eagle proved to be a useful combination for road racing in the hands of Geoff Brabham. Mike Mosley put the same car on the front row at Indy. *(above left)*.
Photo: Mark Clifford
Bobby Unser continued to set a ruthless pace in his Penske PC9B, but elected to go into semi-retirement at the end of the season *(below left)*.
Photo: David Hutson

The beautifully prepared Group 44 Jaguar XJS of Bob Tullius won the TransAm round at Brainerd, Minnesota. *(right)*.
Photo: David Hutson
The pugnacious A.J. Foyt crashed heavily at Michigan. *(below left)*.

puted number one driver at Penske Racing in 1982 while Unser's seat was taken over by Kevin Cogan.

There were a further half-a-dozen car and driver combinations which could match and often outpace the Penske PC9Bs but for reasons of luck and reliability none of them were able to muster a season-long threat to the Penske outfit. Indeed, it was Pancho Carter and the privately-run Alex Foods team which came closest to beating Mears as Carter was very competitive on the fastest high-banked ovals and scored the first win of his eight-year Indy car career with the team's two-year-old Penske PC7 in the fire and accident-ravaged Michigan 500.

1980 CART Champion Johnny Rutherford and the Chaparral team had the worst kind of luck with crashes, tyre blow-outs and engine failures. The team's three 2K chassis were all built in 1979 but they have been steadily developed and modified so that they were the lightest and trimmest machines on last year's Indy car circuit. Rutherford was fast everywhere and won the Phoenix season-opener but he finished no better than fifth in the point standings.

In much the same way, the Bignotti-Cotter team made a promising debut on the Indy car circuit with Tom Sneva hustling the team's March 81Cs into the

lead of most races. He led strongly in both the Indianapolis and Michigan 500s only to drop out with troubles inside the March's aerodynamically-surfaced, transverse Weismann gearbox. The 81Cs also suffered some damaging structural failures as team manager George Bignotti steadily 'Americanised' his British-built chassis. At the end of the year Bignotti's cars appeared in Texaco colours as the oil company announced a two-car sponsorship package for 1982.

The new Wildcat Mk.8s run by the STP-backed Patrick Racing Team also showed a lot of speed as Mario Andretti and Gordon Johncock ran with the leaders in most races. Somehow they too had the worst of luck although Andretti was twice a close second to Mears as well as being the disputed winner of the Indy 500......

The other chassis that was a potential winner in 1981 was the unique Eagle which generated ground effect-style download without the use of bulky side-pods. Driven by Mike Mosley and equipped with a 5.8-litre, 640 BHP all-aluminium Chevrolet 'stock-block', the works Eagle was a threat on all types of tracks and also proved to be a very useful road racing chassis and engine combination in the hands of Geoff Brabham and Rocky Moran. Mosley, meanwhile, was on the front row at Indy, won at Milwaukee in June and also led the Michigan 500.

An interesting exercise was the Longhorn team's attempt to make an Indy car out of the 1980 World Championship-winning Williams FWO7B. After fielding their own version of a Williams in 1980 the Longhorn team produced a faithful reproduction of an FWO7B for the '81 season only to find the resulting Longhorn LRO2 just wasn't suitable for the faster, high-banked tracks. Al Unser continued with the team and on short tracks he was able to give a good account of himself as the braking and tractive capabilities of the car showed their worth.

Another private team to show well was the outfit organised by second generation driver Tony Bettenhausen Jr who drove an old McLaren M24 and a Phoenix into sixth place in the point standings, with a second in the Michigan 500 being his best result. The Phoenix with which Bettenhausen finished the season was driven for most of the year by Kevin Cogan who took the car to fourth place at Indianapolis and showed himself to be the fastest Rookie newcomer, so much so that in September he was seriously entertaining offers of five salaried driving jobs. Another Rookie to show well was Super Vee graduate Josele Garza who won the Rookie-of-the-Year award at Indy after a strong drive with a privately-run Penske PC9.

Among the veterans to have a tough time of it in 1981 were A.J. Foyt and Danny Ongais. Foyt made the debut of a new, ground-effect Coyote at Indy but had little success with the car and switched to a March 81C for June's USAC-sanctioned 500-miler at Pocono. Foyt beat Geoff Brabham and an otherwise weak field (most CART teams refused to go to the race) while recording his 67th Indy car win but a month later he crashed heavily at Michigan while racing his Coyote. Foyt broke his right elbow and arm and also took a hard knock on the head which kept him out of racing for the rest of the season. In mid-September, mind you, the 46-year-old Texan announced that he would be back on a full-time basis in 1982 with a pair of new March chassis.

Danny Ongais was injured more seriously than Foyt when he crashed his neat, new Interscope 002 while giving the long-awaited car its race debut in the Indianapolis 500. After a terrible 1980 season, caused by politics and the unreliability of Porsche's still-born Indy engine, Ongais looked like he was ready to return to the limelight following a couple of 200mph practice laps at Indy. As it was, he was to collect the third turn wall in the race, break both legs badly and miss the balance of the season while trying to rehabilitate himself.

For much of the season there was a dispute over USAC's attempts to outlaw the Cosworth DFX from Indy in 1982 although after trumpeting their 'stock-block' plan for two-and-a-half years USAC quietly acquiesced in August and confirmed that the 2.65-litre

Who's on First?

FOR THE INDIANAPOLIS MOTOR SPEEDWAY AND USAC, the running of the 65th Annual Indianapolis 500 was nothing less than a disaster. First of all the result of the race was changed early the following morning with Bobby Unser being moved back to second place and Mario Andretti being declared the winner. Following a series of appeals and a lengthy hearing Unser was reinstated as the winner in mid-October – 137 days after the race! – only to have Andretti appeal the decision. As *Autocourse* went to press the matter was far from being resolved and in the eyes of the public, motor racing had once again been made to look like a fools' ship ruled by perversely incompetent officials.

The tragicomedy that was the 1981 Indianapolis 500 began with a botched start wherein both the starter and a back-up man located along the pitwall waved yellow flags as the field responded to the chief steward's green light! Just past the 100-mile mark a fire enveloped Rick Mears' pit area while his car was being refuelled and as the fire burned, Danny Ongais' Interscope crashed heavily into the third turn wall. Both of Ongais' legs were smashed in what was one of the worst accidents in recent history at Indianapolis while Mears escaped with some facial burns and two of his mechanics were burned more seriously, one around his head and the other over much of his back and legs.

Later the race settled down with Bobby Unser finally scoring his third win by a wide margin from Mario Andretti who had come through from the back row only to lose time near the end with a flat tyre and fading engine. But on lap 150 as Unser and Andretti raced out of the pits under a yellow flag, Unser passed half-a-dozen cars along the pit exit 'apron' which extends to the end of the second turn. In the eyes of Andretti this manoeuvre violated the 'blending-in' rule and he promptly radioed his pit crew to complain. They in turn relayed Andretti's message to the stewards who found no record of Unser's move.

So it was that Unser and his Penske PC9B went on to beat Andretti's Wildcat Mk.8 to the flag and claim all the usual applause and awards until the posting of the official results the following morning when a long evening of videotape-watching and rule-reviewing resulted in Unser being penalised one lap and Andretti assuming the winner's role. The Penske team immediately initiated a round of appeals which culminated in a long hearing before a specially-appointed three-man appeal board. However, the 23-page document describing Unser's reinstatement as the winner (along with a $40,000 fine) was accepted with little enthusiasm by Andretti.

"If they let this go by it sets a terrible precedent," suggested Andretti. "Either they're going to enforce the rules as they're written, within the framework of the supplementary regulations or they're going to leave themselves wide open for all kinds of legal trouble."

Unser meanwhile was equally convinced of his position and as autumn drifted into winter the fast-waning United States Auto Club and its lone ally, the Indianapolis Motor Speedway, were drifting into precariously black waters.

QUAKER
STATE
SCCA
44
Jaguar
GOODYEAR

NISSAN
Coors
GOODYEAR
GOODYEAR
3

Geoff Brabham clinched the Can Am Championship at Las Vegas with the Tony Cicale/Trevor Harris designed VDS 001 of Count Rudi van der Straten.
Photo: Nigel Snowdon

NASCAR introduced 'downsizing' in 1981. Although cars were smaller in profile with shorter wheelbases, the average speeds remained much as before. Darrell Waltrip, pictured at Daytona, drove the Junior Johnson Buick into the lead of the championship towards the end of the season.

turbo racing engine category would continue to operate under the limits of 48ins Hg boost restrictions, much as CART had agreed on until the end of 1983.

USAC's Gold Crown Championship consisted of only two races – Indianapolis, where everyone was in attendance, and Pocono, where eight front-engined, dirt track cars helped pad-out the field! The 1982 Indy 500 is the third and final round of USAC's futilely-organised Championship series so we'll have to wait until then to see who USAC 1981-82 Champion might be......

Supporting event at most CART races last year was a round of the Bosch/Gold Cup Super Vee championship which also reached new heights of competitiveness. There were full fields everywhere with Ralt RT5s dominating the proceedings and the championship being fought-out between 19-year-old Al Unser Jr and the more experienced Pete Halsmer. Unser Jr showed himself to be a major talent as he won both road and oval races while the presence of Bobby Unser Jr, Roger Penske Jr, and Mike Andretti made the Super Vee series into a more respectable training ground than ever.

ALLISON vs WALTRIP

Down in Grand National land there were some substantial changes for 1981 as NASCAR introduced 'downsizing' to their premier category. The new season brought a five ins reduction in wheelbase and cars that were generally smaller in profile and frontal area. These changes resulted in little or no change in lap times although a lot of political argy-bargy developed over what was the 'right' bodyshape to use.

In the early part of the season the Grand National championship was dominated by veteran Bobby Allison who raced a unique Pontiac Grand Le Mans for coal-mining magnate Harry Ranier. Allison has always been at odds with NASCAR boss Bill France and right from the start of the season he was embroiled in a controversy over the shape of his Pontiac's tail and the size of the spoiler it was required to use. After the Daytona 500, NASCAR decreed that the Pontiac must use a much taller spoiler than any other car and after fighting with NASCAR for a few months, Allison finally acquiesed and exchanged his Grand Le Mans for a Buick Regal which was the bodyshape used by most of the other frontrunners.

As this controversy carried on, Darrell Waltrip began to emerge as the Grand National pacesetter in his first year in the Junior Johnson seat previously occupied by Cale Yarborough. Many people had predicted that Waltrip's move into Johnson's cockpit would soon make for an unbeatable combination and as Johnson's team began to sort-out the various different types of chassis they had built to suit the new regulations, Waltrip began to close in on Allison's comfortable-looking point lead. In mid-September Waltrip was able to overhaul Allison as he scored his ninth win of the season and at press time, looked like finally taking his long-sought first Grand National title.

A solid third in the point standings was Harry Gant who had moved into GN racing in 1980 after a long career on the Late Model Sportsman circuit. Gant showed his stuff immediately and, early in the past season, he was offered the job of driving a second car to LSR contender StaneNTAtan Barrett in the Burt Reynolds/Hal Needham GN team. Gant quickly established himself as a frontrunner as he lead race after race only to suffer all manner of problems and find himself constantly settling for second place. One of these days......

No other team or driver was able to mount a consistent effort last season. Defending Champion Dale Earnhardt found himself caught in the web of politics as the Osterlund team pulled out of the sport in mid-season and left him to rebuild a new team with backing from Wrangler Jeans. Earnhardt doggedly stayed with it but by press time he had not won a single race.

Nor did Richard Petty have a very good season as his reliability record fell far below his usual standards. The same problems affected his son Kyle who campaigned the complete 31-round schedule for the first time. Mind you, King Richard did manage to pull off a few wins in 1981, including his seventh victory in the classic Daytona 500.

The other traditional stars of NASCAR also had a thin time of it in 1981 with Cale Yarborough being the most successful at the wheel of M.C. Anderson's Buick which he raced in only 22 of the championship rounds. It took a few races for the Yarborough-Anderson combination to gell but by mid-season they were in full flight and managed to win the July 4 Firecracker 400 at Daytona. Others to win races in 1981 included the Ford T-Birds driven by Neil Bonnett (for the Wood Bros), Benny Parsons (Bud Moore) and Jody Ridley.

A couple of rookies also scored GN wins last season. Morgan Shepherd and Ron Bouchard came into GN racing after many years in the lesser leagues of stock cars racing but both men immediately proved themselves capable of running at the front. Shepherd won an April race at Martinsville with his privately-run Buick while Bouchard won the Talladega 500 in mid-summer and chased Shepherd hard in the Rookie-of-the-Year standings.

With Winston cigarettes continuing to back the GN championship for the eleventh successive year and newspaper, radio and television coverage of the series maintaining NASCAR's high visibility in the marketplace, the leading form of America's vast sport of stock car racing was as healthy as ever. At the same time a variety of series catering for lightweight, more modified stockers began to establish themselves with

Bobby Unser was at the centre of a controversy over the Indy 500 *(below)*.
Likely Lads. 19-year-old Al Unser Jnr talks shop with his Formula Super Vee cousin Bobby Unser Jnr *(below middle)*.
The March 81A may not have been the best chassis in Formula Atlantic but the combination of Jacques Villeneuve and Doug Shierson's preparation carried off the championship. *(below bottom)*.

solid purses and promotion. Series sanctioned by the ASA, All-Pro and ARTGO produced a good living for a core of competitors and certainly helped to keep Big Bill France and NASCAR on their toes.

SPORTS CAR FEVER

The traditional forms of American road racing took something of a back seat to both Formula 1 and Indy car racing in 1981 as the Grand Prix world began to move seriously into North America and CART started to establish their own very sound group of road races. Once again IMSA's Camel cigarettes-sponsored GT series was the most successful road racing series with seventeen championship rounds and large crowds at most races. Contrastingly, the SCCA's CanAm series made little gain in terms of pulling crowds and plumbed new depths as far as the narrowness of its fields. Once again the SCCA did little to help Formula Atlantic while the TransAm series emerged as their most worthwhile form of racing.

The IMSA GT title was won by the ever-enthusiastic Brian Redman who teamed up with Bobby Rahal and Bob Garretson to win the season-opening Daytona 24 Hrs with a Porsche 935 and then made the debut of the Cooke-Woods Racing Lola-Chevy T600 in victorious style at Laguna Seca in May. Redman was to win three more races and sew-up the title at Atlanta in September.

Redman's major competitors included defending champion John Fitzpatrick (Porsche 935), John Paul Jr (Porsche 935 and Lola T600), Bobby Rahal (various 935s), Klaus Ludwig (Zakspeed/Bill Scott Ford Mustang). Rolf Stommelen put it to the IMSA regulars by winning three mid-season long distance races in company with Harald Grohs (twice) and Derek Bell (once).

The big change in IMSA was the introduction of the prototype-like GTP category which differed from the FISA's Group C regulations as far as engine and aerodynamic rules were concerned. In the hands of Redman, Paul Jr and others, the Lola T600 proved itself to be more than a match for the traditional IMSA-winning Porsche 935 on most circuits while the only other serious GTP contender to appear was the David Hobbs March-BMW M1C which started life with a 3.5-litre straight six engine and was later modified to accept a 2.0-litre, four-cylinder turbocharged lump.

With only half-a-dozen cars seriously contesting the 1981 CanAm series and various ancient, oily stop-gappers filling out the fields (to as many as 18 starters!) there wasn't much pleasure to be had from the ill-conceived series. All of this tended to detract from the fine performances turned in by the likes of Teo Fabi, Geoff Brabham and Danny Sullivan. Fabi led Paul Newman's works March team, initially with Al Unser backing him up and later with Bobby Rahal filling-in. Brabham drove the Team VDS much-modified Lola T530 and later in the season he appeared with the beautifully conceived and constructed VDS 001. Sullivan drove a Lola T530 and then a Frissbee for Garvin Brown Racing while other contenders included Al Holbert (CAC-2), Jeff Wood (Carl Haas Lola), Rocky Moran (Frissbee) and Tom Klausler (Frissbee/Prophet).

Despite a huge crash at Elkhart Lake in July when something broke in the back of his March, and an attack of appendicitis later in the year, Fabi was usually the mercurial pacesetter of the CanAm although Brabham was superb when he and the VDS team were on form while Al Holbert also sparkled from time to time.

A far better series was the TransAm which usually attracted forty-car fields of Corvettes, Mustangs, Camaros, Jaguars and Porsches. Helped by the backing of CRC Chemicals, the TransAm made a good deal of

Gordon Johncock passes Tom Sneva's stalled March in the Indy pit lane *(left)*.

The Cooke-Woods Lola T-600 Chevrolet won the IMSA Championship after an impressive season *(below)*.

Brian Redman takes over the wheel of the Cooke-Woods Porsche 935 to win the Daytona 24hrs. The ever-enthusiastic Englishman went on to win the IMSA GT Championship. *(below left)*.

financial sense to many teams and the title was fought-out primarily between F5000 veteran Eppie Wietzes' beautifully-driven Corvette and Bob Tullius' cagily-driven Jaguar V12. Other contenders included John Bauer (Porsche 911SC), Tom Gloy (Ford Mustang), Monte Shelton (Porsche 930) and Greg Pickett (Corvette).

With no organisational or promotional assistance from the SCCA, the North American Formula Atlantic Championship has begun to suffer seriously from the effects of inflation over the past few years. The result of this is that the series is now beyond the reach of many talented drivers and the furiously hectic competition of four and five years ago is no longer

there. However, the Atlantic fields were still bigger than those seen in the CanAm and they were infinitely superior in the quality of driving and preparation.

Jacques Villeneuve used his exceptional reflexes and incomparable bravery to carry off his second NAFAC title, once again at the wheel of one of Doug Shierson's well-prepared and tested March 81As. Jacques won four races in 1981, including a faultless title-winning victory at Trois Rivieres in early September. Other drivers to win races were Geoff Brabham, Whitney Ganz, Tim Coconis, Rogelio Rodriguez and Kevin Cogan (all of them in Ralt RT4s!) while the series' Rookie-of-the-Year award went to Norm Hunter who showed a lot of skill and intelligence at the wheel of yet another Ralt RT4.

WHO RUNS BIG BILL'S POND?

With the arrival in 1980 on the American national scene of John Cooper as President of the Indianapolis Motor Speedway, Jim Melvin as the Executive Director of the SCCA and John Frasco as CART's Chairman of the Board, there was a lot of interest in watching these men find their feet.

Cooper had a hard time of it as he walked squarely into the middle of the CART/USAC war and soon found himself in deep trouble as he championed USAC's attempts to outlaw the widely used turbo-charged Cosworth DFX. Cooper was finally forced to renege on USAC's 'stock-block' formula as the weight of CART devotees and the organisations strengthening schedule compelled him to retreat from the brink of disaster.

Meanwhile, CART Chairman John Frasco was making steady progress what with a million dollars in purse and point fund money from series sponsor PPG Industries and the establishment of races like the Michigan 500 which offered more than half-a-million dollars in prize money in its first year.

Also doing well was the SCCA's Jim Melvin who weathered a series of internal political squabbles within the club and then brought some worthwhile cashflow and strengthened political clout by helping the Formula 1 circus to establish the Las Vegas Grand Prix.

1981 results

A detailed summary of the season

Formula 2

MARLBORO/DAILY EXPRESS INTERNATIONAL TROPHY, Silverstone Grand Prix Circuit, Great Britain March 29. European Formula 2 Championship, round 1. 47 laps of the 2·932-mile/4·719-km circuit, 137·80 miles/221·79 km.

1 Mike Thackwell, NZ (Ralt RH6-Honda), 1h 11m 44·67s, 115·67 mph/186·15 km/h.
2 Riccardo Paletti, I (March 812-BMW), 1h 12m 20·86s.
3 Corrado Fabi, I (March 812-BMW), 46 laps.
4 Jim Crawford, GB (Toleman TG280-Hart), 46.
5 Carlo Rossi, I (Toleman TG280-Hart), 46.
6 Brian Robinson, GB (Chevron B42-Hart), 46.
7 Geoff Lees, GB (Ralt RH6-Honda), 45 – not running at finish; **8** Ray Mallock, GB (Ralt RT4-Ford BDX), 45; **9** Stefan Johansson, S (Toleman T850-Hart), 45; **10** Christian Danner, D (March 812-BMW), 45; **11** Michele Alboreto, I (Minardi FLY281-BMW), 45; **12** Jurg Leinhard, CH (March 812-BMW), 45; **13** Sewi Hopfer, A (Toleman TG280-Hart), 44; **14** Johnny Cecotto, YV (Minardi FLY281-BMW), 44; **15** Fredy Schnarwiler, CH (Toleman T850-BMW), 43; **16** Warren Booth, GB (Chevron B48C-Hart), 43; **17** Guido Dacco, I (Minardi GM75-BMW), 42; **18** Eje Elgh, S (Maurer MM81-BMW). 42; **19** Kenny Acheson, GB (Toleman T850-Hart), 41.
Running but not classified: Gianfranco Trombetti, I (March 812-BMW), 39.
Fastest lap: Lees, 1m 23·82s, 125·93 mph/202·66 km/h.
Retired: Paul Smith, GB (March 782-Hart), 8 laps, engine; Richard Dallest, F (AGS JH17-BMW), 8, accident; Roberto Guerrero, COL (Maurer MM81-BMW), 21, electrics; Kim Mather, GB (March 792-Hart), 24, wheel bearing; Guido Pardini, I (Toleman T850-BMW), 24, CWP; Thierry Boutsen, B (March 812-BMW), 36, spin; Geoff Lees, 45, spin.
Did not start: Jochen Dauer, D (GRS TC001-BMW), no engine; Bob Howlings, GB (Chevron B42-Hart), did not qualify; Arturo Merzario, I (Merzario M1-BMW), did not qualify; Roy Baker, GB (Chevron B48CTG-Hart), did not qualify.
Championship points: **1** Thackwell, 9; **2** Paletti, 6; **3** Fabi, 4; **4** Crawford, 3; **5** Rossi, 2; **6** Robinson, 1.

JIM CLARK RENNEN, Hockenheim-Ring, German Federal Republic, April 5. European Formula 2 Championship, round 2. 30 laps of the 4·2x9-mile/6·789-km circuit, 126·57 miles/203·67 km.

1 Stefan Johansson, S (Toleman T850-Hart), 1h 00m 28·05s, 125·591 mph/202·119 km/h.
2 Manfred Winkelhock, D (Ralt RT2-BMW), 1h 00m 29·19s.
3 Mike Thackwell, NZ (Ralt RH6-Honda), 1h 00m 42·62s.
4 Eje Elgh, S (Maurer MM81-BMW), 1h 00m 44·87s.
5 Geoff Lees, GB (Ralt RH6-Honda), 1h 00m 45·79s.
6 Carlo Rossi, I (Toleman TG280-Hart), 1h 00m 56·00s.
7 Jim Crawford, GB (Toleman TG280-Hart), 1h 00m 58·31s; **8** Michele Alboreto, I (Minardi FLY281-BMW), 1h 01m 14·11s; **9** Christian Danner, D (March 812-BMW), 1h 02m 02·31s; **10** Roberto Guerrero, COL (Maurer MM81-BMW), 1h 02m 05·23s; **11** Guido Dacco, I (Minardi GM75-BMW), 1h 02m 06·78s; **12** Fredy Schnarwiler, CH (Toleman T850-BMW), 1h 02m 27·93s; **13** Sewi Hopfer, A (Toleman TG280-Hart), 28 laps.
Fastest Lap: Riccardo Paletti, I (March 812-BMW), 1m 59·26s, 127·171 mph/204·662 km/h.
Retired: Johnny Cecotto, YV (Minardi FLY281-BMW), 1 lap, ignition; Richard Dallest, F (AGS JH18-BMW), 1, driver unwell; Marc Surer, CH (March 812-BMW), 1, damaged nosecone; Corrado Fabi, I (March 812-BMW), 3, accident; Gianfranco Trombetti, I (March 812-BMW), 6, electrics; Thierry Boutsen, B (March 812-BMW), 8, accident; Guido Pardini, I (Toleman T850-BMW), 9, oil union; Jochen Dauer, D (GRS TC001-BMW), 15, engine; Harald Brutschin, D (March 802-BMW), 15, throttle cable; Jurg Leinhard, CH (March 812-BMW), 17, engine; Riccardo Paletti, I (March 812-BMW), 23, alternator.
Championship points: **1** Thackwell, 13; **2** Johansson, 9; **3** Paletti and Winkelhock, 6; **5** Fabi, 4; **6** Crawford and Elgh, 3.

P & O FERRIES/JOCHEN RINDT TROPHY, Thruxton Circuit, Great Britain, April 20. European Formula 2 Championship, round 3. 55 laps of the 2·356-mile/3·792-km circuit, 129·58 miles/208·54 km.

1 Roberto Guerrero, COL (Maurer MM81-BMW), 1h 04m 02·40s, 121·41 mph/195·39 km/h.
2 Riccardo Paletti, I (March 812-BMW), 1h 04m 43·60s.
3 Johnny Cecotto, YV (Minardi FLY281-BMW), 1h 04m 59·61s.
4 Christian Danner, D (March 812-BMW), 1h 06m 01·69s.
5 Piero Necchi, I (March 812-BMW), 54 laps.
6 Stefan Johansson, S (Toleman T850-Hart), 53.
7 Bernd Brutschin, D (March 802-BMW), 52; **8** Fredy Schnarwiler, CH (Toleman T850-BMW), 52; **9** Paul Smith, GB (March 802/812-Hart), 52; **10** Warren Booth, GB (Chevron B48CD-Hart), 52; **11** Marc Surer, CH (March 812-BMW), 50 – not running at finish.
Running but not classified: Geoff Lees, GB (Ralt RH6-Honda), 40.
Disqualified: Eje Elgh, S (Maurer MM81-BMW), finished second on the road in 1h 04m 11·69s but disqualified due to over high rear wing.
Fastest lap: Surer, 1m 08·00s, 124·73 mph/200·73 km/h (outright record).
Retired: Michele Alboreto, I (Minardi FLY281-BMW), 8 laps, piston; Richard Dallest, F (AGS JH18-BMW), 10, driver unwell; Thierry Boutsen, B (March 812-BMW), 12, engine; Corrado Fabi, I (March 812-BMW), 15, accident; Guido Pardini, I (Toleman T850-BMW), 15, fuel pressure; Jim Crawford, GB (Toleman TG280-Hart), 19, engine; Manfred Winkelhock, D (Ralt RT2-BMW), 27, engine frame; Gianfranco Trombetti, I (March 812-BMW), 31, rear wheel; Sewi Hopfer, A (Toleman TG280-Hart), 32, engine mount; Carlo Rossi, I (Toleman TG280-Hart), 33, water leak; Kenny Acheson, GB (Toleman T850-Hart), 36, metering unit; Surer, 40, engine.
Did not start: Brian Robinson, GB (Chevron B42-Hart), withdrawn after first practice session; Roy Baker, GB (March 802-Hart), did not qualify; Arturo Merzario, I (Merzario M1-BMW), fuel injection failure on warm up lap.
Championship points: **1** Thackwell, 13; **2** Paletti, 12; **3** Johansson, 10; **4** Guerrero, 9; **5** Winkelhock, 6; **6** Fabi and Cecotto, 4.

EIFELRENNEN, Nürburgring Nordschleife, German Federal Republic, April 26. European Formula 2 Championship, round 4. 9 laps of the 14·189-mile/22·835-km circuit, 127·70 miles/205·52 km.

1 Thierry Boutsen, B (March 812-BMW), 1h 05m 04·63s, 117·74 mph/189·48 km/h.
2 Eje Elgh, S (Maurer MM81-BMW), 1h 06m 06·56s.

3 Corrado Fabi, I (March 812-BMW), 1h 06m 06·81s.
4 Stefan Johansson, S (Toleman T850-Hart), 1h 06m 10·26s.
5 Geoff Lees, GB (Ralt RH6-Honda), 1h 06m 37·78s.
6 Kenny Acheson, GB (Toleman T850-Hart), 1h 07m 05·24s.
7 Jo Gartner, A (Toleman TG280-BMW), 1h 07m 05·46s; **8** Michele Alboreto, I (Minardi FLY281-BMW), 1h 07m 53·25s; **9** Guido Pardini, I (Toleman, T850-BMW), 1h 07m 55·37s; **10** Christian Danner, D (March 812-BMW), 1h 08m 55·99s; **11** Franz Konrad, D (March 802-BMW), 1h 09m 15·57s; **12** Loris Kessel, CH (March 812-BMW), 1h 10m 23·03s; **13** Bernd Bruschin, D (March 802-BMW), 1h 10m 54·66s; **14** Sewi Hopfer, A (Toleman TG280-Hart), 8 laps; **15** Roberto Guerrero, COL (Maurer MM81-BMW), 7 – not running at finish; **16** Piero Necchi, I (March 812-BMW), 7 – not running at finish; **17** Harald Brutschin, D (March 812-BMW), 7.
Fastest lap: Boutsen, 7m 10·33s, 118·70 mph/191·03 km/h.
Retired: Riccardo Paletti, I (March 812-BMW), 0 laps, fuel pump; Carlo Rossi, I (Toleman TG280-Hart), 0, misfire; Manfred Winkelhock, D (Ralt RT2-BMW), 0, gearbox; Jim Crawford, GB (Toleman TG280-Hart), 1, suspension failure; Helmut Kalenborn, D (March 752-BMW), 2, engine; Jurg Leinhard, CH (March 812-BMW), 2, electrics; John Nielson, DK (March 792-BMW), 2, engine; Guido Dacco, I (Minardi GM75-BMW), 4, accident; Arturo Merzario, I (March 812-BMW), 4, suspension; Patrick Gaillard, F (AGS JH17-BMW), 4, oil pressure; Piero Necchi, 7, accident; Roberto Guerrero, 7, accident.
Did not start: Johnny Cecotto, YV (Minardi FLY280-BMW), accident in practice.
Championship points: **1** Thackwell and Johansson, 13; **3** Paletti, 12; **4** Elgh, Guerrero and Boutsen, 9.

31 GRAN PRIMIO ROMA, Autodromo di Vallelunga, Italy, May 10. European Formula 2 Championship, round 5. 65 laps of the 1·988-mile/3·200-km circuit, 129·24 miles/208·00 km.

1 Eje Elgh, S (Maurer MM81-BMW), 1h 16m 01·14s, 100·15 mph/161·18 km/h.
2 Stefan Johansson, S (Toleman T850-Hart), 1h 16m 04·42s.
3 Thierry Boutsen, B (March 812-BMW), 1h 16m 07·74s.
4 Corrado Fabi, I (March 812-BMW), 1h 16m 13·19s.
5 Geoff Lees, GB (Ralt RH6-Honda), 1h 16m 24·13s.
6 Riccardo Paletti, I (March 812-BMW), 1h 16m 53·09s.
7 Guido Pardini, I (Toleman T850-BMW), 1h 17m 00·76s; **8** Carlo Rossi, I (Toleman TG280-Hart), 64 laps; **9** Jim Crawford, GB (Toleman TG280-Hart), 63; **10** Kenny Acheson, GB (Toleman T850-Hart), 63; **11** Sewi Hopfer, A (Toleman TG280-Hart), 62; **12** Guido Dacco, I (Minardi GM75-BMW), 62; **13** Paul Smith, GB (March 812-Hart), 52; **14** Fredy Schnarwiler, CH (Toleman T850-BMW), 39 – not running at finish; **15** Roberto Guerrero, COL (Maurer MM81-BMW), 38 – not running at finish.
Fastest lap: Fabi, 1m 09·06s, 103·65 mph/166·81 km/h (record).
Retired: Christian Danner, D (March 812-BMW), 0 laps, accident; Jurg Leinhard, CH (March 812-BMW), 1, accident; Harald Brutschin, D (March 812-BMW), 1, accident; Richard Dallest, F (AGS JH18-BMW), 2, engine; Michele Alboreto, I (Minardi FLY281-BMW), 7, accident; Piero Necchi, I (March 812-BMW), 9, accident; Johnny Cecotto, YV (Minardi FLY281-BMW), 21, fuel blockage; Roberto Guerrero, 38, gearbox; Fredy Schnarwiler, 39, misfire.
Did not start: Gianfranco Trombetti, I (March 812-BMW), did not qualify; Oscar Pedersoli, I (Ralt RT2-BMW), did not qualify; Bernd Brutschin, D (March 802-BMW), did not qualify; Piero Nappi, I (Ralt RT2-Hart), did not qualify; Marco Brand, I (Merzario M2-BMW), did not qualify.
Championship points: **1** Johansson, 19; **2** Elgh, 18; **3** Thackwell, Paletti and Bousen, 13; **6** Fabi, 11.

EUROPEAN FORMULA 2 CHAMPIONSHIP RACE, Autodromo Internazionale del Mugello, Italy, May 24. European Formula 2 Championship, round 6. 42 laps of the 3·259-mile/5·245-km circuit, 136·88 miles/220·29 km.

1 Corrado Fabi, I (March 812-BMW), 1h 15m 20·99s, 109·00 mph/175·42 km/h.
2 Geoff Lees, GB (Ralt RH6-Honda), 1h 15m 22·40s.
3 Piero Necchi, I (March 812-BMW), 1h 15m 31·82s.
4 Eje Elgh, S (Maurer MM81-BMW), 1h 15m 32·95s.
5 Mike Thackwell, NZ (Ralt RH6-Honda), 1h 15m 57·14s.
6 Roberto Guerrero, COL (Maurer MM81-BMW), 1h 16m 08·59s.
7 Richard Dallest, F (AGS JH18-BMW), 1h 16m 13·20s; **8** Carlo Rossi, I (Toleman TG280-Hart), 1h 16m 16·76s; **9** Jo Gartner, A (Toleman TG280-BMW), 1h 16m 17·50s; **10** Riccardo Paletti, I (March 812-BMW), 1h 16m 39·77s; **11** Jim Crawford, GB (Toleman TG280-Hart), 1h 16m 44·73s; **12** Guido Pardini, I (Toleman T850-BMW), 1h 16m 57·50s; **13** Johnny Cecotto, YV (March 802-BMW), 41 laps; **14** Michele Alboreto, I (Minardi FLY281-BMW), 41; **15** Kenny Acheson, GB (Toleman T850-Hart), 41; **16** Christian Danner, D (March 812-BMW), 41; **17** Jurg Leinhard, CH (March 812-BMW), 41; **18** Roberto Del Castello, I (March 782-BMW), 40; **19** Paul Smith, GB (March 812-Hart), 40; **20** Guido Dacco, I (Minardi GM75-BMW), 40; **21** Loris Kessel, CH (March 812-BMW), 27 – not running at finish; **22** Stefan Johansson, S (Toleman T850-Hart), 22 – not running at finish.
Fastest lap: Necchi, 1m 46·27s, 110·50 mph/117·83 km/h.
Retired: Fredy Schnarwiler, CH (Toleman T850-BMW), 6 laps, puncture; Sewi Hopfer, A (Toleman TG280-BMW), 7, engine; Thierry Boutsen, B (March 812-BMW), 7, engine; Oscar Pedersoli, I (Ralt RT2-BMW), 9, engine; Piero Nappi, I (Ralt RT2-Hart), 11, gearbox; Gianfranco Trombetti, I (March 812-BMW), 12, accident; Johansson, 22, engine; Kessel, 27, engine.
Did not start: Roy Baker, GB (March 802-Hart), did not qualify.
Championship points: **1** Elgh, 21; **2** Fabi, 20; **3** Johansson, 19; **4** Thackwell, 15; **5** Paletti and Boutsen, 13.

41 GRAND PRIX DE PAU, Circuit de Pau, France, June 8. European Formula 2 Championship, round 7. 73 laps of the 1.715-mile/2.760-km circuit, 125.19 miles/201.48 km.

1 Geoff Lees, GB (Ralt RH6-Honda), 1h 33m 13.91s, 80.569 mph/129.663 km/h.
2 Thierry Boutsen, B (March 812-BMW), 1h 33m 14.43s.
3 Piero Necchi, I (March 812-BMW), 1h 34m 11.87s.
4 Carlo Rossi, I (Toleman TG280-Hart), 72 laps.
5 Eje Elgh, S (Maurer MM81-BMW), 72.
6 Mike Thackwell, NZ (Ralt RH6-Honda), 72.
7 Johnny Cecotto, YV (March 812-BMW), 72; **8** Stefan Johansson, S (Toleman T850-Hart), 71; **9** Ricardo Londono, COL (Toleman TG280-Hart), 70; **10** Jim Crawford, GB (Toleman TG280-Hart), 69.
Fastest lap: Lees, 1m 15.0s, 82.319 mph/132.48 km/h.
Retired: Oscar Pedersoli, I (Ralt RT2-BMW), 1 lap, accident; Kenny Acheson, GB (Toleman T850-Hart), 2, accident; Michele Alboreto, I (Minardi FLY281-BMW), 3, accident; Christian Danner, D (March 812-BMW), 15, accident; Corrado Fabi, I (March 812-BMW), 36, brakes; Richard Dallest, F (AGS JH18-BMW), 39, brakes; Roberto Guerrero, COL (Maurer MM81-BMW), 44, accident; Riccardo Paletti, I (March 812-BMW), 47, engine.
Did not start: Guido Pardini, I (Toleman T850-BMW), crashed on warm up lap; Ray Mallock, GB (Ralt RT4-Hart), did not qualify; Harald Brutschin, D (March 812-BMW), did not qualify; Paul Smith, GB (March 802/812-Hart), did not qualify; Bernd Brutschin, D (March 802-BMW), did not qualify.
Championship points: **1** Elgh, 23; **2** Lees, 21; **3** Fabi, 20; **4** Johansson and Boutsen, 19; **6** Thackwell, 16.

19 GRAN PREMIO DEL MEDITERRANEO, Ente Autodromo di Pergusa, Enna, Sicily, July 26. European Formula 2 Championship, round 8. 45 laps of the 3.076-mile/4.950-km circuit, 138.42 miles/ 222.85 km.
1 Thierry Boutsen, B (March 812-BMW), 1h 10m 09.82s, 118.36 mph/190.48 km/h.
2 Huub Rothengatter, NL (March 812-BMW), 1h 10m 13.12s.
3 Michele Alboreto, I (Minardi FLY281-BMW), 1h 10m 24.58s.
4 Roberto Guerrero, COL (Maurer MM81-BMW), 1h 10m 28.63s.
5 Eje Elgh, S (Maurer MM81-BMW), 1h 10m 37.44s.
6 Jo Gartner, A (Toleman TG280-BMW), 1h 11m 18.66s.
7 Fredy Schnarwiler, CH (Toleman TG850-BMW), 44 laps; **8** Paul Smith, GB (March 812-Hart), 43; **9** Richard Dallest, F (AGS JH15-BMW), 43; **10** Roberto del Castello, I (March 782-BMW), 42; **11** Piero Necchi, I (March 812-BMW), 42; **12** Gianfranco Trombetti, I (March 812-BMW), 41.
Fastest lap: Boutsen, 1m 32.05s, 120.30 mph/193.60 km/h.
Retired: Stefan Johansson, S (Toleman T850-Hart), 0 laps, accident; Carlo Rossi, I (Toleman TG280-Hart), 3, fuel pressure; Loris Kesell, CH (March 802-BMW), 4, electrics; Paolo Barilla, I (Minardi FLY281-Ferrari), 7, suspension; Geoff Lees, GB (Ralt RH6-Honda), 10, tyre; Christian Danner, D (March 812-BMW), 13, accident; Guido Pardini, I (Toleman TG850-BMW), 13, accident; Riccardo Paletti, I (March 812-BMW), 13, accident; Johnny Cecotto, YV (March 812-BMW), 14, engine; Guido Dacco, I (Merzario M2-BMW), 20, engine; Ricardo Londono, COL (Toleman TG280-Hart), engine; Corrado Fabi, I (March 812-BMW), 35, engine; Mike Tackwell, NZ (Ralt RH6-Honda), 39, tyres.
Championship points: 1 Boutsen, 28; **2** Elgh, 25; **3** Lees, 21; **4** Fabi, 20; **5** Johansson, 19; **6** Thackwell, 16.

GRAND PRIX de FORMULE 2, Spa-Francorchamps, Belgium, August 9. European Formula 2 Championship, round 9. 30 laps of the 4.332-mile/6.972-km circuit, 129.96 miles/209.16 km.
1 Geoff Lees, GB (Ralt RH6-Honda), 1h 10m 02.68s, 111.392 mph/179.268 km/h.
2 Thierry Boutsen, B (March 812-BMW), 1h 10m 11.65s.
3 Eje Elgh, S (Maurer MM81-BMW), 1h 10m 47.18s.
4 Corrado Fabi, I (March 812-BMW), 1h 10m 48.95s.
5 Manfred Winkelhock, D (Maurer MM81-BMW), 1h 10m 57.46s.
6 Jim Crawford, GB (Toleman TG280-Hart), 1h 11m 19.35s.
7 Piero Necchi, I (March 812-BMW), 1h 11m 36.78s; **8** Michele Alboreto, I (Minardi FLY281-BMW), 1h 11m 42.76s; **9** Ray Mallock, GB (Ralt RT4-Hart), 29 laps, **10** Paul Smith, GB (March 812-Hart), 29; **11** Sewi Hopfer, A (Toleman TG280-Hart), 29; **12** Gianfranco Trombetti, I (March 812-BMW), 29; **13** Huub Rothengatter, NL (March 812-BMW), 29; **14** Stefan Johansson, S (Toleman T850B-Hart), 28; **15** Guido Dacco, I (Minardi GM75-BMW), 27; **16** Richard Dallest, F (AGS JH18-BMW), 3.
Fastest lap: Lees, 2m 16.81s, 114.062 mph/183.565 km/h (record).
Retired: Hervé Regout, B (Ralt RT2-BMW), 0 laps, accident; Carlo Rossi, I (Toleman TG280-Hart), 2, accident; Mike Thackwell, GB (Ralt RH6-Honda), 3, accident; Guido Pardini, I (Toleman T850-BMW), 6, engine; Roberto Guerrero, COL (Maurer MM81-BMW), 11, fuel pump; Fredy Schnarwiler, CH (Toleman T850-BMW), 12, suspension; Ricardo Londono, COL (Toleman TG280-Hart), 15, flywheel; Patrick Gaillard, F (March 802-BMW), 19, engine; Marco Brand, I (Merzario M2-BMW), 23, oil pressure; Johnny Cecotto, YV (March 812-BMW), 24, electrics; Jo Gartner, A (Toleman TG280-BMW), 25, suspension; Harald Brutschin, D (March 802-BMW), 27, engine; Riccardo Paletti, I (March 812-BMW), 27, engine.
Did not start: John Nielsen, DK (March 792-BMW), accident in practice; Roy Baker, GB (March 802-Hart), did not qualify.
Championship points: 1 Boutsen, 34; **2** Lees, 30; **3** Elgh, 29; **4** Fabi, 23; **5** Johansson, 19; **6** Thackwell, 16.

JOHN HOWITT TROPHY RACE, Donington Park Circuit, Great Britain, August 16. European Formula 2 Championship, round 10. 70 laps of the 1.9573-mile/3.150-km circuit, 137.01 miles/220.50 km.
1 Geoff Lees, GB (Ralt RH6-Honda), 1h 16m 49.82s, 107.00 mph/172.20 km/h.
2 Corrado Fabi, I (March 812-BMW), 1h 17m 00.58s.
3 Manfred Winkelhock, D (Maurer MM81-BMW), 1h 17m 18.58s.
4 Stefan Johansson, S (Toleman TG280B-Hart), 1h 17m 41.10s.
5 Mike Thackwell, NZ (Ralt RH6-Honda), 1h 17m 45.49s.
6 Johnny Cecotto, YV (March 812-BMW), 1h 17m 54.78s.
7 Eje Elgh, S (Maurer MM81-BMW), 69 laps; **8** Huub Rothengatter, NL (March 812-BMW), 69, **9** Jim Crawford, GB (Toleman TG280-Hart), 69; **10** Paolo Barilla, I (Minardi FLY281-BMW), 69; **11** Tiff Needell, GB (AGS JH18-BMW), 69; **12** Thierry Boutsen, B (March 812-BMW), 69; **13** Guido Pardini, I (Toleman T850-BMW), 69; **14** Christian Danner, D (March 812-BMW), 69; **15** Keiji Matsumoto, J (March 802-BMW), 68; **16** Fredy Schnarwiler, CH (Toleman T850-BMW), 68; **17** Paul Smith, GB (March 812-Hart), 68; **18** Kim Mather, GB (March 792-Hart), 65; **19** Loris Kessel, CH (March 812-BMW), 64.
Fastest lap: Lees and Fabi, 1m 05.10s, 108.24 mph/174.19 km/h.
Retired: Roberto Guerrero, COL (Maurer MM81-BMW), 1 lap, suspension; Carlo Rossi, I (Toleman TG280-Hart), 9, nosecone; Ray Mallock, GB (Ralt RT4-Hart), 14, stub axle; Riccardo Paletti, I (March 812-BMW), 29, engine; Piero Necchi, I (March 812-BMW), 42, misfire; Sewi Hopfer, A (Toleman TG280-Hart), 44, handling; Guido Dacco, I (Minardi GM75-BMW), 48, engine; Jo Gartner, A (Toleman TG280-BMW), 51, engine.
Did not start: Richard Dallest, F (AGS JH18-BMW), driver unwell; Ricardo Londono, COL (Toleman TG280-Hart), accident in warm up; Brian Robinson, GB (Chevron B48-Hart), did not qualify; Roy Baker, GB (March 802-Hart), did not qualify.
Championship points: 1 Lees, 39; **2** Boutsen, 34; **3** Fabi and Elgh, 29; **5** Johansson, 22; **6** Thackwell, 18.

5th GRAN PREMIO DEL ADRIATICO, Autodromo Santamonica Misano, Italy, September 6. European Formula 2 Championship, round 11. 60 laps of the 2.167-mile/3.488-km circuit, 130.02 miles/209.28 km.
1 Michele Alboreto, I (Minardi FLY281-BMW), 1h 12m 03.74s, 106.41 mph/171.25 km/h.
2 Geoff Lees, GB (Ralt RH6-Honda), 1h 12m 12.90s.
3 Mike Thackwell, NZ (Ralt RH6-Honda), 1h 12m 54.50s.
4 Roberto Guerrero, COL (Maurer MM81-BMW), 1h 12m 55.01s.
5 Richard Dallest, F (AGS JH18-BMW), 1h 12m 55.32s.
6 Johnny Cecotto, YV (March 812-BMW), 1h 13m 15.33s.
7 Jim Crawford, GB (Toleman TG230-Hart), 1h 13m 22.48s; **8** Thierry Boutsen, B (March 812-BMW), 59 laps; **9** Stefan Johansson, S (Toleman TG280B-Hart), 59; **10** Carlo Rossi, I (Toleman TG280-Hart), 59; **11** Huub Rothengatter, NL (March 812-BMW), 59; **12** Gianfranco Trombetti, I (March 812-BMW), 58; **13** Angel Guerra, RA (Minardi FLY281-Ferrari), 56.
Fastest lap: Alboreto and Lees, 1m 11.01s, 109.88 mph/176.83 km/h (record).
Retired: Riccardo Paletti, I (March 812-BMW), 0 laps, accident; Christian Danner, D (March 812-BMW), 0, accident; Oscar Pedersoli, I (Ralt RT2-BMW), 8, engine; Roberto Del Castello, I (March 782-BMW), 26, gearbox; Roberto Farnetti, I (Minardi FLY281-BMW), 29, engine; Eje Elgh, S (Maurer MM81-BMW), 33, brakes; Guido Pardini, I (Toleman T850-BMW), 46, engine; Anders Olofsson, S (March 792-Hart), 46, engine.
Did not start: Jo Gartner, A (March 812-BMW), did not qualify; Paul Smith, GB (March 812-Hart), did not qualify; Guido Dacco, I (Minardi GM75-BMW), did not qualify; Sewi Hopfer, A (Toleman TG280-Hart), did not qualify.
Championship points: 1 Lees, 45; **2** Boutsen, 34; **3** Elgh and Fabi, 29; **5** Thackwell and Johansson, 22.

EUROPEAN FORMULA 2 CHAMPIONSHIP RACE, Mantorp Park, Sweden, September 20. European Formula 2 Championship, round 12. 65 laps of the 1.942-mile/3.125-km circuit, 126.23 miles/204.00 km.
1 Stefan Johansson, S (Toleman TG280B-Hart), 1h 20m 08.8s, 94.50 mph/152.08 km/h.
2 Geoff Lees, GB (Ralt RH6-Honda), 1h 20m 15.3s.
3 Kenny Acheson, GB (Toleman T850-Hart), 1h 20m 44.5s.
4 Thierry Boutsen, B (March 812-BMW), 1h 20m 45.8s.
5 Richard Dallest, F (AGS JH18-BMW), 1h 21m 05.3s.
6 Johnny Cecotto, YV (March 812-BMW), 1h 21m 20.5s.
7 Corrado Fabi, I (March 812-BMW), 64 laps; **8** Jo Gartner, A (March 812-BMW), 64; **9** Anders Olofsson, S (March 792-Hart), 64; **10** Jim Crawford, GB (Toleman TG280-Hart), 64; **11** Christian Danner, D (March 812-BMW), 64; **12** Guido Dacco, I (Minardi GM75-BMW), 64; **13** Gianfranco Trombetti, I (March 812-BMW), 64; **14** Paul Smith, GB (March 812-Hart), 63; **15** Mike Thackwell, NZ (Ralt RH6-Honda), 63; **16** Umberto Calvo, I (Toleman TG280-BMW), 63; **17** Eje Elgh, S (Maurer MM81-BMW), 62; **18** Stanley Dickens, GB (March 802-BMW), 60.
Fastest lap: Cecotto, 1m 11.69s, 97.52 mph/156.94 km/h (record).
Retired: Arturo Merzario, I (Merzario M2-BMW), 13 laps, not competitive; Huub Rothengatter, NL (March 812-BMW), 29, engine; Roberto Guerrero, COL (Maurer MM81-BMW), 43, gear linkage; Riccardo Paletti, I (March 812-BMW), 55, spin.
Final Championship points (following the reinstatement of Eje Elgh in second place at Thruxton):

1	Geoff Lees, GB	51
2	Thierry Boutsen, B	37
3	Eje Elgh, S	35
4	Stefan Johansson, S	30
5	Corrado Fabi, I	29
6	Mike Thackwell, NZ	22

7 Roberto Guerrero, COL, 16; **8** Michele Alboreto, I, 13; **9** Manfred Winkelhock, D, 12; **10** Riccardo Paletti, I, 11; **11** Piero Necchi, I, 9; **12**= Carlo Rossi, I, 6; **12**= Johnny Cecotto, YV, 6; **12**= Huub Rothengatter, NL, 6; **15** Kenny Acheson, GB, 5; **16**= Jim Crawford, GB, 4; **16**= Richard Dallest, F, 4; **18** Christian Danner, D, 2; **19**= Brian Robinson, GB, 1; **19**= Jo Gartner, A, 1.

Formula 3

MARLBORO CHAMPIONSHIP RACE, Silverstone Short Circuit, Great Britain, March 1. Marlboro British Formula 3 Championship, round 1. 20 laps of the 1·608-mile/2·588-km circuit, 32·16 miles/51·76 km.
1 Jonathan Palmer, GB (Ralt RT3-Toyota), 21m 08·22s, 91·29 mph/146·92 km/h.
2 Mike White, ZA (March 813-Alfa Romeo), 21m 08·59s.
3 Raul Boesel, BR (Ralt RT3/81-Toyota), 21m 12·69s.
4 Michael Bleekemolen, NL (Ralt RT3/81-Toyota), 21m 24·62s.
5 Thierry Tassin, B (Argo JM8-Toyota), 21m 31·22s.
6 Kurt Thiim, DK (March 813-Toyota), 21m 32·72s.
7 James Weaver, GB (Ralt RT3-Toyota), 21m 39·09s; **8** Toshio Suzuki, J (March 813-Toyota), 21m 45·74s; **9** John Booth, GB (Argo JM8-Toyota), 22m 06·08s; **10** David Sears, GB (Ralt RT3/81-Toyota), 19 laps.
Fastest lap: White, 1m 01·63s, 93·93 mph/151·17 km/h.
Marlboro Championship points: 1 Palmer, 9; **2** White, 7; **3** Boesel, 4; **4** Bleekemolen, 3; **5** Tassin, 2; **6** Thiim, 1.

MARLBORO CHAMPIONSHIP RACE, Thruxton Circuit, Great Britain, March 8. Marlboro British Formula 3 Championship, round 2. 15 laps of the 2·356-mile/3·792-km circuit, 35·34 miles/56·88 km.
1 Jonathan Palmer, GB (Ralt RT3-Toyota), 19m 10·14s, 110·62 mph/178·03 km/h.
2 David Sears, GB (Ralt RT3/81-Toyota), 19m 12·91s.
3 Michael Bleekemolen, NL (Ralt RT3/81-Toyota), 19m 14·06s.
4 James Weaver, GB (Ralt RT3-Toyota), 19m 20·27s.
5 Thierry Tassin, B (Argo JM8-Toyota), 19m 20·83s.
6 Richard Trott, GB (Ralt RT3/81-Toyota), 19m 26·21s.
7 Raul Boesel, BR (Ralt RT3/81-Toyota), 19m 34·65s; **8** Cliff Hansen, USA (Ralt RT3/81-Toyota), 19m 36·76s; **9** Toshio Suzuki, J (March 813-Toyota), 19m 39·15s; **10** Dave Scott, GB (Argo JM6-Toyota), 19m 40·32s.
Fastest lap: Palmer, 1m 15·96s, 111·86 mph/180·02 km/h.
Marlboro Championship points: 1 Palmer, 19; **2** White and Bleekemolen, 7; **4** Sears, 6; **5** Boesel and Tassin, 4.

EUROPEAN FORMULA 3 CHAMPIONSHIP RACE, Autodromo di Vallelunga, Italy, March 15. European Formula 3 Championship, round 1. Two 15 lap heats of the 1·988-mile/3·200-km circuit, 30 lap final, 59·64 miles/96·00 km.
1 Mauro Baldi, I (March 813-Alfa Romeo), 37m 11·38s, 96·24 mph/154·88 km/h.
2 Enzo Coloni, I (Ralt RT3/81-Toyota), 37m 11·95s.
3 Alain Ferte, F (Martini Mk34-Alfa Romeo), 37m 16·80s.
4 Oscar Larrauri, RA (March 813-Toyota), 37m 17·64s.
5 Philippe Alliot, F (Martini Mk34-Alfa Romeo), 37m 28·01s.
6 Jean-Louis Schlesser, F (Martini Mk34-Alfa Romeo), 37m 28·86s.
7 Paolo Barilla, I (Martini Mk34-Alfa Romeo), 37m 42·06s; **8** Pascal Fabre, F (Martini Mk34-Alfa Romeo), 37m 48·02s; Fabio Mancini, I (March 813-Alfa Romeo), 37m 53·17s; **10** Frank Jelinski, D (Ralt RT3-Toyota), 37m 59·01s.
Fastest lap: Larrauri, 1m 13·65s, 97·19 mph/156·41 km/h.
Heat 1: 1 Ferte, 18m 33·45s, 96·35 mph/155·04 km/h; **2** Coloni; **3** Larrauri; **4** Barilla; **5** Mancini; **6** Peter Schindler, A (Ralt RT3-Toyota).
Fastest lap: Coloni, 1m 13·59s, 97·27 mph/156·54 km/h (record).
Heat 2: 1 Baldi, 18m 41·19s, 95·77 mph/154·13 km/h; **2** Alliot; **3** Schlesser; **4** Eddy Bianchi, I (Martini Mk34-Toyota); **5** Emanuele Pirro, I (Martini Mk34-Toyota); **6** Fabre.
Fastest lap: Baldi, 1m 13·93s, 96·82 mph/155·82 km/h.
European Championship points: 1 Baldi, 9; **2** Coloni, 6; **3** Ferte, 4; **4** Larrauri, 3; **5** Alliot, 2; **6** Schlesser, 1.

MARLBORO CHAMPIONSHIP RACE, Silverstone Grand Prix Circuit, Great Britain, March 29. Marlboro British Formula 3 Championship, round 3. 20 laps of the 2·932-mile/4·719-km circuit, 58·64 miles/94·38 km.
1 Jonathan Palmer, GB (Ralt RT3-Toyota), 33m 16·42s, 105·74 mph/170·17 km/h.
2 Kurt Thiim, DK (March 813-Toyota), 33m 16·49s.
3 Raul Boesel, BR (Ralt RT3/81-Toyota), 33m 24·74s.
4 James Weaver, GB (Ralt RT3-Toyota), 33m 27·60s.
5 Michael Bleekemolen, NL (Ralt RT3/81-Toyota), 33m 32·74s.
6 David Leslie, GB (Ralt RT3/81-Toyota), 33m 32·93s.
7 Mike White, ZA (March 813-Alfa Romeo), 33m 34·84s; **8** Terry Gray, GB (Ralt RT3-Toyota), 33m 35·32s; **9** Toshio Suzuki, J (March 813-Toyota), 33m 53·37s; **10** Mike O'Brian, GB (March 803C-Toyota), 34m 24·71s.
Fastest lap: Boesel, 1m 38·03s, 107·67 mph/173·28 km/h.
Marlboro Championship points: 1 Palmer, 28; **2** Boesel and Bleekemolen, 9; **4** White and Thiim, 7; **6** Sears and Weaver, 6.

EUROPEAN FORMULA 3 CHAMPIONSHIP RACE, Nürburgring Sprint Circuit, German Federal Republic, March 29. European Formula 3 Championship, round 2. Two 18 lap heats of the 1·370-mile/2·205-km circuit, 40 lap final, 54·80 miles/88·20 km.
1 Oscar Larrauri, RA (March 813-Toyota), 34m 50·50s, 98·101 mph/157·878 km/h.
2 Philippe Alliot, F (Martini Mk34-Alfa Romeo), 34m 52·24s.
3 Alain Ferte, F (Martini Mk34-Alfa Romeo), 34m 54·12s.
4 Jean-Louis Schlesser, F (Martini Mk34-Alfa Romeo), 35m 01·51s.
5 Mauro Baldi, I (March 813-Alfa Romeo), 35m 19·92s.
6 Harald Brutschin, D (Ralt RT3-Toyota), 35m 25·37s.
7 Frank Jelinski, D (Ralt RT3-Toyota), 35m 27·60s; **8** Denis Morin, F (Martini Mk31-Toyota), 35m 32·66s; **9** Fabio Mancini, I (March 813-Alfa Romeo), 35m 33·11s; **10** Franz Konrad, D (March 803B-Toyota), 35m 35·91s.
Fastest lap: Larrauri, 51·51s, 99·535 mph/160.192 km/h.
Heat 1: 1 Baldi, 15m 36·61s, 98·533 mph/158·573 km/h; **2** Ferte; **3** Schlesser; **4** Philippe Streiff, F (Martini Mk34-Alfa Romeo); **5** Pascal Fabre, F (Martini Mk34-Alfa Romeo); **6** Konrad.
Fastest lap: Baldi, 51·06s, 101·412 mph/163·206 km/h (record).
Heat 2: 1 Larrauri, 15m 40·55s, 98·120 mph/157·908 km/h; **2** Alliott; **3** Jelinski; **4** Morin; **5** Peter Schindler, A (Ralt RT3-Toyota); **6** Jo Zeller, CH (March 793-Toyota).
Fastest lap: Alliot, 51·44s, 99·670 mph/160·403 km/h.
European Championship points: 1 Larrauri, 12; **2** Balci, 11; **3** Ferte and Alliot, 8; **5** Coloni, 6; **6** Schlesser, 4.

EUROPEAN FORMULA 3 CHAMPIONSHIP RACE, Donington Park Circuit, Great Britain, April 5. European Formula 3 Championship, round 3. 32 laps of the 1·9573-mile/3·150-km circuit, 62·63 miles/ 100·80 km.
1 Mike White, ZA (March 813-Alfa Romeo), 37m 16·97s, 100·80 mph/162·22 km/h.
2 Alain Ferte, F (Martini Mk34-Alfa Romeo), 37m 29·30s.
3 Oscar Larrauri, RA (March 813-Toyota), 37m 30·08s.
4 Toshio Suzuki, J (March 813-Toyota), 37m 39·78s.
5 Philippe Alliot, F (Martini Mk34-Alfa Romeo), 37m 41·09s.
6 Mauro Baldi, I (March 813-Alfa Romeo), 37m 41·33s.
7 Kurt Thiim, DK (March 813-Toyota), 37m 46·42s; **8** Frank Jelinski, D (Ralt RT3-Toyota), 38m 04·31s; **9** Philippe Streiff, F (Martini Mk34-Alfa Romeo), 38m 08·29s; **10** Pascal Fabre, F (Martini Mk34-Alfa Romeo), 38m 09·05s.
Fastest lap: White, 1m 09·15s, 101·90 mph/163·99 km/h (record).
European Championship points: 1 Larrauri, 16; **2** Ferte, 14; **3** Baldi, 12; **4** Alliot, 10; **5** White, 9; **6** Coloni, 6.

MARLBORO CHAMPIONSHIP RACE, Mallory Park Circuit, Great Britain, April 12. Marlboro British Formula 3 Championship, round 4. 25 laps of the 1·350-mile/2·173-km circuit, 33·75 miles/54·33 km.
1 Jonathan Palmer, GB (Ralt RT3-Toyota), 18m 12·39s, 111·22 mph/178·99 km/h.
2 Mike White, ZA (March 813-Alfa Romeo), 18m 12·65s.
3 Raul Boesel, BR (Ralt RT3/81-Toyota), 18m 21·55s.
4 David Leslie, GB (Ralt RT3/81-Toyta), 18m 21·90s.
5 Cliff Hansen, USA (Ralt RT3/81-Toyota), 18m 23·82s.
6 Thierry Tassin, B (Ralt RT3/81-Toyota), 18m 24·22s.
7 Richard Trott, GB (Ralt RT3/81-Toyota), 18m 31·19s; **8** Michael Bleekemolen, NL (Ralt RT3/81-Toyota), 18m 39·92s; **9** Jon Beekhuis, USA (Arge JM8-Toyota), 18m 51·05s; **10** Kees Nierop, CDN (Ralt RT3/81-Toyota), 24 laps.
Fastest lap: White, 42·95s, 113·95 mph/183·38 km/h (record).
Marlboro Championship points: 1 Palmer, 37; **2** White, 14; **3** Boesel, 13; **4** Bleekemolen, 9; **5** Thiim, 7; **6** Sears and Weaver, 6.

EUROPEAN FORMULA 3 CHAMPIONSHIP RACE, Osterreichring, Austria, April 19. European Formula 3 Championship, round 4. 18 laps of the 3·692-mile/5·942-km circuit, 66·46 miles/106.96 km.
1 Mauro Baldi, I (March 813-Alfa Romeo), 33m 28·25s, 119·14 mph/191·74 km/h.
2 Oscar Larrauri, RA (March 813-Toyota), 33m 48·74s.
3 Philippe Alliot, F (Martini Mk34-Alfa Romeo), 33m 48·97s.
4 Frank Jelinski, D (Ralt RT3-Toyota), 33m 55·31s.
5 Franz Konrad, A (March 813-Toyota), 33m 57·20s.
6 Philippe Streiff, F (Martini Mk34-Alfa Romeo), 33m 57·37s.
7 Peter Schindler, A (Ralt RT3-Toyota), 33m 57·98s; **8** Fabio Mancini, I (March 813-Alfa Romeo), 33m 58·57s; **9** Alain Ferte, F (Martini Mk34-Alfa Romeo), 34m 02·73s; **10** Emanuele Pirro, I (Martini Mk34-Toyota), 34m 13·88s.
Fastest lap: Baldi, 1m 50·33s, 120·47 mph/193·88 km/h (record).
European Championship points: 1 Larrauri, 22; **2** Baldi, 21; **3** Ferte and Alliot, 14; **5** White, 9; **6** Coloni, 6.

MARLBORO CHAMPIONSHIP RACE, Thruxton Circuit, Great Britain, April 20. Marlboro British Formula 3 Championship, round 5. 15 laps of the 2·356-mile/3·792-km circuit, 35·34 miles/56·88 km.
1 Thierry Tassin, B (Ralt RT3/81-Toyota), 18m 40·59s, 113·53 mph/182·71 km/h.
2 David Leslie, GB (Ralt RT3/81-Toyota), 18m 41·70s.
3 Raul Boesel, BR (Ralt RT3/81-Toyota), 18m 45·76s.
4 Cliff Hansen, USA (Ralt RT3/81-Toyota), 18m 55·15s.
5 Michael Bleekemolen, NL (Ralt RT3/81-Toyota), 19m 01·63s.
6 James Weaver, GB (Ralt RT3-Toyota), 19m 02·19s.
7 Toshio Suzuki, J (March 813-Toyota), 19m 02·19s; **8** Dave Scott, GB (Argo JM6-Toyota), 19m 14·87s; **9** Kurt Thiim, DK (March 813-Toyota), 19m 15·13s; **10** Shuroku Sasaki, J (Ralt RT3/81-Toyota), 19m 17·66s.
Fastest lap: Tassin, 1m 13·93s, 114·72 mph/184·62 km/h.
Marlboro Championship points: 1 Palmer, 37; **2** Boesel, 17; **3** Tassin, 15; **4** White, 14; **5** Bleekemolen, 11; **6** Leslie, 10.

GROTE PRIJS VAN ZOLDER, Omloop van Zolder, Belgium, April 26. European Formula 3 Championship, round 5. 22 laps of the 2·648-mile/4·262-km circuit, 58·26 miles/93·76 km.
1 Mauro Baldi, I (March 813-Alfa Romeo), 33m 58·1s, 102·91 mph/165·62 km/h.
2 Philippe Streiff, F (Martini Mk34-Alfa Romeo), 34m 12·4s.
3 Oscar Larrauri, RA (March 813-Toyota), 34m 13·0s.
4 Phillipe Alliot, F (Martini Mk34-Alfa Romeo), 34m 13·1s.
5 Alain Ferte, F (Martini Mk34-Alfa Romeo), 34m 31·0s.
6 Fabio Mancini, I (March 813-Alfa Romeo), 34m 34·0s.
7 Peter Schindler, A (Ralt RT3-Toyota), 34m 37·8s; **8** Denis Morin, F (Martini Mk34-Toyota), 34m 38·2s; **9** Pascal Fabre, F (Martini Mk34-Alfa Romeo), 34m 43·6s; **10** Didier Theys, B (Martini Mk34-Alfa Romeo), 34m 44·7s.
Fastest lap: Baldi, 1m 31·7s, 103·96 mph/167·31 km/h (record).
European Championship points: 1 Baldi, 30; **2** Larrauri, 26; **3** Alliot, 17; **4** Ferte, 16; **5** White, 9; **6** Streiff, 7.

EUROPEAN FORMULA 3 CHAMPIONSHIP RACE, Magny Cours, France, May 3. European Formula 3 Championship, round 6. 26 laps of the 2·361-mile/3·800-km circuit, 61·39 miles/98·90 km.
1 Philippe Alliot, F (Martini Mk34-Alfa Romeo), 36m 50·16s, 101·31 mph/163·04 km/h.
2 Mauro Baldi, I (March 813-Alfa Romeo), 36m 50·68s.
3 Alain Ferte, F (Martini Mk34-Alfa Romeo), 36m 53·84s.
4 Philippe Streiff, F (Martini Mk34-Alfa Romeo), 36m 56·08s.
5 Jean-Louis Schlesser, F (Martini Mk34-Alfa Romeo), 36m 56·94s.
6 Jean-Michel Neyerial, F (Martini Mk31-Toyota), 37m 19·21s.
7 Oscar Larrauri, RA (March 813-Toyota), 37m 21·45s; **8** Didier Theys, B (Martini Mk34-Alfa Romeo), 37m 23·84s; **9** Frank Jelinski, D (Ralt RT3-Toyota), 37m 28·30s; **10** Pascal Fabre, F (Martini Mk34-Alfa Romeo), 37m 34·08s.
Fastest lap: Baldi, 1m 24·20s, 102·28 mph/164·60 km/h (record).
European Championship points: 1 Baldi, 36; **2** Larrauri and Alliot, 26; **4** Ferte, 20; **5** Streiff, 10; **6** White, 9.

MARLBORO CHAMPIONSHIP RACE, Thruxton Circuit, Great Britain, May 4. Marlboro British Formula 3 Championship, round 6. 15 laps of the 2·356-mile/3·792-km circuit, 35·34 miles/56·88 km.
1 Mike White, ZA (March 813-Alfa Romeo), 18m 53·66s, 112·22 mph/180·60 km/h.
2 Thierry Tassin, B (Ralt RT3/81-Toyota), 18m 55·54s.
3 David Leslie, GB (Ralt RT3/81-Toyota), 18m 56·52s.
4 Kurt Thiim, DK (March 813-Toyota), 18m 58·02s.
5 Jonathan Palmer, GB (Ralt RT3-Toyota), 18m 58·25s.
6 Cliff Hansen, USA (Ralt RT3/81-Toyota), 19m 03·78s.
7 Richard Trott, GB (Ralt RT3/81-Toyota), 19m 08·42s; **8** Enrique Benamo, RA (Ralt RT3/81-Toyota), 19m 10·39s; **9** Michael Bleekemolen, NL (Ralt RT3/81-Toyota), 19m 10·41s; **10** Toshio Suzuki, J (March 813-Toyota), 19m 12·52s.
Fastest lap: Palmer, 1m 14·53s, 113·80 mph/183·14 km/h.
Marlboro Championship points: 1 Palmer, 40; **2** White, 23; **3** Tassin, 21; **4** Boesel, 17; **5** Leslie, 14; **6** Bleekemolen, 11.

MARLBORO CHAMPIONSHIP RACE, Snetterton Circuit, Great Britain, May 10. Marlboro British Formula 3 Championship, round 7. 25 laps of the 1·917-mile/3·085-km circuit, 47·925 miles/77·125 km.
1 James Weaver, GB (Ralt RT3/81-Toyota), 26m 23·60s, 108·95 mph/175·34 km/h.
2 Jonathan Palmer, GB (Ralt RT3-Toyota), 26m 28·52s.
3 Thierry Tassin, B (Ralt RT3/81-Toyota), 26m 29·61s.
4 David Leslie, GB (Ralt RT3/81-Toyota), 26m 33·80s.
5 Cliff Hansen, USA (Ralt RT3/81-Toyota), 26m 37·40s.
6 David Sears, GB (Ralt RT3/81-Toyota), 26m 38·76s.
7 Richard Trott, GB (Ralt RT3/81-Toyota), 26m 44·60s; **8** Toshio Suzuki, J (March 813-Toyota), 26m 49·24s; **9** Mike White, ZA (March 813-Alfa Romeo), 26m 52·19s; **10** Enrique Benamo, RA (Ralt RT3/81-Toyota), 26m 57·91s.
Fastest lap: Weaver, 1m 02·68s, 110·10 mph/117·19 km/h (record).
Marlboro Championship points: 1 Palmer, 46; **2** Tassin, 25; **3** White, 23; **4** Boesel, Weaver and Leslie, 17.

EUROPEAN FORMULA 3 CHAMPIONSHIP RACE, La Charte Circuit, France, May 24. European Formula 3 Championship, round 7. Two 18 lap heats of the 1·445-mile/2·325-km circuit; 40 lap final, 57·80 miles/93·00 km.
1 Philippe Alliot, F (Martini Mk34-Alfa Romeo), 43m 03·25s, 80·53 mph/129·60 km/h.
2 Alain Ferte, F (Martini Mk34-Alfa Romeo), 43m 03·65s.
3 Oscar Larrauri, RA (March 813-Toyota), 43m 18·51s.
4 Philippe Streiff, F (Martini Mk34-Alfa Romeo), 43m 19·80s.
5 Jean-Louis Schlesser, F (Martini Mk34-Alfa Romeo), 43m 20·19s.
6 Mauro Baldi, I (March 813-Alfa Romeo), 43m 24·91s.
7 Jean-Michel Neyrial, F (Martini Mk34-Toyota), 43m 34·55s; **8** Frank Jelinski, D (Ralt RT3-Toyota), 43m 36·19s; **9** Kurt Thiim, DK (March 813-Alfa Romeo), 43m 39·13s; **10** Didier Theys, B (Martini Mk34-Alfa Romeo), 43m 58·40s.
Fastest lap: Ferte, 1m 03·91s, 81·38 mph/130·97 km/h.
Heat 1: 1 Alliot, 19m 22·64s, 80·52 mph/129·58 km/h; **2** Ferte; **3** Schlesser; **4** Jelinski; **5** Alain Abdel, F (Ralt RT3-Toyota); **6** Thiim.
Fastest lap: Ferte, 1m 03·92s, 81·36 mph/130·94 km/h.
Heat 2: 1 Larrauri, 19m 31·75s, 79·89 mph/128·57 km/h; **2** Streiff; **3** Baldi; **4** Pierre Petit, F (Martini Mk31-Alfa Romeo); **5** Neyrial; **6** Theys.
Fastest lap: Baldi, 1m 04·45s, 80·70 mph/129·87 km/h.
European Championship points: 1 Baldi, 37; **2** Alliot, 35; **3** Larrauri, 30; **4** Ferte, 26; **5** Streiff, 13; **6** White, 9.

MARLBORO CHAMPIONSHIP RACE, Silverstone Short Circuit, Great Britain, May 25. Marlboro British Formula 3 Championship, round 8. 25 laps of the 1·608-mile/2·588-km circuit, 40·20 miles/64·70 km.
1 Thierry Tassin, B (Ralt RT3/81-Toyota), 25m 44·52s, 93·70 mph/150·80 km/h.
2 Raul Boesel, BR (Ralt RT3/81-Toyota), 25m 48·19s.
3 Jonathan Palmer, GB (Ralt RT3-Toyota), 25m 48·34s.
4 Roberto Moreno, BR (Ralt RT3/81-Toyota), 25m 58·36s.
5 David Leslie, GB (Ralt RT3/81-Toyota), 25m 59·78s.
6 James Weaver, GB (Ralt RT3/81-Toyota), 26m 04·89s.
7 Shuroku Sasaki, J (Ralt RT3/81-Toyota), 26m 14·97s; **8** Kees Nierop, CDN (Ralt RT3/81-Toyota), 26m 15·31s; **9** Enrique Benamo, RA (Ralt RT3/81-Toyota), 26m 23·88s; **10** Claus Schinkel, MEX (Ralt RT3/81-Toyota), 26m 26·96s.
Fastest lap: Tassin, 1m 01·03s, 94·85 mph/152·65 km/h.
Marlboro Championship points: 1 Palmer, 50; **2** Tassin, 35; **3** White and Boesel, 23; **5** Leslie, 19; **6** Weaver, 18.

23 GRAND PRIX DE MONACO F3, Monte Carlo, May 30. 24 laps of the 2·058-mile/3·312-km circuit. 49·39 miles/79·49 km.
1 Alain Ferte, F (Martini Mk34-Alfa Romeo), 38m 21·87s, 77·24 mph/124·31 km/h.
2 Oscar Larrauri, RA (March 813-Toyota), 38m 28·15s.
3 Jean-Louis Schlesser, F (Martini Mk34-Alfa Romeo), 38m 52·38s.
4 Kurt Thiim, DK (March 813-Alfa Romeo), 38m 52·58s.
5 Fernando Cazzaniga, I (March 813-Toyota), 38m 52·97s.
6 Paolo Barilla, I (Martini Mk34-Alfa Romeo), 38m 59·61s.
7 Thierry Tassin, B (Ralt RT3/81-Toyota), 39m 05·26s; **8** Brett Riley, NZ (Ralt RT3/81-Toyota), 39m 32·82s; **9** James Weaver, GB (Ralt RT3/81-Toyota), 39m 44·80s; **10** Philippe Alliot, F (Martini Mk34-Alfa Romeo), 39m 47·92s.
Fastest lap: Ferte, 1m 34·466s, 78·427 mph/126·216 km/h.

EUROPEAN FORMULA 3 CHAMPIONSHIP RACE, Circuit van Zandvoort, Holland, June 8. European Formula 3 Championship, round 8. 22 laps of the 2.626-mile/4.226-km circuit, 57.77 miles/92.97 km.
1 Mauro Baldi, I (March 813-Alfa Romeo), 33m 58.0s, 102.68 mph/165.24 km/h.
2 Alain Ferte, F (Martini Mk34-Alfa Romeo), 34m 07.7s.
3 Philippe Streiff, F (Martini Mk34-Alfa Romeo), 34m 17.8s.
4 Kurt Thiim, DK (March 813-Toyota), 34m 17.8s.
5 Philippe Alliot, F (Martini Mk34-Alfa Romeo), 34m 22.0s.
6 Didier Theys, B (Martini Mk34-Alfa Romeo), 34m 22.9s.
7 Oscar Larrauri, RA (March 813-Toyota), 34m 23.8s; **8** Pascal Fabre, F (Martini Mk34-Alfa Romeo), 34m 23.9s; **9** Frank Jelinski, D (Ralt RT3-Toyota), 34m 25.4s; **10** Riccardo Galiano Ramos, E (Martini Mk31-Alfa Romeo), 34m 41.8s.
Fastest lap: Baldi and Ferte, 1m 31.7s, 103.73 mph/166.93 km/h (record).
European Championship points: 1 Baldi, 46; **2** Alliot, 37; **3** Ferte, 32; **4** Larrauri, 30; **5** Streiff, 17; **6** White, 9.

MARLBORO CHAMPIONSHIP RACE, Cadwell Park Circuit, Great Britain, June 14. Marlboro British Formula 3 Championship, round 9. 20 laps of the 2.250-mile/3.621-km circuit, 45.00 miles/72.42 km.
1 Jonathan Palmer, GB (Ralt RT3-Toyota), 28m 23.66s, 95.09 mph/153.03 km/h.
2 Thierry Tassin, B (Ralt RT3/81-Toyota), 28m 36.62s.
3 Raul Boesel, BR (Ralt RT3/81-Toyota), 28m 44.96s.
4 Mike White, ZA (March 813-Alfa Romeo), 28m 46.61s.
5 David Leslie, GB (Ralt RT3/81-Toyota), 28m 53.15s.
6 Roberto Moreno, BR (Ralt RT3/81-Toyota), 28m 55.57s.
7 Victor Rosso, RA (March 813-Toyota), 29m 14.51s; **8** Kees Nierop, CDN (Ralt RT3/81-Toyota), 29m 15.78s; **9** Jon Beekhuis, USA (Argo JM6-Toyota), 29m 16.04s; **10** Mike O'Brian, GB (March 803B-Toyota), 29m 35.51s.
Fastest lap: Palmer, 1m 24.31s, 96.07 mph/154.61 km/h (outright record).
Marlboro Championship points: 1 Palmer, 60; **2** Tassin, 41; **3** Boesel, 27; **4** White, 26; **5** Leslie, 21; **6** Weaver, 18.

EUROPEAN FORMULA 3 CHAMPIONSHIP RACE, Silverstone Grand Prix Circuit, Great Britain, June 21. European Formula 3 Championship, round 9, Marlboro British Formula 3 Championship, round 10. 20 laps of the 2.932-mile/4.719-km circuit, 58.64 miles/94.38 km.
1 Roberto Moreno, BR (Ralt RT3/81-Toyota), 28m 41.42s, 122.63 mph/197.35 km/h.
2 Mauro Baldi, I (March 813-Alfa Romeo), 28m 43.08s.
3 Jonathan Palmer, GB (Ralt RT3-Toyota), 28m 58.57s.
4 Raul Boesel, BR (Ralt RT3/81-Toyota), 29m 11.77s.
5 Shuroku Sasaki, J (Ralt RT3/81-Toyota), 29m 13.52s.
6 Mike White, ZA (March 813-Alfa Romeo), 29m 13.84s.
7 Thierry Tassin, B (Ralt RT3/81-Toyota), 29m, 14.15s; **8** Oscar Larrauri, RA (March 813-Toyota), 29m 18.16s; **9** Philippe Alliot, F (Martini Mk34-Alfa Romeo), 29m 23.34s; **10** Cliff Hansen, USA (Ralt RT3/81-Toyota), 29m 25.36s.
Overall fastest lap: Baldi, 1m 25.07s, 124.08 mph/199.69 km/h (record).
Marlboro Championship fastest lap: Palmer, 1m 25.89s, 122.89 mph/197.77 km/h.
European Championship points: 1 Baldi, 52; **2** Alliot, 37; **3** Ferte, 32; **4** Larrauri, 30; **5** Streiff, 17; **6** White, 10.
Marlboro Championship points: 1 Palmer, 70; **2** Tassin, 44; **3** Boesel, 33; **4** White, 30; **5** Leslie, 21; **6** Weaver, 18.

EUROPEAN FORMULA 3 CHAMPIONSHIP RACE, Croix-en-Ternois, France, June 28. European Formula 3 Championship, round 10. Two 25 lap heats of the 1.181-mile/1.900-km circuit, 48 lap final, 56.69 miles/91.20 km.
1 Mauro Baldi, I (March 813-Alfa Romeo), 43m 37.03s, 77.95 mph/125.45 km/h.
2 Alain Ferte, F (Martini Mk34-Alfa Romeo), 43m 43.89s.
3 Emanuele Pirro, I (Martini Mk34-Alfa Romeo), 43m 46.07s.
4 Kurt Thiim, DK (March 813-Alfa Romeo), 43m 48.12s.
5 Philippe Streiff, F (Martini Mk34-Alfa Romeo), 44m 02.54s.
6 Patrick Teillet, F (Martini Mk34-Toyota), 44m 21.27s.
7 Dominique Tiercelin, F (Martini Mk34-Toyota), 44m 29.89s; **8** Oscar Larrauri, RA (March 813-Toyota), 47 laps; **9** Pierre Petit, F (Martini Mk31-Toyota), 47; **10** Riccardo Galiano Ramos, E (Martini Mk31-Alfa Romeo), 46.
Fastest lap: Ferte, 53.19s, 79.90 mph/128.59 km/h (record).
Heat 1: 1 Philippe Alliot, F (Martini Mk34-Alfa Romeo), 26m 32.57s, 66.67 mph/107.29 km/h; **2** Baldi; **3** Didier Theys, B (Martini Mk34-Alfa Romeo); **4** Larrauri; **5** Jean-Michel Neyrial, F (Martini Mk31-Toyota); **6** Alain Abdel, F (Ralt RT3-Toyota).
Fastest lap: Alliot, 1m 02.40s, 68.11 mph/109.61 km/h.
Heat 2: 1 Pirro, 26m 01.60s, 68.04 mph/109.50 km/h; **2** Jean-Louis Schlesser, F (Martini Mk34-Alfa Romeo); **3** Streiff; **4** Pascal Fabre, F (Martini Mk34-Alfa Romeo); **5** Ramos; **6** Tiercelin.
Fastest lap: Schlesser, 1m 01.24s, 69.40 mph/111.69 km/h.
European Championship points: 1 Baldi, 61; **2** Ferte, 38; **3** Alliot, 37; **4** Larrauri, 30; **5** Streiff, 19; **6** White, 10.

MARLBORO CHAMPIONSHIP RACE, Silverstone Short Circuit, Great Britain, July 5. Marlboro British Formula 3 Championship, round 11. 20 laps of the 1.608-mile/2.588-km circuit, 32.16 miles/64.70 km.
1 Raul Boesel, BR (Ralt RT3/81-Toyota), 18m 19.35s, 105.31 mph/169.48 km/h.
2 Jonathan Palmer, GB (Ralt RT3-Toyota), 18m 19.54s.
3 Thierry Tassin, B (Ralt RT3/81-VW), 18m 23.98s.
4 Cliff Hansen, USA (Ralt RT3/81-Toyota), 18m 31.20s.
5 Richard Trott, GB (Ralt RT3/81-Toyota), 18m 33.11s.
6 Roberto Moreno, BR (Ralt RT3/81-Toyota), 18m 35.49s.
7 Dave Scott, GB (Ralt RT3/81-Toyota), 18m 37.06s; **8** Kees Nierop, CDN (Ralt RT3/81-Toyota), 18m 38.99s; **9** Fred Krab, NL (Ralt RT3/81-Toyota), 18m 39.65s; **10** Claus Schinkel, MEX (Ralt RT3/81-Toyota), 18m 41.64s.
Fastest lap: Palmer, 54.10s, 107.00 mph/172.20 km/h (record).
Marlboro Championship points: 1 Palmer, 77; **2** Tassin, 48; **3** Boesel, 42; **4** White, 30; **5** Leslie, 21; **6** Weaver, 18.

MARLBORO CHAMPIONSHIP RACE, Brands Hatch Indy Circuit, Great Britain, July 12. Marlboro British Formula 3 Championship, round 12. 25 laps of the 1.2035-mile/1.936-km circuit, 30.09 miles/48.40 km.
1 Thierry Tassin, B (Ralt RT3/81-Toyota), 18m 41.31s, 96.60 mph/155.46 km/h.
2 Jonathan Palmer, GB (Ralt RT3-Toyota), 18m 42.37s.
3 Dave Scott, GB (Ralt RT3/81-Toyota), 18m 42.92s.
4 Richard Trott, GB (Ralt RT3/81-Toyota), 18m 46.0Cs.
5 Fred Krab, NL (Ralt RT3/81-Toyota), 18m 47.50s.
6 Raul Boesel, BR (Ralt RT3/81-Toyota), 18m 50.98s.
7 Brett Riley, NZ (Ralt RT3/81-Toyota), 18m 51.68s; **8** Cliff Hansen, USA (Ralt RT3/81-Toyota), 18m 57.41s; **9** Mike White, ZA (March 813-Alfa Romeo), 18m 58.43s; **10** Shuroku Sasaki, J (Ralt RT3/81-Toyota), 18m 58.95s.
Fastest lap: Scott, 44.32s, 97.77 mph/157.35 km/h.
Marlboro Championship points: 1 Palmer, 83; **2** Tassin, 57; **3** Boesel, 43; **4** White, 30; **5** Leslie, 21; **6** Weaver, 18.

MARLBORO CHAMPIONSHIP RACE, Silverstone Grand Prix Circuit, Great Britain, July 18. Marlboro British Formula 3 Championship, round 13. 20 laps of the 2.932-mile/4.719-km circuit, 58.64 miles/94.38 km.
1 Thierry Tassin, B (Ralt RT3/81-Toyota), 28m 55.52s, 121.64 mph/195.76 km/h.
2 Raul Boesel, BR (Ralt RT3/81-Toyota), 29m 05.64s.
3 Jonathan Palmer, GB (Ralt RT3-Toyota), 29m 12.1 s.
4 Fred Krab, NL (Ralt RT3/81-Toyota), 29m 15.42s.
5 Toshio Suzuki, J (March 813-Toyota), 29m 17.73s.
6 Richard Trott, GB (Ralt RT3/81-Toyota), 29m 19.25s.
7 James Weaver, GB (Ralt RT3/81-Toyota), 29m 21.46s; **8** Shuroku Sasaki, J (Ralt RT3/81-Toyota), 29m 22.22s; **9** Dave Scott, GB (Ralt RT3/81-Toyota), 29m 24.55s; **10** David Leslie, GB (Ralt RT3/81-Toyota), 29m 35.65s.
Fastest lap: Tassin, 1m 26.01s, 122.72 mph/197.50 km/h.
Disqualified: Roberto Moreno, BR (Ralt RT3/81-Toyota) crossed the line 1st in 28m 53.40s, 121.79 mph/196.00 km/h but was disqualified and fined 18 championship points due to over high octane rating of fuel.
Marlboro Championship points: 1 Palmer, 87; **2** Tassin, 67; **3** Boesel, 49; **4** White, 30; **5** Leslie, 21; **6** Weaver, 18.

EUROPEAN FORMULA 3 CHAMPIONSHIP RACE, Autodromo Santamonica, Misano, Italy, July 19. European Formula 3 Championship, round 11. Two 12 lap heats of the 2.167-mile/3.488-km circuit, 26 lap final, 56.34 miles/90.69 km.
1 Mauro Baldi, I (March 813-Alfa Romeo), 38m 47.06s, 87.159 mph/140.269 km/h.
2 Alain Ferte, F (Martini Mk34-Alfa Romeo), 26 laps.
3 Jean-Louis Schlesser, F (Martini Mk34-Alfa Romeo), 26.
4 Philippe Streiff, F (Martini Mk34-Alfa Romeo), 26.
5 Emanuele Pirro, I (Martini Mk34-Toyota), 26.
6 Didier Theys, B (Martini Mk34-Alfa Romeo), 26.
7 Paolo Giangrossi, I (Martini Mk34-Alfa Romeo), 26; **8** Enzo Coloni, I (March 813-Alfa Romeo), 26; **9** Pascal Fabre, F (Martini Mk34-Alfa Romeo), 25; **10** Philippe Alliot, F (Martini Mk34-Alfa Romeo), 25.
Fastest lap: Streiff, 1m 25.34s, 91.41 mph/147.12 km/h.
Heat 1: 1 Baldi; **2** Eddy Bianchi, I (Martini Mk34-Alfa Romeo); **3** Streiff; **4** Coloni; **5** Giangrossi; **6** Alliot.
Heat 2: 1 Ferte; **2** Pirro; **3** Schlesser; **4** Vinicio Salmi, I (Martini Mk34-Toyota); **5** Fabre; **6** Theys.
European Championship points: 1 Baldi, 70; **2** Ferte, 44; **3** Alliot, 37; **4** Larrauri, 30; **5** Streiff, 22; **6** Schlesser, 12.

MARLBORO CHAMPIONSHIP RACE, Mallory Park Circuit, Great Britain, August 2. Marlboro British Formula 3 Championship, round 14. 25 laps of the 1.350-mile/2.173-km circuit, 33.75 miles/54.33 km.
1 Roberto Moreno, BR (Ralt RT3/81-Toyota), 18m 10.61s, 111.41 mph/179.30 km/h.
2 Raul Boesel, BR (Ralt RT3/81-Toyota), 18m 11.55s.
3 Mike White, ZA (March 813-Alfa Romeo), 18m 20.56s.
4 Jonathan Palmer, GB (Ralt RT3-Toyota), 18m 21.07s.
5 Kurt Thiim, DK (March 813-Toyota), 18m 26.06s.
6 Dave Scott, GB (Ralt RT3/81-Toyota), 18m 26.45s.
7 David Leslie, GB (Ralt RT3/81-Toyota), 18m 26.94s; **8** Thierry Tassin, B (Ralt RT3/81-Toyota), 18m 28.79s; **9** Victor Rosso, RA (March 813-Toyota), 18m 30.74s; **10** Cliff Hanson, USA (Ralt RT3/81-Toyota), 18m 31.25s.
Fastest lap: Boesel, 42.79s, 113.58 mph/182.79 km/h (record).
Marlboro Championship points: 1 Palmer, 90; **2** Tassin, 67; **3** Boesel, 56; **4** White, 34; **5** Leslie, 21; **6** Weaver, 18.

EUROPEAN FORMULA 3 CHAMPIONSHIP RACE, Ring Knutstorp, Sweden, August 9. European Formula 3 Championship, round 12. Two 20 lap heats of the 1.292-mile/2.079-km circuit, 45 lap final, 58.14 miles/93.56 km.
1 Mauro Baldi, I (March 813-Alfa Romeo), 43m 35.097s, 80.03 mph/128.80 km/h.
2 Alain Ferte, F (Martini Mk34-Alfa Romeo), 43m 49.013s.
3 Philippe Streiff, F (Martini Mk34-Alfa Romeo), 43m 57.269s.
4 Jean-Louis Schlesser, F (Martini Mk34-Alfa Romeo), 44m 02.25s.

5 Kurt Thiim, DK (March 813-Alfa Romeo), 44m 02.62s.
6 Emanuele Pirro, I (Martini Mk34-Toyota), 44m 09.90s.
7 Riccardo Galiano Ramos, E (Martini Mk31-Alfa Romeo), 44m 27.88s; **8** Thomas Kaiser, D (Ralt RT3-Toyota), 44m 35.29s; **9** Jo Zeller, CH (March 793-Toyota), 44 laps; **10** Jan Ridell, S (Argo JM6-Toyota), 44.
Fastest lap: Ferte, 56.801s, 81.86 mph/131.74 km/h (record).
Heat 1: 1 Ferte, 19m 30.61s, 76.46 mph/123.05 km/h; **2** Schlesser; **3** Pascal Fabre, F (Martini Mk34-Alfa Romeo); **4** Kaiser; **5** Olav Ronningen, S (Ralt RT1-Toyota); **6** Zeller.
Fastest lap: Ferte, 57.68s, 80.62 mph/129.74 km/h.
Heat 2: 1 Baldi, 19m 33.39s, 79.27 mph/127.57 km/h; **2** Thiim; **3** Philippe Alliot, F (Martini Mk34-Alfa Romeo); **4** Pirro; **5** Ramos; **6** Leo Andersson, S (Ralt RT1-Toyota).
Fastest lap: Baldi, 57.70s, 80.59 mph/129.70 km/h.
European Championship points: 1 Baldi, 79; **2** Ferte, 50; **3** Alliot, 37; **4** Larrauri, 30; **5** Streiff, 26; **6** Schlesser, 15.

MARLBORO CHAMPIONSHIP RACE, Oulton Park Circuit, Great Britain, August 15. Marlboro British Formula 3 Championship, round 15. 25 laps of the 1.654-mile/2.662-km circuit, 41.35 miles/66.55 km.
1 Raul Boesel, BR (Ralt RT3/81-Toyota), 27m 15.57s, 91.01 mph/146.47 km/h.
2 Jonathan Palmer, GB (Ralt RT3-Toyota), 27m 18.81s.
3 Shuroku Sasaki, J (Ralt RT3-/81-Toyota), 27m 29.44s.
4 David Leslie, GB (Ralt RT3/81-Toyota), 27m 36.57s.
5 Mike White, ZA (March 813-Alfa Romeo), 28m 05.30s.
6 Toshio Suzuki, J (March 813-Toyota), 28m 08.17s.
7 Claus Schinkel, MEX (Ralt RT3/81-Toyota), 28m 38.00s; **8** Fred Krab, NL (Ralt RT3/81-Toyota), 24 laps; **9** Richard Trott, GB (Ralt RT3/81-Toyota), 24; **10** Kees Nierop, CDN (Ralt RT3/81-Toyota), 24.
Fastest lap: Palmer, 58.44s, 101.89 mph/163.98 km/h.
Marlboro Championship points: 1 Palmer, 97; **2** Tassin, 67; **3** Boesel, 65; **4** White, 36; **5** Leslie, 24; **6** Weaver, 18.

MARLBORO CHAMPIONSHIP RACE, Silverstone Short Circuit, Great Britain, August 31. Marlboro British Formula 3 Championship, round 16. 25 laps of the 1.608-mile/2.588-km circuit, 40.20 miles/64.70 km.
1 Dave Scott, GB (Ralt RT3/81-Toyota), 22m 44.37s, 106.07 mph/170.70 km/h.
2 Thierry Tassin, B (Ralt RT3/81-Toyota), 22m 53.76s.
3 Jonathan Palmer, GB (Ralt RT3-Toyota), 22m 54.88s.
4 Raul Boesel, BR (Ralt RT3/81-Toyota), 23m 02.02s.
5 Mike White, ZA (March 813-Alfa Romeo), 23m 02.74s.
6 Shuroku Sasaki, J (Ralt RT3/81-Toyota), 23m 05.85s.
7 Fred Krab, NL (Ralt RT3/81-Toyota), 23m 06.51s; **8** Roberto Moreno, BR (Ralt RT3/81-Toyota), 23m 06.81s; **9** Richard Trott, GB (Ralt RT3/81-Toyota), 23m 09.49s; **10** Cliff Hansen, USA (Ralt RT3/81-Toyota), 23m 09.68s.
Fastest lap: Palmer, 55.03s, 107.14 mph/172.42 km/h (record).
Marlboro Championship points: 1 Palmer, 102; **2** Tassin, 73; **3** Boesel, 68; **4** White, 38; **5** Leslie, 24; **6** Weaver, 18.

TROFEO VILLA DE MADRID, Circuito Permanente del Jarama, Spain, September 6. European Formula 3 Championship, round 13. 30 laps of the 2.115-mile/3.404-km circuit, 63.46 miles/102.13 km.
1 Alain Ferte, F (Martini Mk34-Alfa Romeo), 42m 38.47s, 86.87 mph/139.80 km/h.
2 Mauro Baldi, I (March 813-Alfa Romeo), 42m 50.55s.
3 Philippe Alliot, F (Martini Mk34-Alfa Romeo), 42m 55.11s.
4 Emanuele Pirro, I (Martini Mk34-Toyota), 43m 03.80s.
5 Oscar Larrauri, RA (March 813-Toyota), 43m 12.30s.
6 Didier Theys, B (Martini Mk34-Alfa Romeo), 43m 13.33s.
7 Peter Schindler, A (Ralt RT3-Toyota), 43m 19.49s; **8** Ricardo Galiano Ramos, E (Martini Mk34-Alfa Romeo), 43m 30.18s; **9** Jean-Louis Schlesser, F (Martini Mk34-Alfa Romeo), 27 laps. No other finishers.
Fastest lap: Baldi, 1m 24.30s, 87.89 mph/141.44 km/h (record).
European Championship points: 1 Baldi, 85; **2** Ferte, 59; **3** Alliot, 41; **4** Larrauri, 32; **5** Streiff, 26; **6** Schlesser, 15.

EUROPEAN FORMULA 3 CHAMPIONSHIP RACE, Autodromo Dino Ferrari, Imola, Italy, September 20. European Formula 3 Championship, round 14. Two 8 lap heats of the 3.132-mile/5.040-km circuit, 20 lap final, 62.64 miles/100.80 km.
1 Mauro Baldi, I (March 813-Alfa Romeo), 36m 56.28s, 101.74 mph/163.73 km/h.
2 Philippe Streiff, F (Martini Mk34-Alfa Romeo), 37m 17.49s.
3 Alain Ferte, F (Martini Mk34-Alfa Romeo), 37m 18.79s.
4 Jean-Louis Schlesser, F (Martini Mk34-Alfa Romeo), 37m 22.34s.
5 Guido Cappellotto, I (Ralt RT3-Toyota), 37m 27.40s.
6 Didier Theys, B (Martini Mk34-Alfa Romeo), 37m 32.89s.
7 Oscar Larrauri, RA (March 813-Toyota), 37m 33.12s; **8** Roberto Campominosi, I (Dallara 381-Toyota), 37m 39.13s; **9** Kurt Thiim, DK (March 813-Alfa Romeo), 37m 40.25s; **10** Pier-Luigi Martini, I (Dallara 381-Toyota), 37m 52.70s.
Fastest lap: Baldi, 1m 49.94s, 102.55 mph/165.04 km/h.
Heat 1: 1 Philippe Alliot, F (Martini Mk34-Alfa Romeo), 14m 55.15s, 100.76 mph/162.16 km/h; **2** Peter Schindler, A (Ralt RT3-Toyota); **3** Roberto Ravaglia, I (Dallara 381-Toyota); **4** Roberto Farneti, I (March 783/793-Toyota); **5** Cappellotto; **6** Larrauri.
Fastest lap: Ravaglia, 1m 50.33s, 102.19 mph/164.46 km/h.
Heat 2: 1 Baldi, 14m 52.44s, 101.06 mph/162.64 km/h; **2** Emanuele Pirro, I (Martini Mk34-Alfa Romeo); **3** Streiff **4** Enzo Coloni, I (March 813-Alfa Romeo); **5** Schlesser; **6** Paolo Giangrossi, I (Martini Mk34-Alfa Romeo).
Fastest lap: Baldi, 1m 49.98s, 102.51 mph/164.97 km/h.
European Championship points: 1 Baldi, 94; **2** Ferte, 63; **3** Alliot, 41; **4** Larrauri and Streiff, 32; **6** Schlesser, 18.

MARLBORO CHAMPIONSHIP RACE, Oulton Park Circuit, Great Britain, September 27. Marlboro British Formula 3 Championship, round 17. 25 laps of the 1.654-mile/2.662-km circuit, 41.35 miles/66.55 km.
1 Jonathan Palmer, GB (Ralt RT3-Toyota), 28m 54.76s, 85.81 mph/138.10 km/h.
2 Thierry Tassin, B (Ralt RT3/81-Toyota), 28m 56.58s.
3 Roberto Moreno, BR (Ralt RT3/81-Toyota), 28m 56.74s.
4 David Leslie, GB (Ralt RT3/81-Toyota), 29m 00.06s.
5 David Scott, GB (Ralt RT3/81-Toyota), 29m 30.29s.
6 Raul Boesel, BR (Ralt RT3/81-Toyota), 29m 34.15s.
7 Kees Nierop, CDN (Ralt RT3/81-Toyota), 29m 57.55s; **8** Claus Schinkel, MEX (Ralt RT3/81-Toyota), 24 laps; **9** Rick Whyman, GB (Pilbeam MP51-Toyota), 24; **10** Mike O'Brian, GB (Ralt RT3/81-Toyota), 23.
Fastest lap: Palmer, 1m 08.18s, 87.33 mph/140.54 km/h.
Marlboro Championship points: 1 Palmer, 112; **2** Tassin, 79; **3** Boesel, 69; **4** White, 38; **5** Leslie, 27; **6** Weaver and Scott, 18.

MARLBORO CHAMPIONSHIP RACE, Silverstone Grand Prix Circuit, Great Britain, October 4. Marlboro British Formula 3 Championship, round 18. 20 laps of the 2.932-mile/4.719-km circuit, 58.64 miles/94.37 km.
1 Raul Boesel, BR (Ralt RT3-Toyota), 28m 52.64s, 121.84 mph/196.08 km/h.
2 Dave Scott, GB (Ralt RT3/81-Toyota), 29m 22.66s.
3 Thierry Tassin, B (Ralt RT3/81-Toyota), 29m 26.41s.
4 Mike Blanchet, GB (Ralt RT3/81-Toyota), 29m 26.93s.
5 David Leslie, GB (Ralt RT3/81-Toyota), 29m 36.87s.
6 Claus Schinkel, MEX (Ralt RT3/81-Toyota), 29m 39.91s.
7 Fred Krab, NL (Ralt RT3/81-Toyota), 29m 40.89s; **8** Enrique Benamo, BR (Ralt RT3/81-Toyota), 29m 42.89s; **9** Ian Shaw, GB (Ralt RT3/81-Toyota), 29m 59.33s; **10** Kees Nierop, CDN (Ralt RT3/81-Toyota), 30m 00.14s.
Fastest lap: Boesel, 0m 00.00s, 000.00 mph/000.00 km/h.
Disqualified: Jonathan Palmer finished 2nd in 28m 55.28s and did fastest lap in 1m 25.80s, 123.02 mph/197.98 km/h (record). Roberto Moreno finished 6th in 29m 32.34s. Both were disqualified and fined 18 points due to too wide body work. Palmer's team appealed but the appeal had not been heard when Autocourse 1981/82 went to press.
Marlboro Championship points (pending appeal): 1 Palmer, 94; **2** Tassin, 83; **3** Boesel, 79; **4** White, 38; **5** Leslie, 29; **6** Scott, 24.

EUROPEAN FORMULA 3 CHAMPIONSHIP RACE, Autodromo Internazionale del Mugello, Italy, October 4. European Formula 3 Championship, round 15. Two 10 lap heats of the 3.259-mile/5.245-km circuit, 18 lap final, 58.66 miles/94.41 km.
1 Emanuele Pirro, I (Martini Mk34-Toyota), 34m 14.47s, 102.79 mph/165.42 km/h.
2 Kurt Thiim, DK (March 813-Alfa Romeo), 34m 14.89s.
3 Philippe Streiff, F (Martini Mk34-Alfa Romeo), 34m 27.97s.
4 Guido Cappellotto, I (Ralt RT3-Toyota), 34m 28.97s.
5 Enzo Coloni, I (March 813-Alfa Romeo), 34m 30.97s.
6 Pascal Fabre, F (Martini Mk34-Alfa Romeo), 34m 38.10s.
7 Paolo Barilla, I (Martini Mk34-Alfa Romeo), 34m 40.19s; **8** Roberto Ravaglia, I (Dallara 381-Alfa Romeo), 34m 40.76s; **9** Paolo Giangrossi, I (Martini Mk34-Alfa Romeo), 34m 55.65s; **10** Didier Theys, B (Martini Mk34-Alfa Romeo), 35m 01.25s.
Fastest lap: Theys, 1m 53.09s, 103.83 mph/167.10 km/h (record).
Heat 1: 1 Cappellotto, 19m 13.97s, 101.67 mph/163.62 km/h; **2** Eddy Bianchi, I (Martini Mk34-Alfa Romeo); **3** Theys; **4** Fabre; **5** Ravaglia; **6** Giangrossi.
Fastest lap: Bianchi, 1m 53.67s, 103.30 mph/166.24 km/h.
Heat 2: 1 Pirro, 19m 04.39s, 102.53 mph/165.00 km/h; **2** Streiff; **3** Thiim; **4** Peter Schindler, A (Ralt RT3-Toyota); **5** Coloni; **6** Vinicio Salmi, I (Martini Mk34-Toyota).
Fastest lap: Pirro, 1m 53.28s, 103.65 mph/166.81 km/h.
Final European Formula 3 Championship points:

1 Mauro Baldi, I	94
2 Alain Ferte, F	63
3 Philippe Alliot, F	41
4 Philippe Streiff, F	36
5 Oscar Larrauri, RA	32
6 Emanuele Pirro, I	19

7 Jean-Louis Schlesser, F, 18; **8** Kurt Thiim, DK, 14; **9** Mike White, ZA, 10; **10** Roberto Moreno, BR, 9; **11** Enzo Coloni, I, 8; **12** Guido Cappelletto, I, 5; **13** = Didier Theys, B, 4; **13** = Jonathan Palmer, GB, 4; **15** = Toshio Suzuki, J, 3; **15** = Frank Jelinski, D, 3; **15** = Raul Boesel, BR, 3; **18** = Franz Conrad, D, 2; **18** = Shuroku Sasaki, J, 2; **20** = Harald Brutschin, D, 1; **20** = Fabio Mancini, I, 1; **20** = Jean-Michel Neyerial, F, 1; **20** = Patrick Teillet, F, 1; **20** = Pascal Fabre, F, 1.

MARLBORO CHAMPIONSHIP RACE, Snetterton Circuit, Great Britain, October 11. Marlboro British Formula 3 Championship, round 19. 25 laps of the 1.917-mile/3.085-km circuit, 47.93 miles/77.13 km.
1 Jonathan Palmer, GB (Ralt RT3-Toyota), 26m 31.25s, 108.42 mph/174.48 km/h.
2 Roberto Moreno, BR (Ralt RT3/81-Toyota), 26m 43.79s.
3 Fred Krab, NL (Ralt RT3/81-Toyota), 26m 45.80s.
4 James Weaver, GB (Tiga F381-Toyota), 26m 50.59s.
5 Victor Rosso, RA (March 813-Toyota), 26m 50.86s.
6 Dave Coyne, GB (Anson SA3C-Toyota), 27m 02.67s.
7 Kees Nierop, CDN (Ralt RT3/81-Toyota), 27m 16.45s; **8** Claus Schinkel, MEX (Ralt RT3/81-Toyota), 20 laps. No other finishers.
Fastest lap: Palmer, 1m 02.86s, 109.79 mph/176.69 km/h.
Marlboro Championship points: 1 Palmer, 104; **2** Tassin, 83; **3** Boesel, 79; **4** White, 38; **5** Leslie, 29; **6** Scott, 24.

MARLBORO CHAMPIONSHIP RACE, Thruxton Circuit, Great Britain, October 25. Marlboro British Formula 3 Championship, round 20. 15 laps of the 2.356-mile/3.792-km circuit, 35.34 miles/56.88 km.
1 Thierry Tassin, B (Ralt RT3/81-Toyota), 20m 36.12s, 102.92 mph/165.63 km/h.
2 Bengt Tragardh, S (Ralt RT3/81-Toyota), 20m 36.55s.
3 Dave Scott, GB (Ralt RT3/81-Toyota), 20m 38.71s.
4 Roberto Moreno, BR (Ralt RT3/81-Toyota), 20m 45.41s.
5 Raul Boesel, BR (Ralt RT3/81-Toyota), 20m 46.21s.
6 Jonathan Palmer, GB (Ralt RT3-Toyota), 20m 46.81s.
7 Dave Coyne, GB (Anson SA3C-Toyota), 20m 54.71s; **8** Mike White, ZA (March 813-Toyota), 20m 59.24s; **9** Kees Nierop, CDN (Ralt RT3/81-Toyota), 21m 00.10s; **10** Richard Trott, GB (Ralt RT3/81-Toyota), 21m 00.26s.
Fastest lap: Tragardh, 1m 20.36s, 105.55 mph/169.87 km/h.
Final Marlboro Championship points (pending appeal):

1 Jonathan Palmer, GB	105
2 Thierry Tassin, B	92
3 Raul Boesel, BR	81
4 Mike White, ZA	38
5 David Leslie, GB	29
6 Dave Scott, GB	28

7 James Weaver, GB, 21; **8** Cliff Hanson, USA, 13; **9** Kurt Thiim, DK, 12; **10** Michael Bleekemolen, NL, 11; **11** Fred Krab, NL, 9; **12** = David Sears, GB, 7; **12** = Richard Trott, GB, 7; **12** = Bengt Tragardh, S, 7; **15** Shuroku Sasaki, J, 5; **16** = Toshio Suzuki, J, 3; **16** = Mike Blanchet, GB, 3; **18** Victor Rosso, RA, 2; **19** = Dave Coyne, GB, 1; **19** = Claus Schinkel, MEX, 1.

World Endurance Championship of Makes/ World Endurance Championship for Drivers

20 PEPSI DAYTONA 24 HOURS, Daytona International Speedway, Florida, United States of America, January 31/February 1. World Endurance Championship of Makes, round 1, World Endurance Championship for Drivers, round 1. 708 laps of the 3.840-mile/6.180-km circuit, 2718.72 miles/4375.44 km.
1 Bob Garretson/Bobby Rahal/Brian Redman, USA/USA/GB (3.2 t/c Porsche 935), 24h 01m 36.871s, 113.153 mph/182.102 km/h.
2 Bob Akin/Derek Bell/Craig Siebert, USA/GB/USA (2.8 t/c Porsche 935), 695 laps.
3 William Koll/Jeff Kline/Rob McFarlin, USA/USA/USA (2.5 Porsche 911SC), 644.
4 Frank Carney/Dick Davenport/Rameau Johnson, USA/USA/USA (2.5 Datsun ZX), 626.
5 Carlo Facetti/Martino Finotto/Emanuele Pirro, I/I/I (1.4 t/c Lancia Beta Monte Carlo), 609.
6 Hans Stuck/Alf Gebhardt/Walter Brun, D/USA/CH (3.5 BMW M1), 608.
7 Lee Mueller/Kathy Rude/Philippe Martin, USA/USA/B (2.3 Mazda RX-7), 606; **8** Carlos Gonzalez/Eduardo Barrientos/"Jamsel", ES/ES/ES (3.0 t/c Porsche 935), 595; **9** Roger Manderville/Amos Johnson/Diego Febles, USA/USA/PR (2.3 Mazda RX-7), 595; **10** Jim Mullen/Walt Bohren/J. Kurt Roehrig, USA/USA/USA (2.3 Mazda RX-7), 589.
Fastest lap: Carlo Facetti, I (Ferrari 308 Turbo), 1m 48.14s, 127.834 mph/205.728 km/h.

29 SEBRING 12 HOUR ENDURANCE RACE, Sebring Grand Prix Circuit, Florida, United States of America, March 21. World Endurance Championship for Drivers, round 2. 245 laps of the 5.200-mile/8.399-km circuit, 1274.00 miles/2050.30 km.
1 Bruce Leven/Hurley Haywood/Al Holbert, USA/USA/USA (3.0 t/c Porsche 935), 12h 00m 49.855s, 106.044 mph/170.661 km/h.
2 Roy Woods/Ralph Kent-Cooke/Skeeter McKitterick, USA/USA/USA (3.0 t/c Porsche 935), 242 laps.
3 Marty Hinze/Milt Minter/Bill Whittington, USA/USA/USA (3.0 t/c Porsche 935), 240.
4 Howard Meister/Rolf Strommelen/Harald Grohs, USA/D/D (3.0 t/c Porsche 935), 233.
5 Chuck Kendall/Pete Smith/Dennis Aase, USA/USA/USA (3.0 Porsche Carrera RSR), 218.
6 Gianpiero Moretti/Charles Mendez/Mauricio DeNarvaez, I/USA/COL (3.0 t/c Porsche 935), 213.
7 Timothy Selby/Earl Roe, USA/USA (3.0 Porsche Carrera RSR), 212; **8** M.L. Speer/Eddy Joosen/Dirk Vermeersch, USA/B/B (2.3 Mazda RX-7), 212; **9** Lee Mueller/Walt Bohren, USA/USA (2.3 Mazda RX-7), 211; **10** Bob Tullius/Bill Adam, USA/CDN (4.0 Triumph TR-8), 208.
Fastest lap: John Paul Jnr, USA (3.0 t/c Porsche 935), 2m 28.65s, 125.959 mph/202.912 km/h (record).

6 ORE DI MUGELLO, Autodromo Internazionale Mugello, Italy, April 12. World Endurance Championship for Drivers, round 3. 177 laps of the 3.259-mile/5.245-km circuit, 576.84 miles/928.33 km.
1 Lella Lombardi/Giorgio Francia, I/I (2.0 Osella PA9-BMW), 6h 00m 24.74s, 96.03 mph/154.54 km/h.
2 John Cooper/Dudley Wood, GB/GB (3.2 t/c Porsche 935), 168 laps.
3 Toni Fischaber/Mario Ketterer, D/D (2.0 BMW 320i), 160.
4 Christian Bussi/Jacques Guerin, F/F (3.2 t/c Porsche 935), 160.
5 François Servanin/Laurent Ferrier/Pierre-François Rousselot, F/F/F (3.5 BMW M1), 160.
6 Mario Benusiglio/Luigi de Angelis, I/I (1.6 Osella PA8-Ford), 160.
7 Ruggeri Parpinelli/Silvano Frisori, I/I (1.6 Osella PA6-Ford), 158; **8** Corrado Fabi/Christian Danner, I/D (BMW M1), 155; **9** Del Bueno/Goroni, I/I (4.9 Ferrari 512BB), 155; **10** Veninata/Cascone-Lacono, I/I (2.0 Osella PA7-BMW), 154.
Fastest lap: Michele Alboreto/Piercarlo Ghinzani, I/I (1.4 t/c Lancia Beta Monte Carlo), 1m 56.79s, 100.53 mph/161.79 km/h.

MONZA 1000 KM, Autodromo Nazionale di Monza, Italy, April 26. World Endurance Championship of Makes, round 2, World Endurance Championship for Drivers, round 4. 173 laps of the 3.604-mile/5.800-km circuit, 623.49 miles/1003.40 km.
1 Edgar Doren/Jurgen Lassig/Gerhard Holup, D/D/D (3.3 t/c Porsche 935), 6h 33m 49.09s, 94.99 mph/152.87 km/h.
2 Lella Lombardi/Giorgio Francia, I/I (2.0 Osella PA9-BMW), 172 laps.
3 "Gimax"/Luigi Moreschi, I/I (2.0 Osella PA9-BMW), 171.
4 Teo Fabi/Dieter Quester, I/A (3.5 BMW M1), 170.
5 Siegfried Brun/Eddie Jordan, D/IRL (2.1 t/c Porsche 908/3), 170.
6 François Servanin/Laurent Ferrier/Pierre-François Rousselot, F/F/F (3.5 BMW M1), 167.
7 Germano Nataloni/Gianfranco Ricci, I/I (1.4 t/c Lancia Beta Monte Carlo), 162; **8** Richard Lloyd/Tony Dron, GB/GB (2.0 t/c Porsche 924 Carrera GTR), 161; **9** Gabriele Gottifredi/Giancarlo Galimberti, I/I (2.8 Porsche Carrera RSR), 157; **10** Umberto Grano/Marco Vanoli, I/I (3.5 BMW M1), 156.
Fastest lap: Harald Grohs, D (3.3 t/c Porsche 935), 2m 01.8s, 106.53 mph/171.44 km/h.

LOS ANGELES TIMES/TOYOTA 6 HOUR GRAND PRIX OF ENDURANCE, Riverside International Raceway, California, United States of America, April 26. World Endurance Championship for Drivers, round 5. 199 laps of the 3.30-mile/5.31-km circuit, 656.70 miles/1056.69 km.
1 John Fitzpatrick/Jim Busby, GB/USA (3.0 t/c Porsche 935K3), 6h 00m 46.0s, 109.217 mph/175.761 km/h.
2 John Paul/John Paul Jnr, USA/USA (3.0 t/c Porsche 935), 6h 01m 18.88s.
3 Bobby Rahal/Brian Redman, USA/GB (3.0 t/c Porsche 935), 197 laps.
4 Bob Garretson/Roy Woods/Ralph Kent-Cooke, USA/USA/USA (3.0 t/c Porsche 935), 190.
5 Hurley Haywood/Bruce Leven, USA/USA (3.0 Porsche 935), 189.
6 David Hobbs/Marc Surer, GB/CH (3.5 BMW M1C), 188.
7 Dave Cowart/Kenper Miller, USA/USA (3.5 BMW M1), 183; **8** Tony Garcia/Albert Naon/Hiram Cruz, USA/USA/USA (3.5 BMW M1), 181; **9** Chris Cord/Jim Adams, USA/USA (5.8 Chevrolet Monza), 178; **10** Carlos Moran/Karen Erstad, USA/USA (3.0 Porsche 935), 178.
Fastest lap: Paul Jnr, 1m 40.71s, 117.962 mph/189.841 km/h.

SILVERSTONE 6 HOURS, Silverstone Grand Prix Circuit, Great Britain. May 10. World Endurance Championship of Makes, round 3, World Endurance Championship for Drivers, round 6. Race distance calculated at exact 6 hour mark. 2.932-mile/4.719-km circuit.
1 Dieter Schornstein/Harald Grohs/Walter Rohrl, D/D/D (3.2 t/c Porsche 935), 205.35 laps. 602.08 miles/968.95 km, 100.35 mph/161.50 km/h.
2 Derek Bell/Steve O'Rourke/David Hobbs, GB/GB/GB (3.5 BMW M1), 596.65/960.70.
3 Siegfried Brunn/Eddie Jordan, D/IRL (2.1 t/c Porsche 908/3), 596.08/959.30.
4 Lella Lombardi/Giorgio Francia, I/I (2.0 Osella PA9-BMW), 586.89/944.51.
5 Edgar Doren/Jurgen Lassig, D/D (3.3 t/c Porche 935), 583.68/939.34.
6 Bob Akin/Bobby Rahal/Peter Lovett, USA/USA/GB (3.3 t/c Porsche 935), 582.47/937.39.
7 Beppe Gabbiani/Giorgio Schon/Giorgio Pianta, I/I/I (1.4 t/c Lancia Beta Monte Carlo), 571.10/919.09; **8** Yojiro Terada/Win Percy, J/GB (2.6 Mazda 253i), 569.98/917.29; **9** Peter Zbinden/Edi Kofel/Marco Vanoli, CH/CH/CH (2.0 t/c Porche 924 Carrera GTR), 566.76/912.11; **10** Jacques Guerin/Christian Bussi/Jean-Pierre Delaunay, F/F/F (3.0 t/c Porsche 935), 562.91/905.91.
Fastest lap: Jordan, 1m 26.02s, 122.71 mph/197.48 km/h.

27 ADAC 1000 KM, Nürburgring Nordschleife, German Federal Republic, May 24. World Endurance Championship of Makes, round 4. World Endurance Championship for Drivers, round 7. Race stopped after 17 laps of the 14.189-mile/22.835-km circuit, 241.21 miles/388.195 km.
1 Hans Stuck/Nelson Piquet, D/BR (3.5 BMW M1), 2h 16m 50.86s, 105.796 mph/170.262 km/h.
2 Reinhold Jost/Jochen Mass, D/D (2.1 t/c Porsche 908/80), 2h 17m 10.85s.
3 Bob Wollek, F (3.3 t/c Porsche 935), 2h 18m 15.59s.
4 Hans Heyer/Piercarlo Ghinzani, D/I (1.7 t/c Lancia Beta Monte Carlo), 2h 18m 18.70s.
5 Edgar Doren/Jurgen Lassig, D/D (3.3 t/c Porsche 935K3), 2h 21m 05.72s.
6 Volkert Merl/Jurgen Barth, D/D (2.1 t/c Porsche 908/3), 16 laps.
7 Dieter Schornstein/Walter Rohrl/Harald Grohs, D/D/D (3.3 t/c Porsche 935), 16; **8** Emilio de Villota/Guy Edwards, E/GB (3.3 Lola T600-Cosworth

DFL), 16; **9** John Cooper/Dudley Wood, GB/GB (3.0 t/c Porsche 935), 16; **10** Henri Pescarolo/Andrea de Cesaris, F/I (1.4 t/c Lancia Beta Monte Carlo), 16.
Fastest lap: Mass, 7m 33.53s, 112.627 mph/181.255 km/h.

ENNA 6 HOURS, Ente Autodromo di Pergusa, Enna, Sicily, June 28. World Endurance Championship for Drivers, round 9. 202 laps of the 3.076-mile/4.950-km circuit, 621.35 miles/999.90 km.
1 Guy Edwards/Emilio de Villota, GB/E (3.0 Lola T600-Cosworth DFV), 6h 00m 51.92s, 103.31 mph/166.26 km/h.
2 Giorgio Francia/Lella Lombardi, I/I (2.0 Osella PA9-BMW), 200 laps.
3 "Gimax"/Luigi Moreschi, I/I (2.0 Osella PA9-BMW), 194.
4 Edgar Doren/Angelo Pallavicini, D/CH (3.0 t/c Porche 934), 178.
5 Dullio Truffo/Fabrizio Violati, I/I (4.9 Ferrari 512BB), 173.
6 F. Uncini/G. Ciuti, I/I (2.0 Osella PA7-BMW), 169.
7 Casiglia/Corco, I/I (2.0 Alfa Romeo GT), 162. No other finishers.
Fastest lap: de Villota, 1m 38.45s, 112.47 mph/181.00 km/h.

6 HOURS of DAYTONA CHAMPION SPARK PLUG CHALLENGE, Daytona International Speedway, Florida, United States of America, July 2. World Endurance Championship for Drivers, round 10. 152 laps of the 3.840-mile/6.180-km circuit, 583.68 miles/939.36 km.
1 Roger Manderville/Amos Johnson, USA/USA (2.3 Mazda RX-7), 6h 00m 29.730s, 97.146 mph/156.341 km/h.
2 Jim Downing/Tom Waugh, USA/USA (2.3 Mazda RX-7), 6h 00m 45.550s.
3 Jack Dunham/Hurley Haywood, USA/USA (2.3 Mazda RX-7), 147 laps.
4 Fred Stiff/V.J. Elmore, USA/USA (2.3 Mazda RX-7), 145.
5 Chuck Ulinski/M.L. Speer/Ray Ratcliff, USA/USA/USA (2.3 Mazda RX-7), 145.
6 Jim Nealon/Bill Jobe, USA/USA (2.3 Mazda RX-7), 145.
7 Luis Sereix/Javier Garcia, USA/USA (Buick Skyhawk), 143; **8** Irv Pearce/Rob McFarlin, USA/USA (AMX Spirit), 142; **9** Danny Smith/H.W. Alexander/Phil Elvis, USA/USA/USA (2.3 Mazda RX-7), 140; **10** Paul Lambke/Alf Zeller, CDN/CDN (2.3 Mazda RX-7), 140.
Fastest lap: Downing, 2m 16.62s, 101.186 mph/162.843 km/h.

WATKINS GLEN 6 HOURS, Watkins Glen Grand Prix Circuit, New York, United States of America, July 12. World Endurance Championship of Makes, round 6, World Endurance Championship for Drivers, round 11. 173 laps of the 3.377-mile/5.435-km circuit, 584.22 miles/940.26 km.
1 Riccardo Patrese/Michele Alboreto, I/I (1.4 t/c Lancia Beta Monte Carlo), 6h 19m 04.587s, 92.47 mph/148.82 km/h (Including 19m under yellow flag).
2 Andrea de Cesaris/Henri Pescarolo, I/F (1.4 t/c Lancia Beta Monte Carlo), 171 laps.
3 Rick Mears/Johnny Rutherford/Bob Garretson, USA/USA/USA (3.0 t/c Porche 935K3), 168.
4 John Fitzpatrick/Jim Busby, GB/USA (3.0 t/c Porsche 935K3), 160.
5 Preston Henn/Marty Hinze/Dale Whittington, USA/USA/USA (3.2 t/c Porche 935K3), 157.
6 Gianpiero Moretti/Bobby Rahal, I/USA (3.2 t/c Porsche 935K3), 157.
7 Chet Vincentz/Lance van Every/John Wood, USA/USA/USA (3.0 t/c Porsche 934), 156; **8** Bob Akin/Craig Siebert/Vivian Candy, USA/USA/IRL (3.2 t/c Porsche 935K3), 146; **9** Steve Southard/Mark Altman/Gary Altman, USA/USA/USA (2.0 Porsche 911), 146; **10** Tim Selby/Earl Roe, USA/USA (2.0 Porsche 911SC), 138.
Fastest lap: John Paul Jnr, USA (3.2 t/c Porsche 935K3), 1m 52.831s, 107.75 mph/173.41 km/h.

SPA 24 HOURS, Spa-Francorchamps, Belgium, July 25/26. World Endurance Championship for Drivers, round 12. 456 laps of the 4.332-mile/6.972-km circuit, 1975.39 miles/3179.23 km.
1 Pierre Dieudonne/Tom Walkinshaw, B/GB (2.3 Mazda RX-7), 82.48 mph/132.74 km/h.
2 Eddy Joosen/Jean-Claude Andruet, B/F (3.0 BMW 530i), 454 laps.
3 Vince Woodman/Jonathan Buncombe, GB/GB (3.0 Ford Capri), 453.
4 Jean Xhenceval/Daniel Herregods/Umberto Grano, B/B/I (3.0 BMW 530i), 451.
5 Marc Duez/Jeff Allam/Chuck Nicholson/Win Percy, B/GB/GB/GB (2.3 Mazda RX-7), 445.
6 Holman Blackburn/Bob Akin/John Morrison, GB/USA/GB (3.0 Ford Capri), 435.
7 Jean-Louis Trintignant/Marianne Hoepfner/Alain Cudini, F/F/F (3.0 BMW 530i), 434; **8** Gordon Spice/Thierry Tassin, GB/B (3.0 Ford Capri), 431; **9** Alain Semoulin/Dany Snobeck/"Alain Dex", B/F/B (3.0 Ford Capri), 429; **10** Peter Seikel/Hans Nowak/Fred Rosterg, D/D/D (2.2 Audi 4000), 428.
Fastest lap: Dieudonne/Walkinshaw, 2m 54.5s, 89.37 mph/143.83 km/h.

MOLSON CANADIAN 1000, Mosport Park, Ontario, Canada, August 16. World Endurance Championship for Drivers, round 13. 229 laps of the 2.459-mile/3.957-km circuit, 563.11 miles/906.15 km.
1 Rolf Stommelen/Harald Grohs, D/D (3.2 t/c Porsche 935), 6h 00m 43.0s, 93.661 mph/150.73 km/h.
2 Brian Redman/Eppie Wietzes, GB/CDN (5.7 Lola T600-Chevrolet), 6h 01m 04.0s.
3 Ted Field/Bill Whittington, USA/USA (3.2 t/c Porsche 935), 222 laps.
4 Preston Henn/Edgar Doren, USA/D (3.2 t/c Porsche 935), 219.
5 Dave Cowart/Kenper Miller, USA/USA (3.5 BMW M1), 218.
6 John Fitzpatrick/Jim Busby, GB/USA (3.2 t/c Porsche 935), 217.
7 Bob Garretson/Mauricio DeNarvaez, USA/COL (3.2 t/c Porsche 935), 215; **8** Tony Garcia/Hiram Cruz/Albert Naon, USA/USA/USA (3.5 BMW M1), 210; **9** Lee Mueller/Walt Bohren, USA/USA (2.3 Mazda RX-7), 209; **10** "Jamsal"/Eduardo Barrientos, ES/ES (3.0 t/c Porsche 935), 206.
Fastest lap: Field/Whittington, 1m 20.657s, 109.75 mph/176.63 km/h.

PABST 500, Road America, Elkhart Lake, Wisconsin, United States of America, August 23. World Endurance Championship for Drivers, round 14. 125 laps of the 4.000-mile/6.437-km circuit, 500.00 miles/804.625 km.
1 Rolf Stommelen/Harald Grohs, D/D (3.2 t/c Porsche 935), 4h 44m 35.368s, 105.415 mph/169.649 km/h.
2 Brian Redman/Sam Posey, GB/USA (5.7 Lola T600-Chevrolet), 125 laps.
3 Chris Cord/Jim Adams, USA/USA (5.7 Lola T600-Chevrolet), 122.
4 Bob Garretson/Tom Gloy, USA/USA (3.2 t/c Porsche 935), 119.
5 Gianpiero Moretti/Bobby Rahal, I/USA (3.2 t/c Porsche 935), 118.
6 John Fitzpatrick/Jim Busby, GB/USA (3.2 t/c Porsche 935), 118.
7 Ted Field/Bill Whittington, USA/USA (3.2 t/c Porsche 935), 111; **8** Lee Mueller/Walt Bohren, USA/USA (2.3 Mazda RX-7), 111; **9** Dennis Aase/Chuck Kendall, USA/USA (3.5 BMW M1), 110; **10** Logan Blackburn/Dave Frellsen, USA/USA (2.5 Datsun ZX), 108.
Fastest lap: John Paul Jnr, USA (3.2 t/c Porsche 935), 2m 10.25s, 110.557 mph/177.924 km/h (record).

FLYING TIGERS 1000, Brands Hatch Grand Prix Circuit, Great Britain, September 27. World Endurance Championship for Drivers, round 15. 238 laps of the 2.6136-mile/4.206-km circuit, 622.04 miles/1001.03 km.
1 Guy Edwards/Emilio de Villota, GB/E (3.3 Lola T600-Cosworth DFL), 238 laps.
2 Bob Garretson/Bobby Rahal, USA/USA (3.2 t/c Porsche 935), 230.
3 Derek Bell/Chris Craft, GB/GB (3.5 BMW M1), 227.
4 John Cooper/Dudley Wood, GB/GB (3.2 t/c Porsche 935), 226.
5 Lella Lombardi/Giorgio Francia, I/I (2.0 Osella PA9-BMW), 226.
6 Dieter Schornstein/Harald Grohs, D/D (3.2 t/c Porsche 935), 221.
7 Martin Birrane/Roy Baker/Richard Jones, GB/GB/GB (2.0 Lola T297-Cosworth BDG), 216; **8** Desiré Wilson/Edgar Doren, ZA/D (3.2 t/c Porsche 935), 214; **9** Richard Lloyd/Andy Rouse, GB/GB (2.0 t/c Porsche 924GTR), 213; **10** Richard Eyre/Mike "Jersey" Taylor, GB/GB (2.0 Tiga SC81-Ford), 212.
Fastest lap: Not given.

Final Championship points. World Endurance Championship of Makes

Over 2000cc:	
1 Porsche	100 (107.5)
2 BMW	52
3 Ferrari	18
4 Lancia	6
5 Morgan	2
Up to 2000cc:	
1 Lancia	100 (110)
2 BMW	22.5
3 Opel	6
4 Ford	5
5 Toyota	4
6 Alfa Romeo	3
7 Porsche	2
8 Audi	1.5

Overall Champion Lancia on basis of scoring 6 class victories to Porsche's 5.

Final Championship points. World Endurance Championship for Drivers

1	Bob Garretson	USA	Porsche 935	123
2	Harald Grohs	D	Porsche 935	113½
3	Bobby Rahal	USA	Porsche 935	110
4	Edgar Dören	D	Porsche 934/935	104½
5	Lella Lombardi	I	Osella PA9	101
	Giorgio Francia	I	Osella PA9	101
7	Derek Bell	GB	Porsche 935/936/ BMW M1/530i	85
8	Brian Redman	GB	Porsche 935/ Lola T600	80
9	Bob Akin	USA	Porsche 935/ AMC Spirit/ Ford Capri	78
10	John Cooper	UGB	Porsche 935	73½

Le Mans 24-hours

49 GRAND PRIX D'ENDURANCE, LES 24 HEURES DU MANS, Circuit de la Sarthe, Le Mans, France, June 13/14. World Endurance Championship of Makes, round 5. World Endurance Championship for Drivers, round 8. 8.467-mile/13.626-km circuit. 2996.80 miles/4822.87 km covered in 24 hours (distance calculated at exact 24-hour point).
1 Jacky Ickx/Derek Bell, B/GB (2.6 t/c Porsche 936/81), 354 laps, 124.93 mph/201.05 km/h (1st over 2000cc G6 class).
2 Jacky Haran/Jean-Louis Schlesser/Philippe Streiff, F/F/F (3.0 Rondeau M379C-Cosworth DFV), 340 laps (1st GTP class).
3 Gordon Spice/François Migault, GB/F (3.0 Rondeau M379C-Cosworth DFV), 335.
4 John Cooper/Dudley Wood/Claude Bourgoignie, GB/GB/B (3.0 t/c Porsche 935K3), 330 (1st over 2000cc G5 class).
5 Claude Ballot-Lena/Jean-Claude Andruet/Hervé Regout, F/F/B (4.9 Ferrari 512BB), 328 (1st IMSA GTX class).
6 Anny-Charlotte Verney/Ralph Kent-Cooke/Bob Garretson, F/USA/USA (3.2 t/c Porsche 935K3), 327.
7 Walter Rohrl/Jurgen Barth, D/D (2.5 t/c Porsche 944LM), 323; **8** Michele Alboreto/Carlo Facetti/Eddie Cheever, I/I/USA (1.4 t/c Lancia Beta Monte Carlo), 322 (1st up to 2000cc G5 class); **9** Pierre Dieudonne/Jean Xhenceval/Jean-Paul Liberti, B/B/B (4.9 Ferrari 512BB), 320; **10** Harald Grohs/Gotz von Tschirnhaus/Dieter Schornstein, D/D/D (3.0 t/c Porsche 935), 320; **11** Manfred Schurti/Andy Rouse, FL/GB (2.0 t/c Porsche 924 Carrera GTR), 315 (1st IMSA GTO class); **12** Jochen Mass/Vern Schuppan/Hurley Haywood, D/AUS/USA (2.6 t/c Porsche 936/81), 312; **13** Xavier Mathiot/Denis Morin/Charles Mendez, F/F/USA (2.7 t/c WM P79/80-Peugeot), 307; **14** Martino Finotto/Giorgio Pianta/Giorgio Schon, I/I/I (1.4 t/c Lancia Beta Monte Carlo), 292; **15** Guy Edwards/Emilio de Villota/Juan Fernandez, GB/E/E (3.3 Lola T600-Cosworth DFL), 287; **16** Philippe Alliot/Bernard Darniche/Johnny Cecotto, F/F/YV (3.5 BMW M1), 277; **17** Valentin Bertapelle/Thierry Perrier/Bernard Salam, F/F/F (3.0 t/c Porsche 934), 274 (1st G4 class); **18** Yves Courage/Jean-Philippe Grand, F/F (2.0 Lola T298-BMW), 272 (1st up to 2000cc G6 class). **19** Pierre Yver/Michel Dubois/Jacques Heuclin, F/F/F (2.0 Lola T298-BMW), 203; **20** Hervé Bayard/Louis Descartes/Bruno Preschey, F/F/F (2.0 Renard Delmas RD31-Simca), 187.
Fastest lap: Not given.
Retired: Cale Yarborough/Bill Cooper/Bob Hagen, USA/USA/USA (6.4 Chevrolet Camero), 13 laps, accident; Michel Pignard/Serge Saulnier/Thierry Boutsen, F/F/B (2.7 t/c WM P81-Peugeot), 15, accident; Win Percy/Yojiro Terada/Hiroshi Fushida, GB/J/J (2.6 Mazda 253i), 25, transmission; Jean Ragnotti/Jean-Louis Lafosse, F/F (3.0 Rondeau M379C-Cosworth DFV), 28,

accident; Jacques Almeras/Jean-Marie Almeras/Jean-Pierre Sivel, F/F/F (2.0 t/c Porsche 924 Carrera GTR), 30, gearbox; Henri Pescarolo/Patrick Tambay, F/F (3.3 Rondeau M379C-Cosworth DFL), 41, flat battery; Marcel Mignot/Michael Chandler/Preston Henn, F/USA/USA (3.0 t/c Porsche 935K3), 45, breakdown; Guy Frequelin/Roger Dorchy, F/F (2.7 t/c WM P79/80-Peugeot), 46, engine; Beppe Gabbiani/Emanuele Pirro, I/I (1.4 t/c Lancia Beta Monte Carlo), 47, accident; Edgar Doren/Jurgen Lassig/Gerhard Holup, D/D/D (3.0 t/c Porsche 935K3), 48, breakdown; Christian Danner/Leopold von Bayern/Peter Oberndofer, D/D/D (3.5 BMW M1), 49, crankshaft damper; Axel Plankenhorn/Jan Lundgardh/Mike Wilds, D/S/GB (1.4 t/c Porsche 935L1), 49, engine; Jean-Daniel Raulet/Max Mamers, F/F (2.7 t/c WM P81-Peugeot), 50, accident; Ted Field/Don Whittington/Bill Whittington, USA/USA/USA (3.2 t/c Porsche 935K3), 57, engine; Hans Stuck/Jean-Pierre Jarier/Helmut Henzler, D/F/D (3.5 BMW M1), 57, accident damage; Jean-Pierre Jaussaud/Jean Rondeau, F/F (3.3 Rondeau M379C-Cosworth DFL), 58, handling; Reinhold Jost/Dale Whittington/Klaus Niedzwiedz, D/USA/D (2.1 t/c Porsche 908/80), 60, accident; Xavier Lapeyre/Bob Wollek/Guy Chasseuil, F/F/F (4.9 Porsche 917K/81), 82, engine frame; Tiff Needell/Tony Trimmer, GB/GB (3.0 Ibec P6-Cosworth DFV), 95, head gasket; Max Cohen-Olivar/Jean-Marie Lemerle/Alain Levie, MOR/F/F (2.0 Lola T298-BMW), 104, electrics; Tom Walkinshaw/Tetsu Ikusawa/Peter Lovett, GB/J/GB (2.6 Mazda 253i), 107, engine/gearbox; Patrick Gaillard/Bruno Sotty/André Chevalley, F/F/CH (3.0 ACR 80B-Cosworth DFV), 114, clutch; Maurizio Flammini/Dullio Truffo/Fabrizio Violati, I/I/I (4.9 Ferrari 512BB), 118, breakdown; Mike Salmon/Steve Earle/Simon Phillips, GB/USA/GB (4.9 Ferrari 512BB), 140, structural failure; Gunther Steckkonig/Kenper Miller/Mauricio DeNarvaez, D/USA/COL (2.8 t/c Porsche 935), 152, fire; Bob Evans/Chris Craft, GB/GB (3.0 Dome Zero RL81-Cosworth DFV), 154, engine; Nick Faure/Martin Birrane/Vivian Candy, GB/GB/IRL (3.0 De Cadenet LM-Cosworth DFV), 171, gearbox casing; Piercarlo Ghinzani/Hans Heyer/Riccardo Patrese, I/D/I (1.4 t/c Lancia Beta Monte Carlo), 186, head gasket; Marc Surer/Dieter Quester/David Deacon, CH/A/CDN (3.5 BMW M1), 207, engine; Alain de Cadenet/Philippe Martin/Jean-Michel Martin, GB/B/B (3.3 De Cadenet LM-Cosworth DFL), 210, engine; Pierre-François Rousselot/Laurent Ferrier/François Servanin, F/F/F (3.5 BMW M1), 212, engine; David Hobbs/Eddie Jordan/Steve O'Rourke, GB/IRL/GB (3.5 BMW M1), 236, engine; Alain Cudini/John Morton/Philippe Gurdian, F/USA/F (4.9 Ferrari 512BB), 247, accident; Claude Haldi/Mark Thatcher/Hervé Poulain, CH/GB/F (3.0 t/c Porsche 935), 260, accident; Bob Akin/Paul Miller/Craig Siebert, USA/USA/USA (3.0 t/c Porsche 935K3), 320, electrical fire on last lap.

Robert Bosch/ VW Super Vee

GOODY'S 500, Charlotte Motor Speedway, Harrisburg, North Carolina, United States of America, May 17. Robert Bosch/VW Super Vee Championship, round 1. 28 laps of the 2.250-mile/3.621-km circuit, 63.00 miles/101.39 km.
1 Al Unser Jnr, USA (Ralt RT5-VW), 34m 10.089s, 110.629 mph/178.040 km/h.
2 John Paul Jnr, USA (Ralt RT5-VW), 34m 14.724s.
3 Bob Earl, USA (Ralt RT5-VW), 28 laps.
4 Jim Hickman, USA (Ralt RT5-VW), 28.
5 Chip Ganassi, USA (March 79V-VW), 28.
6 Arie Luyendyk, NL (March 81SV-VW), 28.
7 Stuart Moore, USA (Ralt RT5-VW), 28; **8** Scott Miller, USA (March 81SV-VW), 28; **9** Dave Dickerson, USA (Ralt RT5-VW), 28; **10** Gary Pratt, USA (Protofab-VW), 27.
Fastest lap: Unser Jnr, 1m 10.537s, 114.883 mph/184.886 km/h (record).
Championship points: 1 Unser Jnr, 14; **2** Paul Jnr, 11; **3** Earl, 10; **4** Hickman, 9; **5** Ganassi, 8; **6** Luyendyk, 7.

ROBERT BOSCH/VW SUPER VEE RACE, Wisconsin State Fair Park Speedway, Milwaukee, United States of America, June 7. Robert Bosch/VW Super Vee Championship, round 2. 62 laps of the 1.000-mile/1.609-km circuit, 62.00 miles/99.76 km.
1 Al Unser Jnr, USA (Ralt RT5-VW), 36m 44.98s, 101.225 mph/162.905 km/h.
2 Pete Halsmer, USA (Ralt RT5-VW), 36m 45.98s.
3 Dave McMillen, NZ (Autoresearch-VW), 62 laps.
4 Bob Cicconi, USA (Ralt RT5-VW), 62.
5 John Paul Jnr, USA (Ralt RT5-VW), 62.
6 Bob Earl, USA (Ralt RT5-VW), 62.
7 Roger Penske Jnr, USA (Ralt RT5-VW), 62; **8** Chip Ganassi, USA (Ralt RT5-VW), 62; **9** Larry Skipsey, MEX (Ralt RT1-VW), 62; **10** Jerrill Rice, USA (March 81SV-VW), 62.
Fastest lap: Not given.
Championship points: 1 Unser Jnr, 28; **2** Paul Jnr, 19; **3** Earl, 17; **4** Ganassi, 13; **5** Halsmer, 11; **6** McMillen, 10.

ROBERT BOSCH/VW SUPER VEE RACE, Watkins Glen Grand Prix Circuit, New York, United States of America, July 11. Robert Bosch/VW Super Vee Championship, round 3. 18 laps of the 3.377-mile/5.435-km circuit, 60.79 miles/97.83 km.
1 Pete Halsmer, USA (Ralt RT5-VW), 33m 55.058s, 107.53 mph/173.05 km/h.
2 Dave McMillen, NZ (Autoresearch-VW), 34m 20.995s.
3 Al Unser Jnr, USA (Ralt RT5-VW), 18 laps.
4 Greg Atwell, USA (Ralt RT5-VW), 18.
5 Mike Rosen, USA (Ralt RT5-VW), 18.
6 Arie Luyendyk, NL (March 81SV-VW), 18.
7 Larry Skipsey, MEX (Ralt RT5-VW), 18; **8** Dave Dickerson, USA (Ralt RT5-VW), 17; **9** Dr Curt Erwin, USA (March 80V-VW), 17; **10** Doug Clark, USA (Ralt RT1-VW), 17.
Fastest lap: Halsmer, 1m 51.910s, 108.63 mph/174.82 km/h.
Championship points: 1 Unser Jnr, 38; **2** Halsmer, 25; **3** McMillen, 21; **4** Paul Jnr, 19; **5** Earl, 17; **6** Luyendyk, 15.

ROBERT BOSCH/VW SUPER VEE RACE, Road America, Elkhart Lake, Wisconsin, United States of America, July 26. Robert Bosch/VW Super Vee Championship, round 4. 15 laps of the 4.000-mile/6.437-km circuit, 60.00 miles/96.56 km.
1 Pete Halsmer, USA (Ralt RT5-VW), 33m 31.78s, 107.368 mph/172.79 km/h.
2 Al Unser Jnr, USA (Ralt RT5-VW), 33m 35.64s.
3 Arie Luyendyk, NL (March 81SV-VW), 15 laps.
4 Bob Earl, USA (Ralt RT5-VW), 15.
5 Dave McMillen, NZ (Autoresearch-VW), 15.
6 Jim Hickman, USA (Ralt RT5-VW), 15.
7 Chip Ganassi, USA (Ralt RT5-VW), 15; **8** Stuart Moore, USA (Ralt RT5-VW), 15; **9** Bob Schader, USA (Autoresearch-VW), 15; **10** Jerry Knapp, USA (Ralt RT5-VW), 15.
Fastest lap: Unser Jnr, 2m 12.394s, 108.766 mph/175.041 km/h (record).
Championship points: 1 Unser Jnr, 49; **2** Halsmer, 39; **3** McMillen, 29; **4** Earl, 26; **5** Luyendyk, 25; **6** Paul Jnr, 25.

ROBERT BOSCH/VW SUPER VEE RACE, Brainerd International Raceway, Minnesota, United States of America, August 9. Robert Bosch/VW Super Vee Championship, round 5. 21 laps of the 3.000-mile/4.828-km circuit, 63.00 miles/101.39 km.
1 Al Unser Jnr, USA (Ralt RT5-VW), 35m 56.45s, 105.173 mph/169.259 km/h.
2 Pete Halsmer, USA (Ralt RT5-VW), 35m 59.27s.
3 Arie Luyendyk, NL (March 81SV-VW), 21 laps.
4 Chip Ganassi, USA (Ralt RT5-VW), 21.
5 Stuart Moore, USA (Ralt RT5-VW), 21.
6 Dave Dickerson, USA (Ralt RT5-VW), 21.
7 Mike Rosen, USA (Ralt RT5-VW), 21; **8** Dave McMillen, NZ (Autoresearch-VW), 21; **9** Bob Schader, USA (Autoresearch-VW), 21; **10** Jerry Knapp, USA (Ralt RT5-VW), 21.
Fastest lap: Unser Jnr, 1m 34.873s, 113.836 mph/183.201 km/h (record).
Championship points: 1 Unser Jnr, 63; **2** Halsmer, 50; **3** Luyendyk, 35; **4** McMillen, 34; **5** Ganassi, 28; **6** Earl, 26.

ROBERT BOSCH/VW SUPER VEE RACE, Wisconsin State Fair Park Speedway, Milwaukee, United States of America, September 5. Robert Bosch/VW Super Vee Championship, round 6. 62 laps of the 1.000-mile/1.609-km circuit, 62.00 miles/99.76 km.
1 Al Unser Jnr, USA (Ralt RT5-VW), 33m 46.0s, 110.167 mph/177.296 km/h.
2 Pete Halsmer, USA (Ralt RT5-VW), 33m 49.0s.
3 Chip Ganassi, USA (Ralt RT5-VW), 62.
4 John Kalagian, USA (Ralt RT5-VW), 62.
5 Jim Hickman, USA (Ralt RT5-VW), 62.
6 Dave Dickerson, USA (Ralt RT5-VW), 62.
7 Greg Atwell, USA (Ralt RT5-VW), 61; **8** Bob Earl, USA (Ralt RT5-VW), 61; **9** Mike Rosen, USA (Ralt RT5-VW), 61; **10** Bob Cicconi, USA (Ralt RT5-VW), 61.
Fastest lap: Not given.
Championship points: 1 Unser Jnr, 77; **2** Halsmer, 61; **3** Ganassi, 38; **4** Luyendyk, 35; **5** McMillen, 34; **6** Earl, 31.

ROBERT BOSCH/VW SUPER VEE RACE, Michigan International Speedway, Brooklyn, United States of America, September 19. Robert Bosch/VW Super Vee Championship, round 7. 32 laps of the 2.000-mile/3.219-km circuit, 64.00 miles/103.01 km.
1 Bob Cicconi, USA (Ralt RT5-VW), 29m 50.0s, 128.142 mph/206.224 km/h.
2 Bob Earl, USA (Ralt RT5-VW), 32 laps.
3 Al Unser, USA (Ralt RT5-VW), 32.
4 Roger Penske Jnr, USA (Ralt RT5-VW), 32.
5 Pete Halsmer, USA (Ralt RT5-VW), 32.
6 Fred Phillips, USA (Ralt RT5-VW), 32.
7 Greg Atwell, USA (Ralt RT5-VW), 32; **8** John Kalagian, USA (Ralt RT5-VW), 32; **9** Larry Skipsey, MEX (Ralt RT5-VW), 32; **10** Arie Luyendyk, NL (March 81SV-VW), 32.
Fastest lap: Not given.
Championship points: 1 Unser Jnr, 87; **2** Halsmer, 69; **3** Earl, 42; **4** Ganassi and Luyendyk, 38; **6** McMillen, 34.

ROBERT BOSCH/VW SUPER VEE RACE, Riverside International Raceway, California, United States of America, October 4. Robert Bosch/VW Super Vee Championship, round 8. 24 laps of the 2.547-mile/4.099-km circuit, 61.13 miles/98.38 km.
1 Bob Earl, USA (Ralt RT5-VW), 32m 12.921s, 113.846 mph/183.217 km/h.
2 Pete Halsmer, USA (Ralt RT5-VW), 32m 16.652s.
3 Arie Luyendyk, NL (March 81SV-VW), 24 laps.
4 Fred Phillips, USA (Ralt RT5-VW), 24.
5 Mike Rosen, USA (Ralt RT5-VW), 24.
6 Greg Atwell, USA (Ralt RT5-VW), 24.
7 John Kalagian, USA (Ralt RT5-VW), 24; **8** Jerril Rice, USA (March 79SV-VW), 24; **9** Stuart Moore, USA (Ralt RT5-VW), 24; **10** Jerry Knapp, USA (Ralt RT5-VW), 24.
Fastest lap: Earl, 1m 17.310s, 115.017 mph/185.101 km/h.
Championship points: 1 Unser Jnr, 87; **2** Halsmer, 80; **3** Earl, 56; **4** Luyendyk, 48; **5** Ganassi, 38; **6** McMillen, 34.

ROBERT BOSCH/VW SUPER VEE RACE, Phoenix International Raceway, Arizona, United States of America, October 31. Robert Bosch/VW Super Vee Championship, round 9. 60 laps of the 1.000-mile/1.609-km circuit, 60.00 miles/96.54 km.
1 Pete Halsmer, USA (Ralt RT5-VW), 40m 59.996s, 87.805 mph/141.308 km/h.
2 Al Unser Jnr, USA (Ralt RT5-VW), 60 laps.
3 Bob Cicconi, USA (Ralt RT5-VW), 60.
4 Dave McMillen, NZ (Autoresearch-VW), 60.
5 John Kalagian, USA (Ralt RT5-VW), 60.
6 Jerry Knapp, USA (Ralt RT5-VW), 60.
7 Greg Atwell, USA (Ralt RT5-VW), 60; **8** Larry Skipsey, MEX (Ralt RT5-VW), 60; **9** Stan Fox, USA (Autoresearch-VW), 59; **10** Jim Harvey, USA (March 79SV-VW), 58.
Fastest lap: Not given.
Final Championship points:

1 Al Unser Jnr, USA	98
2 Pete Halsmer, USA	94
3 Bob Earl, USA	56
4 Arie Luyendyk, NL	48
5 Dave McMillen, NL	43
6 Chip Ganassi, USA	38

7 Bob Cicconi, USA, 36; **8** Greg Atwell, USA, 34; **9** John Kalagian, USA, 30; **10** Mike Rosen, USA, 29; **11** Jim Hickman, USA, 24; **12 =** Stuart Moore, USA, 23; **12 =** Dave Dickerson, USA, 23; **14 =** John Paul Jnr, USA, 21; **14 =** Larry Skipsey, MEX, 21.

USAC Gold Crown National Championship 1981/82

INDIANAPOLIS 500, Indianapolis Motor Speedway, Indiana, United States of America, May 24. USAC Gold Crown National Championship 1981/82, round 1. 200 laps of the 2.500-mile/4.023-km circuit, 500.00 miles/804.67 km.
1 Bobby Unser, USA (Penske PC9B-Cosworth DFX), 3h 35m 41.78s, 139.084 mph/223.833 km/h.
2 Mario Andretti, USA (Wildcat Mk8-Cosworth DFX), 3h 35m 46.96s.
3 Vern Schuppan, AUS (McLaren M24B-Cosworth DFX), 199 laps.
4 Kevin Cogan, USA (Phoenix-Cosworth DFX), 197.
5 Geoff Brabham, AUS (Penske PC9-Cosworth DFX), 197.
6 Sheldon Kinser, USA (Longhorn LR01-Cosworth DFX), 195.
7 Tony Bettenhausen, USA (McLaren M24-Cosworth DFX), 195; **8** Steve Krisiloff, USA (Penske PC7-Cosworth DFX), 194; **9** Gordon Johncock, USA (Wildcat Mk8-Cosworth DFX), 194 (DNF, engine); **10** Dennis Firestone, USA (Wildcat Mk8-Cosworth DFX), 193 (DNF, engine); **11** Bill Alsup, USA (Penske PC9B-Cosworth DFX), 193; **12** Mike Chandler, USA (Penske PC7-Cosworth DFX), 192; **13** A.J. Foyt, USA (Coyote 80-Cosworth DFX), 191; **14** Tim Richmond, USA (Parnelli VPJ6C-Cosworth DFX), 191; **15** Jerry Karl, USA (McLaren M16E-Chevrolet), 189; **16** Scott Brayton, USA (Penske PC6-Cosworth DFX), 174 (DNF, driveshaft); **17** Al Unser, USA (Longhorn LR02-Cosworth DFX), 166; **18** Larry Dickson, USA (Penske PC7-Cosworth DFX), 165 (DNF, engine); **19** Bob Lazier, USA (Penske PC7-Cosworth DFX), 154 (DNF, engine); **20** Tom Bigelow, USA (Penske PC7-Chevrolet), 152 (DNF, engine); **21** Bill Whittington, USA (March 81C-Cosworth DFX), 146 (DNF, gearbox); **22** Gordon Smiley, USA (Wildcat Mk8-Cosworth DFX), 141 (DNF, accident); **23** Josele Garza, MEX (Penske PC9-Cosworth DFX), 138 (DNF, rear suspension, accident); **24** Pete Halsmer, USA (Penske PC7-Cosworth DFX), 123 (DNF, accident); **25** Tom Sneva, USA (March 81C-Cosworth DFX), 96 (DNF, gearbox); **26** Gary Bettenhausen, USA (Lightning-Cosworth DFX), 69 (DNF, engine); **27** Danny Ongais, USA (Interscope 022-Cosworth DFX), 64 (DNF, accident); **28** Pancho Carter, USA (Penske PC7-Cosworth DFX), 62 (DNF, turbocharger); **29** Tom Klauser, USA (Lightning-Chevrolet), 60 (DNF, gearbox); **30** Rick Mears, USA (Penske PC9B-Cosworth DFX), 58 (DNF, fire in pits); **31** Don Whittington, USA (March 81C-Cosworth DFX), 32 (DNF, accident); **32** Johnny Rutherford, USA (Chaparral 2K-Cosworth DFX), 25 (DNF, accessory belt); **33** Mike Mosley, USA (Eagle 81-Chevrolet), 16 (DNF, engine).
Fastest Qualifier: B. Unser, 200.545 mph/322.745 km/h.
USAC Championship points: 1 Andretti, 800; **2** Schuppan, 700; **3** Brabham, 500; **4** Kinser, 400; **5** T. Bettenhausen, 300; **6** Firestone, 150.

VAN SCOY DIAMOND MINE 500, Pocono International Raceway, Pennsylvania, United States of America, June 21. USAC Gold Crown National Championship 1981/2, round 2. 122 laps of the 2.500-mile/4.023-km circuit, 305.00 miles/490.81 km (race stopped due to rain).
1 A.J. Foyt, USA (March 81C-Cosworth DFX), 2h 13m 23.16s, 137.196 mph/220.795 km/h.
2 Geoff Brabham, AUS (Penske PC9-Cosworth DFX), 122 laps.
3 Tom Bigelow, USA (Penske PC7-Chevrolet), 122.
4 George Snider, USA (Coyote 81-Cosworth DFX), 121.
5 Harry McDonald, USA (Lola T500B-Cosworth DFX), 120.
6 Billy Vukovich, USA (Watson-Offenhauser), 119.
7 Jim McElreath, USA (Eagle 73-Offenhauser), 118; **8** Roger Rager, USA (Wildcat Mk3-Chevrolet), 113 (DNF, broken wing); **9** Chip Mead, USA (Eagle 81-Cosworth DFX), 106 (DNF, suspension); **10** Bill Henderson, USA (Eagle 73-Offenhauser), 105.
Fastest Qualifier: none – starting positions drawn by lot.
USAC Championship points: 1 Brabham, 1300; **2** Foyt, 1025; **3** Andretti, 800; **4** Schuppan and Bigelow, 720; **6** Snider, 600.
Final round of USAC Gold Star National Championship 1981/82 is the 1982 Indianapolis 500 – final results will be given in Autocourse 1982/83.

North American Formula Atlantic Championship

NORTH AMERICAN FORMULA ATLANTIC CHAMPIONSHIP RACE, Long Beach Grand Prix Circuit, United States of America, March 14. North American Formula Atlantic Championship, round 1. 50.5 laps of the 2.020-mile/3.251-km circuit, 102.01 miles/164.18 km.
1 Geoff Brabham, AUS (Ralt RT4-Ford BDN), 1h 14m 56.81s, 80.86 mph/130.13 km/h.
2 Jacques Villeneuve, CDN (March 81A-Ford BDN), 1h 15m 13.08s.
3 Danny Sullivan, USA (Ralt RT4-Ford BDN), 50.5 laps.
4 Rogelio Rodrigues, MEX (Ralt RT4-Ford BDN), 50.5.
5 Price Cobb, USA (March 80A-Ford BDN), 50.5.
6 John David Briggs, USA (March 79B-Ford BDN), 48.5.
7 Ed Midgley, USA (March 80A-Ford BDN), 48.5; **8** Chris Kneifel, USA (March 81A-Ford BDN), 48.5; **9** Ken Dunn, USA (Ralt RT1-Ford BDN), 48.5; **10** Joe Castellano, USA (Ralt RT1-Ford BDN), 47.5.
Fastest lap: Brabham, 1m 27.232s, 83.364 mph/134.161 km/h.
Championship points: 1 Brabham, 30; **2** Villeneuve, 24; **3** Sullivan, 19; **4** Rodriguez, 15; **5** Cobb, 12; **6** Briggs, 10.

NORTH AMERICAN FORMULA ATLANTIC CHAMPIONSHIP RACE, Ricardo Rodriguez Autodrome, Mexico City, Mexico, April 5. North American Formula Atlantic Championship, round 2. 40 laps of the 2.48-mile/3.99-km circuit, 99.20 miles/159.60 km.
1 Jacques Villeneuve, CDN (March 81A-Ford BDN), 52m 59.196s, 112.33 mph/180.78 km/h.
2 Rogelio Rodriguez, MEX (Ralt RT4-Ford BDN), 53m 29.372s.
3 Norm Hunter, USA (Ralt RT4-Ford BDN), 40 laps.
4 Mike Rosen, USA (Ralt RT4-Ford BDN), 40.
5 Dan Marvin, USA (Ralt RT1-Ford BDN), 40.
6 Tommy Grunnah, USA (March 81A-Ford BDN), 40.
7 Danny Sullivan, USA (Ralt RT4-Ford BDN), 40; **8** Miguel Muniz, MEX (Ralt RT1-Ford BDN), 39; **9** Hubert Phipps, USA (March 80A-Ford BDN), 39; **10** Juan Carlos Bolanos, MEX (Ralt RT1-Ford BDN), 38.
Fastest lap: Villeneuve, 1m 18.216s, 114.15 mph/183.71 km/h.
Championship points: 1 Villeneuve, 54; **2** Rodriguez, 39; **3** Brabham, 30; **4** Sullivan, 28; **5** Hunter, 24; **6** Rosen, 15.

NORTH AMERICAN FORMULA ATLANTIC CHAMPIONSHIP RACE, Mosport Park Circuit, Ontario, Canada, June 13. North American Formula Atlantic Championship, round 3. 40 laps of the 2.459-mile/3.957-km circuit, 98.36 miles/158.28 km.
1 Jacques Villeneuve, CDN (March 81A-Ford BDN), 58m 49.054s, 111.49 mph/179.43 km/h.
2 Whitney Ganz, USA (Ralt RT4-Ford BDN), 58m 55.318s.
3 Allen Berg, CDN (Ralt RT4-Ford BDN), 40 laps.
4 Norm Hunter, USA (Ralt RT4-Ford BDN), 40.
5 Billy Scyphers, USA (Ralt RT4-Ford BDN), 40.
6 Rogelio Rodriguez, MEX (Ralt RT4-Ford BDN), 40 (includes 90s penalty for passing pace car).
7 Chris Kneifel, USA (March 81A-Ford BDN), 39; **8** Tommy Grunnah, USA (March 81A-Ford BDN), 39; **9** James Oppermann, USA (March 81A-Ford BDN), 38; **10** Jeremy Hill, CDN (March 78B-Ford BDN), 38.
Fastest lap: Villeneuve, 1m 18.340s, 113.00 mph/181.86 km/h (record).
Championship points: 1 Villeneuve, 84; **2** Rodriguez, 49; **3** Hunter, 39; **4** Brabham, 30; **5** Sullivan, 28; **6** Ganz, 27.

RED ROOF INNS SPRINT, Mid-Ohio Sports Car Course, Lexington, Ohio, United States of America, June 28. North American Formula Atlantic Championship, round 4. 42 laps of the 2.400-mile/3.862-km circuit, 100.80 miles/162.20 km.
1 Jacques Villeneuve, CDN (March 81A-Ford BDN), 1h 01m 13.93s, 98.80 mph/159.00 km/h.
2 Whitney Ganz, USA (Ralt RT4-Ford BDN), 1h 01m 51.58s.
3 Tim Coconis, USA (Ralt RT4-Ford BDN), 42 laps.
4 Dan Marvin, USA (Ralt RT4-Ford BDN), 42.
5 Rogelio Rodriguez, MEX (Ralt RT4-Ford BDN), 41.
6 Allen Berg, CDN (Ralt RT4-Ford BDN), 41.
7 Mike Rosen, USA (Ralt RT4-Ford BDN), 41; **8** Patrick Garmyn, USA (March 80A-Ford BDN), 41; **9** Ed Midgley, USA (March 80A-Ford BDN), 41; **10** Mark Moore, USA (March 79A-Ford BDN), 41.
Fastest lap: Villeneuve, 1m 26.35s, 100.10 mph/161.09 km/h.
Championship points: 1 Villeneuve, 114; **2** Rodriguez, 61; **3** Ganz, 51; **4** Hunter, 39; **5** Brabham, 30; **6** Berg, 29.

NORTH AMERICAN FORMULA ATLANTIC CHAMPIONSHIP RACE, Road America, Elkhart Lake, Wisconsin, United States of America, July 26. North American Formula Atlantic Championship, round 5. 25 laps of the 4.000-mile/6.437-km circuit, 100.00 miles/160.93 km.
1 Whitney Ganz, USA (Ralt RT4-Ford BDN), 55m 52.06s, 107.897 mph/173.643 km/h.
2 Tommy Grunnah, USA (March 81A-Ford BDN), 56m 00.26s.
3 Tim Coconis, USA (Ralt RT4-Ford BDN), 25 laps.
4 Chris Kneifel, USA (March 81A-Ford BDN), 25.
5 Rogelio Rodriguez, MEX (Ralt RT4-Ford BDN), 25.
6 Allen Berg, CDN (Ralt RT4-Ford BDN), 25.
7 James King, USA (March 79B-Ford BDN), 25; **8** Mike Rosen, USA (Ralt RT4-Ford BDN), 25; **9** Hubert Phipps, USA (Ralt RT4-Ford BDN), 25; **10** Carl Libbich, USA (March 79B-Ford BDN), 25.
Fastest lap: Coconis, 2m 11.350s, 109.631 mph/176.434 km/h (record).
Championship points: 1 Villeneuve, 117; **2** Ganz, 81; **3** Rodriguez, 73; **4** Grunnah, 42; **5** Hunter, 40; **6** Berg, 39.

NORTH AMERICAN FORMULA ATLANTIC CHAMPIONSHIP RACE, Edmonton International Speedway, Edmonton, Alberta, Canada, August 15. North American Formula Atlantic Championship, round 6. 40 laps of the 2.527-mile/4.067-km circuit, 101.08 miles/162.68 km.
1 Tim Coconis, USA (Ralt RT4-Ford BDN), 59m 41.229s, 101.61 mph/163.53 km/h.
2 Rogelio Rodriguez, MEX (Ralt RT4-Ford BDN), 59m 49.741s.
3 Jacques Villeneuve, CDN (March 81A-Ford BDN), 40 laps.
4 Tommy Grunnah, USA (March 81A-Ford BDN), 40.
5 Norm Hunter, USA (Ralt RT4-Ford BDN), 40.
6 Chris Kneifel, USA (March 81A-Ford, BDN), 40.
7 Mike Rosen, USA (Ralt RT4-Ford BDN), 40; **8** Dan Marvin, USA (Ralt RT4-Ford BDN), 39; **9** Colin Tuckey, USA (Magnum-Ford BDN), 39; **10** Bob McGregor, CDN (March 79A-Ford BDN), 36.
Fastest lap: Coconis, 1m 27.457s, 104.02 mph/167.40 km/h.
Championship points: 1 Villeneuve, 136; **2** Rodriguez, 97; **3** Ganz, 81; **4** Coconis, 68; **5** Grunnah, 57; **6** Hunter, 52.

NORTH AMERICAN FORMULA ATLANTIC CHAMPIONSHIP RACE, Westwood Motorsport Park, British Columbia, Canada, August 23. North American Formula Atlantic Championship, round 7. 56 laps of the 1.800-mile/2.897-km circuit, 100.80 miles/162.22 km.
1 Rogelio Rodriguez, MEX (Ralt RT4-Ford BDN), 59m 37.15s, 101.44 mph/163.25 km/h.
2 Allen Berg, CDN (Ralt RT4-Ford BDN), 59m 41.05s.
3 Norm Hunter, USA (Ralt RT4-Ford BDN), 56 laps.
4 Hubert Phipps, USA (Ralt RT4-Ford BDN), 56.
5 Tommy Phillips, USA (March 81A-Ford BDN), 56.
6 Dan Marvin, USA (Ralt RT4-Ford BDN), 56.
7 Mike Rosen, USA (Ralt RT4-Ford BDN), 55; **8** Tommy Grunnah, USA (March 81A-Ford BDN), 55; **9** Riley Hopkins, USA (Ralt RT4-Ford BDN), 55; **10** Tom Klauser, USA (HR 220A-Ford BDN), 55.
Fastest lap: Marvin, 1m 02.97s, 102.91 mph/165.62 km/h.
Championship points: 1 Villeneuve, 136; **2** Rodriguez, 127; **3** Ganz, 81; **4** Hunter, 71; **5** Coconis, 68; **6** Grunnah, 65.

NORTH AMERICAN FORMULA ATLANTIC CHAMPIONSHIP RACE, Trois Rivieres, Quebec, Canada, September 6. North American Formula Atlantic Championship, round 8. 48 laps of the 2.100-mile/3.380-km circuit, 100.80 miles/162.22 km.
1 Jacques Villeneuve, CDN (March 81A-Ford BDN), 1h 11m 05.332s, 85.08 mph/136.92 km/h.
2 Whitney Ganz, USA (Ralt RT4-Ford BDN), 1h 11m 30.961s.
3 Dan Marvin, USA (Ralt RT4-Ford BDN), 48 laps.
4 Allen Berg, CDN (Ralt RT4-Ford BDN), 48.
5 Mark Moore, USA (Ralt RT4-Ford BDN), 47.
6 Norm Hunter, USA (Ralt RT4-Ford BDN), 47.
7 Rick Bell, USA (Ralt RT4-Ford BDN), 47; **8** John David Briggs, USA (March 81A-Ford BDN), 47; **9** Mike Rosen, USA (Ralt RT4-Ford BDN), 45; **10** Mauro Lanaro, USA (March 79A-Ford BDN), 44.
Fastest lap: Villeneuve, 1m 27.806s, 86.10 mph/138.56 km/h.
Championship points: 1 Villeneuve, 166; **2** Rodriguez, 130; **3** Ganz, 105; **4** Hunter, 81; **5** Berg, 78; **6** Coconis, 68.

NORTH AMERICAN FORMULA ATLANTIC CHAMPIONSHIP RACE, Ile Notre-Dame Circuit, Montreal, Canada, September 26. North American Formula Atlantic Championship, round 9. 37 laps of the 2.74-mile/4.41-km circuit, 101.38 miles/163.17 km.
1 Kevin Cogan, USA (Ralt RT4-Ford BDN), 1h 02m 56.431s, 96.64 mph/155.53 km/h.
2 Norm Hunter, USA (Ralt RT4-Ford BDN), 1h 03m 23.899s.
3 Whitney Ganz, USA (Ralt RT4-Ford BDN), 37 laps.
4 Tommy Grunnah, USA (March 81A-Ford BDN), 37.
5 Rick Bell, USA (Ralt RT4-Ford BDN), 37.
6 John David Briggs, USA (March 81A-Ford BDN), 37.
7 Mike Rosen, USA (Ralt RT4-Ford BDN), 36; **8** Steve Shelton, USA (Ralt RT4-Ford BDN), 36; **9** Tom Shelton, USA (Ralt RT4-Ford BDN), 36; **10** Allen Berg, USA (Ralt RT4-Ford BDN), 36.
Fastest lap: Cogan, 1m 40.771s, 97.89 mph/157.54 km/h.
Final Championship points:

1 Jacques Villenenuve, CDN	166
2 Rogelio Rodriguez, MEX	130
3 Whitney Ganz, USA	124
4 Norm Hunter, USA	105
5 Allen Berg, CDN	84
6 Tommy Grunnah, USA	82

7 Tim Coconis, USA, 68; **8 =** Dan Marvin, USA, 66; **8 =** Mike Rosen, USA, 66; **10** Chris Kneifel, USA, 56; **11** Hubert Phipps, USA, 34; **12** John David Briggs, USA, 33; **13 =** Geoff Brabham, AUS, 30; **13 =** Kevin Cogan, USA, 30; **15** Danny Sullivan, USA, 28.

Can-Am

SCCA CAN-AM CHALLENGE RACE, Mosport Park Circuit, Ontario, Canada, June 14. SCCA Can-Am Challenge, round 1. 60 laps of the 2.459-mile/3.957-km circuit, 147.54 miles/237.42 km.
1 Teo Fabi, I (5.0 March 817-Chevrolet), 1h 16m 36.617s, 115.526 mph/185.921 km/h.
2 Geoff Brabham, AUS (5.0 Lola T530-Chevrolet), 1h 17m 00.268s.
3 Danny Sullivan, USA (5.0 Lola T530-Chevrolet), 60 laps.
4 Jeff Wood, USA (5.0 Lola T530-Chevrolet), 58.
5 Al Holbert, USA (5.0 CAC 2-Chevrolet), 57.
6 Horst Kroll, CDN (5.0 Lola T332-Chevrolet), 54.
7 Richard Guider, USA (2.0 Marguey-Ford BDG), 54; **8** Mike Freberg, CDN (5.0 Lola T300/332-Chevrolet), 53; **9** Roman Pechmann, CDN (2.0 Lola T290-Ford BDG), 52; **10** S. Peter Smith, USA (2.0 Bobsy-Hart), 49.
Fastest lap: Fabi, 1m 13.102s, 121.090 mph/194.875 km/h (record).
Championship points: 1 Fabi, 90; **2** Brabham, 60; **3** Sullivan, 40; **4** Wood, 30; **5** Holbert, 20; **6** Kroll, 10.

SCCA CAN-AM CHALLENGE RACE, Mid-Ohio Sports Car Course, Lexington, Ohio, United States of America, June 28. SCCA Can-Am Challenge, round 2. 63 laps of the 2.400-mile/3.862-km circuit, 151.20 miles/243.31 km.
1 Teo Fabi, I (5.0 March 817-Chevrolet), 1h 30m 22.884s, 100.42 mph/161.61 km/h.
2 Geoff Brabham, AUS (5.0 Lola T530-Chevrolet), 1h 30m 27.002s.
3 Rocky Moran, USA (5.0 Frissbee-Chevrolet), 63 laps.
4 Al Holbert, USA (5.0 CAC 2-Chevrolet), 63.
5 Danny Sullivan, USA (5.0 Lola T530-Chevrolet), 62.
6 Jeff Wood, USA (5.0 Lola T530-Chevrolet), 62.
7 Randy Lewis, USA (5.0 CAC 1-Chevrolet), 61; **8** Gary Gove, USA (3.0 Williams FW07S-Cosworth DFV), 60; **9** Jim Trueman, USA (2.0 Ralt RT2-Hart), 60; **10** Richard Guider, USA (2.0 Marguey-Ford BDG), 59.
Fastest lap: Fabi, 1m 22.60s, 104.60 mph/168.34 km/h.
Championship points: 1 Fabi, 180; **2** Brabham, 120; **3** Sullivan, 60; **4** Holbert, 50; **5** Wood and Moran, 40.

SCCA CAN-AM CHALLENGE RACE, Watkins Glen Grand Prix Circuit, New York, United States of America, July 11. SCCA Can-Am Challenge, round 3. 55 laps of the 3.377-mile/5.435-km circuit, 185.735 miles/298.925 km.
1 Al Holbert, USA (5.0 CAC 2-Chevrolet), 1h 39m 03.7s, 112.50 mph/181.05 km/h.
2 Danny Sullivan, USA (5.0 Lola T530-Chevrolet), 1h 39m 17.5s.

3 Rocky Moran, USA (5.0 Frissbee-Chevrolet), 55 laps.
4 David Kennedy, IRL (5.0 Frissbee-Chevrolet), 53.
5 Randy Lewis, USA (5.0 CAC 1-Chevrolet), 52.
6 Jim Trueman, USA (2.0 Ralt RT2-Hart), 51.
7 Richard Guider, USA (2.0 Marguey-Ford BDG), 49; **8** Roman Pechman, CDN (2.0 Lola T290-Ford BDG), 47; **9** Dave Hoover, USA (5.0 Lola T333-Chevrolet), 45; **10** Greg Sorrentino, USA (2.0 March 79S-Ford BDG), 43.
Fastest lap: Geoff Brabham, AUS (5.0 Lola T530-Chevrolet), 1m 40.746s, 120.67 mph/194.199 km/h (record).
Championship points: 1 Fabi, 181; **2** Holbert, 140; **3** Brabham, 124; **4** Sullivan, 120; **5** Moran, 80; **6** Wood, 40.

SCCA CAN-AM CHALLENGE RACE, Road America, Elkhart Lake, Wisconsin, United States of America, July 26. SCCA Can-Am Challenge, round 4. 40 laps of the 4.000-mile/6.437-km circuit, 160.00 miles/257.49 km.
1 Geoff Brabham, AUS (5.0 Lola T530-Chevrolet), 1h 23m 21.34s, 115.169 mph/185.346 km/h.
2 Jeff Wood, USA (5.0 Lola T530-Chevrolet), 1h 23m 35.54s.
3 Al Unser, USA (5.0 March 817-Chevrolet), 39 laps.
4 Al Holbert, USA (5.0 CAC 2-Chevrolet), 39.
5 Jim Trueman, USA (2.0 Ralt RT2-Hart), 37.
6 Richard Guider, USA (2.0 Marguey-Ford BDG), 36.
7 Mike Freberg, CDN (5.0 Lola T332-Chevrolet), 36; **8** Horst Kroll, CDN (5.0 Lola T332-Chevrolet), 34; **9** John Graham, USA (2.0 Midland Special), 34; **10** Randy Lewis, USA (5.0 CAC 1-Chevrolet), 34.
Fastest lap: Brabham, 2m 00.268s, 119.773 mph/192.755 km/h (record).
Championship points: 1 Brabham, 214; **2** Fabi, 181; **3** Holbert, 170; **4** Sullivan, 123; **5** Wood, 100; **6** Moran, 84.

SCCA CAN-AM CHALLENGE RACE, Edmonton International Speedway, Edmonton, Alberta, Canada, August 16. SCCA Can-Am

Challenge, round 5. 60 laps of the 2.527-mile/4.067-km circuit, 151.62 miles/244.02 km.
1 Geoff Brabham, AUS (5.0 VDS 001-Chevrolet), 1h 25m 40.837s, 106.176 mph/170.873 km/h.
2 Danny Sullivan, USA (5.0 Lola T530-Chevrolet), 1h 26m 18.130s.
3 Rocky Moran, USA (5.0 Frissbee-Chevrolet), 60 laps.
4 Jeff Wood, USA (5.0 Lola T530-Chevrolet), 59.
5 Danny Johnson, USA (5.0 Chevron B34-Chevrolet), 57.
6 Jim Trueman, USA (2.0 Ralt RT2-Hart), 56.
7 John Morton, USA (5.0 Frissbee-Chevrolet), 55; **8** Richard Guider, USA (2.0 Marguey-Ford BDG), 55; **9** Horst Kroll, CDN (5.0 Lola T332-Chevrolet), 54; **10** John Graham, CDN (2.0 Midland Special), 51.
Fastest lap: Teo Fabi, I (5.0 March 817-Chevrolet), 1m 22.106s, 110.82 mph/178.35 km/h.
Championship points: 1 Brabham, 304; **2** Fabi, 185; **3** Sullivan, 183; **4** Holbert, 170; **5** Wood, 130; **6** Moran, 124.

SCCA CAN-AM CHALLENGE RACE, Trois Rivieres, Quebec, Canada, September 6. SCCA Can-Am Challenge, round 6. 42 laps of the 2.100-mile/3.380-km circuit, 88.20 miles/141.94 km.
1 Al Holbert, USA (5.0 CAC 2-Chevrolet), 1h 04m 11.353s, 82.44 mph/132.674 km/h.
2 Geoff Brabham, AUS (5.0 Lola T530-Chevrolet), 1h 04m 24.0s.
3 Jeff Wood, USA (5.0 Lola T532-Chevrolet), 42 laps.
4 Teo Fabi, I (5.0 March 817-Chevrolet), 42.
5 Danny Sullivan, USA (5.0 Lola T530-Chevrolet), 42.
6 Jim Trueman, USA (2.0 Ralt RT2-Hart), 41.
7 Richard Guider, USA (2.0 Marguey-Ford BDG), 40; **8** Danny Johnson, USA (5.0 Chevron B34-Chevrolet), 40; **9** Cliff Dawson, CDN (2.0 Brabham-Ford BDG), 38; **10** John Graham, CDN (2.0 Midland Special), 29.
Fastest lap: Sullivan, 1m 25.93s, 87.979 mph/141.588 km/h.
Championship points: 1 Brabham, 364; **2** Holbert, 260; **3** Fabi, 215; **4** Sullivan, 203; **5** Wood, 178; **6** Moran, 124.

SCCA CAN-AM CHALLENGE RACE, Mosport Park Circuit, Ontario, Canada, September 13. SCCA Can-Am Challenge, round 7. 60 laps of the 2.459-mile/3.957-km circuit, 147.54 miles/237.42 km.
1 Teo Fabi, I (5.0 March 817-Chevrolet), 1h 15m 27.667s, 117.279 mph/188.771 km/h.
2 Bobby Rahal, USA (5.0 March 817-Chevrolet), 1h 15m 27.713s.
3 Geoff Brabham, AUS (5.0 VDS 001-Chevrolet), 60 laps.
4 Tom Klauser, USA (5.0 Frissbee-Chevrolet), 58.
5 Paul Macey, CDN (2.0 Lola T294-Ford), 52.
6 John Graham, CDN (2.0 Midland Special), 51.
7 Danny Sullivan, USA (5.0 Lola T530-Chevrolet), 50; **8** Jeff Wood, USA (5.0 Lola T530-Chevrolet), 49; **9** Jim Trueman, USA (2.0 Ralt RT2-Hart), 49; **10** Danny Johnson, USA (5.0 Chevron B34-Chevrolet), 49.
Fastest lap: Fabi, 1m 12.708s, 121.754 mph/195.944 km/h (record).
Championship points: 1 Brabham, 404; **2** Fabi, 305; **3** Holbert, 261; **4** Sullivan, 212; **5** Wood, 178; **6** Moran, 124.

SCCA CAN-AM CHALLENGE RACE, Riverside International Raceway, California, United States of America, October 4. SCCA Can-Am Challenge, round 8. 60 laps of the 2.547-mile/4.099-km circuit, 152.82 miles/245.94 km.
1 Al Holbert, USA (5.0 CAC 2-Chevrolet), 1h 16m 50.868s, 119.319 mph/192.025 km/h.
2 Jeff Wood, USA (5.0 Lola T530-Chevrolet), 1h 16m 51.876s.
3 Tom Klauser, USA (5.0 Frissbee-Chevrolet), 60 laps.
4 Randy Lewis, USA (5.0 CAC 1-Chevrolet), 57.
5 John Morton, USA (5.0 Frissbee-Chevrolet), 57.
6 Mike Allen, USA (5.0 Lola T332-Chevrolet), 56.
7 Graham McRea, NZ (5.0 McRea GM5-Chevrolet), 56; **8** John Gunn, USA (5.0 Lola T332-Chevrolet), 56; **9** Richard Guider, USA (2.0 Ralt RT2-Hart), 56; **10** Tim Evans, USA (2.0 Cicale-Hart), 55.
Fastest lap: Not given.
Championship points: 1 Brabham, 407; **2** Holbert, 351; **3** Fabi, 306; **4** Wood, 238; **5** Sullivan, 212; **6** Moran, 124.

SCCA CAN-AM CHALLENGE RACE, Laguna Seca Raceway, California, United States of America, October 12. SCCA Can-Am Challenge, round 9. 50 laps of the 1.900-mile/3.058-km circuit, 95.00 miles/152.90 km.
1 Teo Fabi, I (5.0 March 817-Chevrolet), 49m 10.950s, 115.895 mph/186.514 km/h.
2 Al Holbert, USA (5.0 CAC 2-Chevrolet), 49m 16.150s.
3 Geoff Brabham, AUS (5.0 VDS 001-Chevrolet), 50 laps.
4 Ricky Moran, USA (5.0 Frissbee-Chevrolet), 50.
5 Tom Klauser, USA (5.0 Frissbee-Chevrolet), 49.
6 Jeff Wood, USA (5.0 Lola T530-Chevrolet), 49.
7 Jim Trueman, USA (2.0 Ralt RT2-Hart), 46; **8** John Gunn, USA (5.0 Lola T332-Chevrolet), 46; **9** Bobby Rahal, USA (5.0 March 817-Chevrolet), 46; **10** Mike Allen, USA (5.0 Lola T332-Chevrolet), 45.
Fastest lap: Sullivan, 57.470s, 119.018 mph/191.540 km/h (record).
Championship points: 1 Brabham, 447; **2** Holbert, 411; **3** Fabi, 396; **4** Wood, 248; **5** Sullivan, 213; **6** Moran, 154.

SCCA CAN-AM CHALLENGE RACE, Las Vegas Grand Prix Circuit, Nevada, United States of America, October 16. SCCA Can-Am Challenge, round 10. 38 laps of the 2.268-mile/3.650-km circuit, 86.18 miles/138.70 km.
1 Danny Sullivan, USA (5.0 Frissbee-Chevrolet), 54m 28.962s, 94.58 mph/152.21 km/h.
2 Teo Fabi, I (5.0 March 817-Chevrolet), 54m 31.209s.
3 Geoff Brabham, AUS (5.0 VDS 001-Chevrolet), 38 laps.
4 Bobby Rahal, USA (5.0 March 817-Chevrolet), 38.
5 John Morton, USA (5.0 Frissbee-Chevrolet), 38.
6 Tom Klauser, USA (5.0 Frissbee-Chevrolet), 38.
7 Al Holbert, USA (5.0 CAC 2-Chevrolet), 37; **8** Jeff Wood, USA (5.0 Lola T530-Chevrolet), 37; **9** Randy Lewis, USA (5.0 CAC 1-Chevrolet), 36; **10** Jim Trueman, USA (2.0 Ralt RT2-Hart), 36.
Fastest lap: Fabi, 1m 24.105s, 97.078 mph/156. 234 km/h (record).

Final Championship points:

1 Geoff Brabham, AUS	487
2 Teo Fabi, I	456
3 Al Holbert, USA	420
4 Danny Sullivan, USA	403
5 Jeff Wood, USA	256
6 Rocky Moran, USA	154

7 Tom Klauser, USA, 100; **8** Bobby Rahal, USA, 97; **9** Jim Trueman, USA, 88; **10** Randy Lewis, USA, 72; **11** Richard Guider, USA, 67; **12** John Morton, USA, 49; **13** Al Unser, USA, 43; **14** John Graham, CDN, 40; **15** Danny Johnson, USA, 35; **16** Horst Kroll, CDN, 34; **17** David Kennady, IRL, 30; **18** Mike Freburg, CDN, 24; **19** Paul Macey, CDN, 20; **20** John Gunn, USA, 17.

CART PPG Indy Car World Series

1980 RESULTS

The final round of the 1980 CART PPG Indy Car World Series was run after Autocourse 1980/81 went to press.

MILLER HIGH LIFE 150, Phoenix International Raceway, Arizona, United States of America, November 8. CART PPG Indy Car World Series, round 12. 150 laps of the 1·000-mile/1·609-km circuit, 150·00 miles/241·40 km.
1 Tom Sneva, USA (Phoenix-Cosworth DFX), 1h 30m 04s, 99·925 mph/160·813 km/h.
2 Mario Andretti, USA (Penske PC9-Cosworth DFX), 1h 30m 13s.
3 Gary Bettenhausen, USA (Orbiter-Cosworth DFX), 146 laps.
4 Sheldon Kinser, USA (Watson-Cosworth DFX), 146.
5 Dennis Firestone, USA (Penske PC6-Cosworth DFX), 145.
6 Pete Halsmer, USA (McLaren M24-Cosworth DFX), 145.
7 Rick Mears, USA (Penske PC9-Cosworth DFX), 143; **8** Herm Johnson, USA (Lightning-Offenhauser), 143; **9** Jerry Karl, USA (Karl-Chevrolet), 130; **10** Roger Rager, USA (Wildcat-Chevrolet), 110; **11** Bill Tempero, USA (Eagle-Chevrolet), 104; **12** Bill Vukovich, USA (Eagle-Offenhauser), 97.
Fastest Qualifier: Andretti, 142·891 mph/229·960 km/h.

Final Championship points:

1 Johnny Rutherford, USA	4723
2 Bobby Unser, USA	3714
3 Tom Sneva, USA	2930
4 Rick Mears, USA	2866
5 Pancho Carter, USA	1855
6 Gordon Johncock, USA	1572

7 Bill Alsup, USA, 1214; **8** Al Unser, USA, 1153; **9** Gary Bettenhausen, USA, 1057; **10** Vern Schuppan, AUS, 806; **11** Tom Bagley, USA, 794; **12** Dennis Firestone, USA, 743; **13** Sheldon Kinser, USA, 697; **14** Tom Gloy, USA, 680; **15** Danny Ongais, USA, 601; **16** Mario Andretti, USA, 580; **17** Spike Gehlhausen, USA, 473; **18** Roger Rager, USA, 381; **19** Rick Muther, USA, 356; **20** Bill Tempero, USA, 331.

1981 RESULTS

KRAKO CAR STEREO 150, Phoenix International Raceway, Arizona, United States of America, March 22. CART PPG Indy Car World Series, round 1. 150 laps of the 1·000-mile/1·609-km circuit, 150·00 miles/241·40 km.
1 Johnny Rutherford, USA (Chaparral 2K-Cosworth DFX), 1h 17m 08·0s, 116·681 mph/187·779 km/h.
2 Bobby Unser, USA (Penske PC9B-Cosworth DFX), 1h 17m 30·0s.
3 Tom Sneva, USA (Phoenix-Cosworth DFX), 149 laps.
4 Rick Mears, USA (Penske PC9B-Cosworth DFX), 147.
5 Bill Alsup, USA (Penske PC7-Cosworth DFX), 145.
6 Gordon Johncock, USA (Wildcat Mk8-Cosworth DFX), 144.
7 Pancho Carter, USA (Penske PC7-Cosworth DFX), 114; **8** Jerry Karl, USA (McLaren M24-Chevrolet), 144; **9** Geoff Brabham, AUS (Penske PC7-Cosworth DFX), 144; **10** Dick Simon, USA (Watson-Cosworth DFX), 140; **11** Mario Andretti, USA (Wildcat Mk8-Cosworth DFX), 139; **12** Bob Lazier, USA (Penske PC7-Cosworth DFX), 136.
Fastest Qualifier: Unser, 25·165s, 143·055 mph/230·224 km/h.
Championship points: 1 Rutherford, 21; **2** Unser, 17; **3** Sneva, 14; **4** Mears, 12; **5** Alsup, 10; **6** Johncock, 8.

GOULD REX MAYS 150, Wisconsin State Fair Park Speedway, Milwaukee, Wisconsin, United States of America, June 7. CART PPG Indy Car World Series, round 2. 150 laps of the 1·000-mile/1·609-km circuit, 150·00 miles/241·40 km.
1 Mike Mosley, USA (Eagle 81-Chevrolet), 1h 19m 03·55s, 113·838 mph/183·204 km/h.
2 Kevin Cogan, USA (Phoenix 80-Cosworth DFX), 149 laps.
3 Mario Andretti, USA (Wildcat Mk8-Cosworth DFX), 148.
4 Tom Sneva, USA (Phoenix 80-Cosworth DFX), 147.
5 Al Unser, USA (Longhorn LR02-Cosworth DFX), 146.
6 Johnny Rutherford, USA (Chaparral 2K-Cosworth DFX), 146.
7 Dick Simon, USA (Watson-Cosworth DFX), 144; **8** Billy Engelhart, USA (McLaren M24-Cosworth DFX), 144; **9** Tom Bigelow, USA (Penske PC7-Chevrolet), 144; **10** Larry Dickson, USA (Penske PC7-Cosworth DFX), 144; **11** Scott Brayton, USA (Penske PC7-Cosworth DFX), 144; **12** Tony Bettenhausen, USA (McLaren M24B-Cosworth DFX), 143.
Fastest Qualifier: Gordon Johncock, USA (Wildcat Mk8-Cosworth DFX), 26·726s, 134·700 mph/216·778 km/h.
Championship points: 1 Rutherford, 29; **2** Sneva, 26; **3** Mosley, 21; **4** Unser, 17; **5** Andretti and Cogan, 16.

KRAKO TWIN 125 RACE ONE, Atlanta International Raceway, Georgia, United States of America, June 28. CART PPG Indy Car World Series, round 3. 83 laps of the 1·522-mile/2·449-km circuit, 126·33 miles/203·27 km.
1 Rick Mears, USA (Penske PC9B-Cosworth DFX), 51m 29·0s, 150·139 mph/241·625 km/h.
2 Johnny Rutherford, USA (Chaparral 2K-Cosworth DFX), 51m 32·0s.
3 Mario Andretti, USA (Wildcat Mk8-Cosworth DFX), 83 laps.
4 Gordon Johncock, USA (Wildcat Mk8-Cosworth DFX), 83.
5 Pancho Carter, USA (Penske PC7-Cosworth DFX), 83.
6 Al Unser, USA (Longhorn LR02-Cosworth DFX), 83.
7 Tony Bettenhausen, USA (McLaren M24B-Cosworth DFX), 82; **8** Bill Alsup, USA (Penske PC9B-Cosworth DFX), 82; **9** Scott Brayton, USA (Penske PC7-Cosworth DFX), 82; **10** Larry Dickson, USA (Penske PC7-Cosworth DFX), 81; **11** Larry Cannon, USA (Penske PC7-Cosworth DFX), 81; **12** Josele Garza, MEX (Penske PC9-Cosworth DFX), 81.
Fastest Qualifier: Rutherford, 27·326s, 200·512 mph/322·692 km/h.
Championship points: 1 Rutherford, 47; **2** Mears, 32; **3** Andretti, 30; **4** Sneva, 26; **5** Johncock, 22; **6** Mosley, 21.

KRAKO TWIN 125 RACE TWO, Atlanta International Raceway, Georgia, United States of America, June 28. CART PPG Indy Car World Series, round 4. 83 laps of the 1·522-mile/2·449-km circuit, 126·33 miles/203·27 km.
1 Rick Mears, USA (Penske PC9B-Cosworth DFX), 45m 20·0s, 167·073 mph/268·877 km/h.
2 Mario Andretti, USA (Wildcat Mk8-Cosworth DFX), 45m 21·7s.
3 Johnny Rutherford, USA (Chaparral 2K-Cosworth DFX), 83 laps.
4 Gordon Johncock, USA (Wildcat Mk8-Cosworth DFX), 83.
5 Pancho Carter, USA (Penske PC7-Cosworth DFX), 83.
6 Bobby Unser, USA (Penske PC9B-Cosworth DFX), 83.
7 Al Unser, USA (Longhorn LR02-Cosworth DFX), 82; **8** Bill Alsup, USA (Penske PC9B-Cosworth DFX), 81; **9** Bob Lazier, USA (Penske PC7-Cosworth DFX), 81; **10** Scott Brayton, USA (Penske PC7-Cosworth DFX), 81; **11** Tony Bettenhausen, USA (McLaren M24B-Cosworth DFX), 80; **12** Larry Dickson, USA (Penske PC7-Cosworth DFX), 79.
Fastest Qualifier: Rutherford, 27·326s, 200·512 mph/322·692 km/h.
Pole position taken by winner of race one.
Championship points: 1 Rutherford, 61; **2** Mears, 53; **3** Andretti, 46; **4** Johncock, 34; **5** Carter, 27; **6** Sneva and B. Unser, 26.

NORTON-MICHIGAN 500, Michigan International Speedway, Brooklyn, United States of America, July 25. CART PPG Indy Car World Series, round 5. 250 laps of the 2.000-mile/3.219-km circuit, 500.00 miles/804.75 km.
1 Pancho Carter, USA (Penske PC7-Cosworth DFX), 3h 45m 45s, 132.890 mph/213.868 km/h.
2 Tony Bettenhausen, USA (McLaren M24B-Cosworth DFX), 3h 45m 47s.
3 Rick Mears, USA (Penske PC9B-Cosworth DFX), 248 laps.
4 Bill Alsup, USA (Penske PC9B-Cosworth DFX), 247.
5 Tom Bigelow, USA (Penske PC7-Chevrolet), 247.
6 Gary Bettenhausen, USA (Wildcat Mk8-Cosworth DFX), 243.
7 Scott Brayton, USA (Penske PC7-Cosworth DFX), 238; **8** Phil Caliva, USA (McLaren M16-Chevrolet), 235; **9** Larry Dickson, USA (Penske PC7-Cosworth DFX), 227; **10** Bob Lazier, USA (Penske PC7-Cosworth DFX), 225 (DNF, vibration); **11** Al Unser, USA (Longhorn LR02-Cosworth DFX), 196 (DNF, engine); **12** Larry Cannon, USA (Penske PC7-Cosworth DFX), 190 (DNF, lost wheel).
Fastest Qualifier: Tom Sneva, USA (March 81C-Cosworth DFX), 35.757s, 201.359 mph/324.055 km/h.
Championship points: 1 Carter, 132; **2** Mears, 123; **3** T. Bettenhausen, 89; **4** Alsup, 80; **5** Rutherford, 61; **6** Bigelow, 54.

LOS ANGELES TIMES CALIFORNIA 500, Riverside International Raceway, California, United States of America, August 30. CART PPG Indy Car World Series, round 6. 95 laps of the 3.30-mile/5.31-km circuit, 313.50 miles/504.45 km.
1 Rick Mears, USA (Penske PC9B-Cosworth DFX), 2h 43m 40.98s, 108.300 mph/174.292 km/h.
2 Gordon Johncock, USA (Wildcat Mk8-Cosworth DFX), 2h 43m 42.37s.
3 Bill Alsup, USA (Penske PC9B-Cosworth DFX), 94 laps.
4 Mike Chandler, USA (Penske PC7-Cosworth DFX), 94.
5 Bob Lazier, USA (Penske PC7-Cosworth DFX), 92.
6 Dick Simon, USA (Watson-Cosworth DFX), 90.
7 Herm Johnson, USA (Lightning-Chevrolet), 88; **8** Scott Brayton, USA (Penske PC7-Cosworth DFX), 87; **9** Bobby Unser, USA (Penske PC9B-Cosworth DFX), 84; **10** Pancho Carter, USA (Penske PC7-Cosworth DFX), 63 (DNF, engine); **11** Kevin Cogan, USA (Phoenix-Cosworth DFX), 53 (DNF, accident); **12** Josele Garza, MEX (Penske PC9-Cosworth DFX), 52 (DNF, fuel injection pump).
Fastest Qualifier: Geoff Brabham, AUS (Eagle 81-Chevrolet), 1m 31.695s, 129.560 mph/208.506 km/h.
Championship points: 1 Mears, 186; **2** Carter, 141; **3** Alsup, 122; **4** T. Bettenhausen, 84; **5** Johncock, 82; **6** Rutherford, 63.

A B DICK/TONY BETTENHAUSEN 200, Wisconsin State Fair Park Speedway, Milwaukee, United States of America, September 5. CART PPG Indy Car World Series, round 7. 200 laps of the 1.000-mile/1.609-km circuit, 200.00 miles/321.87 km.
1 Tom Sneva, USA (March 81C-Cosworth DFX), 1h 41m 41.00s, 118.013 mph/189.923 km/h.
2 Rick Mears, USA (Penske PC9B-Cosworth DFX), 1h 41m 45s.
3 Bobby Unser, USA (Penske PC9B-Cosworth DFX), 199 laps.

4 Johnny Rutherford, USA (Chaparral 2K-Cosworth DFX), 198.
5 Al Unser, USA (Longhorn, LR02-Cosworth DFX), 197.
6 Gordon Johncock, USA (Wildcat Mk8-Cosworth DFX), 197.
7 Steve Krisiloff, USA (Wildcat Mk8-Cosworth DFX), 194; 8 Josele Garza, MEX (Penske PC9-Cosworth DFX), 193; 9 Billy Engelhardt, USA (McLaren M24-Cosworth DFX), 191; 10 Pancho Carter, USA (Penske PC7-Cosworth DFX), 190; 11 Bill Alsup, USA (Penske PC9B-Cosworth DFX), 190; 12 Larry Dickson, USA (Penske PC7-Cosworth DFX), 189.
Fastest Qualifier: Rutherford, 26.492s, 135.890 mph/218.693 km/h.
Championship points: 1 Mears, 218; 2 Carter, 147; 3 Alsup, 126; 4 Johncock, 98; 5 T. Bettenhausen, 91; 6 Rutherford, 87.

DETROIT NEWS GRAND PRIX, Michigan International Speedway, Brooklyn, United States of America, September 20. CART PPG Indy Car World Series, round 8. 74 laps of the 2.000-mile/3.219-km circuit, 148.00 miles/238.21 km.
1 Rick Mears, USA (Penske PC9B-Cosworth DFX), 1h 10m 30.0s, 125.957 mph/202.708 km/h.
2 Mario Andretti, USA (Wildcat Mk8-Cosworth DFX), 74 laps.
3 Al Unser, USA (Eagle 81-Cosworth DFX), 74.
4 Bill Alsup, USA (Penske PC9B-Cosworth DFX), 74.
5 Gordon Johncock, USA (Wildcat Mk8-Cosworth DFX), 74.
6 Dick Ferguson, USA (Penske PC7-Cosworth DFX), 74.
7 Bobby Unser, USA (Penske PC9B-Cosworth DFX), 74; 8 Larry Dickson, USA (Penske PC7-Cosworth DFX), 73; 9 Tom Bigelow, USA (Penske PC7-Chevrolet), 73; 10 Tony Bettenhausen, USA (Phoenix-Cosworth DFX), 73; 11 Jim McElreath, USA (Eagle 73-Offenhauser), 72; 12 Steve Chassey, USA (Eagle 81-Chevrolet), 71.
Fastest Qualifier: Mears, 35.980s, 200.111 mph/322.047 km/h.
Championship points: 1 Mears, 239; 2 Carter, 148; 3 Alsup, 138; 4 Johncock, 108; 5 T. Bettenhausen, 94; 6 Rutherford, 87.

WATKINS GLEN 200, Watkins Glen Grand Prix Circuit, New York, United States of America, October 4. CART PPG Indy Car World Series, round 9. 60 laps of the 3.377-mile/5.435-km circuit, 202.62 miles/326.10 km.
1 Rick Mears, USA (Penske PC9B-Cosworth DFX), 1h 52m 17.0s, 108.273 mph/174.248 km/h.
2 Johnny Rutherford, USA (Chaparral 2K-Cosworth DFX), 59 laps.
3 Bill Alsup, USA (Penske PC7-Cosworth DFX), 59.
4 Bob Lazier, USA (Penske PC7-Cosworth DFX), 58.
5 Steve Chassey, USA (Eagle 81-Chevrolet), 56.
6 Rocky Moran, USA (Eagle 81-Chevrolet), 55 (DNF – out of fuel).
7 Larry Dickson, USA (Penske PC7-Cosworth DFX), 55; 8 Tony Bettenhausen, USA (Phoenix-Cosworth DFX), 54; 9 Herm Johnson, USA (Eagle 81-Chevrolet), 54; 10 Gordon Johncock, USA (Wildcat Mk8-Cosworth DFX), 52; 11 Dick Simon, USA (Watson-Cosworth DFX), 50; 12 Hurley Haywood, USA (Eagle 81-Cosworth DFX), 48.
Fastest Qualifier: Mario Andretti, USA (Wildcat Mk8-Cosworth DFX), 1m 56.167s, 104.653 mph/168.422 km/h.
Championship points: 1 Mears, 279; 2 Alsup, 166; 3 Carter, 150; 4 Rutherford, 119; 5 Johncock, 114; 6 T. Bettenhausen, 104.

COPA MEXICO, Mexico City, Mexico, October 18. CART PPG Indy Car World Series, round 10. 59 laps of the 2.48-mile/3.99-km circuit, 146.32 miles/235.41 km.
1 Rick Mears, USA (Penske PC9B-Cosworth DFX), 1h 24m 48.0s, 104.363 mph/167.956 km/h.
2 Al Unser, USA (Longhorn LR02-Cosworth DFX), 1h 24m 53.0s.
3 Gordon Johncock, USA (Wildcat Mk8-Cosworth DFX), 59 laps.
4 Bob Lazier, USA (March 81C-Cosworth DFX), 58.
5 Bill Alsup, USA (Penske PC9B-Cosworth DFX), 58.
6 Pancho Carter, USA (Penske PC7-Cosworth DFX), 58.
7 Mike Mosley, USA (Penske PC6-Cosworth DFX), 58; 8 Herm Johnson, USA (Eagle 81-Chevrolet), 58; 9 Geoff Brabham, AUS (Eagle 81-Chevrolet), 57; 10 Dick Ferguson, USA (Penske PC7-Cosworth DFX), 57; 11 Tony Bettenhausen, USA (Phoenix-Cosworth DFX), 56; 12 Bill Tempero, USA (McLaren M24-Chevrolet), 55.
Fastest Qualifier: Bobby Unser, USA (Penske PC9B-Cosworth DFX), 1m 11.538s, 124.800 mph/200.846 km/h.
Championship points: 1 Mears, 299; 2 Alsup, 176; 3 Carter, 158; 4 Johncock, 128; 5 Rutherford, 119; 6 Bettenhausen, 106.

MILLER HIGH LIFE 150, Phoenix International Raceway, Arizona, United States of America, October 31. CART PPG Indy Car World Series, round 11. 150 laps of the 1.000-mile/1.609-km circuit, 150.00 miles/241.40 km.
1 Tom Sneva, USA (March 81C-Cosworth DFX), 1h 20m 10.0s, 112.226 mph/180.610 km/h.
2 Bobby Unser, USA (Penske PC9B-Cosworth DFX), 1h 20m 11.0s.
3 Gordon Johncock, USA (Wildcat Mk8-Cosworth), 150 laps.
4 Mario Andretti, USA (Wildcat Mk8-Cosworth), 150.
5 Pancho Carter, USA (Penske PC7-Cosworth DFX), 148.
6 Josele Garza, MEX (Penske PC9-Cosworth DFX), 148.
7 Dick Ferguson, USA (Penske PC7-Cosworth DFX), 148; 8 Rick Mears, USA (Penske PC9B-Cosworth DFX), 145; 9 Herm Johnson, USA (Eagle 81-Chevrolet), 144; 10 Gordon Smiley, USA (Wildcat Mk8-Cosworth DFX), 144; 11 Tom Bigelow, USA (Penske PC7-Chevrolet), 143; 12 Jerry Sneva, USA (Vollstedt-Offenhauser), 143.
Fastest Qualifier: B. Unser, 24.211s, 148.693 mph/239.298 km/h.
Final Championship points:

1 Rick Mears, USA	304
2 Bill Alsup, USA	177
3 Pancho Carter, USA	168
4 Gordon Johncock, USA	142
5 Johnny Rutherford, USA	120
6 Tony Bettenhausen, USA	107

7 Bobby Unser, USA, 99; 8 Tom Sneva, USA, 96; 9 Bob Lazier, USA, 92; 10 Al Unser, USA, 90; 11 Mario Andretti, USA, 81; 12 Tom Bigelow, USA, 60; 13 Scott Brayton, USA, 57; 14 Larry Dickson, USA, 49; 15 Gary Bettenhausen, USA, 42.

NASCAR Winston Cup Grand National

1980 RESULTS

The final rounds of the 1980 NASCAR Winston Cup Grand National series were run after Autocourse 1980/81 went to press.

ATLANTA JOURNAL 500, Atlanta International Raceway, Georgia, United States of America, November 2. NASCAR Winston Cup Grand National, round 30. 328 laps of the 1·522-mile/2·449-km circuit, 499·22 miles/803·41 km.
1 Cale Yarborough, USA (Chevrolet), 3h 48m 19s, 131·190 mph/211·129 km/h.
2 Neil Bonnett, USA (Mercury), 328 laps.
3 Dale Earnhardt, USA (Chevrolet), 327.
4 Buddy Baker, USA (Buick), 327.
5 Terry Labonte, USA (Chevrolet), 327.
6 Jody Ridley, USA (Ford), 326.
7 Lennie Pond, USA (Chevrolet), 326; 8 Ronnie Thomas, USA (Chevrolet), 323; 9 Richard Childress, USA (Chevrolet), 322; 10 Stan Barrett, USA (Chevrolet), 321.
Fastest Qualifier: Bobby Allison, USA (Mercury), 33·083s, 165·620 mph/266·539 km/h.
Championship points. Drivers: 1 Earnhardt, 4501; 2 Yarborough, 4472; 3 Petty, 4182; 4 Waltrip, 4141; 5 Parsons, 4098; 6 Ridley, 3863.
Manufacturers: 1 Chevrolet, 217; 2 Mercury, 63; 3 Ford, 58; 4 Oldsmobile, 48; 5 Buick, 13; 6 Dodge, 1.

LOS ANGELES TIMES 500, Ontario Motor Speedway, California, United States of America, November 15. NASCAR Winston Cup Grand National, round 31. 200 laps of the 2·500-mile/4·023-km circuit, 500·00 miles/804·67 km.
1 Benny Parsons, USA (Chevrolet), 3h 51m 46s, 129·441 mph/208·315 km/h.
2 Neil Bonnett, USA (Mercury), 200 laps.
3 Cale Yarborough, USA (Chevrolet), 200.
4 Bobby Allison, USA (Ford), 200.
5 Dale Earnhardt, USA (Chevrolet), 200.
6 Lake Speed, USA (Chevrolet), 199.
7 Joe Millikan, USA (Chevrolet, 199; 8 Terry Labonte, USA (Chevrolet), 198; 9 John Anderson, USA (Chevrolet, 197; 10 Buddy Arrington, USA (Dodge), 196.
Fastest Qualifier: Yarborough, 57·878s, 155·499 mph/250·251 km/h.

Winston Cup Grand National, third leg points:

1 Cale Yarborough, USA	1540
2 Dale Earnhardt, USA	1526
3 Dave Marcis, USA	1377
4 Darrell Waltrip, USA	1360
5 Benny Parsons, USA	1344
6 Jody Ridley, USA	1330

7 Terry Labonte, USA, 1329; 8 Bobby Allison, USA, 1245; 9 Richard Petty, USA, 1223; 10 Buddy Arrington, USA, 1208; 11 Harry Gant, USA, 1200; 12 Richard Childress, USA, 1180; 13 James Hylton, USA, 1132; 14 Cecil Gordon, USA, 1093; 15 Tommy Gale, USA, 1021.

Final Championship points. Drivers:

1 Dale Earnhardt, USA	4661
2 Cale Yarborough, USA	4642
3 Benny Parsons, USA	4278
4 Richard Petty, USA	4255
5 Darrell Waltrip, USA	4239
6 Bobby Allison, USA	4019

7 Jody Ridley, USA, 3972; 8 Terry Labonte, USA, 3766; 9 Dave Marcis, USA, 3745; 10 Richard Childress, USA, 3742; 11 Harry Gant, USA, 3703; 12 Buddy Arrington, USA, 3461; 13 James Hylton, USA, 3449; 14 Ronnie Thomas, USA, 3066; 15 Cecil Gordon, USA, 2993; 16 J.D. McDuffie, USA, 2968; 17 Jimmy Means, USA, 2947; 18 Tommy Gale, USA, 2885; 19 Neil Bonnett, USA, 2865; 20 Roger Hamby, USA, 2606.
Manufacturers:

1 Chevrolet	226
2 Mercury	69
3 Ford	61
4 Oldsmobile	48
5 Buick	13
6 Dodge	1

1981 RESULTS

WINSTON WESTERN 500, Riverside International Raceway, California, United States of America, January 11. NASCAR Winston Cup Grand National, round 1. 119 laps of the 2·620-mile/4·216-km circuit, 311·78 miles/501·76 km.
1 Bobby Allison, USA (Chevrolet), 3h 16m 18s, 95·263 mph/153·311 km/h.
2 Terry Labonte, USA (Chevrolet), 119 laps.
3 Dale Earnhardt, USA (Pontiac), 119.
4 Richard Childress, USA (Chevrolet), 119.
5 Richard Petty, USA (Chevrolet), 119.
6 Jim Robinson, USA (Chevrolet), 118.
7 Jody Ridley, USA (Ford), 117; 8 Elliott Forbes-Robinson, USA (Buick), 117; 9 Buddy Arrington, USA (Dodge), 117; 10 Don Waterman, USA (Oldsmobile), 117.
Fastest Qualifier: Darrell Waltrip, USA (Chevrolet), 1m 22·195s, 114·711 mph/184·609 km/h.
Championship points. Drivers: 1 B. Allison, 185; 2 Labonte, 175; 3 Earnhardt and Childress, 165; 5 Petty, 160; 6 Robinson, 150.
Manufacturers: 1 Chevrolet, 9; 2 Pontiac, 4.

DAYTONA 500, Daytona International Speedway, Florida, United States of America, February 15. NASCAR Winston Cup Grand National, round 2. 200 laps of the 2·500-mile/4·023-km circuit, 500·00 miles/804·67 km.
1 Richard Petty, USA (Buick), 2h 56m 50s, 169·651 mph/273·026 km/h.
2 Bobby Allison, USA (Pontiac), 200 laps.
3 Ricky Rudd, USA (Oldsmobile), 200.
4 Buddy Baker, USA (Oldsmobile), 200.
5 Dale Earnhardt, USA (Pontiac), 200.
6 Bill Elliott, USA (Ford), 199.
7 Jody Ridley, USA (Ford), 198; 8 Cale Yarborough, USA (Oldsmobile), 197; 9 Joe Millikan, USA (Buick), 197; 10 Johnny Rutherford, USA (Pontiac), 195.
Fastest Qualifier: B. Allison, 46·243s, 194·624 mph/313·216 km/h.
Championship points. Drivers: 1 B. Allison, 365; 2 Petty, 340; 3 Earnhardt, 325; 4 Ridley, 292; 5 Rudd, 281; 6 Millikan, 267.
Manufacturers: 1 Pontiac, 10; 2 Buick and Chevrolet, 9; 4 Oldsmobile, 4; 5 Ford, 1.

RICHMOND 400, Richmond Fairgrounds Raceway, Virginia, United States of America, February 22. NASCAR Winston Cup Grand National, round 3. 400 laps of the 0·542-mile/0·872-km circuit, 216·80 miles/348·90 km.
1 Darrell Waltrip, USA (Buick), 2h 49m 53s, 76·570 mph/123·227 km/h.
2 Ricky Rudd, USA (Oldsmobile), 400 laps.
3 Richard Petty, USA (Buick), 399.
4 Morgan Shepherd, USA (Pontiac), 399.
5 Benny Parsons, USA (Ford), 399.
6 Harry Gant, USA (Buick), 399.
7 Dale Earnhardt, USA (Pontiac), 397; 8 Jody Ridley, USA (Ford), 397; 9 Joe Millikan, USA (Buick), 396; 10 J.D. McDuffie, USA (Pontiac), 395.
Fastest Qualifier: Shepherd, 21·021s, 92·821 mph/149·381 km/h.
Championship points. Drivers: 1 Petty, 510; 2 Earnhardt, 471; 3 B. Allison, 459; 4 Rudd, 456; 5 Ridley, 434; 6 Millikan, 405.
Manufacturers: 1 Buick, 18; 2 Pontiac, 13; 3 Oldsmobile, 10; 4 Chevrolet, 9; 5 Ford, 3.

CAROLINA 500, North Carolina Motor Speedway, Rockingham, United States of America, March 1. NASCAR Winston Cup Grand National, round 4. 492 laps of the 1·017-mile/1·637-km circuit, 500·36 miles/805·26 km.
1 Darrell Waltrip, USA (Buick), 4h 21m 59s, 114·594 mph/184·421 km/h.
2 Cale Yarborough, USA (Buick), 492 laps.
3 Richard Petty, USA (Buick), 492.
4 Neil Bonnett, USA (Ford), 492.
5 Buddy Baker, USA (Oldsmobile), 491.
6 Bobby Allison, USA (Pontiac), 491.
7 Joe Millikan, USA (Chevrolet), 488; 8 Kyle Petty, USA (Buick), 486; 9 Lake Speed, USA (Buick), 482; 10 Elliott Forbes-Robinson, USA (Buick), 477.
Fastest Qualifier: Yarborough, 26·068s, 140·448 mph/226·029 km/h.
Championship points. Drivers: 1 Petty, 680; 2 B. Allison, 614; 3 Earnhardt and Millikan, 556; 5 Ridley, 546; 6 Waltrip, 537.
Manufacturers: 1 Buick, 27; 2 Pontiac, 14; 3 Oldsmobile, 12; 4 Chevrolet, 9; 5 Ford, 6.

COCA-COLA 500, Atlanta International Raceway, Georgia, United States of America, March 15. NASCAR Winston Cup Grand National, round 5. 328 laps of the 1·522-mile/2·449-km circuit, 499·22 miles/803·41 km.
1 Cale Yarborough, USA (Buick), 3h 44m 10s, 133·619 mph/215·038 km/h.
2 Harry Gant, USA (Buick), 328 laps.
3 Dale Earnhardt, USA (Pontiac), 327.
4 Bobby Allison, USA (Pontiac), 327.
5 Benny Parsons, USA (Ford), 326.
6 Jody Ridley, USA (Ford), 326.
7 A.J. Foyt, USA (Oldsmobile), 325; 8 Morgan Shepherd, USA (Pontiac), 325; 9 Bill Elliott, USA (Ford), 323; 10 Joe Ruttman, USA (Buick), 322.
Fastest Qualifier: Terry Labonte, USA (Buick), 33·627s, 162·509 mph/261·532 km/h.
Championship points. Drivers: 1 B. Allison, 779; 2 Petty, 734; 3 Earnhardt, 721; 4 Ridley, 696; 5 Millikan, 674; 6 Gant, 656.
Manufacturers: 1 Buick, 36; 2 Pontiac, 18; 3 Oldsmobile, 12; 4 Chevrolet, 9; 5 Ford, 8.

VALLEYDALE 500, Bristol International Raceway, Tennessee, United States of America, March 29. NASCAR Winston Cup Grand National, round 6. 500 laps of the 0·533-mile/0·858-km circuit, 266·50 miles/428·89 km.
1 Darrell Waltrip, USA (Buick), 2h 58m 36s, 89·530 mph/144·084 km/h.
2 Ricky Rudd, USA (Oldsmobile), 500 laps.
3 Bobby Allison, USA (Pontiac), 500.
4 Morgan Shepherd, USA (Pontiac), 500.
5 Benny Parsons, USA (Ford), 499.
6 Jody Ridley, USA (Ford), 497.
7 Terry Labonte, USA (Buick), 495; 8 Harry Gant, USA (Pontiac), 493; 9 Lake Speed, USA (Oldsmobile), 491; 10 Tim Richmond, USA (Buick), 491.
Fastest Qualifier: Waltrip, 17·113s, 112·125 mph/180·447 km/h.
Championship points. Drivers: 1 B. Allison, 944; 2 Ridley, 846; 3 Petty, 815; 4 Earnhardt, 805; 5 Gant, 803; 6 Rudd, 798.
Manufacturers: 1 Buick, 45; 2 Pontiac, 22; 3 Oldsmobile, 18; 4 Ford, 10; 5 Chevrolet, 9.

NORTHWESTERN BANK 400, North Wilkesboro Speedway, North Carolina, United States of America, April 5. NASCAR Winston Cup Grand National, round 7. 400 laps of the 0·625-mile/1·006-km circuit, 250·00 miles/402·34 km.
1 Richard Petty, USA (Buick), 2h 55m 41s, 85·381 mph/137·407 km/h.
2 Bobby Allison, USA (Pontiac), 400 laps.
3 Darrell Waltrip, USA (Buick), 400.
4 Dave Marcis, USA (Chevrolet), 400
5 Harry Gant, USA (Oldsmobile), 400.
6 Ricky Rudd, USA (Buick), 399.
7 Terry Labonte, USA (Buick), 399; 8 Ron Bouchard, USA (Buick), 399; 9 Morgan Shepherd, USA (Pontiac), 399; 10 Dale Earnhardt, USA (Pontiac), 395.
Fastest Qualifier: Marcis, 39·251s, 114·647 mph/184·506 km/h.
Championship points. Drivers: 1 B. Allison, 1124; 2 Petty, 995; 3 Gant, 958; 4 Waltrip, 952; 5 Rudd, 948; 6 Earnhardt, 939.
Manufacturers: 1 Buick, 54; 2 Pontiac, 28; 3 Oldsmobile, 20; 4 Chevrolet, 12; 5 Ford, 10.

CRC CHEMICALS REBEL 500, Darlington International Raceway, South Carolina, United States of America, April 12. NASCAR Winston Cup Grand National, round 8. 367 laps of the 1·366-mile/2·198-km circuit, 501·32 miles/806·67 km.
1 Darrell Waltrip, USA (Buick), 3h 57m 24s, 126·703 mph/203·908 km/h.
2 Harry Gant, USA (Pontiac), 367 laps.
3 Dave Marcis, USA (Chevrolet), 366.
4 Bill Elliott, USA (Ford), 366.
5 Benny Parsons, USA (Ford), 365.
6 Buddy Baker, USA (Buick), 365.
7 Jody Ridley, USA (Ford), 365; 8 David Pearson, USA (Chevrolet), 365; 9 Bobby Allison, USA (Buick), 364; 10 Joe Millikan, USA (Buick), 361.
Fastest Qualifier: Elliott, 31·954s, 153·896 mph/247·671 km/h.
Championship points. Drivers: 1 B. Allison, 1262; 2 Waltrip, 1137; 3 Gant, 1133; 4 Rudd, 1078; 5 Ridley, 1071; 6 Petty, 1059.
Manufacturers: 1 Buick, 63; 2 Pontiac, 34; 3 Oldsmobile, 20; 4 Chevrolet, 16; 5 Ford, 13.

VIRGINIA 500, Martinsville Speedway, Virginia, United States of America, April 26. NASCAR Winston Cup Grand National, round 9. 500 laps of the 0·525-mile/0·845-km circuit, 262·50 miles/422·45 km.
1 Morgan Shepherd, USA (Pontiac), 3h 30m 10s, 75·019 mph/120·73 km/h.
2 Neil Bonnett, USA (Ford), 500 laps.
3 Ricky Rudd, USA (Buick), 499.
4 Harry Gant, USA (Pontiac), 497.
5 Terry Labonte, USA (Buick), 497.
6 Jody Ridley, USA (Ford), 494.
7 Lake Speed, USA (Buick), 493; 8 Buddy Arrington, USA (Dodge), 492; 9 Ron Bouchard, USA (Buick), 491; 10 Mike Alexander, USA (Oldsmobile), 486.
Fastest Qualifier: Alexander, 21·236s, 89·094 mph/143·38 km/h.
Championship points. Drivers: 1 B. Allison, 1386; 2 Gant, 1297; 3 Rudd, 1248; 4 Waltrip, 1222; 5 Ridley, 1221; 6 Earnhardt, 1139.
Manufacturers: 1 Buick, 67; 2 Pontiac, 43; 3 Oldsmobile, 23; 4 Ford, 19; 5 Chevrolet, 16.

WINSTON 500, Alabama International Motor Speedway, Talladega, United States of America, May 3. NASCAR Winston Cup Grand National, round 10. 188 laps of the 2·660-mile/4·281-km circuit, 500·08 miles/804·80 km.
1 Bobby Allison, USA (Buick), 3h 20m 52s, 149·376 mph/240·397 km/h.
2 Buddy Baker, USA (Buick), 188 laps.
3 Darrell Waltrip, USA (Buick), 188.
4 Ricky Rudd, USA (Oldsmobile), 188.
5 Donnie Allison, USA (Oldsmobile), 187.
6 Tim Richmond, USA (Buick), 185.
7 Terry Labonte, USA (Buick), 185; 8 Dale Earnhardt, USA (Pontiac), 183; 9 Dick May, USA (Dodge), 183; 10 Bobby Wawak, USA (Buick), 183.
Fastest Qualifier: B. Allison, 48·891s, 195·864 mph/315·212 km/h.
Winston Cup Grand National, first leg points. Drivers:

1 Bobby Allison, USA	1566
2 Ricky Rudd, USA	1413
3 Darrell Waltrip, USA	1392
4 Harry Gant, USA	1359
5 Jody Ridley, USA	1291
6 Dale Earnhardt, USA	1286

7 Terry Labonte, USA, 1238; 8 Richard Petty, USA, 1184; 9 Dave Marcis, USA, 1160; 10 Benny Parsons, USA 1155; 11 Joe Millikan, USA, 1135; 12 Tim Richmond, USA, 1102.
Manufacturers: 1 Buick, 76; 2 Pontiac, 43; 3 Oldsmobile, 26; 4 Ford, 19; 5 Chevrolet, 16.

MELLING TOOL 420, Nashville International Raceway, Tennessee, United States of America, May 9. NASCAR Winston Cup Grand National, round 11. 420 laps of the 0·596-mile/0·959-km circuit, 230·32 miles/402·85 km.
1 Benny Parsons, USA (Ford), 2h 47m 02s, 89·756 mph/144·448 km/h.
2 Darrell Waltrip, USA (Buick), 420 laps.
3 Bobby Allison, USA (Pontiac), 420.
4 Richard Petty, USA (Buick), 419.
5 Ricky Rudd, USA (Buick), 419.
6 Terry Labonte, USA (Buick), 418.
7 Kyle Petty, USA (Buick), 417; 8 Morgan Shepherd, USA (Pontiac), 416; 9 Buddy Arrington, USA (Dodge), 414; 10 Dave Marcis, USA (Chevrolet), 413.
Fastest Qualifier: Rudd, 20·550s, 104·409 mph/168·030 km/h.
Championship points. Drivers: 1 B. Allison, 1731; 2 Rudd, 1573; 3 Waltrip, 1567; 4 Gant, 1456; 5 Earnhardt, 1389; 6 Labonte, 1388.
Manufacturers: 1 Buick, 82; 2 Pontiac, 47; 3 Ford, 28; 4 Oldsmobile, 26; 5 Chevrolet, 16.

MASON-DIXON 500, Dover Downs International Speedway, Delaware, United States of America, May 17. NASCAR Winston Cup Grand National, round 12. 500 laps of the 1·000-mile/1·604-km circuit, 500·00 miles/804·67 km.
1 Jody Ridley, USA (Ford), 4h 17m 18s, 116·595 mph/187·641 km/h.
2 Bobby Allison, USA (Buick), 500 laps.
3 Dale Earnhardt, USA (Pontiac), 499.
4 D.K. Ulrich, USA (Buick), 491.
5 Ricky Rudd, USA (Buick), 490.
6 Morgan Shepherd, USA (Pontiac), 489.
7 Buddy Arrington, USA (Dodge), 488; 8 Terry Labonte, USA (Buick), 486; 9 Jimmy Means, USA (Pontiac), 481; 10 Cale Yarborough, USA (Buick), 480.
Fastest Qualifier: David Pearson, USA (Oldsmobile), 26·007s, 138·425 mph/222·773 km/h.
Championship points. Drivers: 1 B. Allison, 1901; 2 Rudd, 1733; 3 Waltrip, 1694; 4 Gant, 1571; 5 Ridley, 1559; 6 Earnhardt, 1554.
Manufacturers: 1 Buick, 88; 2 Pontiac, 51; 3 Ford, 37; 4 Oldsmobile, 26; 5 Chevrolet, 16.

WORLD 600, Charlotte Motor Speedway, North Carolina, United States of America, May 24. NASCAR Winston Cup Grand National, round 13. 400 laps of the 1·500-mile/2·414-km circuit, 600·00 miles/965·80 km.
1 Bobby Allison, USA (Buick), 4h 38m 22s, 129·326 mph/208·130 km/h.
2 Harry Gant, USA (Chevrolet), 400 laps.
3 Cale Yarborough, USA (Buick), 398.
4 Ricky Rudd, USA (Buick), 397.
5 Kyle Petty, USA (Buick), 396.
6 Morgan Shepherd, USA (Pontiac), 395.
7 Joe Ruttman, USA (Buick), 395; 8 Joe Millikan, USA (Chevrolet), 393; 9 Darrell Waltrip, USA (Buick), 392; 10 Elliott Forbes-Robinson, USA (Buick), 390.
Fastest Qualifier: Neil Bonnett, USA (Ford), 2m 16·610s, 158·115 mph/254·461 km/h – 4 laps average.
Championship points. Drivers: 1 B. Allison, 2086; 2 Rudd, 1893; 3 Waltrip, 1837; 4 Gant, 1746; 5 Earnhardt, 1668; 6 Ridley, 1662.
Manufacturers: 1 Buick, 97; 2 Pontiac, 52; 3 Ford, 37; 4 Oldsmobile 26; 5 Chevrolet, 22.

BUDWEISER NASCAR 400, Texas World Speedway, College Station, Texas, United States of America, June 7. NASCAR Winston Cup Grand National, round 14. 200 laps of the 2·000-mile/3·219-km circuit, 400·00 miles/643·80 km.
1 Benny Parsons, USA (Ford), 3h 01m 10s, 132·475 mph/213·197 km/h.
2 Dale Earnhardt, USA (Pontiac), 200 laps.
3 Bobby Allison, USA (Buick), 200.
4 Richard Petty, USA (Buick), 199.
5 Dave Marcis, USA (Buick), 198.
6 Jody Ridley, USA (Ford), 198.
7 Tim Richmond, USA (Oldsmobile), 196; 8 Lake Speed, USA (Oldsmobile), 196; 9 Joe Ruttman, USA (Buick), 195; 10 Harry Gant, USA (Pontiac), 193.
Fastest Qualifier: Terry Labonte, USA (Buick), 42·974s, 167·543 mph/269·634 km/h.
Championship points. Drivers: 1 B. Allison, 2256; 2 Rudd, 1984; 3 Waltrip, 1915; 4 Gant, 1885; 5 Earnhardt, 1848; 6 Ridley, 1817.
Manufacturers: 1 Buick, 101; 2 Pontiac, 58; 3 Ford 46; 4 Oldsmobile, 26; 5 Chevrolet, 22.

WARNER W. HODGDON 400, Riverside International Raceway, California, United States of America, June 14. NASCAR Winston Cup Grand National, round 15. 95 laps of the 2·620-mile/4·216-km circuit, 248·90 miles/400·56 km.
1 Darrell Waltrip, USA (Buick), 2h 39m 30s, 93·597 mph/150·629 km/h.
2 Dale Earnhardt, USA (Pontiac), 95 laps.
3 Richard Petty, USA (Buick), 95.
4 Neil Bonnett, USA (Ford), 95.
5 Ricky Rudd, USA (Buick), 95.
6 Kyle Petty, USA (Buick), 95.
7 Jody Ridley, USA (Ford), 95; 8 Roy Smith, USA (Buick), 95; 9 Dave Marcis, USA (Chevrolet), 95; 10 Jim Robinson, USA (Oldsmobile), 93.
Fastest Qualifier: Waltrip, 1m 22·434s, 114·378 mph/184·073 km/h.
Championship points. Drivers: 1 B. Allison, 2332; 2 Rudd, 2139; 3 Waltrip, 2100; 4 Earnhardt, 2023; 5 Ridley, 1963; 6 Gant, 1955.
Manufacturers: 1 Buick, 110; 2 Pontiac, 64; 3 Ford, 49; 4 Oldsmobile, 26; 5 Chevrolet, 22.

GABRIEL 400, Michigan International Speedway, Brooklyn, Michigan, United States of America, June 21. NASCAR Winston Cup Grand National, round 16. 200 laps of the 2.000-mile/3.219-km circuit, 400.00 miles/643.80 km.
1 Bobby Allison, USA (Buick), 3h 03m 47s, 130.589 mph/210.162 km/h.
2 Harry Gant, USA (Pontiac), 200 laps.
3 Benny Parsons, USA (Ford), 200.
4 Jody Ridley, USA (Ford), 200.
5 Dale Earnhardt, USA (Pontiac), 200.
6 Richard Petty, USA (Buick), 200.
7 Darrell Waltrip, USA (Buick), 200; 8 Cale Yarborough, USA (Buick), 200; 9 Neil Bonnett, USA (Ford), 199; 10 Ron Bouchard, USA (Buick), 199.
Fastest Qualifier: Waltrip, 44.868s, 160.471 mph/258.252 km/h.
Championship points. Drivers: 1 B. Allison, 2512; 2 Waltrip, 2256; 3 Rudd, 2217; 4 Earnhardt, 2183; 5 Gant, 2130; 6 Ridley, 2123.
Manufacturers: 1 Buick, 119; 2 Pontiac, 70; 3 Ford, 53; 4 Oldsmobile, 26; 5 Chevrolet, 22.

FIRECRACKER 400, Daytona International Speedway, Florida, United States of America, July 4. NASCAR Winston Cup Grand National, round 17. 160 laps of the 2.500-mile/4.023-km circuit, 400.00 miles/643.74 km.
1 Cale Yarborough, USA (Buick), 2h 48m 32s, 142.588 mph/229.473 km/h.
2 Harry Gant, USA (Buick), 160 laps.
3 Richard Petty, USA (Buick), 160.
4 Buddy Baker, USA (Oldsmobile), 160.
5 Johnny Rutherford, USA (Pontiac), 160.
6 Kyle Petty, USA (Buick), 160.
7 Mike Alexander, USA (Buick), 160; **8** Terry Labonte, USA (Buick), 159; **9** Ron Bouchard, USA (Buick), 159; **10** Darrell Waltrip, USA (Buick), 159.
Fastest Qualifier: Yarborough, 46.668s, 192.852 mph/310.364 km/h.
Championship points. Drivers: 1 B. Allison, 2596; **2** Waltrip, 2390; **3** Gant, 2305; **4** Rudd, 2260; **5** Earnhardt, 2246; **6** R. Petty, 2206.
Manufacturers: 1 Buick, 128; **2** Pontiac, 72; **3** Ford, 53; **4** Oldsmobile, 29; **5** Chevrolet, 22.

BUSCH NASHVILLE 420, Nashville International Raceway, Tennessee, United States of America, July 11. NASCAR Winston Cup Grand National, round 18. 420 laps of the 0.595-mile/0.959-km circuit, 250.32 miles/402.85 km.
1 Darrell Waltrip, USA (Buick), 2h 46m 47s, 90.052 mph/144.924 km/h.
2 Bobby Allison, USA (Buick), 420 laps.
3 Benny Parsons, USA (Ford), 420.
4 Ricky Rudd, USA (Chevrolet), 419.
5 Terry Labonte, USA (Buick), 418.
6 Kyle Petty, USA (Buick), 418.
7 Dale Earnhardt, USA (Pontiac), 418; **8** Harry Gant, USA (Pontiac), 417; **9** Richard Petty, USA (Buick), 417; **10** Jody Ridley, USA (Ford), 416.
Fastest Qualifier: Mark Martin, USA (Pontiac), 20.561s, 104.353 mph/167.939 km/h.
Championship points. Drivers: 1 B. Allison, 2771; **2** Waltrip, 2575; **3** Gant, 2447; **4** Rudd, 2420; **5** Earnhardt, 2392; **6** R. Petty, 2344.
Manufacturers: 1 Buick, 137; **2** Pontiac, 72; **3** Ford, 57; **4** Oldsmobile, 29; **5** Chevrolet, 25.

MOUNTAIN DEW 500, Pocono International Raceway, Pennsylvania, United States of America, July 26. NASCAR Winston Cup Grand National, round 19. 200 laps of the 2.500-mile/4.023-km circuit, 500.00 miles/804.67 km.
1 Darrell Waltrip, USA (Buick), 4h 11m 52s, 119.111 mph/191.690 km/h.
2 Richard Petty, USA (Buick), 200 laps.
3 Benny Parsons, USA (Ford), 200.
4 Harry Gant, USA (Pontiac), 200.
5 Cale Yarborough, USA (Buick), 200.
6 Ricky Rudd, USA (Chevrolet), 199.
7 Buddy Baker, USA (Buick), 199; **8** Kyle Petty, USA (Buick), 198; **9** Tim Richmond, USA (Oldsmobile), 198; **10** Ron Bouchard, USA (Buick), 198.
Fastest Qualifier: Waltrip, 59.941s, 150.148 mph/241.639 km/h.
Championship points. Drivers: 1 B. Allison, 2864; **2** Waltrip, 2760; **3** Gant, 2612; **4** Rudd, 2570; **5** Earnhardt, 2527; **6** R. Petty, 2519.
Manufacturers: 1 Buick, 146; **2** Pontiac, 75; **3** Ford, 61; **4** Oldsmobile, 29; **5** Chevrolet, 26.

Talladega 500, Alabama International Motor Speedway, Alabama, United States of America, August 2. NASCAR Winston Cup Grand National, round 20. 188 laps of the 2.660-mile/4.281-km circuit, 500.08 miles/804.80 km.
1 Ron Bouchard, USA (Buick), 3h 11m 24s, 156.737 mph/252.243 km/h.
2 Darrell Waltrip, USA (Buick), 188 laps.
3 Terry Labonte, USA (Buick), 188.
4 Harry Gant, USA (Buick), 188.
5 Bobby Allison, USA (Buick), 188.
6 Lake Speed, USA (Buick), 187.
7 Kyle Petty, USA (Buick), 187; **8** Jody Ridley, USA (Ford), 187; **9** Stan Barrett, USA (Pontiac), 186; **10** Dave Marcis, USA (Buick), 185.
Fastest Qualifier: Gant, 48.883s, 195.897 mph/315.265 km/h.
Championship points. Drivers: 1 B. Allison, 3029; **2** Waltrip, 2935; **3** Gant, 2777; **4** Rudd, 2664; **5** Earnhardt, 2608; **6** Labonte, 2573.
Manufacturers: 1 Buick, 155; **2** Pontiac, 75; **3** Ford, 61; **4** Oldsmobile, 29; **5** Chevrolet, 26.

CHAMPION SPARK PLUG 400, Michigan International Speedway, Brooklyn, Michigan, United States of America, August 16. NASCAR Winston Cup Grand National, round 21. 200 laps of the 2.000-mile/3.219-km circuit, 400.00 miles/643.74 km.
1 Richard Petty, USA (Buick), 3h 14m 24s, 123.457 mph/198.684 km/h.
2 Darrell Waltrip, USA (Buick), 200 laps.
3 Ricky Rudd, USA (Chevrolet), 200.
4 Harry Gant, USA (Pontiac), 200.
5 Buddy Baker, USA (Buick), 200.
6 Joe Ruttman, USA (Pontiac), 200.
7 Bobby Allison, USA (Buick), 200; **8** Bill Elliott, USA (Ford), 200; **9** Dale Earnhardt, USA (Pontiac), 200; **10** Mike Alexander, USA (Buick), 200.
Fastest Qualifier: Ron Bouchard, USA (Buick), 44.582s, 161.501 mph/259.910 km/h.

Winston Cup Grand National, second leg points:

1 Darrell Waltrip, USA	1718
2 Bobby Allison, USA	1614
3 Harry Gant, USA	1583
4 Richard Petty, USA	1563
5 Terry Labonte, USA	1461
6 Dale Earnhardt, USA	1460

7 Kyle Petty, USA, 1429; **8** Ricky Rudd, USA, 1416; **9** Jody Ridley, USA, 1407; **10** Benny Parsons, USA, 1352; **11** Dave Marcis, USA, 1191; **12** Jimmy Means, USA, 1153.
Championship points. Drivers: 1 B. Allison, 3180; **2** Waltrip, 3110; **3** Gant, 2942; **4** Rudd, 2829; **5** R. Petty, 2747; **6** Earnhardt, 2746.
Manufacturers: 1 Buick, 164; **2** Pontiac, 78; **3** Ford, 61; **4** Chevrolet, 30; **5** Oldsmobile, 29.

BUSCH 500, Bristol International Raceway, Tennessee, United States of America, August 22. NASCAR Winston Cup Grand National, round 22. 500 laps of the 0.533-mile/0.858-km circuit, 266.50 miles/428.89 km.
1 Darrell Waltrip, USA (Buick), 3h 08m 44s, 84.723 mph/136.348 km/h.
2 Ricky Rudd, USA (Chevrolet), 499 laps.
3 Terry Labonte, USA (Buick), 498.
4 Bobby Allison, USA (Buick), 497.
5 Ron Bouchard, USA (Buick), 497.
6 Benny Parsons, USA (Ford), 497.
7 Lake Speed, USA (Oldsmobile), 493; **8** Tim Richmond, USA (Oldsmobile), 488; **9** Dave Marcis, USA (Buick), 487; **10** Buddy Arrington, USA (Dodge), 486.
Fastest Qualifiers: Waltrip, 17.315s, 110.818 mph/178.344 km/h.
Championship points. Drivers: 1 B. Allison, 3345; **2** Waltrip, 3295; **3** Gant, 3072; **4** Rudd, 3004; **5** Labonte, 2864; **6** R. Petty, 2838.
Manufacturers: 1 Buick, 173; **2** Pontiac, 78; **3** Ford, 62; **4** Chevrolet, 36; **5** Oldsmobile, 29.

SOUTHERN 500, Darlington International Raceway, South Carolina, United States of America, September 7. NASCAR Winston Cup Grand National, round 23. 367 laps of the 1.366-mile/2.198-km circuit, 501.32 miles/806.80 km.
1 Neil Bonnett, USA (Ford), 3h 57m 57s, 126.410 mph/203.437 km/h.
2 Darrell Waltrip, USA (Buick), 367 laps.
3 Dave Marcis, USA (Buick, 367.
4 Terry Labonte, USA (Buick), 367.
5 Buddy Baker, USA (Buick), 367.
6 Dale Earnhardt, USA (Pontiac), 366.
7 Bill Elliott, USA (Ford), 366; **8** David Pearson, USA (Buick), 365; **9** Bobby Allison, USA (Chevrolet), 365; **10** Cale Yarborough, USA (Buick), 363.
Fastest Qualifier: Harry Gant, USA (Pontiac), 32.206s, 152.693 mph/245.735 km/h.
Championship points. Drivers: 1 B. Allison, 3488; **2** Waltrip, 3470; **3** Gant, 3198; **4** Rudd, 3098; **5** Labonte, 3029; **6** Earnhardt, 2978.
Manufacturers: 1 Buick, 179; **2** Pontiac, 79; **3** Ford, 71; **4** Chevrolet, 36; **5** Oldsmobile, 29.

WRANGLER SANFORSET 400, Richmond Fairgrounds Raceway, Virginia, United States of America, September 13. NASCAR Winston Cup Grand National, round 24. 400 laps of the 0.542-mile/0.972-km circuit), 216.80 miles/348.90 km.
1 Benny Parsons, USA (Ford), 3h 05m 50s, 69.998 mph/112.65 km/h.
2 Harry Gant, USA (Pontiac), 400 laps.
3 Darrell Waltrip, USA (Buick), 400.
4 Terry Labonte, USA (Buick), 400.
5 Bobby Allison, USA (Buick), 400.
6 Dale Earnhardt, USA (Pontiac), 398.
7 Mark Martin, USA (Pontiac), 398; **8** Joe Millikan, USA (Pontiac), 397; **9** Jody Ridley, USA (Ford), 396; **10** Gary Balough, USA (Buick), 395.
Fastest Qualifier: Martin, 20.882s, 93.453 mph/150.398 km/h.
Championship points. Drivers: 1 B. Allison, 3648; **2** Waltrip, 3645; **3** Gant, 3373; **4** Rudd, 3225; **5** Labonte, 3194, **6** Earnhardt, 3128.
Manufacturers: 1 Buick, 183; **2** Pontiac, 85; **3** Ford, 80; **4** Chevrolet, 36; **5** Oldsmobile, 29.

CRC CHEMICALS 500, Dover Downs International Speedway, Delaware, United States of America, September 20. NASCAR Winston Cup Grand National, round 25. 500 laps of the 1.000-mile/1.609-km circuit, 500.00 miles/804.67 km.
1 Neil Bonnett, USA (Ford), 4h 10m 55s, 119.561 mph/192.414 km/h.
2 Darrell Waltrip, USA (Buick), 499 laps.
3 Bobby Allison, USA (Buick), 499.
4 Ron Bouchard, USA (Buick), 495.
5 Ricky Rudd, USA (Chevrolet), 495.
6 Joe Ruttman, USA (Pontiac), 495.
7 Kyle Petty, USA (Buick), 496; **8** Dave Marcis, USA (Chevrolet), 495; **9** Tim Richmond, USA (Buick), 494; **10** Richard Petty USA (Buick), 494.
Fastest Qualifier: Rudd, 26.324s, 136.757 mph/220.09 km/h.
Championship points. Drivers: 1 Waltrip, 3820; **2** B. Allison, 3818; **3** Gant, 3472; **4** Rudd, 3385; **5** Labonte, 3275; **6** Earnhardt, 3246.
Manufacturers: 1 Buick, 189; **2** Ford, 89; **3** Pontiac, 86; **4** Chevrolet, 38; **5** Oldsmobile, 29.

OLD DOMINION 500, Martinsville Speedway, Virginia, United States of America, September 27. NASCAR Winston Cup Grand National, round 26. 500 laps of the 0.525-mile/0.845-km circuit, 262.50 miles/422.25 km.
1 Darrell Waltrip, USA (Buick), 3h 44m 57s, 70.089 mph/112.797 km/h.
2 Harry Gant, USA (Pontiac), 500 laps.
3 Mark Martin, USA (Pontiac), 497.
4 Neil Bonnett, USA (Ford), 497.
5 Joe Millikan, USA (Pontiac), 497.
6 Ron Bouchard, USA (Buick), 494.
7 Jimmy Hensley, USA (Buick), 487; **8** Ricky Rudd, USA (Chevrolet), 486; **9** Terry Labonte, USA (Buick), 481; **10** Bobby Allison, USA (Buick), 479.
Fastest Qualifier: Waltrip, 21.255s, 89.014 mph/143 254 km/h.
Championship points. Drivers: 1 Waltrip, 4000; **2** B. Allison, 3957; **3** Gant, 3652; **4** Rudd, 3532; **5** Labonte, 3413; **6** Earnhardt, 3331.
Manufacturers: 1 Buick, 198; **2** Pontiac, 92; **3** Ford, 91; **4** Chevrolet, 38; **5** Oldsmobile, 29.

HOLLY FARMS 400, North Wilkesboro Speedway, North Carolina, United States of America, October 4. NASCAR Winston Cup Grand National, round 27. 400 laps of the 0.625-mile/1.006-km circuit, 250.00 miles/402.34 km.
1 Darrell Waltrip, USA (Buick), 2h 41m 08s, 93.091 mph/149.815 km/h.
2 Bobby Allison, USA (Buick), 399 laps.
3 Joe Millikan, USA (Pontiac), 399.

4 Dale Earnhardt, USA (Pontiac), 399.
5 Ron Bouchard, USA (Buick), 398.
6 Morgan Shepherd, USA (Buick), 393.
7 Jody Ridley, USA (Ford), 391; **8** Bob McElwee, USA (Buick), 389; **9** Jimmy Means, USA (Chevrolet), 386; **10** Buddy Arrington, USA (Dodge), 386.
Fastest Qualifier: Waltrip, 37.431s, 14.065 mph/183.569 km/h.
Championship points. Drivers: 1 Waltrip, 4185; **2** B. Allison, 4132; **3** Gant, 3743; **4** Rudd, 3620; **5** Earnhardt, 3491; **6** Labonte, 3486.
Manufacturers: 1 Buick, 207; **2** Pontiac, 96; **3** Ford, 91; **4** Chevrolet, 38; **5** Oldsmobile, 29.

NATIONAL 500, Charlotte Motor Speedway, North Carolina, United States of America, October 11. NASCAR Winston Cup Grand National, round 28. 334 laps of the 1.500-mile/2.414-km circuit, 501.00 miles/806.28 km.
1 Darrell Waltrip, USA (Buick), 4h 15m 52s, 117.483 mph/189.070 km/h.
2 Bobby Allison, USA (Chevrolet), 334 laps.
3 Ricky Rudd, USA (Chevrolet), 334.
4 Tommy Ellis, USA (Chevrolet), 333.
5 Ron Bouchard, USA (Buick), 332.
6 Rusty Wallace, USA (Buick), 331.
7 Geoff Bodine, USA (Buick), 331; **8** Morgan Shepherd, USA (Buick), 331; **9** Jack Ingram, USA (Ford), 329; **10** Buddy Arrington, USA (Dodge), 328.
Fastest Qualifier: Waltrip, 33.181s, 162.744 mph/261.910 km/h.
Championship points. Drivers: 1 Waltrip, 4365; **2** B. Allison, 4307; **3** Gant, 3788; **4** Rudd, 3785; **5** Labonte, 3585; **6** Earnhardt, 3584.
Manufacturers: 1 Buick, 216; **2** Pontiac, 96; **3** Ford, 92; **4** Chevrolet, 42; **5** Oldsmobile, 29.

AMERICAN 500, North Carolina Motor Speedway, Rockingham, North Carolina, United States of America, October 31. NASCAR Winston Cup Grand National, round 29. 492 laps of the 1.017-mile/1.637-km circuit, 500.36 miles/805.26 km.
1 Darrell Waltrip, USA (Buick), 4h 39m 32s, 107.399 mph/172.842 km/h.
2 Bobby Allison, USA (Buick), 492 laps.
3 Harry Gant, USA (Pontiac), 492.
4 Richard Petty, USA (Buick), 492.
5 Joe Ruttman, USA (Buick), 492.
6 Benny Parsons, USA (Ford), 491.
7 Terry Labonte, USA (Buick), 490; **8** Bill Elliott, USA (Ford), 490; **9** Dale Earnhardt, USA (Pontiac), 488; **10** Jody Ridley, USA (Ford), 488.
Fastest Qualifier: Waltrip, 26.499s, 138.165 mph/222.354 km/h.
Championship points (prior to November 8 and November 22 rounds):
Drivers:

1 Darrell Waltrip, USA	4550
2 Bobby Allison, USA	4482
3 Harry Gant, USA	3958
Manufacturers:	
1 Buick	225
2 Pontiac	100
3 Ford	93
4 Chevrolet	42
5 Oldsmobile	29

Final results will be given in Autocourse 1982/83.

IMSA GT Championship

1980 RESULTS

The final round of the 1980 IMSA GT Challenge was run after Autocourse 1980/81 went to press.

DAYTONA GT 250 IMSA RACE, Daytona International Speedway, Florida, United States of America, November 30. IMSA GT Challenge, round 14. 65 laps of the 3·840-mile/6·180-km circuit, 249·600 miles/401·700 km.
1 Gianpiero Moretti/Reinhold Jost, I/D (Porsche 935), 2h 11m 30·780s, 113·874 mph/183·262 km/h.
2 John Paul/John Paul Jnr, USA/USA (Porsche 935), 64 laps.
3 Volkert Merl/Mauricio DeNarvaez, D/COL (Porsche 935), 63.
4 Maurice Carter, USA (Chevrolet Camero), 63.
5 Marty Hinze/Gary Belcher, USA/USA (Porsche 935), 62.
6 David Cowart/Kenper Miller, USA/USA (BMW M1), 62.
7 Bill Adam, CDN (Triumph TR-8), 61 (1st over 2500 cc GT class); **8** Bob Tullius, USA (Triumph TR-8), 61; **9** Carl Shafer, USA (Chevrolet Camero), 60; **10** Roger Schramm/Werner Frank, USA/USA (Porsche Carrera RSR), 59. 1st up to 2500 cc GT class: George Alderman, USA (Datsun Z), 58.
Fastest Qualifier: Danny Ongais, USA (Porsche 935), 1m 43·073s, 134·119 mph/215·843 km/h (record).
Fastest lap: Ongais, 1m 46·342s, 129·996 mph/209·208 km/h.
Final Championship points:

1 John Fitzpatrick, GB	179.5
2 John Paul, USA	158
3 Ted Field, USA	99.5
4 John Paul Jnr, USA	94
5 Hurley Haywood, USA	73
6 Gianpiero Moretti, I	65

7 Danny Ongais, USA, 59; **8** Dale Whittington, USA, 48.5; **9** Bobby Rahal, USA, 48; **10** Peter Gregg, USA, 47.

Over 2500 cc GT class	
1 Luis Mendez, DOM	153.5
2 Bob Tullius, USA	135
3 Tony Garcia, USA	134
4 Bill Adam, CDN	116
5 Phil Currin, USA	77.5
6 Terry Herman, USA	72
Up to 2500 cc GT class	
1 Walt Bohren, USA	157
2 Jeff Kline, USA	133
3 Brad Frisselle, USA	129
4 Don Devendorf, USA	93
5 William Koll, USA	71
6 Roger Manderville, USA	69

IMSA CAMEL GT Championship

1981 RESULTS

20 PEPSI DAYTONA 24 HOURS, Daytona International Speedway, Florida, United States of America, January 31/February 1. IMSA CAMEL GT Championship, round 1. 708 laps of the 3·840-mile/6·180-km circuit, 2718·72 miles/4375·44 km.
1 Bob Garretson/Bobby Rahal/Brian Redman, USA/USA/GB (Porsche 935), 24h 01m 36·871s, 113·153 mph/182·102 km/h.
2 Bob Akin/Derek Bell/Craig Siebert, USA/GB/USA (Porsche 935), 695 laps.
3 William Koll/Jeff Kline/Rob McFarlin, USA/USA/USA (Porsche 911SC), 644 (1st up to 2500 cc GT class).
4 Frank Carney/Dick Davenport/Rameau Johnson, USA/USA/USA (Datsun ZX), 626.
5 Carlo Facetti/Martino Finotto/Emanuele Pirro, I/I/I (Lancia Beta Monte Carlo), 609.
6 Hans Stuck/Alf Gebhardt/Walter Brun, D/USA/CH (BMW M1), 608 (1st over 2500 cc GT class).
7 Lee Mueller/Kathy Rude/Philippe Martin, USA/USA/B (Mazda RX-7), 606; **8** Carlos Gonzalez/Eduardo Barrientos/"Jamsal", ES/ES/ES (Porsche 935), 595; **9** Roger Manderville/Amos Johnson/Diego Febles, USA/USA/PR (Mazda RX-7), 595; **10** Jim Mullen/Walt Bohren/J. Kurt Roehrig, USA/USA/USA (Mazda RX-7), 589.
Fastest Qualifier: Rolf Stommelen, D (Porsche 935), 1m 43·104s, 134·078 mph/215·771 km/h (record).
Fastest lap: Carlo Facetti, I (Ferrari 308 Turbo), 1m 48·14s, 127·834 mph/205·728 km/h.
Championship points. Overall: 1 Garretson, Rahal and Redman, 20; **4** Akin, Bell and Siebert, 15. GT over 2500 cc: **1** Stuck, 21; **2** Brun, 20; **3** Kendall, Smith and Earle, 15. GT up to 2500 cc: **1** Koll, Kline and McFarlin, 20.

29 SEBRING 12 HOUR ENDURANCE RACE, Sebring Grand Prix Circuit, Florida, United States of America, March 21. IMSA CAMEL GT Championship, round 2. 245 laps of the 5·200-mile/8·399-km circuit, 1274·00 miles/2050·30 km.
1 Bruce Leven/Hurley Haywood/Al Holbert, USA/USA/USA (Porsche 935), 12h 00m 49·855s, 106·044 mph/170·661 km/h.
2 Roy Woods/Ralph Kent-Cooke/Skeeter McKitterick, USA/USA/USA (Porsche 935), 242 laps.
3 Marty Hinze/Milt Minter/Bill Whittington, USA/USA/USA (Porsche 935), 240.
4 Howard Meister/Rolf Stommelen/Harald Grohs, USA/D/D (Porsche 935), 233.
5 Chuck Kendall/Pete Smith/Dennis Aase, USA/USA/USA (Porsche Carrera RSR), 218 (1st over 2500 cc GT class).
6 Gianpiero Moretti/Charles Mendez/Mauricio DeNarvaez, I/USA/COL (Porsche 935), 213.
7 Timothy Selby/Earl Roe, USA/USA (Porsche Carrera RSR), 212; **8** M.L. Speer/Eddy Joosen/Dirk Vermeersch, USA/B/B (Mazda RX-7), 212; **9** Lee Mueller/Walt Bohren, USA/USA (Mazda RX-7), 211 (1st up to 2500 cc GT class); **10** Bob Tullius/Bill Adam, USA/CDN (Triumph TR-8), 208.
Fastest Qualifier: John Fitzpatrick, GB (Porsche 935), 2m 28·675s, 125·912 mph/202·635 km/h (record).
Fastest lap: John Paul Jnr, USA (Porsche 935), 2m 28·65s, 125·959 mph/202·711 km/h (record).
Championship points. Overall: 1 Rahal and Redman, 26; **3** Garretson, Haywood and Holbert, 20; **6** Akin, Bell, Siebert, Kent-Cooke and McKitterick, 15. GT over 2500 cc: **1** Kendall and Smith, 35; **3** Stuck, 21. GT up to 2500 cc: **1** Mueller, 32; **2** Bohren, 28; **3** Koll, Kline and McFarlin, 20.

IMSA CAMEL GT RACE, Road Atlanta, Georgia, United States of America, April 12. IMSA CAMEL GT Championship, round 3. 40 laps of the 2·520-mile/4·055-km circuit, 100·80 miles/162·20 km.
1 John Fitzpatrick, GB (Porsche 935), 56m 05·984s, 107·808 mph/173·450 km/h.
2 Klaus Ludwig, D (Ford Mustang Turbo), 56m 06·128s.
3 Bobby Rahal, USA (Porsche 935), 40 laps.
4 Danny Ongais, USA (Porsche 935), 40.
5 Dale Whittington, USA (Porsche 935), 40.
6 Hurley Haywood, USA (Porsche 935), 40.
7 Ted Field, USA (Porsche 935), 40; **8** John Paul Jnr, USA (Porsche 935), 39; **9** Gianpiero Moretti, I (Porsche 935), 39; **10** Paul Newman, USA (Datsun ZX Turbo), 39.
1st over 2500 cc GT class: David Cowert, USA (BMW M1), 38.
Fastest Qualifier: Paul Jnr, 1m 18·122s, 116·126 mph/186·886 km/h (record).
Fastest lap: Paul Jnr, 1m 20·00s, 113·400 mph/182·499 km/h.
2500 cc race (30 laps, 75·60 miles/121·65 km): 1 Walt Bohren, USA (Mazda RX-7), 46m 35·140s, 97·369 mph/156·700 km/h; **2** Lee Mueller, USA (Mazda RX-7), 46m 37·630s; **3** Patrick Jacquemart, USA (Renault 5 Turbo), 30 laps; **4** Dave White, USA (BMW 320i), 30; **5** Frank Carney, USA (Datsun ZX), 30; **6** Wayne Baker, USA (Porsche 914/4), 30.
Fastest Qualifier: Mueller, 1m 30·801s, 99·911 mph/160·791 km/h (record).
Fastest lap: Mueller, 1m 31·21s, 99·463 mph/160·070 km/h (record).
Championship points. Overall: 1 Rahal, 38; **2** Redman and Haywood, 26; **4** Fitzpatrick, 21; **5** Garretson and Holbert, 20. GT over 2500 cc: **1** Kendall and Smith, 35; **3** Rodriguez, 22. GT up to 2500 cc: **1** Mueller and Bohren, 48; **3** Carney, 23.

LOS ANGELES TIMES/TOYOTA 6 HOUR GRAND PRIX OF ENDURANCE, Riverside International Raceway, California, United States of America, April 26. IMSA CAMEL GT Championship, round 4. 199 laps of the 3·30-mile/5·31-km circuit, 656·70 miles/1056·69 km.
1 John Fitzpatrick/Jim Busby, GB/USA (Porsche 935), 6h 00m 46·0s, 109·217 mph/175·767 km/h.
2 John Paul/John Paul Jnr, USA/USA (Porsche 935), 6h 01m 18·88s.
3 Bobby Rahal/Brian Redman, USA/GB (Porsche 935), 197 laps.
4 Bob Garretson/Roy Woods/Ralph Kent-Cooke, USA/USA/USA (Porsche 935), 190.
5 Hurley Haywood/Bruce Leven, USA/USA (Porsche 935), 189.
6 David Hobbs/Marc Surer, GB/CH (BMW M1C), 188.
7 David Cowart/Kenper Miller, USA/USA (BMW M1), 183 (1st over 2500 cc GT class); **8** Albert Naon/Tony Garcia/Hiram Cruz, USA/USA/USA (BMW M1), 181; **9** Chris Cord/Jim Adams, USA/USA (Chevrolet Monza), 178; **10** Carlos Moran/Karen Erstad, USA/USA (Porshe 935), 178. **1st up to 2500 cc GT class**: Frank Carney/Dick Davenport, USA/USA (Datsun ZX), 173.
Fastest Qualifier: Paul Jnr, 1m 38·090s, 121·113 mph/194·912 km/h (record).
Fastest lap: Paul Jnr, 1m 40·71s, 117·962 mph/189·841 km/h.
Championship points. Overall: 1 Rahal, 50; **2** Fitzpatrick, 41; **3** Redman, 38; **4** Haywood, 34; **5** Garretson, 30; **6** Kent-Cooke, 25. **GT over 2500cc: 1** Cowart, 42; **2** Kendall and Smith, 35. **GT up to 2500cc: 1** Mueller, 49; **2** Bohren, 48; **3** Carney, 43.

MONTEREY TRIPLE CROWN, Laguna Seca Raceway, California, United States of America, May 3. IMSA CAMEL GT Championship, round 5. 53 laps of the 1·900-mile/3·058-km circuit, 100·70 miles/162·061 km.
1 Brian Redman, GB (Lola T600-Chevrolet), 57m 27·462s, 105·157 mph/169·233 km/h.
2 John Paul Jnr, USA (Porsche 935), 57m 38·478s.
3 John Fitzpatrick, GB (Porsche 935), 53 laps.
4 Bobby Rahal, USA (Porsche 935), 53.
5 Danny Ongais, USA (Porsche 935), 53.
6 David Hobbs, GB (BMW M1C), 52.
7 Ted Fields, USA (Porsche 935), 52; **8** Gianpiero Moretti, I (Porsche 935), 52; **9** Hurley Haywood, USA (Porsche 935), 52; **10** Chris Cord, USA (Chevrolet Monza), 51. **1st over 2500cc GT class**: David Cowart, USA (BMW M1), 49.
Fastest Qualifier: Fitzpatrick, 1m 01·145s, 111·145 mph/178·870 km/h (record).
Fastest lap: Redman, 1m 03·02s, 108·537 mph/174·673 km/h (record).
2500cc race (39 laps, 74·10 miles/119·25 km): 1 Lee Mueller, USA (Mazda RX-7), 46m 48·633s, 94·979 mph/152·854 km/h; **2** Walt Bohren, USA (Mazda RX-7), 47m 16·590s; **3** Patrick Jacquemart, USA (Renault 5 Turbo), 39 laps; **4** Jack Dunham, USA (Mazda RX-7), 38; **5** Wayne Baker, USA (Porsche 914/4), 37; **6** John Johnson, USA (Porsche 911), 37.
Fastest Qualifier: Mueller, 1m 10·916s, 96·452 mph/155·224 km/h.
Fastest lap: Mueller, 1m 11·03s, 96·297 mph/154·975 km/h.
Championship points. Overall: 1 Rahal, 60; **2** Redman, 58; **3** Fitzpatrick, 54; **4** Haywood, 36; **5** Paul Jnr, 35; **6** Garretson, 30. **GT over 2500cc: 1** Cowart, 63; **2** Kendall and Smith, 35. **GT up to 2500cc: 1** Mueller, 70; **2** Bohren, 63; **3** Carney, 43.

COCA-COLA 400 CAMEL GT RACE, Lime Rock Park, Connecticut, United States of America, May 25. IMSA CAMEL GT Championship, round 6. 132 laps of the 1·530-mile/2·462-km circuit, 210·96 miles/324·98 km.
1 Brian Redman, GB (Lola T600-Chevrolet), 2h 00m 01·393s, 100·960 mph/162·479 km/h.
2 Ted Field/Bobby Rahal, USA/USA (Porsche 935), 128 laps.
3 Rolf Stommelen, D (Porsche 935), 128.
4 Gianpiero Moretti/Al Holbert, I/USA (Porsche 935), 125.
5 David Cowart/Kenper Miller, USA/USA (BMW M1), 123 (1st over 2500cc GT class).
6 John Paul Jnr, USA (Porsche 935), 123.
7 Sam Posey, USA (Datsun ZX Turbo), 119; **8** Joe Crevier/Al Unser Jnr, USA/USA (BMW M1), 119; **9** John Carusso/Phil Currin, USA/USA (Chevrolet Corvette), 117; **10** René Rodriguez/Tico Almeida, USA/USA (Porsche Carrera RSR), 115.
Fastest Qualifier: Klass Ludwig, D (Ford Mustang Turbo), 49·742s, 110·731 mph/178·204 km/h (record).
Fastest lap: David Hobbs, GB (BMW M1), 52·22s, 105·477 mph/169·748 km/h (record).
2500cc race (47 laps, 71·91 miles/115·71 km): 1 Walt Bohren, USA (Mazda RX-7), 45m 57·498s, 93·877 mph/151·08 km/h; **2** Lee Mueller, USA (Mazda RX-7), 46m 03·802s; **3** Logan Blackburn, USA (Datsun ZX), 47 laps; **4** Jim Mullem, USA (Mazda RX-7), 47; **5** Bob Leitzinger, USA (Datsun ZX), 47; **6** Jim Cook, USA (Mazda RX-7), 46.
Fastest Qualifier: Bohren, 57·049s, 96·549 mph/155·380 km/h.
Fastest lap: Blackburn, 57·17s, 96·344 mph/155·050 km/h.
Championship points. Overall: 1 Redman, 78; **2** Rahal, 75; **3** Fitzpatrick, 54; **4** Paul Jnr, 43; **5** Haywood, 36; **6** Garretson and Holbert, 30. **GT over 2500cc: 1** Cowart, 84; **2** Miller, 40; **3** Unser Jnr, 39. **GT up to 2500cc: 1** Mueller, 85; **2** Bohren, 84; **3** Carney, 45.

RED ROOF INNS 200 CAMEL GT RACE, Mid-Ohio Sports Car Course, Ohio, United States of America, May 31. IMSA CAMEL GT Championship, round 7. 84 laps of the 2·400-mile/3·862-km circuit, 201·60 miles/324·41 km.
1 Brian Redman, GB (Lola T600-Chevrolet), 2h 08m 38·927s, 94·023 mph/151·315 km/h.
2 Gianpiero Moretti/Bobby Rahal, I/USA (Porsche 935), 2h 09m 09·831s.
3 John Paul Jnr, USA (Porsche 935), 84 laps.
4 John Fitzpatrick, GB (Porsche 935), 82.
5 David Hobbs, GB (BMW M1C), 82.
6 Ted Field/Bill Whittington, USA/USA (Porsche 935), 80.
7 David Cowart/Kenper Miller, USA/USA (BMW M1), 78 (1st over 2500cc GT class); **8** Joe Crevier/Al Unser Jnr, USA/USA (BMW M1), 78; **9** Logan Blackburn, USA (Datsun ZX), 77 (1st up to 2500cc GT class); **10** Lee Mueller, USA (Mazda RX-7), 76.
Fastest Qualifier: Paul Jnr, 1m 29·170s, 96·894 mph/155·935 km/h (record).
Fastest lap: Redman, 1m 28·52s, 97·605 mph/157·080 km/h (record).
Championship points. Overall: 1 Redman, 98; **2** Rahal, 75; **3** Fitzpatrick, 64; **4** Paul Jnr, 56; **5** Moretti, 40; **6** Haywood, 36. **GT over 2500cc: 1** Cowart, 104; **2** Unser Jnr, 55; **3** Miller, 40. **GT up to 2500cc: 1** Mueller, 100; **2** Bohren, 96; **3** Carney, 49.

PEPSI GRAND PRIX CAMEL GT RACE, Brainerd International Raceway, Minnesota, United States of America, June 14. IMSA CAMEL GT Championship, round 8. 42 laps of the 3·000-mile/4·828-km circuit, 126·00 miles/202·78 km.
1 Klaus Ludwig, D (Ford Mustang Turbo), 1h 08m 44·106s, 109·987 mph/177·006 km/h.
2 John Fitzpatrick, GB (Porsche 935), 1h 09m 47·579s.
3 John Paul Jnr, USA (Porsche 935), 42 laps.
4 Bruce Leven, USA (Porsche 935), 41.
5 David Cowart, USA (BMW M1), 39 (1st over 2500cc GT class).
6 Lee Mueller, USA (Mazda RX-7), 39 (1st up to 2500cc GT class).
7 Logan Blackburn, USA (Datsun ZX), 39; **8** Wayne Baker, USA (Porsche 914/4), 39; **9** Dick Davenport, USA (Datsun ZX), 38; **10** William Koll, USA (Porsche 911), 38.
Fastest Qualifier: John Paul Jnr, USA (Lola T600-Chevrolet), 1m 47·518s, 100·448 mph/161·655 km/h.
Fastest lap: Paul Jnr, 1m 34·17s, 114·686 mph/184·569 km/h.
Championship points. Overall: 1 Redman, 98; **2** Fitzpatrick, 79; **3** Rahal, 75; **4** Paul Jnr, 57; **5** Moretti, 40; **6** Haywood, 36. **GT over 2500cc: 1** Cowart, 125; **2** Unser Jnr, 55; **3** Miller, 40. **GT up to 2500cc: 1** Mueller, 120; **2** Bohren, 96; **3** Carney, 49.

PAUL REVERE 250, Daytona International Speedway, Florida, United States of America, July 4. IMSA CAMEL GT Championship, round 9. 65 laps of the 3.840-mile/6.180-km circuit, 249.60 miles/401.69 km.
1 Mauricio DeNarvaez/Hurley Haywood, COL/USA (Porsche 935), 2h 17m 30.113s, 108.914 mph/175.280 km/h.
2 David Cowart/Kenper Miller, USA/USA (BMW M1), 63 laps (1st over 2500cc GT class).
3 John Paul Jnr, USA (Porsche 935), 62.
4 Ren Tilton, USA (Porsche 934), 60.
5 Dick Davenport, USA (Datsun ZX), 59 (1st up to 2500cc GT class).
6 Logan Blackburn, USA (Datsun ZX), 58.
7 Ted Field/Bill Whittington, USA/USA (Porsche 935), 57; **8** Roger Manderville/Amos Johnson, USA/USA (Mazda RX-7), 56; **9** Jim Cook/John Casey, USA/USA (Mazda RX-7), 56; **10** Jim Downing, USA (Mazda RX-7), 56.
Fastest Qualifier: Haywood, 1m 45.423s, 131.129 mph/211.031 km/h.
Fastest lap: B. Whittington, 1m 47.18s, 128.979 mph/207.571 km/h.
Championship points. Overall: 1 Redman, 98; **2** Rahal, 83; **3** Fitzpatrick, 79; **4** Paul Jnr, 72; **5** Haywood, 57; **6** Field, 41. **GT over 2500cc: 1** Cowart, 146; **2** Miller, 60; **3** Unser Jnr, 55. **GT up to 2500cc: 1** Mueller, 120; **2** Bohren, 96; **3** Davenport, 66.

DATSUN CAMEL GT RACE, Sears Point International Raceway, Sonoma, California, United States of America, July 26. IMSA CAMEL GT Championship, round 10. 40 laps of the 2.523-mile/4.060-km circuit, 100.92 miles/162.40 km.
1 Klaus Ludwig, D (Ford Mustang Turbo), 1h 05m 09.489s, 92.931 mph/149.558 km/h.
2 Brian Redman, GB (Lola T600-Chevrolet), 1h 05m 12.605s.
3 John Paul Jnr, USA (Lola T600-Chevrolet), 40 laps.
4 Gianpiero Moretti, I (Porsche 935), 39.
5 Maurizio DeNarvaez, COL (Porsche 935), 39.
6 Dennis Aase, USA (BMW M1), 38 (1st over 2500cc GT class).
7 David Cowart, USA (BMW M1), 38; **8** Paul Newman, USA (Datsun ZX Turbo), 37; **9** Bruce Canepa, USA (Porsche 935), 36; **10** Frank Leary, USA (Porsche Carrera RSR), 34.
Fastest Qualifier: Paul Jnr, 1m 33.559s, 97.081 mph/156.236 km/h (record).
Fastest lap: Redman, 1m 35.71s, 94.899 mph/152.725 km/h (record).

2500cc race (30 laps, 75.69 miles/121.81 km): 1 Wayne Baker, USA (Porsche 914/4), 53m 41.064s, 84.594 mph/136.141 km/h; **2** William Koll, USA (Porsche 911), 54m 09.757s; **3** Walt Bohren, USA (Mazda RX-7), 30 laps; **4** Lee Mueller, USA (Mazda RX-7), 30; **5** Frank Carney, USA (Datsun ZX), 30; **6** Jim Cook, USA (Mazda RX-7), 29.
Fastest Qualifier: Cook, 1m 45.194s, 86.343 mph/138.955 km/h (record).
Fastest lap: Baker, 1m 45.26s, 86.289 mph/138.868 km/h (record).
Championship points. Overall: 1 Redman, 113; **2** Paul Jnr, 85; **3** Rahal, 83; **4** Fitzpatrick, 79; **5** Haywood, 57; **6** Ludwig, 56. **GT over 2500cc: 1** Cowart, 161; **2** Miller, 60; **3** Aase and Unser Jnr, 55. **GT up to 2500cc: 1** Mueller, 131; **2** Bohren, 108; **3** Davenport, 66.

G.I. JOE'S GRAND PRIX IMSA CAMEL GT RACE, Portland International Raceway, Oregon, United States of America, August 2. IMSA CAMEL GT Championship, round 11. 53 laps of the 1.915-mile/3.082-km circuit, 101.495 miles/163.346 km.
1 Brian Redman, GB (Lola T600-Chevrolet), 1h 00m 07.34s, 101.288 mph/163.007 km/h.
2 Gianpiero Moretti, I (Porsche 935), 1h 00m 40.30s.
3 Bobby Rahal, USA (Porsche 935), 52 laps.
4 David Hobbs, GB (BMW M1C), 52.
5 Ted Field, USA (Porsche 935), 52.
6 Paul Newman, USA (Datsun ZX Turbo), 50.
7 Mauricio DeNarvaez, COL (Porsche 935), 50; **8** David Cowart, USA (BMW M1), 49 (1st over 2500cc GT class); **9** Neil Shelton, USA (Porsche Carrara RSR), 49; **10** Don Devendorf, USA (Datsun ZX Turbo), 48.
Fastest Qualifier: John Paul Jnr, USA (Lola T600-Chevrolet), 1m 05.15s, 105.817 mph/170.296 km/h.
Fastest lap: Paul Jnr, 1m 06.14s, 104.233 mph/167.746 km/h.
2500cc race (37 laps, 70.86 miles/114.03 km): 1 Lee Mueller, USA (Mazda RX-7), 46m 10.55s, 92.068 mph/148.169 km/h; **2** Walt Bohren, USA (Mazda RX-7), 46m 19.81s; **3** Wayne Baker, USA (Porsche 914/4), 37 laps; **4** Jim Cook, USA (Mazda RX-7), 37; **5** Jeff Kline, USA (Mazda RX-7), 37; **6** William Koll, USA (Porsche 911), 37.
Fastest Qualifier: Mueller, 1m 13.866s, 93.331 mph/150.201 km/h.
Fastest lap: Mueller, 1m 13.95s, 93.225 mph/148.421 km/h.
Championship points. Overall: 1 Redman, 133; **2** Rahal, 95; **3** Paul Jnr, 86; **4** Fitzpatrick, 79; **5** Moretti, 65; **6** Haywood, 57. **GT over 2500cc: 1** Cowart, 181; **2** Miller, 60; **3** Aase and Unser Jnr, 55. **GT up to 2500cc: 1** Mueller, 151; **2** Bohren, 123; **3** Davenport, 66.

MOLSON 1000 6 HOUR ENDURANCE RACE, Mosport Park Circuit, Ontario, Canada, August 16. IMSA CAMEL GT Championship, round 12. 229 laps of the 2.459-mile/3.957-km circuit, 563.11 miles/906.153 km.
1 Rolf Stommelen/Harald Grohs, D/D (Porsche 935), 6h 00m 43.0s, 93.661 mph/150.732 km/h.
2 Brian Redman/Eppie Wietzes, GB/CDN (Lola T600-Chevrolet), 6h 01m 04.0s.
3 Ted Field/Bill Whittington, USA/USA (Porsche 935), 222 laps.
4 Preston Henn/Edgar Doren, USA/D (Porsche 935), 219.
5 David Cowart/Kenper Miller, USA/USA (BMW M1), 218 (1st over 2500cc GT class).
6 John Fitzpatrick/Jim Busby, GB/USA (Porsche 935), 217.
7 Bob Garretson/Mauricio DeNarvaez, USA/COL (Porsche 935), 215; **8** Tony Garcia/Hiram Cruz/Albert Naon, USA/USA/USA (BMW M1), 210; **9** Lee Mueller/Walt Bohren, USA/USA (Mazda RX-7), 209 (1st up to 2500cc GT class; **10** "Jamsal"/Eduardo Barrientos, ES/ES (Porsche 935), 206.
Fastest Qualifier: Stommelen, 1m 18.956s, 112.118 mph/180.436 km/h.
Fastest lap: Field/Whittington, 1m 20.657s, 109.75 mph/176.63 km/h.
Championship points. Overall: 1 Redman, 148; **2** Rahal, 95; **3** Fitzpatrick, 87; **4** Paul Jnr, 85; **5** Moretti, 65; **6** Haywood, 59. **GT over 2500cc: 1** Cowart, 197; **2** Miller, 77; **3** Aase and Unser Jnr, 55. **GT up to 2500cc: 1** Mueller, 171; **2** Bohren, 144; **3** Davenport, 81.

PABST 500 IMSA CAMEL GT RACE, Road America, Elkhart Lake, Wisconsin, United Stated of America, August 23. IMSA CAMEL GT Championship, round 13. 125 laps of the 4.000-mile/6.437-km circuit, 500.00 miles/804.625 km.
1 Rolf Stommelen/Harald Grohs, D/D (Porsche 935), 4h 44m 35.380s, 105.415 mph/169.649 km/h.
2 Brian Redman/Sam Posey, GB/USA (Lola T600-Chevrolet), 4h 46m 26.000s.
3 Chris Cord/Jim Adams, USA/USA (Lola T600-Chevrolet), 121 laps.
4 Bob Garretson/Tom Gloy, USA/USA (Porsche 935), 119.
5 Gianpiero Moretti/Bobby Rahal, I/USA (Porsche 935), 118.
6 John Fitzpatrick/Jim Busby, GB/USA (Porsche 935), 118.
7 Ted Field/Bill Whittington, USA/USA (Porsche 935), 111; **8** Walt Bohren/Lee Mueller, USA/USA (Mazda RX-7), 111 (1st up to 2500cc GT class); **9** Dennis Aase/Chuck Kendall/Pete Smith, USA/USA/USA (BMW M1), 110 (1st over 2500cc GT class); **10** Logan Blackburn/Dave Frellsen, USA/USA (Datsun ZX), 109.
Fastest Qualifier: Stommelen, 2m 08.359s, 112.185 mph/180.544 km/h (record).
Fastest lap: John Paul Jnr, USA (Porsche 935), 2m 10.25s, 110.557 mph/177.924 km/h (record).
Championship points. Overall: 1 Redman, 163; **2** Rahal, 103; **3** Fitzpatrick, 93; **4** Paul Jnr, 89; **5** Moretti, 73; **6** Stommelen, 67. **GT over 2500cc: 1** Cowart, 201; **2** Miller, 82; **3** Aase, 75. **GT up to 2500cc: 1** Mueller, 191; **2** Bohren, 164; **3** Davenport, 82.

LUMBERMAN'S 500, Mid-Ohio Sports Car Course, Ohio, United States of America, August 30. 130 laps of the 2.400-mile/3.862-km circuit, 312.00 miles/502.06 km.
1 Rolf Stommelen/Derek Bell, D/GB (Porsche 935), 3h 21m 43.28s, 92.801 mph/149.348 km/h.
2 John Fitzpatrick/Jim Busby, GB/USA (Porsche 935), 129 laps.
3 Richard Guider/Bertil Roos, USA/S (Cicale-Hart), 129.
4 Dennis Aase/Jim Cook, USA/USA (BMW M1), 124.
5 Jim Trueman/Bobby Rahal, USA/USA (Ralt RT2-Hart), 123 (DNF, vapour lock).
6 Al Holbert/Doc Bundy, USA/USA (Porsche 924 Carrera RSR), 121.
7 Chester Vincentz/John Wood, USA/USA (Porsche 934), 117; **8** Bob Bergstrom/Tom Winters, USA/USA (Porsche 924 Carrera RSR), 117; **9** Ray Radcliff/M.L. Speer, USA/USA (Porsche 935), 116; **10** Bob Beasley/George Stone, USA/USA (Porsche Carrera RSR), 115.
Fastest Qualifier: John Morton/Tom Klauser, USA/USA (Frissbee-Chevrolet), 1m 24.477s, 102.276 mph/164.597 km/h.
Fastest lap: Trueman, 1m 27.26s, 99.014 mph/159.35 km/h.

IMSA CAMEL GT RACES, Road Atlanta, Georgia, United States of America, September 13. IMSA CAMEL GT Championship, round 14. 60 laps of the 2.520-mile/4.056-km circuit, 151.20 miles/243.36 km.
1 Brian Redman, GB (Lola T600-Chevrolet), 1h 03m 24.433s, 73.512 mph/118.306 km/h.
2 Ted Field, USA (Porsche 935), 59 laps.
3 Mauricio DeNarvaez, COL (Porsche 935), 58.
4 Kenper Miller, USA (BMW M1), 58 (1st over 2500cc GT class).
5 Dennis Aase, USA (BMW M1), 58.
6 Hershel McGriff, USA (Chevrolet Corvette), 57.
7 Denny Wilson, USA (BMW M1), 55; **8** Tony Garcia, USA (BMW M1), 55; **9** Don Devendorf, USA (Datsun ZX Turbo), 55; **10** Jo Crevier, USA (BMW M1), 53.
Fastest Qualifier: John Fitzpatrick, GB (Porsche 935), 1m 18.825s, 115.090 mph/185.220 km/h.
Fastest lap: John Paul Jnr, USA (Lola T600-Chevrolet), 1m 20.46s, 112.752 mph/181.456 km/h.
2500cc race (30 laps, 75.60 miles/121.68 km): 1 Walt Bohren, USA (Mazda RX-7), 46m 16.365s, 98.027 mph/157.759 km/h; **2** Lee Mueller, USA (Mazda RX-7), 46m 27.003s; **3** Jim Cook, USA (Mazda RX-7), 30 laps; **4** Logan Blackburn, USA (Datsun ZX), 30; **5** George Alderman, USA (Datsun ZX), 30; **6** Charles Morgan, USA (Datsun ZX), 30.
Fastest Qualifier: Mueller, 1m 30.162s, 100.619 mph/161.930 km/h.
Fastest lap: Bohren, 1m 31.57s, 99.072 mph/159.441 km/h.
Championship points. Overall: 1 Redman, 183; **2** Rahal, 103; **3** Fitzpatrick, 94; **4** Paul Jnr, 89; **5** Field, 80; **6** Moretti, 73. **GT over 2500cc: 1** Cowart, 201; **2** Miller, 103; **3** Aase, 90. **GT up to 2500cc: 1** Mueller, 207; **2** Bohren, 184; **3** Blackburn, 87.

KENWOOD STEREO 500 CAMEL GT RACE, Pocono International Raceway, Pennsylvania, United States of America, September 27. IMSA CAMEL GT Championship, round 15. 150 laps of the 2.800-mile/4.506-km circuit, 420.00 miles/675.90 km.
1 John Paul/John Paul Jnr, USA/USA (Porsche 935), 4h 02m 12.400s, 104.902 mph/168.823 km/h.
2 Brian Redman/Ralph Kent-Cooke, GB/USA (Lola T600-Chevrolet), 4h 04m 19.606s.
3 John Fitzpatrick/Jim Busby, GB/USA (Porsche 935), 148 laps.
4 Chris Cord/Jim Adams, USA/USA (Lola T600-Chevrolet), 147.
5 David Cowart/Kenper Miller, USA/USA (BMW M1), 145 (1st over 2500cc GT class).
6 Bruce Leven/Hurley Haywood, USA/USA (Porsche 935), 145.
7 Tony Garcia/Albert Naon, USA/USA (BMW M1), 142; **8** Walt Bohren/Rick Knoop, USA/USA (Mazda RX-7), 137 (1st up to 2500cc GT class); **9** Lee Mueller/Kathy Rude, USA/USA (Mazda RX-7), 137; **10** Jim Cook/John Casey, USA/USA (Mazda RX-7), 136.
Fastest Qualifier: Paul Jnr, 1m 25.186s, 118.330 mph/190.433 km/h (record).
Fastest lap: Adams, 1m 26.94s, 115.942 mph/186.590 km/h (record).
Championship points (prior to final round at Daytona on November 29):

1 Brian Redman, GB	198
2 John Paul Jnr, USA	110
3 John Fiztpatrick, GB	106
4 Bobby Rahal, USA	103
5 Ted Field, USA	80
6 Gianpiero Moretti, I	73

7 Rolf Stommelen, D, 67; **8** Hurley Haywood, USA, 65; **9** Mauricio DeNarvaez, COL, 59; **10** Klaus Ludwig, D, 56.
GT over 2500cc class: 1 David Cowart, USA, 221; **2** Kenper Miller, USA, 124; **3** Dennis Aase, USA, 90; **4** Tony Garcia, USA, 71; **5** Albert Naon, USA, 61; **6**= Al Unser Jnr, USA, 55; **6**= Chuck Kendall, USA, 55; **6**= Rene Rodriguez, USA, 55. **GT up to 2500cc class: 1** Lee Mueller, USA, 222; **2** Walt Bohren, USA, 204; **3** Logan Blackburn, USA, 87; **4** Wayne Baker, USA, 84; **5** Dick Davenport, USA, 82; **6** Frank Carney, USA, 78.
Final results will be given in Autocourse 1982/83.